True Christianity

A collection of Bible Studies

by

Bro. Steve Winter

True Christianity

A Collection of Bible Studies

by

Bro. Steve Winter

Table of Contents:

The Word of God

Rightly Dividing

The job of a real preacher is not to "interpret" the Bible, but rather to "rightly divide" or "portion out in bite sized portions". Notice that the same Bible that says the scripture is not open to private interpretation also advocates it's being "rightly divided" by a preacher.

> II Timothy 2:15 Study to shew thyself approved unto God, a workman that needeth not to be ashamed, rightly dividing the word of truth.

> II Peter 1:20 Knowing this first, that no prophecy of the scripture is of any private interpretation.

* I hope to cover just a few basics here that will help arm our readers against deceivers. We need to understand that a deceiver will also be quoting scriptures, but the bottom line will be that the false preacher will be teaching why it is not essential to obey the Bible. Two men will use the exact same Bible. One will use it to deceive folks into disobeying it, the other will use it in an attempt to get people to see the importance of obeying God. Here are some important points to consider:*

1. Matthew, Mark, Luke and John were not penned until well after the churches were established (as recorded in the book of Acts), AND they tell the history of a time right BEFORE the new testament church was born. During these books, Jesus always referred to His church in future tense and that conversion" was something that would come later. Jesus did not consider Peter "converted" even though Peter had been with Him for quite a while as a disciple. *

> Matthew 16:18 And I say also unto thee, That thou art Peter, and upon this rock I will build my church; and the gates of hell shall not prevail against it.

* (The "ROCK" was the revelation that Jesus was God Himself (the messiah). *

> Luke 22:32 But I have prayed for thee, that thy faith fail not: and when thou art converted, strengthen thy brethren.

(Peter was not "converted" until he was re-born in Acts 2:4)

2. Jesus chose to use Apostles to teach His message. The ONLY record that we have of anything that Jesus said is what an Apostle wrote down. People who received the doctrine of the Apostles were said to have received "the word" or "Word of the Lord Jesus". (Receiver=Obeyer) *

> Acts 2:41 Then they that gladly received his word were baptized: and the same day there were added [unto them] about three thousand souls.
>
> Acts 19:9 But when divers were hardened, and believed not, but spake evil of that way before the multitude, he departed from them, and separated the disciples, disputing daily in the school of one Tyrannus.
>
> Acts 19:10 And this continued by the space of two years; so that all they which dwelt in Asia heard the word of the Lord Jesus, both Jews and Greeks.
>
> Acts 19:11 And God wrought special miracles by the hands of Paul:

* Paul preached the same Acts 2:38 message that Peter preached on the birthday of the new testament church. Notice that Paul disputed daily with those that opposed the "word of the Lord Jesus". *

> Acts 2:38 Then Peter said unto them, Repent, and be baptized every one of you in the name of Jesus Christ for the remission of sins, and ye shall receive the gift of the Holy Ghost.

* Noticing above that I started at Acts 19:9 where the Bible speaks of those who "believed not" and spoke evil of the "way" that Paul was preaching. Let us go back further and see what the "non-believers" were speaking evil of! Notice carefully that Paul followed the Acts 2:38 formula exactly, even re-baptizing John's disciples: *

Acts 19:1 And it came to pass, that, while Apollos was at Corinth, Paul having passed through the upper coasts came to Ephesus: and finding certain disciples,

Acts 19:2 He said unto them, Have ye received the Holy Ghost since ye believed? And they said unto him, We have not so much as heard whether there be any Holy Ghost.

Acts 19:3 And he said unto them, Unto what then were ye baptized? And they said, Unto John's baptism.

Acts 19:4 Then said Paul, John verily baptized with the baptism of repentance, saying unto the people, that they should believe on him which should come after him, that is, on Christ Jesus.

Acts 19:5 When they heard [this], they were baptized in the name of the Lord Jesus.

Acts 19:6 And when Paul had laid [his] hands upon them, the Holy Ghost came on them; and they spake with tongues, and prophesied.

Acts 19:7 And all the men were about twelve.

Acts 19:8 And he went into the synagogue, and spake boldly for the space of three months, disputing and persuading the things concerning the kingdom of God.

* Now go back and look again at Acts 19:9 concerning those "non-believers" that were speaking evil of the "Word of the Lord Jesus" that Paul was preaching. We have people on this network who also speak evil of the "Word of the Lord Jesus". Look at what Paul has to say about them:

Gal 1:8 But though we, or an angel from heaven, preach any other gospel unto you than that which we have preached unto you, let him be accursed.

3. Remember that the book of Romans forward were letters (epistles) written to those who had obeyed the "Word of the Lord Jesus" that the Apostles had preached.

Exegesis

I have come to notice something. When most people use the term "exegesis". They are often just trying to justify whatever perversion of scripture that they are following, what they *really* mean is a "twisting" and "philophosizing" of the scripture to nullify it's plain clear meaning, to support some religious tradition into which they have themselves become ensnared.

Sooo, instead of simply taking the Word of God as a face value book to be obeyed or disobeyed, they will throw up huge smoke screens of GREAT EXEGESIS, to explain why God "didn't really mean what he said", and then, quite often, they will refer us to some "world renown" "teacher" whose authority is (of course) much greater than some simple Bible commandment because of their fame and recognition (even though in many cases the "great authority" has never bothered to even really obey Acts 2:38 to even become a Christian in the first place). And lemme tell you something! Any "big name" preacher that the average household regards as a "man of Gawd"; is probably (like 99.998%) a FAKE, and the Bible forewarned you about that! Note carefully:

> I John 4:5 They are of the world: therefore speak they of the world, and the world heareth them.

* The false preachers KNOW how to tell people what they want to hear. They know how to "seem spiritual" AND LISTEN!! They KNOW how to tweak your emotions...Just because some turkey can give you goose bumps and make you dewey eyed DOES NOT mean that that person is of GOD! The question to ask is "Is that man preaching the original Acts 2:38 plan of salvation AND the rest of the HOLINESS teachings of the Bible?"* Sooo, those that have always considered baptism as a "spare tire" or "nice thing to maybe do after salvation"... and Ooooooo do they cling to their groundless "doctrine" that whenever someone "believes" then BAM they're saved no matter what they do,,blah blah... IGNORING multitudes of warnings in the Bible (in letters written to saints), that those who do certain things (including heresy) WILL NOT inherit the kingdom of God. And the further they go, the deeper they get, and the more scripture that they must "exegesis" into something DIFFERENT.

However!!! these same "believe only" adherents will often add their own "qualifications" for salvation, which, of course, still do not agree with the Biblical simplicity of the Acts 2:38 method of being born again spiritually (by the NEW Birth of water and spirit)

* "Hey Noah!! What makes you think that *your* boat is the only one that will float, that's just your 'terpretation' , Noah. Hey, Noah, your boat stinks........"*

> Genesis 7:16 And they that went in, went in male and female of all flesh, as God had commanded him: and the LORD shut him in.

*"Hey Noah! Open Up! The water's rising. Noah, we got kids out here!!"

* But it was not in Noah's power to open the door *

> Genesis 7:23 And every living substance was destroyed which was upon the face of the ground, both man, and cattle, and the creeping things, and the fowl of the heaven; and they were destroyed from the earth: and Noah only remained [alive], and they that [were] with him in the ark.

> Matthew 24:37 But as the days of Noe [were], so shall also the coming of the Son of man be.

> Luke 17:26 And as it was in the days of Noe, so shall it be also in the days of the Son of man.

* Listen, folks, this is no game. These filthy false preachers with their smooth words are NOT your friend. The scripture is not here for you to "exegise", it's here for you to obey or disobey...And lemme tell you something! IN JUDGMENT there will be no religious filth to "explain away" the teachings of the Bible. The books will be OPENED and YOU will face God alone... It's gonna be YOU, GOD, and A BOOK, and you will be without excuse, because God has given you a copy of the book in advance. And I pray that you'll simply accept it and obey it...and folks, it's a preacher's job to PREACH IT, not "exegesis" it.

II Timothy 4:2 Preach the word; be instant in season, out of season; reprove, rebuke, exhort with all longsuffering and doctrine.

* PREACH THE WORD!!, Not some watered down, philophised, twisted, humanized, sugar coated VARIATION!!! (that couldn't save a gnat!)*

II Timothy 4:3 For the time will come when they will not endure sound doctrine; but after their own lusts shall they heap to themselves teachers, having itching ears;

II Timothy 4:4 And they shall turn away [their] ears from the truth, and shall be turned unto fables.

James 1:21 Wherefore lay apart all filthiness and superfluity of naughtiness, and receive with meekness the engrafted word, which is able to save your souls.

James 1:22 But be ye doers of the word, and not hearers only, deceiving your own selves.

Acts 2:38 Then Peter said unto them, Repent, and be baptized every one of you in the name of Jesus Christ for the remission of sins, and ye shall receive the gift of the Holy Ghost.

Acts 2:39 For the promise is unto you, and to your children, and to all that are afar off, [even] as many as the Lord our God shall call.

Foundation of Theology

> Mark 12:29 And Jesus answered him, The first of all the commandments is, Hear, O Israel; The Lord our God is one Lord:
>
> 30 And thou shalt love the Lord thy God with all thy heart, and with all thy soul, and with all thy mind, and with all thy strength: this is the first commandment.

But who are we to love? Can we just make up our own gods and worship whoever and however we please?

> Jeremiah 2:11 Hath a nation changed their gods, which are yet no gods? but my people have changed their glory for that which doth not profit.
>
> Jeremiah 5:7 How shall I pardon thee for this? thy children have forsaken me, and sworn by them that are no gods: when I had fed them to the full, they then committed adultery, and assembled themselves by troops in the harlots' houses.
>
> Jeremiah 16:20 Shall a man make gods unto himself, and they are no gods?

Guess not, eh? Well how about if we just follow our hearts to lead us to the right thing to do?

> Proverbs 28:26 He that trusteth in his own heart is a fool: but whoso walketh wisely, he shall be delivered.

Oops, trusting one's own heart isn't highly recommended either now is it?

> Psalms 119:89 LAMED. For ever, O LORD, thy word is settled in heaven.

So we can trust in the Word of God.

> Matthew 24:35 Heaven and earth shall pass away, but my words shall not pass away.

Foundation of Theology

The identity of the God or "god" or "gods" being worshiped is of utmost importance to any religion. If the head of the religion is fake then the whole religion is fake regardless of whether it has positive disciplines and "self-improvement".

Most of the modern "false-christianities" of this hour worship a man made "trinity" of separate persons invented for them by the early Roman Catholic Church. All trinitarians are either Roman Catholic or "catholic lite"<tm>. At the core of these false religions is the teaching that their god squad consists of three separate persons but is still a belief in only one "god". Huh? That doesn't even make sense. Ah, but it must be a "MYSTERY". Anyway, you can read all about MYSTERY BABYLON in the book of Rev.

Let us now instead focus on the truth regarding the identity of Jesus Christ and the counterfeits will be easy to spot.

While we humans (created in God's image) certainly have body, soul and spirit we are not each "three separate persons". Though God manifested Himself as "Father, Son, and Holy Ghost" he is not "three separate persons" either. When society encounters a man or woman who truly is three separate persons what does society do? That's right we lock 'em up for their good and the good of society. God did NOT create a man as three separate persons.

1) God is a Spirit.

> John 4:24 God [is] a Spirit: and they that worship him must worship [him] in spirit and in truth.

2) God is holy.

> I Samuel 2:2 [There is] none holy as the LORD: for [there is] none beside thee: neither [is there] any rock like our God.

3) God is a "Holy Spirit".

4) Jesus is the "Spirit of truth"

John 14:6 Jesus saith unto him, I am the way, the truth, and the life:no man cometh unto the Father, but by me.

5) Jesus was "dwelling with them" and promised to be "in them".

John 14:17 [Even] the Spirit of truth; whom the world cannot receive, because it seeth him not, neither knoweth him: but ye know him; for he dwelleth with you, and shall be in you.

6) The "comforter" is the "Spirit of Christ"

John 14:18 I will not leave you comfortless: I will come to you.

7) The "Spirit of Christ" is the "Holy Spirit" is the "Spirit of Truth"

John 14:26 But the Comforter, [which is] the Holy Ghost, whom the Father will send in my name, he shall teach you all things, and bring all things to your remembrance, whatsoever I have said unto you.

8) The Spirit of God visited His creation robed in flesh as the "Son".

I Timothy 3:16 And without controversy great is the mystery of godliness: God was manifest in the flesh, justified in the Spirit, seen of angels, preached unto the Gentiles, believed on in the world, received up into glory.

9) The fullness of God is in Jesus Christ

Colossians 2:9 For in him dwelleth all the fulness of the Godhead bodily.

Colossians 2:10 And ye are complete in him, which is the head of all principality and power:

10) Jesus IS the "everlasting Father".

> Isaiah 9:6 For unto us a child is born, unto us a son is given: and the government shall be upon his shoulder: and his name shall be called Wonderful, Counsellor, The mighty God, The everlasting Father, The Prince of Peace.

11) Those who believe that Jesus is a "separate person" from the "Father" don't really know Jesus at all.

> John 14:9 Jesus saith unto him, Have I been so long time with you, and yet hast thou not known me, Philip? he that hath seen me hath seen the Father; and how sayest thou [then], Shew us the Father?

> 1 Corinthians 2:8 Which none of the princes of this world knew: for had they known it, they would not have crucified the Lord of glory.

It was none other than the Lord of Glory, Jehovah Himself, on the cross.

There is a problem for those who believe a lie.

> 2 Thessalonians 2:11 And for this cause God shall send them strong delusion, that they should believe a lie:
>
> 12 That they all might be damned who believed not the truth, but had pleasure in unrighteousness.

Now, as an aside here, let me share something that I noticed. If you take the phrase "a lie" and say it with a good southern accent it sounds like the false god of one of the false religions. Is it not astounding that so many follow a religion where the name of their "god" is "a lie" (allah). But I am dealing more with exposing counterfeit christianity rather than the other false religions.

It is essential to know and believe the truth.

> John 4:24 God is a Spirit: and they that worship him must worship him in spirit and in truth.

> Isaiah 48:11 For mine own sake, even for mine own sake, will I do it: for how should my name be polluted? and I will not give my glory unto another.

God said that He would not give His Glory to another. That really was Him, in the flesh, on the cross.

> 1 John 3:16 Hereby perceive we the love of God, because he laid down his life for us: and we ought to lay down our lives for the brethren.

According to the Bible God Himself laid down his life. Does that mean that God died? Keep in mind that God is the inventor of life and death. He can live and die as He pleases because He is God.

> John 2:19 Jesus answered and said unto them, Destroy this temple, and in three days I will raise it up.
>
> 20 Then said the Jews, Forty and six years was this temple in building, and wilt thou rear it up in three days?
>
> 21 But he spake of the temple of his body.
>
> 22 When therefore he was risen from the dead, his disciples remembered that he had said this unto them; and they believed the scripture, and the word which Jesus had said.

Jesus could raise Himself from the dead because He is God. To God both life and death are under His complete control. That is why as real Christians we can understand that it really was God Himself on the Cross, God manifest in the flesh.

Not some junior second person in a Roman god squad!

If Jesus was not God the Father, how could he have said:

> John 14:9 Jesus saith unto him, Have I been so long time with you, and yet hast thou not known me, Philip? he that hath seen me hath seen the Father; and how sayest thou then, Shew us the Father?

When they looked at Jesus, they saw God manifest in the flesh.

> Acts 22:6 And it came to pass, that, as I made my journey, and was come nigh unto Damascus about noon, suddenly there shone from heaven a great light round about me.
>
> Acts 22:7 And I fell unto the ground, and heard a voice saying unto me, Saul, Saul, why persecutest thou me?
>
> Acts 22:8 And I answered, Who art thou, Lord? And he said unto me, I am Jesus of Nazareth, whom thou persecutest.

Notice that the Lord in heaven claimed to be Jesus of Nazareth! None other than the Lord Jesus Christ.

> Acts 22:9 And they that were with me saw indeed the light, and were afraid; but they heard not the voice of him that spake to me.
>
> Acts 22:10 And I said, What shall I do, Lord? And the Lord said unto me, Arise, and go into Damascus; and there it shall be told thee of all things which are appointed for thee to do.

Notice that the Lord (Jesus Christ) spoke to Paul/Saul.

> Acts 22:11 And when I could not see for the glory of that light, being led by the hand of them that were with me, I came into Damascus.
>
> Acts 22:12 And one Ananias, a devout man according to the law, having a good report of all the Jews which dwelt [there],
>
> Acts 22:13 Came unto me, and stood, and said unto me, Brother Saul, receive thy sight. And the same hour I looked up upon him.
>
> Acts 22:14 And he said, The God of our fathers hath chosen thee, that thou shouldest know his will, and see that Just One, and shouldest hear the voice of his mouth.

NOW NOTICE CAREFULLY PLEASE! He said that it was the "God of our Fathers" that had chosen him, but we just read that it was "Jesus Christ" that chose him. JESUS CHRIST is the God of Abraham, Issac and Jacob.

> Acts 22:15 For thou shalt be his witness unto all men of what thou hast seen and heard.
>
> Acts 22:16 And now why tarriest thou? arise, and be baptized, and wash away thy sins, calling on the name of the Lord.

Also, notice, that just a few verses earlier that the "Lord" had declared His Name to be "Jesus of Nazareth".

Jesus Christ is NOT the "second person" in a Roman imaginary "god squad". Jesus Christ is the "Everlasting Father".

> Isaiah 9:6 For unto us a child is born, unto us a son is given: and the government shall be upon his shoulder: and his name shall be called Wonderful, Counsellor, The mighty God, The everlasting Father, The Prince of Peace.

Jesus Christ is the "Mighty God", He is NOT the "second person" of the Roman Catholic trinity, as Satan and his preachers would have you to believe.

> Exodus 3:14 And God said unto Moses, I AM THAT I AM: and he said, Thus shalt thou say unto the children of Israel, I AM hath sent me unto you.
>
> John 8:58 Jesus said unto them, Verily, verily, I say unto you, Before Abraham was, I am.
>
> 59 Then took they up stones to cast at him: but Jesus hid himself, and went out of the temple, going through the midst of them, and so passed by.

The true Christian Church is the bride of one husband only, the bride of Jesus only.

> Isaiah 9:6 For unto us a child is born, unto us a son is given: and the government shall be upon his shoulder: and his name shall be called Wonderful, Counsellor, The mighty God, The everlasting Father, The Prince of Peace.

Spirit of Truth

John 14:17 Even the Spirit of truth; whom the world cannot receive, because it seeth him not, neither knoweth him: but ye know him; for he dwelleth with you, and shall be in you.

John 14:18 I will not leave you comfortless: I will come to you.

John 15:26 But when the Comforter is come, whom I will send unto you from the Father, even the Spirit of truth, which proceedeth from the Father, he shall testify of me:

John 16:13 Howbeit when he, the Spirit of truth, is come, he will guide you into all truth: for he shall not speak of himself; but whatsoever he shall hear, that shall he speak: and he will shew you things to come.

1 John 4:6 We are of God: he that knoweth God heareth us; he that is not of God heareth not us. Hereby know we the spirit of truth, and the spirit of error.

Titus 3:10 A man that is an heretick after the first and second admonition reject;

Invisible Friend

We often hear doubters and non-believers talk about Christians as having an "invisible friend" and they mean that mockingly, comparing us like the children that make up imaginary friends etc. But I believe they have overlooked something.

> Colossians 1:16 For by him were all things created, that are in heaven, and that are in earth, visible and invisible, whether they be thrones, or dominions, or principalities, or powers: all things were created by him, and for him:

However, those same doubters have no problem having faith in many invisible things. They want to reject God while they continue in their own faith in invisible things.

In healthy environments air is invisible but I submit that even the most devout atheist will only hold their breath but for so long.

The atheist will often, by faith in the invisible, turn on a light switch and have faith that the light will come on. We all exercise faith in invisible things every day.

As a side note, if a wire is charged with electricity and an atheist does not believe that the electricity is on and touches the wire, their doubt will not save them.

It's the brick that you don't believe is there that hurts your toe the most.

We have many invisible friends and invisible enemies in this life. But visibility is hardly the measuring stick to determine reality. Actual life itself is invisible.

Let us consider something else. The things that we can see are all temporary and will eventually pass away. Who among us, even the atheist, believes that their physical body will last forever?

> 2 Corinthians 4:18 While we look not at the things which are seen, but at the things which are not seen: for the things which are seen are temporal; but the things which are not seen are eternal.

In dealing with matters of eternity you'd better have an invisible friend.

> Hebrews 11:1 Now faith is the substance of things hoped for, the evidence of things not seen.
>
> 1 Peter 1:8 Whom having not seen, ye love; in whom, though now ye see him not, yet believing, ye rejoice with joy unspeakable and full of glory:

The real Acts 2:38 Oneness Christian has a lot to look forward to.

> John 20:29 Jesus saith unto him, Thomas, because thou hast seen me, thou hast believed: blessed are they that have not seen, and yet have believed.
>
> 1 Corinthians 2:9 But as it is written, Eye hath not seen, nor ear heard, neither have entered into the heart of man, the things which God hath prepared for them that love him.
>
> 1 John 3:16 Hereby perceive we the love of God, because he laid down his life for us: and we ought to lay down our lives for the brethren.

Love is invisible, but do not even the atheists seek it?

We real Acts 2:38 Christians have nothing to be ashamed of for having an invisible friend.

> John 20:29 Jesus saith unto him, Thomas, because thou hast seen me, thou hast believed: blessed are they that have not seen, and yet have believed.

Do you want to be a real Biblical believer, a real Bible Christian? Find a real Church that teaches the real Acts 2:38 salvation message so that your belief won't be in vain.

1 Corinthians 15:2 By which also ye are saved, if ye keep in memory what I preached unto you, unless ye have believed in vain.

Acts 2:38 Then Peter said unto them, Repent, and be baptized every one of you in the name of Jesus Christ for the remission of sins, and ye shall receive the gift of the Holy Ghost.

Acts 2:39 For the promise is unto you, and to your children, and to all that are afar off, even as many as the Lord our God shall call.

Measure of Faith

Every man has a measure of faith but some put their faith in false things.

> Romans 12:3 For I say, through the grace given unto me, to every man that is among you, not to think of himself more highly than he ought to think; but to think soberly, according as God hath dealt to every man the measure of faith.

Even the atheist has faith. He has faith that somehow everything is going to work out OK and he has faith that no belief in God or service to God is of value.

The false-christians have faith, they just have faith that a corrupt council years ago was correct when they invented a "trinity" of god persons to worship.

Many people in Germany a few years ago had great faith in the leader of their country, but it didn't work out.

Many things can be harmful, faith in an unsafe bridge, faith that it is safe to cross the street when it is not, faith that bad potato salad is still good. The point? You can have great faith in something and be so totally wrong.

The alcoholic has faith that his bottle will provide him relief, and it does, at a price. The drug addict has faith in his supplier and in a substance to produce a predictable result that will provide him a measure of satisfaction.

There certainly are pleasures in this life but they are a poor choice upon which to use your measure of faith.

> Luke 8:14 And that which fell among thorns are they, which, when they have heard, go forth, and are choked with cares and riches and pleasures of this life, and bring no fruit to perfection.

Where can we get more faith?

> Romans 10:17 So then faith cometh by hearing, and hearing by the word of God.

How important is faith?

> Hebrews 11:6 But without faith it is impossible to please him: for he that cometh to God must believe that he is, and that he is a rewarder of them that diligently seek him.
>
> 7 By faith Noah, being warned of God of things not seen as yet, moved with fear, prepared an ark to the saving of his house; by the which he condemned the world, and became heir of the righteousness which is by faith.
>
> 8 By faith Abraham, when he was called to go out into a place which he should after receive for an inheritance, obeyed; and he went out, not knowing whither he went.
>
> 9 By faith he sojourned in the land of promise, as in a strange country, dwelling in tabernacles with Isaac and Jacob, the heirs with him of the same promise:
>
> 10 For he looked for a city which hath foundations, whose builder and maker is God.
>
> 11 Through faith also Sara herself received strength to conceive seed, and was delivered of a child when she was past age, because she judged him faithful who had promised.
>
> 12 Therefore sprang there even of one, and him as good as dead, so many as the stars of the sky in multitude, and as the sand which is by the sea shore innumerable.
>
> 13 These all died in faith, not having received the promises, but having seen them afar off, and were persuaded of them, and embraced them, and confessed that they were strangers and pilgrims on the earth.
>
> 14 For they that say such things declare plainly that they seek a country.

15 And truly, if they had been mindful of that country from whence they came out, they might have had opportunity to have returned.

16 But now they desire a better country, that is, an heavenly: wherefore God is not ashamed to be called their God: for he hath prepared for them a city.

17 By faith Abraham, when he was tried, offered up Isaac: and he that had received the promises offered up his only begotten son,

18 Of whom it was said, That in Isaac shall thy seed be called:

19 Accounting that God was able to raise him up, even from the dead; from whence also he received him in a figure.

20 By faith Isaac blessed Jacob and Esau concerning things to come.

21 By faith Jacob, when he was a dying, blessed both the sons of Joseph; and worshipped, leaning upon the top of his staff.

22 By faith Joseph, when he died, made mention of the departing of the children of Israel; and gave commandment concerning his bones.

23 By faith Moses, when he was born, was hid three months of his parents, because they saw he was a proper child; and they were not afraid of the king's commandment.

24 By faith Moses, when he was come to years, refused to be called the son of Pharaoh's daughter;

25 Choosing rather to suffer affliction with the people of God, than to enjoy the pleasures of sin for a season;

26 Esteeming the reproach of Christ greater riches than the treasures in Egypt: for he had respect unto the recompence of the reward.

27 By faith he forsook Egypt, not fearing the wrath of the king: for he endured, as seeing him who is invisible.

Faith involves action. Even the foolish faith of the alcoholic in his bottle will not achieve results unless he exercises his faith and drinks.

How many (don't answer) can relate to this next one:

> Proverbs 25:19 Confidence in an unfaithful man in time of trouble is like a broken tooth, and a foot out of joint.

Even the atheist has faith in his beliefs and in himself, and that faith is valid but only up to a point.

People have faith in their doctors, what about faith in a quack doctor? What about faith in a quack preacher like the trinity preacher? Do not people receive a measure of satisfaction from faith in a quack doctor or a con man? But they lose out in the end of a matter. It is the same with placing faith in a false-christian preacher like some trinity cultist.

Who among us has ever put their life on the line like the Islamic suicide terrorists? They had tremendous faith. One can have tremendous faith and still be tremendously stupid. Their "Allah" is "a lie". One can have tremendous and steadfast faith in a lie. Just look at all the trinity churches. Many of them have great faith and works as well to a false MYSTERY god squad.

> Revelation 17:5 And upon her forehead was a name written, MYSTERY, BABYLON THE GREAT, THE MOTHER OF HARLOTS AND ABOMINATIONS OF THE EARTH.

In some of the more pathetic Roman Catholic cults men have actually had the faith to allow themselves to be crucified. Hey, stupid is as stupid does, eh?

Voodoo victims have great faith in their leaders etc and etc....

Every man has a measure of faith and most put their faith in false things.

On the other hand, the real Christians put their faith in the Word of God.

> Romans 10:11 For the scripture saith, Whosoever believeth on him shall not be ashamed.

"Believeth" does not mean the shallow "claim to believe" of the modern false-christianity. Biblical "believers" are "obeyers".

> Acts 2:38 Then Peter said unto them, Repent, and be baptized every one of you in the name of Jesus Christ for the remission of sins, and ye shall receive the gift of the Holy Ghost.
>
> 39 For the promise is unto you, and to your children, and to all that are afar off, even as many as the Lord our God shall call.
>
> 40 And with many other words did he testify and exhort, saying, Save yourselves from this untoward generation.
>
> 41 Then they that gladly received his word were baptized: and the same day there were added unto them about three thousand souls.

Those who "believed" the Apostles, "obeyed" the Apostles.

> Romans 10:16 But they have not all obeyed the gospel. For Esaias saith, Lord, who hath believed our report?

The Apostles counted people who would not obey as "non-believers".

Remember the very next verse that I read before?

> Romans 10:17 So then faith cometh by hearing, and hearing by the word of God.

I preach this Word to you so that your faith will be increased but you have to take the step of faith in obedience to the Word. Otherwise it is wasted.

> James 2:20 But wilt thou know, O vain man, that faith without works is dead?

> James 2:26 For as the body without the spirit is dead, so faith without works is dead also.
>
> James 1:22 But be ye doers of the word, and not hearers only, deceiving your own selves.

Jesus is only the author of eternal salvation for those who obey His Word.

> Hebrews 5:9 And being made perfect, he became the author of eternal salvation unto all them that obey him;

We all have a measure of faith. God help us all that we put our faith into that which is true so that it be a blessing rather than a curse.

A man who puts his faith in a lie will die.

Refuse

* Well, there are a few scenarios that come to mind as to why some refuse the Word of God. *

> II Timothy 4:2 Preach the word; be instant in season, out of season; reprove, rebuke, exhort with all longsuffering and doctrine.
>
> II Timothy 4:3 For the time will come when they will not endure sound doctrine; but after their own lusts shall they heap to themselves teachers, having itching ears;
>
> II Timothy 4:4 And they shall turn away [their] ears from the truth, and shall be turned unto fables.

*Some have turned away from God already and chosen "fables". *

> Romans 8:5 For they that are after the flesh do mind the things of the flesh; but they that are after the Spirit the things of the Spirit.
>
> Romans 8:6 For to be carnally minded [is] death; but to be spiritually minded [is] life and peace.
>
> Romans 8:7 Because the carnal mind [is] enmity against God: for it is not subject to the law of God, neither indeed can be.
>
> Romans 8:8 So then they that are in the flesh cannot please God.

* Some are just too carnal to perceive spiritual things. *

> I Timothy 3:16 And without controversy great is the mystery of godliness: God was manifest in the flesh, justified in the Spirit, seen of angels, preached unto the Gentiles, believed on in the world, received up into glory.

I Timothy 4:1 Now the Spirit speaketh expressly, that in the latter times some shall depart from the faith, giving heed to seducing spirits, and doctrines of devils;

I Timothy 4:2 Speaking lies in hypocrisy; having their conscience seared with a hot iron;

* Some have been seduced by spirits (cults etc) *

Luke 8:11 Now the parable is this: The seed is the word of God.

Luke 8:12 Those by the way side are they that hear; then cometh the devil, and taketh away the word out of their hearts, lest they should believe and be saved.

Luke 8:13 They on the rock [are they], which, when they hear, receive the word with joy; and these have no root, which for a while believe, and in time of temptation fall away.

Luke 8:14 And that which fell among thorns are they, which, when they have heard, go forth, and are choked with cares and riches and pleasures of [this] life, and bring no fruit to perfection.

Luke 8:15 But that on the good ground are they, which in an honest and good heart, having heard the word, keep [it], and bring forth fruit with patience.

* Some are simply not "good ground" *

II Thessalonians 2:10 And with all deceivableness of unrighteousness in them that perish; because they received not the love of the truth, that they might be saved.

II Thessalonians 2:11 And for this cause God shall send them strong delusion, that they should believe a lie:

II Thessalonians 2:12 That they all might be damned who believed not the truth, but had pleasure in unrighteousness.

* Most grievous are those who have simply refused the truth one too many times, and God Himself has sent them delusion so that they will be damned. I believe that there are some represented here on this echo that have crossed that line. *

> II Thessalonians 2:13 But we are bound to give thanks alway to God for you, brethren beloved of the Lord, because God hath from the beginning chosen you to salvation through sanctification of the Spirit and belief of the truth:

* And here we see that belief of the TRUTH is essential for salvation.*

Love of God

Luke 6:27 But I say unto you which hear, Love your enemies, do good to them which hate you,

28 Bless them that curse you, and pray for them which despitefully use you.

29 And unto him that smiteth thee on the one cheek offer also the other; and him that taketh away thy cloke forbid not to take thy coat also.

30 Give to every man that asketh of thee; and of him that taketh away thy goods ask them not again.

31 And as ye would that men should do to you, do ye also to them likewise.

32 For if ye love them which love you, what thank have ye? for sinners also love those that love them.

33 And if ye do good to them which do good to you, what thank have ye? for sinners also do even the same.

34 And if ye lend to them of whom ye hope to receive, what thank have ye? for sinners also lend to sinners, to receive as much again.

35 But love ye your enemies, and do good, and lend, hoping for nothing again; and your reward shall be great, and ye shall be the children of the Highest: for he is kind unto the unthankful and to the evil.

36 Be ye therefore merciful, as your Father also is merciful.

Exodus 34:6 And the LORD passed by before him, and proclaimed, The LORD, The LORD God, merciful and gracious, longsuffering, and abundant in goodness and truth,

Numbers 14:18 The LORD is longsuffering, and of great mercy, forgiving iniquity and transgression, and by no means clearing the guilty, visiting the iniquity of the fathers upon the children unto the third and fourth generation.

Psalms 86:15 But thou, O Lord, art a God full of compassion, and gracious, longsuffering, and plenteous in mercy and truth.

Romans 2:4 Or despisest thou the riches of his goodness and forbearance and longsuffering; not knowing that the goodness of God leadeth thee to repentance?

Romans 9:22 What if God, willing to shew his wrath, and to make his power known, endured with much longsuffering the vessels of wrath fitted to destruction:

2 Corinthians 6:6 By pureness, by knowledge, by longsuffering, by kindness, by the Holy Ghost, by love unfeigned,

Galatians 5:22 But the fruit of the Spirit is love, joy, peace, longsuffering, gentleness, goodness, faith,

1 John 2:5 But whoso keepeth his word, in him verily is the love of God perfected: hereby know we that we are in him.

1 Corinthians 13:4 Charity suffereth long, and is kind; charity envieth not; charity vaunteth not itself, is not puffed up,

5 Doth not behave itself unseemly, seeketh not her own, is not easily provoked, thinketh no evil;

6 Rejoiceth not in iniquity, but rejoiceth in the truth;

2 John 1:6 And this is love, that we walk after his commandments. This is the commandment, That, as ye have heard from the beginning, ye should walk in it.

1 John 2:5 But whoso keepeth his word, in him verily is the love of God perfected: hereby know we that we are in him.

1 John 2:15 Love not the world, neither the things that are in the world. If any man love the world, the love of the Father is not in him.

Galatians 4:16 Am I therefore become your enemy, because I tell you the truth?

Paul's Gospel

Those who reject Paul, reject the Bible. When one rejects the epistles of Paul, one has rejected Christianity.

Jesus said to Peter:

> MAT 16:19 And I will give unto thee the keys of the kingdom of heaven: and whatsoever thou shalt bind on earth shall be bound in heaven: and whatsoever thou shalt loose on earth shall be loosed in heaven.

So if you reject Peter, you reject Christ. Peter said of Paul, accounting Paul's words as scripture:

> 2PETER 3:15 And account [that] the longsuffering of our Lord [is] salvation; even as our beloved brother Paul also according to the wisdom given unto him hath written unto you;
>
> 2PETER 3:16 As also in all [his] epistles, speaking in them of these things; in which are some things hard to be understood, which they that are unlearned and unstable wrest, as [they do] also the other scriptures, unto their own destruction.

The rejectors of Paul are simply rejectors of the Bible and the God of the Bible and do not in any way represent Bible Christianity.

Seeing

Did you ever wonder why some Biblical truths are just incomprehensible to some people? Well, it was designed to be that way:

> Deuteronomy 29:4 Yet the LORD hath not given you an heart to perceive, and eyes to see, and ears to hear, unto this day.

> Jeremiah 5:21 Hear now this, O foolish people, and without understanding; which have eyes, and see not; which have ears, and hear not:

> Matthew 5:18 For verily I say unto you, Till heaven and earth pass, one jot or one tittle shall in no wise pass from the law, till all be fulfilled.

> Matthew 13:11 He answered and said unto them, Because it is given unto you to know the mysteries of the kingdom of heaven, but to them it is not given.
>
> Matthew 13:12 For whosoever hath, to him shall be given, and he shall have more abundance: but whosoever hath not, from him shall be taken away even that he hath.
>
> Matthew 13:13 Therefore speak I to them in parables: because they seeing see not; and hearing they hear not, neither do they understand.
>
> Matthew 13:14 And in them is fulfilled the prophecy of Esaias, which saith, By hearing ye shall hear, and shall not understand; and seeing ye shall see, and shall not perceive:
>
> Matthew 13:15 For this people's heart is waxed gross, and [their] ears are dull of hearing, and their eyes they have closed; lest at any time they should see with [their] eyes and hear with [their] ears, and should understand with [their] heart, and should be converted, and I should heal them.

Matthew 13:16 But blessed [are] your eyes, for they see: and your ears, for they hear.

Matthew 16:17 And Jesus answered and said unto him, Blessed art thou, Simon Bar-jona: for flesh and blood hath not revealed [it] unto thee, but my Father which is in heaven.

John 1:5 And the light shineth in darkness; and the darkness comprehended it not.

John 1:13 Which were born, not of blood, nor of the will of the flesh, nor of the will of man, but of God.

John 3:5 Jesus answered, Verily, verily, I say unto thee, Except a man be born of water and [of] the Spirit, he cannot enter into the kingdom of God.

** Acts 2:38 also contains the elements of "water" and "Spirit" **

John 3:6 That which is born of the flesh is flesh; and that which is born of the Spirit is spirit.

** Now John 3:6 should dispel the myth that the "birth of water" was the natural human birth. (The birth of water is baptism in water in the name of Jesus Christ see Acts 2:38,39)**

Acts 2:38 Then Peter said unto them, Repent, and be baptized every one of you in the name of Jesus Christ for the remission of sins, and ye shall receive the gift of the Holy Ghost.

Acts 2:39 For the promise is unto you, and to your children, and to all that are afar off, [even] as many as the Lord our God shall call.

John 12:40 He hath blinded their eyes, and hardened their heart; that they should not see with [their] eyes, nor understand with [their] heart, and be converted, and I should heal them.

II Corinthians 4:4 In whom the god of this world hath blinded the minds of them which believe not, lest the light of the glorious gospel of Christ, who is the image of God, should shine unto them.

I John 5:18 We know that whosoever is born of God sinneth not; but he that is begotten of God keepeth himself, and that wicked one toucheth him not.

** Some people will begrudgingly "tolerate" truth, but they don't love it, it is an annoyance to them to have certain truths preached. **

II Thessalonians 2:10 And with all deceivableness of unrighteousness in them that perish; because they received not the love of the truth, that they might be saved.

II Thessalonians 2:11 And for this cause God shall send them strong delusion, that they should believe a lie:

II Thessalonians 2:12 That they all might be damned who believed not the truth, but had pleasure in unrighteousness.

II Thessalonians 2:13 But we are bound to give thanks alway to God for you, brethren beloved of the Lord, because God hath from the beginning chosen you to salvation through sanctification of the Spirit and belief of the truth:

** This seems to say that salvation hinges on belief of the truth, so, once again, I submit that if 2 churches are preaching different doctrines then NO WAY could they both really be saved. (and maybe neither one!).**

Tradition

Matthew 15:3 But he answered and said unto them, Why do ye also transgress the commandment of God by your tradition?

Matthew 15:7 [Ye] hypocrites, well did Esaias prophesy of you, saying,

Matthew 15:8 This people draweth nigh unto me with their mouth, and honoureth me with [their] lips; but their heart is far from me.

Matthew 15:9 But in vain they do worship me, teaching [for] doctrines the commandments of men.

Mark 7:13 Making the word of God of none effect through your tradition, which ye have delivered: and many such like things do ye.

Colossians 2:4 And this I say, lest any man should beguile you with enticing words.

Colossians 2:8 Beware lest any man spoil you through philosophy and vain deceit, after the tradition of men, after the rudiments of the world, and not after Christ.

Colossians 2:9 For in him dwelleth all the fulness of the Godhead bodily.

Colossians 2:10 And ye are complete in him, which is the head of all principality and power:

Colossians 2:12 Buried with him in baptism, wherein also ye are risen with [him] through the faith of the operation of God, who hath raised him from the dead.

I Corinthians 15:1 Moreover, brethren, I declare unto you the gospel which I preached unto you, which also ye have received, and wherein ye stand;

I Corinthians 15:2 By which also ye are saved, if ye keep in memory what I preached unto you, unless ye have believed in vain.

Whale Ride

Many are aware of how someone that does not answer the call of God can end up with a whale of a problem on their hands. But I believe that the Lord has given me another insight regarding the matter.

> Jonah 1:1 Now the word of the LORD came unto Jonah the son of Amittai, saying,
>
> 2 Arise, go to Nineveh, that great city, and cry against it; for their wickedness is come up before me.
>
> 3 But Jonah rose up to flee unto Tarshish from the presence of the LORD, and went down to Joppa; and he found a ship going to Tarshish: so he paid the fare thereof, and went down into it, to go with them unto Tarshish from the presence of the LORD.
>
> 4 ¶ But the LORD sent out a great wind into the sea, and there was a mighty tempest in the sea, so that the ship was like to be broken.
>
> 5 Then the mariners were afraid, and cried every man unto his god, and cast forth the wares that were in the ship into the sea, to lighten it of them. But Jonah was gone down into the sides of the ship; and he lay, and was fast asleep.
>
> 6 So the shipmaster came to him, and said unto him, What meanest thou, O sleeper? arise, call upon thy God, if so be that God will think upon us, that we perish not.
>
> 7 And they said every one to his fellow, Come, and let us cast lots, that we may know for whose cause this evil is upon us. So they cast lots, and the lot fell upon Jonah.
>
> 8 Then said they unto him, Tell us, we pray thee, for whose cause this evil is upon us; What is thine occupation? and whence comest thou? what is thy country? and of what people art thou?

9 And he said unto them, I am an Hebrew; and I fear the LORD, the God of heaven, which hath made the sea and the dry land.

10 Then were the men exceedingly afraid, and said unto him, Why hast thou done this? For the men knew that he fled from the presence of the LORD, because he had told them.

11 ¶ Then said they unto him, What shall we do unto thee, that the sea may be calm unto us? for the sea wrought, and was tempestuous.

12 And he said unto them, Take me up, and cast me forth into the sea; so shall the sea be calm unto you: for I know that for my sake this great tempest is upon you.

13 Nevertheless the men rowed hard to bring it to the land; but they could not: for the sea wrought, and was tempestuous against them.

14 Wherefore they cried unto the LORD, and said, We beseech thee, O LORD, we beseech thee, let us not perish for this man's life, and lay not upon us innocent blood: for thou, O LORD, hast done as it pleased thee.

15 So they took up Jonah, and cast him forth into the sea: and the sea ceased from her raging.

16 Then the men feared the LORD exceedingly, and offered a sacrifice unto the LORD, and made vows.

17 Now the LORD had prepared a great fish to swallow up Jonah. And Jonah was in the belly of the fish three days and three nights.

1 ¶ Then Jonah prayed unto the LORD his God out of the fish's belly,

Many are familiar of the events regarding Jonah and the whale and his hardship because of his refusal to obey God. But do we consider that the whale was Jonah's salvation. Without that whale he would have been history, well I mean he is history now but without that fish he would have been history a lot sooner.

What is the point here? I believe the point is that we should be always thankful even during times that are unpleasant to us.

> 1 Thessalonians 5:18 In every thing give thanks: for this is the will of God in Christ Jesus concerning you.

That is the verse right after verse 5:17 Pray without ceasing.

It is God's will for us to be thankful regardless of circumstance or situation.

Let us consider Jonah. When he was trapped inside of that whale he did not know that he was going to not only survive but get to be this real famous guy and even get his name in the Bible and everything. At the time it probably appeared to him that things were not going well and there was no happy ending in site. Was he thinking wow this is great I'll probably be a famous preacher and save thousands from destruction by preaching them into repentance. I doubt it, and there is a good possibility that he was depressed and sad.

This was probably unpleasant for him and as we all know fish are seldom harvested for their aroma. The air in there must have been like an un burped fish burp.

Of course we know that Jonah prayed to God from the belly of the fish. He didn't just sit there (assuming he could sit, eh?) in his misery, he prayed to God. Note that nothing got resolved until Jonah prayed, eh?

> Jonah 2:1 Then Jonah prayed unto the LORD his God out of the fish's belly,

But as we say the rest is history, Jonah hit some bumps in the road but he recovered and prayed to God, obeyed God and ended up even getting his name in the Bible, yea even a whole book of the Bible named after him and him as a successful preacher who saved many a soul from destruction.

What of Joseph? Do you think it seemed to him when he was cast into a pit by his unfaithful brethren that he was taking the first steps to ruling Egypt? But he stayed faithful to God through all (and we know he was not happy about being in prison and stuff) and he ended up being a famous ruler and getting his name in the Bible too as one of the "good guys."

Remember, though, when these guys were going through some very hard times the parts of the Bible they are in had not been written yet so they did not know where they were headed and I don't find where God told them what was going to happen.

Did God tell Jonah in advance that he would be successful and Nineveh would repent?

Did God tell Joseph that he would rule Egypt? Now I know that Joseph did have dreams to encourage him but none of these had promises equal to that which we have been promised. The New Testament Church had not yet begun. Think about it, we have greater promises and much greater blessings than they did.

While these guys were famous and got their names in the Bible an stuff are we not better off than they? We are in the Rapture generation and have the Gift of the Holy Ghost speaking in tongues available. We have Jesus Name Baptism available so that every past sin can be simply washed away. Would they not trade places with us if they could? There was no Acts 2:38 new birth available to them.

> 1 Thessalonians 5:18 In every thing give thanks: for this is the will of God in Christ Jesus concerning you.

We are a blessed people. Even when we have major challenges we usually have a roof over our heads and something to eat while we endure them.

It is important to be faithful and thankful regardless of circumstance. God may just have a greater blessing for us right around the corner.

The Fullness of the Godhead

Roots

Genesis 1:1 In the beginning God created the heaven and the earth.

Genesis 1:2 And the earth was without form, and void; and darkness [was] upon the face of the deep. And the Spirit of God moved upon the face of the waters.

Genesis 1:3 And God said, Let there be light: and there was light.

Genesis 1:4 And God saw the light, that [it was] good: and God divided the light from the darkness.

Genesis 1:5 And God called the light Day, and the darkness he called Night. And the evening and the morning were the first day.

Genesis 1:6 And God said, Let there be a firmament in the midst of the waters, and let it divide the waters from the waters.

Genesis 1:7 And God made the firmament, and divided the waters which [were] under the firmament from the waters which [were] above the firmament: and it was so.

Genesis 1:8 And God called the firmament Heaven. And the evening and the morning were the second day.

Genesis 1:9 And God said, Let the waters under the heaven be gathered together unto one place, and let the dry [land] appear: and it was so.

Genesis 1:10 And God called the dry [land] Earth; and the gathering together of the waters called he Seas: and God saw that [it was] good.

Genesis 1:11 And God said, Let the earth bring forth grass, the herb yielding seed, [and] the fruit tree yielding fruit after his kind, whose seed [is] in itself, upon the earth: and it was so.

Genesis 1:12 And the earth brought forth grass, [and] herb yielding seed after his kind, and the tree yielding fruit, whose seed [was] in itself, after his kind: and God saw that [it was] good.

Genesis 1:13 And the evening and the morning were the third day.

Genesis 1:14 And God said, Let there be lights in the firmament of the heaven to divide the day from the night; and let them be for signs, and for seasons, and for days, and years:

Genesis 1:15 And let them be for lights in the firmament of the heaven to give light upon the earth: and it was so.

Genesis 1:16 And God made two great lights; the greater light to rule the day, and the lesser light to rule the night: [he made] the stars also.

Genesis 1:17 And God set them in the firmament of the heaven to give light upon the earth,

Genesis 1:18 And to rule over the day and over the night, and to divide the light from the darkness: and God saw that [it was] good.

Genesis 1:19 And the evening and the morning were the fourth day.

Genesis 1:20 And God said, Let the waters bring forth abundantly the moving creature that hath life, and fowl [that] may fly above the earth in the open firmament of heaven.

Genesis 1:21 And God created great whales, and every living creature that moveth, which the waters brought forth abundantly, after their kind, and every winged fowl after his kind: and God saw that [it was] good.

Genesis 1:22 And God blessed them, saying, Be fruitful, and multiply, and fill the waters in the seas, and let fowl multiply in the earth.

Genesis 1:23 And the evening and the morning were the fifth day.

Genesis 1:24 And God said, Let the earth bring forth the living creature after his kind, cattle, and creeping thing, and beast of the earth after his kind: and it was so.

Genesis 1:25 And God made the beast of the earth after his kind, and cattle after their kind, and every thing that creepeth upon the earth after his kind: and God saw that [it was] good.

Genesis 1:26 And God said, Let us make man in our image, after our likeness: and let them have dominion over the fish of the sea, and over the fowl of the air, and over the cattle, and over all the earth, and over every creeping thing that creepeth upon the earth.

Genesis 1:27 So God created man in his [own] image, in the image of God created he him; male and female created he them.

Isaiah 44:24 Thus saith the LORD, thy redeemer, and he that formed thee from the womb, I [am] the LORD that maketh all [things]; that stretcheth forth the heavens alone; that spreadeth abroad the earth by myself;

Isaiah 45:23 I have sworn by myself, the word is gone out of my mouth [in] righteousness, and shall not return, That unto me every knee shall bow, every tongue shall swear.

John 1:1 In the beginning was the Word, and the Word was with God, and the Word was God.

John 1:2 The same was in the beginning with God.

John 1:3 All things were made by him; and without him was not any thing made that was made.

John 1:14 And the Word was made flesh, and dwelt among us, (and we beheld his glory, the glory as of the only begotten of the Father,) full of grace and truth.

And Son

> II John 1:9 Whosoever transgresseth, and abideth not in the doctrine of Christ, hath not God. He that abideth in the doctrine of Christ, he hath both the Father and the Son.

Those who obey Acts 2:38 have both the flesh and Spirit of God. They have both the 'Son' (flesh) and the Spirit (Father) of the ONE GOD named "Jesus".

> Acts 19:10 And this continued by the space of two years; so that all they which dwelt in Asia heard the word of the Lord Jesus, both Jews and Greeks.

The Word of the Lord Jesus IS the Acts 2:38 message:

> Acts 2:38 Then Peter said unto them, Repent, and be baptized every one of you in the name of Jesus Christ for the remission of sins, and ye shall receive the gift of the Holy Ghost. Acts 2:39 For the promise is unto you, and to your children, and to all that are afar off, [even] as many as the Lord our God shall call.

Notice carefully, please, that the doctrine that Paul referred to in Acts 19:10 as "the word of the Lord Jesus" was the Acts 2:38 salvation plan. Backing up a few verses we see that Paul founded the Ephesian Church on the "word of the Lord Jesus". See how they OBEYED Acts 2:38:

> Acts 19:2 He said unto them, Have ye received the Holy Ghost since ye believed? And they said unto him, We have not so much as heard whether there be any Holy Ghost.

> Acts 19:3 And he said unto them, Unto what then were ye baptized? And they said, Unto John's baptism.

> Acts 19:4 Then said Paul, John verily baptized with the baptism of repentance, saying unto the people, that they should believe on him which should come after him, that is, on Christ Jesus.

> Acts 19:5 When they heard [this], they were baptized in the name of the Lord Jesus.

> Acts 19:6 And when Paul had laid [his] hands upon them, the Holy Ghost came on them; and they spake with tongues, and prophesied.

> Galatians 3:27 For as many of you as have been baptized into Christ have put on Christ.

Through Jesus name baptism, one "puts on Christ" or the "Son". Jesus name water baptism IS the re-birth of flesh that Jesus referred to in John 3:5.

> John 3:5 Jesus answered, Verily, verily, I say unto thee, Except a man be born of water and [of] the Spirit, he cannot enter into the kingdom of God.

Notice that the Acts 2:38 salvation (referred to as "the word of the Lord Jesus" in Acts 19:10) contains BOTH the elements "water" and "Spirit", which are BOTH essential for salvation.

> John 4:24 God [is] a Spirit: and they that worship him must worship [him] in spirit and in truth.

God the Father is the Spirit that came to earth in the form of the Lord Jesus Christ, or the "Son of man".

> 1 Tim 3:16 And without controversy great is the mystery of godliness: God was manifest in the flesh, justified in the Spirit, seen of angels, preached unto the Gentiles, believed on in the world, received up into glory.

Look at this next verse, note that the Spirit of God IS the Spirit of Christ.

> Rom 8:9 But ye are not in the flesh, but in the Spirit, if so be that the Spirit of God dwell in you. Now if any man have not the Spirit of Christ, he is none of his.

God the Father is a Spirit (remember John 4:24). God is holy! God is a "Holy Spirit". The Spirit of God IS the Spirit of Christ IS the Holy Spirit.

Those who obey (receive) Acts 2:38 receive the 'Son' (the flesh) AND the "Father" (the Spirit, remember, that sent forth His flesh).

> Luke 9:48 And said unto them, Whosoever shall receive this child in my name receiveth me: and whosoever shall receive me receiveth him that sent me: for he that is least among you all, the same shall be great.

The Spirit of truth was dwelling WITH them in the flesh body of the Lord

Jesus Christ BECAUSE: The Spirit of Truth IS the Spirit of Christ IS the Spirit of God IS the Holy Spirit (AKA the "Holy Ghost"). Yes, ONE God, and ONE ONLY!

> John 14:17 [Even] the Spirit of truth; whom the world cannot receive, because it seeth him not, neither knoweth him: but ye know him; for he dwelleth with you, and shall be in you.

Jesus said that HE was dwelling with them and that He would be IN THEM.

When a person receives the Holy Ghost speaking in tongues, they receive the Spirit of God the Father, which IS the Spirit of Christ. When a person is baptized in Jesus name they "put on Christ", they put o "the Son".

> Gal 3:27 For as many of you as have been baptized into Christ have put on Christ.

> II John 1:9 Whosoever transgresseth, and abideth not in the doctrine of Christ, hath not God. He that abideth in the doctrine of Christ, he hath both the Father and the Son.

Those who reject Acts 2:38 salvation (the doctrine of Christ) reject BOTH the Spirit (Father) and flesh (Son) of the ONE GOD named Jesus.

I Am

John 8:58 Jesus said unto them, Verily, verily, I say unto you, Before Abraham was, I am.

Exodus 3:14 And God said unto Moses, I AM THAT I AM: and he said, Thus shalt thou say unto the children of Israel, I AM hath sent me unto you.

Matthew 13:13 Therefore speak I to them in parables: because they seeing see not; and hearing they hear not, neither do they understand.

Revelation 1:8 I am Alpha and Omega, the beginning and the ending, saith the Lord, which is, and which was, and which is to come, the Almighty.

Revelation 1:11 Saying, I am Alpha and Omega, the first and the last: and, What thou seest, write in a book, and send *it* unto the seven churches which are in Asia; unto Ephesus, and unto Smyrna, and unto Pergamos, and unto Thyatira, and unto Sardis, and unto Philadelphia, and unto Laodicea.

Revelation 1:17-18 And when I saw him, I fell at his feet as dead. And he laid his right hand upon me, saying unto me, Fear not; I am the first and the last: I *am* he that liveth, and was dead; and, behold, I am alive for evermore, Amen; and have the keys of hell and of death.

Revelation 2:23 And I will kill her children with death; and all the churches shall know that I am he which searcheth the reins and hearts: and I will give unto every one of you according to your works.

Revelation 21:6 And he said unto me, It is done. I am Alpha and Omega, the beginning and the end. I will give unto him that is athirst of the fountain of the water of life freely.

Revelation 22:13 I am Alpha and Omega, the beginning and the end, the first and the last.

Revelation 22:16 I Jesus have sent mine angel to testify unto you these things in the churches. I am the root and the offspring of David, *and* the bright and morning star.

Savior

John 8:58 Jesus said unto them, Verily, verily, I say unto you, Before Abraham was, I am.

Exodus 3:14 And God said unto Moses, I AM THAT I AM: and he said, Thus shalt thou say unto the children of Israel, I AM hath sent me unto you.

Matthew 13:13 Therefore speak I to them in parables: because they seeing see not; and hearing they hear not, neither do they understand.

Isaiah 43:11 I, [even] I, [am] the LORD; and beside me [there is] no saviour.

Isaiah 45:21 Tell ye, and bring [them] near; yea, let them take counsel together: who hath declared this from ancient time? [who] hath told it from that time? [have] not I the LORD? and [there is] no God else beside me; a just God and a Saviour; [there is] none beside me.

Hosea 13:4 Yet I [am] the LORD thy God from the land of Egypt, and thou shalt know no god but me: for [there is] no saviour beside me.

Luke 2:11 For unto you is born this day in the city of David a Saviour, which is Christ the Lord.

*** Since there is no saviour except for Jehovah,it must have been Jehovah God coming to earth in a human form as "the son".

> John 14:9 Jesus saith unto him, Have I been so long time with you, and yet hast thou not known me, Philip? he that hath seen me hath seen the Father; and how sayest thou [then], Shew us the Father?

> John 10:30 I and [my] Father are one.

> John 8:58 Jesus said unto them, Verily, verily, I say unto you, Before Abraham was, I am.

*** Jesus revealed that he really was the Father, the "I AM" ***

Isaiah 44:8 Fear ye not, neither be afraid: have not I told thee from that time, and have declared [it]? ye [are] even my witnesses. Is there a God beside me? yea, [there is] no God; I know not [any].

*** I believe that if there had been any other "personages" here that Jehovah would have been aware of them. ***

> II John 1:7 For many deceivers are entered into the world, who confess not that Jesus Christ is come in the flesh. This is a deceiver and an antichrist.

*** Those who deny that "Jehovah saviour" came "in the flesh" are of the antichrist spirit. That is why both the Baha's and the trinitarian's are antichrist deceivers. The trinitarian teaches that only a "junior member" or "second person" of a "family" or "group" of gods came to earth. And, many other antichrist religions teach that Jesus was just one of several "saviors".

Three Records

> 1 John 5:7 For there are three that bear record in heaven, the Father, the Word, and the Holy Ghost: and these three are one.

Since the verse declares that it is only speaking of one being, then it is not stretching things to state that it is referring to three records in heaven of that single being.

The very next verse goes on to describe three separate items that are separate, but in agreement.

> 1 John 5:8 And there are three that bear witness in earth, the Spirit, and the water, and the blood: and these three agree in one.

There is a distinct difference between three records of one God and three separate witnesses of that one God.

Many confuse the aspects of these verses and try to mix them up to promote polytheism.

Created

John 1:10 He was in the world, and the world was made by him, and the world knew him not.

*** So Jesus created the world ***

John 1:11 He came unto his own, and his own received him not.

*** Jehovah came to the Jews but they didn't recognize Him. ***

Isaiah 44:24 Thus saith the LORD, thy redeemer, and he that formed thee from the womb, I [am] the LORD that maketh all [things]; that stretcheth forth the heavens alone; that spreadeth abroad the earth by myself;

*** Here Jesus explains that he created the earth ALONE ***

Zechariah 12:1 The burden of the word of the LORD for Israel, saith the LORD, which stretcheth forth the heavens, and layeth the foundation of the earth, and formeth the spirit of man within him.

Malachi 3:1 Behold, I will send my messenger, and he shall prepare the way before me: and the Lord, whom ye seek, shall suddenly come to his temple, even the messenger of the covenant, whom ye delight in: behold, he shall come, saith the LORD of hosts.

*** Jehovah came suddenly to His temple. ****

Jesus Christ, Jehovah God manifest in the flesh. Jesus Christ is God!

Flesh & Spirit

In this post I will attempt to explain how the son could pray to the father and still not be two separate gods (or persons). The key to understanding this is understanding "flesh" and "spirit":...... Here, we see that God the Father of the old testament does NOT have flesh and bone (so consider also "The Right Hand" does not mean a big ole arm)..See, God is a Spirit and a spirit hath NOT flesh and bone.

> Luke 24:39 Behold my hands and my feet, that it is I myself: handle me, and see; for a spirit hath not flesh and bones, as ye see me have.
>
> John 4:24 God [is] a Spirit: and they that worship him must worship [him] in spirit and in truth....

Also notice the importance of TRUTH in worshiping God, We MUST know WHO we are worshiping! God of the old testament came to earth in human form, he did NOT have blood to shed for anyone; sooooo he took on a human body and came to his people:......

> John 1:11 He came unto his own, and his own received him not.
>
> II Corinthians 5:19 To wit, that God was in Christ, reconciling the world unto himself, not imputing their trespasses unto them; and hath committed unto us the word of reconciliation.

In other words God came in the form of Christ, not a "second person" or "Jehovah Jr.", but God HIMSELF in a human body..the Lord of Glory himself....

> I Corinthians 2:8 Which none of the princes of this world knew: for had they known [it], they would not have crucified the Lord of glory.

God did not send anyone else to "do the dirty work"; HE CAME HIMSELF and took on a life and then gave up that life for us!!

> I John 3:16 Hereby perceive we the love [of God], because he laid down his life for us...."

God himself in a human body, but even then the Spirit of God was greater than the flesh of God..even God had to keep his flesh in subjection to his Spirit..It was not the flesh body of God that did the miracles, but rather the Spirit that was in the body...and, in the garden it was flesh praying to Spirit (not one god praying to another)

> John 14:10 Believest thou not that I am in the Father, and the Father in me? the words that I speak unto you I speak not of myself: but the Father that dwelleth in me, he doeth the works.
>
> John 5:37 And the Father himself, which hath sent me, hath borne witness of me. Ye have neither heard his voice at any time, nor seen his shape.

(The Father IN the son = The Spirit in the flesh)

> Matthew 13:17 For verily I say unto you, That many prophets and righteous [men] have desired to see [those things] which ye see, and have not seen [them]; and to hear [those things] which ye hear, and have not heard [them].
>
> Matthew 17:5 While he yet spake, behold, a bright cloud overshadowed them: and behold a voice out of the cloud, which said, This is my beloved Son, in whom I am well pleased; hear ye him.
>
> Mark 1:11 And there came a voice from heaven, [saying], Thou art my beloved Son, in whom I am well pleased.
>
> II Peter 1:17 For he received from God the Father honour and glory, when there came such a voice to him from the excellent glory, This is my beloved Son, in whom I am well pleased.

(Notice "IN WHOM" in each verse, the Father (spirit) was IN the son (flesh)).

> John 14:9 Jesus saith unto him, Have I been so long time with you, and yet hast thou not known me, Philip? he that hath seen me hath seen the Father; and how sayest thou [then], Shew us the Father?

> John 14:10 Believest thou not that I am in the Father, and the Father in me? the words that I speak unto you I speak not of myself: but the Father that dwelleth in me, he doeth the works.....

Jesus Christ, Jehovah God in the flesh....Why is this so important?!?

> Mark 12:29 And Jesus answered him, The first of all the commandments [is], Hear, O Israel; The Lord our God is one Lord:

Not three lords, not "three separate persons", ONE GOD: JESUS!!.....

Fullness

Colossians 2:8 Beware lest any man spoil you through philosophy and vain deceit, after the tradition of men, after the rudiments of the world, and not after Christ.

Colossians 2:9 For in him dwelleth all the fullness of the Godhead bodily.

Colossians 2:10 And ye are complete in him, which is the head of all principality and power:

John 14:9 Jesus saith unto him, Have I been so long time with you, and yet hast thou not known me, Philip? he that hath seen me hath seen the Father; and how sayest thou [then], Shew us the Father?

Holy One

I Timothy 3:16 And without controversy great is the mystery of godliness: God was manifest in the flesh, justified in the Spirit, seen of angels, preached unto the Gentiles, believed on in the world, received up into glory.

Revelation 1:8 I am Alpha and Omega, the beginning and the ending, saith the Lord, which is, and which was, and which is to come, the Almighty.

Revelation 1:11 Saying, I am Alpha and Omega, the first and the last: and, What thou seest, write in a book, and send [it] unto the seven churches which are in Asia; unto Ephesus, and unto Smyrna, and unto Pergamos, and unto Thyatira, and unto Sardis, unto Philadelphia, and unto Laodicea.

Revelation 21:6 And he said unto me, It is done. I am Alpha and Omega, the beginning and the end. I will give unto him that is athirst of the fountain of the water of life freely.

Revelation 22:13 I am Alpha and Omega, the beginning and the end, the first and the last.

Isaiah 45:6 That they may know from the rising of the sun, and from the west, that [there is] none beside me. I [am] the LORD, and [there is] none else.

Isaiah 45:21 Tell ye, and bring [them] near; yea, let them take counsel together: who hath declared this from ancient time? [who] hath told it from that time? [have] not I the LORD? and [there is] no God else beside me; a just God and a Saviour; [there is] none beside me.

John 4:24 God [is] a Spirit: and they that worship him must worship [him] in spirit and in truth.

* God is a Spirit (who became flesh) *

I Samuel 6:20 And the men of Beth-shemesh said, Who is able to stand before this holy LORD God? and to whom shall he go up from us?

Isaiah 54:5 For thy Maker [is] thine husband; the LORD of hosts [is] his name; and thy Redeemer the Holy One of Israel; The God of the whole earth shall he be called.

* God is holy. *

* God is a Spirit. God is holy. God is a Holy Spirit. *

Philippians 1:19 For I know that this shall turn to my salvation through your prayer, and the supply of the Spirit of Jesus Christ,

Romans 8:9 But ye are not in the flesh, but in the Spirit, if so be that the Spirit of God dwell in you. Now if any man have not the Spirit of Christ, he is none of his.

The Spirit of God was manifest in the flesh. The Spirit of Christ was manifest in the flesh. The Spirit of God is the Spirit of Christ which is a Holy Spirit. *

I Timothy 3:16 And without controversy great is the mystery of godliness: God was manifest in the flesh, justified in the Spirit, seen of angels, preached unto the Gentiles, believed on in the world, received up into glory.

God Jesus

Deut 4:39 Know therefore this day, and consider it in thine heart, that the Lord he is God in heaven above, and upon the earth beneath; there is none else.

Deut 6:4 Hear, O Israel: The Lord our God is one Lord:

Deut 32:39 See now that I, even I, am he, and THERE IS NO GOD WITH ME: I kill, and I make alive; I wound and I heal: neither is there any that can deliver out of my hand.

Psalms 86:10 For thou art great, and doest wonderous things: THOU ART GOD ALONE.

Isaiah 43:3 For I am the Lord thy God, the Holy One of Israel, THY SAVIOR: I gave Egypt for thy ransom, Ethiopia and Seba for thee.

Isaiah 43:10 Ye are my witnesses, sayeth the Lord, and my servant whom I have chosen; that ye may know and believe me, and understand that I am he: before me there was no God formed, neither shall there be after me.

Isaiah 43:11 I, even I, am the Lord, and BESIDES ME THERE IS NO SAVIOR.

Isaiah 44:6 Thus saith the Lord, the King of Israel, and his redeemer the Lord of hosts: I am the first, and I am the last, and BESIDE ME THERE IS NO GOD.

Isaiah 44:24 Thus saith the Lord, thy redeemer, and he that formed thee from the womb, I am the Lord that maketh all things; that stretcheth forth the heavens ALONE; that spreadeth abroad the earth BY MYSELF;

Isaiah 45:5 ¶ I am the LORD, and there is none else, there is no God beside me: I girded thee, though thou hast not known me:

6 That they may know from the rising of the sun, and from the west, that there is none beside me. I am the LORD, and there is none else.

Isaiah 45:18 For thus saith the LORD that created the heavens; God himself that formed the earth and made it; he hath established it, he created it not in vain, he formed it to be inhabited: I am the LORD; and there is none else.

Isaiah 45:21 Tell ye, and bring them near; yea, let them take counsel together: who hath declared this from ancient time? who hath told it from that time? have not I the LORD? and there is no God else beside me; a just God and a Saviour; there is none beside me.

22 Look unto me, and be ye saved, all the ends of the earth: for I am God, and there is none else.

23 I have sworn by myself, the word is gone out of my mouth in righteousness, and shall not return, That unto me every knee shall bow, every tongue shall swear.

Isaiah 46:5 ¶ To whom will ye liken me, and make me equal, and compare me, that we may be like?

Isaiah 46:9 Remember the former things of old: for I am God, and there is none else; I am God, and there is none like me,

Isaiah 47:10 For thou hast trusted in thy wickedness: thou hast said, None seeth me. Thy wisdom and thy knowledge, it hath perverted thee; and thou hast said in thine heart, I am, and none else beside me.

Isaiah 48:11 For mine own sake, even for mine own sake, will I do it: for how should my name be polluted? and I will not give my glory unto another.

Titus 1:3 But hath in due times manifested his word through preaching, which is committed unto me according to the commandment of GOD OUR SAVIOR.

Titus 3:4 But after that the kindness and love of GOD OUR SAVIOR toward man appeared,

Mark 12:29 And Jesus answered him, The first of all the commandments is, Hear, O Israel; the Lord our God is one Lord.

Ephesians 4:5 ONE LORD, one faith, one baptism.

I Tim 3:16 And without controversy great is the mystery of godliness: GOD WAS MANIFEST IN THE FLESH, justified in the Spirit, seen of angels, preached unto the Gentiles, believed on in the world, received up into glory.

I John 3:16 Hereby perceive we the love of God, because he laid down HIS LIFE for us: and we ought to lay down our lives for the brethren.

St. John 14:9 Jesus saith unto him, Have I been so long time with you, and yet HAST THOU NOT KNOWN ME, Phillip? HE THAT HATH SEEN ME HATH SEEN THE FATHER; and how sayest thou then, Shew us the Father?

Isaiah 9:6 For unto us a CHILD is born, unto us a SON is given: and the government shall be upon his shoulder: and his name shall be called Wonderful, Counsellor, THE MIGHTY GOD, THE EVERLASTING FATHER, the Prince of Peace.

Jude 25 To the only wise GOD OUR SAVIOR, be glory and majesty, dominion and power, both now and forever. Amen..................

It was God on the Cross

The Oneness belief, the religion of the Bible, has at its core, the belief that Jesus Christ is Jehovah God, the Everlasting Father, the Lord of Glory.

Jesus has existed as "I AM" and "Alpha & Omega". While the flesh human body of Jesus was created, "made of a woman", the individual who inhabited that body was none other than the Lord of Glory, Jehovah Saviour.

> 1 Corinthians 2:8 Which none of the princes of this world knew: for had they known it , they would not have crucified the Lord of glory.

It was God Himself on the cross, the Great "I AM", the "Alpha & Omega". The Great "I AM", The Alpha and Omega, allowed Himself to be crucified.

> 1 John 3:16 Hereby perceive we the love of God, because he laid down his life for us: and we ought to lay down our lives for the brethren.

God provided Himself as a sacrifice.

> Genesis 22:8 And Abraham said, My son, God will provide himself a lamb for a burnt offering: so they went both of them together.

God became the lamb. And that is the foundation core of real, Acts 2:38, Oneness Christianity.

Jesus is God

Let us consider that some things in the word of God are clear and absolute. There are other things that, if not viewed in the light of the absolutes can infer heretical conclusions. Now, there has never been an heretic who was not convinced he was right (and saved); and there was never an heretic who did not have scripture that seemed to infer his correctness......But TRUTH is essential for salvation!! Not just accepting truth, but LOVING IT!!!

> II Thessalonians 2:9 [Even him], whose coming is after the working of Satan with all power and signs and lying wonders,
>
> II Thessalonians 2:10 And with all deceivableness of unrighteousness in them that perish; because they received not the LOVE OF THE TRUTH, that they might be saved.
>
> II Thessalonians 2:11 And for this cause GOD SHALL SEND THEM STRONG DELUSION, that they should believe a lie:
>
> II Thessalonians 2:12 That they all might be DAMNED WHO BELIEVED NOT THE TRUTH, but had pleasure in unrighteousness.

Now, friend, this says that if you don't love the truth, then God himself will send you STRONG DELUSION!! If you don't believe the truth you will be damned...So that is how important accuracy in doctrine is!! It is a matter of HEAVEN or HELL! NOW, there are many scriptures, if viewed carnally without knowledge, that can be misconstrued and a false doctrine built:

> Exodus 3:4 And when the LORD saw that he turned aside to see, God called unto him out of the midst of the bush, and said, Moses, Moses. And he said, Here [am] I.
>
> Exodus 3:5 And he said, Draw not nigh hither: put off thy shoes from off thy feet, for the place whereon thou standest [is] holy ground.

> Exodus 3:6 Moreover he said, I [am] the God of thy father, the God of Abraham, the God of Isaac, and the God of Jacob. And Moses hid his face; for he was afraid to look upon God.

NOW, does this mean that there is a "bush" in the GodHead? Are we to infer that God is a bush?? Did Moses really SEE God??

> I John 4:12 No man hath seen God at any time.... Because of the ABSOLUTE in John 4:12 we see that Moses only saw a manifestation of God... NOW, it is essential to know who God is because MANY are merely worshipping figments of human imagination. We must know God, by his WORD!!:..

> Jeremiah 16:20 Shall a man make gods unto himself, and they[are] no gods?....

NOW...

> John 4:24 God [is] a Spirit: and they that worship him must worship [him] in spirit and in truth.

> Luke 24:39 Behold my hands and my feet, that it is I myself: handle me, and see; for a spirit hath not flesh and bones, as ye see me have.

....God is a SPIRIT and a SPIRIT HATH NOT FLESH AND BONE....Consider God's flesh and God's Spirit...Flesh and Spirit... Jesus prayed to the Father. Jesus said that the Father was greater. There was a voice from heaven at his baptism. When Jesus prayed, It was flesh praying to Spirit, flesh yielding to Spirit (in the garden)...Jesus said that the Father was greater (of course the Spirit is greater than the flesh)...A voice from heaven for men to hear, a voice from an animal, a voice from a bush.

John 8:58 Jesus said unto them, Verily, verily, I say unto you, Before Abraham was, I am.

(It was Jesus SPEAKING out of the burning bush).....NOW these things can infer more than one person in the GodHead UNLESS we view them in the Light of some other ABSOLUTES:

Deut 4:35 Unto thee it was shewed, that thou mightest know that the Lord he is God; there is none else beside him.

Deut 4:39 Know therefore this day, and consider it in thine heart, that the Lord he is God in heaven above, and upon the earth beneath; there is none else.

Deut 6:4 Hear, O Israel: The Lord our God is one Lord:

Deut 32:39 See now that I, even I, am he, and THERE IS NO GOD WITH ME: I kill, and I make alive; I wound and I heal: neither is there any that can deliver out of my hand.

Psalms 86:10 For thou art great, and doest wondrous things: THOU ART GOD ALONE.

Isaiah 43:3 For I am the Lord thy God, the Holy One of Israel, THY SAVIOR: I gave Egypt for thy ransom, Ethiopia and Seba for thee.

Isaiah 43:10 Ye are my witnesses, sayeth the Lord, and my servant whom I have chosen; that ye may know and believe me, and understand that I am he: before me there was no God formed, neither shall there be after me.

Isaiah 43:11 I, even I, am the Lord, and BESIDES ME THERE IS NO SAVIOR.

Isaiah 44:6 Thus saith the Lord, the King of Israel, and his redeemer the Lord of hosts: I am the first, and I am the last, and BESIDE ME THERE IS NO GOD.

Isaiah 44:24 Thus saith the Lord, thy redeemer, and he that formed thee from the womb, I am the Lord that maketh all things; that stretcheth forth the heavens ALONE; that spreadeth abroad the earth BY MYSELF;

See also: Isaiah 45:5, 6, 18, 21, 22, CH 46:5, 9, CH 47:10, CH 48:11

Titus 1:3 But hath in due times manifested his word through preaching, which is committed unto me according to the commandment of GOD OUR SAVIOR.

Titus 3:4 But after that the kindness and love of GOD OUR SAVIOR toward man appeared,

Mark 12:29 And Jesus answered him, The first of all the commandments is, Hear, O Israel; the Lord our God is one Lord.

Ephesians 4:5 ONE LORD, one faith, one baptism.

I Tim 3:16 And without controversy great is the mystery of godliness: GOD WAS MANIFEST IN THE FLESH, justified in the Spirit, seen of angels, preached unto the Gentiles, believed on in the world, received up into glory.

I John 3:16 Hereby perceive we the love of God, because he laid down HIS LIFE for us: and we ought to lay down our lives for the brethren.

St. John 14:9 Jesus saith unto him, Have I been so long time with you, and yet HAST THOU NOT KNOWN ME, Phillip? HE THAT HATH SEEN ME HATH SEEN THE FATHER; and how sayest thou then, Shew us the Father?

Isaiah 9:6 For unto us a CHILD is born, unto us a SON is given: and the government shall be upon his shoulder: and his name shall be called Wonderful, Counsellor, THE MIGHTY GOD, THE EVERLASTING FATHER, the Prince of Peace.

Jude 25 To the only wise GOD OUR SAVIOR, be glory and majesty, dominion and power, both now and forever. Amen

John 1:1-14

The trinity philosophy deceives the gullible into thinking that there are three gods, but a quick look John 1 and a few other verses shows the truth of the matter. John 1:1-14 refers to Jehovah God (the Father).

> John 1:1 In the beginning was the Word, and the Word was with God, and the Word was God.
>
> John 1:2 The same was in the beginning with God.
>
> John 1:3 All things were made by him; and without him was not any thing made that was made.

* We see here in Isaiah that Jehovah God stretched forth the heavens by Himself, so verses 1-3 were clearly talking about Jehovah. *

> Isaiah 44:24 Thus saith the LORD, thy redeemer, and he that formed thee from the womb, I [am] the LORD that maketh all [things]; that stretcheth forth the heavens alone; that spreadeth abroad the earth by myself;
>
> Isaiah 44:25 That frustrateth the tokens of the liars, and maketh diviners mad; that turneth wise [men] backward, and maketh their knowledge foolish;

> John 1:4 In him was life; and the life was the light of men.
>
> John 1:5 And the light shineth in darkness; and the darkness comprehended it not.
>
> John 1:6 There was a man sent from God, whose name [was] John.
>
> John 1:7 The same came for a witness, to bear witness of the Light, that all [men] through him might believe.
>
> John 1:8 He was not that Light, but [was sent] to bear witness of that Light.

John 1:9 [That] was the true Light, which lighteth every man that cometh into the world.

I Timothy 3:16 And without controversy great is the mystery of godliness: God was manifest in the flesh, justified in the Spirit, seen of angels, preached unto the Gentiles, believed on in the world, received up into glory.

* Here we see where Jehovah came into the world that He had made. *

John 1:10 He was in the world, and the world was made by him, and the world knew him not.

John 1:11 He came unto his own, and his own received him not.

Malachi 3:1 Behold, I will send my messenger, and he shall prepare the way before me: and the Lord, whom ye seek, shall suddenly come to his temple, even the messenger of the covenant, whom ye delight in: behold, he shall come, saith the LORD of hosts.

Luke 2:46 And it came to pass, that after three days they found him in the temple, sitting in the midst of the doctors, both hearing them, and asking them questions.

* Jesus came suddenly to His temple. They just weren't expecting Him to be in the body of a twelve year old boy. *

John 1:12 But as many as received him, to them gave he power to become the sons of God, [even] to them that believe on his name:

Matthew 1:21 And she shall bring forth a son, and thou shalt call his name JESUS: for he shall save his people from their sins.

Luke 1:31 And, behold, thou shalt conceive in thy womb, and bring forth a son, and shalt call his name JESUS.

* We see here that when the everlasting Father (God) came to earth His name was revealed to be "Jesus" (the definition of the word "Jesus" translates as "Jehovah Saviour" or "Jehovah has become our Salvation") *

Isaiah 9:6 For unto us a child is born, unto us a son is given: and the government shall be upon his shoulder: and his name shall be called Wonderful, Counsellor, The mighty God, The everlasting Father, The Prince of Peace.

John 1:13 Which were born, not of blood, nor of the will of the flesh, nor of the will of man, but of God.

John 1:14 And the Word was made flesh, and dwelt among us, (and we beheld his glory, the glory as of the only begotten of the Father,) full of grace and truth.

* Jehovah God (who created the world by Himself) became flesh, a flesh that was the only begotten of the Spirit of God.*

Made

The flesh of Jehovah was "made" or "created".

> Gal 4:4 But when the fulness of the time was come, God sent forth his Son, made of a woman, made under the law,

The Son, or "flesh" was, made, begotten.

> 1 Tim 3:16 And without controversy great is the mystery of godliness: God was manifest in the flesh, justified in the Spirit, seen of angels, preached unto the Gentiles, believed on in the world, received up into glory.

That "flesh" or "SON" housed Jesus Christ (Jehovah Saviour), the "I AM"

> John 14:9 Jesus saith unto him, Have I been so long time with you, and yet hast thou not known me, Philip? he that hath seen me hath seen the Father; and how sayest thou then, Show us the Father?

The "I AM" of the burning bush came to Earth, in the flesh, as the "Son".

> John 8:58 Jesus said unto them, Verily , verily, I say unto you, Before Abraham was, I am.

Those who do not recognize Jesus as "I AM" will see no need to be baptized in His name for the remission of their sins and will die in their sins.

> John 8:24 I said therefore unto you, that ye shall die in your sins: for if ye believe not that I am he, ye shall die in your sins.

And we recall this exhortation:

> Acts 22:16 And now why tarriest thou? arise, and be baptized, and wash away thy sins, calling on the name of the Lord.

Manifest

I Timothy 3:16 And without controversy great is the mystery of godliness: God was manifest in the flesh, justified in the Spirit, seen of angels, preached unto the Gentiles, believed on in the world, received up into glory.

I John 3:16 Hereby perceive we the love [of God], because he laid down his life for us: and we ought to lay down [our] lives for the brethren.

I Timothy 4:1 Now the Spirit speaketh expressly, that in the latter times some shall depart from the faith, giving heed to seducing spirits, and doctrines of devils;

I Timothy 4:2 Speaking lies in hypocrisy; having their conscience seared with a hot iron;

II Timothy 4:4 And they shall turn away [their] ears from the truth, and shall be turned unto fables.

Jude 1:25 To the only wise God our Saviour, [be] glory and majesty, dominion and power, both now and for ever. Amen.

Who?

Who is God?

> 1 Corinthians 2:8 Which none of the princes of this world knew: for had they known it, they would not have crucified the Lord of glory.

It was none other than the Lord of Glory, Jehovah Himself, on the cross.

There is a problem for those who believe a lie.

> 2 Thessalonians 2:11 And for this cause God shall send them strong delusion, that they should believe a lie:
>
> 12 That they all might be damned who believed not the truth, but had pleasure in unrighteousness.

Now, as an aside here, let me share something that I noticed. If you take the phrase "a lie" and say it with a good southern accent it sounds like the false god of one of the false religions. Is it not astounding that so many follow a religion where the name of their "god" is "a lie" (allah). But I am dealing more with exposing counterfeit christianity rather than the other false religions.

It is essential to know and believe the truth.

> John 4:24 God is a Spirit: and they that worship him must worship him in spirit and in truth.
>
> Isaiah 48:11 For mine own sake, even for mine own sake, will I do it: for how should my name be polluted? and I will not give my glory unto another.

God said that He would not give His Glory to another. That really was Him, in the flesh, on the cross.

1 John 3:16 Hereby perceive we the love of God, because he laid down his life for us: and we ought to lay down our lives for the brethren.

According to the Bible God Himself laid down his life. Does that mean that God died? Keep in mind that God is the inventor of life and death. He can live and die as He pleases because He is God.

> John 2:19 Jesus answered and said unto them, Destroy this temple, and in three days I will raise it up.
>
> 20 Then said the Jews, Forty and six years was this temple in building, and wilt thou rear it up in three days?
>
> 21 But he spake of the temple of his body.
>
> 22 When therefore he was risen from the dead, his disciples remembered that he had said this unto them; and they believed the scripture, and the word which Jesus had said.

Jesus could raise Himself from the dead because He is God. To God both life and death are under His complete control. That is why as real Christians we can understand that it really was God Himself on the Cross, God manifest in the flesh. Not some junior second person in a Roman god squad! If Jesus was not God the Father, how could he have said:

> John 14:9 Jesus saith unto him, Have I been so long time with you, and yet hast thou not known me, Philip? he that hath seen me hath seen the Father; and how sayest thou then, Shew us the Father?

When they looked at Jesus, they saw God manifest in the flesh.

> Acts 22:6 And it came to pass, that, as I made my journey, and was come nigh unto Damascus about noon, suddenly there shone from heaven a great light round about me.
>
> Acts 22:7 And I fell unto the ground, and heard a voice saying unto me, Saul, Saul, why persecutest thou me?
>
> Acts 22:8 And I answered, Who art thou, Lord? And he said unto me, I am Jesus of Nazareth, whom thou persecutest.

Notice that the Lord in heaven claimed to be Jesus of Nazareth! None other than the Lord Jesus Christ.

> Acts 22:9 And they that were with me saw indeed the light, and were afraid; but they heard not the voice of him that spake to me.
>
> Acts 22:10 And I said, What shall I do, Lord? And the Lord said unto me, Arise, and go into Damascus; and there it shall be told thee of all things which are appointed for thee to do.

Notice that the Lord (Jesus Christ) spoke to Paul/Saul.

> Acts 22:11 And when I could not see for the glory of that light, being led by the hand of them that were with me, I came into Damascus.
>
> Acts 22:12 And one Ananias, a devout man according to the law, having a good report of all the Jews which dwelt [there],
>
> Acts 22:13 Came unto me, and stood, and said unto me, Brother Saul, receive thy sight. And the same hour I looked up upon him.
>
> Acts 22:14 And he said, The God of our fathers hath chosen thee, that thou shouldest know his will, and see that Just One, and shouldest hear the voice of his mouth.

NOW NOTICE CAREFULLY PLEASE! He said that it was the "God of our Fathers" that had chosen him, but we just read that it was "Jesus Christ" that chose him. JESUS CHRIST is the God of Abraham, Issac and Jacob.

> Acts 22:15 For thou shalt be his witness unto all men of what thou hast seen and heard.
>
> Acts 22:16 And now why tarriest thou? arise, and be baptized, and wash away thy sins, calling on the name of the Lord.

Also, notice, that just a few verses earlier that the "Lord" had declared His Name to be "Jesus of Nazareth".

Jesus Christ is NOT the "second person" in a Roman imaginary "god squad". Jesus Christ is the "Everlasting Father".

> Isaiah 9:6 For unto us a child is born, unto us a son is given: and the government shall be upon his shoulder: and his name shall be called Wonderful, Counsellor, The mighty God, The everlasting Father, The Prince of Peace.

Jesus Christ is the "Mighty God", He is NOT the "second person" of the Roman Catholic trinity, as Satan and his preachers would have you to believe.

> Exodus 3:14 And God said unto Moses, I AM THAT I AM: and he said, Thus shalt thou say unto the children of Israel, I AM hath sent me unto you.
>
> John 8:58 Jesus said unto them, Verily, verily, I say unto you, Before Abraham was, I am.
>
> 59 Then took they up stones to cast at him: but Jesus hid himself, and went out of the temple, going through the midst of them, and so passed by.

The true Christian Church is the bride of one husband only, the bride of Jesus only.

> Isaiah 9:6 For unto us a child is born, unto us a son is given: and the government shall be upon his shoulder: and his name shall be called Wonderful, Counsellor, The mighty God, The everlasting Father, The Prince of Peace.

Trinity polytheism

We see many different flavors of trinitarian in the world, and they are certainly "of the world". Some of them will be quite honest regarding their polytheism but others will try to appear to be monotheistic even as they launch into "great swelling words" to try to defend their triunity.

God is not the author of confusion! You cannot be trinitarian and monotheistic at the same time. A brief "one god" disclaimer at the end of a lengthy three person discourse does NOT a monotheist make! If you have three separate persons in a god squad that agree together, how can you even imagine yourself as a monotheist.

Who will be the Bridegroom of the Church? Would it be "god person #1", "god person #2", or "god person #3"? Think about it, sinner friend, your SOUL is at stake here and wicked sly men are making merchandise of your immortal SOUL!

People accuse me of being intolerant. Well I certainly hope I am intolerant towards those who want to destroy the souls of my neighbors!

> Joshua 24:15 And if it seem evil unto you to serve the LORD, choose you this day whom ye will serve; whether the gods which your fathers served that were on the other side of the flood, or the gods of the Amorites, in whose land ye dwell: but as for me and my house, we will serve the LORD.
>
> 2 Corinthians 6:17 Wherefore come out from among them, and be ye separate, saith the Lord, and touch not the unclean thing; and I will receive you,

The bride of Christ is the bride of one Husband only. The true bride of Jesus Christ is the bride of Jesus Only. True monotheists know that Jesus is God the Father manifest in the flesh and not some "second anything". Jesus Christ is the alpha and the omega but He is not "second person" of some Roman god squad.

Revelation 1:8 I am Alpha and Omega, the beginning and the ending, saith the Lord, which is, and which was, and which is to come, the Almighty.

The phrase "Who art thou, Lord?" appears as a question only three times in the Holy Bible. The answer is the same each time!

Acts 9:5 And he said, Who art thou, Lord? And the Lord said, I am Jesus whom thou persecutest: it is hard for thee to kick against the pricks.

Acts 22:8 And I answered, Who art thou, Lord? And he said unto me, I am Jesus of Nazareth, whom thou persecutest.

Acts 26:15 And I said, Who art thou, Lord? And he said, I am Jesus whom thou persecutest.

John 20:26 ¶ And after eight days again his disciples were within, and Thomas with them: then came Jesus, the doors being shut, and stood in the midst, and said, Peace be unto you.

27 Then saith he to Thomas, Reach hither thy finger, and behold my hands; and reach hither thy hand, and thrust it into my side: and be not faithless, but believing.

28 And Thomas answered and said unto him, My Lord and my God.

29 Jesus saith unto him, Thomas, because thou hast seen me, thou hast believed: blessed are they that have not seen, and yet have believed.

That is NOT the religion called the "trinity" regardless of how crafty deceivers try to make it appear so. Notice this next verse that really nails it down that if you believe that Jesus is not the Father, then you really don't know Jesus!

John 14:9 Jesus saith unto him, Have I been so long time with you, and yet hast thou not known me, Philip? he that hath seen me hath seen the Father; and how sayest thou then, Shew us the Father?

Trinity polytheism

I know there are verses that the trinitarians will use to try to justify their polytheism (even as they themselves will so try to deny their polytheism), but if we have a firm knowledge of truth from the Word of God then we will not fall prey to the crafty deceptions of the deceiver.

If you think this is not essential or important, why would Jesus have stated that:

> Mark 12:29 And Jesus answered him, The first of all the commandments is, Hear, O Israel; The Lord our God is one Lord:

Though we humans (created in God's image) have body, soul and spirit we are not each "three separate persons". Though God manifested Himself as "Father, Son, and Holy Ghost" he is not "three separate persons".

1) God is a Spirit.

> John 4:24 God [is] a Spirit: and they that worship him must worship [him] in spirit and in truth.

2) God is holy.

> I Samuel 2:2 [There is] none holy as the LORD: for [there is] none beside thee: neither [is there] any rock like our God.

3) God is a "Holy Spirit".

4) Jesus is the "Spirit of truth"

> John 14:6 Jesus saith unto him, I am the way, the truth, and the life: no man cometh unto the Father, but by me.

5) Jesus was "dwelling with them" and promised to be "in them".

> John 14:17 [Even] the Spirit of truth; whom the world cannot receive, because it seeth him not, neither knoweth him: but ye know him; for he dwelleth with you, and shall be in you.

6) The "comforter" is the "Spirit of Christ"

> John 14:18 I will not leave you comfortless: I will come to you.

7) The "Spirit of Christ" is the "Holy Spirit" is the "Spirit of Truth"

> John 14:26 But the Comforter, [which is] the Holy Ghost, whom the Father will send in my name, he shall teach you all things, and bring all things to your remembrance, whatsoever I have said unto you.

8) The Spirit of God visited His creation robed in flesh as the "Son".

> I Timothy 3:16 And without controversy great is the mystery of godliness: God was manifest in the flesh, justified in the Spirit, seen of angels, preached unto the Gentiles, believed on in the world, received up into glory.

9) The fullness of God is in Jesus Christ

> Colossians 2:9 For in him dwelleth all the fulness of the Godhead bodily.
>
> Colossians 2:10 And ye are complete in him, which is the head of all principality and power:

10) Jesus IS the "everlasting Father".

> Isaiah 9:6 For unto us a child is born, unto us a son is given: and the government shall be upon his shoulder: and his name shall be called Wonderful, Counsellor, The mighty God, The everlasting Father, The Prince of Peace.

11) Those who believe that Jesus is a "separate person" from the "Father" don't really know Jesus at all.

> John 14:9 Jesus saith unto him, Have I been so long time with you, and yet hast thou not known me, Philip? he that hath seen me hath seen the Father; and how sayest thou [then], Shew us the Father?

One God

Jeremiah 16: 20 Shall a man make gods unto himself, and they are no Gods?"

Deut 4:35 Unto thee it was shewed, that thou mightest know that the Lord he is God; there is none else beside him.

Deut 4:39 Know therefore this day, and consider it in thine heart, that the Lord he is God in heaven above, and upon the earth beneath; there is none else.

Deut 6:4 Hear, O Israel: The Lord our God is one Lord:

Deut 32:39 See now that I, even I, am he, and THERE IS NO GOD WITH ME: I kill, and I make alive; I wound and I heal: neither is there any that can deliver out of my hand.

Psalms 86:10 For thou art great, and doest wonderous things: THOU ART GOD ALONE.

Isaiah 43:3 For I am the Lord thy God, the Holy One of Israel, THY SAVIOR: I gave Egypt for thy ransom, Ethiopia and Seba for thee.

Isaiah 43:10 Ye are my witnesses, sayeth the Lord, and my servant whom I have chosen; that ye may know and believe me, and understand that I am he: before me there was no God formed, neither shall there be after me.

Isaiah 43:11 I, even I, am the Lord, and BESIDES ME THERE IS NO SAVIOR.

Isaiah 44:6 Thus saith the Lord, the King of Israel, and his redeemer the Lord of hosts: I am the first, and I am the last, and BESIDE ME THERE IS NO GOD.

Isaiah 44:24 Thus saith the Lord, thy redeemer, and he that formed thee from the womb, I am the Lord that maketh all things; that stretcheth forth the heavens ALONE; that spreadeth abroad the earth BY MYSELF;

Isaiah 45:5, 6, 18, 21, 22, CH 46:5, 9, CH 47:10, CH 48:11

Titus 1:3 But hath in due times manifested his word through preaching, which is committed unto me according to the commandment of GOD OUR SAVIOR.

Titus 3:4 But after that the kindness and love of GOD OUR SAVIOR toward man appeared,

Mark 12:29 And Jesus answered him, The first of all the commandments is, Hear, O Israel; the Lord our God is one Lord.

Ephesians 4:5 ONE LORD, one faith, one baptism.

I Tim 3:16 And without controversy great is the mystery of godliness: GOD WAS MANIFEST IN THE FLESH, justified in the Spirit, seen of angels, preached unto the Gentiles, believed on in the world, received up into glory.

I John 3:16 Hereby perceive we the love of God, because he laid down HIS LIFE for us: and we ought to lay down our lives for the brethren.

St. John 14:9 Jesus saith unto him, Have I been so long time with you, and yet HAST THOU NOT KNOWN ME, Phillip? HE THAT HATH SEEN ME HATH SEEN THE FATHER; and how sayest thou then, Shew us the Father?

Isaiah 9:6 For unto us a CHILD is born, unto us a SON is given: and the government shall be upon his shoulder: and his name shall be called Wonderful, Counsellor, THE MIGHTY GOD, THE EVERLASTING FATHER, the Prince of Peace.

Jude 25 To the only wise GOD OUR SAVIOR, be glory and majesty, dominion and power, both now and forever. Amen

Salvation

Faith Step

Deuteronomy 32:20 And he said, I will hide my face from them, I will see what their end shall be: for they are a very froward generation, children in whom is no faith.

Habakkuk 2:4 Behold, his soul which is lifted up is not upright in him: but the just shall live by his faith.

Matthew 6:24 No man can serve two masters: for either he will hate the one, and love the other; or else he will hold to the one, and despise the other. Ye cannot serve God and mammon.

25 ¶ Therefore I say unto you, Take no thought for your life, what ye shall eat, or what ye shall drink; nor yet for your body, what ye shall put on. Is not the life more than meat, and the body than raiment?

26 Behold the fowls of the air: for they sow not, neither do they reap, nor gather into barns; yet your heavenly Father feedeth them. Are ye not much better than they?

27 Which of you by taking thought can add one cubit unto his stature?

28 And why take ye thought for raiment? Consider the lilies of the field, how they grow; they toil not, neither do they spin:

29 And yet I say unto you, That even Solomon in all his glory was not arrayed like one of these.

30 Wherefore, if God so clothe the grass of the field, which to day is, and to morrow is cast into the oven, shall he not much more clothe you, O ye of little faith?

31 Therefore take no thought, saying, What shall we eat? or, What shall we drink? or, Wherewithal shall we be clothed?

32 (For after all these things do the Gentiles seek:) for your heavenly Father knoweth that ye have need of all these things.

33 But seek ye first the kingdom of God, and his righteousness; and all these things shall be added unto you.

34 Take therefore no thought for the morrow: for the morrow shall take thought for the things of itself. Sufficient unto the day is the evil thereof.

The faith of the Bible is not a "do nothing" faith. While we should have faith and not worry that does not mean that we should not be diligent in our business and work.

So in order to, by faith, obey the Bible, you will work hard and be diligent.

Ephesians 6:7 With good will doing service, as to the Lord, and not to men:

Colossians 3:23 And whatsoever ye do, do it heartily, as to the Lord, and not unto men;

Proverbs 22:29 Seest thou a man diligent in his business? he shall stand before kings; he shall not stand before mean men.

Paul was an independent business owner. He was a tentmaker and he continued this business of his. In fact that is how he came in contact with Aquila and Priscilla and abode with them. It started as a business relationship.

Acts 18:1 ¶ After these things Paul departed from Athens, and came to Corinth;

2 And found a certain Jew named Aquila, born in Pontus, lately come from Italy, with his wife Priscilla; (because that Claudius had commanded all Jews to depart from Rome:) and came unto them.

3 And because he was of the same craft, he abode with them, and wrought: for by their occupation they were tentmakers.

How important is faith?

> Hebrews 11:6 But without faith it is impossible to please him: for he that cometh to God must believe that he is, and that he is a rewarder of them that diligently seek him.

Where can you get it?

> Romans 12:3 For I say, through the grace given unto me, to every man that is among you, not to think of himself more highly than he ought to think; but to think soberly, according as God hath dealt to every man the measure of faith.

and

> Romans 10:17 So then faith cometh by hearing, and hearing by the word of God.

> Ephesians 2:8 For by grace are ye saved through faith; and that not of yourselves: it is the gift of God:

Of course we need to keep in mind that the faith of the Ephesians was not the empty claim of faith of false-christianity today, but rather the faith that caused them to obey Paul and to be baptized in Jesus name and to receive the Holy Spirit, which was an opportunity provided to them purely by the grace of God.

Look back at the birth of that Ephesian Church when the people there obeyed Paul and were baptized in Jesus Name. They had the faith to obey!

> Acts 19:4 Then said Paul, John verily baptized with the baptism of repentance, saying unto the people, that they should believe on him which should come after him, that is, on Christ Jesus.

> 5 When they heard this, they were baptized in the name of the Lord Jesus.

> 6 And when Paul had laid his hands upon them, the Holy Ghost came on them; and they spake with tongues, and prophesied.

Faith is a shield for you!

> Ephesians 6:16 Above all, taking the shield of faith, wherewith ye shall be able to quench all the fiery darts of the wicked.

There is a joy associated with faith!

> Philippians 1:25 And having this confidence, I know that I shall abide and continue with you all for your furtherance and joy of faith;
>
> 1 Thessalonians 1:3 Remembering without ceasing your work of faith, and labour of love, and patience of hope in our Lord Jesus Christ, in the sight of God and our Father;

Now I would point out here for any trinitarian that this does not mean that "God" and "Father" are two separate persons any more than "Father" and "Son" are two separate persons. But, if you have "Son" and "Father" as separate persons, by the same logic you would need to also have "Father" and "God" as two separate persons as well. But you really knew that already, didn't you?

But notice it speaks of "work of faith", that just doesn't jive with the "do nothing but claim to believe" false doctrines of the modern false-christian cults now does it?

James had an interesting way of phrasing it:

> James 2:20 But wilt thou know, O vain man, that faith without works is dead?
>
> James 2:26 For as the body without the spirit is dead, so faith without works is dead also.

Be Saved?

Well, the question really needs to be "What does the Bible say?", because a true preacher's job is to show you things that the Bible teaches. God commands a preacher:

> II Timothy 3:16 All scripture [is] given by inspiration of God, and [is] profitable for doctrine, for reproof, for correction, for instruction in righteousness:
>
> II Timothy 3:17 That the man of God may be perfect, throughly furnished unto all good works.
>
> II Timothy 4:1 I charge [thee] therefore before God, and the Lord Jesus Christ, who shall judge the quick and the dead at his appearing and his kingdom;
>
> II Timothy 4:2 Preach the word; be instant in season, out of season; reprove, rebuke, exhort with all longsuffering and doctrine.
>
> II Timothy 4:3 For the time will come when they will not endure sound doctrine; but after their own lusts shall they heap to themselves teachers, having itching ears;
>
> II Timothy 4:4 And they shall turn away [their] ears from the truth, and shall be turned unto fables.

So it is my job as a preacher to "preach the word" and expose popular "fables".

In the Bible when sinners asked "what shall we do?" the Apostles responded (with Peter as the spokesman) and said:

> Acts 2:38 Then Peter said unto them, Repent, and be baptized every one of you in the name of Jesus Christ for the remission of sins, and ye shall receive the gift of the Holy Ghost.

They were told to repent, be water baptized in Jesus name to have their past sins remitted, and to receive the gift of the Holy Ghost.

> Acts 2:39 For the promise is unto you, and to your children, and to all that are afar off, [even] as many as the Lord our God shall call.

Then Peter went on to say that this was the plan for "as many as the Lord our God shall call".

> Acts 2:40 And with many other words did he testify and exhort, saying, Save yourselves from this untoward generation.

> Acts 2:41 Then they that gladly received his word were baptized: and the same day there were added [unto them] about three thousand souls.

Then about 3000 that received the "word" were water baptized in Jesus name to have all of their past sins remitted. Sins are actually washed away when people are baptized using the NAME of the Lord (His name is Jesus).

> Acts 22:16 And now why tarriest thou? arise, and be baptized, and wash away thy sins, calling on the name of the Lord.

The other "epistles" like Romans and Ephesians are letters to people who were already Christians telling them how to "stay Christian". Acts 2:38 tells you how to BECOME a Christian, then you need the other books to learn what God expects of Christians.

Unless you first become a Christian by obeying Acts 2:38, the other epistles aren't really addressed to you and the promises aren't for you.

Notice how the Apostles founded the churches and what they told people to do to become Christians.

** Jews when they received the Holy Ghost **

> Acts 2:4 And they were all filled with the Holy Ghost, and began to speak with other tongues, as the Spirit gave them utterance.

** Samaritans when they received the Holy Ghost **

Acts 8:14 Now when the apostles which were at Jerusalem heard that Samaria had received the word of God, they sent unto them Peter and John:

Acts 8:15 Who, when they were come down, prayed for them, that they might receive the Holy Ghost:

Acts 8:16 (For as yet he was fallen upon none of them: only they were baptized in the name of the Lord Jesus.)

Acts 8:17 Then laid they [their] hands on them, and they received the Holy Ghost.

** There was a clear instant sign so that the Apostles knew that they had received the same Holy Ghost that the Apostles had *

** Gentiles when they received the Holy Ghost **

Acts 10:45 And they of the circumcision which believed were astonished, as many as came with Peter, because that on the Gentiles also was poured out the gift of the Holy Ghost.

Acts 10:46 For they heard them speak with tongues, and magnify God. Then answered Peter,

Acts 10:47 Can any man forbid water, that these should not be baptized, which have received the Holy Ghost as well as we?

Acts 10:48 And he commanded them to be baptized in the name of the Lord. Then prayed they him to tarry certain days.

** John the Baptist's disciples had to be RE- baptized and then they received the same Holy Ghost **

Acts 19:2 He said unto them, Have ye received the Holy Ghost since ye believed? And they said unto him, We have not so much as heard whether there be any Holy Ghost.

Acts 19:3 And he said unto them, Unto what then were ye baptized? And they said, Unto John's baptism.

> Acts 19:4 Then said Paul, John verily baptized with the baptism of repentance, saying unto the people, that they should believe on him which should come after him, that is, on Christ Jesus.
>
> Acts 19:5 When they heard [this], they were baptized in the name of the Lord Jesus.
>
> Acts 19:6 And when Paul had laid [his] hands upon them, the Holy Ghost came on them; and they spake with tongues, and prophesied.

Jews, gentiles, Samaritans; all baptized in JESUS name, all spoke in tongues when they received the Holy Ghost.

Acts 2:38

Ever wonder why deceivers, and fake christians in general, single out Acts 2:38 as the verse that "need not be obeyed"? It is because Acts 2:38 is the plan of salvation for the new testament church. Notice that Jesus had personally given Peter the keys to the kingdom of heaven:

> Matt 16:19 And I will give unto thee the keys of the kingdom of heaven: and whatsoever thou shalt bind on earth shall be bound in heaven: and whatsoever thou shalt loose on earth shall be loosed in heaven.

Let us also notice that when sinners were "pricked in their hearts" and asked Peter what they could do, that Peter unlocked the kingdom of heaven for "as many as the Lord our God shall call"

> Acts 2:36 Therefore let all the house of Israel know assuredly, that God hath made that same Jesus, whom ye have crucified, both Lord and Christ.
>
> Acts 2:37 Now when they heard [this], they were pricked in their
>
> heart, and said unto Peter and to the rest of the apostles, Men [and] brethren, what shall we do?
>
> Acts 2:38 Then Peter said unto them, Repent, and be baptized every one of you in the name of Jesus Christ for the remission of sins, and ye shall receive the gift of the Holy Ghost.
>
> Acts 2:39 For the promise is unto you, and to your children, and to all that are afar off, [even] as many as the Lord our God shall call.
>
> Acts 2:40 And with many other words did he testify and exhort, saying, Save yourselves from this untoward generation.
>
> Acts 2:41 Then they that gladly received his word were baptized: and the same day there were added [unto them] about three thousand souls.

Notice, there were 3000 there that elected to have their sins remitted. So you better believe that the minister of Satan will do just about anything that he can to try to downplay Acts 2:38. Paul mentions that there will be those that come along and preach "another gospel."

> Galatians 1:8 But though we, or an angel from heaven, preach any other gospel unto you than that which we have preached unto you, let him be accursed.

Paul also didn't leave us in ignorance that when Satan's ministers come, they come masquerading as "ministers of righteousness", as smooth talking false preachers saying "Just claim belief and you are saved."

> II Corinthians 11:13 For such [are] false apostles, deceitful workers, transforming themselves into the apostles of Christ.

> II Corinthians 11:14 And no marvel; for Satan himself is transformed into an angel of light.

> II Corinthians 11:15 Therefore [it is] no great thing if his ministers also be transformed as the ministers of righteousness; whose end shall be according to their works.

It is the job of the false preacher to cause YOU to be among those that don't obey Acts 2:38.

> II Thessalonians 1:7 And to you who are troubled rest with us, when the Lord Jesus shall be revealed from heaven with his mighty angels,

> II Thessalonians 1:8 In flaming fire taking vengeance on them that know not God, and that obey not the gospel of our Lord Jesus Christ:

Notice that there are TWO groups mentioned in verse 8, those that don't know God, AND those that know him BUT REFUSE TO OBEY HIM.

> II Thessalonians 1:9 Who shall be punished with everlasting destruction from the presence of the Lord, and from the glory of his power;

> James 1:22 But be ye doers of the word, and not hearers only,

> deceiving your own selves.

> Hebrews 5:9 And being made perfect, he became the author of eternal salvation unto all them that obey him;

> Acts 22:16 And now why tarriest thou? arise, and be baptized, and wash away thy sins, calling on the name of the Lord.

Water Baptism in Jesus name remits sins BECAUSE of Jesus finished work on the cross. It is the re-birth of water (see John 3:5).

> Matthew 1:21 And she shall bring forth a son, and thou shalt call his name JESUS: for he shall save his people from their sins.

> Acts 4:12 Neither is there salvation in any other: for there is none other name under heaven given among men, whereby we must be saved.

> Galatians 3:27 For as many of you as have been baptized into Christ have put on Christ.

The devil's servants don't want you to "put on Christ". They want you to reject Jesus name baptism. Is the man in the pulpit of your church just there to soothe you into hell? Is your preacher stressing the URGENCY of obeying the Bible or is he/she/it selling a fable of a false grace that ignores obedience to the Bible.

> II Timothy 4:2 Preach the word; be instant in season, out of season; reprove, rebuke, exhort with all longsuffering and doctrine.

> II Timothy 4:3 For the time will come when they will not endure sound doctrine; but after their own lusts shall they heap to themselves teachers, having itching ears;

> II Timothy 4:4 And they shall turn away [their] ears from the truth, and shall be turned unto fables.

Is your preacher preaching Acts 2:38, or soothing fables?

Salvation

Salvation. All churches claim to have it, but if we look at what they are teaching we see that many of them have starkly different requirements for salvation. Can two groups of people saying opposite things both be right? If two groups are teaching opposite things then at least one and possibly both of them are wrong. What is a person to do to secure true Biblical salvation?

I believe that the safest path would be to simply obey what the Apostles preached and practiced, to obey the Bible.

Now I know the devil has a lot of his PR folks teaching that the Bible is so complicated that you cannot know it so you might as well not try. If you fall for that then he gotcha!

> Isaiah 35:8 And an highway shall be there, and a way, and it shall be called The way of holiness; the unclean shall not pass over it; but it shall be for those: the wayfaring men, though fools, shall not err therein.

God did not give his Word to confuse or alienate people. He gave it to show us the way and give us true light and understanding.

> Psalms 119:105 NUN. Thy word is a lamp unto my feet, and a light unto my path.

If we want true salvation then we must look at what was taught by Jesus Christ, then preached upon His authority by Peter, and then practiced by the apostles consistently. If we do that then we see two essential elements that make up the Christian new birth.

> John 3:5 Jesus answered, Verily, verily, I say unto thee, Except a man be born of water and of the Spirit, he cannot enter into the kingdom of God.

Those essential elements are: WATER and SPIRIT. We should take note that a grown man was told by God manifest in the flesh that he had to be born of water and that he had to be born of the Spirit.

> Hebrews 5:9 And being made perfect, he became the author of eternal salvation unto all them that obey him;

I believe it is important that we remember who was being addressed and why by Jesus. Jesus told a grown man that he still needed to be born of water and of Spirit. We who are "Apostolic" or in other words teach what the Apostles taught know that the "birth of water" is Jesus Name water baptism.

> Gal 3:27 For as many of you as have been baptized into Christ have put on Christ.

The devil's PR folks who fight against the importance of Jesus Name baptism are not being honest with you or themselves.

> Mark 16:16 He that believeth and is baptized shall be saved; but he that believeth not shall be damned.

Yet even with that verse we still have the devil's crowd deceiving souls. Look at that verse. Is it telling you to do one thing or two things? I will give you a hint, please carefully note God's choice of words when he said the word "and".

Let me try to really break this down. If mama sends you to go to the store and says to buy eggs and milk does that mean that she only wants eggs?

We know that Jesus gave Peter the keys to the kingdom of God. Why reject what Peter did with those keys. I have actually had some of the more ignorant of the devil's PR guys try to teach people that Peter disobeyed Jesus. He said something like, "Well I will take Jesus's words over Peter's any day." as he was trying to justify his defiance of the Bible. The devil sure is fishing for fools in this hour.

If we can't trust the Apostles we have a big problem. Just who do the devil's PR guys think it was that kept track of what Jesus said? Do they really think people are stupid enough to believe that Jesus just penned in the red words Himself?

Speaking of the devil's servants, I feel I should point out something here. Note that the Word of God does not teach tolerance towards ministers of Satan.

> 2 Cor 11:12 But what I do, that I will do, that I may cut off occasion from them which desire occasion; that wherein they glory, they may be found even as we.
>
> 13 For such are false apostles, deceitful workers, transforming themselves into the apostles of Christ.
>
> 14 And no marvel; for Satan himself is transformed into an angel of light.
>
> 15 Therefore it is no great thing if his ministers also be transformed as the ministers of righteousness; whose end shall be according to their works.

Notice also what role that Satan's crew will try to play. They will pretend to be teaching righteousness. Let's get back to talking about Peter and Jesus.

> Matthew 16:18 And I say also unto thee, That thou art Peter, and upon this rock I will build my church; and the gates of hell shall not prevail against it.
>
> 19 And I will give unto thee the keys of the kingdom of heaven: and whatsoever thou shalt bind on earth shall be bound in heaven: and whatsoever thou shalt loose on earth shall be loosed in heaven.

How can the devil's servants figure that people will be so stupid that they think they can somehow reject Peter's teachings because their modern

Satanic preacher knows Jesus better? Satan's boys are really fishing for fools these days.

Anyway, back to our topic of salvation. Peter preached the "Apostolic" salvation on the Day of Pentecost and the Apostles adhered to it from then on. That is where we get the concept "Apostolic Pentecostal". It is really very simple. Those who are preaching the Pentecostal message that the Apostles preached are ta da, "Apostolic Pentecostal". I know there are liars who claim to be who aren't preaching the original message but why would we be surprised that Satan's crew would lie? Is he not the father of it? Jesus said to some people:

> John 8:44 Ye are of your father the devil, and the lusts of your father ye will do. He was a murderer from the beginning, and abode not in the truth, because there is no truth in him. When he speaketh a lie, he speaketh of his own: for he is a liar, and the father of it.

So we don't need to be surprised when the devil's servants lie, OK?

Back to our salvation topic. We have established that one can't reject Peter without rejecting the one who gave Peter the keys to the kingdom of heaven. So let's have a look at what Peter taught.

> Acts 2:36 Therefore let all the house of Israel know assuredly, that God hath made that same Jesus, whom ye have crucified, both Lord and Christ.
>
> 37 ¶ Now when they heard this, they were pricked in their heart, and said unto Peter and to the rest of the apostles, Men and brethren, what shall we do?
>
> 38 Then Peter said unto them, Repent, and be baptized every one of you in the name of Jesus Christ for the remission of sins, and ye shall receive the gift of the Holy Ghost.
>
> 39 For the promise is unto you, and to your children, and to all that are afar off, even as many as the Lord our God shall call.

How can someone in their wildest imagination think that they are among the "called of God" when they reject the Acts 2:38 salvation that Peter preached on the authority of the Lord Jesus Christ?

Let me also point out something else here. We see that baptism is to be done in Jesus Name. Monotheists have no problem with that, but Satan's polytheistic PR guys really stumble on that and so often expose themselves that they truly are polytheistic and really are teaching three god squad members. Something else to consider is that when people receive the Holy Ghost, they speak with other tongues.

I know a lot of people fight against this because the devil's PR guys have found that the best way to keep people from seeking the baptism of the Holy Ghost is to convince them they already have it and then just hold them by their pride. But why would someone desiring and claiming a true Biblical experience be so adamantly against such a basic Bible principle.

> Acts 2:4 And they were all filled with the Holy Ghost, and began to speak with other tongues, as the Spirit gave them utterance.
>
> Acts 19:6 And when Paul had laid his hands upon them, the Holy Ghost came on them; and they spake with tongues, and prophesied

I have heard the devil's PR guys teaching that Paul didn't believe in tongues, but Paul said:

> 1 Corinthians 14:18 I thank my God, I speak with tongues more than ye all:

There are examples in the Bible where people received the Holy Ghost before they were baptized in Jesus Name. There are also other examples where people were baptized in Jesus Name before they received the Holy Ghost.

Looking back, Jesus did not say that the order of the birth of water and birth of spirit was important.

> John 3:5 Jesus answered, Verily, verily, I say unto thee, Except a man be born of water and of the Spirit, he cannot enter into the kingdom of God.

Whenever either ingredient of the Christian New Birth was missing, the apostles IMMEDIATELY added the missing one. If a person was baptized in Jesus Name then the Apostles prayed for them to receive the Holy Spirit. (that also proves that people don't automatically receive the Holy Ghost when they "believe" as some of Satan's PR guys teach. When people received the Holy Ghost with the evidence of speaking in tongues, the Apostles immediately baptized them in Jesus Name.

> Acts 8:12 But when they believed Philip preaching the things concerning the kingdom of God, and the name of Jesus Christ, they were baptized, both men and women.
>
> 13 Then Simon himself believed also: and when he was baptized, he continued with Philip, and wondered, beholding the miracles and signs which were done.
>
> 14 ¶ Now when the apostles which were at Jerusalem heard that Samaria had received the word of God, they sent unto them Peter and John:
>
> 15 Who, when they were come down, prayed for them, that they might receive the Holy Ghost:
>
> 16 (For as yet he was fallen upon none of them: only they were baptized in the name of the Lord Jesus.)
>
> 17 Then laid they their hands on them, and they received the Holy Ghost.

Note how they had been baptized.

> Acts 10:44 ¶ While Peter yet spake these words, the Holy Ghost fell on all them which heard the word.

45 And they of the circumcision which believed were astonished, as many as came with Peter, because that on the Gentiles also was poured out the gift of the Holy Ghost.

46 For they heard them speak with tongues, and magnify God. Then answered Peter,

47 Can any man forbid water, that these should not be baptized, which have received the Holy Ghost as well as we?

48 And he commanded them to be baptized in the name of the Lord. Then prayed they him to tarry certain days.

So how did the Apostles know that Gentiles had received the same Holy Ghost they had? Now think about all this. Why would anyone who really loved God and the Bible fight so hard against basic Bible doctrines? Well, it is because they have become quite comfortable listening to Satan's sugar coated lies and Satan just uses their pride like strings to play with them like puppets.

Those who had even been baptized personally by John the Baptist were re-baptized in Jesus name for the remission of their sins. John's baptism was only for a temporary period of time. Jesus Name baptism does remit sins by the POWER of the shed blood of God.

Acts 19:1 And it came to pass, that, while Apollos was at Corinth, Paul having passed through the upper coasts came to Ephesus: and finding certain disciples,

2 He said unto them, Have ye received the Holy Ghost since ye believed? And they said unto him, We have not so much as heard whether there be any Holy Ghost.

3 And he said unto them, Unto what then were ye baptized? And they said, Unto John's baptism.

4 Then said Paul, John verily baptized with the baptism of repentance, saying unto the people, that they should believe on him which should come after him, that is, on Christ Jesus.

5 When they heard this, they were baptized in the name of the Lord Jesus.

> 6 And when Paul had laid his hands upon them, the Holy Ghost came on them; and they spake with tongues, and prophesied.
>
> 7 And all the men were about twelve.

So with that verse 2 up there, how are Satan's PR guys still convincing people that they automatically receive the Holy Ghost when they first "believe"? Hell is going to have a big bunch of really embarrassed people, eh?

> Acts 22:16 And now why tarriest thou? arise, and be baptized, and wash away thy sins, calling on the name of the Lord.

How does a person have their sins washed away? Clearly it is by being baptized in Jesus Name which is the METHOD whereby one calls on the Name of the Lord. That is the reason that trinitarians will all die in their sins because they reject Jesus Name water baptism.

> Colossians 2:12 Buried with him in baptism, wherein also ye are risen with him through the faith of the operation of God, who hath raised him from the dead.

Note the essentiality of both WATER and SPIRIT:

> Romans 8:9 But ye are not in the flesh, but in the Spirit, if so be that the Spirit of God dwell in you. Now if any man have not the Spirit of Christ, he is none of his.

Notice here that the Bible speaks of the Spirit of God and the Spirit of Christ as EXACTLY the same Spirit.

> Mark 16:16 He that believeth and is baptized shall be saved; but he that believeth not shall be damned.

How could Jesus have been more clear regarding the essentiality of Jesus Name baptism? False-christians are simply not being honest with themselves.

> James 1:22 But be ye doers of the word, and not hearers only, deceiving your own selves.

> John 3:5 Jesus answered, Verily, verily, I say unto thee, Except a man be born of water and [of] the Spirit, he cannot enter into the kingdom of God.
>
> 6 That which is born of the flesh is flesh; and that which is born of the Spirit is spirit.
>
> 7 Marvel not that I said unto thee, Ye must be born again.

Remember here that Jesus was telling a grown man what he STILL needed to do in order to be saved. The grown man still had to be reborn of WATER and of the SPIRIT.

This is totally consistent with the plan of salvation that the "man with the keys to the kingdom" preached on the birthday of the New Testament Church.

> Matthew 16:18 And I say also unto thee, That thou art Peter, and upon this rock I will build my church; and the gates of hell shall not prevail against it.
>
> 19 And I will give unto thee the keys of the kingdom of heaven: and whatsoever thou shalt bind on earth shall be bound in heaven: and whatsoever thou shalt loose on earth shall be loosed in heaven.

> Acts 2:38 Then Peter said unto them, Repent, and be baptized every one of you in the name of Jesus Christ for the remission of sins, and ye shall receive the gift of the Holy Ghost.

Acts 2:39 For the promise is unto you, and to your children, and to all that are afar off, [even] as many as the Lord our God shall call.

Acts 2:40 And with many other words did he testify and exhort, saying, Save yourselves from this untoward generation.

Acts 2:41 Then they that gladly received his word were baptized: and the same day there were added [unto them] about three thousand souls.

Here is an example where the re-birth of WATER preceded the re-birth of SPIRIT

Acts 8:14 Now when the apostles which were at Jerusalem heard that Samaria had received the word of God, they sent unto them Peter and John:

Acts 8:15 Who, when they were come down, prayed for them, that they might receive the Holy Ghost:

Acts 8:16 (For as yet he was fallen upon none of them: only they were baptized in the name of the Lord Jesus.)

Acts 8:17 Then laid they [their] hands on them, and they received the Holy Ghost.

Here is one where the re-birth of SPIRIT preceded the re-birth of WATER:

Acts 10:45 And they of the circumcision which believed were

astonished, as many as came with Peter, because that on the Gentiles also was poured out the gift of the Holy Ghost.

Acts 10:46 For they heard them speak with tongues, and magnify God. Then answered Peter,

Acts 10:47 Can any man forbid water, that these should not be baptized, which have received the Holy Ghost as well as we?

> Acts 10:48 And he commanded them to be baptized in the name of the Lord. Then prayed they him to tarry certain days.

Another here where the re-birth of the WATER preceded re-birth of SPIRIT.

> Acts 19:1 And it came to pass, that, while Apollos was at Corinth, Paul having passed through the upper coasts came to Ephesus: and finding certain disciples,
>
> Acts 19:2 He said unto them, Have ye received the Holy Ghost since ye believed? And they said unto him, We have not so much as heard whether there be any Holy Ghost.
>
> Acts 19:3 And he said unto them, Unto what then were ye baptized? And they said, Unto John's baptism.
>
> Acts 19:4 Then said Paul, John verily baptized with the baptism of repentance, saying unto the people, that they should believe on him which should come after him, that is, on Christ Jesus.
>
> Acts 19:5 When they heard [this], they were baptized in the name of the Lord Jesus.
>
> Acts 19:6 And when Paul had laid [his] hands upon them, the Holy Ghost came on them; and they spake with tongues, and prophesied.

The apostles made sure that folks had been re-born both of the WATER and re-born of the SPIRIT, the Acts 2:38 plan of salvation that has always been adhered to by true Christianity.

> 2 Thessalonians 1:7 And to you who are troubled rest with us, when the Lord Jesus shall be revealed from heaven with his mighty angels,
>
> 8 In flaming fire taking vengeance on them that know not God, and that obey not the gospel of our Lord Jesus Christ:

9 Who shall be punished with everlasting destruction from the presence of the Lord, and from the glory of his power;

1 Peter 4:17 For the time is come that judgment must begin at the house of God: and if it first begin at us, what shall the end be of them that obey not the gospel of God?

Romans 10:16 But they have not all obeyed the gospel. For Esaias saith, Lord, who hath believed our report?

Galatians 3:27 For as many of you as have been baptized into Christ have put on Christ.

True Bible Salvation

True Bible salvation is a hotly debated subject with many diverse opinions and beliefs. I submit that it is very important what we believe.

> 1 Corinthians 15:2 By which also ye are saved, if ye keep in memory what I preached unto you, unless ye have believed in vain.

If what we believe is not accurate then our belief is in vain. You owe it to yourself and to your family to make sure that what you believe is the same as what the Bible teaches.

Satan is in the ministry business and he has many diligent, dedicated workers.

> 2 Timothy 3:13 But evil men and seducers shall wax worse and worse, deceiving, and being deceived.

Many of Satan's ministers really think that they are "Christian preachers" and have no clue that they are deceiving souls into hell. That will be no excuse for them in judgment, however.

Why would someone think that they could be saved without being baptized in Jesus Name and receiving the real Holy Ghost of the Bible. Almost anyone in any church of any kind will claim to have the Holy Ghost because they read about it! But the only evidence that the Apostles accepted was that they heard them speak with tongues.

> John 3:5 Jesus answered, Verily, verily, I say unto thee, Except a man be born of water and of the Spirit, he cannot enter into the kingdom of God.

Basic essential elements of salvation after repentance are: WATER and SPIRIT. We should take note that a grown man was told by God manifest in the flesh that he had to be born of water and that he had to be born of the Spirit.

> Hebrews 5:9 And being made perfect, he became the author of eternal salvation unto all them that obey him;

How can anyone continue to believe the false preachers who teach that grace means nothing to obey?

> Gal 3:27 For as many of you as have been baptized into Christ have put on Christ.

Consider here, why would any real man of God try to talk you OUT of putting on Christ as so many of the false-christian preachers do when they fight against Jesus Name Baptism?

> Mark 16:16 He that believeth and is baptized shall be saved; but he that believeth not shall be damned.

Yes even with that verse we still have the devil's ministers deceiving multitudes of souls. Look at that verse. Is it telling you to do one thing or to do two things? What part of the word "and" do you not understand?

If you pay good money for a wash AND wax for your car, don't you expect both to be done?

Jesus Christ gave the Apostle Peter the keys to the kingdom of God. What will become of those who choose to reject what Peter did with those keys. It has become commonplace that the devil's workmen go so far as to teach people that Peter disobeyed Jesus. They say something like, "Well I will take Jesus's words over Peter's any day." They are fishing for fools and catching a plenty!

If we can't trust the Apostles we have a big problem. Was it not the Apostles themselves who told us what Jesus said? Who else do we have to refer to but the Apostles to even have a clue what Jesus said?

Many attack me for being less than tolerant towards the devils's deceivers, but what does Paul tell the Christians to do regarding deceivers?

> 2 Cor 11:12 But what I do, that I will do, that I may cut off occasion from them which desire occasion; that wherein they glory, they may be found even as we.
>
> 13 For such are false apostles, deceitful workers, transforming themselves into the apostles of Christ.
>
> 14 And no marvel; for Satan himself is transformed into an angel of light.
>
> 15 Therefore it is no great thing if his ministers also be transformed as the ministers of righteousness; whose end shall be according to their works.

Again consider what role that Satan's servants will play. They will pretend to be teaching righteousness. They will get jobs as preachers.

Can we reject Peter's Acts 2:38 message without rejecting the One who sent him?

> Matthew 16:18 And I say also unto thee, That thou art Peter, and upon this rock I will build my church; and the gates of hell shall not prevail against it.
>
> 19 And I will give unto thee the keys of the kingdom of heaven: and whatsoever thou shalt bind on earth shall be bound in heaven: and whatsoever thou shalt loose on earth shall be loosed in heaven.

Are those false-preachers who want you to disregard Peter's Acts 2:38 salvation message really your friend?

Was Jesus nice to everyone? He didn't coddle false preachers and the falsely religious.

> John 8:44 Ye are of your father the devil, and the lusts of your father ye will do. He was a murderer from the beginning, and abode not in the truth, because there is no truth in him. When he speaketh a lie, he speaketh of his own: for he is a liar, and the father of it.

We should not be surprised when the devil's servants lie! They are just doing their job for the father of lies.

One can't reject Peter without rejecting the Lord Jesus Christ who gave Peter the keys to the kingdom of heaven. So we had better know what Peter taught, and you can know this for yourself.

> Acts 2:36 Therefore let all the house of Israel know assuredly, that God hath made that same Jesus, whom ye have crucified, both Lord and Christ.
>
> 37 ¶ Now when they heard this, they were pricked in their heart, and said unto Peter and to the rest of the apostles, Men and brethren, what shall we do?
>
> 38 Then Peter said unto them, Repent, and be baptized every one of you in the name of Jesus Christ for the remission of sins, and ye shall receive the gift of the Holy Ghost.
>
> 39 For the promise is unto you, and to your children, and to all that are afar off, even as many as the Lord our God shall call.

How can anyone even imagine that they would be among the "called of God" when they reject the Acts 2:38 salvation that Peter preached on the authority of the Lord Jesus Christ?

We need to also know that water baptism is to be done in Jesus Name. We monotheists have no problem with that, but polytheists really stumble on that and actually show us that they truly are polytheistic and really are teaching three god squad members.

Satan's servants, the false-christian preachers have found that the best way to keep people from seeking the real Baptism of the Holy Ghost is to convince them they already have it and then just hold them by their religious pride.

> Acts 2:4 And they were all filled with the Holy Ghost, and began to speak with other tongues, as the Spirit gave them utterance.

See, we Pentecostals didn't make up the part about other tongues! If you don't like tongues then you have a problem with God and with His Word.

> Acts 19:6 And when Paul had laid his hands upon them, the Holy Ghost came on them; and they spake with tongues, and prophesied

Paul once said:

> 1 Corinthians 14:18 I thank my God, I speak with tongues more than ye all:

We find examples in the Bible where people received the baptism of the Holy Ghost speaking in tongues before they were baptized in Jesus Name. There are other examples where people were baptized in Jesus Name before they received the Holy Ghost. Both are valid salvation experiences since the Bible documents both scenarios as valid.

> John 3:5 Jesus answered, Verily, verily, I say unto thee, Except a man be born of water and of the Spirit, he cannot enter into the kingdom of God.

Whenever either ingredient of the "water and Spirit" Christian New Birth was missing, the Apostles of Jesus IMMEDIATELY added the missing ingredient. If a person was baptized in Jesus Name then the Apostles would pray for them to receive the Holy Spirit. (that also proves that people don't automatically receive the Holy Ghost when they first "believe" as some of Satan's ministers teach. When people received the Holy Ghost with the evidence of speaking in tongues, the Apostles immediately baptized them in Jesus Name.

These are not man made doctrines I am preaching to you!

> Acts 8:12 But when they believed Philip preaching the things concerning the kingdom of God, and the name of Jesus Christ, they were baptized, both men and women.
>
> 13 Then Simon himself believed also: and when he was baptized, he continued with Philip, and wondered, beholding the miracles and signs which were done.
>
> 14 ¶ Now when the apostles which were at Jerusalem heard that Samaria had received the word of God, they sent unto them Peter and John:
>
> 15 Who, when they were come down, prayed for them, that they might receive the Holy Ghost:
>
> 16 (For as yet he was fallen upon none of them: only they were baptized in the name of the Lord Jesus.)
>
> 17 Then laid they their hands on them, and they received the Holy Ghost.

Note how they had been baptized in Jesus Name. Now why would any true Christian fight against Jesus Name water baptism?

> Acts 10:44 ¶ While Peter yet spake these words, the Holy Ghost fell on all them which heard the word.
>
> 45 And they of the circumcision which believed were astonished, as many as came with Peter, because that on the Gentiles also was poured out the gift of the Holy Ghost.
>
> 46 For they heard them speak with tongues, and magnify God. Then answered Peter,
>
> 47 Can any man forbid water, that these should not be baptized, which have received the Holy Ghost as well as we?
>
> 48 And he commanded them to be baptized in the name of the Lord. Then prayed they him to tarry certain days.

So how did the Apostles know that Gentiles had received the same Holy Ghost they had? They heard them speak with tongues. Now why would any real Christian want to deny you the same experience as Biblical Christianity?

> Psalms 119:89 LAMED. For ever, O LORD, thy word is settled in heaven.

Even those souls who had even been baptized personally by John the Baptist were re-baptized in Jesus name for the remission of their sins. John's baptism was only for a temporary period of time. Jesus Name baptism remits sins by the POWER of the shed blood of God. That does not contradict the doctrine of the Blood of God but rather is the method whereby the Blood of God is applied to the repentant believer during their New Birth.

> Acts 19:1 And it came to pass, that, while Apollos was at Corinth, Paul having passed through the upper coasts came to Ephesus: and finding certain disciples,
>
> 2 He said unto them, Have ye received the Holy Ghost since ye believed? And they said unto him, We have not so much as heard whether there be any Holy Ghost.
>
> 3 And he said unto them, Unto what then were ye baptized? And they said, Unto John’s baptism.
>
> 4 Then said Paul, John verily baptized with the baptism of repentance, saying unto the people, that they should believe on him which should come after him, that is, on Christ Jesus.
>
> 5 When they heard this, they were baptized in the name of the Lord Jesus.
>
> 6 And when Paul had laid his hands upon them, the Holy Ghost came on them; and they spake with tongues, and prophesied.
>
> 7 And all the men were about twelve.

So even with that verse 2 up there, Satan's ministers still convince people that they automatically receive the Holy Ghost when they first "believe"? They prey upon the ignorant and carnal.

> Acts 22:16 And now why tarriest thou? arise, and be baptized, and wash away thy sins, calling on the name of the Lord.

Water baptism Jesus Name is the METHOD whereby one calls on the Name of the Lord.

> Colossians 2:12 Buried with him in baptism, wherein also ye are risen with him through the faith of the operation of God, who hath raised him from the dead.

Note the presence of both WATER and SPIRIT:

> Romans 8:9 But ye are not in the flesh, but in the Spirit, if so be that the Spirit of God dwell in you. Now if any man have not the Spirit of Christ, he is none of his.

The Bible speaks of the Spirit of God and the Spirit of Christ as EXACTLY the same Spirit.

> Mark 16:16 He that believeth and is baptized shall be saved; but he that believeth not shall be damned.
>
> James 1:22 But be ye doers of the word, and not hearers only, deceiving your own selves.
>
> John 3:5 Jesus answered, Verily, verily, I say unto thee, Except a man be born of water and [of] the Spirit, he cannot enter into the kingdom of God.
>
> 6 That which is born of the flesh is flesh; and that which is born of the Spirit is spirit.
>
> 7 Marvel not that I said unto thee, Ye must be born again.

Jesus was telling a grown man what he STILL needed to do in order to be saved. The grown man still had to be reborn of WATER and of the SPIRIT.

This is totally consistent with the plan of salvation that Peter, the "man with the keys to the kingdom from Jesus Himself" preached on the birthday of the New Testament Church.

> Matthew 16:18 And I say also unto thee, That thou art Peter, and upon this rock I will build my church; and the gates of hell shall not prevail against it.
>
> 19 And I will give unto thee the keys of the kingdom of heaven: and whatsoever thou shalt bind on earth shall be bound in heaven: and whatsoever thou shalt loose on earth shall be loosed in heaven.

> Acts 2:38 Then Peter said unto them, Repent, and be baptized every one of you in the name of Jesus Christ for the remission of sins, and ye shall receive the gift of the Holy Ghost.
>
> Acts 2:39 For the promise is unto you, and to your children, and to all that are afar off, [even] as many as the Lord our God shall call.
>
> Acts 2:40 And with many other words did he testify and exhort, saying, Save yourselves from this untoward generation.
>
> Acts 2:41 Then they that gladly received his word were baptized: and the same day there were added [unto them] about three thousand souls.

If your preacher told you that you don't need to obey Acts 2:38, I want you to consider these next verses.

> 2 Thessalonians 1:7 And to you who are troubled rest with us, when the Lord Jesus shall be revealed from heaven with his mighty angels,

> 8 In flaming fire taking vengeance on them that know not God, and that obey not the gospel of our Lord Jesus Christ:
>
> 9 Who shall be punished with everlasting destruction from the presence of the Lord, and from the glory of his power;

How can people be so deceived that they don't think they need to obey the Gospel?

> 1 Peter 4:17 For the time is come that judgment must begin at the house of God: and if it first begin at us, what shall the end be of them that obey not the gospel of God?
>
> Romans 10:16 But they have not all obeyed the gospel. For Esaias saith, Lord, who hath believed our report?

See in the above verse how the Apostles considered a "non-obeyer" to be a "non-believer"?

> Galatians 3:27 For as many of you as have been baptized into Christ have put on Christ.

Repentance

> 2 Corinthians 7:10 For godly sorrow worketh repentance to salvation not to be repented of: but the sorrow of the world worketh death.

There are different types of sorrow. Some are sorry for something that they did purely because of the consequences. Many in prison are very sorry that they got caught doing some crime and are sorry that they did what they got caught for, but they are not at all repentant. They are not at all sorry for the crimes they got away with. There is a difference between godly sorrow and the sorrow of the world. Many are very sorry that they are reaping that which they sowed. That is not to say that some who have that same worldly sorry will not turn to godly sorrow. What makes the difference? Repentance

> 1 Peter 2:20 For what glory is it, if, when ye be buffeted for your faults, ye shall take it patiently? but if, when ye do well, and suffer for it, ye take it patiently, this is acceptable with God.
>
> 21 For even hereunto were ye called: because Christ also suffered for us, leaving us an example, that ye should follow his steps:
>
> 22 Who did no sin, neither was guile found in his mouth:

> 1 Peter 3:10 For he that will love life, and see good days, let him refrain his tongue from evil, and his lips that they speak no guile:
>
> 11 Let him eschew evil, and do good; let him seek peace, and ensue it.
>
> 12 For the eyes of the Lord are over the righteous, and his ears are open unto their prayers: but the face of the Lord is against them that do evil.

13 And who is he that will harm you, if ye be followers of that which is good?

14 But and if ye suffer for righteousness' sake, happy are ye: and be not afraid of their terror, neither be troubled;

15 But sanctify the Lord God in your hearts: and be ready always to give an answer to every man that asketh you a reason of the hope that is in you with meekness and fear:

16 ¶ Having a good conscience; that, whereas they speak evil of you, as of evildoers, they may be ashamed that falsely accuse your good conversation in Christ.

17 For it is better, if the will of God be so, that ye suffer for well doing, than for evil doing.

So there are some who will suffer for doing good, but with that comes a blessing from God.

Let us look deeper at repentance. Repentance is the first step in the New Testament plan of salvation

Looking at the new testament plan of salvation from the AV and the Darby Bibles (indexed to Strong's concordance) we see:

Ac 2:38 Then <1161> Peter <4074> said <5346> (5713) to <4314> them <846>, Repent ye <3340> (5657), and <2532> each one <1538> of you <5216> be baptized <907> (5682) in <1909> the name <3686> of Jesus <2424> Christ <5547> for <1519> the remission <859> of sins <266>, and <2532> ye shall receive <2983> (5695) the gift <1431> of the Holy <40> Spirit <4151>.

Ac 2:38 And Peter said to them, Repent, and be baptized, each one of you, in the name of Jesus Christ, for remission of sins, and ye will receive the gift of the Holy Spirit.

The first step in the new testament plan of salvation is repentance.

Repentance

This means a turning away from sin. A painter who repents of painting QUITS painting; if he truly repented of painting, he doesn't continue to paint.

> 3340 metanoeo met-an-o-eh'-o
>
> from 3326 and 3539; TDNT - 4:975,636; v
>
> AV - repent 34; 34
>
> 1) to change one's mind, i.e. to repent
>
> 2) to change one's mind for better, heartily to amend with abhorrence of one's past sins

The first step of faith in becoming a Christian is to repent of one's sins. Always repentance involves a change of mind and a change of lifestyle.

> Ezekiel 14:6 Therefore say unto the house of Israel, Thus saith the Lord GOD; Repent, and turn yourselves from your idols; and turn away your faces from all your abominations.
>
> Ezekiel 18:30 Therefore I will judge you, O house of Israel, every one according to his ways, saith the Lord GOD. Repent, and turn yourselves from all your transgressions; so iniquity shall not be your ruin.
>
> Ezekiel 24:14 I the LORD have spoken it: it shall come to pass, and I will do it; I will not go back, neither will I spare, neither will I repent ; according to thy ways, and according to thy doings, shall they judge thee, saith the Lord GOD.

Noting the Lord's statement that He will not repent of His position gives us insight into the meaning of the word, "repent". Remember that repentance from sin is the first step of faith that a man takes towards salvation.

> Matthew 4:17 From that time Jesus began to preach, and to say, Repent: for the kingdom of heaven is at hand.

Repentance

Jesus clearly preached repentance.

> Mark 1:15 And saying, The time is fulfilled, and the kingdom of God is at hand: repent ye, and believe the gospel.

Notice repent AND believe.

> Luke 13:3 I tell you, Nay: but, except ye repent, ye shall all likewise perish.
>
> Luke 13:5 I tell you, Nay: but, except ye repent, ye shall all likewise perish.

> Acts 2:38 Then Peter said unto them, Repent, and be baptized every one of you in the name of Jesus Christ for the remission of sins, and ye shall receive the gift of the Holy Ghost.

Repentance, the first step of faith of salvation.

> Acts 3:19 Repent ye therefore, and be converted, that your sins may be blotted out, when the times of refreshing shall come from the presence of the Lord;

Notice that it says repent AND be converted. There is more to Christian conversion than repentance, though repentance is a necessary FIRST STEP.

> Acts 17:30 And the times of this ignorance God winked at; but now commandeth all men every where to repent:

There is no question that in the New Testament Church dispensation that repentance is essential.

> Acts 26:20 But shewed first unto them of Damascus, and at Jerusalem, and throughout all the coasts of Judaea, and then to the Gentiles, that they should repent and turn to God, and do works meet for repentance.

Even Churches exhorted to repentance.

> Revelation 2:5 Remember therefore from whence thou art fallen, and repent, and do the first works; or else I will come unto thee quickly, and will remove thy candlestick out of his place, except thou repent.
>
> Revelation 2:16 Repent; or else I will come unto thee quickly, and will fight against them with the sword of my mouth.

We look back even at John the Baptist when the multitude came to be baptized. He demanded to see proof of their repentance.

> Luke 3:7 Then said he to the multitude that came forth to be baptized of him, O generation of vipers, who hath warned you to flee from the wrath to come?
>
> 8 Bring forth therefore fruits worthy of repentance, and begin not to say within yourselves, We have Abraham to our father: for I say unto you, That God is able of these stones to raise up children unto Abraham.

There is a sorrow of the world that is not really repentance. Many a criminal is sorry because they got caught or people are sorry because of the results of sin, but that, in itself, is not repentance.

> 2 Corinthians 7:10 For godly sorrow worketh repentance to salvation not to be repented of: but the sorrow of the world worketh death.

To repent from something one quits doing whatever it was.

Receiving the Holy Ghost

** Jews when they received the Holy Ghost **

Acts 2:4 And they were all filled with the Holy Ghost, and began to speak with other tongues, as the Spirit gave them utterance.

** Samaritans when they received the Holy Ghost **

Acts 8:14 Now when the apostles which were at Jerusalem heard that Samaria had received the word of God, they sent unto them Peter and John:

Acts 8:15 Who, when they were come down, prayed for them, that they might receive the Holy Ghost:

Acts 8:16 (For as yet he was fallen upon none of them: only they were baptized in the name of the Lord Jesus.)

Acts 8:17 Then laid they [their] hands on them, and they received the Holy Ghost.

Gentiles when they received the Holy Ghost

Acts 10:45 And they of the circumcision which believed were astonished, as many as came with Peter, because that on the Gentiles also was poured out the gift of the Holy Ghost.

Acts 10:46 For they heard them speak with tongues, and magnify God. Then answered Peter,

Acts 10:47 Can any man forbid water, that these should not be baptized, which have received the Holy Ghost as well as we?

Acts 10:48 And he commanded them to be baptized in the name of the Lord. Then prayed they him to tarry certain days.

John the Baptist's disciples when they were RE- baptized and received the Holy Ghost.

> Acts 19:2 He said unto them, Have ye received the Holy Ghost since ye believed? And they said unto him, We have not so much as heard whether there be any Holy Ghost.
>
> Acts 19:3 And he said unto them, Unto what then were ye baptized? And they said, Unto John's baptism.
>
> Acts 19:4 Then said Paul, John verily baptized with the baptism of repentance, saying unto the people, that they should believe on him which should come after him, that is, on Christ Jesus.
>
> Acts 19:5 When they heard [this], they were baptized in the name of the Lord Jesus.
>
> Acts 19:6 And when Paul had laid [his] hands upon them, the Holy Ghost came on them; and they spake with tongues, and prophesied.

Jews, gentiles, Samaritans; all baptized in JESUS name, all spoke in tongues when they received the Holy Ghost.

> Romans 8:9 But ye are not in the flesh, but in the Spirit, if so be that the Spirit of God dwell in you. Now if any man have not the Spirit of Christ, he is none of his.
>
> Acts 1:8 But ye shall receive power, after that the Holy Ghost is come upon you: and ye shall be witnesses unto me both in Jerusalem, and in all Judaea, and in Samaria, and unto the uttermost part of the earth

In You

The Holy Ghost most certainly is the Spirit of Christ.

** Jesus told the disciples to WAIT for POWER. **

> Luke 24:49 And, behold, I send the promise of my Father upon you: but tarry ye in the city of Jerusalem, until ye be endued with power from on high.
>
> Acts 1:8 But ye shall receive power, after that the Holy Ghost is come upon you: and ye shall be witnesses unto me both in Jerusalem, and in all Judaea, and in Samaria, and unto the uttermost part of the earth.

** When they received POWER they ALL spoke in tongues. **

> Acts 2:4 And they were all filled with the Holy Ghost, and began to speak with other tongues, as the Spirit gave them utterance.

** Speaking in tongues is the sign of a true believer. **

> Mark 16:17 And these signs shall follow them that believe; In my name shall they cast out devils; they shall speak with new tongues;

Many prefer false preachers instead of the truth.

> II Timothy 4:3 For the time will come when they will not endure sound doctrine; but after their own lusts shall they heap to themselves teachers, having itching ears;

They have the form (church services, appearing "good", etc.), but deny "tongues" (denying the POWER) **

> II Timothy 3:5 Having a form of godliness, but denying the power thereof: from such turn away.

If you don't have the Spirit (POWER), you're NONE OF HIS. **

> Romans 8:9 But ye are not in the flesh, but in the Spirit, if so be that the Spirit of God dwell in you. Now if any man have not the Spirit of Christ, he is none of his.

Jesus declaring HIMSELF to be the Spirit of Truth (the Holy Ghost, the POWER). Look closely! **

> John 14:17 [Even] the Spirit of truth; whom the world cannot receive, because it seeth him not, neither knoweth him: but ye know him; for he dwelleth with you, and shall be in you.

The Spirit of Truth (the Holy Ghost) is the form that Jesus is manifesting Himself in, in this dispensation. Those that deny tongues, deny Christ. They are only holding to the form of religion, but they don't have the real thing, they don't have the POWER. When they rejected the Holy Ghost speaking in tongues; they rejected Jesus Christ. **

Jesus identified Himself as the comforter.

> John 14:18 I will not leave you comfortless: I will come to you.

John 3:16

> John 3:16 For God so loved the world, that he gave his only begotten Son, that whosoever believeth in him should not perish, but have everlasting life.

That is a beautiful verse, but it is abused by many false preachers to promote false christianity and lies. John 3:16 was only PART of a conversation which INCLUDED John 3:5.

> John 3:1 There was a man of the Pharisees, named Nicodemus, a ruler of the Jews:
>
> John 3:2 The same came to Jesus by night, and said unto him, Rabbi, we know that thou art a teacher come from God: for no man can do these miracles that thou doest, except God be with him.
>
> John 3:3 Jesus answered and said unto him, Verily, verily, I say unto thee, Except a man be born again, he cannot see the kingdom of God.
>
> John 3:4 Nicodemus saith unto him, How can a man be born when he is old? can he enter the second time into his mother's womb, and be born?
>
> John 3:5 Jesus answered, Verily, verily, I say unto thee, Except a man be born of water and [of] the Spirit, he cannot enter into the kingdom of God.

Jesus declared that salvation required a re-birth of water and Spirit.

> John 3:6 That which is born of the flesh is flesh; and that which is born of the Spirit is spirit.
>
> John 3:7 Marvel not that I said unto thee, Ye must be born again.
>
> John 3:8 The wind bloweth where it listeth, and thou hearest the sound thereof, but canst not tell whence it cometh, and whither it goeth: so is every one that is born of the Spirit.

John 3:9 Nicodemus answered and said unto him, How can these things be?

John 3:10 Jesus answered and said unto him, Art thou a master of Israel, and knowest not these things?

John 3:11 Verily, verily, I say unto thee, We speak that we do know, and testify that we have seen; and ye receive not our witness.

John 3:12 If I have told you earthly things, and ye believe not, how shall ye believe, if I tell you [of] heavenly things?

John 3:13 And no man hath ascended up to heaven, but he that came down from heaven, [even] the Son of man which is in heaven.

John 3:14 And as Moses lifted up the serpent in the wilderness, even so must the Son of man be lifted up:

John 3:15 That whosoever believeth in him should not perish, but have eternal life.

Jesus knew that anyone who *really* believed in Him would OBEY. The example that Jesus used regarding the serpent was a situation where only the obedient were saved! Jesus used an example that stressed OBEDIENCE!

Here is the situation that Jesus cited.

Numbers 21:8 And the LORD said unto Moses, Make thee a fiery serpent, and set it upon a pole: and it shall come to pass, that every one that is bitten, when he looketh upon it, shall live.

Here is the whole context.

Numbers 21:5 And the people spake against God, and against Moses, Wherefore have ye brought us up out of Egypt to die in the wilderness? for there is no bread, neither is there any water; and our soul loatheth this light bread.

6 And the LORD sent fiery serpents among the people, and they bit the people; and much people of Israel died.

> 7 Therefore the people came to Moses, and said, We have sinned, for we have spoken against the LORD, and against thee; pray unto the LORD, that he take away the serpents from us. And Moses prayed for the people.
>
> 8 And the LORD said unto Moses, Make thee a fiery serpent, and set it upon a pole: and it shall come to pass, that every one that is bitten, when he looketh upon it, shall live.
>
> 9 And Moses made a serpent of brass, and put it upon a pole, and it came to pass, that if a serpent had bitten any man, when he beheld the serpent of brass, he lived.

Jesus used an example of a sinful people who were, by grace, given an opportunity to OBEY and be saved.

> John 3:16 For God so loved the world, that he gave his only begotten Son, that whosoever believeth in him should not perish, but have everlasting life.

When the plan of salvation was preached on the birthday of the Church, it was based on the two elements that Jesus had declared essential. Notice "water" (baptism) and "Spirit" (Holy Ghost), John 3:5 in ACTion.

> Acts 2:38 Then Peter said unto them, Repent, and be baptized every one of you in the name of Jesus Christ for the remission of sins, and ye shall receive the gift of the Holy Ghost.
>
> Acts 2:39 For the promise is unto you, and to your children, and to all that are afar off, [even] as many as the Lord our God shall call.
>
> Acts 2:40 And with many other words did he testify and exhort, saying, Save yourselves from this untoward generation.
>
> Acts 2:41 Then they that gladly received his word were baptized: and the same day there were added [unto them] about three thousand souls.

Those who "believed" were baptized in Jesus name.

> Acts 8:12 But when they believed Philip preaching the things concerning the kingdom of God, and the name of Jesus Christ, they were baptized, both men and women.
>
> Acts 8:13 Then Simon himself believed also: and when he was baptized, he continued with Philip, and wondered, beholding the miracles and signs which were done.

Those who "believed" the apostles, "obeyed" the apostles.

> Acts 18:8 And Crispus, the chief ruler of the synagogue, believed on the Lord with all his house; and many of the Corinthians hearing believed, and were baptized.

Those who "believed" the apostles, "obeyed" the apostles.

> Acts 19:4 Then said Paul, John verily baptized with the baptism of repentance, saying unto the people, that they should believe on him which should come after him, that is, on Christ Jesus.
>
> Acts 19:5 When they heard [this], they were baptized in the name of the Lord Jesus.

Anyone who would not obey Acts 2:38 was counted to be a NON-BELIEVER.

> Romans 10:16 But they have not all obeyed the gospel. For Esaias saith, Lord, who hath believed our report?
>
> Hebrews 5:9 And being made perfect, he became the author of eternal salvation unto all them that obey him;

What is promised to those who refuse to obey the Gospel? Remember Jesus used in His discussion about salvation a situation where any non-obeyer DIED.

John 3:14 And as Moses lifted up the serpent in the wilderness, even so must the Son of man be lifted up:

The serpent was lifted up to provide an option for the people to obey and be saved.

2 Thessalonians 1:7 And to you who are troubled rest with us, when the Lord Jesus shall be revealed from heaven with his mighty angels,

8 In flaming fire taking vengeance on them that know not God, and that obey not the gospel of our Lord Jesus Christ:

9 Who shall be punished with everlasting destruction from the presence of the Lord, and from the glory of his power;

1 Peter 4:17 For the time is come that judgment must begin at the house of God: and if it first begin at us, what shall the end be of them that obey not the gospel of God?

18 And if the righteous scarcely be saved, where shall the ungodly and the sinner appear?

Hebrews 5:9 And being made perfect, he became the author of eternal salvation unto all them that obey him;

All things work together

Looking at the verse, we see that there is a very important qualifier.

> Romans 8:28 And we know that all things work together for good to them that love God, to them who are the called according to his purpose.

It is important to understand who this was addressed to. "Those who love god and those who are called according to His purpose." Romans is an epistle, a letter, that was addressed to those at Rome who had obeyed Acts 2:38.

Regarding who is "called" we see verse 39 and that there is a very important qualifier.

> Acts 2:38 Then Peter said unto them, Repent, and be baptized every one of you in the name of Jesus Christ for the remission of sins, and ye shall receive the gift of the Holy Ghost.
>
> Acts 2:39 For the promise is unto you, and to your children, and to all that are afar off, even as many as the Lord our God shall call.

So Romans 8:28 is not referring to just anyone, but rather to those who are real Acts 2:38 Christians, baptized in Jesus Name, having the Holy Ghost speaking in tongues and living a holy life.

I hope this helps.

Gospel

The gospel is the death, burial, and resurrection of the Lord Jesus Christ. This gospel (good news) is to be preached in all nations (beginning at Jerusalem). The gospel was first preached at Jerusalem on the the day of Pentecost.

All are commanded to OBEY the gospel:

> 2 Th 1:8 In flaming fire taking vengeance on them that know not God, and that obey not the gospel of our Lord Jesus Christ:
>
> 1 Pet 4:17 For the time is come that judgment must begin at the house of God: and if it first begin at us, what shall the end be of them that obey not the gospel of God?

Now..how does one OBEY the death, burial, and resurrection?

> John 3:5 Jesus answered, Verily , verily, I say unto thee, Except a man be born of water and of the Spirit, he cannot enter into the kingdom of God.

Of course if someone did not believe, they would have no desire to obey..Jesus told Nicodemus a couple of very important things in John 3:16 and John 3:5, he said that those who believeth SHOULD not perish. He had just told Nicodemus that he HAD to be born AGAIN two ways. One water, one of Spirit. What does water and spirit have to do with the gospel? Well the first gospel sermon preached to sinners was:

> Acts 2:38 Then Peter said unto them, Repent, and be baptized every one of you in the name of Jesus Christ for the remission of sins, and ye shall receive the gift of the Holy Ghost.

Here we are: water (baptism) and Spirit (the gift of the Holy Ghost)..and in repentance a person dies to sin..the old man dies. The Bible says that we are "buried with Christ in baptism" (Romans 6:4) or baptized into his death.

The Holy Ghost is Christ in you the hope of glory ..the hope of resurrection.

> Rom 8:9 But ye are not in the flesh, but in the Spirit, if so be that the Spirit of God dwell in you. Now if any man have not the Spirit of Christ, he is none of his.

So there you have death, burial, and resurrection..the gospel.

And the way that the apostles taught to obey it.

Have you obeyed the gospel of the Lord Jesus Christ?

See also Gal 1:8, Acts 2:39, Acts 10:44-48, Acts 11:5, Acts 19:1-6.

Matthew 28:19

> John 5:43 I am come in my Father's name, and ye receive me not: if another shall come in his own name, him ye will receive.
>
> Matthew 1:21 And she shall bring forth a son, and thou shalt call his name JESUS: for he shall save his people from their sins.
>
> Luke 1:31 And, behold, thou shalt conceive in thy womb, and bring forth a son, and shalt call his name JESUS.
>
> Matthew 28:19 Go ye therefore, and teach all nations, baptizing them in the name of the Father, and of the Son, and of the Holy Ghost:

In order to obey Matt 28:19 one MUST be aware of the name that Jesus was referring to. Merely chanting the Bible verse is not the same as obeying it.

The Apostles obeyed Jesus and used the NAME that Jesus was referring to. Father, Son, and Holy Ghost are not names but rather they are used to specify which NAME that Jesus wanted to be used.

"Father" is not a NAME, there are many fathers (who also have names). "Son" is not a NAME, there are many sons (who also have names). "Holy Spirit" is not a NAME, and Lord knows that there are a *bunch* of demons and spirits running around "pretending" to be "holy" (to numerous to name, but one third of the angels).

Jesus Christ is a NAME. And it is a name that the false churches hate (at least in baptism, where it counts!).

Look also at the previous verse:

> Matthew 28:18 And Jesus came and spake unto them, saying, All power is given unto me in heaven and in earth.

If there were any other "god squad members" they would be powerless.

Some 3 god cultists will actually use the name of Jesus in what they perceive to be an insult. They will call the true ONE GOD Apostolic Christians "Jesus only" (and they mean it as an insult because they actually believe in three separate Catholic gods).

Notice carefully that in Matt 28:19 Jesus said 'name' (singular) and not 'names' (plural). For those (like the Apostles) that only believe in ONE GOD, baptism in a singular name does not present a problem (ONE GOD, ONE NAME).

To find out what the NAME is that fits the ONE GOD who manifested Himself as "Father"(Spirit) and as "Son"(Flesh) and as "Holy Spirit"(Spirit of Christ to indwell saints); we can look and see how the Apostles baptized. The Apostles always baptized in the name of their God. The Bible says that there is only one name that can save:

> Acts 4:10 Be it known unto you all, and to all the people of Israel, that by the name of Jesus Christ of Nazareth, whom ye crucified, whom God raised from the dead, [even] by him doth this man stand here before you whole.
>
> Acts 4:11 This is the stone which was set at nought of you builders, which is become the head of the corner.
>
> Acts 4:12 Neither is there salvation in any other: for there is none other name under heaven given among men, whereby we must be saved.

There is only one God, and there is only one saving NAME.

> Acts 2:38 Then Peter said unto them, Repent, and be baptized every one of you in the name of Jesus Christ for the remission of sins, and ye shall receive the gift of the Holy Ghost.

Water Baptism in Jesus name remits sins.

Acts 8:12 But when they believed Philip preaching the things

concerning the kingdom of God, and the name of Jesus Christ, they

were baptized, both men and women.

People who BELIEVE in the NAME are baptized in that NAME. The next verse shows how the folks in verse 12 were baptized

Acts 8:16 (For as yet he was fallen upon none of them: only they were baptized in the name of the Lord Jesus.)

Acts 15:26 Men that have hazarded their lives for the name of our Lord Jesus Christ.

Acts 16:18 And this did she many days. But Paul, being grieved, turned and said to the spirit, I command thee in the name of Jesus Christ to come out of her. And he came out the same hour.

There is POWER in the NAME (that is why the devil and his ministers fight against Jesus name baptism).

Acts 19:4 Then said Paul, John verily baptized with the baptism of repentance, saying unto the people, that they should believe on him which should come after him, that is, on Christ Jesus.

Acts 19:5 When they heard [this], they were baptized in the name of the Lord Jesus.

Those who "believed on the name" were baptized in that name.

Acts 19:6 And when Paul had laid [his] hands upon them, the Holy Ghost came on them; and they spake with tongues, and prophesied.

> Acts 19:17 And this was known to all the Jews and Greeks also dwelling at Ephesus; and fear fell on them all, and the name of the Lord Jesus was magnified.

Notice also the dire warning against the trinity in the Word of God and how it is a SPOILER of the souls of men.

> Colossians 2:8 Beware lest any man spoil you through philosophy and vain deceit, after the tradition of men, after the rudiments of the world, and not after Christ.
>
> 9 For in him dwelleth all the fulness of the Godhead bodily.
>
> 10 And ye are complete in him, which is the head of all principality and power:
>
> 11 In whom also ye are circumcised with the circumcision made without hands, in putting off the body of the sins of the flesh by the circumcision of Christ:
>
> 12 Buried with him in baptism, wherein also ye are risen with him through the faith of the operation of God, who hath raised him from the dead.

How do we know we're saved?

Someone once asked me: “Problem is I bet both you and I know in our hearts that we are saved, how do we know we aren't deceiving ourselves?”

Excellent point! That is why it is so important to be a part of the SAME Church that was started in the book of Acts. I find myself sometimes wondering why people who don't believe what the Apostles preached, don't obey what the Apostles preached and don't experience what the early Church experienced would ever imagine in their wildest dreams that they are "Christian" anyway (of course I know that some gainsayer was paid to convince them).

One needs to measure one's religion and see if it is the exact same "Jesus name baptizing", "Holy Ghost tongue talking" religion of the Bible, or just some modern "man pleasing" counterfeit.

Men are lured into denominal polytheism by the treachery of others, but they are retained therein by their own pride.

I find it interesting that the Bible would be so clear in its warning regarding the "last days" religious climate.

> 2 Tim 4:3 For the time will come when they will not endure sound doctrine; but after their own lusts shall they heap to themselves teachers, having itching ears;
>
> 2 Tim 4:4 And they shall turn away their ears from the truth, and shall be turned unto fables.

There is also a rather blatant warning against denominal polytheism with their "separate persons" mystery religion.

> Col 2:8 Beware lest any man spoil you through philosophy and vain deceit, after the tradition of men, after the rudiments of the world, and not after Christ.
>
> Col 2:9 For in him dwelleth all the fulness of the Godhead bodily.

> Col 2:10 And ye are complete in him, which is the head of all principality and power:

A study of the book of Acts reveals that the criteria that the Apostles used for determining the new birth (or lack thereof) was "Jesus name water baptism" and "The baptism of the Holy Ghost with the evidence of speaking with other tongues". So, I believe that it would be a good question to ask of oneself whether the Apostles would have considered you a brother or a candidate for brotherhood.

Saved as the Devils in Legion

There are many today who claim to be "Christian" and "saved" because they got a prayer answered. If God did not hear the prayers of sinners then there wouldn't be any Christians. If God did not fill sinners with the Holy Ghost then we would not have examples in the Bible where people received the Holy Ghost baptism with the initial evidence of speaking in other tongues

BEFORE they were baptized in Jesus Name to have their sins washed away.

Let's look at a situation where Jesus was acknowledged as Lord and answered prayers and then compare that with the salvation experience that so many will claim today.

> Mark 5:2 And when he was come out of the ship, immediately there met him out of the tombs a man with an unclean spirit,
>
> 3 Who had his dwelling among the tombs; and no man could bind him, no, not with chains:
>
> 4 Because that he had been often bound with fetters and chains, and the chains had been plucked asunder by him, and the fetters broken in pieces: neither could any man tame him.
>
> 5 And always, night and day, he was in the mountains, and in the tombs, crying, and cutting himself with stones.
>
> 6 But when he saw Jesus afar off, he ran and worshipped him,
>
> 7 And cried with a loud voice, and said, What have I to do with thee, Jesus, thou Son of the most high God? I adjure thee by God, that thou torment me not.

Notice that the devils confessed Jesus as Lord (and even PRAYED to Him, eh?). This is important because at that point the devils fulfilled the salvation requirements of most if not all denominal trinitarian false-christian cults in this city, yea even in this world.

> 8 For he said unto him, Come out of the man, thou unclean spirit.
>
> 9 And he asked him, What is thy name? And he answered, saying, My name is Legion: for we are many.
>
> 10 And he besought him much that he would not send them away out of the country.

The devils prayed to Jesus after acknowledging Him as Lord God. They prayed a specific prayer request directly to the Lord Jesus Christ.

> 11 Now there was there nigh unto the mountains a great herd of swine feeding.
>
> 12 And all the devils besought him, saying, Send us into the swine, that we may enter into them.

More praying to Jesus by the devils!

> 13 And forthwith Jesus gave them leave. And the unclean spirits went out, and entered into the swine: and the herd ran violently down a steep place into the sea, (they were about two thousand;) and were choked in the sea.

Jesus GRANTED their prayer request. He answered their prayer.

> 14 And they that fed the swine fled, and told it in the city, and in the country. And they went out to see what it was that was done.
>
> 15 And they come to Jesus, and see him that was possessed with the devil, and had the legion, sitting, and clothed, and in his right mind: and they were afraid.
>
> 16 And they that saw it told them how it befell to him that was possessed with the devil, and also concerning the swine.

17 And they began to pray him to depart out of their coasts.

The townspeople asked Jesus to leave and He granted their prayer request as well. Jesus honors the prayer requests of the false-christian cults that don't want Him around. (in this day Jesus comes to us as the Holy Ghost and His infilling always has the initial evidence of speaking in other tongues.) The false-christian cults pray Him to depart and He does.

Are you a Baptist, Presbyterian, Methodist, Lutheran etc? If so and if you have followed your denominational doctrines, you are just as saved as the devils in Legion! There are a lot of deceived good people out there!

The townspeople asking Jesus to leave is a sermon in itself, but my point here is that false churches are lying to you when they tell you that if you just "believe" or "pray", or "acknowledge Jesus as Lord" that you are "saved". Did not the devils in Legion do those things?

Jesus gave the Apostle Peter the keys to the kingdom of heaven.

> Matt 16:19 And I will give unto thee the keys of the kingdom of heaven: and whatsoever thou shalt bind on earth shall be bound in heaven: and whatsoever thou shalt loose on earth shall be loosed in heaven.

Peter was no pope but he was the man with the keys to the kingdom. You cannot reject Peter and claim to retain Jesus who gave Peter the keys. (and Peter also affirmed Paul too).

> 2 Peter 3:15 And account that the longsuffering of our Lord is salvation; even as our beloved brother Paul also according to the wisdom given unto him hath written unto you;

> 2 Peter 3:16 As also in all his epistles, speaking in them of these things; in which are some things hard to be understood, which they that are unlearned and unstable wrest, as they do also the other scriptures, unto their own destruction.

That again is another sermon in itself.

Then when men were honest and asked Peter what they could do, Peter unlocked the kingdom of heaven.

> Acts 2:36 Therefore let all the house of Israel know assuredly, that God hath made that same Jesus, whom ye have crucified, both Lord and Christ.
>
> Acts 2:37 Now when they heard [this], they were pricked in their heart, and said unto Peter and to the rest of the apostles, Men [and] brethren, what shall we do?
>
> Acts 2:38 Then Peter said unto them, Repent, and be baptized every one of you in the name of Jesus Christ for the remission of sins, and ye shall receive the gift of the Holy Ghost.
>
> Acts 2:39 For the promise is unto you, and to your children, and to all that are afar off, [even] as many as the Lord our God shall call.
>
> Acts 2:40 And with many other words did he testify and exhort, saying, Save yourselves from this untoward generation.
>
> Acts 2:41 Then they that gladly received his word were baptized: and the same day there were added [unto them] about three thousand souls.

Notice there were 3000 there that elected to have their sins remitted or "washed away" by being baptized in the Name of Jesus.

So you'd better believe that the minister of Satan will do just about anything that he can to try to downplay Acts 2:38. Paul mentions that there will be those that come along and preach "another gospel."

> Gal 1:8 But though we, or an angel from heaven, preach any other gospel unto you than that which we have preached unto you, let him be accursed.

Paul also didn't leave us in ignorance that when Satan's ministers come, they come masquerading as "ministers of righteousness", as smooth talking false preachers saying things like, "Just claim belief and you are saved."

> II Corinthians 11:13 For such [are] false apostles, deceitful workers, transforming themselves into the apostles of Christ.
>
> II Corinthians 11:14 And no marvel; for Satan himself is transformed into an angel of light.
>
> II Corinthians 11:15 Therefore [it is] no great thing if his ministers also be transformed as the ministers of righteousness; whose end shall be according to their works.

Did you ever wonder why there are so many "churches" claiming to be "christian" but preaching totally different salvation doctrines.

It is the job of the false preacher to cause YOU to be among those that don't obey Acts 2:38.

> II Thessalonians 1:7 And to you who are troubled rest with us, when the Lord Jesus shall be revealed from heaven with his mighty angels,
>
> II Thessalonians 1:8 In flaming fire taking vengeance on them that know not God, and that obey not the gospel of our Lord Jesus Christ:
>
> II Thessalonians 1:9 Who shall be punished with everlasting destruction from the presence of the Lord, and from the glory of his power;

> James 1:22 But be ye doers of the word, and not hearers only, deceiving your own selves.

> Hebrews 5:9 And being made perfect, he became the author of eternal salvation unto all them that obey him;

> Acts 22:16 And now why tarriest thou? arise, and be baptized, and wash away thy sins, calling on the name of the Lord.

Just having the same salvation experience and foundation as the devils in Legion will leave you eternally challenged.

Not Yet

Acts 2:38 is only "infamous" among the fake christians who refuse to obey it.

> Romans 1:6 Among whom are ye also the called of Jesus Christ:
>
> Romans 1:7 To all that be in Rome, beloved of God, called [to be] saints: Grace to you and peace from God our Father, and the Lord Jesus Christ.
>
> Romans 1:8 First, I thank my God through Jesus Christ for you all, that your faith is spoken of throughout the whole world.

Romans was written to the "saints" at Rome, the "called of Jesus Christ". It is not addressed those of you who have not yet obeyed Acts 2:38 to become a real Christian.

> I Corinthians 1:1 Paul, called [to be] an apostle of Jesus Christ through the will of God, and Sosthenes [our] brother,
>
> I Corinthians 1:2 Unto the church of God which is at Corinth, to them that are sanctified in Christ Jesus, called [to be] saints, with all that in every place call upon the name of Jesus Christ our Lord, both theirs and ours:

Corinthians was written to the "Church of Jesus". It is not addressed to those who have not been born again

> Galatians 1:1 Paul, an apostle, (not of men, neither by man, but by Jesus Christ, and God the Father, who raised him from the dead;)
>
> Galatians 1:2 And all the brethren which are with me, unto the churches of Galatia:

Galatians was written to the churches of Galatia, it was not addressed to you who have not obeyed the Gospel.

> Ephesians 1:1 Paul, an apostle of Jesus Christ by the will of God, to the saints which are at Ephesus, and to the faithful in Christ Jesus:

The book of Ephesians was written to the "saints" at Ephesus. Look at Acts 19 and see how the saints at Ephesus became Christian by OBEYING Acts 2:38.

> Acts 19:1 And it came to pass, that, while Apollos was at Corinth, Paul having passed through the upper coasts came to Ephesus: and finding certain disciples,
>
> Acts 19:2 He said unto them, Have ye received the Holy Ghost since ye believed? And they said unto him, We have not so much as heard whether there be any Holy Ghost.
>
> Acts 19:3 And he said unto them, Unto what then were ye baptized? And they said, Unto John's baptism.
>
> Acts 19:4 Then said Paul, John verily baptized with the baptism of repentance, saying unto the people, that they should believe on him which should come after him, that is, on Christ Jesus.
>
> Acts 19:5 When they heard [this], they were baptized in the name of the Lord Jesus.
>
> Acts 19:6 And when Paul had laid [his] hands upon them, the Holy Ghost came on them; and they spake with tongues, and prophesied.

The "saints" at Ephesus became Christians by obeying Acts 2:38, just like every other person who will ever become a real Christian.

Letters

The epistles of the Bible are letters that were addressed to those who had received the preaching of the Apostles. The "receiving" or "believing" was determined by whether or not the hearers of the Apostles obeyed the word preached by the Apostles. One who would not obey was considered a "non-believer".

> Romans 10:16 But they have not all obeyed the gospel. For Esaias saith, Lord, who hath believed our report?

Some will claim to be "believers" even though they never obeyed the Gospel that the Apostles preached (some say there is nothing to obey). Before continuing, let's make it perfectly clear what Jesus Christ has in store for any and all who do not obey the Gospel that the Apostles preached.

> 2THES 1:7 And to you who are troubled rest with us, when the Lord Jesus shall be revealed from heaven with his mighty angels,
>
> 2THES 1:8 In flaming fire taking vengeance on them that know not God, and that obey not the gospel of our Lord Jesus Christ:
>
> 2THES 1:9 Who shall be punished with everlasting destruction from the presence of the Lord, and from the glory of his power;

So we see that obedience is a requirement for Biblical salvation. False preachers have their favorite verses that they use to deceive souls into a comfortable disobedience to the Bible. But once one understands that the ones the epistles were addressed to had already obeyed then the false preachers are easier to spot.

For example, the book of Romans was addressed to Christians who were known for their obedience. (also demonstrating that they had obeyed).

Romans 1:5 By whom we have received grace and apostleship, for obedience to the faith among all nations, for his name:

Romans 16:19 For your obedience is come abroad unto all [men]. I am glad therefore on your behalf: but yet I would have you wise unto that which is good, and simple concerning evil.

The book of Ephesians is also a favorite of the false preacher, but we just need to look at how the Ephesian Church was founded on obedience to Acts 2:38. (also notice that the people knew that believing on Jesus included being baptized in Jesus Name)

Acts 19:1 And it came to pass, that, while Apollos was at Corinth, Paul having passed through the upper coasts came to Ephesus: and finding certain disciples,

Acts 19:2 He said unto them, Have ye received the Holy Ghost since ye believed? And they said unto him, We have not so much as heard whether there be any Holy Ghost.

Acts 19:3 And he said unto them, Unto what then were ye baptized? And they said, Unto John's baptism.

Notice what they did when Paul told them to believe on Jesus.

Acts 19:4 Then said Paul, John verily baptized with the baptism of repentance, saying unto the people, that they should believe on him which should come after him, that is, on Christ Jesus.

Acts 19:5 When they heard [this], they were baptized in the name of the Lord Jesus.

Acts 19:6 And when Paul had laid [his] hands upon them, the Holy Ghost came on them; and they spake with tongues, and prophesied.

The epistles are letters written to those who had obeyed the word that the Apostles preached. Let us look at the birthday of the Church. Notice how they measured whether someone had received the word or not.

> Acts 2:41 Then they that gladly received his word were baptized: and the same day there were added [unto them] about three thousand souls.

Receivers of the word, obeyed the word that they received. Let's back up and see exactly what Peter had preached (some claim Peter as pope but do not obey the message he preached).

> Acts 2:38 Then Peter said unto them, Repent, and be baptized every one of you in the name of Jesus Christ for the remission of sins, and ye shall receive the gift of the Holy Ghost.
>
> Acts 2:39 For the promise is unto you, and to your children, and to all that are afar off, [even] as many as the Lord our God shall call.
>
> Acts 2:40 And with many other words did he testify and exhort, saying, Save yourselves from this untoward generation.
>
> Acts 2:41 Then they that gladly received his word were baptized: and the same day there were added [unto them] about three thousand souls.
>
> Acts 2:42 And they continued stedfastly in the apostles' doctrine and fellowship, and in breaking of bread, and in prayers.

In the Bible believer equals obeyer. One calls on Jesus Name by being baptized in Jesus Name. Grace offers that opportunity to have one's sins remitted. Baptism is not a "work" because you don't do it, rather it is something that you submit to through obedience to God. Don't let some crafty false preacher con you into rejecting Acts 2:38 salvation.

> Acts 22:16 And now why tarriest thou? arise, and be baptized, and wash away thy sins, calling on the name of the Lord.

Paul Said

2 Peter 3:15 And account that the longsuffering of our Lord is salvation; even as our beloved brother Paul also according to the wisdom given unto him hath written unto you;

16 As also in all his epistles, speaking in them of these things; in which are some things hard to be understood, which they that are unlearned and unstable wrest, as they do also the other scriptures, unto their own destruction.

17 Ye therefore, beloved, seeing ye know these things before, beware lest ye also, being led away with the error of the wicked, fall from your own stedfastness.

18 But grow in grace, and in the knowledge of our Lord and Saviour Jesus Christ. To him be glory both now and for ever. Amen.

One calls on the Name of Jesus by being water baptized in the Name of Jesus.

Acts 22:16 And now why tarriest thou? arise, and be baptized, and wash away thy sins, calling on the name of the Lord.

The Apostle Paul preached the Acts 2:38 message. Notice how it is referred to as the word of the Lord Jesus.

Please examine carefully the account when Paul founded the Ephesian church.

Acts 19:1 And it came to pass, that, while Apollos was at Corinth, Paul having passed through the upper coasts came to Ephesus: and finding certain disciples,

Acts 19:2 He said unto them, Have ye received the Holy Ghost since ye believed? And they said unto him, We have not so much as heard whether there be any Holy Ghost.

* Notice that "believers" did not yet have the Holy Ghost. *

> Acts 19:3 And he said unto them, Unto what then were ye baptized? And they said, Unto John's baptism.

* Notice that Paul questioned the validity of their baptism. *

> Acts 19:4 Then said Paul, John verily baptized with the baptism of repentance, saying unto the people, that they should believe on him which should come after him, that is, on Christ Jesus.

Note what the people IMMEDIATELY did when Paul told them to believe on Jesus.

> Acts 19:5 When they heard [this], they were baptized in the name of the Lord Jesus.

* Notice that they were re-baptized the Christian way. *

> Acts 19:6 And when Paul had laid [his] hands upon them, the Holy Ghost came on them; and they spake with tongues, and prophesied.

* Notice that when they did receive the Holy Ghost that they spoke in tongues just like every other real Christian. *

> Acts 19:7 And all the men were about twelve.

> Acts 19:8 And he went into the synagogue, and spake boldly for the space of three months, disputing and persuading the things concerning the kingdom of God.

> Acts 19:9 But when divers were hardened, and believed not, but spake evil of that way before the multitude, he departed from them, and separated the disciples, disputing daily in the school of one Tyrannus.

They had those even back then who opposed the Acts 2:38 message.

> Acts 19:10 And this continued by the space of two years; so that all they which dwelt in Asia heard the word of the Lord Jesus, both Jews and Greeks.

Notice that Paul was preaching the word of the Lord Jesus.

Notice also the instructions Paul gave for dealing with any who would preach otherwise.

> Gal 1:8 But though we, or an angel from heaven, preach any other gospel unto you than that which we have preached unto you, let him be accursed.

Notice the plan of salvation for as many as "our God" (Jesus) shall call.

> Acts 2:38 Then Peter said unto them, Repent, and be baptized every one of you in the name of Jesus Christ for the remission of sins, and ye shall receive the gift of the Holy Ghost.
>
> 39 For the promise is unto you, and to your children, and to all that are afar off, [even] as many as the Lord our God shall call.
>
> 40 And with many other words did he testify and exhort, saying, Save yourselves from this untoward generation.
>
> 41 Then they that gladly received his word were baptized: and the same day there were added unto them about three thousand souls.

Philip Said

Philip also preached Jesus Name Baptism.

> Acts 8:12 But when they believed Philip preaching the things concerning the kingdom of God, and the name of Jesus Christ, they were baptized, both men and women.

Notice the similarity between them and those before who received the Word of God.

> Acts 2:41 Then they that gladly received his word were baptized: and the same day there were added unto them about three thousand souls.

How were the people that Philip preached to baptized?

> Acts 8:14 Now when the apostles which were at Jerusalem heard that Samaria had received the word of God, they sent unto them Peter and John:
>
> 15 Who, when they were come down, prayed for them, that they might receive the Holy Ghost:
>
> 16 (For as yet he was fallen upon none of them: only they were baptized in the name of the Lord Jesus.)

Again the Apostles used the fact that they had been baptized in Jesus Name to determine that they had received the Word of God.

Peter we remember preached Jesus Name baptism

> Acts 2:38 Then Peter said unto them, Repent, and be baptized every one of you in the name of Jesus Christ for the remission of sins, and ye shall receive the gift of the Holy Ghost.

Paul preached Jesus Name Baptism too.

The Apostle Paul preached the Acts 2:38 message. Notice how it is referred to as the word of the Lord Jesus.

Examine carefully the account when Paul founded the Ephesian church.

> Acts 19:1 And it came to pass, that, while Apollos was at Corinth, Paul having passed through the upper coasts came to Ephesus: and finding certain disciples,
>
> Acts 19:2 He said unto them, Have ye received the Holy Ghost since ye believed? And they said unto him, We have not so much as heard whether there be any Holy Ghost.

* Notice that "believers" did not yet have the Holy Ghost. *

> Acts 19:3 And he said unto them, Unto what then were ye baptized? And they said, Unto John's baptism.

* Notice that Paul questioned the validity of their baptism. *

> Acts 19:4 Then said Paul, John verily baptized with the baptism of repentance, saying unto the people, that they should believe on him which should come after him, that is, on Christ Jesus.
>
> Acts 19:5 When they heard [this], they were baptized in the name of the Lord Jesus.

* Notice that they were re-baptized the Christian way. *

> Acts 19:6 And when Paul had laid [his] hands upon them, the Holy Ghost came on them; and they spake with tongues, and prophesied.

Notice that when they did receive the Holy Ghost that they spoke in tongues just like every other real Christian.

Acts 19:7 And all the men were about twelve.

Acts 19:8 And he went into the synagogue, and spake boldly for the space of three months, disputing and persuading the things concerning the kingdom of God.

Acts 19:9 But when divers were hardened, and believed not, but spake evil of that way before the multitude, he departed from them, and separated the disciples, disputing daily in the school of one Tyrannus.

* They had those even back then who opposed the Acts 2:38 message. *

Acts 19:10 And this continued by the space of two years; so that all they which dwelt in Asia heard the word of the Lord Jesus, both Jews and Greeks.

* Notice that Paul was preaching the word of the Lord Jesus. *

* Notice also the instructions Paul gave for dealing with any who would preach otherwise. *

Galatians 1:8 But though we, or an angel from heaven, preach any other gospel unto you than that which we have preached unto you, let him be accursed.

* Notice the plan of salvation for as many as "our God" (Jesus) shall call.*

Acts 2:38 Then Peter said unto them, Repent, and be baptized every one of you in the name of Jesus Christ for the remission of sins, and ye shall receive the gift of the Holy Ghost.

Acts 2:39 For the promise is unto you, and to your children, and to all that are afar off, [even] as many as the Lord our God shall call.

Corner

I wish to point out something that may be helpful to those who are reading here. In one corner we have those like myself that are teaching the basic plan of salvation that the apostles taught to everyone that they encountered, we also point out that the apostles even said that anyone preaching anything else was "accursed". (Acts 2:38, Gal 1:8)

In the opposite corner we have the "majority" who are teaching that a simple mental affirmation of Jesus' existence gives them "eternal security" (except they will often exclude those of us preaching the Bible from the "eternally secure"<grin>).

Both sides seem to have no shortage of Bible verses that seem to prove their point. That is where "rightly dividing" comes in. "Rightly dividing" has more to do with "portioning", "presenting" or "explaining" rather than "interpreting". If I point out that "Noah's ark" came before "John the Baptist", I am not "interpreting", but merely pointing out a chronological order.

An important point to consider is that those that "believed" the apostles "obeyed" the apostles. Notice here in Romans that if someone refused to obey the apostles, it was because they didn't "believe" the apostles.

> Romans 10:16 But they have not all obeyed the gospel. For Esaias saith, Lord, who hath believed our report?

Those that received the Word of God "obeyed" it.

> Acts 2:41 Then they that gladly received his word were baptized: and the same day there were added [unto them] about three thousand souls.

Those that "believed" the apostles, "obeyed" the apostles.

> Acts 8:12 But when they believed Philip preaching the things concerning the kingdom of God, and the name of Jesus Christ, they were baptized, both men and women.

> Acts 8:13 Then Simon himself believed also: and when he was baptized, he continued with Philip, and wondered, beholding the miracles and signs which were done.
>
> Acts 8:14 Now when the apostles which were at Jerusalem heard that Samaria had received the word of God, they sent unto them Peter and John:

Folks who "obeyed" the Word of God, were considered to have "received" the Word of God.

So, in the Bible, when someone is referred to as a "believer", it is because they obeyed the apostles doctrine (Acts 2:38). The books of Romans forward are letters (epistles) that the apostles wrote to the "believers" (the ones who had obeyed them).

The "claim to believe only" heresy is based upon a rather silly foundation that the apostles accepted folks who had rejected them and refused to obey them, and that the apostles still accepted the "Christ rejectors" as brethren and saints.

So let us keep in mind that when the apostles commented to their converts about their "belief", that they were writing letters to the folks who had obeyed them.

> Mark 16:16 He that believeth and is baptized shall be saved; but he that believeth not shall be damned.
>
> Hebrews 5:9 And being made perfect, he became the author of eternal salvation unto all them that obey him;
>
> II Thessalonians 1:7 And to you who are troubled rest with us, when the Lord Jesus shall be revealed from heaven with his mighty angels,
>
> II Thessalonians 1:8 In flaming fire taking vengeance on them that know not God, and that obey not the gospel of our Lord Jesus Christ:

II Thessalonians 1:9 Who shall be punished with everlasting destruction from the presence of the Lord, and from the glory of his power;

II Thessalonians 1:10 When he shall come to be glorified in his saints, and to be admired in all them that believe (because our testimony among you was believed) in that day.

Satan's preachers teach that people don't need to "obey", and they twist the Word of God to try to prove it; but just look at what Jesus has promised to the disobeying "claim to believe" group.

Repent & Baptize

Acts 2:38

Then <1161> Peter <4074> said <5346> unto them, Repent,<3340> and be baptized <907> every <1538> one of you in the name <3686> of Jesus <2424> Christ <5547> for the remission <859> of sins <266>, and ye shall receive <2983> the gift <1431> of the Holy <40> Ghost <4151>.

From the Greek

3340 metanœo 3326, 3539

AV - repent (34)

1) to change one's mind, i.e. to repent; to change one's mind for better, heartily to amend with abhorrence of one's past sins

0907 baptizo 911

AV - baptize (76)

- wash (2)
- baptist (1)
- baptized + 2258 (1) [80]

1) to dip repeatedly, to immerse, to submerge (of vessels sunk)

2) to cleanse by dipping or submerging, to wash, to make clean with water, to wash one's self, bathe

Be Baptized

Many false preachers (who are to be accursed according to Galatians 1:8) teach that Jesus name baptism is not essential for salvation. They teach that baptism is "An outward profession of inward faith" or some such deceptive garbage. Water baptism (in Jesus name) is the re-birth of Water referred to in John 3:5.

Jesus declared baptism to be essential:

> Mark 16:16 He that believeth and is baptized shall be saved; but he that believeth not shall be damned.

The plan of salvation includes baptism as the method whereby sins are remitted.

> Acts 2:38 Then Peter said unto them, Repent, and be baptized every one of you in the name of Jesus Christ for the remission of sins, and ye shall receive the gift of the Holy Ghost.

> Acts 2:41 Then they that gladly received his word were baptized: and the same day there were added [unto them] about three thousand souls.

There were 3000 baptized in Jesus name on the birthday of the Church.

Notice here, when.the first Gentiles became Christian:

> Acts 10:45 And they of the circumcision which believed were astonished, as many as came with Peter, because that on the Gentiles also was poured out the gift of the Holy Ghost.

> Acts 10:46 For they heard them speak with tongues, and magnify God. Then answered Peter,

> Acts 10:47 Can any man forbid water, that these should not be baptized, which have received the Holy Ghost as well as we?

Acts 10:48 And he commanded them to be baptized in the name of the Lord. Then prayed they him to tarry certain days.

Acts 19:4 Then said Paul, John verily baptized with the baptism of repentance, saying unto the people, that they should believe on him which should come after him, that is, on Christ Jesus.

Acts 19:5 When they heard [this], they were baptized in the name of the Lord Jesus.

Acts 22:16 And now why tarriest thou? arise, and be baptized, and wash away thy sins, calling on the name of the Lord.

Sins are washed away in Jesus' name baptism

Romans 6:3 Know ye not, that so many of us as were baptized into Jesus Christ were baptized into his death?

Galatians 3:27 For as many of you as have been baptized into Christ have put on Christ.

OF COURSE Satan's ministers want to downplay Jesus NAME water baptism!

Naaman

A consideration about receiving the Holy Ghost speaking in other tongues is that there are cases in the Bible where folks were water baptized in Jesus name before they received the Holy Spirit and also where they received the Holy Spirit before they were water baptized in Jesus name. In both cases the Apostles immediately added in the missing element of the new birth.

In John 3:5 (which was the early part of the conversation that included John 3:16), Jesus spoke of a re-birth of water and a re-birth of Spirit.

> John 3:5 Jesus answered, Verily, verily, I say unto thee, Except a man be born of water and [of] the Spirit, he cannot enter into the kingdom of God.

Notice carefully a re-birth of "water" and a re-birth of "Spirit". When Peter preached the salvation sermon to sinners on the birthday of the new testament (or "new covenant") church, he preached a plan of salvation (for as many as God would call) that included Jesus's essential elements of water and Spirit.

> Acts 2:38 Then Peter said unto them, Repent, and be baptized every one of you in the name of Jesus Christ for the remission of sins, and ye shall receive the gift of the Holy Ghost.

> Acts 2:39 For the promise is unto you, and to your children, and to all that are afar off, [even] as many as the Lord our God shall call.

Notice:

Water baptism in Jesus name = The re-birth of water.

The Holy Ghost speaking in tongues = The re-birth of the Spirit.

Water baptism must be administered in the only saving name:

> Acts 4:12 Neither is there salvation in any other: for there is none other name under heaven given among men, whereby we must be saved.
>
> I Peter 3:21 The like figure whereunto [even] baptism doth also now save us (not the putting away of the filth of the flesh, but the answer of a good conscience toward God,) by the resurrection of Jesus Christ:

Baptism in Jesus name apples the blood of Christ to the repentant believer. It is not that the physical dirt is washed away, but that the spiritual dirt of sin is washed away. This is not inconsistent with types in the old testament wherein Naaman was commanded to dip into a river 7 times to have his leprosy cured (leprosy was an old testament 'type' of SIN. The water didn't cure him, his works didn't cure him, but his OBEDIENCE enabled him to receive a free gift given by the grace of God.

I HOPE that you ALL will take the time to read these few verses because there is a POWERFUL message here:

> II Kings 5:8 And it was [so], when Elisha the man of God had heard that the king of Israel had rent his clothes, that he sent to the king, saying, Wherefore hast thou rent thy clothes? let him come now to me, and he shall know that there is a prophet in Israel.
>
> II Kings 5:9 So Naaman came with his horses and with his chariot, and stood at the door of the house of Elisha.
>
> II Kings 5:10 And Elisha sent a messenger unto him, saying, Go and wash in Jordan seven times, and thy flesh shall come again to thee, and thou shalt be clean.
>
> II Kings 5:11 But Naaman was wroth, and went away, and said, Behold, I thought, He will surely come out to me, and stand, and call on the name of the LORD his God, and strike his hand over the place, and recover the leper.
>
> II Kings 5:12 [Are] not Abana and Pharpar, rivers of Damascus, better than all the waters of Israel? may I not wash in them, and be clean? So he turned and went away in a rage.

II Kings 5:13 And his servants came near, and spake unto him, and said, My father, [if] the prophet had bid thee [do some] great thing, wouldest thou not have done [it]? how much rather then, when he saith to thee, Wash, and be clean?

II Kings 5:14 Then went he down, and dipped himself seven times in Jordan, according to the saying of the man of God: and his flesh came again like unto the flesh of a little child, and he was clean.

Acts 22:16 And now why tarriest thou? arise, and be baptized, and wash away thy sins, calling on the name of the Lord.

Faith – Works

Sermon preached 8/14/2004.

There is much discussion in religious circles regarding faith and works. Most would agree that no one is justified by their works in the sight of God. Do we not know of many who think that because they do "good works" that they will somehow compensate for their sins? For anyone trying to do that I would offer:

> Isaiah 64:6 But we are all as an unclean thing, and all our righteousnesses are as filthy rags; and we all do fade as a leaf; and our iniquities, like the wind, have taken us away.

> Romans 4:2 For if Abraham were justified by works, he hath whereof to glory; but not before God.

> 3 For what saith the scripture? Abraham believed God, and it was counted unto him for righteousness.

Of course, we must consider how did God know that Abraham "believed" Him? Certainly it was because Abraham "obeyed" him.

> Genesis 26:5 Because that Abraham obeyed my voice, and kept my charge, my commandments, my statutes, and my laws.

Here is another scriptural example of how obedience is a measuring stick for belief or lack thereof.

> Romans 10:16 But they have not all obeyed the gospel. For Esaias saith, Lord, who hath believed our report?

Another example I feel to mention here is that many consider baptism to be a "work" so they believe that it is not part of salvation (though many will concede that it is a "good thing to do". But we find Jesus saying:

> Mark 16:16 He that believeth and is baptized shall be saved; but he that believeth not shall be damned.

Sure seems like a quick trip to join the eternally challenged to reject baptism, eh?

But, consider this little mentioned fact: Baptism is not something you "do" or in any way a "work" that you do. Baptism is something that you allow a preacher to do to you because the Bible says to in order to have your sins washed away or remitted. So clearly Baptism is God's work.

> Acts 22:16 And now why tarriest thou? arise, and be baptized, and wash away thy sins, calling on the name of the Lord.

> Acts 2:38 Then Peter said unto them, Repent, and be baptized every one of you in the name of Jesus Christ for the remission of sins, and ye shall receive the gift of the Holy Ghost.39 For the promise is unto you, and to your children, and to all that are afar off, even as many as the Lord our God shall call.

Pretty blunt for anyone with any sincerity regarding the Word of God, eh? "as many as the Lord our God shall call" doesn't leave a whole lot of wiggle room does it? Water baptism in Jesus Name being a part of the Christian rebirth is not a "salvation by works" doctrine, just as receiving the Holy Spirit baptism is not a "work". It is God who does the "filling". These are things that one "obeys".

Dare we change the salvation plan from Word of God simply to fit some human tradition to which we have become accustomed? Some most certainly do dare, but not I.

Involvement of the believer in their salvation through obedience does not equal "works".

> Romans 2:8 But unto them that are contentious, and do not obey the truth, but obey unrighteousness, indignation and wrath,

> Galatians 3:1 O foolish Galatians, who hath bewitched you, that ye should not obey the truth, before whose eyes Jesus Christ hath been evidently set forth, crucified among you?

Many confuse obedience with works, however. Here is another clear example of how man benefits from God's works by OBEDIENCE.

> John 9:2 And his disciples asked him, saying, Master, who did sin, this man, or his parents, that he was born blind?John 9:3 Jesus answered, Neither hath this man sinned, nor his parents: but that the works of God should be made manifest in him.

Notice carefully that Jesus declared twice that God's works would be demonstrated.

> John 9:4 I must work the works of him that sent me, while it is day: the night cometh, when no man can work.

> John 9:5 As long as I am in the world, I am the light of the world.
>
> John 9:6 When he had thus spoken, he spat on the ground, and made clay of the spittle, and he anointed the eyes of the blind man with the clay,
>
> John 9:7 And said unto him, Go, wash in the pool of Siloam, (which is by interpretation, Sent.) He went his way therefore, and washed, and came seeing.

Here is a strong Biblical foundational principle for your consideration. God's works did not benefit the man UNTIL he OBEYED what God told him.

> John 9:8 The neighbours therefore, and they which before had seen him that he was blind, said, Is not this he that sat and begged?John 9:9 Some said, This is he: others [said], He is like him: [but] he said, I am [he].
>
> John 9:10 Therefore said they unto him, How were thine eyes opened?
>
> John 9:11 He answered and said, A man that is called Jesus made clay, and anointed mine eyes, and said unto me, Go to the pool of Siloam, and wash: and I went and washed, and I received sight.

The blind man's "OBEDIENCE" did not in any way "cheapen the grace of God" (as some false preachers imply when they confuse "works" with "OBEDIENCE".)

The blind man was saved by FAITH, through GRACE and not of his own works.

People who obey Acts 2:38 become Christians by FAITH, through GRACE.

> Acts 2:38 Then Peter said unto them, Repent, and be baptized every one of you in the name of Jesus Christ for the remission of sins, and ye shall receive the gift of the Holy Ghost.
>
> Acts 2:39 For the promise is unto you, and to your children, and to all that are afar off, [even] as many as the Lord our God shall call.

We see many commandments with a promise. Just as Jesus commanded the blind man to wash (and he was not healed until he obeyed); people are commanded to be baptized in Jesus name "for the remission of sins" (and they remain "in their sins" until they obey.)

Hopefully any honest heart will see now that the preaching of obedience to the Word of God is not a "salvation by works" doctrine. But that also does not negate the fact that we do benefit from good works.

Now that we understand that obedience is not works, let us take a quick look at how important works are.

> Matthew 5:16 Let your light so shine before men, that they may see your good works, and glorify your Father which is in heaven.

> Titus 2:14 Who gave himself for us, that he might redeem us from all iniquity, and purify unto himself a peculiar people, zealous of good works.

> Titus 3:8 This is a faithful saying, and these things I will that thou affirm constantly, that they which have believed in God might be careful to maintain good works. These things are good and profitable unto men.

So while none attains salvation by "good works", one who has salvation will do good works. All who do good works don't have salvation, but all who have salvation have good works.

> James 2:20 But wilt thou know, O vain man, that faith without works is dead?

> James 2:26 For as the body without the spirit is dead, so faith without works is dead also.

> Revelation 20:12 And I saw the dead, small and great, stand before God; and the books were opened: and another book was opened, which is the book of life: and the dead were judged out of those things which were written in the books, according to their works.

> Revelation 20:13 And the sea gave up the dead which were in it; and death and hell delivered up the dead which were in them: and they were judged every man according to their works.

So while we would never teach "salvation by works" we should not ignore the importance of good works.

Blessed is the soul who does good works based upon the rock of true salvation and holiness.

Grace

Luke 17:26 And as it was in the days of Noe, so shall it be also in the days of the Son of man.

Luke 17:27 They did eat, they drank, they married wives, they were given in marriage, until the day that Noe entered into the ark, and the flood came, and destroyed them all.

Genesis 6:7 And the LORD said, I will destroy man whom I have created from the face of the earth; both man, and beast, and the creeping thing, and the fowls of the air; for it repenteth me that I have made them.

Genesis 6:8 But Noah found GRACE in the eyes of the LORD.

Now, the enemies of God would have us to believe that the GRACE of God means "Man doing nothing but believing (or CLAIMING to believe)....Noah believed God; that is why he built the ark...Noah was SAVED BY GRACE, it was through GRACE that Noah was advised to OBEY GOD and build an ark...Was Noah saved by his own works?? NO! Noah was saved by the GRACE of God.

It is purely the GRACE of God that offers Repentance, Baptism in Jesus name, and the infilling of the Holy Ghost WITH the evidence of speaking in other tongues...The new testament plan of salvation.

Acts 2:38 Then Peter said unto them, Repent, and be baptized every one of you in the name of Jesus Christ for the remission of sins, and ye shall receive the gift of the Holy Ghost.

Ephesians 2:8 For by grace are ye saved through faith; and that not of yourselves: [it is] the gift of God:..

You are saved if you have the FAITH to obey and avail yourself of the free gift of salvation. It is GRACE that gives man the ability to repent of sin. It is GRACE that gives man the privilege to have all his past sins washed away in baptism in Jesus name. It is GRACE that a man can be filled with the Spirit of Jesus (the Baptism of the Holy Ghost)....It is the sermon preached at Pentecost, Acts 2:38, the new testament plan of salvation, for Jew and gentile alike.

The enemies of God with their "believe only" heresy don't like Acts 2:38, they don't like "tongues", they don't really believe the word of God. They take verses written to SAINTS that had ALLREADY OBEYED Acts 2:38/John 3:5 and try to build false doctrine that excludes Acts 2:38...but remember by GRACE Noah OBEYED God and was saved, and all others that obeyed were saved also. Those that disobeyed and were deceived, DIED by the hand of an angry Jesus.

> Galatians 1:6 I marvel that ye are so soon removed from him that called you into the grace of Christ unto another gospel:
>
> Galatians 1:8 But though we, or an angel from heaven, preach any other gospel unto you than that which we have preached unto you, let him be accursed.

Remember ALL the Apostles were present when Peter preached Acts 2:38..Jesus had given Peter the keys to the kingdom..Acts 2:38 is the basic apostolic message...If your preacher is not preaching Acts 2:38 as the plan of salvation read Galatians 1:8,9.

Become

One major issue that many appear to be negligently overlooking is that one must first BECOME a Christian before one can "remain" a Christian.

Some very foolish and some wicked people are quoting from letters written to Christian people to instruct them of how to remain Christian and trying to twist those verses to a false conclusion.

The Epistles are letters written to people who had obeyed Acts 2:38. They are not letters to the lost on "how to be saved". The Bible is quite clear that Acts 2:38 is for ALL that God will call.

> Acts 2:38 Then Peter said unto them, Repent, and be baptized every one of you in the name of Jesus Christ for the remission of sins, and ye shall receive the gift of the Holy Ghost.
>
> Acts 2:39 For the promise is unto you, and to your children, and to all that are afar off, even as many as the Lord our God shall call.

All of the whining in the world is not going to change the fact that a person must first BECOME a Christian in order to "BE" a Christian or to "remain" a Christian.

** Jews when they received the Holy Ghost **

> Acts 2:4 And they were all filled with the Holy Ghost, and began to speak with other tongues, as the Spirit gave them utterance.

** Samaritans when they received the Holy Ghost **

> Acts 8:14 Now when the apostles which were at Jerusalem heard that Samaria had received the word of God, they sent unto them Peter and John:
>
> Acts 8:15 Who, when they were come down, prayed for them, that they might receive the Holy Ghost:

Acts 8:16 (For as yet he was fallen upon none of them: only they were baptized in the name of the Lord Jesus.)

Acts 8:17 Then laid they [their] hands on them, and they received the Holy Ghost.

** I wonder how the apostles knew they had received the Holy Ghost?

** Gentiles when they received the Holy Ghost **

Acts 10:45 And they of the circumcision which believed were astonished, as many as came with Peter, because that on the Gentiles also was poured out the gift of the Holy Ghost.

Acts 10:46 For they heard them speak with tongues, and magnify God. Then answered Peter,

Acts 10:47 Can any man forbid water, that these should not be baptized, which have received the Holy Ghost as well as we?

Acts 10:48 And he commanded them to be baptized in the name of the Lord. Then prayed they him to tarry certain days.

** John the Baptist's disciples when they were RE- baptized and received the Holy Ghost **

Acts 19:2 He said unto them, Have ye received the Holy Ghost since ye believed? And they said unto him, We have not so much as heard whether there be any Holy Ghost.

Acts 19:3 And he said unto them, Unto what then were ye baptized? And they said, Unto John's baptism.

Acts 19:4 Then said Paul, John verily baptized with the baptism of repentance, saying unto the people, that they should believe on him which should come after him, that is, on Christ Jesus.

Acts 19:5 When they heard [this], they were baptized in the name of the Lord Jesus.

> Acts 19:6 And when Paul had laid [his] hands upon them, the Holy Ghost came on them; and they spake with tongues, and prophesied.

Jews, gentiles, Samaritans; all baptized in JESUS name, all spoke in tongues when they received the Holy Ghost.

** Have YOU received the Holy Ghost since YOU believed? **

** Have YOU been baptized in JESUS name? **

If not, what would *ever* lead you to imagine that you could be saved without being born again of the Water and of the Spirit? (John 3:5)

The epistles of the Bible are letters that were addressed to those who had received the preaching of the Apostles. The "receiving" or "believing" was determined by whether or not the hearers of the Apostles obeyed the word preached by the Apostles. One who would not obey was considered a "non-believer".

> Romans 10:16 But they have not all obeyed the gospel. For Esaias saith, Lord, who hath believed our report?

Some will claim to be "believers" even though they never obeyed the Gospel that the Apostles preached (some say there is nothing to obey). Before continuing, let's make it perfectly clear what Jesus Christ has in store for any and all who do not obey the Gospel that the Apostles preached.

> 2THES 1:7 And to you who are troubled rest with us, when the Lord Jesus shall be revealed from heaven with his mighty angels,
>
> 2THES 1:8 In flaming fire taking vengeance on them that know not God, and that obey not the gospel of our Lord Jesus Christ:
>
> 2THES 1:9 Who shall be punished with everlasting destruction from the presence of the Lord, and from the glory of his power;

So we see that obedience is a requirement for Biblical salvation. False preachers have their favorite verses that they use to deceive souls into a comfortable disobedience to the Bible. But once one understands that the ones the epistles were addressed to had already obeyed then the false preachers are easier to spot.

For example, the book of Romans was addressed to Christians who were known for their obedience. (also demonstrating that they had obeyed).

> Romans 1:5 By whom we have received grace and apostleship, for obedience to the faith among all nations, for his name:
>
> Romans 16:19 For your obedience is come abroad unto all [men]. I am glad therefore on your behalf: but yet I would have you wise unto that which is good, and simple concerning evil.

The book of Ephesians is also a favorite of the false preacher, but we just need to look at how the Ephesian Church was founded on obedience to Acts 2:38. (also notice that the people knew that believing on Jesus included being baptized in Jesus Name)

> Acts 19:1 And it came to pass, that, while Apollos was at Corinth, Paul having passed through the upper coasts came to Ephesus: and finding certain disciples,
>
> Acts 19:2 He said unto them, Have ye received the Holy Ghost since ye believed? And they said unto him, We have not so much as heard whether there be any Holy Ghost.
>
> Acts 19:3 And he said unto them, Unto what then were ye baptized? And they said, Unto John's baptism.

Notice what they did when Paul told them to believe on Jesus.

> Acts 19:4 Then said Paul, John verily baptized with the baptism of repentance, saying unto the people, that they should believe on him which should come after him, that is, on Christ Jesus.
>
> Acts 19:5 When they heard [this], they were baptized in the name of the Lord Jesus.

> Acts 19:6 And when Paul had laid [his] hands upon them, the Holy Ghost came on them; and they spake with tongues, and prophesied.

The epistles are letters written to those who had obeyed the word that the Apostles preached. Let us look at the birthday of the Church. Notice how they measured whether someone had received the word or not.

> Acts 2:41 Then they that gladly received his word were baptized: and the same day there were added [unto them] about three thousand souls.

Receivers of the word, obeyed the word that they received. Let's back up and see exactly what Peter had preached (some claim Peter as pope but do not obey the message he preached).

> Acts 2:38 Then Peter said unto them, Repent, and be baptized every one of you in the name of Jesus Christ for the remission of sins, and ye shall receive the gift of the Holy Ghost.
>
> Acts 2:39 For the promise is unto you, and to your children, and to all that are afar off, [even] as many as the Lord our God shall call.
>
> Acts 2:40 And with many other words did he testify and exhort, saying, Save yourselves from this untoward generation.
>
> Acts 2:41 Then they that gladly received his word were baptized: and the same day there were added [unto them] about three thousand souls.
>
> Acts 2:42 And they continued steadfastly in the apostles' doctrine and fellowship, and in breaking of bread, and in prayers.

In the Bible believer equals obeyer. One calls on Jesus Name by being baptized in Jesus Name. Grace offers that opportunity to have one's sins remitted. Baptism is not a "work" because you don't do it, rather it is something that you submit to through obedience to God. Don't let some crafty false preacher con you into rejecting Acts 2:38 salvation.

Acts 22:16 And now why tarriest thou? arise, and be baptized, and wash away thy sins, calling on the name of the Lord.

Baptism

Note when Paul was commanded to be baptized:

> Acts 22:16 And now why tarriest thou? arise, and be baptized, and wash away thy sins, calling on the name of the Lord.

Many false preachers (accursed of God) teach that baptism is merely "An outward profession of inward faith" or some such nonsense... It is a lie from the very pits of hell, a trick of the devil to keep people in their sins. Water baptism is the re-birth of Water referred to in John 3:5.

> Mark 16:16 He that believeth and is baptized shall be saved; but he that believeth not shall be damned.
>
> Acts 2:38 Then Peter said unto them, Repent, and be baptized every one of you in the name of Jesus Christ for the remission of sins, and ye shall receive the gift of the Holy Ghost.
>
> Acts 2:41 Then they that gladly received his word were baptized: and the same day there were added [unto them] about three thousand souls.

> Acts 10:45 And they of the circumcision which believed were astonished, as many as came with Peter, because that on the Gentiles also was poured out the gift of the Holy Ghost.
>
> Acts 10:46 For they heard them speak with tongues, and magnify God. Then answered Peter,
>
> Acts 10:47 Can any man forbid water, that these should not be baptized, which have received the Holy Ghost as well as we?
>
> Acts 10:48 And he commanded them to be baptized in the name of the Lord. Then prayed they him to tarry certain days.

> Acts 19:4 Then said Paul, John verily baptized with the baptism of repentance, saying unto the people, that they

should believe on him which should come after him, that is, on Christ Jesus.

Acts 19:5 When they heard [this], they were baptized in the name of the Lord Jesus.

Acts 22:16 And now why tarriest thou? arise, and be baptized, and wash away thy sins, calling on the name of the Lord.

** Sins are washed away in Jesus' name baptism **

Romans 6:3 Know ye not, that so many of us as were baptized into Jesus Christ were baptized into his death?

Galatians 3:27 For as many of you as have been baptized into Christ have put on Christ.

What Name

> Matthew 28:19 Go ye therefore, and teach all nations, baptizing them in the name of the Father, and of the Son, and of the Holy Ghost:

In order to obey Matt 28:19 we must know the singular Name that Jesus was referring to.

Another place the Bible says: (and I am here only to teach you what the Bible says and not to promote the party line of any organization)

> Acts 4:12 Neither is there salvation in any other: for there is none other name under heaven given among men, whereby we must be saved.

A point for your consideration is what would be a better source to discover the correct "name" to use in water baptism than the Apostles themselves?

If we must know which singular "name" to use, then should we not look and see what the Apostles who heard Jesus speak and then wrote His words down for us, did themselves?

As an aside, if we can not trust the Apostles then we have a problem because the only way we have of knowing what Jesus said is from what the Apostles tell us He said.

There are many examples that prove that the Apostles who heard Jesus speak Matt 28:19 baptized in Jesus Name and preached Jesus Name baptism. Who do we believe? The polytheistic trinity preachers, or Jesus hand picked Apostles? Also consider that the "three person" baptism of the trinitarian really does establish their polytheism

> Acts 2:38 Then Peter said unto them, Repent, and be baptized every one of you in the name of Jesus Christ for the remission of sins, and ye shall receive the gift of the Holy Ghost.

People accuse the real Christians of being hung up on only one verse, but if you don't obey Acts 2:38 it really won't matter what you do with the rest of the verses.

> Acts 8:12 But when they believed Philip preaching the things concerning the kingdom of God, and the name of Jesus Christ, they were baptized, both men and women.

How were they baptized who believed about the singular name?

> Acts 8:16 (For as yet he was fallen upon none of them: only they were baptized in the name of the Lord Jesus.)

Paul told some people to believe on Jesus, then...

> Acts 19:5 When they heard this, they were baptized in the name of the Lord Jesus.

> Colossians 3:17 And whatsoever ye do in word or deed, do all in the name of the Lord Jesus, giving thanks to God and the Father by him.

Look at that verse. Makes you wonder why the trinitarian false-christians don't teach that "God" and "Father" are two separate persons, eh?

> 2 Thessalonians 1:12 That the name of our Lord Jesus Christ may be glorified in you, and ye in him, according to the grace of our God and the Lord Jesus Christ.

Now in that verse they do try to teach two separate persons.

Note that the verse is really saying that Jesus Christ is God and the Lord.

Baptize in the Name

I'm writing this in response to a rather common argument from those that oppose water baptism in Jesus name as commanded in Acts 2:38,Acts 10:48, Acts 19:5, Acts 22:16, Matt 28:19.

> Acts 2:38 Then Peter said unto them, Repent, and be baptized every one of you in the name of Jesus Christ for the remission of sins, and ye shall receive the gift of the Holy Ghost.
>
> Acts 10:48 And he commanded them to be baptized in the name of the Lord. Then prayed they him to tarry certain days.
>
> Acts 19:4 Then said Paul, John verily baptized with the baptism of repentance, saying unto the people, that they should believe on him which should come after him, that is, on Christ Jesus.
>
> Acts 19:5 When they heard [this], they were baptized in the name of the Lord Jesus.
>
> Acts 22:16 And now why tarriest thou? arise, and be baptized, and wash away thy sins, calling on the name of the Lord.
>
> Matthew 28:19 Go ye therefore, and teach all nations, baptizing them in the name of the Father, and of the Son, and of the Holy Ghost:

Oh yes BTW here are some verses that prove that Jesus is the NAME of the Father...

> John5:43 I am come in my Father's name, and ye receive me not: if another shall come in his own name, him ye will receive.
>
> Heb 1:3Who being the brightness of his glory, and the express image of his person, and upholding all things by the word of his power, when he had by himself purged our sins, sat down on the right hand of the Majesty on high;
>
> 4 ¶ Being made so much better than the angels, as he hath by inheritance obtained a more excellent name than they.

If you inherit your name from your father you have your father's name.

> John 17:26 And I have declared unto them thy name, and will declare it: that the love wherewith thou hast loved me may be in them, and I in them.

Here's one that proves that Jesus is the name of the Holy Ghost,

> John 14:26 But the Comforter, which is the Holy Ghost, whom the Father will send in my name, he shall teach you all things, and bring all things to your remembrance, whatsoever I have said unto you.

Many say that the different pronunciation or translation of the name of Jesus somehow nullifies all the scriptures about the importance of the name of Jesus. Different languages do pronounce the name of Jesus differently, Spanish comes to mind as an example. However we should keep in mind that is was God who created the different languages so that different people saying the same thing would use different syllables to say it. When a Spanish speaking person says Jesus, it will sound different than when I say Jesus, this would not nullify the fact that we had both just said Jesus.

The Bible puts a great emphasis and importance on the "name

> Acts 4:12 Neither is there salvation in any other: for there is none other name under heaven given among men, whereby we must be saved.
>
> Matthew 24:5 For many shall come in my name, saying, I am Christ; and shall deceive many.
>
> Matthew 12:21 And in his name shall the Gentiles trust.
>
> Acts 3:16 And his name through faith in his name hath made this man strong, whom ye see and know: yea, the faith which is by him hath given him this perfect soundness in the presence of you all.

Baptize in the Name

The word of God is full of references that prove the importance of the NAME, which is Jesus, it is a privilege (paid for in precious blood) to be baptized in Jesus name and have ones sins remitted

> Acts 2:41 Then they that gladly received his word were baptized: and the same day there were added [unto them] about three thousand souls.
>
> Acts 22:16 And now why tarriest thou? arise, and be baptized, and wash away thy sins, calling on the name of the Lord.
>
> Acts 19:3 And he said unto them, Unto what then were ye baptized? And they said, Unto John's baptism.

Re-baptized in Jesus name.

> Acts 19:4 Then said Paul, John verily baptized with the baptism of repentance, saying unto the people, that they should believe on him which should come after him, that is, on Christ Jesus.
>
> Acts 19:5 When they heard [this], they were baptized in the name of the Lord Jesus.

How do you "put on Christ?

> Galatians 3:27 For as many of you as have been baptized into Christ have put on Christ.

More on Baptism

Water baptism administered in Jesus NAME is the re-birth of Water referred to in John 3:5.

> Mark 16:16 He that believeth and is baptized shall be saved; but he that believeth not shall be damned.

Jesus declared that baptism is a requirement for salvation.

> Acts 2:38 Then Peter said unto them, Repent, and be baptized every one of you in the name of Jesus Christ for the remission of sins, and ye shall receive the gift of the Holy Ghost.

It is through obedience to baptism that an individual accepts Jesus offer to remit their sins through His NAME.

> Acts 2:41 Then they that gladly received his word were baptized: and the same day there were added [unto them] about three thousand souls.

3000 were baptized in Jesus name for the remission of their sins.

> Acts 10:45 And they of the circumcision which believed were astonished, as many as came with Peter, because that on the Gentiles also was poured out the gift of the Holy Ghost.
>
> Acts 10:46 For they heard them speak with tongues, and magnify God. Then answered Peter,
>
> Acts 10:47 Can any man forbid water, that these should not be baptized, which have received the Holy Ghost as well as we?
>
> Acts 10:48 And he commanded them to be baptized in the name of the Lord. Then prayed they him to tarry certain days.

More on Baptism

Those who received the Holy Spirit before baptism were immediately commanded to be water baptized in Jesus NAME. Notice also how the apostles were able to know that Gentiles had really received the same Holy Spirit that they (the apostles) had received.

> Acts 19:4 Then said Paul, John verily baptized with the baptism of repentance, saying unto the people, that they should believe on him which should come after him, that is, on Christ Jesus.
>
> Acts 19:5 When they heard [this], they were baptized in the name of the Lord Jesus.

> Acts 22:16 And now why tarriest thou? arise, and be baptized, and wash away thy sins, calling on the name of the Lord.

** Sins are washed away in Jesus' name baptism **

> Romans 6:3 Know ye not, that so many of us as were baptized into Jesus Christ were baptized into his death?

> Galatians 3:27 For as many of you as have been baptized into Christ have put on Christ.

Those who have not been baptized in Jesus name have not been re-born of the water, have not "put on Christ" and are still in their sins (even if they have received the Holy Spirit). "Half saved" people do not get a cooler shelf in hell.

Name

Why did Jesus tell his followers they would be hated? Was it because they would have worship services or because they would live right? (answer provided at the end of this post)

> Matthew 28:18 And Jesus came and spake unto them, saying, All power is given unto me in heaven and in earth.

Jesus declared that he had ALL POWER by himself, then he commanded that baptism be administered in a singular name.

> Matthew 28:19 Go ye therefore, and teach all nations, baptizing them in the name ...

Notice Jesus said "name" (singular); Then He went on to describe that singular name.

> Matthew 28:19 Go ye therefore, and teach all nations, baptizing them in the name of the Father, and of the Son, and of the Holy Ghost:

When the apostles that heard Jesus speak, baptized; they used a name as Jesus had commanded. They did not "parrot" the description of the name, but, they used the name itself, because,

> Acts 4:12 Neither is there salvation in any other: for there is none other name under heaven given among men, whereby we must be saved.
>
> Acts 2:38 Then Peter said unto them, Repent, and be baptized every one of you in the name of Jesus Christ for the remission of sins, and ye shall receive the gift of the Holy Ghost.
>
> John 20:31 But these are written, that ye might believe that Jesus is the Christ, the Son of God; and that believing ye might have life through his name.

Ye might have life through his NAME.

Acts 4:18 And they called them, and commanded them not to speak at all nor teach in the name of Jesus.

Acts 8:16 (For as yet he was fallen upon none of them: only they were baptized in the name of the Lord Jesus.)

Acts 19:4 Then said Paul, John verily baptized with the baptism of repentance, saying unto the people, that they should believe on him which should come after him, that is, on Christ Jesus.

Acts 19:5 When they heard [this], they were baptized in the name of the Lord Jesus .

Philippians 2:10 That at the name of Jesus every knee should bow, of [things] in heaven, and [things] in earth, and [things] under the earth;

Colossians 3:17 And whatsoever ye do in word or deed, do all in the name of the Lord Jesus, giving thanks to God and the Father by him.

Ooopsie for the trinitarian here. They would now have to declare the "Father" and "God" to be two more separate persons.

The false church refuses to "do all" in the name of Jesus. They refuse to baptize in the name of "Jesus". They refuse the NAME, while parroting or "chanting" the description of the name.

Matthew 10:22 And ye shall be hated of all men for my name's sake: but he that endureth to the end shall be saved.

Mark 13:13 And ye shall be hated of all men for my name's sake: but he that shall endure unto the end, the same shall be saved.

Luke 21:17 And ye shall be hated of all men for my name's sake.

Acts 4:12 Neither is there salvation in any other: for there is none other name under heaven given among men, whereby we must be saved.

Name

The phrase "calling on the name of the Lord" appears only ONCE in the entire Bible.

> Acts 22:16 And now why tarriest thou? arise, and be baptized, and wash away thy sins, calling on the name of the Lord.

So how does one "call on the name of the Lord" and have their sins washed away?

> Acts 2:38 Then Peter said unto them, Repent, and be baptized every one of you in the name of Jesus Christ for the remission of sins, and ye shall receive the gift of the Holy Ghost.
>
> Acts 2:39 For the promise is unto you, and to your children, and to all that are afar off, even as many as the Lord our God shall call.

We can look at the example of the scriptures as well. What did these folks do IMMEDIATELY when Paul told them to believe on Jesus?

> Acts 19:4 Then said Paul, John verily baptized with the baptism of repentance, saying unto the people, that they should believe on him which should come after him, that is, on Christ Jesus.
>
> Acts 19:5 When they heard this, they were baptized in the name of the Lord Jesus.

Basic Salvation

Basic Bible salvation, what subject could be more important in this hour in which

the last moments in the history of mankind fill the headlines with their fury.

What subject angers the sweet talking false preacher like the subject of basic Biblical salvation? There is a reason for that, you know.

Some would teach you that the Bible is not comprehensible so you might as well not try, but I believe that the Bible is there for us to understand.

> Isaiah 35:8 And an highway shall be there, and a way, and it shall be called The way of holiness; the unclean shall not pass over it; but it shall be for those: the wayfaring men, though fools, shall not err therein.

God declares did not give his Word to confuse or alienate people. He gave it to show us the way and give us true light and understanding. Even a fool will stand

before God without excuse.

> Psalms 119:105 NUN. Thy word is a lamp unto my feet, and a light unto my path.

How many have ever walked in an unfamiliar area without any light, yet so many choose to exercise their God given free will to do just that with their spiritual path?

If we want true salvation then we need to reject the man made fables of the worldly man made religions, we must instead look at what was taught by Jesus Christ, then preached upon His authority by Peter, and then practiced by the Apostles faithfully. If we do that then we see two essential elements that make up the Christian new birth. Those elements are water and spirit. These truths do not contradict the scriptures regarding belief but provide the foundation upon which to exercise true Biblical belief, which is based upon obedience (another concept that

the false-christians really hate).

The false-christian needs to face reality. Was Noah saved by grace through faith by the mercy of God? Would not he have drowned if he had refused to obey and build the ark? Was Noah somehow waterproof? Don't let your false preacher take you down, friend.

> John 3:5 Jesus answered, Verily, verily, I say unto thee, Except a man be born of water and of the Spirit, he cannot enter into the kingdom of God.

Those essential elements are: WATER and SPIRIT. We should take note that a grown man was told by God manifest in the flesh that he had to be born of water and that he had to be born of the Spirit.

> Hebrews 5:9 And being made perfect, he became the author of eternal salvation unto all them that obey him;

How can you continue to believe your false preacher that grace means nothing to obey?

> Gal 3:27 For as many of you as have been baptized into Christ have put on Christ.

Why would a real man of God try to talk you OUT of putting on Christ as so many of the false-christian preachers do when they fight against Jesus Name Baptism?

> Mark 16:16 He that believeth and is baptized shall be saved; but he that believeth not shall be damned.

Yes even with that verse we still have the devil's crowd deceiving souls. Look at that verse. Is it telling you to do one thing or to do two things? What part of

the word "and" do you not comprehend?

If you pay good money for a wash AND wax for your car, what do you expect?

Jesus Christ gave Peter the keys to the kingdom of God. What will become of those who reject what Peter did with those keys. It has become common that the devil's workmen try to teach people that Peter disobeyed Jesus. They say something like, "Well I will take Jesus's words over Peter's any day."

If we can't trust the Apostles we have a big problem. Was it not the Apostles

who told us what Jesus said?

Some attack me for being less than tolerant towards the devils's deceivers, but what does Paul tell the Christians to do?

> 2 Cor 11:12 But what I do, that I will do, that I may cut off occasion from them which desire occasion; that wherein they glory, they may be found even as we.
>
> 13 For such are false apostles, deceitful workers, transforming themselves into the apostles of Christ.
>
> 14 And no marvel; for Satan himself is transformed into an angel of light.
>
> 15 Therefore it is no great thing if his ministers also be transformed as the ministers of righteousness; whose end shall be according to their works.

Notice also what role that Satan's servants will play. They will pretend to be teaching righteousness. They will get jobs as preachers.

Can we reject Peter without rejecting the One who sent him?

> Matthew 16:18 And I say also unto thee, That thou art Peter, and upon this rock I will build my church; and the gates of hell shall not prevail against it.
>
> 19 And I will give unto thee the keys of the kingdom of heaven: and whatsoever thou shalt bind on earth shall be bound in heaven: and whatsoever thou shalt loose on earth shall be loosed in heaven.

Are those false-preachers who want you to disregard Peter's salvation message

really your friend? Are they telling you the truth?

> John 8:44 Ye are of your father the devil, and the lusts of your father ye will do. He was a murderer from the beginning, and abode not in the truth, because there is no truth in him. When he speaketh a lie, he speaketh of his own: for he is a liar, and the father of it.

So we don't need to be surprised when the devil's servants lie, OK?

I hope and pray that all can see that one can't reject Peter without rejecting the Lord Jesus Christ who gave Peter the keys to the kingdom of heaven. So let's study what Peter taught.

> Acts 2:36 Therefore let all the house of Israel know assuredly, that God hath made that same Jesus, whom ye have crucified, both Lord and Christ.
>
> 37 ¶ Now when they heard this, they were pricked in their heart, and said unto Peter and to the rest of the apostles, Men and brethren, what shall we do?

> 38 Then Peter said unto them, Repent, and be baptized every one of you in the name of Jesus Christ for the remission of sins, and ye shall receive the gift of the Holy Ghost.
>
> 39 For the promise is unto you, and to your children, and to all that are afar off, even as many as the Lord our God shall call.

How can anyone, even in their wildest imagination, believe that they are among the "called of God" when they reject the Acts 2:38 salvation that Peter preached on the authority of the Lord Jesus Christ?

We need to take note that water baptism is to be done in Jesus Name. Monotheists have no problem with that, but polytheists really stumble on that and thereby expose themselves that they truly are polytheistic and really are teaching three god squad members. In the Bible when people received the Holy Ghost, they spoke with other tongues.

The devil's servants have found that the best way to keep people from seeking the real Baptism of the Holy Ghost is to convince them they already have it and then just hold them by their religious pride. But why would anyone desiring and claiming a true Biblical experience be so adamantly against such a basic Bible principle.

> Acts 2:4 And they were all filled with the Holy Ghost, and began to speak with other tongues, as the Spirit gave them utterance.

> Acts 19:6 And when Paul had laid his hands upon them, the Holy Ghost came on them; and they spake with tongues, and prophesied

Paul also said:

> 1 Corinthians 14:18 I thank my God, I speak with tongues more than ye all:

There are examples in the Bible where people received the Holy Ghost before they

were baptized in Jesus Name. There are also examples where people were baptized in Jesus Name before they received the Holy Ghost. Both are valid salvation experiences since the Bible documents both scenarios as valid.

> John 3:5 Jesus answered, Verily, verily, I say unto thee, Except a man be born of water and of the Spirit, he cannot enter into the kingdom of God.

Whenever either ingredient of the Christian New Birth was missing, the Apostles of Jesus IMMEDIATELY added the missing one. If a person was baptized in Jesus Name then the Apostles prayed for them to receive the Holy Spirit. (that also proves that people don't automatically receive the Holy Ghost when they "believe" as some of Satan's ministers teach. When people received the Holy Ghost with the evidence of speaking in tongues, the Apostles immediately baptized them in Jesus Name.

> Acts 8:12 But when they believed Philip preaching the things concerning the kingdom of God, and the name of Jesus Christ, they were baptized, both men and women.
>
> 13 Then Simon himself believed also: and when he was baptized, he continued with Philip, and wondered, beholding the miracles and signs which were done.
>
> 14 ¶ Now when the apostles which were at Jerusalem heard that Samaria had received the word of God, they sent unto them Peter and John:
>
> 15 Who, when they were come down, prayed for them, that they might receive the Holy Ghost:
>
> 16 (For as yet he was fallen upon none of them: only they were baptized in the name of the Lord Jesus.)
>
> 17 Then laid they their hands on them, and they received the Holy Ghost.

Note how they had been baptized.

> Acts 10:44 ¶ While Peter yet spake these words, the Holy Ghost fell on all them which heard the word.
>
> 45 And they of the circumcision which believed were astonished, as many as came with Peter, because that on the Gentiles also was poured out the gift of the Holy Ghost.
>
> 46 For they heard them speak with tongues, and magnify God. Then answered Peter,
>
> 47 Can any man forbid water, that these should not be baptized, which have received the Holy Ghost as well as we?
>
> 48 And he commanded them to be baptized in the name of the Lord. Then prayed they him to tarry certain days.

So how did the Apostles know that Gentiles had received the same Holy Ghost they had?

Those who had even been baptized personally by John the Baptist were re-baptized in Jesus name for the remission of their sins. John's baptism was only for a temporary period of time. Jesus Name baptism does remit sins by the POWER of the shed blood of God.

> Acts 19:1 And it came to pass, that, while Apollos was at Corinth, Paul having passed through the upper coasts came to Ephesus: and finding certain disciples,
>
> 2 He said unto them, Have ye received the Holy Ghost since ye believed? And they said unto him, We have not so much as heard whether there be any Holy Ghost.
>
> 3 And he said unto them, Unto what then were ye baptized? And they said, Unto John's baptism.
>
> 4 Then said Paul, John verily baptized with the baptism of repentance, saying unto the people, that they should believe on him which should come after him, that is, on Christ Jesus.

> 5 When they heard this, they were baptized in the name of the Lord Jesus.
>
> 6 And when Paul had laid his hands upon them, the Holy Ghost came on them; and they spake with tongues, and prophesied.
>
> 7 And all the men were about twelve.

So with that verse 2 up there, how are Satan's ministers still convincing people that they automatically receive the Holy Ghost when they first "believe"?

> Acts 22:16 And now why tarriest thou? arise, and be baptized, and wash away thy sins, calling on the name of the Lord.

How does a person have their sins washed away? Clearly it is by being baptized in Jesus Name which is the METHOD whereby one calls on the Name of the Lord.

> Colossians 2:12 Buried with him in baptism, wherein also ye are risen with him through the faith of the operation of God, who hath raised him from the dead.

Note the essentiality of both WATER and SPIRIT:

> Romans 8:9 But ye are not in the flesh, but in the Spirit, if so be that the Spirit of God dwell in you. Now if any man have not the Spirit of Christ, he is none of his.

The Bible speaks of the Spirit of God and the Spirit of Christ as EXACTLY the same Spirit.

> Mark 16:16 He that believeth and is baptized shall be saved; but he that believeth not shall be damned.

How could Jesus have been more clear regarding the essentiality of Jesus Name baptism?

> James 1:22 But be ye doers of the word, and not hearers only, deceiving your own selves.

John 3:5 Jesus answered, Verily, verily, I say unto thee, Except a man be born of water and [of] the Spirit, he cannot enter into the kingdom of God.

6 That which is born of the flesh is flesh; and that which is born of the Spirit is spirit.

7 Marvel not that I said unto thee, Ye must be born again.

Remember here that Jesus was telling a grown man what he STILL needed to do in order to be saved. The grown man still had to be reborn of WATER and of the SPIRIT.

This is totally consistent with the plan of salvation that Peter, the "man with the keys to the kingdom" preached on the birthday of the New Testament Church.

> Matthew 16:18 And I say also unto thee, That thou art Peter, and upon this rock I will build my church; and the gates of hell shall not prevail against it.
>
> 19 And I will give unto thee the keys of the kingdom of heaven: and whatsoever thou shalt bind on earth shall be bound in heaven: and whatsoever thou shalt loose on earth shall be loosed in heaven.

> Acts 2:38 Then Peter said unto them, Repent, and be baptized every one of you in the name of Jesus Christ for the remission of sins, and ye shall receive the gift of the Holy Ghost.
>
> Acts 2:39 For the promise is unto you, and to your children, and to all that are afar off, [even] as many as the Lord our God shall call.

Acts 2:40 And with many other words did he testify and exhort, saying, Save yourselves from this untoward generation.

Acts 2:41 Then they that gladly received his word were baptized: and the same day there were added [unto them] about three thousand souls.

If your false-preacher has told you that you don't need to obey Acts 2:38, I want you to consider these next verses.

2 Thessalonians 1:7 And to you who are troubled rest with us, when the Lord Jesus shall be revealed from heaven with his mighty angels,

8 In flaming fire taking vengeance on them that know not God, and that obey not the gospel of our Lord Jesus Christ:

9 Who shall be punished with everlasting destruction from the

presence of the Lord, and from the glory of his power;

How can people be so gullible that they don't think they need to obey the Gospel?

1 Peter 4:17 For the time is come that judgment must begin at the house of God: and if it first begin at us, what shall the end be of them that obey not the gospel of God?

Romans 10:16 But they have not all obeyed the gospel. For Esaias saith, Lord, who hath believed our report?

See in the above verse how the Apostles considered a "non-obeyer" to be a "non-believer"?

Galatians 3:27 For as many of you as have been baptized into Christ have put on Christ.

Remit

It is baptism in Jesus name that remits sins, that is how remission of sins is applied to a believer.

Remission of sins comes to those who believe THROUGH His Name. One calls on the name of the Lord and receives remission of sins through Jesus name baptism.

> Acts 22:16 And now why tarriest thou? arise, and be baptized, and wash away thy sins, calling on the name of the Lord.

It is baptism in the NAME of Jesus that remits sins because God chose to do it that way. One "calls on the name" by being baptized in that name.

> Acts 2:38 Then Peter said unto them, Repent, and be baptized every one of you in the name of Jesus Christ for the remission of sins, and ye shall receive the gift of the Holy Ghost.

One is baptized to have their sins remitted.

> Acts 2:41 Then they that gladly received his word were baptized: and the same day there were added unto them about three thousand souls.

Those who believe are always baptized.

> Acts 8:12 But when they believed Philip preaching the things concerning the kingdom of God, and the name of Jesus Christ, they were baptized, both men and women.

When people believe the gospel, they are baptized in the name of Jesus.

> Acts 8:13 Then Simon himself believed also: and when he was baptized, he continued with Philip, and wondered, beholding the miracles and signs which were done.

When people believe in Jesus name, they get baptized in Jesus name.

> Acts 19:4 Then said Paul, John verily baptized with the baptism of repentance, saying unto the people, that they should believe on him which should come after him, that is, on Christ Jesus.
>
> Acts 19:5 When they heard this, they were baptized in the name of the Lord Jesus.

One "believes on" Jesus , by Obeying Jesus.

> Rom 10:16 But they have not all obeyed the gospel. For Esaias saith, Lord, who hath believed our report?

Those who do not obey are classified by the Bible as "non-believers". Jesus is only the author of salvation for those who obey him.

> Heb 5:9 And being made perfect, he became the author of eternal salvation unto all them that obey him;

What has Jesus promised to the "claim to believe" cults? Read on:

> 2 Th 1:7 And to you who are troubled rest with us, when the Lord Jesus shall be revealed from heaven with his mighty angels,
>
> 2 Th 1:8 In flaming fire taking vengeance on them that know not God, and that obey not the gospel of our Lord Jesus Christ:

I would hate to be in some false christian cult that was basing their salvation on the defective premise that the apostles accepted people who refused to be baptized as "brethren", and that the apostles then wrote the epistles to people who "claimed to believe" while refusing to obey.

False religion

We see so many claiming this and that, but we do have Bibles so we will be without excuse if we follow a religion that doesn't match up.

SO WHAT DID THE APOSTLES TEACH?

1) Acts 2:1-4..."And they were ALL filled with the Holy Ghost and began to speak with other tongues, as the Spirit gave them utterance."(This was in the upper room where 120, including MARY the mother of Jesus, were gathered Acts 1:14-15). many false preachers teach that "tongues were just for the 12 apostles" .ever heard that?

2) Acts 2:38. "Then Peter said unto them, repent and be baptized in the name of Jesus Christ for the remission of sins, and ye shall receive the gift of the Holy Ghost". the next verse mentions that this promise is to "as many as the Lord our God shall call."...most false preachers do not baptize in Jesus name they just use "titles"

3)Acts 8: 15-17 (Samaria) "Who, when they were come down, prayed for them that they might receive the Holy Ghost: (For as yet he was fallen on none of them: only they were baptized in the name of the Lord Jesus.) Then they laid their hands on them, and they received the Holy Ghost." many false preachers teach that you automatically have the Holy Ghost when you first "believe on the Lord"...ever heard that one?

4) Acts 10: 44-48 (First gentiles saved) "And they of the circumcision (Jews) which believed were astonished, as many as came with Peter, because that on the gentiles also was poured out the gift of the Holy Ghost. FOR THEY HEARD THEM SPEAK WITH TONGUES, and magnify God. Then answered Peter. Can any man forbid water that these should not be baptized which have received the Holy Ghost as well as well as we? And he commanded them to be baptized in the name of the Lord."....false preachers

teach people that they already have the Holy Ghost even though they don't even believe in tongues..ever heard that one?

5) See also Acts 19:1-6...Galatians 3: 27...Acts 22: 16 "As we said before, so say I again, If ANY MAN preach any other gospel unto you than that ye have received, let him be ACCURSED."(Galatians 1:9)

Not the Jesus of the Bible

> Jeremiah 5:7 How shall I pardon thee for this? thy children have forsaken me, and sworn by [them that are] no gods: when I had fed them to the full, they then committed adultery, and assembled themselves by troops in the harlots' houses.

> Jeremiah 16:20 Shall a man make gods unto himself, and they [are] no gods?

I hope that the folks reading here will not be deceived when trinitarians claim to believe in only one god. If you will notice, they will claim to believe in one god and then refer to their god as "they"; and then ignorantly post the scriptures that they perceive teach separate gods. When a trinitarian refers to "one god" what they are referring to is "one committee".

Some have no idea what the trinity is, but their false preacher told them that is what they believe and their definition of their "trinity" is as loose as their whim. What they are is deceived and confused. Deception and confusion are some of the devils main tools.

When the trinitarian claims to believe in one god and sets out to prove three, he/she/it is simply lying and deceived.

It's the devil's business to keep YOU from worshiping Jesus. The "Jesus" of the "trinity" is NOT the Jesus of the Bible. The Jesus of the Bible is the 'I AM' in person (not a "separate jr person).

> John 8:24 I said therefore unto you, that ye shall die in your sins: for if ye believe not that I am [he], ye shall die in your sins.

Those that do not realize that Jesus is the 'I AM' see no need to be baptized in Jesus name. Sins are remitted through Jesus name baptism. Those who do not have their sins remitted, die in their sins.

If the devil can deceive people into refusing Jesus name baptism, he gets their soul for eternity. OF COURSE his preachers say it doesn't matter!!! Just like Satan told Eve about the forbidden fruit.

> John 8:58 Jesus said unto them, Verily, verily, I say unto you, Before Abraham was, I am.
>
> Exodus 3:14 And God said unto Moses, I AM THAT I AM: and he said, Thus shalt thou say unto the children of Israel, I AM hath sent me unto you.

The "I AM" of the burning bush, the God of Abraham, came to earth in the flesh. He didn't send a junior member of a "god squad".

> I Timothy 3:16 And without controversy great is the mystery of godliness: God was manifest in the flesh, justified in the Spirit, seen of angels, preached unto the Gentiles, believed on in the world, received up into glory.

> John 14:9 Jesus saith unto him, Have I been so long time with you, and yet hast thou not known me, Philip? he that hath seen me hath seen the Father; and how sayest thou [then], Shew us the Father?

Sins are remitted by Jesus name baptism because that is the way God chose to do it.

> Acts 22:16 And now why tarriest thou? arise, and be baptized, and wash away thy sins, calling on the name of the Lord.

Death Penalty

> Romans 6:23 For the wages of sin is death; but the gift of God is eternal life through Jesus Christ our Lord.

Many think that well if they sin then maybe things won't work out for them as well as they might have hoped or something like that. Sin brings death not inconvenience. The modern false-christian sin cults are just fooling themselves.

It truly was sin that brought death upon mankind.

> Romans 5:12 Wherefore, as by one man sin entered into the world, and death by sin; and so death passed upon all men, for that all have sinned:
>
> Romans 1:18 For the wrath of God is revealed from heaven against all ungodliness and unrighteousness of men, who hold the truth in unrighteousness;
>
> 19 ¶ Because that which may be known of God is manifest in them; for God hath shewed it unto them.
>
> 20 For the invisible things of him from the creation of the world are clearly seen, being understood by the things that are made, even his eternal power and Godhead; so that they are without excuse:
>
> 21 Because that, when they knew God, they glorified him not as God, neither were thankful; but became vain in their imaginations, and their foolish heart was darkened.
>
> 22 Professing themselves to be wise, they became fools,
>
> 23 And changed the glory of the uncorruptible God into an image made like to corruptible man, and to birds, and fourfooted beasts, and creeping things.
>
> 24 Wherefore God also gave them up to uncleanness through the lusts of their own hearts, to dishonour their own bodies between themselves:

25 Who changed the truth of God into a lie, and worshipped and served the creature more than the Creator, who is blessed for ever. Amen.

26 For this cause God gave them up unto vile affections: for even their women did change the natural use into that which is against nature:

27 And likewise also the men, leaving the natural use of the woman, burned in their lust one toward another; men with men working that which is unseemly, and receiving in themselves that recompence of their error which was meet.

28 And even as they did not like to retain God in their knowledge, God gave them over to a reprobate mind, to do those things which are not convenient;

29 Being filled with all unrighteousness, fornication, wickedness, covetousness, maliciousness; full of envy, murder, debate, deceit, malignity; whisperers,

30 Backbiters, haters of God, despiteful, proud, boasters, inventors of evil things, disobedient to parents,

31 Without understanding, covenantbreakers, without natural affection, implacable, unmerciful:

32 Who knowing the judgment of God, that they which commit such things are worthy of death, not only do the same, but have pleasure in them that do them.

Romans 3:23 For all have sinned, and come short of the glory of God;

All have sin in their past but the Bible is clearly not making excuses for sin as many false-christian cults would teach you.

Romans 5:12 Wherefore, as by one man sin entered into the world, and death by sin; and so death passed upon all men, for that all have sinned:

13 (For until the law sin was in the world: but sin is not imputed when there is no law.

14 Nevertheless death reigned from Adam to Moses, even over them that had not sinned after the similitude of Adam's transgression, who is the figure of him that was to come.

15 But not as the offence, so also is the free gift. For if through the offence of one many be dead, much more the grace of God, and the gift by grace, which is by one man, Jesus Christ, hath abounded unto many.

16 And not as it was by one that sinned, so is the gift: for the judgment was by one to condemnation, but the free gift is of many offences unto justification.

17 For if by one man's offence death reigned by one; much more they which receive abundance of grace and of the gift of righteousness shall reign in life by one, Jesus Christ.)

18 Therefore as by the offence of one judgment came upon all men to condemnation; even so by the righteousness of one the free gift came upon all men unto justification of life.

19 For as by one man's disobedience many were made sinners, so by the obedience of one shall many be made righteous.

1 John 3:8 He that committeth sin is of the devil; for the devil sinneth from the beginning. For this purpose the Son of God was manifested, that he might destroy the works of the devil.

9 Whosoever is born of God doth not commit sin; for his seed remaineth in him: and he cannot sin, because he is born of God.

So think about this; are the preachers that teach you that you must sin every day so get used to it really your friend? Oh sure they can make you feel good, but no man can be an effective con man if he can't make you feel good.

Romans 6:16 Know ye not, that to whom ye yield yourselves servants to obey, his servants ye are to whom ye obey; whether of sin unto death, or of obedience unto righteousness?

17 But God be thanked, that ye were the servants of sin, but ye have obeyed from the heart that form of doctrine which was delivered you.

18 Being then made free from sin, ye became the servants of righteousness.

19 I speak after the manner of men because of the infirmity of your flesh: for as ye have yielded your members servants to uncleanness and to iniquity unto iniquity; even so now yield your members servants to righteousness unto holiness.

20 For when ye were the servants of sin, ye were free from righteousness.

21 What fruit had ye then in those things whereof ye are now ashamed? for the end of those things is death.

22 But now being made free from sin, and become servants to God, ye have your fruit unto holiness, and the end everlasting life.

23 For the wages of sin is death; but the gift of God is eternal life through Jesus Christ our Lord.

Hebrews 5:9 And being made perfect, he became the author of eternal salvation unto all them that obey him;

2 Thessalonians 1:8 In flaming fire taking vengeance on them that know not God, and that obey not the gospel of our Lord Jesus Christ:

1 Peter 4:17 For the time is come that judgment must begin at the house of God: and if it first begin at us, what shall the end be of them that obey not the gospel of God?

What is this gospel that we are to obey to receive righteousness as a gift from God?

I would be remiss if I taught you about the horrors of sin without giving you the method whereby you can be saved. Can we really know for sure? Yes, if we just look to the Word of God instead of man made religious traditions. We can easily see that Jesus gave the keys to Peter.

> Matthew 16:18 And I say also unto thee, That thou art Peter, and upon this rock I will build my church; and the gates of hell shall not prevail against it.
>
> 19 And I will give unto thee the keys of the kingdom of heaven: and whatsoever thou shalt bind on earth shall be bound in heaven: and whatsoever thou shalt loose on earth shall be loosed in heaven.

Then we can read what Peter said to do. So you see that you cannot disobey Peter without rejecting Jesus Christ who sent him.

> Acts 2:38 Then Peter said unto them, Repent, and be baptized every one of you in the name of Jesus Christ for the remission of sins, and ye shall receive the gift of the Holy Ghost.
>
> 39 For the promise is unto you, and to your children, and to all that are afar off, even as many as the Lord our God shall call.

If something is for as many as the Lord our God shall call, then that is what you should obey to be safe.

Are the modern false preachers with their sugar coated man made fables really your friend as they scratch your itching ears with "comfortable" anything goes doctrines? Did you know that the Bible mentions them?

> 2 Timothy 4:3 For the time will come when they will not endure sound doctrine; but after their own lusts shall they heap to themselves teachers, having itching ears;
>
> 4 And they shall turn away their ears from the truth, and shall be turned unto fables.

Are these false christian preachers not bringing death itself to their victims?

Converted

We have many people today claiming to be converted or "saved" without ever obeying Acts 2:38/John 3:5. None of them spent time with Jesus. Peter spent quite a bit of time with the Lord, yet, we see that Peter was not completely "converted" or "born again", even though he obviously "believed". We see that Jesus told Peter that WHEN he was converted (future tense)..In fact we notice that Peter even denied the Lord after this conversation:

> Luke 22:31 And the Lord said, Simon, Simon, behold, Satan hath desired [to have] you, that he may sift [you] as wheat:
>
> Luke 22:32 But I have prayed for thee, that thy faith fail not: and WHEN thou art converted, strengthen thy brethren.
>
> Luke 22:33 And he said unto him, Lord, I am ready to go with thee, both into prison, and to death.
>
> Luke 22:34 And he said, I tell thee, Peter, the cock shall not crow this day, before that thou shalt thrice deny that thou knowest me.

The only major "conversion" event that happened to Peter besides baptism was when he was filled with the Holy Ghost in the Upper Room. He never denied the Lord after that. The Holy Ghost speaking in tongues is the "re-birth of the Spirit" that Jesus mentioned in John 3:5. It was in the Upper Room that Peter was "born again of the Spirit." Many today make great swelling claims of Christianity, and claim to be Christian even though they don't even believe in "tongues" But, just as Peter was wrong when he said that he would never deny the Lord....Are also these others wrong, when they claim to be "Christian" without the baptism of the Holy Ghost (with speaking in tongues) and Jesus name water baptism.

The only way to be "converted" is to obey Acts 2:38/John 3:5.

> Romans 8:9 But ye are not in the flesh, but in the Spirit, if so be that the Spirit of God dwell in you. Now if any man have not the Spirit of Christ, he is none of his.

Acts 22:16 And now why tarriest thou? arise, and be baptized, and wash away thy sins, calling on the name of the Lord.

One Way

Jesus Christ declared rather clearly that there was only one "method" of salvation. Also I added the verse 9:41 for the benefit of those "professing" Christianity, while disregarding Biblical salvation.

The false christians teaching their "broad road" are not your friends.

> John 9:41 Jesus said unto them, If ye were blind, ye should have no sin: but now ye say, We see; therefore your sin remaineth.
>
> John 10:1 Verily, verily, I say unto you, He that entereth not by the door into the sheepfold, but climbeth up some other way, the same is a thief and a robber.

The same Jesus that speaks of a door in John 10:1 also spoke of "keys" to that door. Jesus gave those keys to the Apostle Peter.

> Matt 16:19 And I will give unto thee the keys of the kingdom of heaven: and whatsoever thou shalt bind on earth shall be bound in heaven: and whatsoever thou shalt loose on earth shall be loosed in heaven.

Peter then used those keys to unlock the door to the sheepfold, by employing the two essential elements (as declared by Jesus in John 3:5), that is "water"(baptism) and "Spirit"(the baptism of the Holy Ghost).

> John 3:5 Jesus answered, Verily, verily, I say unto thee, Except a man be born of water and [of] the Spirit, he cannot enter into the kingdom of God.
>
> Acts 2:38 Then Peter said unto them, Repent, and be baptized every one of you in the name of Jesus Christ for the remission of sins, and ye shall receive the gift of the Holy Ghost.

Acts 2:39 For the promise is unto you, and to your children, and to all that are afar off, [even] as many as the Lord our God shall call.

*Interestingly enough the keys of the door to the sheepfold also give a method with which man can "obey the Gospel". The Gospel MUST be OBEYED to _really_ become a Christian. *

II Thessalonians 1:7 And to you who are troubled rest with us, when the Lord Jesus shall be revealed from heaven with his mighty angels,

II Thessalonians 1:8 In flaming fire taking vengeance on them that know not God, and that obey not the gospel of our Lord Jesus Christ:

II Thessalonians 1:9 Who shall be punished with everlasting destruction from the presence of the Lord, and from the glory of his power;

The Gospel consists of the Death, Burial and Resurrection. This orchestrates beautifully with the Acts 2:38 "keys to the door of the kingdom"....THE METHOD of OBEYING the Death, burial and resurrection. (and notice how death and burial are intertwined, like repentance and baptism)

1. Death is obeyed through REPENTANCE.

Romans 6:6 Knowing this, that our old man is crucified with [him], that the body of sin might be destroyed, that henceforth we should not serve sin.

* 2. Burial is obeyed through Jesus name baptism.

Romans 6:3 Know ye not, that so many of us as were baptized into Jesus Christ were baptized into his death?

Romans 6:4 Therefore we are buried with him by baptism into death: that like as Christ was raised up from the dead by the glory of the Father, even so we also should walk in newness of life.

Romans 6:5 For if we have been planted together in the likeness of his death, we shall be also [in the likeness] of [his] resurrection:

* 3.The resurrection is obeyed through the baptism of the Holy Ghost.

Romans 8:9 But ye are not in the flesh, but in the Spirit, if so be that the Spirit of God dwell in you. Now if any man have not the Spirit of Christ, he is none of his.

Romans 8:11 But if the Spirit of him that raised up Jesus from the dead dwell in you, he that raised up Christ from the dead shall also quicken your mortal bodies by his Spirit that dwelleth in you.

* The Apostles led folks in through Jesus' door, all through the book of Acts. And then wrote letters to the folks who had OBEYED (the epistles).

** Jews when they received the Holy Ghost **

Acts 2:4 And they were all filled with the Holy Ghost, and began to speak with other tongues, as the Spirit gave them utterance.

** Samaritans when they received the Holy Ghost **

Acts 8:14 Now when the apostles which were at Jerusalem heard that Samaria had received the word of God, they sent unto them Peter and John:

Acts 8:15 Who, when they were come down, prayed for them, that they might receive the Holy Ghost:

Acts 8:16 (For as yet he was fallen upon none of them: only they were baptized in the name of the Lord Jesus.)

Acts 8:17 Then laid they [their] hands on them, and they received the Holy Ghost.

** Gentiles when they received the Holy Ghost **

Acts 10:45 And they of the circumcision which believed were astonished, as many as came with Peter, because that on the Gentiles also was poured out the gift of the Holy Ghost.

Acts 10:46 For they heard them speak with tongues, and magnify God. Then answered Peter,

Acts 10:47 Can any man forbid water, that these should not be baptized, which have received the Holy Ghost as well as we?

Acts 10:48 And he commanded them to be baptized in the name of the Lord. Then prayed they him to tarry certain days.

** John the Baptist's disciples when they were RE- baptized and received the Holy Ghost **

Acts 19:2 He said unto them, Have ye received the Holy Ghost since ye believed? And they said unto him, We have not so much as heard whether there be any Holy Ghost.

Acts 19:3 And he said unto them, Unto what then were ye baptized? And they said, Unto John's baptism.

Acts 19:4 Then said Paul, John verily baptized with the baptism of repentance, saying unto the people, that they should believe on him which should come after him, that is, on Christ Jesus.

Acts 19:5 When they heard [this], they were baptized in the name of the Lord Jesus.

Acts 19:6 And when Paul had laid [his] hands upon them, the Holy Ghost came on them; and they spake with tongues, and prophesied.

* Jews, gentiles, Samaritans; all baptized in JESUS name, all spoke in tongues when they received the Holy Ghost.*

John 10:1 Verily, verily, I say unto you, He that entereth not by the door into the sheepfold, but climbeth up some other way, the same is a thief and a robber.

One Door

> II Timothy 3:16 All scripture [is] given by inspiration of God, and [is] profitable for doctrine, for reproof, for correction, for instruction in righteousness:
>
> II Timothy 3:17 That the man of God may be perfect, throughly furnished unto all good works.
>
> II Timothy 4:1 I charge [thee] therefore before God, and the Lord Jesus Christ, who shall judge the quick and the dead at his appearing and his kingdom;
>
> II Timothy 4:2 Preach the word; be instant in season, out of season; reprove, rebuke, exhort with all longsuffering and doctrine.
>
> II Timothy 4:3 For the time will come when they will not endure sound doctrine; but after their own lusts shall they heap to themselves teachers, having itching ears;
>
> II Timothy 4:4 And they shall turn away [their] ears from the truth, and shall be turned unto fables.

We need to be aware that a great number of people will simply reject the word of God and choose one of the many "fables" being preached by the false churches, or the "Hollywood" type fables etc... The message to any and all sinners is Acts 2:38. It was the original Christian plan of salvation and will be until the Lord comes again for His true church.

> Acts 2:37 Now when they heard [this], they were pricked in their heart, and said unto Peter and to the rest of the apostles, Men [and] brethren, what shall we do?
>
> Acts 2:38 Then Peter said unto them, Repent, and be baptized every one of you in the name of Jesus Christ for the remission of sins, and ye shall receive the gift of the Holy Ghost.

The message to the homosexual is the same message to the denominal preacher, is the same message to the movie star; there is only one door to the sheepfold. To become a Christian a person must (1) Repent of their sins. (2) Be water baptized in the name of Jesus Christ (which is the name of the ONE God who was Father in creation, Son in redemption and the Holy Ghost in the Christian), and (3) Receive the same Holy Ghost that they received in the Bible.

The message in the Bible was the same for the Jew and the Gentile, the GIFT of a plan of salvation, an opportunity given by the Grace of God to OBEY and be SAVED.

> John 10:1 Verily, verily, I say unto you, He that entereth not by the door into the sheepfold, but climbeth up some other way, the same is a thief and a robber. * That same Acts 2:38 message is for: Acts 2:39 For the promise is unto you, and to your children, and to all that are afar off, [even] as many as the Lord our God shall call.

So it doesn't really matter what kind of sinner they are, whether one is witnessing to a denominal preacher or a drag queen (or these days one could be both); the message of God's offer of salvation is the same, regardless of how deep they are in sin. The blood of Jesus when applied through Jesus name water baptism, is able to remit sins.

> Isaiah 1:18 Come now, and let us reason together, saith the LORD: though your sins be as scarlet, they shall be as white as snow; though they be red like crimson, they shall be as wool.

> Acts 22:16 And now why tarriest thou? arise, and be baptized, and wash away thy sins, calling on the name of the Lord.

Romans

Here is a study that I hope will be a blessing to you. We need to remember that Romans is a letter written to people who had already been baptized in Jesus Name and had received the Holy Ghost with the evidence of speaking in other tongues.

Always remember that the book of Romans was a letter that was written to the Church at Rome. It was a letter written to Christians, to people who had ALREADY become Christians.

> Rom 1:6 Among whom are ye also the called of Jesus Christ:
>
> Rom 1:7 To all that be in Rome, beloved of God, called to be saints: Grace to you and peace from God our Father, and the Lord Jesus Christ.
>
> Rom 1:8 First, I thank my God through Jesus Christ for you all, that your faith is spoken of throughout the whole world.

The Epistles of the Bible were all letters written to Christians instructing them how to STAY Christians, and how to please the Lord.

Many antichrist preachers will use verses that were written to people who had ALREADY been "born again". They will use these verses to deceive people who have never become Christians. For example notice these verses that were written to people at Rome who were ALREADY Christians.

> Romans 10:9 That if thou shalt confess with thy mouth the Lord Jesus, and shalt believe in thine heart that God hath raised him from the dead, thou shalt be saved.
>
> Romans 10:10 For with the heart man believeth unto righteousness; and with the mouth confession is made unto salvation.

These verses are excellent instructions for people who have ALREADY obeyed Acts 2:38 and become Christians (we see in Acts 19 that when Paul founded churches he preached Acts 2:38). A Christian that will obey Romans 10:9-10 will remain strong and will endure to the end and will be saved.

The antichrist preacher, though, will use Romans 10:9-10 to deceive sinners into thinking that all they have to do is mouth a few words and they are suddenly "Christian" and "saved".

If we simply understand that Romans was a letter written to people who had ALREADY become Christians by obeying Acts 2:38, then we can spot those accursed false preachers when they attempt to deceive people into disobeying the Word of God.

> Acts 2:38 Then Peter said unto them, Repent, and be baptized every one of you in the name of Jesus Christ for the remission of sins, and ye shall receive the gift of the Holy Ghost.
>
> Acts 2:39 For the promise is unto you, and to your children, and to all that are afar off, [even] as many as the Lord our God shall call.

Notice the phrase, "as many as the Lord our God shall call."

> Galatians 1:8 But though we, or an angel from heaven, preach any other gospel unto you than that which we have preached unto you, let him be accursed.

> II Corinthians 11:12 But what I do, that I will do, that I may cut off occasion from them which desire occasion; that wherein they glory, they may be found even as we.
>
> II Corinthians 11:13 For such [are] false apostles, deceitful workers, transforming themselves into the apostles of Christ.
>
> II Corinthians 11:14 And no marvel; for Satan himself is transformed into an angel of light.

> II Corinthians 11:15 Therefore [it is] no great thing if his ministers also be transformed as the ministers of righteousness; whose end shall be according to their works.

Don't be surprised that Satan's ministers will pretend to be Christian preachers, the Bible says that they will do that; and it is their job to convince YOU that you can be saved without obeying the Bible.

Believe Only

Many of the enemies of God are taking a couple of Bible verses out of letters that were written to SAINTS that had ALREADY OBEYED Acts 2:38. These enemies of God are teaching that if a person simply says that they believe in Jesus, that they are saved simply by "claiming to believe".

If belief ALONE would save then we would have a saved devil.

> James 2:19 Thou believest that there is one God; thou doest well: the devils also believe, and tremble.

The devils in Legion "made public profession" that Jesus was LORD. Jesus even answered their prayer. and allowed them to go into a herd of pigs.

> Mark 5:7 And cried with a loud voice, and said, What have I to do with thee, Jesus, [thou] Son of the most high God? I adjure thee by God, that thou torment me not.
>
> Mark 5:8 For he said unto him, Come out of the man, [thou] unclean spirit.
>
> Mark 5:9 And he asked him, What [is] thy name? And he answered, saying, My name [is] Legion: for we are many.
>
> Mark 5:10 And he besought him much that he would not send them away out of the country.
>
> Mark 5:12 And all the devils besought him, saying, Send us into the swine, that we may enter into them.

Don't let God's enemies deceive you with their "belief only" doctrine. It is such shallow foolishness....

> Acts 2:38 Then Peter said unto them, Repent, and be baptized every one of you in the name of Jesus Christ for the remission of sins, and ye shall receive the gift of the Holy Ghost.

Acts 2:39 For the promise is unto you, and to your children, and to all that are afar off, [even] as many as the Lord our God shall call.

I Corinthians 15:2 By which also ye are saved, if ye keep in memory what I preached unto you, unless ye have believed in vain.

Ephesians

Many are confused by some verses in the book of Ephesians into thinking that they can be saved without obeying the Gospel as revealed in Acts 2:38.

We have verses like:

> 2 Thessalonians 1:8 In flaming fire taking vengeance on them that know not God, and that obey not the gospel of our Lord Jesus Christ:
>
> Ephesians 2:8 For by grace are ye saved through faith; and that not of yourselves: it is the gift of God:

How can this not be a contradiction? Well, obedience and works are simply two different things.

To talk about Ephesians, one needs to know how the Ephesian Church was founded. When Paul wrote the epistle to the Ephesians, he was writing to people who had been baptized in Jesus Name and who had received the Holy Ghost with the evidence of other tongues.

We simply can look to Acts Chapter 19 and find when the Ephesian Church was founded.

> Acts 19:1 And it came to pass, that, while Apollos was at Corinth, Paul having passed through the upper coasts came to Ephesus: and finding certain disciples,
>
> 2 He said unto them, Have ye received the Holy Ghost since ye believed? And they said unto him, We have not so much as heard whether there be any Holy Ghost.
>
> 3 And he said unto them, Unto what then were ye baptized? And they said, Unto John's baptism.
>
> 4 Then said Paul, John verily baptized with the baptism of repentance, saying unto the people, that they should believe on him which should come after him, that is, on Christ Jesus.

> 5 When they heard this, they were baptized in the name of the Lord Jesus.
>
> 6 And when Paul had laid his hands upon them, the Holy Ghost came on them; and they spake with tongues, and prophesied.

It was grace that offered the true Acts 2:38 salvation to the people at Ephesus, not any works that they had done. They were given the opportunity of Acts 2:38 salvation purely by grace alone.

You can obey Acts 2:38 and also be saved by grace.

Ephesians: Grace and Works

Many of the representatives of false Christianity today will quote from the book of Ephesians to explain how they are Christian even though they have never met any of the Biblical criteria for Christianity. Some are audacious enough to suggest that they disobey the commandments of God, so that they will not "cheapen" God's grace.

I suppose they would accuse Noah of cheapening God's grace by obeying and building an Ark.

> Genesis 6:8 But Noah found grace in the eyes of the LORD.
>
> Genesis 6:22 Thus did Noah; according to all that God commanded him, so did he.
>
> Genesis 7:23 And every living substance was destroyed which was upon the face of the ground, both man, and cattle, and the creeping things, and the fowl of the heaven; and they were destroyed from the earth: and Noah only remained [alive], and they that [were] with him in the ark.

* Here are some of the verses from Ephesians that the false preachers will attempt to use to deceive the gullible. *

> Ephesians 2:8 For by grace are ye saved through faith; and that not of yourselves: [it is] the gift of God:
>
> Ephesians 2:9 Not of works, lest any man should boast.

I would call your attention to the founding of the Ephesian Church (to whom these verses were addressed in a letter from Paul, the book of Ephesians is a letter that Paul wrote to a church that he founded in Acts 19., according to Acts 2:38).

> Acts 19:1 And it came to pass, that, while Apollos was at Corinth, Paul having passed through the upper coasts came to Ephesus: and finding certain disciples,

> Acts 19:2 He said unto them, Have ye received the Holy Ghost since ye believed? And they said unto him, We have not so much as heard whether there be any Holy Ghost.
>
> Acts 19:3 And he said unto them, Unto what then were ye baptized? And they said, Unto John's baptism.
>
> Acts 19:4 Then said Paul, John verily baptized with the baptism of repentance, saying unto the people, that they should believe on him which should come after him, that is, on Christ Jesus.
>
> Acts 19:5 When they heard [this], they were baptized in the name of the Lord Jesus.
>
> Acts 19:6 And when Paul had laid [his] hands upon them, the Holy Ghost came on them; and they spake with tongues, and prophesied.
>
> Acts 19:7 And all the men were about twelve.
>
> Acts 19:8 And he went into the synagogue, and spake boldly for the space of three months, disputing and persuading the things concerning the kingdom of God.
>
> Acts 19:9 But when divers were hardened, and believed not, but spake evil of that way before the multitude, he departed from them, and separated the disciples, disputing daily in the school of one Tyrannus.

There are still many who "speak evil" of the way of the apostles which Paul refers to as "the word of the Lord Jesus."

> Acts 19:10 And this continued by the space of two years; so that all they which dwelt in Asia heard the word of the Lord Jesus, both Jews and Greeks.

The Apostles equated the Acts 2:38 plan of salvation (preached by Peter on Jesus' authority) with the "word of the Lord Jesus".

> Acts 2:38 Then Peter said unto them, Repent, and be baptized every one of you in the name of Jesus Christ for the remission of sins, and ye shall receive the gift of the Holy Ghost.

Acts 2:39 For the promise is unto you, and to your children, and to all that are afar off, [even] as many as the Lord our God shall call.

Galatians 1:8 But though we, or an angel from heaven, preach any other gospel unto you than that which we have preached unto you, let him be accursed.

Galatians 1:9 As we said before, so say I now again, If any [man]

preach any other gospel unto you than that ye have received, let him be accursed.

Galatians 1:10 For do I now persuade men, or God? or do I seek to please men? for if I yet pleased men, I should not be the servant of Christ.

* But the world just loves their false preachers!!! *

II Timothy 4:2 Preach the word; be instant in season, out of season; reprove, rebuke, exhort with all longsuffering and doctrine.

II Timothy 4:3 For the time will come when they will not endure sound doctrine; but after their own lusts shall they heap to themselves teachers, having itching ears;

II Timothy 4:4 And they shall turn away [their] ears from the truth, and shall be turned unto fables.

Accepted

There are many today who claim to have "accepted Christ as their personal savior" and they claim to be headed to a heaven that is taught by the Bible. But, the Bible teaches that those who try to enter heaven any other way than the Bible way, will be lost.

> John 10:1 Verily, verily, I say unto you, He that entereth not by the door into the sheepfold, but climbeth up some other way, the same is a thief and a robber.

The Bible makes NO MENTION WHATSOEVER of "accepting Christ as your personal saviour by a mental/verbal affirmation that He exists"; that is a MAN MADE FALSE DOCTRINE. People are being taught everything from "Just flash your headlights twice" (in the drive in "church") to "walk the Roman road and make a public profession" or "Shake the preachers hand" as though these activities could even save a gnat!

> James 2:19 Thou believest that there is one God; thou doest well: the devils also believe, and tremble.

It is not real brilliant to want to be just as "saved" as the devils.

It is notable that the devils in Legion confessed that Jesus was God and even made a prayer request. Jesus even granted their prayer request!

> Mark 5:2 And when he was come out of the ship, immediately there met him out of the tombs a man with an unclean spirit,
>
> 3 Who had his dwelling among the tombs; and no man could bind him, no, not with chains:
>
> 4 Because that he had been often bound with fetters and chains, and the chains had been plucked asunder by him, and the fetters broken in pieces: neither could any man tame him.
>
> 5 And always, night and day, he was in the mountains, and in the tombs, crying, and cutting himself with stones.

> 6 But when he saw Jesus afar off, he ran and worshipped him,
>
> 7 And cried with a loud voice, and said, What have I to do with thee, Jesus, thou Son of the most high God? I adjure thee by God, that thou torment me not.
>
> 8 For he said unto him, Come out of the man, thou unclean spirit.
>
> 9 And he asked him, What is thy name? And he answered, saying, My name is Legion: for we are many.
>
> 10 And he besought him much that he would not send them away out of the country.
>
> 11 Now there was there nigh unto the mountains a great herd of swine feeding.
>
> 12 And all the devils besought him, saying, Send us into the swine, that we may enter into them.
>
> 13 And forthwith Jesus gave them leave. And the unclean spirits went out, and entered into the swine: and the herd ran violently down a steep place into the sea, (they were about two thousand;) and were choked in the sea.

So if we follow the doctrine of 90% of the so called "christian" churches, we end up just as saved as the devils in Legion. Someone is lying to someone folks, and it is the con game of con games because people are loosing their souls. Some deceiving trinity preacher goes to jail for cheating some old women out of their savings and no one gives any thought for their souls. Do you think the "Jim & Tammy" followers are going to worry about the money when they find themselves in hell?

When people are decived by a false-preacher there is no happy ending.

> Matthew 15:14 Let them alone: they be blind leaders of the blind. And if the blind lead the blind, both shall fall into the ditch.
>
> Luke 6:39 And he spake a parable unto them, Can the blind lead the blind? shall they not both fall into the ditch?

2 Corinthians 11:14 And no marvel; for Satan himself is transformed into an angel of light.

15 Therefore it is no great thing if his ministers also be transformed as the ministers of righteousness; whose end shall be according to their works.

The plan of salvation taught by Jesus' disciples is:

Acts 2:38 Then Peter said unto them, Repent, and be baptized every one of you in the name of Jesus Christ for the remission of sins, and ye shall receive the gift of the Holy Ghost.

Acts 2:39 For the promise is unto you, and to your children, and to all that are afar off, [even] as many as the Lord our God shall call.

Note the 39th verse "as many as the Lord our God shall call" Now, if your preacher is teaching anything other than the apostles doctrine (Acts 2:38), then YOUR BIBLE says to "let him be accursed"

Galatians 1:8 But though we, or an angel from heaven, preach any other gospel unto you than that which we have preached unto you, let him be accursed.

The gospel that they had received was clearly Acts 2:38. So, do you really think that a man that God calls accursed can really be trusted?

Matthew 15:14 Let them alone: they be blind leaders of the blind. And if the blind lead the blind, both shall fall into the ditch.

Luke 6:39 And he spake a parable unto them, Can the blind lead the blind? shall they not both fall into the ditch?

The ditch is hell. If you're following a false preacher you will BOTH end up in hell. How can a man, accursed of God, tell you how to be saved. Do you really think that God will honor a LIE just to save a

bunch of people that chose tradition instead of the word of God??

II Corinthians 11:14 And no marvel; for Satan himself is transformed into an angel of light.

II Corinthians 11:15 Therefore [it is] no great thing if his ministers also be transformed as the ministers of righteousness; whose end shall be according to their works.

Satan's ministers CLAIM to be ministers of righteousness... They are of the world, and the worldly LOVE to hear them preach..

> II Peter 2:17 These are wells without water, clouds that are carried with a tempest; to whom the mist of darkness is reserved for ever.

> II Peter 2:18 For when they speak great swelling [words] of vanity, they allure through the lusts of the flesh, [through much] wantonness, those that were clean escaped from them who live in error.

> Romans 16:18 For they that are such serve not our Lord Jesus Christ, but their own belly; and by good words and fair speeches deceive the hearts of the simple.

If you obey HIS word, then, and only then, have you "accepted Christ". The multitudes who claim to have accepted him, while rejecting his word are merely decieved..OR WORSE:

> II Thessalonians 2:10 And with all deceivableness of unrighteousness in them that perish; because they received not the love of the truth, that they might be saved.

> II Thessalonians 2:11 And for this cause God shall send them strong delusion, that they should believe a lie:

> II Thessalonians 2:12 That they all might be damned who believed not the truth, but had pleasure in unrighteousness.

God WILL not only *let* truth haters believe a lie, he will even send them STRONG DELUSION...Read 2 :12 again, Who does God say will be damned??

> Matthew 7:13 Enter ye in at the strait gate: for wide [is] the gate, and broad [is] the way, that leadeth to destruction, and many there be which go in thereat:

> Matthew 7:14 Because strait [is] the gate, and narrow [is] the way, which leadeth unto life, and few there be that find it.

> Matthew 7:15 Beware of false prophets, which come to you in sheep's clothing, but inwardly they are ravening wolves.

So, we see trinity denominations with their broad roads, and many who claim to be saved. Yet they have abandoned Biblical salvation..Is the Bible right?

Denominal preachers are going to their pulpits with a book under their arm that teaches that they, and those that hear them, are damned...

Mary spoke in Tongues

Here we have the birth of the new testament church when the Baptism of the Holy Ghost was first given.

> Acts 2:1 And when the day of Pentecost was fully come, they were all with one accord in one place.
>
> Acts 2:2 And suddenly there came a sound from heaven as of a rushing mighty wind, and it filled all the house where they were sitting.
>
> Acts 2:3 And there appeared unto them cloven tongues like as of fire, and it sat upon each of them.
>
> Acts 2:4 And they were all filled with the Holy Ghost, and began to speak with other tongues, as the Spirit gave them utterance.

Let us look back and establish who was present in the Upper Room.

Looking back we see that Jesus told a crowd of people that they all should not depart from Jerusalem until they all were baptized with the Holy Ghost.

> Acts 1:4 And, being assembled together with [them], commanded them that they should not depart from Jerusalem, but wait for the promise of the Father, which, [saith he], ye have heard of me.
>
> Acts 1:5 For John truly baptized with water; but ye shall be baptized with the Holy Ghost not many days hence.

Then the whole crowd watched Jesus go up into the sky.

> Acts 1:9 And when he had spoken these things, while they beheld, he was taken up; and a cloud received him out of their sight.

> Acts 1:10 And while they looked stedfastly toward heaven as he went up, behold, two men stood by them in white apparel;
>
> Acts 1:11 Which also said, Ye men of Galilee, why stand ye gazing up into heaven? this same Jesus, which is taken up from you into heaven, shall so come in like manner as ye have seen him go into heaven.

Then the crowd returned to Jerusalem.

> Acts 1:12 Then returned they unto Jerusalem from the mount called Olivet, which is from Jerusalem a sabbath day's journey.

The crowd that Jesus had commanded to wait for the Holy Ghost went into the Upper Room and were numbered at about 120.

> Acts 1:13 And when they were come in, they went up into an upper room, where abode both Peter, and James, and John, and Andrew, Philip, and Thomas, Bartholomew, and Matthew, James [the son] of Alphaeus, and Simon Zelotes, and Judas [the brother] of James.
>
> Acts 1:14 These all continued with one accord in prayer and supplication, with the women, and Mary the mother of Jesus, and with his brethren.
>
> Acts 1:15 And in those days Peter stood up in the midst of the disciples, and said, (the number of names together were about an hundred and twenty,)

Notice that we have followed the crowd from when Jesus told them to all wait in Jerusalem until they received the Baptism of the Holy Ghost. We see that the crowd was numbered at about 120 and included Mary. These people had been commanded by Jesus to WAIT for several days, and they had just seen Him go up into the sky.

The book of Acts then gives the account of another Apostle being selected to replace Judas. There is NO MENTION of any of the 120 leaving the Upper Room. Jesus had told them to wait, "not many days" and who would have left while another Apostle was being selected?

Then we see that all those 120 that Jesus had promised the Holy Ghost to, did receive the baptism of the Holy Ghost and that they ALL (including Mary) spoke in "other tongues" when they received the Holy Ghost (soon after Matthias was named as the 12th Apostle)

> Acts 1:26 And they gave forth their lots; and the lot fell upon Matthias; and he was numbered with the eleven apostles.

> Acts 2:1 And when the day of Pentecost was fully come, they were all with one accord in one place.

The crowd (of 120) were ALL together in one place.

> Acts 2:2 And suddenly there came a sound from heaven as of a rushing mighty wind, and it filled all the house where they were sitting.

> Acts 2:3 And there appeared unto them cloven tongues like as of fire, and it sat upon each of them.

> Acts 2:4 And they were all filled with the Holy Ghost, and began to speak with other tongues, as the Spirit gave them utterance.

120 people INCLUDING Mary the mother of Jesus were filled with the Holy Ghost and ALL spoke in tongues.

Peter Walked on Water

> Mat 14:23 And when he had sent the multitudes away, he went up into a mountain apart to pray: and when the evening was come, he was there alone.
>
> Mat 14:24 But the ship was now in the midst of the sea, tossed with waves: for the wind was contrary.
>
> Mat 14:25 And in the fourth watch of the night Jesus went unto them, walking on the sea.
>
> Mat 14:26 And when the disciples saw him walking on the sea, they were troubled, saying, It is a spirit; and they cried out for fear.

The disciples (who had just witnessed a miracle) were crying out in fear just a short time later. Interesting...

> Mat 14:27 But straightway Jesus spake unto them, saying, Be of good cheer; it is I; be not afraid.
>
> Mat 14:28 And Peter answered him and said, Lord, if it be thou, bid me come unto thee on the water.

Now here it was really good for Peter that it was, in fact, Jesus.

> Mat 14:29 And he said, Come . And when Peter was come down out of the ship, he walked on the water, to go to Jesus.

Peter walked on water by faith. How many of us had the faith to walk on water?

When Peter walked on water by faith it was before he became a Christian and was converted to salvation. Think about that now. He had enough faith to walk on water but he was not yet saved.

We have many people today claiming to be converted or "saved" without ever obeying Acts 2:38/John 3:5. None of them spent time with Jesus. Peter spent quite a bit of time with the Lord and obeying Him. You need to see the empty claims of the false christian for what they are.

Yet, we see that Peter was not "converted" or "born again", even though he obviously "believed" enough to walk on water. We see that Jesus told Peter that WHEN he was converted (future tense). We should also notice that Peter even denied the Lord after this conversation:

> Luke 22:31 And the Lord said, Simon, Simon, behold, Satan hath desired [to have] you, that he may sift [you] as wheat:
>
> Luke 22:32 But I have prayed for thee, that thy faith fail not: and WHEN thou art converted, strengthen thy brethren.
>
> Luke 22:33 And he said unto him, Lord, I am ready to go with thee, both into prison, and to death.
>
> Luke 22:34 And he said, I tell thee, Peter, the cock shall not crow this day, before that thou shalt thrice deny that thou knowest me.

The only major conversion event that happened to Peter besides baptism was when he was filled with the Holy Ghost speaking in other tongues in the Upper Room. He never denied the Lord after that. The Holy Ghost speaking in tongues is the "re-birth of the Spirit" that Jesus mentioned in John 3:5. It was in the Upper Room that Peter was "born again of the Spirit."

Many today make great swelling claims of Christianity, and claim to be Christian even though they don't even believe in "tongues". But, just as Peter was wrong when he said that he would never deny the Lord....Are also these others wrong, when they claim to be "Christian" without the baptism of the Holy Ghost (with speaking in tongues) and Jesus name water baptism.

The only way to be "converted" is to obey Acts 2:38/John 3:5.

> Romans 8:9 But ye are not in the flesh, but in the Spirit, if so be that the Spirit of God dwell in you. Now if any man have not the Spirit of Christ, he is none of his.

Those who have not the Holy Spirit (the Spirit of Christ) are none of His.

> Acts 22:16 And now why tarriest thou? arise, and be baptized, and wash away thy sins, calling on the name of the Lord.

Be baptized in Jesus Name to have your sins remitted.

Consider that when Peter walked on the water it was BEFORE he became converted!

> Luke 22:32 But I have prayed for thee, that thy faith fail not: and when thou art converted, strengthen thy brethren.

See, future tense? Peter had NOT yet been converted or Jesus could not have spoken those words to him.

Consider also that the epistles are letters to Christians and not letters to the lost telling them how to become Christian. The epistles are letters to people who have been converted. So if even walking with Jesus and serving Jesus did not equal salvation I must submit that no amount of attendance in a false church gives salvation either.

True Biblical salvation was important enough for Jesus to state that Peter didn't have it yet!

The false preacher in the false church is NOT your friend regardless of how dewy eyed they can get you with sympathetic stories. I could tell you emotional sad stories like that and probably not be able to finish without crying myself too, but that won't save you!!!

A preacher is to "preach the word", not scratch itching ears with emotional fables as has become so much the norm in this hour.

> 2 Timothy 4:2 Preach the word; be instant in season, out of season; reprove, rebuke, exhort with all longsuffering and doctrine.
>
> 1 Corinthians 1:21 For after that in the wisdom of God the world by wisdom knew not God, it pleased God by the foolishness of preaching to save them that believe.

If the false preacher can get the crowd stirred up then they think they have been fed spiritually but its just empty calories brethren!

> 2 Timothy 4:3 For the time will come when they will not endure sound doctrine; but after their own lusts shall they heap to themselves teachers, having itching ears;
>
> 4 And they shall turn away their ears from the truth, and shall be turned unto fables.

What powerful verses describing the hour in which we now live! Have you ever wondered why there could be so many churches all teaching completely different things?

While the worldly false preachers are teaching more and more that the commandments of the Bible don't matter and such like doctrines of devils, the Word of God speaks to the real Acts 2:38 Christian with an awesome commandment and responsibility:

> Romans 12:2 And be not conformed to this world: but be ye transformed by the renewing of your mind, that ye may prove what is that good, and acceptable, and perfect, will of God.

Tongues

James 3:1 ¶ My brethren, be not many masters, knowing that we shall receive the greater condemnation.

2 For in many things we offend all. If any man offend not in word, the same is a perfect man, and able also to bridle the whole body.

3 Behold, we put bits in the horses' mouths, that they may obey us; and we turn about their whole body.

4 Behold also the ships, which though they be so great, and are driven of fierce winds, yet are they turned about with a very small helm, whithersoever the governor listeth.

5 Even so the tongue is a little member, and boasteth great things. Behold, how great a matter a little fire kindleth!

6 And the tongue is a fire, a world of iniquity: so is the tongue among our members, that it defileth the whole body, and setteth on fire the course of nature; and it is set on fire of hell.

7 For every kind of beasts, and of birds, and of serpents, and of things in the sea, is tamed, and hath been tamed of mankind:

8 But the tongue can no man tame; it is an unruly evil, full of deadly poison.

9 Therewith bless we God, even the Father; and therewith curse we men, which are made after the similitude of God.

10 Out of the same mouth proceedeth blessing and cursing. My brethren, these things ought not so to be.

11 Doth a fountain send forth at the same place sweet water and bitter?

James 4:11 ¶ Speak not evil one of another, brethren. He that speaketh evil of his brother, and judgeth his brother, speaketh evil of the law, and judgeth the law: but if thou judge the law, thou art not a doer of the law, but a judge.

12 There is one lawgiver, who is able to save and to destroy: who art thou that judgest another?

13 Go to now, ye that say, To day or to morrow we will go into such a city, and continue there a year, and buy and sell, and get gain:

14 Whereas ye know not what shall be on the morrow. For what is your life? It is even a vapour, that appeareth for a little time, and then vanisheth away.

15 For that ye ought to say, If the Lord will, we shall live, and do this, or that.

16 But now ye rejoice in your boastings: all such rejoicing is evil.

Proverbs 25:23 The north wind driveth away rain: so doth an angry countenance a backbiting tongue.

Matthew 12:34 O generation of vipers, how can ye, being evil, speak good things? for out of the abundance of the heart the mouth speaketh.

35 A good man out of the good treasure of the heart bringeth forth good things: and an evil man out of the evil treasure bringeth forth evil things.

36 But I say unto you, That every idle word that men shall speak, they shall give account thereof in the day of judgment.

37 For by thy words thou shalt be justified, and by thy words thou shalt be condemned.

Two types of tongues

IT IS ESSENTIAL to understand that there are TWO COMPLETELY DIFFERENT KINDS OF TONGUES in the Bible. #1: Other Tongues and #2: The Gift of Tongues (Unknown tongues).

When the 120 in the upper room were filled with the Holy Ghost they spoke in other tongues(#1).

> Acts 1:15 And in those days Peter stood up in the midst of the disciples, and said, (the number of names together were about an hundred and twenty,)

Other tongues(#1) WAS UNDERSTOOD by men

> Acts 2:5 ¶ And there were dwelling at Jerusalem Jews, devout men, out of every nation under heaven.
>
> 6 Now when this was noised abroad, the multitude came together, and were confounded, because that every man heard them speak in his own language.
>
> 7 And they were all amazed and marvelled, saying one to another, Behold, are not all these which speak Galilaeans?

> Acts 2:11 Cretes and Arabians, we do hear them speak in our tongues the wonderful works of God.

In I Cor 14:2 however it says that when a man speaks in "unknown tongues (#2)" that NO MAN UNDERSTANDS him.

> 1 Corinthians 14:2 For he that speaketh in an unknown tongue speaketh not unto men, but unto God: for no man understandeth him; howbeit in the spirit he speaketh mysteries.

Two types of tongues

In I Cor 12: 29,30 Paul is speaking concerning "the Gift of Tongues(unknown tongues #2)" when he asks "Do all speak with tongues(#2)?", the group that he was addressing all had spoken in "other tongues(#1)" when they had received the Holy Ghost.

> 1 Corinthians 12:29 Are all apostles? are all prophets? are all teachers? are all workers of miracles?
>
> 30 Have all the gifts of healing? do all speak with tongues? do all interpret?

> 1 Corinthians 12:4 Now there are diversities of gifts, but the same Spirit.
>
> 5 And there are differences of administrations, but the same Lord.
>
> 6 And there are diversities of operations, but it is the same God which worketh all in all.
>
> 7 But the manifestation of the Spirit is given to every man to profit withal.
>
> 8 For to one is given by the Spirit the word of wisdom; to another the word of knowledge by the same Spirit;
>
> 9 To another faith by the same Spirit; to another the gifts of healing by the same Spirit;
>
> 10 To another the working of miracles; to another prophecy; to another discerning of spirits; to another divers kinds of tongues; to another the interpretation of tongues:
>
> 11 But all these worketh that one and the selfsame Spirit, dividing to every man severally as he will.

Though ALL that receive the Holy Ghost DO SPEAK IN OTHER TONGUES(#1). Of these not everyone will be used in the "Gift of Tongues(#2)". Every new-testament Christian will speak in "other tongues(#1)", but every Christian will not be used in the "Gift of tongues(#2)"

Other tongues(#1) is, however, only the initial evidence that a person has been "reborn of the Spirit". It is not an end unto itself, but rather the beginning of a Christian life that should go "on to perfection" and manifest the full "fruit of the Spirit" in due season. Also essential is repentance from sin and baptism in water in the NAME of Jesus.

> Acts 2:38 Then Peter said unto them, Repent, and be baptized every one of you in the name of Jesus Christ for the remission of sins, and ye shall receive the gift of the Holy Ghost.

Everyone in the new testament (including Mary the mother of Jesus) spoke in "other tongues(#1)" when they received the Holy Ghost.

> Acts 1:12 ¶ Then returned they unto Jerusalem from the mount called Olivet, which is from Jerusalem a sabbath day's journey.
>
> 13 And when they were come in, they went up into an upper room, where abode both Peter, and James, and John, and Andrew, Philip, and Thomas, Bartholomew, and Matthew, James the son of Alphaeus, and Simon Zelotes, and Judas the brother of James.
>
> 14 These all continued with one accord in prayer and supplication, with the women, and Mary the mother of Jesus, and with his brethren.
>
> 15 ¶ And in those days Peter stood up in the midst of the disciples, and said, (the number of names together were about an hundred and twenty,)

So we see that Mary, the mother of Jesus was among the 120 in the Upper Room. Then we see that they were ALL filled with the Holy Ghost and began to speak with other tongues.

> Acts 2:1 ¶ And when the day of Pentecost was fully come, they were all with one accord in one place.

> 2 And suddenly there came a sound from heaven as of a rushing mighty wind, and it filled all the house where they were sitting.
>
> 3 And there appeared unto them cloven tongues like as of fire, and it sat upon each of them.
>
> 4 And they were all filled with the Holy Ghost, and began to speak with other tongues, as the Spirit gave them utterance.

Remember that the only way that the Apostles knew that Gentiles had received the same Holy Ghost that they had was because they heard them speak in tongues.

> Acts 10:45 And they of the circumcision which believed were astonished, as many as came with Peter, because that on the Gentiles also was poured out the gift of the Holy Ghost.
>
> 46 For they heard them speak with tongues, and magnify God. Then answered Peter,
>
> 47 Can any man forbid water, that these should not be baptized, which have received the Holy Ghost as well as we?

> Acts 2:1 ¶ And when the day of Pentecost was fully come, they were all with one accord in one place.
>
> 2 And suddenly there came a sound from heaven as of a rushing mighty wind, and it filled all the house where they were sitting.
>
> 3 And there appeared unto them cloven tongues like as of fire, and it sat upon each of them.
>
> 4 And they were all filled with the Holy Ghost, and began to speak with other tongues, as the Spirit gave them utterance.

> Acts 19:4 Then said Paul, John verily baptized with the baptism of repentance, saying unto the people, that they

> should believe on him which should come after him, that is, on Christ Jesus.
>
> 5 When they heard this, they were baptized in the name of the Lord Jesus.
>
> 6 And when Paul had laid his hands upon them, the Holy Ghost came on them; and they spake with tongues, and prophesied.

Those who don't believe in Jesus Name water baptism and speaking in other tongues don't really believe the Bible at all and are not a part of the religion of the Bible.

Tongue Types

We see false christians often pointing to verses like this when they want to claim to have the Holy Spirit even though they never spoke with tongues.

> 1 Cor 12:30 Have all the gifts of healing? do all speak with tongues? do all interpret?

The teaching of this verse is clear, but what we must know is what kind of tongues were being discussed. I believe that I can prove that there are two distinct different kinds of tongues. In other words, the "other tongues" that a person speaks in when they are filled with the Holy Spirit is NOT the "Gift of Tongues" that is one of the 9 spiritual gifts for the true Church.

Just as the measure of faith that is given to all men is NOT the "Gift of Faith" that only some Christians receive. All Christians have faith, but all Christians do not receive the "Gift of Faith".

Just as all Christians have knowledge, but not all Christians receive the "Word of Knowledge".

> 1 Cor 12:7 But the manifestation of the Spirit is given to every man to profit withal.
>
> 1 Cor 12:8 For to one is given by the Spirit the word of wisdom; to another the word of knowledge by the same Spirit;
>
> 1 Cor 12:9 To another faith by the same Spirit; to another the gifts of healing by the same Spirit;
>
> 1 Cor 12:10 To another the working of miracles; to another prophecy; to another discerning of spirits; to another divers kinds of tongues; to another the interpretation of tongues:
>
> 1 Cor 12:11 But all these worketh that one and the selfsame Spirit, dividing to every man severally as he will.

Tongue Types

The difference between the two types of tongues is really quite simple to prove. One type could be understood by men who happened to speak the language, the other could not be understood by any man.

One (the "Pentecost" tongues that is the initial evidence of the Holy Spirit) was understood by men. Therefore it was a language of Earth, though not known by the speaker. These verses prove that.

> Acts 2:4 And they were all filled with the Holy Ghost, and began to speak with other tongues, as the Spirit gave them utterance.
>
> Acts 2:5 And there were dwelling at Jerusalem Jews, devout men, out of every nation under heaven.
>
> Acts 2:6 Now when this was noised abroad, the multitude came together, and were confounded, because that every man heard them speak in his own language.
>
> Acts 2:7 And they were all amazed and marvelled, saying one to another, Behold, are not all these which speak Galilaeans?
>
> Acts 2:8 And how hear we every man in our own tongue, wherein we were born?

When, however, we read of the Gift of Tongues we discover that it is not a language of the Earth because no man understands it.

> 1 Cor 14:2 For he that speaketh in an unknown tongue speaketh not unto men, but unto God: for no man understandeth him; howbeit in the spirit he speaketh mysteries.

"Unknown tongues" is NOT the same thing as "Other tongues".

It is important that we not confuse the two completely different types of tongues.

Gift of Tongues

Consider, that the languages that the Apostles spoke in when they were filled with the Holy Ghost were actually "known" rather than "unknown". If they had been speaking in "unknown tongues", then no one would have been able to understand them. So the Apostles did not receive the "gift of tongues" when they were filled with the Holy Spirit. The fact that they *were* understood by men (without interpretation) proves that. People do not receive the "gift of tongues" when they are filled with the Holy Spirit, but rather they speak in "other tongues". It is important to understand the difference lest one could be confused by the teachings in Corinthians.

> I Corinthians 14:2 For he that speaketh in an [unknown] tongue speaketh not unto men, but unto God: for no man understandeth [him]; howbeit in the spirit he speaketh mysteries.

When the "gift of tongues" is manifested, NO MAN understands unless the spiritual gift of "interpretation" is also present.

Corinthians also speaks of the "gift of faith" that not all saints receive, yet we know that God has given to every man (both saint and sinner) a "measure of faith". Every man has a "measure of faith" but every saint will not receive the "gift of faith".

This is very important to understand because the false preachers prey on peoples lack of knowledge and misuse the verses in Corinthians to deceive people concerning tongues.

When Paul said "do all speak with tongues?" he was clearly referring to the "gift of tongues" that not every saint receives.

Everyone has some "knowledge"(saint and sinner alike), but not every saint receives the "gift of knowledge".

Gift of Tongues

Everyone who receives the Baptism of the Holy Spirit like in the Bible, speaks in "other tongues" like in the Bible. Of these, only a few will receive the entirely different "gift of tongues".

It is as if false preachers are using a verse about "ice cubes" to try to explain away "drinking water".

The "other" tongues mentioned in Acts were not "unknown tongues" (the "gift of tongues") that were taught about in I Cor 14. If they had been, then "NO MAN" would have been able to understand them.

Deliverance

Salvation means "deliverance from sin". God has a method whereby this is accomplished (if you've been taught different, then just go spit in that old false preacher's face who tried to kill you).

> John 10:1 Verily , verily, I say unto you, He that entereth not by the door into the sheepfold, but climbeth up some other way, the same is a thief and a robber.

You go God's way, or you don't go.

> 2 Th 1:8 In flaming fire taking vengeance on them that know not God, and that obey not the gospel of our Lord Jesus Christ:
>
> 2 Th 1:9 Who shall be punished with everlasting destruction from the presence of the Lord, and from the glory of his power;

God provided a re-birth of water and Spirit to deliver from sin:

> Acts 2:38 Then Peter said unto them, Repent, and be baptized every one of you in the name of Jesus Christ for the remission of sins, and ye shall receive the gift of the Holy Ghost.
>
> Acts 2:39 For the promise is unto you, and to your children, and to all that are afar off, even as many as the Lord our God shall call.

This plan is for as many as God will call, it is all inclusive (including you). Three steps: Repentance, Jesus name water baptism, and the Baptism of the Holy Ghost (speaking in tongues) The order of obedience is not important, but rather the COMPLETENESS of your deliverance from sin, or "salvation"

First, you must of your free will want to repent.

Second God provides the remission of all of your past sins through applying His shed blood through baptism in His name. That is how you actually "call on the name of the Lord".

> Acts 22:16 And now why tarriest thou? arise, and be baptized, and wash away thy sins, calling on the name of the Lord.

Then God provides POWER for an individual to have victory OVER temptation.

> Acts 10:46 For they heard them speak with tongues, and magnify God. Then answered Peter,
>
> Acts 10:47 Can any man forbid water, that these should not be baptized, which have received the Holy Ghost as well as we?

That is how God, through grace and through nothing that man deserves, offers "deliverance from sin" or "salvation".

That is the re-birth of water and Spirit that Jesus taught before He started the new testament Church.

> John 3:5 Jesus answered, Verily , verily, I say unto thee, Except a man be born of water and of the Spirit, he cannot enter into the kingdom of God.

Oh yeah, actually the Bible doesn't say to spit in your false preachers' face, BUT it does actually give instructions of how to relate to them:

> Gal 1:8 But though we, or an angel from heaven, preach any other gospel unto you than that which we have preached unto you, let him be accursed.

And, just in case the first verse was not specific enough, Paul said in the next verse:

> Gal 1:9 As we said before, so say I now again, If any man preach any other gospel unto you than that ye have received, let him be accursed.

I hope this helps you obtain deliverance from sin...

Knowledge

There are several areas of ignorance that most false preachers are taking advantage of as they "explain" to people why they do not need to obey the Bible.

We have had as filthy a false preacher as has ever walked the earth posting verses here like these beautiful verses.

> Matthew 7:7 Ask, and it shall be given you; seek, and ye shall find; knock, and it shall be opened unto you:
>
> Matthew 7:8 For every one that asketh receiveth; and he that seeketh findeth; and to him that knocketh it shall be opened.

The false preacher was trying to promote a false religion that teaches that men need merely to "claim to believe" to become "instant christians". But, if we simply keep reading we see that there is more to it than what the devil's servant wanted you to notice. Let's look down five verses later when Jesus warns that salvation is a NARROW and STRAIGHT way that very few would find. (Doesn't quite fit with the false preacher's lie)

> Matthew 7:13 Enter ye in at the strait gate: for wide [is] the gate, and broad [is] the way, that leadeth to destruction, and many there be which go in thereat:
>
> Matthew 7:14 Because strait [is] the gate, and narrow [is] the way, which leadeth unto life, and few there be that find it.
>
> Matthew 7:15 Beware of false prophets, which come to you in sheep's clothing, but inwardly they are ravening wolves.

The false preachers like to try to appear real kind and "lovey dovey", but they preach a lie. One of the things that can help you arm yourself against the "believe only" and other filthy false preachers is to have a knowledge of the scripture. Please understand that the "Church" that Jesus came to build was not "started" until the book of Acts. Notice that Jesus spoke in FUTURE TENSE about His church (and Jesus knew that the people who "believed" in Him would obey His Apostles and obey Acts 2:38 to become Christians") When Jesus was still on the earth in the flesh the Apostles had no idea that salvation would even be available to a Gentile. Notice "will build".

> Matthew 16:18 And I say also unto thee, That thou art Peter, and upon this rock I will build my church; and the gates of hell shall not prevail against it.

Notice here that Jesus had not yet built His church. The new testament was NOT in place yet. Acts 2:38 salvation was NOT available yet.

> Hebrews 9:15 And for this cause he is the mediator of the new testament, that by means of death, for the redemption of the transgressions [that were] under the first testament, they which are called might receive the promise of eternal inheritance.
>
> Hebrews 9:16 For where a testament [is], there must also of necessity be the death of the testator.
>
> Hebrews 9:17 For a testament [is] of force after men are dead: otherwise it is of no strength at all while the testator liveth.

False preachers will abuse and twist Jesus' words that were spoken BEFORE the "new testament" was actually started. They will use those words to convince people that they do not need to be a part of the REAL Church that Jesus gave His life for.

That is why I labor to expose the vile deceivers.

But there is still one MAJOR thing that will help you to spot the filth when they come with sweet words and fake love to deceive you and yours. Their LIE is based on the fool's premise that those who "believed" in Jesus refused to obey Him or His apostles as THEY refuse to obey His apostles as they teach that all one needs to do is "claim to believe"

In the Bible when men "believed", men "obeyed".

> Acts 8:12 But when they believed Philip preaching the things concerning the kingdom of God, and the name of Jesus Christ, they were baptized, both men and women.

Acts 19:4 Then said Paul, John verily baptized with the baptism of repentance, saying unto the people, that they should believe on him which should come after him, that is, on Christ Jesus.

Acts 19:5 When they heard [this], they were baptized in the name of the Lord Jesus.

Acts 19:6 And when Paul had laid [his] hands upon them, the Holy Ghost came on them; and they spake with tongues, and prophesied.

Acts 2:38 Then Peter said unto them, Repent, and be baptized every one of you in the name of Jesus Christ for the remission of sins, and ye shall receive the gift of the Holy Ghost.

Acts 2:39 For the promise is unto you, and to your children, and to all that are afar off, [even] as many as the Lord our God shall call.

Acts 2:40 And with many other words did he testify and exhort, saying, Save yourselves from this untoward generation.

Acts 2:41 Then they that gladly received his word were baptized: and the same day there were added [unto them] about three thousand souls.

Acts 22:16 And now why tarriest thou? arise, and be baptized, and wash away thy sins, calling on the name of the Lord.

Amazed

I am amazed at the audacity of some of the false christians that we encounter from time to time. Not only will they teach disobedience

to the Bible, but, they will question the salvation of the people that really believe in only ONE God (Jesus), and DO obey Acts 2:38.

We should not forget that the Bible warned us against such like and teaches that true Christians should NOT coddle such deceivers.

> II Corinthians 11:12 But what I do, that I will do, that I may cut off occasion from them which desire occasion; that wherein they glory,
>
> they may be found even as we.
>
> II Corinthians 11:13 For such [are] false apostles, deceitful workers, transforming themselves into the apostles of Christ.
>
> II Corinthians 11:14 And no marvel; for Satan himself is transformed into an angel of light.
>
> II Corinthians 11:15 Therefore [it is] no great thing if his ministers also be transformed as the ministers of righteousness; whose end shall be according to their works.

Now common sense should make us aware that Satan is going to have his servants pretending to be "christian teachers", the difference will be that their teaching will be to undermine the importance of knowing who Jesus is, AND to undermine the importance of obeying His Word.

It's the same old story. God says do something, and the devil teaches that it doesn't really matter.

God says be baptized in Jesus name; the devil's ministers teach that it doesn't really matter.

> Acts 2:38 Then Peter said unto them, Repent, and be baptized every one of you in the name of Jesus Christ for the

> remission of sins, and ye shall receive the gift of the Holy Ghost.
>
> Acts 2:39 For the promise is unto you, and to your children, and to all that are afar off, [even] as many as the Lord our God shall call.

God says that Jesus name baptism remits the sins of as many as God will call. The religious filth will come along and say "Oh, our glorious and wonderful god doesn't really mean that" and then they will manufacture some emotionally titillating fable of whatabout this or that...

> II Peter 2:18 For when they speak great swelling [words] of vanity, they allure through the lusts of the flesh, [through much] wantonness, those that were clean escaped from them who live in error.
>
> II Peter 2:19 While they promise them liberty, they themselves are the servants of corruption: for of whom a man is overcome, of the same is he brought in bondage.

It is a real preachers' job to convince you to obey the Bible, it's the false preachers job to teach you that you really don't need to obey the Bible.

Forget the devil's fairy tales, salvation is only for the obedient.

> Hebrews 5:9 And being made perfect, he became the author of eternal salvation unto all them that obey him;
>
> Acts 22:16 And now why tarriest thou? arise, and be baptized, and wash away thy sins, calling on the name of the Lord.

Almost

> Mark 16:16 He that believeth and is baptized shall be saved; but he that believeth not shall be damned.

Jesus declared that baptism is a requirement for salvation. Maybe that is why false preachers fight against it so and try to relegate it to a "nice thing to do if you happen to feel like it".

> Acts 2:38 Then Peter said unto them, Repent, and be baptized every one of you in the name of Jesus Christ for the remission of sins, and ye shall receive the gift of the Holy Ghost.

It is through obediance to Jesus name baptism that an individual accepts Jesus offer to remit their sins through His NAME.

> Acts 2:41 Then they that gladly received his word were baptized: and the same day there were added [unto them] about three thousand souls.

3000 were baptized in Jesus name to have their sins remitted by the power of His NAME.

> Acts 10:45 And they of the circumcision which believed were astonished, as many as came with Peter, because that on the Gentiles also was poured out the gift of the Holy Ghost.
>
> Acts 10:46 For they heard them speak with tongues, and magnify God.
>
> Then answered Peter,

The apostles noticed that Gentiles had received the Spirit of Christ.

> Acts 10:47 Can any man forbid water, that these should not be baptized, which have received the Holy Ghost as well as we?
>
> Acts 10:48 And he commanded them to be baptized in the name of the Lord. Then prayed they him to tarry certain days.

Those who received the Holy Spirit were immediately commanded to be water baptized in Jesus NAME. Note that the apostles were able to know that Gentiles had received the SAME Holy Spirit that the apostles had received.

> Acts 19:4 Then said Paul, John verily baptized with the baptism of repentance, saying unto the people, that they should believe on him which should come after him, that is, on Christ Jesus.
>
> Acts 19:5 When they heard [this], they were baptized in the name of the Lord Jesus.

Real true belief ALWAYS includes obediance.

> Acts 22:16 And now why tarriest thou? arise, and be baptized, and wash away thy sins, calling on the name of the Lord.

Sins are washed away by Jesus' name baptism. Why? Because that is the way that God chose to do it.

> Romans 6:3 Know ye not, that so many of us as were baptized into Jesus Christ were baptized into his death?

> Galatians 3:27 For as many of you as have been baptized into Christ have put on Christ.

They who have not been water baptized in Jesus name have not been re-born of the water, the have not "put on Christ" and they are still in their sins (even if they have received the Holy Spirit). "Half

saved" people do not get a cooler spot in the lake of fire.

> Acts 26:28 Then Agrippa said unto Paul, Almost thou persuadest me to be a Christian.

> Acts 26:29 And Paul said, I would to God, that not only thou, but also all that hear me this day, were both almost, and altogether such as I am, except these bonds.

Where do "almost" Christians spend eternity? They spend it with all the others who "almost" decided to obey.

> Hebrews 5:9 And being made perfect, he became the author of eternal salvation unto all them that obey him;

Faith, Works, Grace

> James 2:14 What [doth it] profit, my brethren, though a man say he hath faith, and have not works? can faith save him?
>
> James 2:17 Even so faith, if it hath not works, is dead, being alone.
>
> James 2:18 Yea, a man may say, Thou hast faith, and I have works: shew me thy faith without thy works, and I will shew thee my faith by my works.
>
> James 2:20 But wilt thou know, O vain man, that faith without works is dead?...............

There are many that teach that if you obey the Word of God, then you are trying to be saved by your own personal works....So they teach that you are saved no matter whether you obey or not....In other words they are saying that if Noah had not "by faith" gone into the ark, that he would have been saved anyway....But they are very confused. They don't understand faith at all. It is because of faith that a person will obey the Word of God, accepting that God's works on the cross is enough to remit sins (through Jesus NAME baptism)

> Acts 2:38 "Then Peter said unto them, Repent, and be baptized every one of you in the name of Jesus Christ for the remission of sins, and ye shall receive the gift of the Holy Ghost."

For a man to partake of salvation, through obedience to the Word of God, is NOT AT ALL a man trying to be saved by his own works, RATHER it is a man who through FAITH is obeying in order to apply the free gift of salvation to his own life..consider Naaman the leper, he almost disobeyed....

> II Kings 5:13 And his servants came near, and spake unto him, and said, My father, [if] the prophet had bid thee [do some] great thing, wouldest thou not have done [it]? how much rather then, when he saith to thee, Wash, and be clean?
>
> II Kings 5:14 Then went he down, and dipped himself seven times in Jordan, according to the saying of the man of God: and his flesh came again like unto the flesh of a little child, and he was clean....

Now Naaman was not healed until he dipped the seventh time!! Was he healed by his own WORKS??? OF COURSE NOT!! He was "saved" by FAITH through his obedience THROUGH the GRACE of God..If he had not obeyed, he would NOT have been healed, even though obediance was VERY EASY..

Likewise YOU will NOT be saved if you don't OBEY the word of God and apply the free gift of salvation to your OWN soul...When you repent of sins it's GOD'S WORKS that enable you to do so, when one is baptized in Jesus NAME for the remission of sins it's GOD'S WORKS that remits the sins through His shed blood on the cross...When a person is filled with the Holy Ghost and speaks in tongues IT'S GOD doing it... What I have just referred to is the birth of water(baptism) and the birth of the Spirit (the Holy Ghost baptism), Jesus spoke of this in John 3:5

> John 3:5 "Jesus answered, Verily, verily, I say unto thee, Except a man be born of water and [of] the Spirit, he cannot enter into the kingdom of God."

....The Bible also teaches that holiness is essential for salvation....

> Hebrews 12:14 Follow peace with all [men], and holiness, without which no man shall see the Lord:

...You must live a HOLY CLEAN life in order to be saved..and this is impossible EXCEPT through the POWER of the Holy Ghost....Notice that the same preachers that deny that a person can live above sin, are also the same preachers that deny tongues, and deny the importance of Jesus NAME baptism!!! They go to church they have a religious form, they go through the motion, BUT they don't believe in POWER over sin, or POWER to speak in tongues, or POWER to live a HOLY separated, unspotted life.....But the Bible mentioned them.....In the last days that they would come...

> II Timothy 3:5 Having a form of godliness, but denying the POWER thereof: from such turn away.

> II Timothy 3:8 Now as Jannes and Jambres withstood Moses, so do these also RESIST the truth: men of corrupt minds, REPROBATE concerning the faith...

They have the FORM of Godliness, they have church services, BUT they deny the POWER...and they twist the scriptures that were written to SAINTS who had ALLREADY OBEYED Acts 2:38, and they use these to deceive sinners into thinking that they are already saved. ie Romans was written to the SAINTS at Rome, one of the churches that started in Acts. Remember Romans through Rev was written to Saints who were ALLREADY in the Apostolic Church..they had ALLREADY OBEYED Acts 2:38!!! These were letters giving instruction to the churches on how to continue on to be saved....Paul was very clear in his letter to the Galatian church concerning the subject of men changing the original APOSTOLIC doctrine.

> Galatians 1:8 But though we, or an angel from heaven, preach any other gospel unto you than that which we have preached unto you, let him be accursed.

So don't believe these false preachers that try to modify the original plan, Paul knew that they would, it was even going on then.

> Romans 16:17 Now I beseech you, brethren, mark them which cause divisions and offenses contrary to the DOCTRINE which ye have learned; and avoid them.

(the doctrine they had was the Acts 2:38 message)

> Romans 16:18 For they that are such serve not our Lord Jesus Christ, but their own belly; and by GOOD WORDS and fair speeches DECIEVE the hearts of the simple.

Obedience - Works

There seems to be some confusion (from the author of confusion) concerning faith and works. Many confuse obedience with works. Here is a clear example of how man benefits from God's works by OBEDIANCE. Obedience is not "works" in the sense that some perceive it to be. To hear some talk, they fear that God would be offended if they were to obey Him; I believe the opposite to be the case. God is offended when men reject His Acts 2:38 salvation (for *whatever* reason).

> John 9:2 And his disciples asked him, saying, Master, who did sin, this man, or his parents, that he was born blind?
>
> John 9:3 Jesus answered, Neither hath this man sinned, nor his parents: but that the works of God should be made manifest in him.

Please notice carefully that the event we are about to study is an example of God's works. Jesus declared that God's works would be demonstrated.

> John 9:4 I must work the works of him that sent me, while it is day: the night cometh, when no man can work.
>
> John 9:5 As long as I am in the world, I am the light of the world.
>
> John 9:6 When he had thus spoken, he spat on the ground, and made clay of the spittle, and he anointed the eyes of the blind man with the clay,
>
> John 9:7 And said unto him, Go, wash in the pool of Siloam, (which is by interpretation, Sent.) He went his way therefore, and washed, and came seeing.

God's works did not benefit the man UNTIL he OBEYED!! Please note that key point. Healing was made available to a man by God's works, but until the man obeyed God, he remained blind.

> John 9:8 The neighbours therefore, and they which before had seen him that he was blind, said, Is not this he that sat and begged?
>
> John 9:9 Some said, This is he: others [said], He is like him: [but] he said, I am [he].
>
> John 9:10 Therefore said they unto him, How were thine eyes opened?
>
> John 9:11 He answered and said, A man that is called Jesus made clay, and anointed mine eyes, and said unto me, Go to the pool of Siloam, and wash: and I went and washed, and I received sight.

The blind man's "obedience" did not "cheapen the grace of God" (as some might imply if they confused "works" with "obedience".) The blind man was saved by FAITH, through GRACE and not because of his own works. He did NOT deserve to be healed.

People who obey Acts 2:38 become Christians by FAITH, through GRACE.

> Acts 2:38 Then Peter said unto them, Repent, and be baptized every one of you in the name of Jesus Christ for the remission of sins, and ye shall receive the gift of the Holy Ghost.
>
> Acts 2:39 For the promise is unto you, and to your children, and to all that are afar off, [even] as many as the Lord our God shall call.

Acts 2:38 is a commandment with a promise. Just as Jesus commanded the blind man to wash (and he was not healed until he obeyed); people are commanded to be baptized in Jesus name "for the remission of sins" (and they remain "in their sins" until they obey.) *

Church

The Bible is quite clear that the new testament Church actually began on the day of Pentecost. Jesus always referred to His church as "future tense"

> Matthew 16:18 And I say also unto thee, That thou art Peter, and upon this rock I will build my church; and the gates of hell shall not prevail against it.
>
> Matthew 16:19 And I will give unto thee the keys of the kingdom of heaven: and whatsoever thou shalt bind on earth shall be bound in heaven: and whatsoever thou shalt loose on earth shall be loosed in heaven.
>
> Notice that Jesus said that Peter would be the man with the keys to the kingdom of heaven. Peter used those keys AFTER he had received power from the baptism of the Holy Spirit.
>
> Luke 24:47 And that repentance and remission of sins should be preached in his name among all nations, beginning at Jerusalem.
>
> Luke 24:48 And ye are witnesses of these things.
>
> Luke 24:49 And, behold, I send the promise of my Father upon you: but tarry ye in the city of Jerusalem, until ye be endued with power from on high.

Notice that according to Jesus that remission of sins through his name was to (future tense again) be preached BEGINNING at Jerusalem, AFTER they were to receive POWER. They received that POWER on the day of Pentecost:

> Acts 2:1 And when the day of Pentecost was fully come, they were all with one accord in one place.
>
> Acts 2:2 And suddenly there came a sound from heaven as of a rushing mighty wind, and it filled all the house where they were sitting.

> Acts 2:3 And there appeared unto them cloven tongues like as of fire, and it sat upon each of them.
>
> Acts 2:4 And they were all filled with the Holy Ghost, and began to speak with other tongues, as the Spirit gave them utterance.

After receiving POWER, Peter began to preach:

> Acts 2:36 Therefore let all the house of Israel know assuredly, that God hath made that same Jesus, whom ye have crucified, both Lord and Christ.
>
> Acts 2:37 Now when they heard [this], they were pricked in their heart, and said unto Peter and to the rest of the apostles, Men [and] brethren, what shall we do?

Convicted sinners asked what they could do (to be saved).

> Acts 2:38 Then Peter said unto them, Repent, and be baptized every one of you in the name of Jesus Christ for the remission of sins, and ye shall receive the gift of the Holy Ghost.

Then the method of remission of sins JESUS NAME BAPTISM was first preached at Jerusalem just as Jesus commanded that it would be.

> Acts 2:39 For the promise is unto you, and to your children, and to all that are afar off, [even] as many as the Lord our God shall call.
>
> Acts 2:38 is the plan of salvation for any and ALL Christianity. Baptism in Jesus name is the only method for the remission of sins through Jesus Name for all Christianity. (as many as God will call)
>
> Acts 2:40 And with many other words did he testify and exhort, saying, Save yourselves from this untoward generation.
>
> Acts 2:41 Then they that gladly received his word were baptized: and the same day there were added [unto them] about three thousand souls.

Those who "believed" were "baptized".

> Acts 2:42 And they continued stedfastly in the apostles' doctrine and fellowship, and in breaking of bread, and in prayers.

One "calls on the name of the Lord" and receives a washing from their sins through Jesus name water baptism. Even though Paul had just spoken directly with God (who identified Himself as "Jesus"), Paul still needed to have his sins remitted and was told by the preacher:

> Acts 22:16 And now why tarriest thou? arise, and be baptized, and wash away thy sins, calling on the name of the Lord.

(the NAME of the Lord is Jesus)

> Acts 22:7 And I fell unto the ground, and heard a voice saying unto me, Saul, Saul, why persecutest thou me?

> Acts 22:8 And I answered, Who art thou, Lord? And he said unto me, I am Jesus of Nazareth, whom thou persecutest.

Anything other than Acts 2:38 salvation is simply not really Christianity, it is something else. Those who promote "something else" are to be "accursed".

> Galatians 1:8 But though we, or an angel from heaven, preach any other gospel unto you than that which we have preached unto you, let him be accursed.

It is to be expected that the "accursed" will have much support:

> II Timothy 4:3 For the time will come when they will not endure sound doctrine; but after their own lusts shall they heap to themselves teachers, having itching ears;

> II Timothy 4:4 And they shall turn away [their] ears from the truth, and shall be turned unto fables.

Option

It is of utmost importance that you find a Church that is preaching the basic Apostolic Acts 2:38 message.

You are offered the option of obeying Acts 2:38 through the grace of God who became human and allowed himself to be sacrificed for you.

> 1 John 3:16 Hereby perceive we the love of God, because he laid down his life for us: and we ought to lay down our lives for the brethren.

It was God's laying down of His human life that made the following option available to you and yours.

> Acts 2:38 Then Peter said unto them, Repent, and be baptized every one of you in the name of Jesus Christ for the remission of sins, and ye shall receive the gift of the Holy Ghost.
>
> Acts 2:39 For the promise is unto you, and to your children, and to all that are afar off, even as many as the Lord our God shall call.

If anyone becomes a Christian it is by obeying Acts 2:38. All other "plans" are deceit.

> John 10:1 Verily , verily, I say unto you, He that entereth not by the door into the sheepfold, but climbeth up some other way, the same is a thief and a robber.

Fool

Why are so many people content in false churches even after they hear about Acts 2:38 and they know that they haven't obeyed it? (and Acts 2:39 states that it is for as many as God will call)

> Acts 2:38 Then Peter said unto them, Repent, and be baptized every one of you in the name of Jesus Christ for the remission of sins, and ye shall receive the gift of the Holy Ghost.
>
> Acts 2:39 For the promise is unto you, and to your children, and to all that are afar off, [even] as many as the Lord our God shall call.

Why are so many people content in three godlet cults even though the Bible warns so clearly against the trinity?

> Colossians 2:8 Beware lest any man spoil you through philosophy and vain deceit, after the tradition of men, after the rudiments of the world, and not after Christ.
>
> Colossians 2:9 For in him dwelleth all the fulness of the Godhead bodily.
>
> Colossians 2:10 And ye are complete in him, which is the head of all principality and power:

I have had many tell me even after I show them scriptures like these that they just KNOW in their heart that they are saved. They just know in their hearts that they are saved and can never be lost because some false preacher has convinced them with some misunderstood scripture.

God has a word that He uses to describe such people. Those people who trust in their own hearts over the Word of God are described by God.

See if you can find the adjective in this next verse to describe the folks in ALL these false churches who are trusting the feelings of their own hearts.

> Proverbs 28:26 He that trusteth in his own heart is a fool: but whoso walketh wisely, he shall be delivered.

Now what does God say that you are if you trust in the feelings of your own heart? That's right! You got it!

Why are these people content in these filthy trinity cults?

It's because they are FOOLS.

Are you a happy catholic, are you a happy trinitarian? Well guess why!

That's right! You got it!

One more time, so that you won't forget it:

> Colossians 2:8 Beware lest any man spoil you through philosophy and vain deceit, after the tradition of men, after the rudiments of the world, and not after Christ.
>
> Colossians 2:9 For in him dwelleth all the fulness of the Godhead bodily.
>
> Colossians 2:10 And ye are complete in him, which is the head of all principality and power:

> Proverbs 28:26 He that trusteth in his own heart is a fool: but whoso walketh wisely, he shall be delivered.

You just KNOW in your HEART that you are SAVED, don't you?

Cursed

I know that most here are aware that the Bible says concerning false preachers "let them be accursed".

> Galatians 1:8 But though we, or an angel from heaven, preach any other gospel unto you than that which we have preached unto you, let him be accursed.

I also know that a lot of people are somewhat shocked to see a false preacher cursed in the name of the Lord; but, let us look into the issue of false preachers.

In the first place, I am surprised that so many who don't believe what the apostles taught, don't obey what the apostles preached, and don't manifest the evidences that the apostles accepted; are being accepted as "Christian" just because they claim to be. The Bible has many many warnings about false preachers, just a few are:

> Matthew 7:15 Beware of false prophets, which come to you in sheep's clothing, but inwardly they are ravening wolves.
>
> Matthew 24:11 And many false prophets shall rise, and shall deceive many.
>
> I John 4:1 Beloved, believe not every spirit, but try the spirits whether they are of God: because many false prophets are gone out into the world.

The Bible warned that there would be a counterfeit church that would deny the "power". Jesus told His apostles and disciples to WAIT for POWER that they.did not yet have (even though they had been with Jesus as His disciples and Apostles).

> Luke 24:49 And, behold, I send the promise of my Father upon you: but tarry ye in the city of Jerusalem, until ye be endued with power from on high.
>
> Acts 1:8 But ye shall receive power, after that the Holy Ghost is come upon you: and ye shall be witnesses unto me both in

> Jerusalem, and in all Judaea, and in Samaria, and unto the uttermost part of the earth.

When they received the "POWER" they ALL spoke in tongues.

> Acts 2:4 And they were all filled with the Holy Ghost, and began to speak with other tongues, as the Spirit gave them utterance.

Speaking in tongues is the sign of a true believer, and is repeatedly referred to in the Bible as the only evidence that the apostles accepted that a person had been "born again" of the Spirit. (remember John 3:5)

> Mark 16:17 And these signs shall follow them that believe; In my name shall they cast out devils; they shall speak with new tongues;

The Bible predicted that many would prefer false preachers instead of wanting the truth, this also explains the popularity of anti-Biblical.

> II Timothy 4:3 For the time will come when they will not endure sound doctrine; but after their own lusts shall they heap to themselves teachers, having itching ears;

The Bible also warned that there would be those that would have the "form" (ie .church services, appearing "good", etc.), but deny "tongues" (denying the POWER). Please notice this next verse carefully:

> II Timothy 3:5 Having a form of godliness, but denying the power thereof: from such turn away.

The Bible teaches that those who don't have the real Spirit of Christ (POWER), are "none of His".

> Romans 8:9 But ye are not in the flesh, but in the Spirit, if so be that the Spirit of God dwell in you. Now if any man have not the Spirit of Christ, he is none of his.

Notice that the Spirit of Christ IS the Spirit of God. I hope that you realize that any deceiver is going to "claim" to have the Spirit of Christ.

Jesus declaring HIMSELF to be the Spirit of Truth (the Holy Ghost, the "Power"). Please look carefully.

> John 14:17 [Even] the Spirit of truth; whom the world cannot receive, because it seeth him not, neither knoweth him: but ye know him; for he dwelleth with you, and shall be in you.

^^

The Spirit of Truth (the Holy Ghost) is the form that Jesus is manifesting Himself in, in this dispensation. Those that deny tongues, deny Christ. They are only holding to the form of religion, but they don't have the real thing, they don't have the "POWER". When someone rejects the Holy Ghost speaking in tongues; they are rejecting Jesus.

Consider that "speaking in tongues" is not the "Power", but rather it is the initial sign or "evidence" that a person has received that power.

Remember, these that are trying to teach against tongues and Jesus name baptism, are simply teaching a different religion than the Bible teaches. They don't have the real thing (don't expect them to admit it) and, they don't want YOU to have it either.

They are claiming to be "Christian", BUT, they don't believe what the apostles believe, they don't teach what the apostles taught, they don't experience what the apostles experienced, and they fight against those who do.

> II Corinthians 11:13 For such [are] false apostles, deceitful workers, transforming themselves into the apostles of Christ.
>
> II Corinthians 11:14 And no marvel; for Satan himself is transformed into an angel of light.
>
> II Corinthians 11:15 Therefore [it is] no great thing if his ministers also be transformed as the ministers of righteousness; whose end shall be according to their works.

So, please, don't be overly upset when you see one of Satan's ministers rebuked or cursed. They are deceiving sincere sweet people who are trying to find God. It is one thing when a person asks questions, or simply doesn't understand something, or even just can't believe; but it is quite another thing when one of Satan's false preachers boldly rises up against the truth.

Anyone who receives the same Holy Ghost that the Bible teaches, will receive it the same WAY that the Bible teaches. God is no respecter of persons. I challenge anyone to find a false Christian on this earth that doesn't claim that they have the Holy Ghost.

Defective Premise

A BASIC DEFECTIVE PREMISE OF THE FALSE CHRISTIAN CULTS

The "believe only" cults are basing their salvation upon the defective premise that the early Christians to whom the original epistles were addressed, "believed" the apostles, but didn't obey them. Then they are also building upon their defective premise that the apostles accepted as "brethren" folks who refused to obey them.

Every time that a deceiving cultist leads a victim to the book of Galatians, or Romans, or Ephesians to "explain" to them why obedience to Acts 2:38 isn't necessary for salvation; they deceptively ignore the fact that the addressees of the epistles of the Bible were those who had OBEYED the Acts 2:38 plan of salvation.

Unless a person BECOMES a Christian, they are NOT even the individuals that epistles containing the benevolent promises are addressed to. It's as if they are holding a promissory note that is addressed to someone else. They rejoice about its promised value (which is real), but don't realize that it's not addressed to them.

The benevolent promises of God are only for those who OBEY Him.

A brief glance at just a couple of scriptures serves to expose the majority of these cultists.

True preachers teach why the Bible needs to be obeyed, while the Satanic cultists "proclaim" their "salvation without obedience".

The book of Romans shows that a "non-believer" was recognized by "lack of obedience" to the original Apostolic message (Acts 2:38)

> Romans 10:16 But they have not all obeyed the gospel. For Esaias saith, Lord, who hath believed our report?

Romans is a letter to OBEYERS, not to "wannabes".

> Romans 1:5 By whom we have received grace and apostleship, for obedience to the faith among all nations, for his name:
>
> 6 Among whom are ye also the called of Jesus Christ:

Deceivers often take verses from Ephesians (a letter to the CHURCH at Ephesus), and ignore the fact that the Ephesian Church was FOUNDED upon the Acts 2:38 plan of salvation. The membership of the Ephesian Church had ALREADY OBEYED Acts 2:38.

Notice carefully the founding of the Ephesian church and pay careful attention to Paul adhering faithfully to the Acts 2:38 plan even though John the Baptist had already baptized those individuals.

> Acts 19:1 And it came to pass, that, while Apollos was at Corinth, Paul having passed through the upper coasts came to Ephesus: and finding certain disciples,
>
> Acts 19:2 He said unto them, Have ye received the Holy Ghost since ye believed? And they said unto him, We have not so much as heard whether there be any Holy Ghost.

Here also is clear proof in verse 2 that a person doesn't receive the Holy Ghost just because they "believe". The "believe only" cultists will often teach that lie.

> Acts 19:3 And he said unto them, Unto what then were ye baptized? And they said, Unto John's baptism.

When Paul saw that they had not received the Spirit (of Christ), he questioned the validity of their baptism.

> Acts 19:4 Then said Paul, John verily baptized with the baptism of repentance, saying unto the people, that they should believe on him which should come after him, that is, on Christ Jesus.

Believers were/are ALWAYS obeyers.

> Acts 19:5 When they heard [this], they were baptized in the name of the Lord Jesus.

Folks who had been baptized by John the Baptist himself had to be RE-baptized in Jesus name in order to become Christians.

> Acts 19:6 And when Paul had laid [his] hands upon them, the Holy Ghost came on them; and they spake with tongues, and prophesied.

After obeying Christian baptism they did receive the same Spirit of Christ that the Apostles had received in Acts 2:4.

> II Peter 3:15 And account [that] the longsuffering of our Lord [is] salvation; even as our beloved brother Paul also according to the wisdom given unto him hath written unto you; 16 As also in all [his] epistles, speaking in them of these things; in which are some things hard to be understood, which they that are unlearned and unstable wrest, as [they do] also the other scriptures, unto their own destruction.

Thief on the Cross

I thought by now all of the false-christians knew better than to try that old "thief on the cross" argument to try to justify their disobedience of the Bible in their false-christian cults.

The thief on the cross died before the New Testament Church was born. The new testament Church was born in Acts 2:4 and the new testament plan of salvation preached in Acts 2:38, confirmed in Acts 2:39 and preached and practiced by the Apostles Acts 19-4-6.

One of the tricks that many false preachers use in their deception is that they use the "thief on the cross" as "proof" that baptism in Jesus name is not required for salvation. They use that one account of the "thief on the cross" to deceive people into flat ignoring *bunches* of verses about baptism, even a verse where the Lord Himself declares baptism as ESSENTIAL, they will ignore ALL these verses:

> Mark 16:16 He that believeth and is baptized shall be saved; but he that believeth not shall be damned.

* Jesus said,"... AND is baptized" *

> Acts 22:16 And now why tarriest thou? arise, and be baptized, and wash away thy sins, calling on the name of the Lord.

* Sins washed away THROUGH baptism *

> Acts 8:12 But when they believed Philip preaching the things concerning the kingdom of God, and the name of Jesus Christ, they were baptized, both men and women.

* Believers were always baptized. *

Acts 19:5 When they heard [this], they were baptized in the name of the Lord Jesus.

Romans 6:3 Know ye not, that so many of us as were baptized into Jesus Christ were baptized into his death?

Galatians 3:27 For as many of you as have been baptized into Christ have put on Christ.

* Just look at those verses about Jesus name baptism! But the false preachers will still proclaim "thief on the cross" and those so deceived will go "amen brother"... BUT!! What the false preachers and those so deceived are overlooking is: The thief DIED BEFORE Baptism in Jesus name was even instituted and preached by the apostle Peter!! When the thief on the cross died, the new testament church had not been born; Jesus had not yet risen from the dead!!! The thief on the cross was dead for over a month BEFORE Acts 2:38 was even preached. *

The thief on the cross was not even in the "church" dispensation, the commandment to be baptized had not been given.

Acts 2:38 Then Peter said unto them, Repent, and be baptized every one of you in the name of Jesus Christ for the remission of sins, and ye shall receive the gift of the Holy Ghost.

Acts 2:39 For the promise is unto you, and to your children, and to all that are afar off, [even] as many as the Lord our God shall call.

Acts 2:40 And with many other words did he testify and exhort, saying, Save yourselves from this untoward generation.

Acts 2:41 Then they that gladly received his word were baptized: and the same day there were added [unto them] about three thousand souls.

I really hope that you can see the deception in the "thief on the cross" argument against baptism. But I hope that if your preacher told you that lie, that you will realize that he has lied to you about other things as well, and is not really a man of God at all.

The Bible warns so many times, in so many places that there will be MANY false preachers leading people to hell. People who are being led into hell by false preachers BELIEVE THAT THEY ARE SAVED; that is the job of the false preacher to keep them feeling "secure".

Does your preacher teach the "thief on the cross" as an excuse to undermine the essentiality of baptism? If so, are you going to follow him/her/it into the pits of hell, anyway?

> Matthew 15:14 Let them alone: they be blind leaders of the blind. And if the blind lead the blind, both shall fall into the ditch.
>
> Luke 6:39 And he spake a parable unto them, Can the blind lead the blind? shall they not both fall into the ditch?

> Romans 16:17 Now I beseech you, brethren, mark them which cause divisions and offenses contrary to the doctrine which ye have learned; and avoid them.
>
> Romans 16:18 For they that are such serve not our Lord Jesus Christ, but their own belly; and by good words and fair speeches deceive the hearts of the simple.

> Acts 2:38 Then Peter said unto them, Repent, and be baptized every one of you in the name of Jesus Christ for the remission of sins, and ye shall receive the gift of the Holy Ghost.
>
> Acts 2:39 For the promise is unto you, and to your children, and to all that are afar off, [even] as many as the Lord our God shall call.

Delusion

There are some who have rejected the Acts 2:38 message once too often.

> II Thessalonians 2:10 And with all deceivableness of unrighteousness in them that perish; because they received not the love of the truth, that they might be saved.

The true Christian loves the truth!

> II Thessalonians 2:11 And for this cause God shall send them strong delusion, that they should believe a lie:
>
> II Thessalonians 2:12 That they all might be damned who believed not the truth, but had pleasure in unrighteousness.

> Acts 2:38 Then Peter said unto them, Repent, and be baptized every one of you in the name of Jesus Christ for the remission of sins, and ye shall receive the gift of the Holy Ghost.
>
> Acts 2:39 For the promise is unto you, and to your children, and to all that are afar off, [even] as many as the Lord our God shall call.
>
> Acts 2:40 And with many other words did he testify and exhort, saying, Save yourselves from this untoward generation.
>
> Acts 2:41 Then they that gladly received his word were baptized: and the same day there were added [unto them] about three thousand souls.

Three thousand baptized in Jesus name, on the birthday of the new testament church.

> Acts 2:42 And they continued stedfastly in the apostles' doctrine and fellowship, and in breaking of bread, and in prayers.

James 1:22 But be ye doers of the word, and not hearers only, deceiving your own selves.

Acts 22:16 And now why tarriest thou? arise, and be baptized, and wash away thy sins, calling on the name of the Lord.

Acts 4:12 Neither is there salvation in any other: for there is none other name under heaven given among men, whereby we must be saved.

Galatians 1:8 But though we, or an angel from heaven, preach any other gospel unto you than that which we have preached unto you, let him be accursed.

Galatians 1:9 As we said before, so say I now again, If any [man] preach any other gospel unto you than that ye have received, let him be accursed.

Galatians 1:10 For do I now persuade men, or God? or do I seek to please men? for if I yet pleased men, I should not be the servant of Christ.

Too Late

There are some who have rejected the Acts 2:38 salvation message once too often and it is too late for them.

> II Thessalonians 2:10 And with all deceivableness of unrighteousness in them that perish; because they received not the love of the truth, that they might be saved.

The true Christian loves the truth!

> II Thessalonians 2:11 And for this cause God shall send them strong delusion, that they should believe a lie:
>
> II Thessalonians 2:12 That they all might be damned who believed not the truth, but had pleasure in unrighteousness.

> Acts 2:38 Then Peter said unto them, Repent, and be baptized every one of you in the name of Jesus Christ for the remission of sins, and ye shall receive the gift of the Holy Ghost.
>
> Acts 2:39 For the promise is unto you, and to your children, and to all that are afar off, [even] as many as the Lord our God shall call.
>
> Acts 2:40 And with many other words did he testify and exhort, saying, Save yourselves from this untoward generation.
>
> Acts 2:41 Then they that gladly received his word were baptized: and the same day there were added [unto them] about three thousand souls.

Three thousand baptized in Jesus name, on the birthday of the new testament church. And to think that some false preachers have actually convinced gullible souls that Oneness Christianity originated only in the 1900s.

> Acts 2:42 And they continued stedfastly in the apostles' doctrine and fellowship, and in breaking of bread, and in prayers.
>
> James 1:22 But be ye doers of the word, and not hearers only, deceiving your own selves.
>
> Acts 22:16 And now why tarriest thou? arise, and be baptized, and wash away thy sins, calling on the name of the Lord.
>
> Acts 4:12 Neither is there salvation in any other: for there is none other name under heaven given among men, whereby we must be saved.

Paul gives the real Christians instructions on how to relate to deceivers.

> Galatians 1:8 But though we, or an angel from heaven, preach any other gospel unto you than that which we have preached unto you, let him be accursed.
>
> Galatians 1:9 As we said before, so say I now again, If any [man] preach any other gospel unto you than that ye have received, let him be accursed.
>
> Galatians 1:10 For do I now persuade men, or God? or do I seek to please men? for if I yet pleased men, I should not be the servant of Christ.

Have you rejected Acts 2:38 once too often? Is it too late for you to find God? If not, you better quit playing with more than you can afford to lose.

> II Thessalonians 2:11 And for this cause God shall send them strong delusion, that they should believe a lie:
>
> II Thessalonians 2:12 That they all might be damned who believed not the truth, but had pleasure in unrighteousness.

Not all who sought repentance found it.

> Hebrews 12:16 Lest there be any fornicator, or profane person, as Esau, who for one morsel of meat sold his birthright.

Too Late

> Hebrews 12:17 For ye know how that afterward, when he would have inherited the blessing, he was rejected: for he found no place of repentance, though he sought it carefully with tears.

Some repentance is too late.

> Matthew 27:3 Then Judas, which had betrayed him, when he saw that he was condemned, repented himself, and brought again the thirty pieces of silver to the chief priests and elders,

The kind reassuring smile of the trinity preacher will appear to you in quite a different light when illuminated by the flames of the lake of fire.

Nothing new under the Sun (issues of our time)

Abortion

If they were not real human babies, there would be no need to kill them. Sacrificing tiny humans at alters of lust is actually not a new practice.

> Leviticus 18:21 And thou shalt not let any of thy seed pass through the fire to Molech, neither shalt thou profane the name of thy God: I am the LORD.

Deuteronomy 18:10 There shall not be found among you any one that maketh his son or his daughter to pass through the fire, or that useth divination, or an observer of times, or an enchanter, or a witch,

> 2 Kings 16:3 But he walked in the way of the kings of Israel, yea, and made his son to pass through the fire, according to the abominations of the heathen, whom the LORD cast out from before the children of Israel.

> 2 Kings 17:17 And they caused their sons and their daughters to pass through the fire, and used divination and enchantments, and sold themselves to do evil in the sight of the LORD, to provoke him to anger.

> 2 Kings 21:6 And he made his son pass through the fire, and observed times, and used enchantments, and dealt with familiar spirits and wizards: he wrought much wickedness in the sight of the LORD, to provoke him to anger.

> 2 Kings 23:10 And he defiled Topheth, which is in the valley of the children of Hinnom, that no man might make his son or his daughter to pass through the fire to Molech.

> 2 Chronicles 33:6 And he caused his children to pass through the fire in the valley of the son of Hinnom: also he observed times, and used enchantments, and used witchcraft, and dealt with a familiar spirit, and with wizards: he wrought much evil in the sight of the LORD, to provoke him to anger.

> Jeremiah 32:35 And they built the high places of Baal, which are in the valley of the son of Hinnom, to cause their sons and their daughters to pass through the fire unto Molech; which I commanded them not, neither came it into my mind, that they should do this abomination, to cause Judah to sin.

Ezekiel 16:21 That thou hast slain my children, and delivered them to cause them to pass through the fire for them?

Ezekiel 20:26 And I polluted them in their own gifts, in that they caused to pass through the fire all that openeth the womb, that I might make them desolate, to the end that they might know that I am the LORD.

Ezekiel 20:31 For when ye offer your gifts, when ye make your sons to pass through the fire, ye pollute yourselves with all your idols, even unto this day: and shall I be enquired of by you, O house of Israel? As I live, saith the Lord GOD, I will not be enquired of by you.

Ezekiel 23:37 That they have committed adultery, and blood is in their hands, and with their idols have they committed adultery, and have also caused their sons, whom they bare unto me, to pass for them through the fire, to devour them.

Adultery

Adultery is a type of pollution.

Exodus 20:14 Thou shalt not commit adultery.

Galatians 5:9 A little leaven leaveneth the whole lump.

adulterate: make impure, to make something less pure by adding inferior or unsuitable elements or substances to it. To change, corrupt.

adulterant: something that makes something else less pure

Leviticus 20:10 And the man that committeth adultery with another man's wife, even he that committeth adultery with his neighbour's wife, the adulterer and the adulteress shall surely be put to death.

Deuteronomy 5:18 Neither shalt thou commit adultery.

Proverbs 6:32 But whoso committeth adultery with a woman lacketh understanding: he that doeth it destroyeth his own soul.

Acts 15:29 That ye abstain from meats offered to idols, and from blood, and from things strangled, and from fornication: from which if ye keep yourselves, ye shall do well. Fare ye well.

Romans 1:29 Being filled with all unrighteousness, fornication, wickedness, covetousness, maliciousness; full of envy, murder, debate, deceit, malignity; whisperers,

30 Backbiters, haters of God, despiteful, proud, boasters, inventors of evil things, disobedient to parents,

31 Without understanding, covenantbreakers, without natural affection, implacable, unmerciful:

32 Who knowing the judgment of God, that they which commit such things are worthy of death, not only do the same, but have pleasure in them that do them.

1 Corinthians 6:9 Know ye not that the unrighteous shall not inherit the kingdom of God? Be not deceived: neither

fornicators, nor idolaters, nor adulterers, nor effeminate, nor abusers of themselves with mankind,

10 Nor thieves, nor covetous, nor drunkards, nor revilers, nor extortioners, shall inherit the kingdom of God.

11 And such were some of you: but ye are washed, but ye are sanctified, but ye are justified in the name of the Lord Jesus, and by the Spirit of our God.

12 All things are lawful unto me, but all things are not expedient: all things are lawful for me, but I will not be brought under the power of any.

13 Meats for the belly, and the belly for meats: but God shall destroy both it and them. Now the body is not for fornication, but for the Lord; and the Lord for the body.

14 And God hath both raised up the Lord, and will also raise up us by his own power.

15 Know ye not that your bodies are the members of Christ? shall I then take the members of Christ, and make them the members of an harlot? God forbid.

16 What? know ye not that he which is joined to an harlot is one body? for two, saith he, shall be one flesh.

17 But he that is joined unto the Lord is one spirit.

18 Flee fornication. Every sin that a man doeth is without the body; but he that committeth fornication sinneth against his own body.

19 What? know ye not that your body is the temple of the Holy Ghost which is in you, which ye have of God, and ye are not your own?

20 For ye are bought with a price: therefore glorify God in your body, and in your spirit, which are God's.

Galatians 5:19 Now the works of the flesh are manifest, which are these; Adultery, fornication, uncleanness, lasciviousness,

20 Idolatry, witchcraft, hatred, variance, emulations, wrath, strife, seditions, heresies,

21 Envyings, murders, drunkenness, revellings, and such like: of the which I tell you before, as I have also told you in time past, that they which do such things shall not inherit the kingdom of God.

Ephesians 5:3 But fornication, and all uncleanness, or covetousness, let it not be once named among you, as becometh saints;

Colossians 3:5 Mortify therefore your members which are upon the earth; fornication, uncleanness, inordinate affection, evil concupiscence, and covetousness, which is idolatry:

1 Thessalonians 4:3 For this is the will of God, even your sanctification, that ye should abstain from fornication:

Jude 1:7 Even as Sodom and Gomorrha, and the cities about them in like manner, giving themselves over to fornication, and going after strange flesh, are set forth for an example, suffering the vengeance of eternal fire.

Revelation 2:14 But I have a few things against thee, because thou hast there them that hold the doctrine of Balaam, who taught Balac to cast a stumblingblock before the children of Israel, to eat things sacrificed unto idols, and to commit fornication.

Revelation 2:20 Notwithstanding I have a few things against thee, because thou sufferest that woman Jezebel, which calleth herself a prophetess, to teach and to seduce my servants to commit fornication, and to eat things sacrificed unto idols.

Revelation 2:21 And I gave her space to repent of her fornication; and she repented not.

Revelation 9:21 Neither repented they of their murders, nor of their sorceries, nor of their fornication, nor of their thefts.

Drug use

> 1 Samuel 15:23 For rebellion is as the sin of witchcraft, and stubbornness is as iniquity and idolatry. Because thou hast rejected the word of the LORD, he hath also rejected thee from being king.
>
> Galatians 5:19 Now the works of the flesh are manifest, which are these; Adultery, fornication, uncleanness, lasciviousness,
>
> 20 Idolatry, witchcraft, hatred, variance, emulations, wrath, strife, seditions, heresies,
>
> 21 Envyings, murders, drunkenness, revellings, and such like: of the which I tell you before, as I have also told you in time past, that they which do such things shall not inherit the kingdom of God.

The word "witchcraft" in verse 20 above translates from pharmakeia which has obvious roots also in the word pharmacy. The use of drugs in witchcraft is not "news". Drug abuse is scripturally related to witchcraft.

> 5331 pharmakeia far-mak-i'-ah
>
> from 5332;; n f
>
> AV - sorcery 2, witchcraft 1; 3
>
> 1. the use or the administering of drugs
> 2. poisoning
> 3. sorcery, magical arts, often found in connection with idolatry and fostered by it
> 4. metaph. the deceptions and seductions of idolatry

There are some herbs that are in a sense poisons or drugs that also are to be avoided. Just because it grows does not mean it is good.

Man did bring a curse on this world when he disobeyed God and brought sin and death into the world.

> Genesis 3:17 And unto Adam he said, Because thou hast hearkened unto the voice of thy wife, and hast eaten of the tree, of which I commanded thee, saying, Thou shalt not eat of it: cursed is the ground for thy sake; in sorrow shalt thou eat of it all the days of thy life;
>
> 18 Thorns also and thistles shall it bring forth to thee; and thou shalt eat the herb of the field;

> 1 Corinthians 3:16 Know ye not that ye are the temple of God, and that the Spirit of God dwelleth in you?
>
> 1 Corinthians 3:17 If any man defile the temple of God, him shall God destroy; for the temple of God is holy, which temple ye are.

Drug abuse, tobacco, alcohol abuse all these things defile the body. Most under the power thereof will admit that they know they are hurting themselves.

> 1 Corinthians 6:19 What? know ye not that your body is the temple of the Holy Ghost which is in you, which ye have of God, and ye are not your own?
>
> 20 For ye are bought with a price: therefore glorify God in your body, and in your spirit, which are God's.

We also see in the Word of God that there are positive references to medicine. The laws of our land as well while being strong against drug abuse have respect for medical use of drugs.

> Proverbs 17:22 A merry heart doeth good like a medicine: but a broken spirit drieth the bones.
>
> Ezekiel 47:12 And by the river upon the bank thereof, on this side and on that side, shall grow all trees for meat, whose leaf shall not fade, neither shall the fruit thereof be consumed: it shall bring forth new fruit according to his months, because their waters they issued out of the sanctuary: and the fruit thereof shall be for meat, and the leaf thereof for medicine.

> Matthew 9:12 But when Jesus heard that, he said unto them, They that be whole need not a physician, but they that are sick.

If Jesus Himself recommended using a physician when sick, then we can hardly preach against medicine.

> Mark 2:17 When Jesus heard it, he saith unto them, They that are whole have no need of the physician, but they that are sick: I came not to call the righteous, but sinners to repentance.

Jesus even used the analogy of a physician to speak of Himself.

> Luke 5:31 And Jesus answering said unto them, They that are whole need not a physician; but they that are sick.

> Colossians 4:14 Luke, the beloved physician, and Demas, greet you.

Luke was a physician and the Bible does not say that he quit practicing medicine to serve God.

> Revelation 22:2 In the midst of the street of it, and on either side of the river, was there the tree of life, which bare twelve manner of fruits, and yielded her fruit every month: and the leaves of the tree were for the healing of the nations.

> 2 Kings 20:5 Turn again, and tell Hezekiah the captain of my people, Thus saith the LORD, the God of David thy father, I have heard thy prayer, I have seen thy tears: behold, I will heal thee: on the third day thou shalt go up unto the house of the LORD.

> 6 And I will add unto thy days fifteen years; and I will deliver thee and this city out of the hand of the king of Assyria; and I will defend this city for mine own sake, and for my servant David's sake.

> 7 And Isaiah said, Take a lump of figs. And they took and laid it on the boil, and he recovered.

Another drug abuse issue is drinking of alcohol.

> Proverbs 20:1 Wine is a mocker, strong drink is raging: and whosoever is deceived thereby is not wise.
>
> Proverbs 31:4 It is not for kings, O Lemuel, it is not for kings to drink wine; nor for princes strong drink:
>
> Isaiah 5:22 Woe unto them that are mighty to drink wine, and men of strength to mingle strong drink:
>
> Galatians 5:23 Meekness, temperance: against such there is no law.

You cannot be "too temperate". I believe that there is strong scriptural support for a Christian to abstain totally from any drug use or alcoholic drinks except in a medical situation. Things like vitamins and herbal things that are good for the body do not fall into those categories.

> 2 Peter 1:1 ¶ Simon Peter, a servant and an apostle of Jesus Christ, to them that have obtained like precious faith with us through the righteousness of God and our Saviour Jesus Christ:
>
> 2 Grace and peace be multiplied unto you through the knowledge of God, and of Jesus our Lord,
>
> 3 According as his divine power hath given unto us all things that pertain unto life and godliness, through the knowledge of him that hath called us to glory and virtue:
>
> 4 Whereby are given unto us exceeding great and precious promises: that by these ye might be partakers of the divine nature, having escaped the corruption that is in the world through lust.
>
> 5 ¶ And beside this, giving all diligence, add to your faith virtue; and to virtue knowledge;
>
> 6 And to knowledge temperance; and to temperance patience; and to patience godliness;
>
> 7 And to godliness brotherly kindness; and to brotherly kindness charity.

8 For if these things be in you, and abound, they make you that ye shall neither be barren nor unfruitful in the knowledge of our Lord Jesus Christ.

9 But he that lacketh these things is blind, and cannot see afar off, and hath forgotten that he was purged from his old sins.

10 Wherefore the rather, brethren, give diligence to make your calling and election sure: for if ye do these things, ye shall never fall:

Homosexuality

It is notable how many of trinity cults are making headlines for their sub-canine morals embracing the "G"ot "A"ids "Y"et crowd.

> Leviticus 18:22 Thou shalt not lie with mankind, as with womankind: it [is] abomination.
>
> Leviticus 20:13 If a man also lie with mankind, as he lieth with a woman, both of them have committed an abomination: they shall surely be put to death; their blood [shall be] upon them.
>
> Romans 1:26 For this cause God gave them up unto vile affections: for even their women did change the natural use into that which is against nature:
>
> Romans 1:27 And likewise also the men, leaving the natural use of the woman, burned in their lust one toward another; men with men working that which is unseemly, and receiving in themselves that recompense of their error which was meet.
>
> Romans 1:28 And even as they did not like to retain God in [their] knowledge, God gave them over to a reprobate mind, to do those things which are not convenient;
>
> I Corinthians 6:9 Know ye not that the unrighteous shall not inherit the kingdom of God? Be not deceived: neither fornicators, nor idolaters, nor adulterers, nor EFFEMINATE, nor abusers of themselves with mankind,

I wonder if I've been "exhaustive" enough here with this brief Bible study. It does seem from these verses that God does have feelings concerning certain matters....

I hope this helps...

Blame

Have we not heard many frustrated people and may even ourselves have wondered how God could allow some of the things that go on in this world, the horrors of war and terrible things that happen to even innocent children? Have we not also heard those who would blame God for the evil that we see?

> Romans 5:12 Wherefore, as by one man sin entered into the world, and death by sin; and so death passed upon all men, for that all have sinned:

It is not God who is to blame but rather sin and the father of it. Many don't realize the godlike powers that God has given to them. Is it not one of the hardest things to get though to young people that they can destroy themselves and others without remedy? If young people could only realize that they have the power to do that which they cannot ever undo. How many in prisons would not give anything to just be able to undo one single thing that they did to another in the heat of the moment thoughtlessly?

Some wonder why some seem to get away with so much for so long, but consider this.

> Luke 13:1 ¶ There were present at that season some that told him of the Galilaeans, whose blood Pilate had mingled with their sacrifices.
>
> Luke 13:2 And Jesus answering said unto them, Suppose ye that these Galilaeans were sinners above all the Galilaeans, because they suffered such things?
>
> Luke 13:3 I tell you, Nay: but, except ye repent, ye shall all likewise perish.
>
> Luke 13:4 Or those eighteen, upon whom the tower in Siloam fell, and slew them, think ye that they were sinners above all men that dwelt in Jerusalem?
>
> Luke 13:5 I tell you, Nay: but, except ye repent, ye shall all likewise perish.

There is an important lesson there that I hope you will receive.

But now what I want to show you is that it was God's will for mankind to be living in paradise. Always remember that! God's will for Adam and Eve was for them to literally be frolicking and ruling in paradise. But God gave them great power and warned them not to misuse it.

> Genesis 1:27 So God created man in his own image, in the image of God created he him; male and female created he them.
>
> Genesis 1:28 And God blessed them, and God said unto them, Be fruitful, and multiply, and replenish the earth, and subdue it: and have dominion over the fish of the sea, and over the fowl of the air, and over every living thing that moveth upon the earth.
>
> Genesis 1:29 ¶ And God said, Behold, I have given you every herb bearing seed, which is upon the face of all the earth, and every tree, in the which is the fruit of a tree yielding seed; to you it shall be for meat.
>
> Genesis 2:8 ¶ And the LORD God planted a garden eastward in Eden; and there he put the man whom he had formed.
>
> Genesis 2:9 And out of the ground made the LORD God to grow every tree that is pleasant to the sight, and good for food; the tree of life also in the midst of the garden, and the tree of knowledge of good and evil.
>
> Genesis 2:16 ¶ And the LORD God commanded the man, saying, Of every tree of the garden thou mayest freely eat:
>
> 17 But of the tree of the knowledge of good and evil, thou shalt not eat of it: for in the day that thou eatest thereof thou shalt surely die.

God warned the man not to eat of the forbidden fruit. It was man (actually woman) who chose to defy God and bring sin into this paradise world that God had created for them. Don't blame God for sin, that was mankind's choice to bring sin into the world and corrupt God's perfect paradise. God really gave mankind free will just as we have free will and great power to do good or evil. Some will say well why did God put that tree there, but how do we know that God might have had great plans for that to be a blessing to them in due season? There are plants on this Earth that are deadly poison if they are eaten before they mature.

We may never know what God had in mind for the tree of the knowledge of good and evil since man used his free will to STEAL from the forbidden tree.

Don't blame God for man's sin! Don't blame God for trusting man!

> John 10:34 Jesus answered them, Is it not written in your law, I said, Ye are gods?

Jesus here reveals that He is the Jehovah God of the Old Testament (notice the "I said", eh?). Don't misunderstand that verse, but consider, does not man not have the power to create life and to kill? God gave mankind a measure of "god like" power. How many are sitting now for the rest of their lives in prison because they made a bad decision and used their "god like" power to destroy.

> Genesis 1:27 So God created man in his own image, in the image of God created he him; male and female created he them.

I would point out that neither man or woman is three separate persons and when we find any that are we lock 'em up or medicate them to protect them and society. God is NOT three separate persons regardless of which false-church says so.

Sin is not fair. Sin was not the will of God. One person drives drunk and an innocent family gets killed on the highway, is that fair? No, but you better believe it happens.

The enemy is sin. Everything from bad breath to pimples to road rage to false churches to robbery and murder all the way to the distinctive aroma of an old wet dog to tooth decay you can trace it all back to sin. Anything that is evil or even unpleasant is the result of man choosing to bring sin into the world.

> Proverbs 14:1 Every wise woman buildeth her house: but the foolish plucketh it down with her hands.

How many women have destroyed their own homes and security with their own hands (or in many cases mouths, and that can be said of men and women.)

How many use their "god like" power of speech to tear down and destroy without really intending to?

> James 3:5 Even so the tongue is a little member, and boasteth great things. Behold, how great a matter a little fire kindleth!
>
> James 3:6 And the tongue is a fire, a world of iniquity: so is the tongue among our members, that it defileth the whole body, and setteth on fire the course of nature; and it is set on fire of hell.
>
> James 3:7 For every kind of beasts, and of birds, and of serpents, and of things in the sea, is tamed, and hath been tamed of mankind:
>
> James 3:8 But the tongue can no man tame; it is an unruly evil, full of deadly poison.
>
> James 3:9 Therewith bless we God, even the Father; and therewith curse we men, which are made after the similitude of God.
>
> James 3:10 Out of the same mouth proceedeth blessing and cursing. My brethren, these things ought not so to be.

(Of course that is not talking about people obeying Gal 1:8 and cursing false preachers, but that is a different topic.)

You want to hear something really scary, pay close attention here:

> Matthew 12:36 But I say unto you, That every idle word that men shall speak, they shall give account thereof in the day of judgment.
>
> Matthew 12:37 For by thy words thou shalt be justified, and by thy words thou shalt be condemned.

We need to be very careful what we say. If we knew a celestial tape recorder was running that would be played before God Himself would we talk any differently? Well guess what?

> Colossians 4:6 Let your speech be alway with grace, seasoned with salt, that ye may know how ye ought to answer every man.
>
> 2 Peter 3:11 Seeing then that all these things shall be dissolved, what manner of persons ought ye to be in all holy conversation and godliness,

Of course "conversation" means much more than "speech" in the above verse but that does not mean that it excludes speech in any way.

Many underestimate the "god like" power that they have with simply their speech. Are men not convicted of crimes based upon the words of witnesses?

Many will be familiar with this next verse:

> Exodus 20:16 Thou shalt not bear false witness against thy neighbour.

Why is that so important? It is because of the power we have to do both good and evil. So many young people are ensnared by the devil because they do not grasp the concept of the power they have to do things that cannot ever be changed and the devil deceives them into destroying their lives and often several other people's.

Did not God speak the world into existence? We, created in the image of God need to be aware of the power of our words and our great responsibility.

> John 10:34 Jesus answered them, Is it not written in your law, I said, Ye are gods?

That does not mean that we are "God" at all. But God did make man in His image and He gave man free will to do good or evil, but man chose to defy God and brought sin into the world.

If this seems like a stretch consider, would you be here if a couple of people had not used their "god like" power to make a baby?

This is not something that gets preached very often and can be misunderstood, but it is important for people to realize their great power AND the responsibility and consequences that will result. Just consider the magnitude of suffering over the years that can be traced back to Eve and Adam and their "error in judgment" or momentary lapse or whatever...

Was the issue of the forbidden tree just a "matter of conscience"? (excuse my little dig against the loose preachers of this hour who want to relegate obedience of the Bible to a "matter of conscience" in their bloated, pride engorged, measure themselves by themselves, corrupt organizations).

If you remember nothing else of what you have heard tonight I want you to really remember that it was man and not God who chose to bring sin and all the suffering that comes with it into the world. Don't blame God for sin; that was your ever so distant relative who made that decision! Why would anyone want to blame God for something one of their relatives did, eh?

So there is another thing I want you to remember and that is the Acts 2:38 salvation plan. I don't want to give you a sermon about sin without giving you the way to escape.

God Himself wasn't happy with the situation that man was in so He came in the flesh and paid with his own Blood to redeem or "buy back" whosoever will choose to avail themselves of his offer.

> 1 John 3:16 Hereby perceive we the love of God, because he laid down his life for us: and we ought to lay down our lives for the brethren.

God made a way for men to be free from sin and it was offered on the birthday of the Church, on the Day of Pentecost when the man with the keys from Jesus Himself unlocked the doors of heaven when he preached Acts 2:38:

> Acts 2:38 Then Peter said unto them, Repent, and be baptized every one of you in the name of Jesus Christ for the remission of sins, and ye shall receive the gift of the Holy Ghost.
>
> 39 For the promise is unto you, and to your children, and to all that are afar off, even as many as the Lord our God shall call.

So remember:

Don't blame God for what a couple of your ancestors did.

> Acts 2:38 is the Biblical plan of salvation for as many as God will call.

And, don't forget about that celestial tape recorder either.

Death

Psalms 48:14 For this God is our God for ever and ever: he will be our guide even unto death.

Psalms 116:15 Precious in the sight of the LORD is the death of his saints.

Proverbs 14:12 There is a way which seemeth right unto a man, but the end thereof are the ways of death.

Proverbs 16:25 There is a way that seemeth right unto a man, but the end thereof are the ways of death.

Ecclesiastes 7:1 A good name is better than precious ointment; and the day of death than the day of one's birth.

Ecclesiastes 8:8 There is no man that hath power over the spirit to retain the spirit; neither hath he power in the day of death: and there is no discharge in that war; neither shall wickedness deliver those that are given to it.

Isaiah 25:8 He will swallow up death in victory; and the Lord GOD will wipe away tears from off all faces; and the rebuke of his people shall he take away from off all the earth: for the LORD hath spoken it.

Isaiah 38:18 For the grave cannot praise thee, death can not celebrate thee: they that go down into the pit cannot hope for thy truth.

Isaiah 53:12 Therefore will I divide him a portion with the great, and he shall divide the spoil with the strong; because he hath poured out his soul unto death: and he was numbered with the transgressors; and he bare the sin of many, and made intercession for the transgressors.

Ezekiel 18:32 For I have no pleasure in the death of him that dieth, saith the Lord GOD: wherefore turn yourselves, and live ye.

Ezekiel 33:11 Say unto them, As I live, saith the Lord GOD, I have no pleasure in the death of the wicked; but that the wicked turn from his way and live: turn ye, turn ye from your evil ways; for why will ye die, O house of Israel?

Hosea 13:14 I will ransom them from the power of the grave; I will redeem them from death: O death, I will be thy plagues; O grave, I will be thy destruction: repentance shall be hid from mine eyes.

Psalms 115:17 The dead praise not the LORD, neither any that go down into silence.

Matthew 8:22 But Jesus said unto him, Follow me; and let the dead bury their dead.

Romans 5:12 Wherefore, as by one man sin entered into the world, and death by sin; and so death passed upon all men, for that all have sinned:

Romans 6:3 Know ye not, that so many of us as were baptized into Jesus Christ were baptized into his death?

Romans 6:4 Therefore we are buried with him by baptism into death: that like as Christ was raised up from the dead by the glory of the Father, even so we also should walk in newness of life.

Romans 6:5 For if we have been planted together in the likeness of his death, we shall be also in the likeness of his resurrection:

Romans 6:9 Knowing that Christ being raised from the dead dieth no more; death hath no more dominion over him.

Romans 6:16 Know ye not, that to whom ye yield yourselves servants to obey, his servants ye are to whom ye obey; whether of sin unto death, or of obedience unto righteousness?

Romans 6:21 What fruit had ye then in those things whereof ye are now ashamed? for the end of those things is death.

Romans 6:23 For the wages of sin is death; but the gift of God is eternal life through Jesus Christ our Lord.

Romans 8:6 For to be carnally minded is death; but to be spiritually minded is life and peace

Romans 8:11 But if the Spirit of him that raised up Jesus from the dead dwell in you, he that raised up Christ from the dead shall also quicken your mortal bodies by his Spirit that dwelleth in you.

2 Corinthians 1:9 But we had the sentence of death in ourselves, that we should not trust in ourselves, but in God which raiseth the dead:

1 Corinthians 15:42 So also is the resurrection of the dead. It is sown in corruption; it is raised in incorruption:

1 Corinthians 15:52 In a moment, in the twinkling of an eye, at the last trump: for the trumpet shall sound, and the dead shall be raised incorruptible, and we shall be changed.

1 Corinthians 15:53 For this corruptible must put on incorruption, and this mortal must put on immortality.

1 Corinthians 15:54 So when this corruptible shall have put on incorruption, and this mortal shall have put on immortality, then shall be brought to pass the saying that is written, Death is swallowed up in victory.

1 Corinthians 15:55 O death, where is thy sting? O grave, where is thy victory?

2 Corinthians 1:9 But we had the sentence of death in ourselves, that we should not trust in ourselves, but in God which raiseth the dead:

2 Corinthians 1:10 Who delivered us from so great a death, and doth deliver: in whom we trust that he will yet deliver us;

2 Corinthians 7:10 For godly sorrow worketh repentance to salvation not to be repented of: but the sorrow of the world worketh death.

2 Timothy 1:10 But is now made manifest by the appearing of our Saviour Jesus Christ, who hath abolished death, and hath brought life and immortality to light through the gospel:

Hebrews 2:14 Forasmuch then as the children are partakers of flesh and blood, he also himself likewise took part of the same; that through death he might destroy him that had the power of death, that is, the devil;

Hebrews 11:5 By faith Enoch was translated that he should not see death; and was not found, because God had translated him: for before his translation he had this testimony, that he pleased God.

James 1:15 Then when lust hath conceived, it bringeth forth sin: and sin, when it is finished, bringeth forth death.

James 5:20 Let him know, that he which converteth the sinner from the error of his way shall save a soul from death, and shall hide a multitude of sins.

Revelation 1:18 I am he that liveth, and was dead; and, behold, I am alive for evermore, Amen; and have the keys of hell and of death.

Revelation 9:6 And in those days shall men seek death, and shall not find it; and shall desire to die, and death shall flee from them.

Revelation 20:14 And death and hell were cast into the lake of fire. This is the second death.

Revelation 21:4 And God shall wipe away all tears from their eyes; and there shall be no more death, neither sorrow, nor crying, neither shall there be any more pain: for the former things are passed away.

Revelation 21:8 But the fearful, and unbelieving, and the abominable, and murderers, and whoremongers, and sorcerers, and idolaters, and all liars, shall have their part in the lake which burneth with fire and brimstone: which is the second death.

Ecclesiastes 9:5 For the living know that they shall die: but the dead know not any thing, neither have they any more a reward; for the memory of them is forgotten.

Hebrews 9:27 And as it is appointed unto men once to die, but after this the judgment:

1 Thessalonians 4:16 For the Lord himself shall descend from heaven with a shout, with the voice of the archangel, and with the trump of God: and the dead in Christ shall rise first:

1 Thessalonians 4:17 Then we which are alive and remain shall be caught up together with them in the clouds, to meet the Lord in the air: and so shall we ever be with the Lord.

Revelation 20:12 And I saw the dead, small and great, stand before God; and the books were opened: and another book was opened, which is the book of life: and the dead were judged out of those things which were written in the books, according to their works.

Revelation 20:13 And the sea gave up the dead which were in it; and death and hell delivered up the dead which were in them: and they were judged every man according to their works.

Healing

Matthew 8:13 And Jesus said unto the centurion, Go thy way; and as thou hast believed, [so] be it done unto thee. And his servant was healed in the selfsame hour.

Matthew 8:16 When the even was come, they brought unto him many that were possessed with devils: and he cast out the spirits with [his] word, and healed all that were sick:

Matthew 12:22 Then was brought unto him one possessed with a devil, blind, and dumb: and he healed him, insomuch that the blind and dumb both spake and saw.

Matthew 14:14 And Jesus went forth, and saw a great multitude, and was moved with compassion toward them, and he healed their sick.

Matthew 15:30 And great multitudes came unto him, having with them [those that were] lame, blind, dumb, maimed, and many others, and cast them down at Jesus' feet; and he healed them:

Matthew 19:2 And great multitudes followed him; and he healed them there.

Matthew 21:14 And the blind and the lame came to him in the temple; and he healed them.

Mark 1:34 And he healed many that were sick of divers diseases, and cast out many devils; and suffered not the devils to speak, because they knew him.

Mark 3:10 For he had healed many; insomuch that they pressed upon him for to touch him, as many as had plagues.

Mark 5:29 And straightway the fountain of her blood was dried up; and she felt in [her] body that she was healed of that plague.

Mark 6:5 And he could there do no mighty work, save that he laid his hands upon a few sick folk, and healed [them].

Luke 4:40 Now when the sun was setting, all they that had any sick with divers diseases brought them unto him; and he laid his hands on every one of them, and healed them.

Acts 8:7 For unclean spirits, crying with loud voice, came out of many that were possessed [with them]: and many taken with palsies, and that were lame, were healed.

Acts 28:8 And it came to pass, that the father of Publius lay sick of a fever and of a bloody flux: to whom Paul entered in, and prayed, and laid his hands on him, and healed him.

Acts 28:9 So when this was done, others also, which had diseases in the island, came, and were healed:

James 5:16 Confess [your] faults one to another, and pray one for another, that ye may be healed. The effectual fervent prayer of a righteous man availeth much.

I Peter 2:24 Who his own self bare our sins in his own body on the tree, that we, being dead to sins, should live unto righteousness: by whose stripes ye were healed.

More on Healing

Isaiah 53:5 But he was wounded for our transgressions, he was bruised for our iniquities: the chastisement of our peace was upon him; and with his stripes we are healed.

1 Peter 2:24 Who his own self bare our sins in his own body on the tree, that we, being dead to sins, should live unto righteousness: by whose stripes ye were healed.

James 5:14 Is any sick among you? let him call for the elders of the church; and let them pray over him, anointing him with oil in the name of the Lord:

James 5:15 And the prayer of faith shall save the sick, and the Lord shall raise him up; and if he have committed sins, they shall be forgiven him.

James 5:16 Confess your faults one to another, and pray one for another, that ye may be healed. The effectual fervent prayer of a righteous man availeth much.

Mark 8:22 ¶ And he cometh to Bethsaida; and they bring a blind man unto him, and besought him to touch him.

23 And he took the blind man by the hand, and led him out of the town; and when he had spit on his eyes, and put his hands upon him, he asked him if he saw ought.

24 And he looked up, and said, I see men as trees, walking.

25 After that he put his hands again upon his eyes, and made him look up: and he was restored, and saw every man clearly.

26 And he sent him away to his house, saying, Neither go into the town, nor tell it to any in the town.

27 ¶ And Jesus went out, and his disciples, into the towns of Caesarea Philippi: and by the way he asked his disciples, saying unto them, Whom do men say that I am?

28 And they answered, John the Baptist: but some say, Elias; and others, One of the prophets.

Mark 8:29 And he saith unto them, But whom say ye that I am? And Peter answereth and saith unto him, Thou art the Christ.

30 And he charged them that they should tell no man of him.

2 Kings 20:6 And I will add unto thy days fifteen years; and I will deliver thee and this city out of the hand of the king of Assyria; and I will defend this city for mine own sake, and for my servant David's sake.

7 And Isaiah said, Take a lump of figs. And they took and laid it on the boil, and he recovered.

Matthew 9:12 But when Jesus heard that, he said unto them, They that be whole need not a physician, but they that are sick.

Luke 5:31 And Jesus answering said unto them, They that are whole need not a physician; but they that are sick.

Colossians 4:14 Luke, the beloved physician, and Demas, greet you.

Buddha

Many false religions are based upon the concept of worshiping a rotting corpse of some "hero" who could say neat things. This is not recommended because for a religion to be practical, the "hero" must be able to handle the death thing.

Now Buddha, for example, could say cool things about being nice, but when it came to the death thing, it was like plop and rot, I mean talk about a big "0" for credibility. Same with Booboo 'lulu et al. Any turkey can say "be nice be happy", but that doesn't make them God.

Worshiping a rotting corpse, is, quite frankly, "un-cool" and not real smart. A rock, however well carved is still "dumb as a rock", and wood is somewhat similar in that regard.

Some will point out similarities in different religions with the basic moral teaching of Christianity as a justification, but remember, the closer a counterfeit is to the original, the more harmful it is.

Jesus, however, proved that He was exactly who He said He was when He allowed his body to be killed and then raised it up after three days

> 1 Cor 15:3 For I delivered unto you first of all that which I also received, how that Christ died for our sins according to the scriptures;
>
> 1 Cor 15:4 And that he was buried, and that he rose again the third day according to the scriptures:
>
> 1 Cor 15:5 And that he was seen of Cephas, then of the twelve:
>
> 1 Cor 15:6 After that, he was seen of above five hundred brethren at once; of whom the greater part remain unto this present, but some are fallen asleep.

Buddha

There was no need for a guard at Buddha's grave.

I hope this helps...

Reincarnation

> Hebrews 9:27 And as it is appointed unto men once to die, but after this the judgment:

The Bible clearly teaches that there is not reincarnation, but rather resurrection and judgment. You cannot be a Christian and believe in reincarnation. Reincarnation is contrary to the word of God.

> John 5:29 And shall come forth; they that have done good, unto the resurrection of life; and they that have done evil, unto the resurrection of damnation.

> John 11:24 Martha saith unto him, I know that he shall rise again in the resurrection at the last day.

> Revelation 20:6 Blessed and holy [is] he that hath part in the first resurrection: on such the second death hath no power, but they shall be priests of God and of Christ, and shall reign with him a thousand years.

Children

Proverbs 13:24 He that spareth his rod hateth his son: but he that loveth him chasteneth him betimes.

Proverbs 22:15 Foolishness [is] bound in the heart of a child; [but] the rod of correction shall drive it far from him.

Proverbs 23:12 Apply thine heart unto instruction, and thine ears to the words of knowledge.

Proverbs 23:13 Withhold not correction from the child: for [if] thou beatest him with the rod, he shall not die.

Proverbs 23:14 Thou shalt beat him with the rod, and shalt deliver his soul from hell.

Mary's Kids

Mary had other kids the "normal" way after Jesus was born.

> Mark 6:3 Is not this the carpenter, the son of Mary, the brother of James, and Joses, and of Juda, and Simon? and are not his sisters here with us? And they were offended at him.
>
> 4 But Jesus said unto them, A prophet is not without honour, but in his own country, and among his own kin, and in his own house.

Note that Jesus did not reply, "Oh, these are just cousins, mom's still a virgin."

> Matthew 12:46 While he yet talked to the people, behold, his mother and his brethren stood without, desiring to speak with him.
>
> 47 Then one said unto him, Behold, thy mother and thy brethren stand without, desiring to speak with thee.

Note that Jesus also here did not reply, "Oh, these are just cousins, mom's still a virgin."

> Matthew 13:55 Is not this the carpenter's son? is not his mother called Mary? and his brethren, James, and Joses, and Simon, and Judas?
>
> 56 And his sisters, are they not all with us? Whence then hath this man all these things?

Note that Jesus also here did not reply, "Oh, these are just cousins, mom's still a virgin."

> Luke 8:19 Then came to him his mother and his brethren, and could not come at him for the press.

> 20 And it was told him by certain which said, Thy mother and thy brethren stand without, desiring to see thee.

Note that Jesus also here did not reply, "Oh, these are just cousins, mom's still a virgin."

> John 2:12 After this he went down to Capernaum, he, and his mother, and his brethren, and his disciples: and they continued there not many days.

Life isn't fair

How many young people miss out with God and mess up their lives because something unfair happened to them?

How many are sitting in prisons today because something unfair happened to them so they felt justified in hurting or killing someone?

I guarantee you that whoever you are unfair things will happen to you. That is not optional and will happen, period.

But, what you do and how you handle it will determine the severity and longevity of the matter.

To many in prison for harming or killing someone, the original "unfair" issue would now seem so trivial.

> Ecclesiastes 1:12 ¶ I the Preacher was king over Israel in Jerusalem.
>
> 13 And I gave my heart to seek and search out by wisdom concerning all things that are done under heaven: this sore travail hath God given to the sons of man to be exercised therewith.
>
> 14 I have seen all the works that are done under the sun; and, behold, all is vanity and vexation of spirit.
>
> 15 That which is crooked cannot be made straight: and that which is wanting cannot be numbered.
>
> 16 I communed with mine own heart, saying, Lo, I am come to great estate, and have gotten more wisdom than all they that have been before me in Jerusalem: yea, my heart had great experience of wisdom and knowledge.
>
> 17 And I gave my heart to know wisdom, and to know madness and folly: I perceived that this also is vexation of spirit.
>
> 18 For in much wisdom is much grief: and he that increaseth knowledge increaseth sorrow.

2: 1 ¶ I said in mine heart, Go to now, I will prove thee with mirth, therefore enjoy pleasure: and, behold, this also is vanity.

2 I said of laughter, It is mad: and of mirth, What doeth it?

Ecclesiastes 2:11 Then I looked on all the works that my hands had wrought, and on the labour that I had laboured to do: and, behold, all was vanity and vexation of spirit, and there was no profit under the sun.

Ecclesiastes 3:12 I know that there is no good in them, but for a man to rejoice, and to do good in his life.

13 And also that every man should eat and drink, and enjoy the good of all his labour, it is the gift of God.

Ecclesiastes 9:10 Whatsoever thy hand findeth to do, do it with thy might; for there is no work, nor device, nor knowledge, nor wisdom, in the grave, whither thou goest.

11 ¶ I returned, and saw under the sun, that the race is not to the swift, nor the battle to the strong, neither yet bread to the wise, nor yet riches to men of understanding, nor yet favour to men of skill; but time and chance happeneth to them all.

12 For man also knoweth not his time: as the fishes that are taken in an evil net, and as the birds that are caught in the snare; so are the sons of men snared in an evil time, when it falleth suddenly upon them.

13 ¶ This wisdom have I seen also under the sun, and it seemed great unto me:

Ecclesiastes 1:9 The thing that hath been, it is that which shall be; and that which is done is that which shall be done: and there is no new thing under the sun.

1 Corinthians 10:13 There hath no temptation taken you but such as is common to man: but God is faithful, who will not suffer you to be tempted above that ye are able; but will with the temptation also make a way to escape, that ye may be able to bear it.

Guess what, there are "no excuses" with God. I have said before and I say again, while I can find numerous accounts of God accepting apologies, even arguments, yea even negotiations from men, I have yet to find a single example of God accepting an excuse from a man for violating His Word. If you can find one please let me know.

My point is that everyone feels justified in anything that they ever do. So much sin from adultery to murder is a result of someone having something they feel is unfair happen to them.

> Ephesians 4:26 Be ye angry, and sin not: let not the sun go down upon your wrath:

I feel to mention that there is great power in thankfulness

> 1 Thessalonians 5:18 In every thing give thanks: for this is the will of God in Christ Jesus concerning you.

> 2 Timothy 3:1 ¶ This know also, that in the last days perilous times shall come.
>
> 2 For men shall be lovers of their own selves, covetous, boasters, proud, blasphemers, disobedient to parents, unthankful, unholy,
>
> 3 Without natural affection, trucebreakers, false accusers, incontinent, fierce, despisers of those that are good,
>
> 4 Traitors, heady, highminded, lovers of pleasures more than lovers of God;
>
> 5 Having a form of godliness, but denying the power thereof: from such turn away.
>
> 6 For of this sort are they which creep into houses, and lead captive silly women laden with sins, led away with divers lusts,
>
> 7 Ever learning, and never able to come to the knowledge of the truth.

> 8 Now as Jannes and Jambres withstood Moses, so do these also resist the truth: men of corrupt minds, reprobate concerning the faith.

I didn't mean to get into TV preachers and such like, but those verses cover a lot of ground. How does this tangent relate to the topic of life not being fair? Note the "unthankful" part early on. It is hard to be thankful when you feel that God is "unfair" or that life is "unfair" to you. Unthankful people are easy prey for the devil. What unthankful person would be concerned with holiness?

When something "unfair" happens to you, and it will, you need to give thanks to God for your blessings. When your mind is dwelling on the blessings of God the devil has a hard time. In time so many of the "unfair" things that happen to us turn out to be very minor. How many fill prison cells because of their overreaction to some trivial matter in their past?

Keep the Faith. Stay prayed up and thankful!

Eli

1Samuel 1:1 ¶ Now there was a certain man of Ramathaimzophim, of mount Ephraim, and his name was Elkanah, the son of Jeroham, the son of Elihu, the son of Tohu, the son of Zuph, an Ephrathite:

2 And he had two wives; the name of the one was Hannah, and the name of the other Peninnah: and Peninnah had children, but Hannah had no children.

3 And this man went up out of his city yearly to worship and to sacrifice unto the LORD of hosts in Shiloh. And the two sons of Eli, Hophni and Phinehas, the priests of the LORD, were there.

4 And when the time was that Elkanah offered, he gave to Peninnah his wife, and to all her sons and her daughters, portions:

5 But unto Hannah he gave a worthy portion; for he loved Hannah: but the LORD had shut up her womb.

6 And her adversary also provoked her sore, for to make her fret, because the LORD had shut up her womb.

7 And as he did so year by year, when she went up to the house of the LORD, so she provoked her; therefore she wept, and did not eat.

8 Then said Elkanah her husband to her, Hannah, why weepest thou? and why eatest thou not? and why is thy heart grieved? am not I better to thee than ten sons?

9 ¶ So Hannah rose up after they had eaten in Shiloh, and after they had drunk. Now Eli the priest sat upon a seat by a post of the temple of the LORD.

10 And she was in bitterness of soul, and prayed unto the LORD, and wept sore.

11 And she vowed a vow, and said, O LORD of hosts, if thou wilt indeed look on the affliction of thine handmaid, and

remember me, and not forget thine handmaid, but wilt give unto thine handmaid a man child, then I will give him unto the LORD all the days of his life, and there shall no razor come upon his head.

12 And it came to pass, as she continued praying before the LORD, that Eli marked her mouth.

13 Now Hannah, she spake in her heart; only her lips moved, but her voice was not heard: therefore Eli thought she had been drunken.

14 And Eli said unto her, How long wilt thou be drunken? put away thy wine from thee.

15 And Hannah answered and said, No, my lord, I am a woman of a sorrowful spirit: I have drunk neither wine nor strong drink, but have poured out my soul before the LORD.

16 Count not thine handmaid for a daughter of Belial: for out of the abundance of my complaint and grief have I spoken hitherto.

17 Then Eli answered and said, Go in peace: and the God of Israel grant thee thy petition that thou hast asked of him.

18 And she said, Let thine handmaid find grace in thy sight. So the woman went her way, and did eat, and her countenance was no more sad.

19 ¶ And they rose up in the morning early, and worshipped before the LORD, and returned, and came to their house to Ramah: and Elkanah knew Hannah his wife; and the LORD remembered her.

20 Wherefore it came to pass, when the time was come about after Hannah had conceived, that she bare a son, and called his name Samuel, saying, Because I have asked him of the LORD.

1Samuel 2:12 Now the sons of Eli were sons of Belial; they knew not the LORD.

13 And the priests' custom with the people was, that, when any man offered sacrifice, the priest's servant came, while the flesh was in seething, with a fleshhook of three teeth in his hand;

14 And he struck it into the pan, or kettle, or caldron, or pot; all that the fleshhook brought up the priest took for himself. So they did in Shiloh unto all the Israelites that came thither.

15 Also before they burnt the fat, the priest's servant came, and said to the man that sacrificed, Give flesh to roast for the priest; for he will not have sodden flesh of thee, but raw.

16 And if any man said unto him, Let them not fail to burn the fat presently, and then take as much as thy soul desireth; then he would answer him, Nay; but thou shalt give it me now: and if not, I will take it by force.

17 Wherefore the sin of the young men was very great before the LORD: for men abhorred the offering of the LORD.

18 But Samuel ministered before the LORD, being a child, girded with a linen ephod.

1Samuel 2:22 Now Eli was very old, and heard all that his sons did unto all Israel; and how they lay with the women that assembled at the door of the tabernacle of the congregation.

23 And he said unto them, Why do ye such things? for I hear of your evil dealings by all this people.

24 Nay, my sons; for it is no good report that I hear: ye make the LORD'S people to transgress.

25 If one man sin against another, the judge shall judge him: but if a man sin against the LORD, who shall intreat for him? Notwithstanding they hearkened not unto the voice of their father, because the LORD would slay them.

26 And the child Samuel grew on, and was in favour both with the LORD, and also with men.

27 ¶ And there came a man of God unto Eli, and said unto him, Thus saith the LORD, Did I plainly appear unto the house of thy father, when they were in Egypt in Pharaoh's house?

28 And did I choose him out of all the tribes of Israel to be my priest, to offer upon mine altar, to burn incense, to wear an ephod before me? and did I give unto the house of thy father all the offerings made by fire of the children of Israel?

29 Wherefore kick ye at my sacrifice and at mine offering, which I have commanded in my habitation; and honourest thy sons above me, to make yourselves fat with the chiefest of all the offerings of Israel my people?

30 Wherefore the LORD God of Israel saith, I said indeed that thy house, and the house of thy father, should walk before me for ever: but now the LORD saith, Be it far from me; for them that honour me I will honour, and they that despise me shall be lightly esteemed.

31 Behold, the days come, that I will cut off thine arm, and the arm of thy father's house, that there shall not be an old man in thine house.

32 And thou shalt see an enemy in my habitation, in all the wealth which God shall give Israel: and there shall not be an old man in thine house for ever.

33 And the man of thine, whom I shall not cut off from mine altar, shall be to consume thine eyes, and to grieve thine heart: and all the increase of thine house shall die in the flower of their age.

34 And this shall be a sign unto thee, that shall come upon thy two sons, on Hophni and Phinehas; in one day they shall die both of them.

35 And I will raise me up a faithful priest, that shall do according to that which is in mine heart and in my mind: and I will build him a sure house; and he shall walk before mine anointed for ever.

36 And it shall come to pass, that every one that is left in thine house shall come and crouch to him for a piece of silver

and a morsel of bread, and shall say, Put me, I pray thee, into one of the priests' offices, that I may eat a piece of bread.

1Samuel 3:11 ¶ And the LORD said to Samuel, Behold, I will do a thing in Israel, at which both the ears of every one that heareth it shall tingle.

12 In that day I will perform against Eli all things which I have spoken concerning his house: when I begin, I will also make an end.

13 For I have told him that I will judge his house for ever for the iniquity which he knoweth; because his sons made themselves vile, and he restrained them not.

14 And therefore I have sworn unto the house of Eli, that the iniquity of Eli's house shall not be purged with sacrifice nor offering for ever.

15 And Samuel lay until the morning, and opened the doors of the house of the LORD. And Samuel feared to shew Eli the vision.

16 Then Eli called Samuel, and said, Samuel, my son. And he answered, Here am I.

17 And he said, What is the thing that the LORD hath said unto thee? I pray thee hide it not from me: God do so to thee, and more also, if thou hide any thing from me of all the things that he said unto thee.

18 And Samuel told him every whit, and hid nothing from him. And he said, It is the LORD: let him do what seemeth him good.

19 ¶ And Samuel grew, and the LORD was with him, and did let none of his words fall to the ground.

1Samuel 4: ¶ And the word of Samuel came to all Israel. Now Israel went out against the Philistines to battle, and pitched beside Ebenezer: and the Philistines pitched in Aphek.

2 And the Philistines put themselves in array against Israel: and when they joined battle, Israel was smitten before the Philistines: and they slew of the army in the field about four thousand men.

3 And when the people were come into the camp, the elders of Israel said, Wherefore hath the LORD smitten us to day before the Philistines? Let us fetch the ark of the covenant of the LORD out of Shiloh unto us, that, when it cometh among us, it may save us out of the hand of our enemies.

5 And when the ark of the covenant of the LORD came into the camp, all Israel shouted with a great shout, so that the earth rang again.

6 And when the Philistines heard the noise of the shout, they said, What meaneth the noise of this great shout in the camp of the Hebrews? And they understood that the ark of the LORD was come into the camp.

7 And the Philistines were afraid, for they said, God is come into the camp. And they said, Woe unto us! for there hath not been such a thing heretofore.

8 Woe unto us! who shall deliver us out of the hand of these mighty Gods? these are the Gods that smote the Egyptians with all the plagues in the wilderness.

9 Be strong, and quit yourselves like men, O ye Philistines, that ye be not servants unto the Hebrews, as they have been to you: quit yourselves like men, and fight.

10 ¶ And the Philistines fought, and Israel was smitten, and they fled every man into his tent: and there was a very great slaughter; for there fell of Israel thirty thousand footmen.

11 And the ark of God was taken; and the two sons of Eli, Hophni and Phinehas, were slain.

12 ¶ And there ran a man of Benjamin out of the army, and came to Shiloh the same day with his clothes rent, and with earth upon his head.

13 And when he came, lo, Eli sat upon a seat by the wayside watching: for his heart trembled for the ark of God. And

when the man came into the city, and told it, all the city cried out.

14 And when Eli heard the noise of the crying, he said, What meaneth the noise of this tumult? And the man came in hastily, and told Eli.

15 Now Eli was ninety and eight years old; and his eyes were dim, that he could not see.

16 And the man said unto Eli, I am he that came out of the army, and I fled to day out of the army. And he said, What is there done, my son?

17 And the messenger answered and said, Israel is fled before the Philistines, and there hath been also a great slaughter among the people, and thy two sons also, Hophni and Phinehas, are dead, and the ark of God is taken.

18 And it came to pass, when he made mention of the ark of God, that he fell from off the seat backward by the side of the gate, and his neck brake, and he died: for he was an old man, and heavy. And he had judged Israel forty years.

19 ¶ And his daughter in law, Phinehas' wife, was with child, near to be delivered: and when she heard the tidings that the ark of God was taken, and that her father in law and her husband were dead, she bowed herself and travailed; for her pains came upon her.

20 And about the time of her death the women that stood by her said unto her, Fear not; for thou hast born a son. But she answered not, neither did she regard it.

21 And she named the child Ichabod, saying, The glory is departed from Israel: because the ark of God was taken, and because of her father in law and her husband.

22 And she said, The glory is departed from Israel: for the ark of God is taken.

1 ¶ And the Philistines took the ark of God, and brought it from Ebenezer unto Ashdod.

Same Devil

Just like when God said one thing, the devil said another:

God said:

> Gen 2:17 But of the tree of the knowledge of good and evil, thou shalt not eat of it: for in the day that thou eatest thereof thou shalt surely die.

The devil said:

> Gen 3:4 And the serpent said unto the woman, Ye shall not surely die:

God said "and is baptized" and "be baptized in the name of Jesus"

> Mark 16:16 He that believeth and is baptized shall be saved; but he that believeth not shall be damned.

> John 3:5 Jesus answered, Verily , verily, I say unto thee, Except a man be born of water and of the Spirit, he cannot enter into the kingdom of God.

> Acts 2:38 Then Peter said unto them, Repent, and be baptized every one of you in the name of Jesus Christ for the remission of sins, and ye shall receive the gift of the Holy Ghost.

> Acts 2:39 For the promise is unto you, and to your children, and to all that are afar off, even as many as the Lord our God shall call.

But the devil says:

"Oh, just claim to believe and ignore the commandments of the Bible."

It's just the same old devil with the same old lies... (spoken, with great swelling "claims" by his ministers of disobedience)

> 2 Tim 3:13 But evil men and seducers shall wax worse and worse, deceiving, and being deceived.

> 2 Cor 11:13 For such are false apostles, deceitful workers, transforming themselves into the apostles of Christ.
>
> 2 Cor 11:14 And no marvel; for Satan himself is transformed into an angel of light.
>
> 2 Cor 11:15 Therefore it is no great thing if his ministers also be transformed as the ministers of righteousness; whose end shall be according to their works.

Sin is not fair

Luke 13:1 ¶ There were present at that season some that told him of the Galilaeans, whose blood Pilate had mingled with their sacrifices.

2 And Jesus answering said unto them, Suppose ye that these Galilaeans were sinners above all the Galilaeans, because they suffered such things?

3 I tell you, Nay: but, except ye repent, ye shall all likewise perish.

4 Or those eighteen, upon whom the tower in Siloam fell, and slew them, think ye that they were sinners above all men that dwelt in Jerusalem?

5 I tell you, Nay: but, except ye repent, ye shall all likewise perish.

Genesis 1:27 So God created man in his own image, in the image of God created he him; male and female created he them.

28 And God blessed them, and God said unto them, Be fruitful, and multiply, and replenish the earth, and subdue it: and have dominion over the fish of the sea, and over the fowl of the air, and over every living thing that moveth upon the earth.

29 ¶ And God said, Behold, I have given you every herb bearing seed, which is upon the face of all the earth, and every tree, in the which is the fruit of a tree yielding seed; to you it shall be for meat.

Genesis 2:8 ¶ And the LORD God planted a garden eastward in Eden; and there he put the man whom he had formed.

> 9 And out of the ground made the LORD God to grow every tree that is pleasant to the sight, and good for food; the tree of life also in the midst of the garden, and the tree of knowledge of good and evil.

> Genesis 2:16 ¶ And the LORD God commanded the man, saying, Of every tree of the garden thou mayest freely eat:
>
> 17 But of the tree of the knowledge of good and evil, thou shalt not eat of it: for in the day that thou eatest thereof thou shalt surely die.

God warned the man not to eat of the forbidden fruit. It was man (actually woman) who chose to defy God and bring sin into this paradise world that God had created for them. Don't blame God for sin, that was mankind's choice to bring sin into the world and corrupt God's perfect paradise. God really gave mankind free will just as we have free will and great power to do good or evil.

> John 10:34 Jesus answered them, Is it not written in your law, I said, Ye are gods?

Jesus here reveals that He is the Jehovah God of the Old Testament. Don't misunderstand that verse, but consider, does not man not have the power to create life and to kill? God gave mankind a measure of "god like" power. How many are sitting now for the rest of their lives in prison because they made a bad decision and used their "god like" power to destroy.

> Genesis 1:27 So God created man in his own image, in the image of God created he him; male and female created he them.

We are responsible for what we do and say.

Sin is not fair

Sin is not fair. Sin was not the will of God. One person drives drunk and an innocent family gets killed on the highway, is that fair? No, but you better believe it happens.

The enemy is sin.

> Proverbs 14:1 Every wise woman buildeth her house: but the foolish plucketh it down with her hands.

How many women have destroyed their own homes and security with their own hands (or in many cases mouths, and that can be said of men and women.) How many use their "god like" power of speech to tear down and destroy without really intending to?

> James 3:5 Even so the tongue is a little member, and boasteth great things. Behold, how great a matter a little fire kindleth!
>
> 6 And the tongue is a fire, a world of iniquity: so is the tongue among our members, that it defileth the whole body, and setteth on fire the course of nature; and it is set on fire of hell.
>
> 7 For every kind of beasts, and of birds, and of serpents, and of things in the sea, is tamed, and hath been tamed of mankind:
>
> 8 But the tongue can no man tame; it is an unruly evil, full of deadly poison.
>
> 9 Therewith bless we God, even the Father; and therewith curse we men, which are made after the similitude of God.
>
> 10 Out of the same mouth proceedeth blessing and cursing. My brethren, these things ought not so to be.

(Of course that is not talking about people obeying Gal 1:8 and cursing false preachers, but that is a different topic.)

You want to hear something really scary, pay close attention here:

> Matthew 12:36 But I say unto you, That every idle word that men shall speak, they shall give account thereof in the day of judgment.
>
> 37 For by thy words thou shalt be justified, and by thy words thou shalt be condemned.

We need to be very careful what we say. If we knew a tape recorder was running that would be played before God Himself would we talk any differently? Well guess what?

> Colossians 4:6 Let your speech be alway with grace, seasoned with salt, that ye may know how ye ought to answer every man.

> 2 Peter 3:11 Seeing then that all these things shall be dissolved, what manner of persons ought ye to be in all holy conversation and godliness,

Of course "conversation" means much more than "speech" in the above verse but that does not mean that it excludes speech in any way.

Many underestimate the "god like" power that they have with simply their speech. Are men not convicted of crimes based upon the words of witnesses?

Many will be familiar with this next verse:

> Exodus 20:16 Thou shalt not bear false witness against thy neighbour.

Why is that so important? It is because of the power we have to do both good and evil. So many young people are ensnared by the devil because they do not grasp the concept of the power they have to do things that cannot ever be changed and the devil deceives them into destroying their lives and often several other people's.

Did not God speak the world into existence? We, created in the image of God need to be aware of the power of our words and our great responsibility.

> John 10:34 Jesus answered them, Is it not written in your law, I said, Ye are gods?

That does not mean that we are "God" at all. But God did make man in His image and He gave man free will to do good or evil.

If this seems like a stretch consider, would you be here if a couple of people had not used their "god like" power to make a baby?

This is not something that gets preached very often and can be misunderstood, but it is important for people to realize their great power AND the responsibility and consequences that will result.

And, don't forget about that tape recorder either.

Division

Luke 12:51 Suppose ye that I am come to give peace on earth? I tell you, Nay; but rather division:

Ecclesiastes 7:5 [It is] better to hear the rebuke of the wise, than for a man to hear the song of fools.

I Timothy 5:20 Them that sin rebuke before all, that others also may fear.

II Timothy 4:2 Preach the word; be instant in season, out of season; reprove, rebuke, exhort with all longsuffering and doctrine.

Titus 1:13 This witness is true. Wherefore rebuke them sharply, that they may be sound in the faith;

Titus 2:15 These things speak, and exhort, and rebuke with all authority. Let no man despise thee.

Revelation 3:19 As many as I love, I rebuke and chasten: be zealous therefore, and repent.

Luke 13:23 Then said one unto him, Lord, are there few that be saved? And he said unto them,

Luke 13:24 Strive to enter in at the strait gate: for many, I say unto you, will seek to enter in, and shall not be able.

Luke 13:25 When once the master of the house is risen up, and hath shut to the door, and ye begin to stand without, and to knock at the door, saying, Lord, Lord, open unto us; and he shall answer and say unto you, I know you not whence ye are:

Luke 13:26 Then shall ye begin to say, We have eaten and drunk in thy presence, and thou hast taught in our streets.

Luke 13:27 But he shall say, I tell you, I know you not whence ye are; depart from me, all ye workers of iniquity.

Paul sets an example of spiritual chastity and makes some fascinating points. He plainly states that Satan is going to have his ministers pretending to be Christian ministers. God wants their to be division between the true Church and the Satanic false church.

> II Corinthians 11:12 But what I do, that I will do, that I may cut off occasion from them which desire occasion; that wherein they glory, they may be found even as we.
>
> II Corinthians 11:13 For such [are] false apostles, deceitful workers, transforming themselves into the apostles of Christ.
>
> II Corinthians 11:14 And no marvel; for Satan himself is transformed into an angel of light.
>
> II Corinthians 11:15 Therefore [it is] no great thing if his ministers also be transformed as the ministers of righteousness; whose end shall be according to their works.

The Bible does not teach that a real Christian should be tolerant towards deceivers.

> Galatians 1:8 But though we, or an angel from heaven, preach any other gospel unto you than that which we have preached unto you, let him be accursed.

Jesus was quite plain about that sort of thing and how He felt about it. So many false christians like to talk of John 3:16 as they promote their sinful false religion, but they don't like to bring up Revelation 3:16.

> Revelation 3:16 So then because thou art lukewarm, and neither cold nor hot, I will spue thee out of my mouth.

Jesus wants us to be divided from the cults that teach that there is nothing you need to obey. He has other plans for them.

> II Thessalonians 1:7 And to you who are troubled rest with us, when the Lord Jesus shall be revealed from heaven with his mighty angels,
>
> II Thessalonians 1:8 In flaming fire taking vengeance on them that know not God, and that obey not the gospel of our Lord Jesus Christ:

> II Thessalonians 1:9 Who shall be punished with everlasting destruction from the presence of the Lord, and from the glory of his power;

God wants division

> II Corinthians 11:2 For I am jealous over you with godly jealousy: forI have espoused you to one husband, that I may present [you as] a chaste virgin to Christ.
>
> II Corinthians 11:3 But I fear, lest by any means, as the serpent beguiled Eve through his subtilty, so your minds should be corrupted from the simplicity that is in Christ.

Notice that Paul fears for their LOSS OF CHASTITY and CORRUPTION

> II Corinthians 11:4 For if he that cometh preacheth another Jesus, whom we have not preached, or [if] ye receive another spirit, which ye have not received, or another gospel, which ye have not accepted, ye might well bear with [him].

Just "bearing with" a trinitarian is defined as the manifestation of whoredom and corruption (lack of chastity is "unchaste" or "whorish". One who lacks "fidelity" is an "infidel").

> II John 1:9 Whosoever transgresseth, and abideth not in the doctrine of Christ, hath not God. He that abideth in the doctrine of Christ, he hath both the Father and the Son.
>
> II John 1:10 If there come any unto you, and bring not this doctrine, receive him not into [your] house, neither bid him God speed:
>
> II John 1:11 For he that biddeth him God speed is partaker of his evil deeds.

So it is a sin to even bid "God speed" to a trinitarian or other false christian that is promoting their doctrines, and that does not mean merely the words "God speed" but it means to offer any Christian greeting or salutation.

5463 chairo khah'-ee-ro

a primary verb; TDNT - 9:359,1298; v

AV - rejoice 42, be glad 14, joy 5, hail 5, greeting 3, God speed 2, all hail 1, joyfully 1, farewell 1; 74

1) to rejoice, be glad
2) to rejoice exceedingly
3) to be well, thrive
4) in salutations, hail!
5) at the beginning of letters: to give one greeting, salute

Yes, that means that it is a SIN to offer greetings or salutations to anyone who is bringing false doctrine.

Let us look back and see what would be the symptoms of the HIGH RISK group for whoredom and infidelity.

> 2 Cor 10:12 For we dare not make ourselves of the number, or compare ourselves with some that commend themselves: but they measuring themselves by themselves, and comparing themselves among themselves, are not wise.

They COMMEND themselves this "high risk" group. They MEASURE THEMSELVES BY THEMSELVES etc .

> 2 Cor 10:17 But he that glorieth, let him glory in the Lord.
>
> 2 Cor 10:18 For not he that commendeth himself is approved, but whom the Lord commendeth.

True Love

True Love was manifest in the flesh to freely (through grace) offer man a plan of salvation.

> 1 Tim 3:16 And without controversy great is the mystery of godliness: God was manifest in the flesh, justified in the Spirit, seen of angels, preached unto the Gentiles, believed on in the world, received up into glory.

The plan of salvation (the WAY or METHOD whereby one accepts God's free offer) is :

> Acts 2:38 Then Peter said unto them, Repent, and be baptized every one of you in the name of Jesus Christ for the remission of sins, and ye shall receive the gift of the Holy Ghost.
>
> Acts 2:39 For the promise is unto you, and to your children, and to all that are afar off, even as many as the Lord our God shall call.

You must repent of your sins, you must be full immersion water baptized in Jesus name, and receive the Holy Ghost (which is ALWAYS accompanied with speaking in other tongues as the Spirit gives the utterance).

If you don't obey, and thereby reject LOVE, then LOVE is going to cast you into a lake of fire!

> 2 Th 1:7 And to you who are troubled rest with us, when the Lord Jesus shall be revealed from heaven with his mighty angels,
>
> 2 Th 1:8 In flaming fire taking vengeance on them that know not God, and that obey not the gospel of our Lord Jesus Christ:

2 Th 1:9 Who shall be punished with everlasting destruction from the presence of the Lord, and from the glory of his power;

Just WHO do YOU think that you are, that you could stand in the presence of LOVE in an unwashed, unregenerate state?? In order to STAND in the presence of LOVE, you MUST be born again of WATER AND of SPIRIT (see Acts 2:38 above!)

John 3:3 Jesus answered and said unto him, Verily , verily, I say unto thee, Except a man be born again, he cannot see the kingdom of God. John

3:5 Jesus answered, Verily , verily, I say unto thee, Except a man be born of water and of the Spirit, he cannot enter into the kingdom of God.

Did some false preacher tell you otherwise?? If you reject Christ, you won't be the first one in hell because of PRIDE!

1 John 2:16 For all that is in the world, the lust of the flesh, and the lust of the eyes, and the pride of life, is not of the Father, but is of the world.

It will be PURE LOVE that casts all Christ rejectors into a lake of fire to burn FOREVER!!

Rev 21:8 But the fearful, and unbelieving, and the abominable, and murderers, and whoremongers, and sorcerers, and idolaters, and all liars, shall have their part in the lake which burneth with fire and brimstone: which is the second death.

It's WAKE UP TIME!! Jesus is COMING SOON!!

Don't face LOVE in JUDGMENT as a filthy trinitarian CHRIST REJECTOR!!

> Acts 22:16 And now why tarriest thou? arise, and be baptized, and wash away thy sins, calling on the name of the Lord.

You "CALL" on the NAME of Jesus by being baptized in the NAME of Jesus!

> Acts 4:12 Neither is there salvation in any other: for there is none other name under heaven given among men, whereby we must be saved.

> Gal 3:27 For as many of you as have been baptized into Christ have put on Christ.

Will you face LOVE in JUDGMENT, as a CHRIST REJECTOR!!!!! or will you find a true Jesus Name / Acts 2:38 Church and OBEY the Gospel??

I hope this helps...

> 2 Tim 4:3 For the time will come when they will not endure sound doctrine; but after their own lusts shall they heap to themselves teachers, having itching ears;
>
> 2 Tim 4:4 And they shall turn away their ears from the truth, and shall be turned unto fables.

False Christianity

In this day and age may "churches" are nothing more than spiritual abortion mills Souls seeking God walk into these dens, but, instead of being born again in the true scriptural way, are poisoned against the truth of the Bible.

Wicked workers, posing as ministers of righteousness, use man-made traditions and doctrines to deceive too many honest souls, just as predicted in the Bible.

> 2 Corinthians 4:4 In whom the god of this world hath blinded the minds of them which believe not, lest the light of the glorious gospel of Christ, who is the image of God, should shine unto them.
>
> 2 Corinthians 11:13 For such are false apostles, deceitful workers, transforming themselves into the apostles of Christ.
>
> 14 And no marvel; for Satan himself is transformed into an angel of light.
>
> 15 Therefore it is no great thing if his ministers also be transformed as the ministers of righteousness; whose end shall be according to their works.

Vain

> Matthew 15:9 {But in vain they do worship me, teaching [for] doctrines the commandments of men.}
>
> Mark 7:7 {Howbeit in vain do they worship me, teaching [for] doctrines the commandments of men.}
>
> I Corinthians 15:2 By which also ye are saved, if ye keep in memory what I preached unto you, unless ye have believed in vain.

I hope that these verses will show that through manmade doctrines it is possible that a persons worship could be IN VAIN, and that a persons sincere belief could also be IN VAIN..I want to expose the "easy-believism preachers" as the accursed satanic workers that they are.

> II Timothy 3:4 Traitors, heady, highminded, lovers of pleasures more than lovers of God;
>
> II Timothy 3:5 Having a form of godliness, but denying the power thereof: from such turn away.

This is a pleasure mad generation even in many so called "churches", they "hold to the form"(in other words they go to church they have the form or ritual) but deny the power..they deny the power to quit sins, they deny tongues (which is the initial power of the Holy Ghost)

> II Timothy 3:6 For of this sort are they which creep into houses, and lead captive silly women laden with sins, led away with divers lusts,
>
> II Timothy 3:7 Ever learning, and never able to come to the knowledge of the truth.
>
> II Timothy 3:8 Now as Jannes and Jambres withstood Moses, so do these also resist the truth: men of corrupt minds, reprobate concerning the faith.

Matthew 7:15 {Beware of false prophets, which come to you in sheep's clothing, but inwardly they are ravening wolves.}

Matthew 24:11 {And many false prophets shall rise, and shall deceive many.}

I John 4:1 Beloved, believe not every spirit, but try the spirits whether they are of God: because many false prophets are gone out into the world.

II Corinthians 11:13 For such [are] false apostles, deceitful workers, transforming themselves into the apostles of Christ.

II Corinthians 11:14 And no marvel; for Satan himself is transformed into an angel of light.

II Corinthians 11:15 Therefore [it is] no great thing if his ministers also be transformed as the ministers of righteousness; whose end shall be according to their work

So Satan's ministers pretend to be Christs ministers..and oh do they speak great swelling words that appear so wise, and they deftly, and masterfully TWIST the scriptures, deceiving the masses....

II Timothy 4:2 Preach the word; be instant in season, out of season; reprove, rebuke, exhort with all longsuffering and doctrine.

II Timothy 4:3 For the time will come when they will not endure sound doctrine; but after their own lusts shall they heap to themselves teachers, having itching ears;

II Timothy 4:4 And they shall turn away [their] ears from the truth, and shall be turned unto fables.

We are at that place where men and women will not endure sound doctrine, but are elevating false preachers that will just call any doctrine "legalism" and "bondage" and will preach a fable that everyone is going to heaven if they just "believe on the Lord" and stuff like that, twisting and perverting the precious word of God....But the Bible WARNED that they would come and deceive MANY.....

> Acts 2:38 Then Peter said unto them, Repent, and be baptized every one of you in the name of Jesus Christ for the remission of sins, and ye shall receive the gift of the Holy Ghost.....
>
> Acts 2:39 For the promise is unto you, and to your children, and to all that are afar off, [even] as many as the Lord our God shall call.

AS MANY AS THE LORD OUR GOD SHALL CALL

> Galatians 1:8 But though we, or an angel from heaven, preach any other gospel unto you than that which we have preached unto you, let him be accursed.
>
> Galatians 1:9 As we said before, so say I now again, If any [man] preach any other gospel unto you than that ye have received, let him be accursed.

(the one that they had received was Acts 2:38)

Alien

"Apostolic" is not a foreign concept to the real Christian, but to many false christians it seems alien and foreign like some "other" religion. Well, for them, Biblical Christianity IS a different religion, because they are not a part of the Body of Christ.

To find out what "Apostolic" is, just study what the Apostles preached and practiced. Anything less is NOT Christianity and the purveyors of these false religions are to be accursed.

> Gal 1:8 But though we, or an angel from heaven, preach any other gospel unto you than that which we have preached unto you, let him be accursed.

> Gal 1:9 As we said before, so say I now again, If any man preach any other gospel unto you than that ye have received, let him be accursed.

So if Apostolic Biblical Christianity seems strange and alien to you, it is because you are being deceived into hell in a false christian cult. To many, the sewers of false christianity are quite comfortable. That is why they hate the real Christians and the Bible so much.

> 2 Tim 4:2 Preach the word; be instant in season, out of season; reprove, rebuke, exhort with all longsuffering and doctrine. 2 Tim 4:3 For the time will come when they will not endure sound doctrine; but after their own lusts shall they heap to themselves teachers, having itching ears;

> 2 Tim 4:3 For the time will come when they will not endure sound doctrine; but after their own lusts shall they heap to themselves teachers, having itching ears;

The Bible warns about Satan's preachers

> 2 Cor 11:13 For such are false apostles, deceitful workers, transforming themselves into the apostles of Christ.

> 2 Cor 11:14 And no marvel; for Satan himself is transformed into an angel of light.

2 Cor 11:15 Therefore it is no great thing if his ministers also be transformed as the ministers of righteousness; whose end shall be according to their works.

Here we have a clear warning against the trinity.

Col 2:8 Beware lest any man spoil you through philosophy and vain deceit, after the tradition of men, after the rudiments of the world, and not after Christ.

Col 2:9 For in him dwelleth all the fulness of the Godhead bodily.

Col 2:10 And ye are complete in him, which is the head of all principality and power:

Does this Apostolic "Jesus" Christianity seem foreign and alien to you?

If so, it just means that you are on the road to hell.

I hope this helps...

Not your friend

II Corinthians 11:14 And no marvel; for Satan himself is transformed into an angel of light.

II Corinthians 11:15 Therefore [it is] no great thing if his ministers also be transformed as the ministers of righteousness; whose end shall be according to their works.

Revelation 14:10 The same shall drink of the wine of the wrath of God, which is poured out without mixture into the cup of his indignation; and he shall be tormented with fire and brimstone in the presence of the holy angels, and in the presence of the Lamb:

Revelation 20:10 And the devil that deceived them was cast into the lake of fire and brimstone, where the beast and the false prophet [are], and shall be tormented day and night for ever and ever.

People deceived; people thinking that everything is OK when everything is NOT OK.

Revelation 21:8 But the fearful, and unbelieving, and the abominable,and murderers, and whoremongers, and sorcerers, and idolaters, and all liars, shall have their part in the lake which burneth with fire and brimstone: which is the second death.

How did the Apostles detect a "non-believer"?

Romans 2:8 But unto them that are contentious, and do not obey the truth, but obey unrighteousness, indignation and wrath,

So, there is a truth that MUST be OBEYED!

> II Thessalonians 1:7 And to you who are troubled rest with us, when the Lord Jesus shall be revealed from heaven with his mighty angels,
>
> II Thessalonians 1:8 In flaming fire taking vengeance on them that know not God, and that obey not the gospel of our Lord Jesus Christ:

So, there is a Gospel that MUST be OBEYED!

> Hebrews 5:9 And being made perfect, he became the author of eternal salvation unto all them that obey him;

> Acts 2:41 Then they that gladly received his word were baptized: and the same day there were added unto them about three thousand souls.

> Acts 8:12 But when they believed Philip preaching the things concerning the kingdom of God, and the name of Jesus Christ, they were baptized, both men and women.

Here is the answer.

> Romans 10:16 But they have not all obeyed the gospel. For Esaias saith, Lord, who hath believed our report?

The Word of God labels "non-obeyers" as "non-believers".

Yet we have entire denominations and an entire "christian industry" that are taught that they do not need to "obey" anything. Why is that?

Well, let us look at how and why Paul related as he did to false preachers.

> II Corinthians 11:12 But what I do, that I will do, that I may cut off occasion from them which desire occasion; that wherein they glory, they may be found even as we.
>
> II Corinthians 11:13 For such [are] false apostles, deceitful workers, transforming themselves into the apostles of Christ.
>
> II Corinthians 11:14 And no marvel; for Satan himself is transformed into an angel of light.
>
> II Corinthians 11:15 Therefore [it is] no great thing if his ministers also be transformed as the ministers of righteousness; whose end shall be according to their works.

So, we see that it is the devil's business to produce counterfeit preachers. Oh they can use such great swelling words and claims of "luv" to explain to you why you don't need to obey Acts 2:38, but the kind reassuring smile of the trinity preacher will be seen in a completely different light when illuminated by the flames of hell.

How does the Word of God command Christians to relate to false preachers?

> Galatians 1:8 But though we, or an angel from heaven, preach any other gospel unto you than that which we have preached unto you, let him be accursed.

What is clearly the end for all who are convinced by their false preacher that they need not obey the Gospel?

> II Thessalonians 1:7 And to you who are troubled rest with us, when the Lord Jesus shall be revealed from heaven with his mighty angels,
>
> II Thessalonians 1:8 In flaming fire taking vengeance on them that know not God, and that obey not the gospel of our Lord Jesus Christ:

> II Thessalonians 1:9 Who shall be punished with everlasting destruction from the presence of the Lord, and from the glory of his power;

The false preacher is not your friend as they labor to convince you why you don't need to obey the Bible.

> Hebrews 11:7 By faith Noah, being warned of God of things not seen as yet, moved with fear, prepared an ark to the saving of his house; by the which he condemned the world, and became heir of the righteousness which is by faith.

By FAITH Noah OBEYED. Noah found grace, but he STILL had to OBEY in order to benefit.

> Hebrews 11:8 By faith Abraham, when he was called to go out into a place which he should after receive for an inheritance, obeyed; and he went out, not knowing whither he went.

Abraham was counted faithful because he OBEYED

> James 1:22 But be ye doers of the word, and not hearers only, deceiving your own selves.

James phrased it rather clearly, didn't he?

Consider the plan of salvation for "as many as the Lord our God shall call.

> Acts 2:38 Then Peter said unto them, Repent, and be baptized every one of you in the name of Jesus Christ for the remission of sins, and ye shall receive the gift of the Holy Ghost.

> Acts 2:39 For the promise is unto you, and to your children, and to all that are afar off, [even] as many as the Lord our God shall call.

Not your friend

The false preacher is not your friend, there is a price.

> Mark 9:43 And if thy hand offend thee, cut it off: it is better for thee to enter into life maimed, than having two hands to go into hell, into the fire that never shall be quenched:
>
> Mark 9:44 Where their worm dieth not, and the fire is not quenched.

So some of the Satanic preachers teach there is no hell or that you would just burn up and be gone, don't count on it...

> Mark 9:45 And if thy foot offend thee, cut it off: it is better for thee to enter halt into life, than having two feet to be cast into hell, into the fire that never shall be quenched:
>
> Mark 9:46 Where their worm dieth not, and the fire is not quenched.
>
> Mark 9:47 And if thine eye offend thee, pluck it out: it is better for thee to enter into the kingdom of God with one eye, than having two eyes to be cast into hell fire:
>
> Mark 9:48 Where their worm dieth not, and the fire is not quenched.

The trinity preacher is NOT your friend.

So how does one obey the Gospel?

The gospel is the death, burial, and resurrection of the Lord Jesus Christ. This gospel (good news) is to be preached in all nations (beginning at Jerusalem). The gospel was first preached at Jerusalem on the day of Pentecost.

All are commanded to OBEY the gospel:

> 2 Th 1:8 In flaming fire taking vengeance on them that know not God, and that obey not the gospel of our Lord Jesus Christ:
>
> 1 Pet 4:17 For the time is come that judgment must begin at the house of God: and if it first begin at us, what shall the end be of them that obey not the gospel of God?

How does one OBEY the death, burial, and resurrection?

> John 3:5 Jesus answered, Verily , verily, I say unto thee, Except a man be born of water and of the Spirit, he cannot enter into the kingdom of God.

Of course if someone did not believe, they would have no desire to obey..Jesus told Nicodemus a couple of very important things in John 3:16 and John 3:5, he said that those who believeth SHOULD not perish. He had just told Nicodemus that he HAD to be born AGAIN two ways. One water, one of Spirit. What does water and spirit have to do with the gospel? Well the first gospel sermon preached to sinners was:

> Acts 2:38 Then Peter said unto them, Repent, and be baptized every one of you in the name of Jesus Christ for the remission of sins, and ye shall receive the gift of the Holy Ghost.

Here we are: water (baptism) and Spirit (the gift of the Holy Ghost)..and in repentance a person dies to sin..the old man dies. The Bible says that we are buried with Christ in baptism or baptized into his death.

> Colossians 2:12 Buried with him in baptism, wherein also ye are risen with him through the faith of the operation of God, who hath raised him from the dead.

You obey burial by Jesus Name Water Baptism.

The Holy Ghost is Christ in you the hope of glory ... the hope of resurrection.

> Rom 8:9 But ye are not in the flesh, but in the Spirit, if so be that the Spirit of God dwell in you. Now if any man have not the Spirit of Christ, he is none of his.

So there you have death, burial, and resurrection, the gospel. You also have the way that the apostles taught to obey it.

You obey death through repentance, burial through Jesus Name Baptism and the resurrection through the Baptism of the Holy Spirit.

Not your friend

Have you obeyed the gospel of the Lord Jesus Christ?

The false preacher is NOT your friend. Hell will be hot and eternity long.

> Mark 9:48 Where their worm dieth not, and the fire is not quenched.

> Matthew7:22 Many will say to me in that day, Lord, Lord, have we not prophesied in thy name? and in thy name have cast out devils? and in thy name done many wonderful works?
>
> 23 And then will I profess unto them, I never knew you: depart from me, ye that work iniquity.

Claimers

There appears to be a lot of confusion coming from people who are claiming to be "christians" even though they never obeyed Acts 2:38. This is quite understandable since there are so many false preachers making money convincing people that a mere 'claim to believe' fills the Biblical criteria for salvation. The Bible predicted that this would happen.

> II Timothy 4:3 For the time will come when they will not endure sound doctrine; but after their own lusts shall they heap to themselves teachers, having itching ears;
>
> II Timothy 4:4 And they shall turn away [their] ears from the truth, and shall be turned unto fables.

The Bible shows us that there will be fake ministers. The job of the fake is simply to convince people that God need not be obeyed. A way to keep souls from obeying God and really becoming Christian is simply to convince them that they already are "christian" and then chain them by their own pride.

> II Corinthians 11:14 And no marvel; for Satan himself is transformed into an angel of light.
>
> II Corinthians 11:15 Therefore [it is] no great thing if his ministers also be transformed as the ministers of righteousness; whose end shall be according to their works.

The Bible is perfectly clear that Acts 2:38 is the plan for as many as God will call. The epistles are simply letters to folks who obeyed Acts 2:38.

> Acts 2:38 Then Peter said unto them, Repent, and be baptized every one of you in the name of Jesus Christ for the remission of sins, and ye shall receive the gift of the Holy Ghost.
>
> Acts 2:39 For the promise is unto you, and to your children, and to all that are afar off, [even] as many as the Lord our God shall call.

Paul mentioned how we should react to those that teach otherwise:

> Gal 1:8 But though we, or an angel from heaven, preach any other gospel unto you than that which we have preached unto you, let him be accursed.

Jesus also warned.

> Matthew7:22 Many will say to me in that day, Lord, Lord, have we not prophesied in thy name? and in thy name have cast out devils? and in thy name done many wonderful works?
>
> 23 And then will I profess unto them, I never knew you: depart from me, ye that work iniquity.

Cling

I am somewhat surprised by the attitudes of many that are the victims of false preachers. They appear to have a verse or two that they misunderstand, yet they cling violently to their misunderstandings while ignoring the verses that describe their false preachers.

> II Corinthians 11:13 For such [are] false apostles, deceitful workers, transforming themselves into the apostles of Christ.
>
> II Corinthians 11:14 And no marvel; for Satan himself is transformed into an angel of light.
>
> II Corinthians 11:15 Therefore [it is] no great thing if his ministers also be transformed as the ministers of righteousness; whose end shall be according to their works.

Somehow these false preachers have convinced them that their "claim to believe" supersedes any clear commandment, which they will then ignorantly label as "legalistic". It is that scenario and other false teachings that the Bible says would have APPEAL to those who don't wish to be bothered with the truth.

> II Timothy 4:2 Preach the word; be instant in season, out of season; reprove, rebuke, exhort with all longsuffering and doctrine.
>
> II Timothy 4:3 For the time will come when they will not endure sound doctrine; but after their own lusts shall they heap to themselves teachers, having itching ears;
>
> II Timothy 4:4 And they shall turn away [their] ears from the truth, and shall be turned unto fables.

People in false churches don't want to "hear the Word", they want more sweet sounding fables about how they are "saved" even though they often haven't even begun to meet the Biblical criteria for salvation. The false preachers have so twisted their minds that I believe some are actually afraid to obey the Bible for fear of losing their "fable religion". What they need to understand is that these "fable denominal religions" do NOT lead anywhere but hell.

> Matthew 15:14 Let them alone: they be blind leaders of the blind. And if the blind lead the blind, both shall fall into the ditch.
>
> Luke 6:39 And he spake a parable unto them, Can the blind lead the blind? shall they not both fall into the ditch?

The sweet reassuring smile of the denominal trinitarian preacher will appear in a whole new light when illuminated by the lake of fire.

So many wrestle with the scripture, but remain in false doctrine.

> II Peter 3:12 Looking for and hasting unto the coming of the day of God, wherein the heavens being on fire shall be dissolved, and the elements shall melt with fervent heat.
>
> II Peter 3:13 Nevertheless we, according to his promise, look for new heavens and a new earth, wherein dwelleth righteousness.
>
> II Peter 3:14 Wherefore, beloved, seeing that ye look for such things, be diligent that ye may be found of him in peace, without spot, and blameless.
>
> II Peter 3:15 And account [that] the longsuffering of our Lord [is] salvation; even as our beloved brother Paul also according to the wisdom given unto him hath written unto you;
>
> * * * * * * * * *
>
> II Peter 3:16 As also in all [his] epistles, speaking in them of these things; in which are some things hard to be understood, which they that are unlearned and unstable wrest, as [they do] also the other scriptures, unto their own destruction.
>
> * * * * * * * * *
>
> II Peter 3:17 Ye therefore, beloved, seeing ye know [these things] before, beware lest ye also, being led away with the error of the wicked, fall from your own stedfastness.

Many false Christians do much study, but are unable to see basic truths, people actually believe that they can be Christian without the Baptism of the Holy Ghost, or they claim to have the Holy Ghost even though they've never spoken in tongues. They really think that their misunderstanding of the scriptures concerning "belief" and "believeth" will save them; and they use that to ignore the truth of the Word of God. They mock at the basic Biblical teachings of holy living and decency, preferring the standards of the "world". And they brazenly lead their families to hell.

> II Timothy 3:7 Ever learning, and never able to come to the knowledge of the truth.
>
> II Timothy 3:8 Now as Jannes and Jambres withstood Moses, so do these also resist the truth: men of corrupt minds, reprobate concerning the faith.
>
> II Timothy 3:13 But evil men and seducers shall wax worse and worse, deceiving, and being deceived.
>
> II Timothy 3:14 But continue thou in the things which thou hast learned and hast been assured of, knowing of whom thou hast learned [them];
>
> II Timothy 3:15 And that from a child thou hast known the holy scriptures, which are able to make thee wise unto salvation through faith which is in Christ Jesus.
>
> II Timothy 3:16 All scripture [is] given by inspiration of God, and [is] profitable for doctrine, for reproof, for correction, for instruction in righteousness:

* Some just want the scriptures that speak of belief, and feel that they can ignore the rest, at will; but they are not really honest. Often they just feel in their hearts that they are "saved" even though they have never really obeyed Acts 2:38. God uses a special word to describe people like that:*

> PRO 28:26 He that trusteth in his own heart is a fool: but whoso walketh wisely, he shall be delivered.

See what God has to say about those who wrest with the scripture rather than simply obeying it because they just know in their heart that they are saved? Did you see what God calls people like that?

Devil

I have noticed a different approach in several of Satan's ministers that I believe is notable. I guess that Satan is noticing that people are starting to read in the book of Acts (in most false churches "Acts" is just a mysterious, obscure book that they just kinda glaze over).

Now that people are starting to take a second look at the book of Acts, Satan's servants are starting to teach that Peter and the rest of the apostles disobeyed Jesus. Now they must really be going after fools as a last ditch effort, because it was the apostles that wrote down Jesus' words in the Bible.

Believe me, when they try to build a case to defend a modern false religion by teaching that the apostles disobeyed Jesus, but that *they* in their great wisdom really know God, they are canvassing for fools.

They know a "god" alright, but it is the god of this world that blinds the eyes of pride filled men. They are simply teaching different religion than the religion of Jesus Christ. They may quote a scripture or two, but they handle the Word of God deceitfully. They even quote the apostles as "evidence" to try to build their case that the apostles weren't really of God, but that they in their anti-apostolic religions have the "true way". (you may have noticed that they teach a "broad road")

> II Corinthians 4:1 Therefore seeing we have this ministry, as we have received mercy, we faint not;
>
> II Corinthians 4:2 But have renounced the hidden things of dishonesty, not walking in craftiness, nor handling the word of God deceitfully; but by manifestation of the truth commending ourselves to every man's conscience in the sight of God.
>
> II Corinthians 4:3 But if our gospel be hid, it is hid to them that are lost:
>
> II Corinthians 4:4 In whom the god of this world hath blinded the minds of them which believe not, lest the light of the

> glorious gospel of Christ, who is the image of God, should shine unto them.
>
> II Corinthians 4:5 For we preach not ourselves, but Christ Jesus the Lord; and ourselves your servants for Jesus' sake.

I believe that we should take the word of Jesus' apostles over the word of modern Satanic filth.

It's the same old thing, are they twisting the Bible to try to teach why it doesn't need to be obeyed? OR are they preaching the necessity of obeying God? Don't be deceived by Satan's "verbose" ministers.

> Acts 2:38 Then Peter said unto them, Repent, and be baptized every one of you in the name of Jesus Christ for the remission of sins, and ye shall receive the gift of the Holy Ghost.
>
> Acts 2:39 For the promise is unto you, and to your children, and to all that are afar off, [even] as many as the Lord our God shall call.

> Galatians 1:8 But though we, or an angel from heaven, preach any other gospel unto you than that which we have preached unto you, let him be accursed.

> Acts 22:16 And now why tarriest thou? arise, and be baptized, and wash away thy sins, calling on the name of the Lord.

Hand

I'd like to also address the point regarding "right hand". "Right hand" symbolizes "POWER" and not a physical hand. To prove that point I offer these verses:

> John 4:24 God is a Spirit: and they that worship him must worship him in spirit and in truth.
>
> Luke 24:39 Behold my hands and my feet, that it is I myself: handle me, and see; for a spirit hath not flesh and bones, as ye see me have.

Now we must keep in mind that Jesus was Jehovah manifest in the flesh:

> Tim 3:16 And without controversy great is the mystery of godliness: God was manifest in the flesh, justified in the Spirit, seen of angels, preached unto the Gentiles, believed on in the world, received up into glory.

As an aside, do you really envision a big ole finger hanging out of the clouds when you read the following verse?

> Luke 11:20 But if I with the finger of God cast out devils, no doubt the kingdom of God is come upon you.

Now, let's look at the verse that false preachers use to deceive good folks like yourself:

> Acts 7:55 But he, being full of the Holy Ghost, looked up stedfastly into heaven, and saw the glory of God, and Jesus standing on the right hand of God,

Now, though, we have ALSO the "glory of God" standing on that hand. Do the trinitarians now apply "personhood" to a fourth separate "glory of God" personager?

Oops! Here we have yet another individual sitting on that big 'ole hand:

> Psa 63:8 My soul followeth hard after thee: thy right hand upholdeth me.

Now, does the above verse place David sitting with Jesus on the hand? Or does it symbolize POWER? If you have ANY doubts about "right hand" meaning power, read this next verse:

> Mark 14:62 And Jesus said, I am: and ye shall see the Son of man sitting on the right hand of power, and coming in the clouds of heaven.

Now, some false preacher has taught you that one junior member of a Roman god squad is sitting on the hand of another god squad member. Now that you see the folly, are you STILL going to follow that trinitarian preacher(s) into the flames of hell?

> 2 Cor 11:13 For such are false apostles, deceitful workers, transforming themselves into the apostles of Christ.
>
> 2 Cor 11:14 And no marvel; for Satan himself is transformed into an angel of light.
>
> 2 Cor 11:15 Therefore it is no great thing if his ministers also be transformed as the ministers of righteousness; whose end shall be according to their works.

Jesus Only

Many of the false preachers from the "three god" churches will use God's name in what they perceive to be a derogatory term. They say that the one God church is "Jesus only" and their victims are conditioned to react "Oh, yeah, "Jesus only"...

Well, if they aren't worshiping "only Jesus", just WHO are those deceivers worshiping, eh? Think about it! When the Christ rejecting trinity cults try to INSULT the real Christians by calling them "Jesus only"; the trinitarians actually EXPOSE themselves as the Christ rejectors that they are!!

> 2 Cor 4:3 But if our gospel be hid, it is hid to them that are lost:
>
> 2 Cor 4:4 In whom the god of this world hath blinded the minds of them which believe not, lest the light of the glorious gospel of Christ, who is the image of God, should shine unto them.
>
> 2 Cor 4:5 For we preach not ourselves, but Christ Jesus the Lord; and ourselves your servants for Jesus' sake.

Satanic deceivers HATE the name of Jesus in baptism!

> Matthew 10:22 And ye shall be hated of all [men] for my name's sake: but he that endureth to the end shall be saved.
>
> Matthew 24:9 Then shall they deliver you up to be afflicted, and shall kill you: and ye shall be hated of all nations for my name's sake.
>
> Mark 13:13 And ye shall be hated of all [men] for my name's sake: but he that shall endure unto the end, the same shall be saved.
>
> Luke 21:17 And ye shall be hated of all [men] for my name's sake.

The false christians hate the name of Jesus so much that they perceive it to be an INSULT to call someone "Jesus only". That ALSO exposes them as POLYTHEISTIC, regardless of vain claims to the contrary.

> Acts 4:12 Neither is there salvation in any other: for there is none other name under heaven given among men, whereby we must be saved.
>
> Ephesians 4:5 One Lord, one faith, one baptism,

And so they take the Lord's name in vain, and use God's name as an insult..Of course Jesus told us (the true Church) that we would be hated "FOR HIS NAME'S SAKE"...The false "three mystery god's of Babylon"(that's where the trinity originated, long before Christ) churches HATE baptism in Jesus name......they hate the name of Jesus so bad that they use it as an insult "Jesus only" they say....so they really don't believe that Jesus is God....they claim to be Christian, but they lie (their father is the father of lies) They are the harlot daughters of a three god whore:

> Revelation 17:1 And there came one of the seven angels which had the seven vials, and talked with me, saying unto me, Come hither; I will shew unto thee the judgment of the great whore that sitteth upon many waters:

The RCC sits on many waters (it's international).

> Revelation 17:2 With whom the kings of the earth have committed fornication, and the inhabitants of the earth have been made drunk with the wine of her fornication.

Many kings and nations deceived by the three god religious system with its "indulgences" and other abominations.

> Revelation 17:3 So he carried me away in the spirit into the wilderness: and I saw a woman sit upon a scarlet coloured beast, full of names of blasphemy, having seven heads and ten horns.

> Revelation 17:4 And the woman was arrayed in purple and scarlet colour, and decked with gold and precious stones and pearls, having a golden cup in her hand full of abominations and filthiness of her fornication:

The pomp and regalia and scarlet robes of the RCC.

> Revelation 17:5 And upon her forehead [was] a name written, MYSTERY, BABYLON THE GREAT, THE MOTHER OF HARLOTS AND ABOMINATIONS OF THE EARTH.

The harlots are ALL trinitarian denominations. All protestant churches are merely wayward harlot daughters of the GREAT WHORE.

> Revelation 17:6 And I saw the woman drunken with the blood of the saints, and with the blood of the martyrs of Jesus: and when I saw her, I wondered with great admiration.

No false church has murdered true Apostolic Christians like the RCC and her harlot daughters.

That is why these false preachers can use the name of God Himself as an insult, they are the harlot daughters of a Great Whore.

Don't be Deceived! The Bible says that the fullness of the Godhead dwelt in Him (Jesus) bodily, and YE ARE COMPLETE IN HIM... He is coming soon, in the clouds for those that LOVE His NAME, and have obeyed His word.

> Colossians 2:6 As ye have therefore received Christ Jesus the Lord, [so] walk ye in him:
>
> Colossians 2:7 Rooted and built up in him, and stablished in the faith, as ye have been taught, abounding therein with thanksgiving.

> Colossians 2:8 Beware lest any man spoil you through philosophy and vain deceit, after the tradition of men, after the rudiments of the world, and not after Christ.
>
> Colossians 2:9 For in him dwelleth all the fulness of the Godhead bodily.
>
> Colossians 2:10 And ye are complete in him, which is the head of all principality and power:

And the false-christians will accuse and mock and say "Jesus Only"; thus betraying their whorish roots and polytheism.

The true bride of Jesus Christ is the bride of one husband only!

The true bride of Jesus Christ is the bride of only Jesus!

Notice below that it says "he" singular.

> Revelation 1:7 Behold, he cometh with clouds; and every eye shall see him, and they also which pierced him: and all kindreds of the earth shall wail because of him. Even so, Amen.
>
> Revelation 1:8 I am Alpha and Omega, the beginning and the ending, saith the Lord, which is, and which was, and which is to come, the Almighty.
>
> Revelation 1:11 Saying, I am Alpha and Omega, the first and the last: and, What thou seest, write in a book, and send it unto the seven churches which are in Asia; unto Ephesus, and unto Smyrna, and unto Pergamos, and unto Thyatira, and unto Sardis, and unto Philadelphia, and unto Laodicea.
>
> Revelation 21:6 And he said unto me, It is done. I am Alpha and Omega, the beginning and the end. I will give unto him that is athirst of the fountain of the water of life freely.
>
> Revelation 22:13 I am Alpha and Omega, the beginning and the end, the first and the last.
>
> John 14:6 Jesus saith unto him, I am the way, the truth, and the life: no man cometh unto the Father, but by me.

John 14:9 Jesus saith unto him, Have I been so long time with you, and yet hast thou not known me, Philip? he that hath seen me hath seen the Father; and how sayest thou then, Shew us the Father?

Blind

Isaiah 9:16 For the leaders of this people cause [them] to err; and [they that are] led of them [are] destroyed.

Isaiah 9:17 Therefore the Lord shall have no joy in their young men, neither shall have mercy on their fatherless and widows: for every one [is] an hypocrite and an evildoer, and every mouth speaketh folly. For all this his anger is not turned away, but his hand [is] stretched out still.

Isaiah 56:10 His watchmen [are] blind: they are all ignorant, they [are] all dumb dogs, they cannot bark; sleeping, lying down, loving to slumber.

Isaiah 56:11 Yea, [they are] greedy dogs [which] can never have enough, and they [are] shepherds [that] cannot understand: they all look to their own way, every one for his gain, from his quarter.

Jeremiah 5:27 As a cage is full of birds, so [are] their houses full of deceit: therefore they are become great, and waxen rich.

Jeremiah 5:28 They are waxen fat, they shine: yea, they overpass the deeds of the wicked: they judge not the cause, the cause of the fatherless, yet they prosper; and the right of the needy do they not judge.

Jeremiah 5:29 Shall I not visit for these [things]? saith the LORD: shall not my soul be avenged on such a nation as this?

Jeremiah 5:30 A wonderful and horrible thing is committed in the land;

Jeremiah 5:31 The prophets prophesy falsely, and the priests bear rule by their means; and my people love [to have it] so: and what will ye do in the end thereof?

Jeremiah 6:13 For from the least of them even unto the greatest of them every one [is] given to covetousness; and from the prophet even unto the priest every one dealeth falsely.

Jeremiah 6:14 They have healed also the hurt [of the daughter] of my people slightly, saying, Peace, peace; when [there is] no peace.

Jeremiah 6:15 Were they ashamed when they had committed abomination? nay, they were not at all ashamed, neither could they blush: therefore they shall fall among them that fall: at the time [that] I visit them they shall be cast down, saith the LORD.

Jeremiah 6:16 Thus saith the LORD, Stand ye in the ways, and see, and ask for the old paths, where [is] the good way, and walk therein, and ye shall find rest for your souls. But they said, We will not walk [therein].

Jeremiah 6:17 Also I set watchmen over you, [saying], Hearken to the sound of the trumpet. But they said, We will not hearken.

Jeremiah 6:18 Therefore hear, ye nations, and know, O congregation, what [is] among them.

Jeremiah 6:19 Hear, O earth: behold, I will bring evil upon this people, [even] the fruit of their thoughts, because they have not hearkened unto my words, nor to my law, but rejected it.

Jeremiah 8:8 How do ye say, We [are] wise, and the law of the LORD [is] with us? Lo, certainly in vain made he [it]; the pen of the scribes [is] in vain.

Jeremiah 8:9 The wise [men] are ashamed, they are dismayed and taken: lo, they have rejected the word of the LORD; and what wisdom [is] in them?

Jeremiah 8:10 Therefore will I give their wives unto others, [and] their fields to them that shall inherit [them]: for every one from the least even unto the greatest is given to covetousness, from the prophet even unto the priest every one dealeth falsely.

Jeremiah 8:11 For they have healed the hurt of the daughter of my people slightly, saying, Peace, peace; when [there is] no peace.

Jeremiah 8:12 Were they ashamed when they had committed abomination? nay, they were not at all ashamed, neither could they blush: therefore shall they fall among them that fall: in the time of their visitation they shall be cast down, saith the LORD.

Ezekiel 14:7 For every one of the house of Israel, or of the stranger that sojourneth in Israel, which separateth himself from me, and setteth up his idols in his heart, and putteth the stumblingblock of his iniquity before his face, and cometh to a prophet to inquire of him concerning me; I the LORD will answer him by myself:

Ezekiel 14:8 And I will set my face against that man, and will make him a sign and a proverb, and I will cut him off from the midst of my people; and ye shall know that I [am] the LORD.

Ezekiel 14:9 And if the prophet be deceived when he hath spoken a thing, I the LORD have deceived that prophet, and I will stretch out my hand upon him, and will destroy him from the midst of my people Israel.

Ezekiel 14:10 And they shall bear the punishment of their iniquity: the punishment of the prophet shall be even as the punishment of him that seeketh [unto him];

Ezekiel 14:11 That the house of Israel may go no more astray from me, neither be polluted any more with all their transgressions; but that they may be my people, and I may be their God, saith the Lord GOD.

Ezekiel 14:6 Therefore say unto the house of Israel, Thus saith the Lord GOD; Repent, and turn [yourselves] from your idols; and turn away your faces from all your abominations.

Luke 6:39 And he spake a parable unto them, Can the blind lead the blind? shall they not both fall into the ditch?

I Timothy 6:5 Perverse disputings of men of corrupt minds, and destitute of the truth, supposing that gain is godliness: from such withdraw thyself.

II Peter 2:1 But there were false prophets also among the people, even as there shall be false teachers among you, who privily shall bring in damnable heresies, even denying the Lord that bought them, and bring upon themselves swift destruction.

II Peter 2:17 These are wells without water, clouds that are carried with a tempest; to whom the mist of darkness is reserved for ever.

Legalism

I guess that the "legalism" cop out is about the most foolish error of the false christian today, but oh how they ignorantly cling to their error.

What a beautiful cop out that just seems to "cancel" any commandment or teaching of the Bible that doesn't tickle their carnal, unregenerate fancy. It is only effective for fools, though, because the scenario that is actual legalism is a scenario of a Judaiser attempting to teach a Gentile that they need to obey the ceremonial Jewish law.

It is only by obeying Acts 2:38 that a person avails themselves of the grace of God and frees their soul from the curse of the law.

The Acts 2:38 plan of salvation is not the "law", but rather it is the door where one can freely escape the debt of the law by having their sins remitted through Jesus Name baptism.

> Mat 5:18 For verily I say unto you, Till heaven and earth pass, one jot or one tittle shall in no wise pass from the law, till all be fulfilled.

Another cry of fools when confronted with the clear teaching of their Bible is that they will whine "Oh, you're just dotting 'I's and crossing 't's", but just look at what Jesus said after verse 18.

> Matthew 5:19 Whosoever therefore shall break one of these least commandments, and shall teach men so, he shall be called the least in the kingdom of heaven: but whosoever shall do and teach [them], the same shall be called great in the kingdom of heaven.

> Matthew 5:20 For I say unto you, That except your righteousness shall exceed [the righteousness] of the scribes and Pharisees, ye shall in no case enter into the kingdom of heaven.

Another consideration is that the scribes and the Pharisees were *very* righteous, disciplined, and holy living people (and they did it without the infilling of the Holy Spirit). When a crowd that had just murdered Jesus Christ and were aware of the "law" asked what they could do (to be saved), Peter preached Acts 2:38 (for as many as God would call).

> Acts 2:38 Then Peter said unto them, Repent, and be baptized every one of you in the name of Jesus Christ for the remission of sins, and ye shall receive the gift of the Holy Ghost.
>
> Acts 2:39 For the promise is unto you, and to your children, and to all that are afar off, [even] as many as the Lord our God shall call.
>
> Acts 2:40 And with many other words did he testify and exhort, saying, Save yourselves from this untoward generation.

One "saves themselves" by obeying Acts 2:38, which is offered as a free gift, and obeyed by FAITH of those that receive the Word of God.

> Acts 2:41 Then they that gladly received his word were baptized: and the same day there were added [unto them] about three thousand souls.

Acts 2:38 is not "legalism", but rather, YOUR ONLY HOPE of avoiding the debt of the law by availing yourself of Jesus's substitutionary payment that is offered to all who will obey.

(Salvation is only to "obeyers").

> Hebrews 5:9 And being made perfect, he became the author of eternal salvation unto all them that obey him;
>
> Matthew 5:17 Think not that I am come to destroy the law, or the prophets: I am not come to destroy, but to fulfil.

The teachings in the epistles are not "legalism" but instructions and warnings to souls who have obeyed Acts 2:38 to become Christians.

> Hebrews 10:26 For if we sin wilfully after that we have received the knowledge of the truth, there remaineth no more sacrifice for sins,
>
> Hebrews 10:27 But a certain fearful looking for of judgment and fiery indignation, which shall devour the adversaries.
>
> Hebrews 10:28 He that despised Moses' law died without mercy under two or three witnesses:
>
> Hebrews 10:29 Of how much sorer punishment, suppose ye, shall he be thought worthy, who hath trodden under foot the Son of God, and hath counted the blood of the covenant, wherewith he was sanctified, an unholy thing, and hath done despite unto the Spirit of grace?
>
> Hebrews 10:30 For we know him that hath said, Vengeance [belongeth] unto me, I will recompense, saith the Lord. And again, The Lord shall judge his people.
>
> Hebrews 10:31 [It is] a fearful thing to fall into the hands of the living God.

Paul warned that the devil would present his deceivers as "preachers".

> II Corinthians 11:12 But what I do, that I will do, that I may cut off occasion from them which desire occasion; that wherein they glory, they may be found even as we.
>
> II Corinthians 11:13 For such [are] false apostles, deceitful workers, transforming themselves into the apostles of Christ.
>
> II Corinthians 11:14 And no marvel; for Satan himself is transformed into an angel of light.
>
> II Corinthians 11:15 Therefore [it is] no great thing if his ministers also be transformed as the ministers of righteousness; whose end shall be according to their works.

Paul also said that people would desire false doctrines (like the fool's cry "legalism" and other false "easy believism" doctrines).

> II Timothy 4:3 For the time will come when they will not endure sound doctrine; but after their own lusts shall they heap to themselves teachers, having itching ears;
>
> II Timothy 4:4 And they shall turn away [their] ears from the truth, and shall be turned unto fables.

Sky Santa

In prayer my heart ached, would it not be wonderful if the "santa in the sky" trinity religion were true and all of the people in the trinity churches and all but the worst of the worst were going to be lovingly welcomed into heaven. Wouldn't it be so much easier for me to be able to embrace all of the trinitarians as brethren and go play music in their churches. No more of the malicious and vicious hateful actions against me by various trinitarians and reprobates, just one big happy family waiting for heaven....

BUT, it is WRITTEN!!!

> Mark 12:29 And Jesus answered him, The first of all the commandments is, Hear, O Israel; The Lord our God is one Lord

How can I be saved if I reject the first of all the commandments?

How can I be saved if I choose the approval of men above the Word of God as so many reprobates have?

> Ezekiel 33:1 ¶ Again the word of the LORD came unto me, saying,
>
> 2 Son of man, speak to the children of thy people, and say unto them, When I bring the sword upon a land, if the people of the land take a man of their coasts, and set him for their watchman:
>
> 3 If when he seeth the sword come upon the land, he blow the trumpet, and warn the people;
>
> 4 Then whosoever heareth the sound of the trumpet, and taketh not warning; if the sword come, and take him away, his blood shall be upon his own head.
>
> 5 He heard the sound of the trumpet, and took not warning; his blood shall be upon him. But he that taketh warning shall deliver his soul.

6 But if the watchman see the sword come, and blow not the trumpet, and the people be not warned; if the sword come, and take any person from among them, he is taken away in his iniquity; but his blood will I require at the watchman's hand.

7 So thou, O son of man, I have set thee a watchman unto the house of Israel; therefore thou shalt hear the word at my mouth, and warn them from me.

8 When I say unto the wicked, O wicked man, thou shalt surely die; if thou dost not speak to warn the wicked from his way, that wicked man shall die in his iniquity; but his blood will I require at thine hand.

9 Nevertheless, if thou warn the wicked of his way to turn from it; if he do not turn from his way, he shall die in his iniquity; but thou hast delivered thy soul.

I cannot take the easy way! I cannot preach the "santa claus in the sky" false-christianity to scratch itching ears and become popular.

2 Timothy 4:2 Preach the word; be instant in season, out of season; reprove, rebuke, exhort with all longsuffering and doctrine.

3 For the time will come when they will not endure sound doctrine; but after their own lusts shall they heap to themselves teachers, having itching ears;

4 And they shall turn away their ears from the truth, and shall be turned unto fables.

The "santa in the sky" religion of the trinitarian is the religion of the prince of the power of the air! You wonder why the broadcast airways are so full of false-christian doctrines of devils?

The "santa in the sky" is the prince of the power of the air!

Ephesians 2:2 Wherein in time past ye walked according to the course of this world, according to the prince of the power of the air, the spirit that now worketh in the children of disobedience:

> 3 Among whom also we all had our conversation in times past in the lusts of our flesh, fulfilling the desires of the flesh and of the mind; and were by nature the children of wrath, even as others.

The santa in the sky trinity religion will let you believe that to obey the Word of the Lord is "legalism".

> 2 Peter 2:19 While they promise them liberty, they themselves are the servants of corruption: for of whom a man is overcome, of the same is he brought in bondage.

The world loves their santa in the sky trinity religion

> Colossians 2:8 Beware lest any man spoil you through philosophy and vain deceit, after the tradition of men, after the rudiments of the world, and not after Christ.
>
> 9 For in him dwelleth all the fulness of the Godhead bodily.
>
> 10 And ye are complete in him, which is the head of all principality and power:

The world loves their santa in the sky preachers!

> 1 John 4:4 ¶ Ye are of God, little children, and have overcome them: because greater is he that is in you, than he that is in the world.
>
> 5 They are of the world: therefore speak they of the world, and the world heareth them.

Kind reassurances whispered to a man asleep in a burning building is not "love", but to so many in the false-christian "sky santa" trinity churches, that is how they have come to define "love".

It would be so easy to join with the santa preachers, but LOVE will NOT allow it!

> 2 John 1:6 And this is love, that we walk after his commandments. This is the commandment, That, as ye have heard from the beginning, ye should walk in it.

I really wish I was wrong, oh how much easier life would be for me.... But I have a calling, I was bought with a price!

> 2 Timothy 4:2 Preach the word; be instant in season, out of season; reprove, rebuke, exhort with all longsuffering and doctrine.
>
> 1 Corinthians 6:20 For ye are bought with a price: therefore glorify God in your body, and in your spirit, which are God's.
>
> 1 Corinthians 7:23 Ye are bought with a price; be not ye the servants of men.
>
> Titus 1:9 Holding fast the faithful word as he hath been taught, that he may be able by sound doctrine both to exhort and to convince the gainsayers.

The god of this world is the prince of the power of the air, is the lying santa in the sky and he and your hirelings cannot save you. The words that scratch your itching ears now will only haunt you in hell.

> John 10:10 The thief cometh not, but for to steal, and to kill, and to destroy: I am come that they might have life, and that they might have it more abundantly.
>
> Acts 2:38 Then Peter said unto them, Repent, and be baptized every one of you in the name of Jesus Christ for the remission of sins, and ye shall receive the gift of the Holy Ghost.
>
> 39 For the promise is unto you, and to your children, and to all that are afar off, even as many as the Lord our God shall call.

Heathen

Psalms 1:5 Therefore the ungodly shall not stand in the judgment, nor sinners in the congregation of the righteous.

Psalms 1:6 For the LORD knoweth the way of the righteous: but the way of the ungodly shall perish.

Psalms 2:1 Why do the heathen rage, and the people imagine a vain thing?

Acts 4:25 Who by the mouth of thy servant David hast said, Why did the heathen rage, and the people imagine vain things?

Matthew 15:7 [Ye] hypocrites, well did Esaias prophesy of you, saying,

Matthew 15:8 This people draweth nigh unto me with their mouth, and honoureth me with [their] lips; but their heart is far from me.

Matthew 15:9 But in vain they do worship me, teaching [for] doctrines the commandments of men.

Mark 7:7 Howbeit in vain do they worship me, teaching [for] doctrines the commandments of men.

Mark 7:8 For laying aside the commandment of God, ye hold the tradition of men, [as] the washing of pots and cups: and many other such like things ye do.

Mark 7:9 And he said unto them, Full well ye reject the commandment of God, that ye may keep your own tradition.

Matthew 7:15 Beware of false prophets, which come to you in sheep's clothing, but inwardly they are ravening wolves.

Matthew 24:11 And many false prophets shall rise, and shall deceive many.

Matthew 24:24 For there shall arise false Christs, and false prophets, and shall shew great signs and wonders; insomuch that, if [it were] possible, they shall deceive the very elect.

Luke 6:22 Blessed are ye, when men shall hate you, and when they shall separate you [from their company], and shall reproach [you], and cast out your name as evil, for the Son of man's sake.

Luke 6:23 Rejoice ye in that day, and leap for joy: for, behold, your reward [is] great in heaven: for in the like manner did their fathers unto the prophets.

Luke 6:26 Woe unto you, when all men shall speak well of you! for so did their fathers to the false prophets.

Fakes

It is the job of the false preacher to convince the damned that they are "saved". It is the job of the false preacher to convince people that God didn't really mean what he said. It is the job of the false preacher to deceive people, to play on their pride and convince them that "it doesn't *really* matter". The Bible speaks of false preachers...

> II Corinthians 11:13 For such [are] false apostles, deceitful workers, transforming themselves into the apostles of Christ.
>
> II Corinthians 11:14 And no marvel; for Satan himself is transformed into an angel of light.
>
> II Corinthians 11:15 Therefore [it is] no great thing if his ministers also be transformed as the ministers of righteousness; whose end shall be according to their works.

So we see that Satan's ministers will pretend to be God's preachers!

> Jeremiah 14:14 Then the LORD said unto me, The prophets prophesy lies in my name: I sent them not, neither have I commanded them, neither spake unto them: they prophesy unto you a false vision and divination, and a thing of nought, and the deceit of their heart.

Have you noticed how the false preachers will point to the multitudes that believe like they teach as "proof"?

> Matthew 7:13 Enter ye in at the strait gate: for wide [is] the gate, and broad [is] the way, that leadeth to destruction, and many there be which go in thereat:
>
> Matthew 7:14 Because strait [is] the gate, and narrow [is] the way, which leadeth unto life, and few there be that find it.
>
> Matthew 7:15 Beware of false prophets, which come to you in sheep's clothing, but inwardly they are ravening wolves.
>
> Matthew 24:11 And many false prophets shall rise, and shall deceive many.
>
> I John 4:5 They are of the world: therefore speak they of the world, and the world heareth them.

The worldly just *love* their false preachers, but...

> Matthew 15:14 Let them alone: they be blind leaders of the blind. And if the blind lead the blind, both shall fall into the ditch.
>
> Luke 6:39 And he spake a parable unto them, Can the blind lead the blind? shall they not both fall into the ditch?

Here's what true preachers teach:

> Acts 2:38 Then Peter said unto them, Repent, and be baptized every one of you in the name of Jesus Christ for the remission of sins, and ye shall receive the gift of the Holy Ghost.
>
> Acts 2:39 For the promise is unto you, and to your children, and to all that are afar off, [even] as many as the Lord our God shall call.
>
> Acts 2:40 And with many other words did he testify and exhort, saying, Save yourselves from this untoward generation.
>
> Acts 2:41 Then they that gladly received his word were baptized: and the same day there were added [unto them] about three thousand souls.
>
> Acts 2:42 And they continued stedfastly in the apostles' doctrine and fellowship, and in breaking of bread, and in prayers.

The Bible mentions those who preach "different things":

> Galatians 1:8 But though we, or an angel from heaven, preach any other gospel unto you than that which we have preached unto you, let him be accursed.
>
> Galatians 1:9 As we said before, so say I now again, If any [man] preach any other gospel unto you than that ye have received, let him be accursed.

Gentiles

Acts 2:39 includes "all that are afar off". That speaks of the Gentiles.

> Acts 2:38 Then Peter said unto them, Repent, and be baptized every one of you in the name of Jesus Christ for the remission of sins, and ye shall receive the gift of the Holy Ghost.
>
> Acts 2:39 For the promise is unto you, and to your children, and to all that are afar off, [even] as many as the Lord our God shall call.

The first Gentiles became Christian by obedience to Acts 2:38:

> Acts 10:44 While Peter yet spake these words, the Holy Ghost fell on all them which heard the word.
>
> Acts 10:45 And they of the circumcision which believed were astonished, as many as came with Peter, because that on the Gentiles also was poured out the gift of the Holy Ghost.
>
> Acts 10:46 For they heard them speak with tongues, and magnify God. Then answered Peter,

The Apostles were able to tell that Gentiles had received the very same Holy Spirit that they had received, because they spoke in other tongues.

> Acts 10:47 Can any man forbid water, that these should not be baptized, which have received the Holy Ghost as well as we?
>
> Acts 10:48 And he commanded them to be baptized in the name of the Lord. Then prayed they him to tarry certain days.

They were baptized in the NAME of the Lord (the name of the Lord is JESUS).

> Acts 11:1 And the apostles and brethren that were in Judaea heard that the Gentiles had also received the word of God.

Gentiles

Gentiles were said to have "received the word of God" because they were baptized in Jesus name and filled with the Holy Spirit.

Gentiles become Christians today, the same way that they became Christians in earlier days of the Church, by obeying Acts 2:38.

Many Gentiles prefer the filth of the denominal cults (as the Bible said that they would).

> II Timothy 4:3 For the time will come when they will not endure sound doctrine; but after their own lusts shall they heap to themselves teachers, having itching ears;
>
> II Timothy 4:4 And they shall turn away [their] ears from the truth, and shall be turned unto fables.

We have such false preachers from various cults (like baptist) in this very echo from time to time.

> II Corinthians 11:13 For such [are] false apostles, deceitful workers, transforming themselves into the apostles of Christ.
>
> II Corinthians 11:14 And no marvel; for Satan himself is transformed into an angel of light.
>
> II Corinthians 11:15 Therefore [it is] no great thing if his ministers also be transformed as the ministers of righteousness; whose end shall be according to their works.

We should not be surprised when Satanic filth come around claiming to be "christian ministers". Of course they will "claim" to be saving souls as they lead them into a comfortable disobedience of the Bible.

We should also remember that they are to be "accursed".

> Galatians 1:8 But though we, or an angel from heaven, preach any other gospel unto you than that which we have preached unto you, let him be accursed.

Galatians 1:9 As we said before, so say I now again, If any [man] preach any other gospel unto you than that ye have received, let him be accursed.

Galatians 1:10 For do I now persuade men, or God? or do I seek to please men? for if I yet pleased men, I should not be the servant of Christ.

We should not be surprised when the world supports the false churches.

I John 4:5 They are of the world: therefore speak they of the world, and the world heareth them.

Awesome

It is awesome to me how many false churches there are. Cults that are so far from true Christianity that the book of Acts appears to them as something strange and foreign and unpleasant.

But THAT (the book of Acts Church) is what REAL Christianity is and always has been!

> 2 Tim 4:3 For the time will come when they will not endure sound doctrine; but after their own lusts shall they heap to themselves teachers, having itching ears; 2 Tim 4:4 And they shall turn away their ears from the truth, and shall be turned unto fables.

False christian fables have become the "norm" and the "standard".

> 2 Tim 3:13 But evil men and seducers shall wax worse and worse, deceiving, and being deceived.

The road to heaven is not a broad road with many "ways"

> Mat 7:13 Enter ye in at the strait gate: for wide is the gate, and broad is the way, that leadeth to destruction, and many there be which go in thereat: Mat 7:14 Because strait is the gate, and narrow is the way, which leadeth unto life, and few there be that find it. Mat 7:15 Beware of false prophets, which come to you in sheep's clothing, but inwardly they are ravening wolves.

The denominal trintarian preacher can appear to be pleasant and "loving", but so must any con man appear in order to be successful.

How could the Bible be ANY clearer about trinitarianism than the following:

> Col 2:8 Beware lest any man spoil you through philosophy and vain deceit, after the tradition of men, after the rudiments of the world, and not after Christ.

> Col 2:9 For in him dwelleth all the fulness of the Godhead bodily. Col 2:10 And ye are complete in him, which is the head of all principality and power:

Him, not "Them"

Don't follow your sly, philosophising, trinity preacher into hell!

> Mat 15:14 Let them alone: they be blind leaders of the blind. And if the blind lead the blind, both shall fall into the ditch.

BOTH, both the false preacher AND their followers..

> Matthew7:22 Many will say to me in that day, Lord, Lord, have we not prophesied in thy name? and in thy name have cast out devils? and in thy name done many wonderful works?
>
> 23 And then will I profess unto them, I never knew you: depart from me, ye that work iniquity.

Consider

The false christian church is likened to a "whore" and a "harlot" by the Word of God.

> Revelation 17:1 And there came one of the seven angels which had the seven vials, and talked with me, saying unto me, Come hither; I will shew unto thee the judgment of the great whore that sitteth upon many waters:
>
> Revelation 17:2 With whom the kings of the earth have committed fornication, and the inhabitants of the earth have been made drunk with the wine of her fornication.
>
> Revelation 17:5 And upon her forehead [was] a name written, MYSTERY, BABYLON THE GREAT, THE MOTHER OF HARLOTS AND ABOMINATIONS OF THE EARTH.
>
> Revelation 17:6 And I saw the woman drunken with the blood of the saints, and with the blood of the martyrs of Jesus: and when I saw her, I wondered with great admiration.

We have/had several representatives of the false christian church posting false doctrines here. Notice the similarity between them and the following verses which apply not only to the physical harlots, but also the spiritual harlots.

> Proverbs 9:13 A foolish woman is clamorous: she is simple, and knoweth nothing.
>
> Proverbs 9:14 For she sitteth at the door of her house, on a seat in the high places of the city,
>
> Proverbs 9:15 To call passengers who go right on their ways:
>
> Proverbs 9:16 Whoso is simple, let him turn in hither: and as for him that wanteth understanding, she saith to him,
>
> Proverbs 9:17 Stolen waters are sweet, and bread eaten in secret is pleasant.
>
> Proverbs 9:18 But he knoweth not that the dead are there; and that her guests are in the depths of hell.

Be Washed

In John 3:5, Jesus told a full grown man that he needed to be born again of a spiritual birth which consisted of water and spirit. (notice two distinct elements WATER and SPIRIT)..

The devil has many false christian preachers that teach that the "birth of the water" refers to a man's physical birth (since there is a watery fluid involved at birth). That teaching is one of the cheapest, cop out, deceptions in Satan's arsenal to deceive people about the IMPORTANCE of baptism.

> John 3:5 Jesus answered, Verily, verily, I say unto thee, Except a man be born of water and [of] the Spirit, he cannot enter into the kingdom of God.

Notice carefully that Jesus was declaring what a MAN had to do (not a baby), and that Jesus was referring to a RE-BIRTH; being BORN AGAIN. He could not have been referring to the fluids of a baby's birth. HE was telling a grown MAN how to be BORN AGAIN. Oh, it sounds real convincing to look at it as "physical birth", unless you consider that he was talking to a MAN, a grown MAN telling him how to be RE-BORN (spiritually). And if that isn't enough to convince you, then just look at how WATER and SPIRIT are BOTH elements in the plan of salvation that was preached at the birth of the church:

> Acts 2:38 Then Peter said unto them, Repent, and be baptized every one of you in the name of Jesus Christ for the remission of sins, and ye shall receive the gift of the Holy Ghost.

Water Baptism in Jesus name is what washes away sins because of the shed blood of God.

> Acts 22:16 And now why tarriest thou? arise, and be baptized, and wash away thy sins, calling on the name of the Lord.

Let's look at another verse that Jesus spoke (and I hope that no one would be so shallow and deceitful to suggest that a non-believer would even consider baptism) *

> Mark 16:16 He that believeth and is baptized shall be saved; but he that believeth not shall be damned.

The same God that said Water was part of the RE-BIRTH also declared "and is baptized" as part of salvation. How could the Bible be any clearer?

In John 3:5 Jesus was talking to a GROWN MAN telling him about a RE-BIRTH. Also, as a matter of fact, a baby are born IN water NOT 'OF' Water. Of course, Jesus was not speaking of a "re-entering" of the womb for the second birth, but rather the spiritual results of baptism.

> John 3:3 Jesus answered and said unto him, Verily , verily, I say unto thee, Except a man be born again, he cannot see the kingdom of God.

> John 3:4 Nicodemus saith unto him, How can a man be born when he is old? can he enter the second time into his mother's womb, and be born?

> John 3:5 Jesus answered, Verily , verily, I say unto thee, Except a man be born of water and of the Spirit, he cannot enter into the kingdom of God.

A MAN is re born of water by being water baptized in Jesus name. (for the remission of sins).

> Acts 22:16 And now why tarriest thou? arise, and be baptized, and wash away thy sins, calling on the name of the Lord.

If you are in the snare of a false preacher, it's not going to be "OK", unless you get away from him/her/it and find a true church. Denominal preachers are only deceiving souls into hell.

> Mat 15:14 Let them alone: they be blind leaders of the blind. And if the blind lead the blind, both shall fall into the ditch.

> Mat 7:13 Enter ye in at the strait gate: for wide is the gate, and broad is the way, that leadeth to destruction, and many there be which go in thereat:
>
> Mat 7:14 Because strait is the gate, and narrow is the way, which leadeth unto life, and few there be that find it.

But some of you like your false preacher, don't you? The Bible addresses that scenario as well.

> 2 Tim 4:3 For the time will come when they will not endure sound doctrine; but after their own lusts shall they heap to themselves teachers, having itching ears;
>
> 2 Tim 4:4 And they shall turn away their ears from the truth, and shall be turned unto fables.

Water

I hope to herein expose one of the filthiest lies that false preachers are teaching these days. If I seem emotional, it's just that I hate to see people so deceived. In John 3:5, Jesus told a full grown man that he needed to be born again of a spiritual birth which consisted of water and spirit...(notice two distinct elements WATER and SPIRIT)..

Satan has many misinformed, and some knowingly deceiving false preachers that teach that the "birth of the water" refers to a man's physical birth (since there is a watery fluid involved at birth). That teaching is one of the cheapest, cop out, deceptions in Satan's arsenal to deceive people about the IMPORTANCE of baptism.

> John 3:5 Jesus answered, Verily, verily, I say unto thee, Except a man be born of water and [of] the Spirit, he cannot enter into the kingdom of God.

Notice that Jesus was declaring what a MAN had to do (not a baby), and that Jesus was referring to a RE-BIRTH; being BORN AGAIN. He could not have been referring to the fluids of a baby's birth. HE was telling a grown MAN how to be BORN AGAIN.

Oh, it sounds real convincing to the shallow and carnal to look at it as "physical birth", unless you consider that he was talking to a MAN, a grown MAN telling him how to be RE-BORN (spiritually). And if that isn't enough to convince you, then just look at how WATER and SPIRIT are BOTH elements in the plan of salvation that was preached at the birth of the church:

> Acts 2:38 Then Peter said unto them, Repent, and be baptized every one of you in the name of Jesus Christ for the remission of sins, and ye shall receive the gift of the Holy Ghost.

* Baptism is what washes away sins!!! Look at this next verse: *

> Acts 22:16 And now why tarriest thou? arise, and be baptized, and wash away thy sins, calling on the name of the Lord.

Then, if you are still not convinced let's look at another verse that Jesus spoke (and I certainly pray that you will not suggest that a non-believer would even consider baptism).

> Mark 16:16 He that believeth and is baptized shall be saved; but he that believeth not shall be damned.

Look how the same God that said Water was part of the RE-BIRTH also declared "and is baptized" How could the Bible be any clearer????

Remember! Jesus was talking to a GROWN MAN telling him about a RE-BIRTH, and as a matter of fact babies are born IN water NOT 'OF' Water.. DON'T BE DECEIVED!!!!

Intolerance

Does the Word of God teach tolerance towards deceivers?

The Bible does NOT teach that we should be tolerant of false christian deceivers that are the vilest of parasites, filth that actually snare souls that are trying to find God, and deceive them with lies.

Nice sweet people are being deceived into a very very real hell by religious filth and deceivers. What viler thing could there be upon the earth than a sweet talking false preacher? Here we have ALL these people that *think* that they have obeyed the Bible and are headed for heaven, YET, the basic Acts 2:38 message sounds strange and foreign to them because some deceiver has preached them full of sugar coated lies, AND has probably already preached some of their older relatives into hell.

Of COURSE these men must oppose the truth! If their congregations find out what true Christianity is, then they will also realize that their preacher has already deceived some of their relatives into hell. THINK ABOUT THAT! They can't admit even what they know because then they would have to admit that everyone who had died in their church so far was in hell. THEY HAVE TO FIGHT THIS Acts 2:38 TRUTH!

It is the job of a TRUE preacher to convince you TO OBEY the Word of God, it is the job of Satan and his servants to explain to you why you really don't need to obey the Word of God and it is the job of the reprobate to muddy the waters between the two.

Look what Paul says about false christian deceivers :

> II Corinthians 11:12 But what I do, that I will do, that I may cut off occasion from them which desire occasion; that wherein they glory, they may be found even as we.
>
> II Corinthians 11:13 For such [are] false apostles, deceitful workers, transforming themselves into the apostles of Christ.

> II Corinthians 11:14 And no marvel; for Satan himself is transformed into an angel of light.
>
> II Corinthians 11:15 Therefore [it is] no great thing if his ministers also be transformed as the ministers of righteousness; whose end shall be according to their works.

That should tell you that Satan is in the religion business. Satan is in the preaching business.

What did Paul command the Christian regarding how to relate to any deceiver?

> Galatians 1:8 But though we, or an angel from heaven, preach any other gospel unto you than that which we have preached unto you, let him be accursed.

Does that sound to you like Paul preached tolerance?

Note that there are disadvantages forecast for those who, for whatever reason, neglect to obey the Gospel that Paul preached.

> II Thessalonians 1:7 And to you who are troubled rest with us, when the Lord Jesus shall be revealed from heaven with his mighty angels,
>
> II Thessalonians 1:8 In flaming fire taking vengeance on them that know not God, and that obey not the gospel of our Lord Jesus Christ:
>
> II Thessalonians 1:9 Who shall be punished with everlasting destruction from the presence of the Lord, and from the glory of his power;

It is such a simple matter. Some preachers are trying to convince you to obey the Bible and others here are trying to convince you why you don't need to obey the Bible.

In case anyone had any doubt about what Paul preached, and you really need to keep in mind that Paul was writing to people who believed "his way", or he would NOT have considered them brethren.

The Apostle Paul preached the same Acts 2:38 salvation message that Peter first preached on the day of Pentecost. Notice how it is even referred to as the word of the Lord Jesus.

Please examine carefully the account when Paul founded the Ephesian church.

> Acts 19:1 And it came to pass, that, while Apollos was at Corinth, Paul having passed through the upper coasts came to Ephesus: and finding certain disciples,
>
> Acts 19:2 He said unto them, Have ye received the Holy Ghost since ye believed? And they said unto him, We have not so much as heard whether there be any Holy Ghost.

Note that "believers" did not yet have the Holy Ghost. That proves that one does not automatically receive the Holy Ghost just when they "believe" as many false preachers teach.

> Acts 19:3 And he said unto them, Unto what then were ye baptized? And they said, Unto John's baptism.

Note that Paul immediately questioned the validity of their baptism when they admitted that they did not have the Holy Ghost.

> Acts 19:4 Then said Paul, John verily baptized with the baptism of repentance, saying unto the people, that they should believe on him which should come after him, that is, on Christ Jesus.
>
> Acts 19:5 When they heard [this], they were baptized in the name of the Lord Jesus.

Note that they were immediately re-baptized the Christian way, in Jesus Name.

> Acts 19:6 And when Paul had laid [his] hands upon them, the Holy Ghost came on them; and they spake with tongues, and prophesied.

When they did receive the Holy Ghost that they spoke in tongues just like every other real Christian.

How did Paul teach us to relate to any preacher who would teach otherwise?

> Galatians 1:8 But though we, or an angel from heaven, preach any other gospel unto you than that which we have preached unto you, let him be accursed.
>
> Galatians 1:9 As we said before, so say I now again, If any man preach any other gospel unto you than that ye have received, let him be accursed.

The phrase "let him be accursed" appears only two times in the Bible. It is not even used to speak of the Sodomite or any other rank sinner, but only regarding anyone who would preach some "alternate" doctrine.

The trinity preacher is lower in the sight of God, much lower than the Sodomite (not withstanding that many trinity cults are even ordaining Sodomites, but that is another sermon).

Accursed

The Bible does give instructions on how Christians are to relate to deceivers, those who teach a false doctrine.

I believe that we need not lose track of the bottom line, regardless of any formality, and that is, the accursedness of any preacher that is preaching other than the Acts 2:38 message.

Technically the word translated as accursed means nailed up on the church wall. "If any man comes preaching any other doctrine, nail him up on the wall of the church" or "let him be nailed up on the wall of the church." I am only pointing this out for academic purposes as I feel that a verbal curse with much prayer is a much more appropriate obedience to the verses. This also has an excellent built in "fuse" as it were, that the Lord will not grant a prayer request that is in error. I believe that our consideration should be more the realization of the accursedness of the false preacher rather than getting hung up over who prays the prayer.

> Gal 1: 8 But though <1437> we, or <2228> an angel <32> from heaven <3772>, preach <2097> any other gospel <2097> unto you than <3844> that which <3739> we have preached <2097> unto you, let him be accursed <331>.

331 anathema an-ath'-em-ah from 394; TDNT - 1:353,57; n n

AV - accursed (4)

- anathema (1)

- bind under a great curse + 332 (1) [6]

1) a thing set up or laid by in order to be kept; specifically an offering resulting from a vow, which after being consecrated to a god was hung upon the walls or columns of the temple, or put in some

other conspicuous place.

2) a thing devoted to God without hope of being redeemed, and if an animal, to be slain; therefore a person or thing doomed to destruction.

2a) a curse

2b) a man accursed, devoted to the direst of woes.

I believe that my perception of Gal 1:8 is quite accurate and preferable to other possible considerations, like for instance: If any man preach another gospel:

1. Hang him up on the church wall or some other conspicuous place.
2. Slay him.
3. Destroy him.

That simply would not be proper Christian behaviour and would violate many Biblical principles (not to mention several laws of the land which Christians are to obey).

But, we as Christians are to commit such details to God in prayer.

I believe that praying a curse against such a person is the only acceptable, proper Christian approach to take. Of course some groups that measure themselves among themselves and as a natural result of that begin to "bear with" those who preach "another Jesus" (for example the "false Jesus" of the trinitarians), soon begin to regard the trinitarians and such like as "wayward brethren" rather than "accursed children".(not saying that they are beyond repentance, but we are talking about preachers and teachers here).

II Corinthians 10:12 For we dare not make ourselves of the number, or compare ourselves with some that commend themselves: but they measuring themselves by themselves, and comparing themselves among themselves, are not wise.

II Corinthians 10:13 But we will not boast of things without [our] measure, but according to the measure of the rule which God hath distributed to us, a measure to reach even unto you.

II Corinthians 10:14 For we stretch not ourselves beyond [our measure], as though we reached not unto you: for we are come as far as to you also in [preaching] the gospel of Christ:

*(just as an added bonus, ponder these next 3 verses in light of what you know has happened recently in regards to recent happenings) *

II Corinthians 10:15 Not boasting of things without [our] measure, [that is], of other men's labours; but having hope, when your faith is

increased, that we shall be enlarged by you according to our rule abundantly,

II Corinthians 10:16 To preach the gospel in the [regions] beyond you, [and] not to boast in another man's line of things made ready to our hand.

II Corinthians 10:17 But he that glorieth, let him glory in the Lord.

II Corinthians 10:18 For not he that commendeth himself is approved, but whom the Lord commendeth.

II Corinthians 11:1 Would to God ye could bear with me a little in

[my] folly: and indeed bear with me.

II Corinthians 11:2 For I am jealous over you with godly jealousy: for I have espoused you to one husband, that I may present [you as]

a chaste virgin to Christ.

II Corinthians 11:3 But I fear, lest by any means, as the serpent beguiled Eve through his subtilty, so your minds should be corrupted

from the simplicity that is in Christ.

II Corinthians 11:4 For if he that cometh preacheth another Jesus, whom we have not preached, or [if] ye receive another spirit, which ye have not received, or another gospel, which ye have not accepted, ye might well bear with [him].

Notice carefully that the ones that measure themselves among themselves are also a "high risk" group as far as "bearing with" those that preach "another Jesus" (not to mention trying to steal another preachers work, eh? did you notice that before?)

God DOES NOT want his people to even "bear with" trinitarian preachers. Your Bible says "let them be accursed", so don't get sidetracked into the mechanics so much that you lose track of the accursedness of these false preachers.

What if I was totally wrong? Would a trinitarian be more or less accused? If God was saying "I will curse them", would my saying "I curse you" lessen the curse upon that person? Would God hold me accountable for agreeing in prayer and in public concerning the accursedness of one that He had declared "accursed"? Will God hold me accountable for praying that His Word be manifest in a direct manner?

Admit

I hope that we would not expect an unrepentant member of a false church to admit that they had done anything wrong.

The Bible (*your* Bible) uses the words "whore" and "harlot" in it's reference to the great false religious system AND to her daughters (or "denominations").

> Revelation 17:1 And there came one of the seven angels which had the seven vials, and talked with me, saying unto me, Come hither; I will shew unto thee the judgment of the great whore that sitteth upon many waters:
>
> Revelation 17:4 And the woman was arrayed in purple and scarlet colour, and decked with gold and precious stones and pearls, having a golden cup in her hand full of abominations and filthiness of her fornication:
>
> Revelation 17:5 And upon her forehead [was] a name written, MYSTERY, BABYLON THE GREAT, THE MOTHER OF HARLOTS AND ABOMINATIONS OF THE EARTH.

The Bible mentions principles of lifestyle:

> Proverbs 30:20 Such [is] the way of an adulterous woman; she eateth, and wipeth her mouth, and saith, I have done no wickedness.

The spiritual "adulteress" or "harlot" will eat (delve into the Word of God), and true to the spirit of "harlotry" will boldly defend their "position" and say "I have done no wickedness". This is to be *expected* from those who reject the true Gospel of Jesus Christ, and cling to the empty lies of the "harlot church"

Faith

Two types of Faith

The Bible speaks of two basic types of faith. (I am not referring to the "Gift of Faith" in this study).

For some groundwork let us note that everyone has the measure of faith from God. This is true for both saint and sinner.

> Rom 12:3 For I say, through the grace given unto me, to every man that is among you, not to think of himself more highly than he ought to think; but to think soberly, according as God hath dealt to every man the measure of faith.

It does not say that "every brother" but rather "every man" is given the measure of faith.

At this point in our study it is important, for a foundation, to be aware of what exactly Paul preached for salvation. We can study Acts 19 to confirm that Paul preached the Acts 2:38 message.

> Acts 19:2 He said unto them, Have ye received the Holy Ghost since ye believed? And they said unto him, We have not so much as heard whether there be any Holy Ghost.

> Acts 19:3 And he said unto them, Unto what then were ye baptized? And they said, Unto John's baptism.

> Acts 19:4 Then said Paul, John verily baptized with the baptism of repentance, saying unto the people, that they should believe on him which should come after him, that is, on Christ Jesus.

> Acts 19:5 When they heard this, they were baptized in the name of the Lord Jesus.

> Acts 19:6 And when Paul had laid his hands upon them, the Holy Ghost came on them; and they spake with tongues, and prophesied.

Please notice that Paul's teaching included water baptism in Jesus Name and receiving the Holy Ghost with the evidence of speaking in other tongues. Having established clearly from the Word of God that the Apostle Paul preached the Acts 2:38 message I call your attention to a clear admonition and warning from Paul.

> 1 Cor 15:1 Moreover, brethren, I declare unto you the gospel which I preached unto you, which also ye have received, and wherein ye stand;
>
> 1 Cor 15:2 By which also ye are saved, if ye keep in memory what I preached unto you, unless ye have believed in vain.

Notice carefully here this next verse that again confirms that the Apostle Paul preached the same Acts 2:38 message that Peter and the other Apostles preached. This also confirms that the Corinthian Church was also founded upon Acts 2:38 salvation as were all true Christian Churches.

> 1 Cor 15:11 Therefore whether it were I or they, so we preach, and so ye believed.

This next verse establishes that the Spirit of God (the Holy Ghost) and the Spirit of Christ are one in the same. (Check it out!)

> Rom 8:9 But ye are not in the flesh, but in the Spirit, if so be that the Spirit of God dwell in you. Now if any man have not the Spirit of Christ, he is none of his.

For those who have obeyed Acts 2:38 by being baptized in Jesus name and having received the Holy Ghost (Spirit of Christ) with the evidence of speaking in tongues, I have some more verses:

> 2 Pet 1:4 Whereby are given unto us exceeding great and precious promises: that by these ye might be partakers of the divine nature, having escaped the corruption that is in the world through lust.
>
> 2 Pet 1:5 And beside this, giving all diligence, add to your faith virtue; and to virtue knowledge;
>
> 2 Pet 1:6 And to knowledge temperance; and to temperance patience; and to patience godliness;
>
> 2 Pet 1:7 And to godliness brotherly kindness; and to brotherly kindness charity.
>
> 2 Pet 1:8 For if these things be in you, and abound, they make you that ye shall neither be barren nor unfruitful in the knowledge of our Lord Jesus Christ.

2 Pet 1:9 But he that lacketh these things is blind, and cannot see afar off, and hath forgotten that he was purged from his old sins.

2 Pet 1:10 Wherefore the rather, brethren, give diligence to make your calling and election sure: for if ye do these things, ye shall never fall:

2 Pet 1:11 For so an entrance shall be ministered unto you abundantly into the everlasting kingdom of our Lord and Saviour Jesus Christ.

2 Pet 1:12 Wherefore I will not be negligent to put you always in remembrance of these things, though ye know them, and be established in the present truth.

Cultists

It is amazing that cultists are able to convince people that the Apostles disobeyed Jesus when they baptized in Jesus name.

It is even more amazing when a simple glance shows that Jesus commanded that a singular name be used in baptism and then the Apostles used a singular name.

The bottom line is that these cults don't really believe that Jesus is God, and they don't really believe in one God.

If they believed in one God, then they would baptise in His name like the Apostles did, but they do not worship the God of the Apostles.

They deny that Jesus gave Peter the keys to the kingdom.

> Matthew 16:19 And I will give unto thee the keys of the kingdom of heaven: and whatsoever thou shalt bind on earth shall be bound in heaven: and whatsoever thou shalt loose on earth shall be loosed in heaven.

Jesus declared that He had ALL POWER. If there were any other 'persons' or 'godlets' they would be powerless because it's all in Jesus.

> Matthew 28:18 And Jesus came and spake unto them, saying, All power is given unto me in heaven and in earth.

Then Jesus told them to use the singular name that fit His different attributes.

> Matthew 28:19 Go ye therefore, and teach all nations, baptizing them in the name of the Father, and of the Son, and of the Holy Ghost:

Then Peter used Jesus's keys to unlock the kingdom of heaven.

> Acts 2:38 Then Peter said unto them, Repent, and be baptized every one of you in the name of Jesus Christ for the remission of sins, and ye shall receive the gift of the Holy Ghost.

Peter is not the Satanic deceiver. The trinitarian preachers are the Satanic deceivers.

Foreign

Regarding the misconception that speaking in other tongues was for "preaching to foreign nations", I find the following scriptures to be helpful.

We see here that "other tongues" (not to be confused with the "gift of tongues") was the evidence that the Apostles accepted that a Gentile had received the same Spirit of Christ that they had received.

> Acts 10:45 And they of the circumcision which believed were astonished, as many as came with Peter, because that on the Gentiles also was poured out the gift of the Holy Ghost.
>
> Acts 10:46 For they heard them speak with tongues, and magnify God. Then answered Peter,
>
> Acts 10:47 Can any man forbid water, that these should not be baptized, which have received the Holy Ghost as well as we?
>
> Acts 10:48 And he commanded them to be baptized in the name of the Lord. Then prayed they him to tarry certain days.

I see no "foreign nations" being preached to. Especially note that the Gentiles were not completely Christians yet as they had not been baptized in Jesus name. Since they were not yet even Christian, they most certainly could not have been "preaching to foreign nations".

I hope you find the above helpful...

Compare

Let's compare what the apostles taught compared to what some of the modern deceivers teach.

The apostles were the ones who wrote down Jesus's words for us to read. The apostles had heard Jesus when he said:

> Mark 16:16 He that believeth and is baptized shall be saved; but he that believeth not shall be damned.

(Notice that Jesus said "and is baptized")

> John 3:16 For God so loved the world, that he gave his only begotten Son, that whosoever believeth in him should not perish, but have everlasting life.
>
> John 5:24 Verily, verily, I say unto you, He that heareth my word, and believeth on him that sent me, hath everlasting life, and shall not come into condemnation; but is passed from death unto life.
>
> John 6:47 Verily, verily, I say unto you, He that believeth on me hath everlasting life.
>
> John 7:38 He that believeth on me, as the scripture hath said, out of his belly shall flow rivers of living water.

The modern false preachers teach that "belief" is merely a mental affirmation but we see from this next verse that the apostles measured a person's "belief" by their "OBEDIANCE" and counted non-obeyers to be "non-believers".

> Romans 10:16 But they have not all obeyed the gospel. For Esaias saith, Lord, who hath believed our report?

Then from this next verse we see a problem with believing a lie.

> II Thessalonians 2:12 That they all might be damned who believed not the truth, but had pleasure in unrighteousness.

Compare

When the apostles who had been WITH JESUS and had heard Him speak about belief were asked what they needed to do (to be saved), Peter responded with the plan of salvation that the modern false preachers hate so much:

> Acts 2:38 Then Peter said unto them, Repent, and be baptized every one of you in the name of Jesus Christ for the remission of sins, and ye shall receive the gift of the Holy Ghost.
>
> Acts 2:39 For the promise is unto you, and to your children, and to all that are afar off, [even] as many as the Lord our God shall call.

The Apostle Peter declared in verse 39 that "Acts 2:38" was for as many as God would call. Paul declared in his letter to the Galatians that anyone preaching some "other" gospel was to be "accursed".

> Galatians 1:8 But though we, or an angel from heaven, preach any other gospel unto you than that which we have preached unto you, let him be accursed.
>
> Galatians 1:9 As we said before, so say I now again, If any [man] preach any other gospel unto you than that ye have received, let him be accursed.

Paul did not embrace false christian teachers and deceivers:

> II Corinthians 11:12 But what I do, that I will do, that I may cut off occasion from them which desire occasion; that wherein they glory, they may be found even as we.
>
> II Corinthians 11:13 For such [are] false apostles, deceitful workers, transforming themselves into the apostles of Christ.
>
> II Corinthians 11:14 And no marvel; for Satan himself is transformed into an angel of light.
>
> II Corinthians 11:15 Therefore [it is] no great thing if his ministers also be transformed as the ministers of righteousness; whose end shall be according to their works.

True believers obey, fake believers don't. True preachers teach obedience to the Bible, false preachers teach that it really doesn't matter.

True preachers lead people to heaven, false preachers lead people to hell.

To listen to some false preachers, you would think that a person would be lost because they obeyed the Bible.

When we who are real Christians teach that you need to obey the Bible to even become a Christian, we are telling you the truth. When the false preachers speak of their fake love and teach that you need not obey the Bible, they are telling you a lie. Don't be deceived.

> James 1:22 But be ye doers of the word, and not hearers only, deceiving your own selves.

Premise

It is amazing how many cults are basing their salvation upon the premise that the early Christians to whom the original epistles were addressed, "believed" the apostles, but didn't obey them. Then they are also counting on the premise that the apostles accepted as "brethren" folks who refused to obey them.

Every time that the "cultist" leads a victim to Galatians, or Romans, or Ephesians to "explain" to them why obedience to Acts 2:38 isn't necessary for salvation; they ignore the fact that the addressees of the epistles of the Bible were those who had OBEYED the Acts 2:38 plan of salvation.

Unless a person BECOMES a Christian, they are NOT even the people that the benevolent promises are addressed to (the benevolent promises in the epistles). It's as if they are holding a valuable check that is made out to someone else. They rant and rave about its promised value (which is real), but don't realize that it's not addressed to them. The benevolent promises of God are only for those who OBEY Him.

Even a perfunctory glance at a couple of scriptures should expose many of these cultists. The battle is a classic one, really. We teach why the Bible needs to be obeyed, while the Satanic folks "proclaim" their "salvation without obedience".

In the book of Romans a "non-believer" was recognized by "lack of obedience".

> Romans 10:16 But they have not all obeyed the gospel. For Esaias saith, Lord, who hath believed our report?

Cultists *love* to take verses from Ephesians, ignoring the fact that the Ephesian Church was FOUNDED upon the Acts 2:38 plan of salvation. and that those folks had ALREADY OBEYED. Let's look at the founding of the Ephesian church and carefully notice how Paul adhered to the Acts 2:38 plan even though John the Baptist had ALREADY baptized them!

> Acts 19:1 And it came to pass, that, while Apollos was at Corinth, Paul having passed through the upper coasts came to Ephesus: and finding certain disciples,
>
> Acts 19:2 He said unto them, Have ye received the Holy Ghost since ye believed? And they said unto him, We have not so much as heard whether there be any Holy Ghost.

Here's clear proof in verse 2 that a person doesn't receive the Holy Ghost just because they "believe" *

> Acts 19:3 And he said unto them, Unto what then were ye baptized? And they said, Unto John's baptism.
>
> Acts 19:4 Then said Paul, John verily baptized with the baptism of repentance, saying unto the people, that they should believe on him which should come after him, that is, on Christ Jesus.
>
> Acts 19:5 When they heard [this], they were baptized in the name of the Lord Jesus.

Even folks who had been baptized by John the Baptist himself had to be RE-Baptized in Jesus name in order to become Christians.

> Acts 19:6 And when Paul had laid [his] hands upon them, the Holy Ghost came on them; and they spake with tongues, and prophesied.

Psalm 23

Psa 23:1 A Psalm of David. The LORD is my shepherd; I shall not want.

Psa 23:2 He maketh me to lie down in green pastures: he leadeth me beside the still waters.

Psa 23:3 He restoreth my soul: he leadeth me in the paths of righteousness for his name's sake.

(It is important to note that the trinity cults reject the name of Jesus in baptism and reject the path of righteousness)

Psa 23:4 Yea, though I walk through the valley of the shadow of death, I will fear no evil: for thou art with me; thy rod and thy staff they comfort me.

Psa 23:5 Thou preparest a table before me in the presence of mine enemies: thou anointest my head with oil; my cup runneth over.

Psa 23:6 Surely goodness and mercy shall follow me all the days of my life: and I will dwell in the house of the LORD for ever.

Heb 5:9 And being made perfect, he became the author of eternal salvation unto all them that obey him;

Acts 2:38 Then Peter said unto them, Repent, and be baptized every one of you in the name of Jesus Christ for the remission of sins, and ye shall receive the gift of the Holy Ghost.

Acts 2:39 For the promise is unto you, and to your children, and to all that are afar off, even as many as the Lord our God shall call.

> Acts 22:16 And now why tarriest thou? arise, and be baptized, and wash away thy sins, calling on the name of the Lord.

One "calls on the name" of Jesus by being BAPTIZED in the NAME of Jesus.

> Gal 3:27 For as many of you as have been baptized into Christ have put on Christ.

Those who have not been baptized in Jesus Christ have not yet put on Christ and are still in their sins (regardless of what some false preacher might have convinced them otherwise)

The rejectors of Jesus name baptism (otherwise known as "Christ rejectors") have certain promises awaiting them.

> 2 Th 1:7 And to you who are troubled rest with us, when the Lord Jesus shall be revealed from heaven with his mighty angels,
>
> 2 Th 1:8 In flaming fire taking vengeance on them that know not God, and that obey not the gospel of our Lord Jesus Christ:
>
> 2 Th 1:9 Who shall be punished with everlasting destruction from the presence of the Lord, and from the glory of his power;

Itching ears

2 Tim 4:3 For the time will come when they will not endure sound doctrine; but after their own lusts shall they heap to themselves teachers, having itching ears;

2 Tim 4:4 And they shall turn away their ears from the truth, and shall be turned unto fables.

Col 2:8 Beware lest any man spoil you through philosophy and vain deceit, after the tradition of men, after the rudiments of the world, and not after Christ.

Col 2:9 For in him dwelleth all the fulness of the Godhead bodily.

Col 2:10 And ye are complete in him, which is the head of all principality and power:

Rev 17:4 And the woman was arrayed in purple and scarlet colour, and decked with gold and precious stones and pearls, having a golden cup in her hand full of abominations and filthiness of her fornication:

Rev 17:5 And upon her forehead was a name written, MYSTERY, BABYLON THE GREAT, THE MOTHER OF HARLOTS AND ABOMINATIONS OF THE EARTH.

False preachers

Concerning the topic of what is the proper way to relate to false preachers, I have several scriptures that have influenced me.

> I Kings 18:26 And they took the bullock which was given them, and they dressed [it], and called on the name of Baal from morning even until noon, saying, O Baal, hear us. But [there was] no voice, nor any that answered. And they leaped upon the altar which was made.
>
> I Kings 18:27 And it came to pass at noon, that Elijah mocked them, and said, Cry aloud: for he [is] a god; either he is talking, or he is pursuing, or he is in a journey, [or] peradventure he sleepeth, and must be awaked.

In the old testament the prophet of God mocked the idol worshipper's preachers .

> Galatians 1:8 But though we, or an angel from heaven, preach any other gospel unto you than that which we have preached unto you, let him be accursed.
>
> Galatians 1:9 As we said before, so say I now again, If any [man] preach any other gospel unto you than that ye have received, let him be accursed.

In the new testament false preachers are to be "accursed". I am also reminded of Paul's prayer against the coppersmith. Let us also consider that just as today the false preachers make money from their idol worship of the trinity and withstand the truth, the coppersmiths made money from the worship of their physical idols and withstood the truth that would have hurt their income. Now, knowing what Paul knew, what worse curse could he have possibly uttered against Alexander:

> II Timothy 4:14 Alexander the coppersmith did me much evil: the Lord reward him according to his works:
>
> II Timothy 4:15 Of whom be thou ware also; for he hath greatly withstood our words.

What words could Paul have said that would have been any worse? Think about it, Paul would have been much kinder to simply curse him in the name of the Lord or to have even prayed blindness upon him.

Also when Paul delivered blasphemers over to Satan:

> I Timothy 1:18 This charge I commit unto thee, son Timothy, according to the prophecies which went before on thee, that thou by them mightest war a good warfare;
>
> I Timothy 1:19 Holding faith, and a good conscience; which some having put away concerning faith have made shipwreck:
>
> I Timothy 1:20 Of whom is Hymenaeus and Alexander; whom I have delivered unto Satan, that they may learn not to blaspheme.

In these new testament examples we are apparently seeing people who had heard the truth but continued in evil, just as we have false preachers on this forum that have now heard the truth but continue to deceive souls into hell in their false churches and labor to deceive souls here as well. This is spiritual warfare. I can not imagine Paul speaking Galatians 1:8 if he did not himself curse false preachers.

Paul speaks of opposing Satan's ministers that would feign Christianity.

> II Corinthians 11:12 But what I do, that I will do, that I may cut off occasion from them which desire occasion; that wherein they glory, they may be found even as we.
>
> II Corinthians 11:13 For such [are] false apostles, deceitful workers, transforming themselves into the apostles of Christ.
>
> II Corinthians 11:14 And no marvel; for Satan himself is transformed into an angel of light.
>
> II Corinthians 11:15 Therefore [it is] no great thing if his ministers also be transformed as the ministers of righteousness; whose end shall be according to their works.

My sympathies and concerns do not go to those that are making their living deceiving souls into hell. My sympathies and concerns go to those that are being deceived.

Paul expressed deep concern that a Christian would even "bear with" someone like a trinitarian that was preaching a "different Jesus".

> II Corinthians 11:2 For I am jealous over you with godly jealousy: for I have espoused you to one husband, that I may present [you as] a chaste virgin to Christ.
>
> II Corinthians 11:3 But I fear, lest by any means, as the serpent beguiled Eve through his subtilty, so your minds should be corrupted from the simplicity that is in Christ.
>
> II Corinthians 11:4 For if he that cometh preacheth another Jesus, whom we have not preached, or [if] ye receive another spirit, which ye have not received, or another gospel, which ye have not accepted, ye might well bear with [him].
>
> II Corinthians 11:5 For I suppose I was not a whit behind the very chiefest apostles.
>
> II Corinthians 11:6 But though [I be] rude in speech, yet not in knowledge; but we have been throughly made manifest among you in all things.

A trinitarian preacher is a servant of Satan as much as any prophet of Baal ever was. The catholic trinity is just as much an idol as Buddha or Krishna.

Carnal

Romans 8:5 For they that are after the flesh do mind the things of the flesh; but they that are after the Spirit the things of the Spirit.

Romans 8:6 For to be carnally minded [is] death; but to be spiritually minded [is] life and peace.

Romans 8:7 Because the carnal mind [is] enmity against God: for it is not subject to the law of God, neither indeed can be.

Romans 8:8 So then they that are in the flesh cannot please God.

I Corinthians 2:12 Now we have received, not the spirit of the world, but the spirit which is of God; that we might know the things that are freely given to us of God.

I Corinthians 2:13 Which things also we speak, not in the words which man's wisdom teacheth, but which the Holy Ghost teacheth; comparing spiritual things with spiritual.

It takes a genuine spiritual rebirth to even be able to understand spiritual things.

I Corinthians 2:14 But the natural man receiveth not the things of the Spirit of God: for they are foolishness unto him: neither can he know [them], because they are spiritually discerned.

I Corinthians 2:15 But he that is spiritual judgeth all things, yet he himself is judged of no man.

***The false preachers will be the ones that teach the popular worldly false doctrines the "mainstream" religions.

I John 4:5 They are of the world: therefore speak they of the world, and the world heareth them.

I John 4:6 We are of God: he that knoweth God heareth us; he that is not of God heareth not us. Hereby know we the spirit of truth, and the spirit of error.

Sins

* Most of the false churches teach that it is "unavoidable" that everyone from the pulpit to the pew will have sin in their lives (and in the false church, it's true, they are, in that respect at least, being honest; they are all living in sin). The main verse that they use to "cover themselves" is usually: *

> I John 1:8 If we say that we have no sin, we deceive ourselves, and the truth is not in us.

* Their contention is that this verse is referring to unrepentant ongoing sin that "can't be helped" and is "normal and unavoidable". So they their false preachers teach the "I sin everyday, you sin everyday we're all just sinners, saved by grace" and if anyone claims to be living clean, they just quote I John 1:8 and say that the individual obviously doesn't have the truth in them. What they are _really_ doing is fullfilling Jude 1:13.*

> Jude 1:13 Raging waves of the sea, foaming out their own shame; wandering stars, to whom is reserved the blackness of darkness for ever.

* Let us look at I John 1:8 IN CONTEXT, and see that it is referring to PAST sins and not ONGOING sins. Everyone has sin in their past and needs to be baptized in Jesus name for the remission of sins. (see Acts 2:38) *

> I John 1:6 If we say that we have fellowship with him, and walk in darkness, we lie, and do not the truth:

* To claim fellowship with Jesus while living in sin (darkness) is to lie. So just the preceding verse of I John 1:6 blows away the false churches "live in sin" doctrine.*

I John 1:7 But if we walk in the light, as he is in the light, we have fellowship one with another, and the blood of Jesus Christ his Son cleanseth us from all sin.

I John 1:8 If we say that we have no sin, we deceive ourselves, and the truth is not in us.

I John 1:9 If we confess our sins, he is faithful and just to forgive us [our] sins, and to cleanse us from all unrighteousness.

I John 1:10 If we say that we have not sinned, we make him a liar, and his word is not in us.

* All have sin in their past, notice the past tense of "have not sinned" this verse does NOT teach that it's "normal" to live in ongoing sin. *

I John 2:1 My little children, these things write I unto you, that ye sin not. And if any man sin, we have an advocate with the Father, Jesus Christ the righteous:

* If a Christian falls from grace (sins), they certainly can (through confession and repentance) be restored to Christianity. *

I John 2:4 He that saith, I know him, and keepeth not his commandments, is a liar, and the truth is not in him.

I John 2:5 But whoso keepeth his word, in him verily is the love of God perfected: hereby know we that we are in him.

* God issued commandments THROUGH His Apostles. Acts 2:38 is just as much a commandment as any other, as are the commandments in Corinthians concerning worship services (which Paul clearly states are "commandments of the Lord"). Here are a few more verses to further knock the props out of the false churches "saved in sin" doctrine. I do want you to remember, though, that sins that have been repented of, and "baptized away through Jesus name baptism" no longer count against you. All "have sinned" but Christians do not continue "in sin". *

I John 3:6 Whosoever abideth in him sinneth not: whosoever sinneth hath not seen him, neither known him.

I John 3:7 Little children, let no man deceive you: he that doeth righteousness is righteous, even as he is righteous.

I John 3:8 He that committeth sin is of the devil; for the devil sinneth from the beginning. For this purpose the Son of God was manifested, that he might destroy the works of the devil. I John 3:9 Whosoever is born of God doth not commit sin; for his seed remaineth in him: and he cannot sin, because he is born of God.

I John 5:18 We know that whosoever is born of God sinneth not; but he that is begotten of God keepeth himself, and that wicked one toucheth him not.

John 8:34 Jesus answered them, Verily, verily, I say unto you, Whosoever committeth sin is the servant of sin.

Romans 6:2 God forbid. How shall we, that are dead to sin, live any longer therein?

Romans 6:6 Knowing this, that our old man is crucified with [him], that the body of sin might be destroyed, that henceforth we should not serve sin.

Romans 6:16 Know ye not, that to whom ye yield yourselves servants to obey, his servants ye are to whom ye obey; whether of sin unto death, or of obedience unto righteousness? Romans 6:17 But God be thanked, that ye were the servants of sin, but ye have obeyed from the heart that form of doctrine which was delivered you.

* False churches also take parts of 'Romans' to try to undermined the importance of obeying doctrine, when Romans declares that it was "obedience to doctrine" that delivered them from their sins. *

I Timothy 5:20 Them that sin rebuke before all, that others also may fear.

Hebrews 10:26 For if we sin wilfully after that we have received the knowledge of the truth, there remaineth no more sacrifice for sins,

* Notice also that the same false churches that teach that living in sin is "normal" are usually the ones that teach that obedience to doctrine is also "unimportant". They hold to a "religious form" they have a "form" or "ritual" of "godliness"; BUT, they deny that Jesus has the strength (or power) to cause people to live above sin. So they just wallow in their shame, denying the "power" to live above sin, while maintaining a "form or ritual of godliness" *

II Timothy 3:1 This know also, that in the last days perilous times shall come.

II Timothy 3:2 For men shall be lovers of their own selves, covetous, boasters, proud, blasphemers, disobedient to parents, unthankful, unholy,

II Timothy 3:3 Without natural affection, trucebreakers, false accusers, incontinent, fierce, despisers of those that are good,

II Timothy 3:4 Traitors, heady, highminded, lovers of pleasures more than lovers of God;

II Timothy 3:5 Having a form of godliness, but denying the power thereof: from such turn away.

II Timothy 3:6 For of this sort are they which creep into houses, and lead captive silly women laden with sins, led away with divers lusts,

II Timothy 3:7 Ever learning, and never able to come to the knowledge of the truth.

II Timothy 3:8 Now as Jannes and Jambres withstood Moses, so do these also resist the truth: men of corrupt minds, reprobate concerning the faith.

Expect

I hope that we would not expect an unrepentant member of a harlot church (or the whore mama) to admit that they were doing anything wrong.

Your Bible uses the words "whore" and "harlot" in it's reference to the great whore's false religious system AND to her denominations.

> Rev 17:1 And there came one of the seven angels which had the seven vials, and talked with me, saying unto me, Come hither; I will shew unto thee the judgment of the great whore that sitteth upon many waters:
>
> Rev 17:4 And the woman was arrayed in purple and scarlet colour, and decked with gold and precious stones and pearls, having a golden cup in her hand full of abominations and filthiness of her fornication:
>
> Rev 17:5 And upon her forehead [was] a name written, MYSTERY, BABYLON THE GREAT, THE MOTHER OF HARLOTS AND ABOMINATIONS OF THE EARTH.

The Bible mentions the principles of a whore's lifestyle:

> Proverbs 30:20 Such [is] the way of an adulterous woman; she eateth, and wipeth her mouth, and saith, I have done no wickedness.

The spiritual "adulteress", "harlot" or "whore" will eat (delve into the Word of God), and true to the spirit of "harlotry" will boldly defend their "position" and say "I have done no wickedness". This is to be *expected* from those who reject the true Gospel of Jesus Christ, and cling to the empty lies of the "harlot church"

Virgin Birth

If Joseph had been having marital relations with Mary before the birth of Jesus Christ, he would not have thought it an irregularity for her to be with child, right?

> Matthew 1:18 ¶ Now the birth of Jesus Christ was on this wise: When as his mother Mary was espoused to Joseph, before they came together, she was found with child of the Holy Ghost.
>
> 19 Then Joseph her husband, being a just man, and not willing to make her a publick example, was minded to put her away privily.
>
> 20 But while he thought on these things, behold, the angel of the Lord appeared unto him in a dream, saying, Joseph, thou son of David, fear not to take unto thee Mary thy wife: for that which is conceived in her is of the Holy Ghost.
>
> 21 And she shall bring forth a son, and thou shalt call his name JESUS: for he shall save his people from their sins.

Mary was a virgin before the birth of Jesus.

After that, she and Joseph had a normal marriage that produced more children the old fashioned way that is still being practiced in this hour.

> Matthew 1:22 Now all this was done, that it might be fulfilled which was spoken of the Lord by the prophet, saying,
>
> 23 Behold, a virgin shall be with child, and shall bring forth a son, and they shall call his name Emmanuel, which being interpreted is, God with us.
>
> 24 Then Joseph being raised from sleep did as the angel of the Lord had bidden him, and took unto him his wife:

> 25 And knew her not till she had brought forth her firstborn son: and he called his name JESUS.

Keyword "till".

> Matthew 13:55 Is not this the carpenter's son? is not his mother called Mary? and his brethren, James, and Joses, and Simon, and Judas?
>
> Mark 3:31 There came then his brethren and his mother, and, standing without, sent unto him, calling him.
>
> Luke 8:19 Then came to him his mother and his brethren, and could not come at him for the press.

Yes, Catholic neighbor, the same ones molesting your boys and covering up for each other were also lying to you about scriptural matters. They are not your friend.

Virgin

While Mary was a virgin at the time of Jesus's birth, she did not remain a virgin, but had normal relations with her husband which is honorable and righteous.

> Luke 1:26 ¶ And in the sixth month the angel Gabriel was sent from God unto a city of Galilee, named Nazareth,
>
> 27 To a virgin espoused to a man whose name was Joseph, of the house of David; and the virgin's name was Mary.
>
> 28 And the angel came in unto her, and said, Hail, thou that art highly favoured, the Lord is with thee: blessed art thou among women.
>
> 29 And when she saw him, she was troubled at his saying, and cast in her mind what manner of salutation this should be.
>
> 30 And the angel said unto her, Fear not, Mary: for thou hast found favour with God.
>
> 31 And, behold, thou shalt conceive in thy womb, and bring forth a son, and shalt call his name JESUS.
>
> 32 He shall be great, and shall be called the Son of the Highest: and the Lord God shall give unto him the throne of his father David:
>
> 33 And he shall reign over the house of Jacob for ever; and of his kingdom there shall be no end.
>
> 34 Then said Mary unto the angel, How shall this be, seeing I know not a man?
>
> 35 And the angel answered and said unto her, The Holy Ghost shall come upon thee, and the power of the Highest shall overshadow thee: therefore also that holy thing which shall be born of thee shall be called the Son of God.

Notice in verse 34 that Mary was quite clear that she had not known a man.

The Bible most certainly does teach that Jesus Christ, God manifest in the flesh, was born of a virgin, a virgin who at first questioned how she could have a child since she was a virgin.

> 1 Timothy 3:16 And without controversy great is the mystery of godliness: God was manifest in the flesh, justified in the Spirit, seen of angels, preached unto the Gentiles, believed on in the world, received up into glory.

However, Mary did not remain a virgin after the birth of Jesus.

> Matthew 1:23 Behold, a virgin shall be with child, and shall bring forth a son, and they shall call his name Emmanuel, which being interpreted is, God with us.
>
> 24 Then Joseph being raised from sleep did as the angel of the Lord had bidden him, and took unto him his wife:
>
> 25 And knew her not till she had brought forth her firstborn son: and he called his name JESUS.

This clearly states that Joseph did know his wife in the physical meaning AFTER Jesus was born.

We see several references to Jesus's brothers.

> Matthew 12:46 While he yet talked to the people, behold, his mother and his brethren stood without, desiring to speak with him.
>
> Matthew 12:47 Then one said unto him, Behold, thy mother and thy brethren stand without, desiring to speak with thee.
>
> Matthew 13:55 Is not this the carpenter’s son? is not his mother called Mary? and his brethren, James, and Joses, and Simon, and Judas?
>
> Mark 3:31 There came then his brethren and his mother, and, standing without, sent unto him, calling him.

> Mark 3:32 And the multitude sat about him, and they said unto him, Behold, thy mother and thy brethren without seek for thee.

And his sisters:

> Mark 6:3 Is not this the carpenter, the son of Mary, the brother of James, and Joses, and of Juda, and Simon? and are not his sisters here with us? And they were offended at him.

Note carefully this was not talking about his disciples.

> John 2:12 After this he went down to Capernaum, he, and his mother, and his brethren, and his disciples: and they continued there not many days.
>
> John 7:3 His brethren therefore said unto him, Depart hence, and go into Judaea, that thy disciples also may see the works that thou doest.
>
> John 7:5 For neither did his brethren believe in him.
>
> John 7:10 But when his brethren were gone up, then went he also up unto the feast, not openly, but as it were in secret.

The Catholics are not being honest with themselves or others.

Also consider that any trinitarian is worshiping the SAME god squad that the pope does and might as well be worshiping Mary too for that matter.

Keys

Many in the false church claim Peter as their "papa" or "pope" even though they reject the Acts 2:38 salvation message that Peter preached when he used the keys that Jesus had given him. Peter certainly was the man with the keys as we will confirm later in this study. Let's look at Peter's salvation

message and note that the other Apostles adhered to this doctrine of Jesus Name Baptism and the Holy Ghost with the initial evidence of speaking in other tongues. Remember that the Apostles had just the same day Peter spoke received the Holy Ghost with the evidence of speaking in other tongues.

> Acts 2:4 And they were all filled with the Holy Ghost, and began to speak with other tongues, as the Spirit gave them utterance.

> Acts 2:38 Then Peter said unto them, Repent, and be baptized every one of you in the name of Jesus Christ for the remission of sins, and ye shall receive the gift of the Holy Ghost.
>
> 39 For the promise is unto you, and to your children, and to all that are afar off, even as many as the Lord our God shall call.
>
> 41 Then they that gladly received his word were baptized: and the same day there were added unto them about three thousand souls.
>
> 42 ¶ And they continued stedfastly in the apostles' doctrine and fellowship, and in breaking of bread, and in prayers.

Why would someone be so silly as to call Peter their "pope" when they don't even obey what he taught? Let us study the foundation of Peter's ministry.

Please notice carefully that Jesus told Peter "when" he was converted (note future tense.) This proves that Peter was not yet "converted" (after Peter *was* converted and received the POWER, he NEVER denied Jesus.)

> Luke 22:31 And the Lord said, Simon, Simon, behold, Satan hath desired [to have] you, that he may sift [you] as wheat:
>
> Luke 22:32 But I have prayed for thee, that thy faith fail not: and when thou art converted, strengthen thy brethren.

Note carefully in the above verse that Jesus did not consider Peter to be converted yet.

> Luke 22:33 And he said unto him, Lord, I am ready to go with thee, both into prison, and to death.
>
> Luke 22:34 And he said, I tell thee, Peter, the cock shall not crow this day, before that thou shalt thrice deny that thou knowest me.

When Jesus spoke of the "church" He spoke of it in "future tense" (the church was not started until the book of Acts).

> Matthew 16:18 And I say also unto thee, That thou art Peter, and upon this rock I will build my church; and the gates of hell shall not prevail against it.

Jesus gave Peter the keys to unlock the door to the new testament church.

> Matthew 16:19 And I will give unto thee the keys of the kingdom of heaven: and whatsoever thou shalt bind on earth shall be bound in heaven: and whatsoever thou shalt loose on earth shall be loosed in heaven.

Peter unlocked the door to the church on the day of Pentecost in approximately 33 AD.

> Acts 2:38 Then Peter said unto them, Repent, and be baptized every one of you in the name of Jesus Christ for the remission of sins, and ye shall receive the gift of the Holy Ghost.

> Acts 2:39 For the promise is unto you, and to your children, and to all that are afar off, [even] as many as the Lord our God shall call.

The man with the keys from Jesus declared that Acts 2:38 was for as many as God would call.

> Acts 2:40 And with many other words did he testify and exhort, saying, Save yourselves from this untoward generation.

> Acts 2:41 Then they that gladly received his word were baptized: and the same day there were added [unto them] about three thousand souls.

Three thousand had their sins remitted by being baptized in Jesus name.

> Acts 2:42 And they continued stedfastly in the apostles' doctrine and fellowship, and in breaking of bread, and in prayers.

They did not depart from that "Apostles' doctrine". But Paul later gave instructions concerning "men pleasing" deceivers that might come along:

> Galatians 1:8 But though we, or an angel from heaven, preach any other gospel unto you than that which we have preached unto you, let him be accursed.

> Galatians 1:9 As we said before, so say I now again, If any [man] preach any other gospel unto you than that ye have received, let him be accursed.

> Galatians 1:10 For do I now persuade men, or God? or do I seek to please men? for if I yet pleased men, I should not be the servant of Christ.

If you are Biblically accursed and not teaching the same message that Peter preached, then you should not call Peter your "first pope". That would simply be dishonest.

Catholic Lite™

The protestants worship the same three headed idol from Rome that the Catholics do. All trinitarians are daughters of the RCC or "Catholic lite"

The false church is following a man made teaching. They have to go to "denominal opinions of men" that originated in the 2nd and 3rd century to explain and discuss their beliefs. It is also interesting that the same bunch at Rome that dreamed up the trinity, also ushered in the dark ages by killing people for possessing Bibles. It is important to realize that the Catholic Church is the "Great Whore" in the book of Rev. and the "mother of harlots" (the harlots being the denominations that retain the trinity heresy). The harlot wants relationship with man, but will not "take the man's name" and will not forsake her worldly loves for her husband. Just as the harlot churches will not use Jesus name in baptism, and will not forsake the sins of the world. Here I will show some of the apostles writing that exposes certain of the false doctrines taught by the harlot churches.:

> Acts 2:38 Then Peter said unto them, Repent, and be baptized every one of you in the name of Jesus Christ for the remission of sins, and ye shall receive the gift of the Holy Ghost.

The harlot churches use the titles of their 3 gods if they even baptize at all. They ignore Matt 28:19 in which Jesus said to use a "name," and they just "parrot" the command instead of obeying it.

Matt 28:19

> Luke 24:47 And that repentance and remission of sins should be preached in his NAME among all nations, beginning at Jerusalem.

Here we have a dire warning against the trinity or anything like it.

> Colossians 2:8 Beware lest any man spoil you through philosophy and vain deceit, after the tradition of men, after

the rudiments of the world, and not after Christ. 9 For in him dwelleth ALL the fulness of the Godhead bodily.

The harlot church doesn't believe that the fulness is in Jesus, they don't believe that "ye are complete in him", they teach the tradition of men from the 2nd and 3rd century.

Colossians 2:10 And ye are complete in HIM, which is the head of all principality and power:

Acts 4:12 Neither is there salvation in any other: for there is none other name under heaven given among men, whereby we must be saved.

Acts 8:16 (For as yet he was fallen upon none of them: only they were baptized in the name of the Lord Jesus.)

17 Then laid they *their* hands on them, and they received the Holy Ghost.

Acts 10:43 To him give all the prophets witness, that through his name whosoever believeth in him shall receive remission of sins.

Acts 10:48 And he commanded them to be baptized in the name of the Lord. Then prayed they him to tarry certain days.

Acts 19:4 Then said Paul, John verily baptized with the baptism of repentance, saying unto the people, that they should believe on him which should come after him, that is, on Christ Jesus.

5 When they heard *this*, they were baptized in the name of the Lord Jesus.

6 And when Paul had laid *his* hands upon them, the Holy Ghost came on them; and they spake with tongues, and prophesied.

Colossians 3:17 And whatsoever ye do in word or deed, *do* all in the name of the Lord Jesus, giving thanks to God and the Father by him.

Here are some historical references showing where tradition replaced apostolic truth:

****

ENCYCLOPEDIA BRITANNICA, 11th Ed. Vol. 3 Page 365-366, "The baptismal formula was changed from the name of Jesus Christ to the words Father, Son, and Holy Ghost by the Catholic Church in the 2nd Century." Vol. 3

Page 82 "Everywhere in the oldest sources it states that baptism took place in the Name of Jesus Christ."

****

CANNEY ENCYCLOPEDIA OF RELIGION, Page 53 -- "The early church always baptized in the Name of Lord Jesus until the development of the trinity doctrine in the 2nd Century."

****

HASTINGS ENCYCLOPEDIA OF RELIGION, Vol. 2 pages 377-378-389, "The Christian baptism was administered using the Name of Jesus. The use of the trinitarian formula of any sort was not suggested in the early church history, baptism was always in the Name of the Lord Jesus, until the time of Justin Martyr when the trinity formula was used."

Hastings also said in Vol. 2 Page 377, commenting on Acts 2:38, "NAME was an ancient synonym for person. Payment was always made in the name of some person referring to ownership. Therefore one being baptized in Jesus Name became his personal property." "Ye are Christ's." I Cor. 3:23.

****

NEW INTERNATIONAL ENCYCLOPEDIA, Vol. 22 Page 477, "The term "trinity" was originated by Tertullain, Roman Catholic Church father."

****

TYNDALE NEW TESTAMENT COMMENTARIES: "... the true explanation why the early church did not at once administer baptism in the threefold name is that the words of Mat 28:19 were not meant as a baptismal formula. [Jesus] was not giving instructions about the actual words to be used in the service of baptism, but, as has already been suggested, was indicating that the baptized

person would by baptism pass into the possession of the Father, the Son, and the Holy Ghost."

****

THE ENCYCLOPEDIA OF RELIGION AND ETHICS, James Hastings, p.384, "there is no evidence [in early church history] for the use of the triune name."

****

> Revelation 17:1 And there came one of the seven angels which had the seven vials, and talked with me, saying unto me, Come hither; I will shew unto thee the judgment of the great whore that sitteth upon many waters:

The RCC "sitteth on many waters", she is international.

> Revelation 17:2 With whom the kings of the earth have committed fornication, and the inhabitants of the earth have been made drunk with the wine of her fornication.

Catholic "indulgences" and false religion have made many "drunk" with her false religion.

> Revelation 17:3 So he carried me away in the spirit into the wilderness: and I saw a woman sit upon a scarlet coloured beast, full of names of blasphemy, having seven heads and ten horns.

The "beast" is the economic community that the "Whore" (the RCC)rides on. The nations support the Vatican.

> Revelation 17:4 And the woman was arrayed in purple and scarlet colour, and decked with gold and precious stones and pearls, having a golden cup in her hand full of abominations and filthiness of her fornication:

The pomp and jewelry and scarlet robes of the RCC.

> Rev 17:5 And upon her forehead [was] a name written, MYSTERY, BABYLON THE GREAT, THE MOTHER OF HARLOTS AND ABOMINATIONS OF THE EARTH.

The RCC is the mother of all of the trinity denominations.

> Revelation 17:6 And I saw the woman drunken with the blood of the saints, and with the blood of the martyrs of Jesus: and when I saw her, I wondered with great admiration.

No organization has murdered (as "heretics") so many real Apostolic Christians as the Roman Catholic Church! History knows no other possible organization than the RCC to fit verse Rev 17:6.

Only Mock

Many of the "three god" cultists mock real Christians and call them "Jesus only" because the real Christians know that there is only one God. The cultists really expose themselves that they are actually polytheistic and that their lord is someone OTHER THAN Jesus.

How can these false christians use the name of Jesus in what they perceive to be an insult and then turn right around and "claim" to be "christian"?

It is important to keep in mind that the Bible likens the daughters of the RCC to "harlot daughters" of the RCC mother church that the Bible calls the Great Whore.

Now whores are certainly not renown for their discretion or scruples, so it is nothing for them to take the Lord's name in vain and then brazenly turn right around and claim that they are His servants.

> Prov 30:20 Such is the way of an adulterous woman; she eateth, and wipeth her mouth, and saith, I have done no wickedness.

We certainly cannot expect those from the "two god" or "three god" harlot cults to admit that they have done anything wrong. "Jesus only" they mock as they attempt to convince others that Jesus isn't really God. That is the gist of their false doctrine, how else could they mock and accuse Jesus's true bride of being "Jesus only".

The true Church is the bride of Christ. Well a bride has only ONE husband, while a whore has several.

Should we be surprised when a "three god" harlot rails at the true bride for having only one husband (Jesus)?

Only Mock

"Jesus only, Jesus only" the harlots will rail at the true bride. The harlots are jealous of the true Christian church.

Of course real Christians are the bride of "one husband only", and that husband is Jesus.

> Exo 34:16 And thou take of their daughters unto thy sons, and their daughters go a whoring after their gods, and make thy sons go a whoring after their gods.
>
> Deu 11:16 Take heed to yourselves, that your heart be not deceived, and ye turn aside, and serve other gods, and worship them;
>
> Deu 11:28 And a curse, if ye will not obey the commandments of the LORD your God, but turn aside out of the way which I command you this day, to go after other gods, which ye have not known.

One thing that typifies the brazenness of the religious harlots is that they will mock at the true bride for having only one husband, saying "Jesus only"; then they will turn right around and "claim" that their "god squad" is only "one god".

Just think about it. The audacity of the "three god" harlot as she mocks and rails at the true bride accusing the bride for only having one husband.

Every time that you see religious filth use the expression "Jesus only" as an insult, just realize that these are the harlot daughters of the "Great Whore", mama trinity herself.

Modalists

We see generic "three god" false christian filth (often without the guts or integrity to even post with their true identity) trying to classify the real "One God" Christian as some sort of cult and they will often bring up some group that the RCC were killing when they had free reign to do so. It is good to remember that the same group doing the killing was also writing history.

Since we know from the Word of God that trinitarians are the spiritual whores and harlots in the Bible, we should also be aware that when such spiritual filth were allowed to murder true Christians, that they would accuse them of some type of "heresy".

One of the names that the whore and harlots would use is "modal monarchist" which basically means that the individual was a monotheist instead of a "three god" whore.

It is not surprising that the "three god" harlots would also "claim" to be "christian" today. It is also not surprising that such spiritual scum would still have nice little "categories" to "categorize" the true Christians as they used to do when they would murder them.

The "harlot daughters" are the denominations that worship the same false gods as the "Great Whore" (the Catholic trinity). Most of the false christian churches are daughters of the RCC. That is another reason that no one can be saved in a trinity church.

The RCC is the mother of all of the trinity denomintations (harlots).

Revelation 17:6 And I saw the woman drunken with the blood of the saints, and with the blood of the martyrs of Jesus: and when I saw her, I wondered with great admiration.

Modalists

When the whore and her harlots would murder the real Christians, they would call them "heretics" also instead of calling them "One God Apostolic Christians" they would call them "modal monarchists". I am sure that some of the souls that the whore murdered were really heretics, but not the majority.

We need to consider also that the whore and her denominations were certainly not above simply LYING about the true saints that they were butchering.

No organization has murdered (as "heretics") so many real Apostolic Christians as the Roman Catholic Church! History knows no other possible organization than the RCC to fit verse Rev 17:6. Her harlot daughters are every bit as filthy as their mother. Speaking of abomination, several of the three god cults are even now ordaining Sodomites.

I guess I find it kind of amazing that, given the historical accounts of the murderous roots of the RCC, AND the blatant disregard for so much of the Bible's commandments; that so many people can be so deceived into a blind loyalty to such a filthy, ungodly cult.

To be a happy catholic or trinitarian one must simply close one's mind to historical events. One must reject most of the Bible that pertains to the new testament church (including the teachings of Peter). The RCC must simultaneously claim Peter as "infallible pope" while declaring that he disobeyed Jesus by teaching JESUS NAME baptism (Acts 2:38). They must teach that Acts 2:38 is disobedience to Matt 28:19 (rather than the FULFILLMENT that it *really* was).

They must disregard the mentions of Jesus' earthly flesh brothers to continue their "mother god" cultism (which is actually the worship of Diana). It is no wonder that they found needful to murder much of the early Christian church (who knew only one God, Jesus[Jehovah Saviour]).

> Galatians 1:19 But other of the apostles saw I none, save James the Lord's brother.

> Acts 1:14 These all continued with one accord in prayer and supplication, with the women, and Mary the mother of Jesus, and with his brethren.

They must attempt to Biblically prove three gods, while knowing that they are going to tack a "one god" disclaimer on the end to try to appear "scriptural". Yet their gods are a "they" rather than a "he".

When pinned down concerning areas of gross disobedience they want to talk about "love" and try to appear gentle and "loving", while their cup still drips with the blood of thousands of true Christians.

There's nothing "Christian" about the RCC OR her harlot denominal daughters.

The RCC is the Great Whore. It is no surprise when her members brazenly blaspheme against God, it is the nature of a harlot.

> Prov 30:20 Such is the way of an adulterous woman; she eateth, and wipeth her mouth, and saith, I have done no wickedness.

> Rev 17:5 And upon her forehead was a name written, MYSTERY, BABYLON THE GREAT, THE MOTHER OF HARLOTS AND ABOMINATIONS OF THE EARTH.

The church of "mystery trinity"

Holy Ghost & Blasphemy

Mat 12:24 But when the Pharisees heard it, they said, This fellow doth not cast out devils, but by Beelzebub the prince of the devils.

Mat 12:28 But if I cast out devils by the Spirit of God, then the kingdom of God is come unto you.

Mat 12:31 Wherefore I say unto you, All manner of sin and blasphemy shall be forgiven unto men: but the blasphemy against the Holy Ghost shall not be forgiven unto men.

Mat 12:32 And whosoever speaketh a word against the Son of man, it shall be forgiven him: but whosoever speaketh against the Holy Ghost, it shall not be forgiven him, neither in this world, neither in the world to come.

Luke 12:10 And whosoever shall speak a word against the Son of man, it shall be forgiven him: but unto him that blasphemeth against the Holy Ghost it shall not be forgiven.

Other Tongues

I am involved with debating a lot of false-christian devils on the internet and various places. One of the fouler devils claims to have obeyed Acts 2:38 which would be a good thing, right? It would be good if he was telling the truth, but he is lying. He claims that he has the Holy Ghost, but when it comes to speaking in other tongues he denies it. He is simply a liar.

You could hardly call a church in the city and ask them if they obeyed any Bible verse and get an honest no answer. Think about it. You call some cult and ask do you obey Acts 2:38 and they would say, "Oh no we don't obey that". Don't hold your breath... Only by asking some questions can we find out if they really are an Acts 2:38 Church. If the preacher or person answering the phone doesn't know what it is, that is not a good sign.

It is the business and calling of the ministers of Satan to pretend to be Christian ministers.

> 2 Corinthians 11:14 And no marvel; for Satan himself is transformed into an angel of light.
>
> 15 Therefore it is no great thing if his ministers also be transformed as the ministers of righteousness; whose end shall be according to their works.

So if we are going to discover the ministers of Satan then we are going to have to know where to look, and that is among the ranks of men calling themselves "Christian minister" or "Christian teacher".

Anyway, the deceiver that I was debating with was claiming to have the Holy Ghost even though he fights against the doctrine of other tongues as the initial evidence of the Holy Ghost baptism. One of the verses he uses to deceive people is:

> 1 Corinthians 12:30 Have all the gifts of healing? do all speak with tongues? do all interpret?

Now that verse is clear that the quoted verse from the Word of God that not all speak with tongues, BUT the type of tongues that Paul was addressing is the "Gift of Tongues", not the "Pentecost tongues" or "other tongues".

What? Am I now saying that there are two completely different types of speaking in tongues? Yes! I believe I can prove it from the scriptures and it is so easy a child could understand it. One type of tongues CAN be understood by men if they happen to speak that language. The other CANNOT be understood by any man and requires a second spiritual gift called "interpretation of tongues".

IT IS ESSENTIAL to understand that there are TWO COMPLETELY DIFFERENT KINDS OF TONGUES in the Bible. #1: Other Tongues and #2: The Gift of Tongues (Unknown tongues).

When the 120 in the upper room were filled with the Holy Ghost they spoke in other tongues(#1).

> Acts 1:15 And in those days Peter stood up in the midst of the disciples, and said, (the number of names together were about an hundred and twenty,)

Other tongues(#1) WAS UNDERSTOOD by men

> Acts 2:5 ¶ And there were dwelling at Jerusalem Jews, devout men, out of every nation under heaven.
>
> 6 Now when this was noised abroad, the multitude came together, and were confounded, because that every man heard them speak in his own language.
>
> 7 And they were all amazed and marvelled, saying one to another, Behold, are not all these which speak Galilaeans?

Acts 2:11 Cretes and Arabians, we do hear them speak in our tongues the wonderful works of God.

In I Cor 14:2 however it says that when a man speaks in "unknown tongues (#2)" that NO MAN UNDERSTANDS him.

1 Corinthians 14:2 For he that speaketh in an unknown tongue speaketh not unto men, but unto God: for no man understandeth him; howbeit in the spirit he speaketh mysteries.

In I Cor 12: 29,30 Paul is speaking concerning "the Gift of Tongues(unknown tongues #2)" when he asks "Do all speak with tongues(#2)?", the group that he was addressing all had spoken in "other tongues(#1)" when they had received the Holy Ghost.

1 Corinthians 12:29 Are all apostles? are all prophets? are all teachers? are all workers of miracles?

30 Have all the gifts of healing? do all speak with tongues? do all interpret?

1 Corinthians 12:4 Now there are diversities of gifts, but the same Spirit.

5 And there are differences of administrations, but the same Lord.

6 And there are diversities of operations, but it is the same God which worketh all in all.

7 But the manifestation of the Spirit is given to every man to profit withal.

8 For to one is given by the Spirit the word of wisdom; to another the word of knowledge by the same Spirit;

> 9 To another faith by the same Spirit; to another the gifts of healing by the same Spirit;
>
> 10 To another the working of miracles; to another prophecy; to another discerning of spirits; to another divers kinds of tongues; to another the interpretation of tongues:
>
> 11 But all these worketh that one and the selfsame Spirit, dividing to every man severally as he will.

Notice in the above verse 9 where Paul is talking about the "Gift of faith" and saying that not all Christians will have it. We don't have the false-christians claiming to be "saved" without faith, though. Faith most certainly is required for salvation but Paul is talking about the "Gift of Faith", not saving Faith! Just like Paul is talking about the "Gift of Tongues" and not "salvation tongues" AKA "other tongues". Think about that! All Christians have faith but not all Christians have the "Gift of Faith".

Though ALL that receive the Holy Ghost DO SPEAK IN OTHER TONGUES(#1). Of these not everyone will be used in the "Gift of Tongues(#2)". Every new-testament Christian will speak in "other tongues(#1)", but every Christian will not be used in the "Gift of tongues(#2)"

Other tongues(#1) is, however, only the initial evidence that a person has been "reborn of the Spirit". It is not an end unto itself, but rather the beginning of a Christian life that should go "on to perfection" and manifest the full "fruit of the Spirit" in due season. Also essential is repentance from sin and baptism in water in the NAME of Jesus.

> Acts 2:38 Then Peter said unto them, Repent, and be baptized every one of you in the name of Jesus Christ for the remission of sins, and ye shall receive the gift of the Holy Ghost.

Everyone in the new testament (including Mary the mother of Jesus) spoke in "other tongues(#1)" when they received the Holy Ghost.

> Acts 1:12 ¶ Then returned they unto Jerusalem from the mount called Olivet, which is from Jerusalem a sabbath day's journey.
>
> 13 And when they were come in, they went up into an upper room, where abode both Peter, and James, and John, and Andrew, Philip, and Thomas, Bartholomew, and Matthew, James the son of Alphaeus, and Simon Zelotes, and Judas the brother of James.
>
> 14 These all continued with one accord in prayer and supplication, with the women, and Mary the mother of Jesus, and with his brethren.
>
> 15 ¶ And in those days Peter stood up in the midst of the disciples, and said, (the number of names together were about an hundred and twenty,)

So we see that Mary, the mother of Jesus was among the 120 in the Upper Room. Then we see that they were ALL filled with the Holy Ghost and began to speak with other tongues.

> Acts 2:1 ¶ And when the day of Pentecost was fully come, they were all with one accord in one place.
>
> 2 And suddenly there came a sound from heaven as of a rushing mighty wind, and it filled all the house where they were sitting.
>
> 3 And there appeared unto them cloven tongues like as of fire, and it sat upon each of them.
>
> 4 And they were all filled with the Holy Ghost, and began to speak with other tongues, as the Spirit gave them utterance.

Remember that the only way that the Apostles knew that Gentiles had received the same Holy Ghost that they had was because they heard them speak in tongues.

> Acts 10:45 And they of the circumcision which believed were astonished, as many as came with Peter, because that on the Gentiles also was poured out the gift of the Holy Ghost.

46 For they heard them speak with tongues, and magnify God. Then answered Peter,

47 Can any man forbid water, that these should not be baptized, which have received the Holy Ghost as well as we?

Acts 2:1 ¶ And when the day of Pentecost was fully come, they were all with one accord in one place.

2 And suddenly there came a sound from heaven as of a rushing mighty wind, and it filled all the house where they were sitting.

3 And there appeared unto them cloven tongues like as of fire, and it sat upon each of them.

4 And they were all filled with the Holy Ghost, and began to speak with other tongues, as the Spirit gave them utterance.

Acts 19:4 Then said Paul, John verily baptized with the baptism of repentance, saying unto the people, that they should believe on him which should come after him, that is, on Christ Jesus.

5 When they heard this, they were baptized in the name of the Lord Jesus.

6 And when Paul had laid his hands upon them, the Holy Ghost came on them; and they spake with tongues, and prophesied.

Those who don't believe in Jesus Name water baptism and speaking in other tongues don't really believe the Bible at all and are not a part of the religion of the Bible. But don't expect ministers of Satan to admit that they are ministers of Satan or in many cases to even realize that they are actually serving the devil.

It does not excuse a false preacher because he is deceived!

> 2 Timothy 3:13 But evil men and seducers shall wax worse and worse, deceiving, and being deceived.

Those who have not received the Holy Ghost speaking in tongues need to quit their lying and claiming to have the Holy Ghost baptism and start seeking God for real Biblical salvation!

The devils that I am debating on the internet can't admit the truth because of their pride. They can't admit that they are not even Christians when they have been playing "christian" for so long! They certainly won't be the first load to hit hell because of their pride. Don't go with them. It's just not a smart thing to do.

Missionary

I just wanted to mention to any of our international readers that if a missionary is claiming to be "christian" but is teaching a "trinity" that they are fakes and are only there to con you. Some of them might be very nice and pleasant, but they are there to poison your souls. They "sugar-coat" their poison lies.

> Col 2:8 Beware lest any man spoil you through philosophy and vain deceit, after the tradition of men, after the rudiments of the world, and not after Christ.
>
> Col 2:9 For in him dwelleth all the fulness of the Godhead bodily.
>
> Col 2:10 And ye are complete in him, which is the head of all principality and power:

The basic thing that these false christian missionaries do is that they teach you that you are "christian" even if you never do what the Bible says. But we see here what Jesus will do to those that the trinity missionaries deceive into disobeying God:

> 2 Th 1:7 And to you who are troubled rest with us, when the Lord Jesus shall be revealed from heaven with his mighty angels,
>
> 2 Th 1:8 In flaming fire taking vengeance on them that know not God, and that obey not the gospel of our Lord Jesus Christ:
>
> 2 Th 1:9 Who shall be punished with everlasting destruction from the presence of the Lord, and from the glory of his power;

The *only* way to *really* be Christian is to do what the Bible says. Why would a missionary tell you not to obey the Bible? Because a trinity missionary is a liar and a devil. The Bible says:

> Acts 2:38 Then Peter said unto them, Repent, and be baptized every one of you in the name of Jesus Christ for the remission of sins, and ye shall receive the gift of the Holy Ghost.
>
> Acts 2:39 For the promise is unto you, and to your children, and to all that are afar off, [even] as many as the Lord our God shall call.

Notice that verse says "as many as the Lord our God shall call."

> Acts 2:40 And with many other words did he testify and exhort, saying, Save yourselves from this untoward generation.
>
> Acts 2:41 Then they that gladly received his word were baptized: and the same day there were added [unto them] about three thousand souls.

Look that 3000 were baptized in Jesus name (no trinity here)

> Galatians 1:8 But though we, or an angel from heaven, preach any other gospel unto you than that which we have preached unto you, let him be accursed.

See here that the trinity missionary is said by the Bible to be "accursed". The Bible also warned that the devil's ministers would pretend to be "christian", just like the trinity missionaries do (actually the trinity cults were the ones who murdered the real Christians in early history)

> II Corinthians 11:13 For such [are] false apostles, deceitful workers, transforming themselves into the apostles of Christ.
>
> II Corinthians 11:14 And no marvel; for Satan himself is transformed into an angel of light.
>
> II Corinthians 11:15 Therefore [it is] no great thing if his ministers also be transformed as the ministers of righteousness; whose end shall be according to their works.

> Revelation 17:4 And the woman was arrayed in purple and scarlet colour, and decked with gold and precious stones and pearls, having a golden cup in her hand full of abominations and filthiness of her fornication:

The Roman Catholic cult with their scarlet robes and stuff is the "Whore"

> Revelation 17:5 And upon her forehead [was] a name written, MYSTERY, BABYLON THE GREAT, THE MOTHER OF HARLOTS AND ABOMINATIONS OF THE EARTH.

The trinity missionaries are part of the "harlot" daughters.

> Revelation 17:6 And I saw the woman drunken with the blood of the saints, and with the blood of the martyrs of Jesus: and when I saw her, I wondered with great admiration.

History clearly tells of how the Roman Catholic cult and her protestant harlot daughters murdered the real Christians (the real saints). They would call them "heretics" and then they would murder them.

Don't be deceived by the harlot trinity missionaries. They are devils.

Find a real Christian preacher that preaches Acts 2:38 like the Apostles preached and baptized in Jesus NAME. (One God, one name)

Judiaser

There are those who like to feign scholarship and play with original languages to kind of gain a "oneupmanship" over people and deceive them. They often get by because their frivolous spewings are so mentally straining to decipher that many just pass it by, but believe that the deceiver is a scholar. In that sense the deceiver has "put himself over" as a scholar, when, in fact, it is just smokescreen and mirrors.

Just because something is lengthy, complicated and mentally excruciating to read, does not at all mean that it is even remotely true. Here are just a couple of Bible verses in regular plain English that pop the tires of the Judaiser.

First of all notice that "Rabbi Paul"...oh yes let's look at that one for a second..Doesn't that sound so spiritual to say "rabbi" and use an original word? Check this plain English verse out:

> Matthew 23:8 But be not ye called Rabbi: for one is your Master, [even] Christ; and all ye are brethren.
>
> Matthew 23:9 And call no [man] your father upon the earth: for one is your Father, which is in heaven.

Also, if you boil it down and skim off all the veneer and smokescreen, the "rabbi paul" crowd is actually worshipping the three headed Roman god called the "Holy Trinity" they just have their own brand of smokescreen and confusion.

Concerning physical circumcision. (all the fake christians just *luv* to cry "legalism" every time a new testament commandment is mentioned, but in truth, "legalism" only applies to the Judaiser trying to get people back under the Jewish ceremonial law.) Look at these plain English verses:

> I Corinthians 7:18 Is any man called being circumcised? let him not become uncircumcised. Is any called in uncircumcision? let him not be circumcised.

> I Corinthians 7:19 Circumcision is nothing, and uncircumcision is nothing, but the keeping of the commandments of God.

To be "circumcised" in the new testament sense means obeying the commandments of God. Salvation is only to the obedient. New testament circumcision is water baptism in the name of Jesus Christ as commanded in Acts 2:38 for the remission of sins.

> Acts 2:38 Then Peter said unto them, Repent, and be baptized every one of you in the name of Jesus Christ for the remission of sins, and ye shall receive the gift of the Holy Ghost.
>
> Acts 2:39 For the promise is unto you, and to your children, and to all that are afar off, [even] as many as the Lord our God shall call.
>
> Acts 22:16 And now why tarriest thou? arise, and be baptized, and wash away thy sins, calling on the name of the Lord.
>
> Colossians 2:11 In whom also ye are circumcised with the circumcision made without hands, in putting off the body of the sins of the flesh by the circumcision of Christ:
>
> Colossians 2:12 Buried with him in baptism, wherein also ye are risen with [him] through the faith of the operation of God, who hath raised him from the dead.

Sins are remitted through the "circumcision of Christ" which IS Jesus name water baptism.

> Colossians 2:13 And you, being dead in your sins and the uncircumcision of your flesh, hath he quickened together with him, having forgiven you all trespasses;
>
> Colossians 2:14 Blotting out the handwriting of ordinances that was against us, which was contrary to us, and took it out of the way, nailing it to his cross;

> Colossians 2:15 [And] having spoiled principalities and powers, he made a shew of them openly, triumphing over them in it.
>
> Colossians 2:16 Let no man therefore judge you in meat, or in drink, or in respect of an holyday, or of the new moon, or of the sabbath [days]:

Notice also that no Christian is required to keep the sabbath. Also, if you study the sabbath you will see that the Judaisers aren't really keeping the sabbath themselves, they are just trying to snow you.

> Revelation 3:9 Behold, I will make them of the synagogue of Satan, which say they are Jews, and are not, but do lie; behold, I will make them to come and worship before thy feet, and to know that I have loved thee.

Posing

The reason that men are posing as "ministers" and preaching against the clear commandments of the Bible is addressed:

II Corinthians 11:12 But what I do, that I will do, that I may cut off occasion from them which desire occasion; that wherein they glory, they may be found even as we.

II Corinthians 11:13 For such [are] false apostles, deceitful workers, transforming themselves into the apostles of Christ.

II Corinthians 11:14 And no marvel; for Satan himself is transformed into an angel of light.

II Corinthians 11:15 Therefore [it is] no great thing if his ministers also be transformed as the ministers of righteousness; whose end shall be according to their works.

II Timothy 3:13 But evil men and seducers shall wax worse and worse, deceiving, and being deceived.

II Timothy 3:14 But continue thou in the things which thou hast learned and hast been assured of, knowing of whom thou hast learned [them];

II Timothy 3:15 And that from a child thou hast known the holy scriptures, which are able to make thee wise unto salvation through faith which is in Christ Jesus.

II Timothy 3:16 All scripture [is] given by inspiration of God, and [is] profitable for doctrine, for reproof, for correction, for instruction in righteousness:

II Timothy 3:17 That the man of God may be perfect, throughly furnished unto all good works.

II Timothy 4:1 I charge [thee] therefore before God, and the Lord Jesus Christ, who shall judge the quick and the dead at his appearing and his kingdom;

II Timothy 4:2 Preach the word; be instant in season, out of season; reprove, rebuke, exhort with all longsuffering and doctrine.

II Timothy 4:3 For the time will come when they will not endure sound doctrine; but after their own lusts shall they heap to themselves teachers, having itching ears;

II Timothy 4:4 And they shall turn away [their] ears from the truth, and shall be turned unto fables.

The False Preacher

> 2 Timothy 4:2 Preach the word; be instant in season, out of season; reprove, rebuke, exhort with all longsuffering and doctrine.

You know that I am not one to preach stories, but I will share with you the following because it is true and it proves my point about the false church.

I found myself seated next to a false preacher at a political function and we were having a conversation. Some of the highlights were as follows.

He asked what Church we were from and I said Jesus Name Apostolic Holiness and I could sense him recoiling in the spirit and some discomfort. I went on to say that we were part of the "back to the Bible" movement because so many churches were not lining up with the Word of God. He made some comment asking if I believed that the Bible had errors in it and I basically ignored his question and continued with my commentary. I went on about how false-christianity was the con game of con games. He commented that I must feel very strongly about it and I mentioned that there was a lot at stake.

I then mentioned how most of the modern religions don't at all match up with the Church of the Book of Acts and they don't believe in Jesus Name baptism or the Holy Ghost speaking in tongues. I told him how in many of the "Bible colleges" run by false churches that sometimes students will read the Bible, seek God on their own and receive the Holy Ghost speaking with tongues but if they tell people about it they are simply kicked out.

I mentioned that many of the false preachers can't allow the truth because they have bills to pay. How can they tell their current congregations that they have already deceived grandmaw and grampa into hell.

About that time he asked me if I was familiar with some genealogy and I said I wasn't. He went on to explain how some linage in the Bible was in error and left.

So here is this guy, supposedly a "christian" preacher betting his eternal soul on the hope that the Bible is in error.

A little later someone came inquiring about the vacant seat beside me and I told them he had left. Then I commented to a man across the table who had been watching all this something like Man that false preacher just tried to convince me that the Bible isn't true and then left. If he doesn't believe the Bible what is he doing claiming to be a preacher?

It is my understanding that the supposed error the supposed preacher had found is one of the many that has been debunked anyway. Something about the variation being caused by one tracing Mary and the other tracing Joseph.

I am really not going to get into all that because:

> 1 Timothy 1:4 Neither give heed to fables and endless genealogies, which minister questions, rather than godly edifying which is in faith: so do.

So many of the false churches know full well that they don't match up with the religion of the Bible but they think that if they can find some error that it justifies them! What a sad state of affairs to be in!

Some other things I mentioned to that false preacher, I told him how the Bible says that Satan's ministers will be false preachers and that Satan is in the false preacher business.

> 2 Corinthians 11:12 But what I do, that I will do, that I may cut off occasion from them which desire occasion; that wherein they glory, they may be found even as we.

> 13 For such are false apostles, deceitful workers, transforming themselves into the apostles of Christ.
>
> 14 And no marvel; for Satan himself is transformed into an angel of light.
>
> 15 Therefore it is no great thing if his ministers also be transformed as the ministers of righteousness; whose end shall be according to their works.

It is a hard thing for so many people because their social identity is so tied up in some false church and they are ensnared. I understand that there are some very fine kind loving people so ensnared.

People just aren't thinking. If we base our hope of heaven on the Bible, but then follow a doctrine contrary to what the Bible teaches based on the hope that the Bible really isn't true are we really being honest?

In the Bible the Apostles baptized in Jesus Name and not in trinity titles. Why would someone choose to trust some modern false preacher more than they trust the Apostles?

> Acts 2:38 Then Peter said unto them, Repent, and be baptized every one of you in the name of Jesus Christ for the remission of sins, and ye shall receive the gift of the Holy Ghost.

If the Bible isn't true, what is the point?

> Acts 8:12 But when they believed Philip preaching the things concerning the kingdom of God, and the name of Jesus Christ, they were baptized, both men and women.

> Acts 8:16 (For as yet he was fallen upon none of them: only they were baptized in the name of the Lord Jesus.)

All these verses that establish that baptism is to be administered in the name of Jesus, but people will choose to reject the Bible because it is not compatible with their church traditions and doctrines.

> Acts 19:4 Then said Paul, John verily baptized with the baptism of repentance, saying unto the people, that they should believe on him which should come after him, that is, on Christ Jesus.
>
> Acts 19:5 When they heard this, they were baptized in the name of the Lord Jesus.

What did the people do when they were told to believe on Jesus? So why are so many in false churches in this hour, churches that don't even remotely resemble the Church in the Bible?

> 2 Timothy 4:3 For the time will come when they will not endure sound doctrine; but after their own lusts shall they heap to themselves teachers, having itching ears;
>
> 3 For the time will come when they will not endure sound doctrine; but after their own lusts shall they heap to themselves teachers, having itching ears;
>
> 4 And they shall turn away their ears from the truth, and shall be turned unto fables.

Sadly they are doing exactly what the Bible said they would do.

Trinity or One God

Spotting the harlots

Of course the harlot churches are going to "claim" to believe in only one god. They will throw up great smoke screens of confusion to mask their polytheism and whoredom.

A *very* easy way to spot most of them (most all trinity cults), is the fact that they reject the name of the Lord in baptism. They lie and spout a multitude of excuses, but the fact remains that their cult doesn't baptize in Jesus name. They merely repeat "titles" (notice the plural, they claim "one god", but need THREE titles in baptism (they confuse these titles as "names")

They are harlots, they see no need in wearing the NAME of the bridegroom.

> Galatians 3:27 For as many of you as have been baptized into Christ have put on Christ.

> Acts 2:38 Then Peter said unto them, Repent, and be baptized every one of you in the name of Jesus Christ for the remission of sins, and ye shall receive the gift of the Holy Ghost.

> Acts 2:39 For the promise is unto you, and to your children, and to all that are afar off, [even] as many as the Lord our God shall call.

The Apostles KNEW the NAME of the Father, Son, and Holy Ghost. They used that NAME when they baptized. It is the ONLY SAVING NAME.

> Acts 4:10 Be it known unto you all, and to all the people of Israel, that by the name of Jesus Christ of Nazareth, whom ye crucified, whom God raised from the dead, [even] by him doth this man stand here before you whole.

> Acts 4:11 This is the stone which was set at nought of you builders, which is become the head of the corner.

> Acts 4:12 Neither is there salvation in any other: for there is none other name under heaven given among men, whereby we must be saved.

Look at the bottom line, folks. Look beyond all the religious claims and fake "lovey dovey". Are they baptizing in Jesus name? Or are they spewing great clouds of reasons why "it doesn't matter"? They are fishing for fools when they teach that the apostles disobeyed Jesus. The apostles baptized in Jesus name (the NAME must be used in order to obey Matt 28:19).

Don't be deceived by the modern religious deceivers who are merely scratching the itching ears of the lost and deceived with "yet another fable".

> II Timothy 4:3 For the time will come when they will not endure sound doctrine; but after their own lusts shall they heap to themselves teachers, having itching ears;
>
> II Timothy 4:4 And they shall turn away [their] ears from the truth, and shall be turned unto fables.

A fable can't save you. Have you been water baptized in Jesus name by a real preacher? If not, you haven't obeyed the Bible at all, don't kid yourself.

Taking on the name of a bridegroom is the difference between a whore and a bride. One calls on Jesus name by being baptized in that name.

> Acts 22:16 And now why tarriest thou? arise, and be baptized, and wash away thy sins, calling on the name of the Lord.
>
> Acts 2:38 Then Peter said unto them, Repent, and be baptized every one of you in the name of Jesus Christ for the remission of sins, and ye shall receive the gift of the Holy Ghost.

> Acts 2:39 For the promise is unto you, and to your children, and to all that are afar off, [even] as many as the Lord our God shall call.

> Acts 2:40 And with many other words did he testify and exhort, saying, Save yourselves from this untoward generation.

> Acts 2:41 Then they that gladly received his word were baptized: and the same day there were added [unto them] about three thousand souls.

> Acts 2:42 And they continued stedfastly in the apostles' doctrine and fellowship, and in breaking of bread, and in prayers.

(The "epistles" of the Bible were letters written to people who had obeyed Acts 2:38 and were continuing in it)

Don't be deceived into fake christianity, they are Satanic souls teaching disobedience to the Bible.

> II Corinthians 11:12 But what I do, that I will do, that I may cut off occasion from them which desire occasion; that wherein they glory, they may be found even as we.

> II Corinthians 11:13 For such [are] false apostles, deceitful workers, transforming themselves into the apostles of Christ.

> II Corinthians 11:14 And no marvel; for Satan himself is transformed into an angel of light.

> II Corinthians 11:15 Therefore [it is] no great thing if his ministers also be transformed as the ministers of righteousness; whose end shall be according to their works.

Don't let these Satanic ministers deceive you. Obey Acts 2:28 to become a Biblical Christian, that's what the apostles taught and practiced, nothing less than that is real.

Catholic Roots

The trinitarian should be aware of their roots. The Apostles knew nothing of any trinity. Jesus was careful to instruct them. Some examples being:

> Mark 12:29 And Jesus answered him, The first of all the commandments is, Hear, O Israel; The Lord our God is one Lord:

That is a commandment to be aware of the Oneness of God.

> John 14:9 Jesus saith unto him, Have I been so long time with you, and yet hast thou not known me, Philip? he that hath seen me hath seen the Father; and how sayest thou then, Shew us the Father?

There Jesus pointed out that someone who thought that the Father was a separate person didn't know Jesus at all. Look carefully.

The RCC is the "Great Whore" in the book of Revelation.

> Revelation 17:1 And there came one of the seven angels which had the seven vials, and talked with me, saying unto me, Come hither; I will shew unto thee the judgment of the great whore that sitteth upon many waters:
>
> 2 With whom the kings of the earth have committed fornication, and the inhabitants of the earth have been made drunk with the wine of her fornication.
>
> 3 So he carried me away in the spirit into the wilderness: and I saw a woman sit upon a scarlet coloured beast, full of names of blasphemy, having seven heads and ten horns.
>
> 4 And the woman was arrayed in purple and scarlet colour, and decked with gold and precious stones and pearls, having a golden cup in her hand full of abominations and filthiness of her fornication:
>
> 5 And upon her forehead was a name written, MYSTERY, BABYLON THE GREAT, THE MOTHER OF HARLOTS AND ABOMINATIONS OF THE EARTH.

> 6 And I saw the woman drunken with the blood of the saints, and with the blood of the martyrs of Jesus: and when I saw her, I wondered with great admiration.

The "harlot daughters" are none other than the denominations that worship the same false gods as the "Great Whore" (the Catholic trinity).

Most all of the false christian churches are daughters of the RCC. That is another reason that no one can be saved in a trinity church.

> Revelation 17:1 And there came one of the seven angels which had the seven vials, and talked with me, saying unto me, Come hither; I will shew unto thee the judgment of the great whore that sitteth upon many waters:

The RCC "sitteth on many waters", she is international.

> Revelation 17:2 With whom the kings of the earth have committed fornication, and the inhabitants of the earth have been made drunk with the wine of her fornication.

Catholic "indulgences" and false religion have made many "drunk" with her false religion.

> Revelation 17:3 So he carried me away in the spirit into the wilderness: and I saw a woman sit upon a scarlet coloured beast, full of names of blasphemy, having seven heads and ten horns.
>
> Revelation 17:4 And the woman was arrayed in purple and scarlet colour, and decked with gold and precious stones and pearls, having a golden cup in her hand full of abominations and filthiness of her fornication:

The pomp and jewelry and purple scarlet robes of the RCC.

> Revelation 17:5 And upon her forehead [was] a name written, MYSTERY, BABYLON THE GREAT, THE MOTHER OF HARLOTS AND ABOMINATIONS OF THE EARTH.

The RCC is the mother of all of the trinity denominations.

> Revelation 17:6 And I saw the woman drunken with the blood of the saints, and with the blood of the martyrs of Jesus: and when I saw her, I wondered with great admiration.

No organization has murdered (as "heretics") so many real Apostolic Christians as the Roman Catholic Church! History knows no other possible organization than the RCC to fit verse Rev 17:6.

There is a judgment ahead for the false church. Consider carefully that there is no false-christian organization on Earth that has EVER slaughtered real Christians like the Roman Catholic Church.

> Revelation 19:1 ¶ And after these things I heard a great voice of much people in heaven, saying, Alleluia; Salvation, and glory, and honour, and power, unto the Lord our God:
>
> 2 For true and righteous are his judgments: for he hath judged the great whore, which did corrupt the earth with her fornication, and hath avenged the blood of his servants at her hand.
>
> 3 And again they said, Alleluia. And her smoke rose up for ever and ever.
>
> 4 And the four and twenty elders and the four beasts fell down and worshipped God that sat on the throne, saying, Amen; Alleluia.
>
> 5 ¶ And a voice came out of the throne, saying, Praise our God, all ye his servants, and ye that fear him, both small and great.
>
> 6 And I heard as it were the voice of a great multitude, and as the voice of many waters, and as the voice of mighty

thunderings, saying, Alleluia: for the Lord God omnipotent reigneth.

7 Let us be glad and rejoice, and give honour to him: for the marriage of the Lamb is come, and his wife hath made herself ready.

8 And to her was granted that she should be arrayed in fine linen, clean and white: for the fine linen is the righteousness of saints.

9 And he saith unto me, Write, Blessed are they which are called unto the marriage supper of the Lamb. And he saith unto me, These are the true sayings of God.

Trinity

The Doctrine of the trinity clearly states that God is three separate persons, co-eternal, co-equal. Many are taught that this theory must be accepted, that it is beyond human understanding, and must be accepted by faith. While I believe that there is much in the word of God that should be accepted by faith, I don't believe that a human theory that contradicts the word of God need be accepted at all.

In Isaiah Chapter 44-46 God clearly declares that there is no God beside him and no god equal to him, that he is alone. According to the trinity the three separate persons are having fellowship together during this period. Is 44: 6,8, 24 Is 45: 5, 6, 18, 21, 22 Is 46: 5, 9. You need to stick with the Bible!

Isaiah 9:6 Clearly states that the child that is to be born is the everlasting Father, the Mighty God. In Matt 28:18 Jesus clearly states that he has ALL POWER, so if there were any separate "persons" they would be powerless. Jesus even told Philip "He that hath seen me hath seen the Father." John 14:9 The doctrine of the trinity is simply carnal ungodly men attempting to explain spiritual things to other carnal men.

In Matt 28:19 Jesus told his disciples to baptize using a name. The apostles did use a name, they used the name of Jesus. Acts 2:38, 8:16, 19:5.

In Acts 9:5 When Saul cried out to God and asked God who he was, God answered and said, "I AM JESUS". The devil has many deceived into thinking that Jesus is a junior one third of god, when in fact JESUS IS THE MIGHTY GOD!

Harlot

The protestants worship the same three headed idol from Rome that the Catholics do. All trinitarians are daughters of the RCC.

The false church is following a man made teaching. They have to go to "denominal opinions of men" that originated in the 2nd and 3rd century to explain and discuss their beliefs. It is also interesting that the same bunch at Rome that dreamed up the trinity, also ushered in the dark ages by killing people for possessing Bibles. It is important to realize that the Catholic Church is the "Great Whore" in the book of Rev. and the "mother of harlots" (the harlots being the denominations that retain the trinity heresy). The harlot wants relationship with man, but will not "take the man's name" and will not forsake her worldly loves for her husband. Just as the harlot churches will not use Jesus name in baptism, and will not forsake the sins of the world.

> Revelation 17:5 And upon her forehead was a name written, MYSTERY, BABYLON THE GREAT, THE MOTHER OF HARLOTS AND ABOMINATIONS OF THE EARTH.

Here I will show some of the apostles writing that exposes certain of the false doctrines taught by the harlot churches.:

> Acts 2:38 Then Peter said unto them, Repent, and be baptized every one of you in the name of Jesus Christ for the remission of sins, and ye shall receive the gift of the Holy Ghost.

The harlot trinity churches use the titles of their 3 gods if they even baptize at all. They ignore Matt 28:19 in which Jesus said to use a "name," and they just "parrot" the command instead of obeying it.

> Luke 24:47 And that repentance and remission of sins should be preached in his NAME among all nations, beginning at Jerusalem.
>
> Colossians 2:8 Beware lest any man spoil you through philosophy and vain deceit, after the tradition of men, after the rudiments of the world, and not after Christ.
>
> Colossians 2:9 For in him dwelleth ALL the fulness of the Godhead bodily.

The harlot trinity church doesn't believe that the fulness is in Jesus, they don't believe that "ye are complete in him", they teach the tradition of men from the 2nd and 3rd century.

> Colossians 2:10 And ye are complete in HIM, which is the head of all principality and power: Acts 4:12 Neither is there salvation in any other: for there is none other name under heaven given among men, whereby we must be saved. Also Acts 8:16, 10:48, 10:43, 19:5, Col 3:17

Also here are some historical references showing where tradition replaced apostolic truth.:

ENCYCLOPEDIA BRITANNICA, 11th Ed. Vol. 3 Page 365-366,

> "The baptismal formula was changed from the name of Jesus Christ to the words Father, Son, and Holy Ghost by the Catholic Church in the 2nd Century." Vol. 3 Page 82 "Everywhere in the oldest sources it states that baptism took place in the Name of Jesus Christ."

CANNEY ENCYCLOPEDIA OF RELIGION, Page 53 --

> "The early church always baptized in the Name of Lord Jesus until the development of the trinity doctrine in the 2nd Century."

HASTINGS ENCYCLOPEDIA OF RELIGION, Vol. 2 pages 377-378-389,

> "The Christian baptism was administered using the Name of Jesus. The use of the trinitarian formula of any sort was not suggested in the early church history, baptism was always in the Name of the Lord Jesus, until the time of Justin Martyr when the trinity formula was used." Hastings also said in Vol. 2 Page 377, commenting on Acts 2:38, "NAME was an ancient synonym for person. Payment was always made in the name of some person referring to ownership. Therefore one being baptized in Jesus Name became his personal property." "Ye are Christ's." I Cor. 3:23.

NEW INTERNATIONAL ENCYCLOPEDIA, Vol. 22 Page 477,

> "The term "trinity" was originated by Tertullain, Roman Catholic Church father."

TYNDALE NEW TESTAMENT COMMENTARIES:

> "... the true explanation why the early church did not at once administer baptism in the threefold name is that the words of Mat 28:19 were not meant as a baptismal formula. [Jesus] was not giving instructions about the actual words to be used in the service of baptism, but, as has already been suggested, was indicating that the baptized person would by baptism pass into the possession of the Father, the Son, and the Holy Ghost."

THE ENCYCLOPEDIA OF RELIGION AND ETHICS, James Hastings, p.384,

> "there is no evidence [in early church history] for the use of the triune name."

And Dad

Just have a look at these verses.

> Ephesians 5:20 Giving thanks always for all things unto God and the Father in the name of our Lord Jesus Christ;
>
> Philippians 4:20 Now unto God and our Father [be] glory for ever and ever. Amen.
>
> Colossians 1:3 We give thanks to God and the Father of our Lord Jesus Christ, praying always for you,
>
> I Thessalonians 1:3 Remembering without ceasing your work of faith, and labour of love, and patience of hope in our Lord Jesus Christ, in the sight of God and our Father;
>
> I Thessalonians 3:11 Now God himself and our Father, and our Lord Jesus Christ, direct our way unto you.

I can't imagine why the trinitarians don't teach that "God" and "Father" are two separate persons.

They didn't follow their thinking to its logical conclusion of a lot more than just three gods in a squad.

They will try to teach that "father" and "son" are separate persons in a god squad, but ignore the verses above that would (if taken in the same ignorance) also teach "Father" and "God" as two separate persons.

Don't let the trinitarians deceive you into hell with their polytheistic foolishness. It's just not a good idea.

Hebrews

Heb 1:1 God, who at sundry times and in divers manners spake in time past unto the fathers by the prophets,

Heb 1:2 Hath in these last days spoken unto us by his Son, whom he hath appointed heir of all things, by whom also he made the worlds;

Heb 1:3 Who being the brightness of his glory, and the express image of his person, and upholding all things by the word of his power, when he had by himself purged our sins, sat down on the right hand of the Majesty on high;

Heb 1:4 Being made so much better than the angels, as he hath by inheritance obtained a more excellent name than they.

Heb 1:5 For unto which of the angels said he at any time, Thou art my Son, this day have I begotten thee? And again, I will be to him a Father, and he shall be to me a Son?

Heb 1:6 And again, when he bringeth in the firstbegotten into the world, he saith, And let all the angels of God worship him.

Heb 1:7 And of the angels he saith, Who maketh his angels spirits, and his ministers a flame of fire.

Heb 1:8 But unto the Son he saith, Thy throne, O God, is for ever and ever: a sceptre of righteousness is the sceptre of thy kingdom.

Heb 1:9 Thou hast loved righteousness, and hated iniquity; therefore God, even thy God, hath anointed thee with the oil of gladness above thy fellows.

Heb 1:10 And, Thou, Lord, in the beginning hast laid the foundation of the earth; and the heavens are the works of thine hands:

It is interesting that some cultists will try to use the above verses (ie. verse 8) to try to prove that the "Son" is a separate god from the "Father". But why would they stop before verse 10 and trying to teach that the "Lord" is also a separate godlet in their god squad?

> Hebrews 1 1:10 are the words of a prophet (and is most assuredly the Word of God, just as the Psalms) and this verse:
>
> 1 Sam 2:2 There is none holy as the LORD: for there is none beside thee: neither is there any rock like our God.

Let' take a brief look at a couple of the verses that many cultists misunderstand and twist.

> Heb 1:2 Hath in these last days spoken unto us by his Son, whom he hath appointed heir of all things, by whom also he made the worlds;

Those of us who are aware that Jesus was God manifest in the flesh see this verse as saying that God has spoken to us by (or through) his begotten flesh body, or "physical being".

> 1 Tim 3:16 And without controversy great is the mystery of godliness: God was manifest in the flesh, justified in the Spirit, seen of angels, preached unto the Gentiles, believed on in the world, received up into glory.

> Heb 1:3 Who being the brightness of his glory, and the express image of his person, and upholding all things by the word of his power, when he had by himself purged our sins, sat down on the right hand of the Majesty on high;

Here is another verse that shows that Jesus Christ is the PERSON God and not a "second person" (as the three god people teach). Would not verse 3 have to read "image of the second person" to fit the trinity cultists whim??? (we'll give them 3 question marks to make them at ease).

Here the prophet equates the "first person" with the "second person".

> Heb 1:8 But unto the Son he saith, Thy throne, O God, is for ever and ever: a sceptre of righteousness is the sceptre of thy kingdom.

Oh my, trinito! This puts god person #2 on the throne instead of god person #1. (Hey maybe they just switched and god #1 is now sitting on god #2's hand, eh???)

Look

Let's look and see how the trinity fits into these BIBLE verses. My point is that Jesus is NOT "person #2" of a Roman, 2nd century "god squad".

> Jeremiah 16: 20 Shall a man make gods unto himself, and they are no Gods?"

* You can't just make them up as you go along. *

> Deut 4:35 Unto thee it was shewed, that thou mightest know that the Lord he is God; there is none else beside him.

* Oops, where are the other persons? I thought the trinity had god #2 sitting on the right hand of god #1.*

> Deut 4:39 Know therefore this day, and consider it in thine heart, that the Lord he is God in heaven above, and upon the earth beneath; there is none else.

* God denying the "other persons"? *

> Deut 6:4 Hear, O Isriael: The Lord our God is one Lord:

* Here, O deceived: the catholic idol, your gods are three lords. *

> Deut 32:39 See now that I, even I, am he, and THERE IS NO GOD WITH ME: I kill, and I make alive; I wound and I heal: neither is there any that can deliver out of my hand.

* What? no co-equal, co-eternal "persons"?

> Psalms 86:10 For thou art great, and doest wonderous things: THOU ART GOD ALONE.

- (alone except for the other "persons", eh?) *
-

Isaiah 43:11 I, even I, am the Lord, and BESIDES ME THERE IS NO SAVIOR.

* Oh my! The 1st member of the trinity squad, claiming to be the 2nd person! Jehovah claiming to be the "saviour".

Isaiah 44:6 Thus saith the Lord, the King of Israel, and his redeemer the Lord of hosts: I am the first, and I am the last, and BESIDE ME THERE IS NO GOD.

* I wonder why he can't see god # 2 sitting on his right hand??*

Isaiah 44:24 Thus saith the Lord, thy redeemer, and he that formed thee from the womb, I am the Lord that maketh all things; that stretcheth forth the heavens ALONE; that spreadeth abroad the earth BY MYSELF;

* The trinity bible probably says "by ourselves". *

Isaiah 45:5, 6, 18, 21, 22, CH 46:5, 9, CH 47:10, CH 48:11

Titus 1:3 But hath in due times manifested his word through preaching, which is committed unto me according to the commandment of GOD OUR SAVIOR.

Titus 3:4 But after that the kindness and love of GOD OUR SAVIOR toward man appeared,

Mark 12:29 And Jesus answered him, The first of all the commandments is, Hear, O Israel; the Lord our God is one Lord.

Ephesians 4:5 ONE LORD, one faith, one baptism.

I Tim 3:16 And without controversy great is the mystery of godliness: GOD WAS MANIFEST IN THE FLESH, justified in the Spirit, seen of angels, preached unto the Gentiles, believed on in the world, received up into glory.

I John 3:16 Hereby perceive we the love of God, because he laid down HIS LIFE for us: and we ought to lay down our lives for the brethren.

St. John 14:9 Jesus saith unto him, Have I been so long time with you, and yet HAST THOU NOT KNOWN ME, Phillip? HE THAT HATH SEEN ME HATH SEEN THE FATHER; and how sayest thou then, Shew us the Father?

Isaiah 9:6 For unto us a CHILD is born, unto us a SON is given: and the government shall be upon his shoulder: and his name shall be called Wonderful, Counsellor, THE MIGHTY GOD, THE EVERLASTING FATHER, the Prince of Peace.

Jude 25 To the only wise GOD OUR SAVIOR, be glory and majesty, dominion and power, both now and forever. Amen.

Beware

> Col 2:7 Rooted and built up in him, and stablished in the faith,as ye have been taught, abounding therein with thanksgiving.
>
> Col 2:8 Beware lest any man spoil you through philosophy and vain deceit, after the tradition of men, after the rudiments of the world,and not after Christ.
>
> Col 2:9 For in him dwelleth all the fulness of the Godhead bodily.
>
> Col 2:10 And ye are complete in him, which is the head of all principality and power:

It is good that the Lord saw fit to warn us against trinitarians and the like, that teach the tradition of men. They simply don't believe the Bible. They often even admit that they don't believe that Jesus is God. Notice how verse 10 says "HIM" not "them".

> Isaiah 44:6 Thus saith the LORD the King of Israel, and his redeemer the LORD of hosts; I [am] the first, and I [am] the last; and beside me [there is] no God. ...
>
> Isaiah 44:8 Fear ye not, neither be afraid: have not I told thee from that time, and have declared [it]? ye [are] even my witnesses. Is there a God beside me? yea, [there is] no God; I know not [any].

Don't you think that if there were any other "persons" or gods here, that God would have known about it. Who is the liar? God or the trinitarian?

> Isaiah 45:5 I [am] the LORD, and [there is] none else, [there is] no God beside me: I girded thee, though thou hast not known me: ...
>
> Isaiah 45:21 Tell ye, and bring [them] near; yea, let them take counsel together: who hath declared this from ancient time? [who] hath told it from that time? [have] not I the LORD? and [there is] no God else beside me; a just God and a Saviour; [there is] none beside me.

> Hosea 13:4 Yet I [am] the LORD thy God from the land of Egypt, and thou shalt know no god but me: for [there is] no saviour beside me.

> Isaiah 44:24 Thus saith the LORD, thy redeemer, and he that formed thee from the womb, I [am] the LORD that maketh all [things]; that stretcheth forth the heavens alone; that spreadeth abroad the earth by myself;

Here this teaches that God created the earth by Himself.

> John 14:9 Jesus saith unto him, Have I been so long time with you, and yet hast thou not known me, Philip? he that hath seen me hath seen the Father; and how sayest thou [then], Shew us the Father?

> Matthew 13:13 Therefore speak I to them in parables: because they seeing see not; and hearing they hear not, neither do they understand.

> Isaiah 9:6 For unto us a child is born, unto us a son is given: and the government shall be upon his shoulder: and his name shall be called Wonderful, Counsellor, The mighty God, The everlasting Father, The Prince of Peace.

Jesus is God, come to the world , in the flesh. I hope the reader can see the ravings of the trinitarian for what they are. They even admit that they don't believe that Jesus is really God, yet they claim to be Christian.

Some of the viler of the "god squad" cultists will attempt to insult real Christians by calling them "Jesus only". In addition to taking the name of the Lord in vain and exposing themselves that Jesus is certainly not their lord, they expose themselves as polytheistic.

The man-made Roman "trinity" is their idol "god squad". The Bible so clearly warns against their polytheistic philosophies.

> Col 2:8 Beware lest any man spoil you through philosophy and vain deceit, after the tradition of men, after the rudiments of the world,and not after Christ.

> Col 2:9 For in him dwelleth all the fullness of the Godhead bodily.
>
> Col 2:10 And ye are complete in him, which is the head of all principality and power:

How could the Bible be any clearer in its warning against the trinity cultists, and their clever sounding, three god, philosophies.

Trinity heresy

> Galatians 5:19 Now the works of the flesh are manifest, which are these; Adultery, fornication, uncleanness, lasciviousness,
>
> 20 Idolatry, witchcraft, hatred, variance, emulations, wrath, strife, seditions, heresies,
>
> 21 Envyings, murders, drunkenness, revellings, and such like: of the which I tell you before, as I have also told you in time past, that they which do such things shall not inherit the kingdom of God.

> 1 Corinthians 11:19 For there must be also heresies among you, that they which are approved may be made manifest among you.

Let me preface this study with the clarification that while I believe the doctrine of the trinity to be heresy, technically one cannot be a heretic without being a real Christian first. So most trinitarians are not heretics because they never ever became Christians to begin with.

One becomes a Christian by obeying Acts 2:38. One "remains" a Christian by living holy and obeying the rest of the Bible.

> Acts 2:38 Then Peter said unto them, Repent, and be baptized every one of you in the name of Jesus Christ for the remission of sins, and ye shall receive the gift of the Holy Ghost.

Some attack me for preaching it straight and narrow, but there is nothing "loving" about deceiving souls with some smooth lie as so many do in this hour.

> Jude 1:23 And others save with fear, pulling them out of the fire; hating even the garment spotted by the flesh.

Strong preaching is scriptural!

> 2 Timothy 4:2 Preach the word; be instant in season, out of season; reprove, rebuke, exhort with all longsuffering and doctrine.

Remission of sins is essential for sinful humanity to be "sin free". The word "salvation" means free from sin.

In Acts 2:38 we see that sins are remitted (washed away) by Jesus name baptism. The "Jesus" of the trinitarian is not really the Jesus of the Bible, so they see no need to be baptized in Jesus name (even though the Bible clearly commands it). They think that their three gods need three separate "titles" in baptism. They relegate their "Jesus" to second person status in their god committee.

Again, let's review the Biblical plan of salvation. If you don't obey these verses it really will not matter what you do with the rest of them.

> Acts 2:38 Then Peter said unto them, Repent, and be baptized every one of you in the name of Jesus Christ for the remission of sins, and ye shall receive the gift of the Holy Ghost.
>
> Acts 2:39 For the promise is unto you, and to your children, and to all that are afar off, even as many as the Lord our God shall call.

This is because Jesus is the Great "I AM" of the Bible. His name is the ONLY saving name.

> Acts 4:12 Neither is there salvation in any other: for there is none other name under heaven given among men, whereby we must be saved. So, you see, trinity preachers really are

> deceiving people into hell. I don't say that to be mean or rude, but because it is true.

Both of the following statements were spoken by the same person:

> Exo 3:14 And God said unto Moses, I AM THAT I AM: and he said, Thus shalt thou say unto the children of Israel, I AM hath sent me unto you.

> John 8:58 Jesus said unto them, Verily , verily, I say unto you, Before Abraham was, I am.

The polytheistic false-christian will not accept that Jesus is "I AM". They "don't believe". They are scripturally "non-believers".

> Romans 10:16 But they have not all obeyed the gospel. For Esaias saith, Lord, who hath believed our report?

See how a persons status as a "believer" is based entirely upon their obedience? That is not a hard concept. Why would someone who really believed the Bible not obey? The test of belief is OBEDIENCE!

Jesus said that those who would not accept that He really was the "I AM" would die in their sins.

1. Those who do not see Jesus as "I AM" see no need to be baptized in the name of Jesus.

> John 8:24 I said therefore unto you, that ye shall die in your sins: for if ye believe not that I am he, ye shall die in your sins.

2. Sins are remitted by Jesus name baptism.

Acts 22:16 And now why tarriest thou? arise, and be baptized, and wash away thy sins, calling on the name of the Lord.

3. Those who don't believe in Jesus will refuse Jesus name baptism and will die with their sins UN-REMITTED.

1 Timothy 5:24 Some men's sins are open beforehand, going before to judgment; and some men they follow after.

That is why Jesus said:

John 8:24 I said therefore unto you, that ye shall die in your sins: for if ye believe not that I am he, ye shall die in your sins.

Mark 16:16 He that believeth and is baptized shall be saved; but he that believeth not shall be damned.

John 3:5 Jesus answered, Verily, verily, I say unto thee, Except a man be born of water and of the Spirit, he cannot enter into the kingdom of God.

Sins are washed away by Jesus name baptism. That is why the Bible commands it, so you can "put on Christ".

Gal 3:27 For as many of you as have been baptized into Christ have put on Christ.

Trinitarians are deceived by their false preachers into refusing to "put on Christ".

Mat 1:21 And she shall bring forth a son, and thou shalt call his name JESUS: for he shall save his people from their sins.

Acts 19:4 Then said Paul, John verily baptized with the baptism of repentance, saying unto the people, that they should believe on him which should come after him, that is, on Christ Jesus.

Acts 19:5 When they heard this, they were baptized in the name of the Lord Jesus.

What did the people do immediately when Paul told them to believe on Jesus?

Acts 22:16 And now why tarriest thou? arise, and be baptized, and wash away thy sins, calling on the name of the Lord.

Acts 8:34 And the eunuch answered Philip, and said, I pray thee, of whom speaketh the prophet this? of himself, or of some other man?

35 Then Philip opened his mouth, and began at the same scripture, and preached unto him Jesus.

36 And as they went on their way, they came unto a certain water: and the eunuch said, See, here is water; what doth hinder me to be baptized?

37 And Philip said, If thou believest with all thine heart, thou mayest. And he answered and said, I believe that Jesus Christ is the Son of God.

38 And he commanded the chariot to stand still: and they went down both into the water, both Philip and the eunuch; and he baptized him.

39 And when they were come up out of the water, the Spirit of the Lord caught away Philip, that the eunuch saw him no more: and he went on his way rejoicing.

> Notice how the eunuch understood that believing on Jesus included being baptized. You now have several examples from the Word of God where hearers of the Word of God knew that belief in Jesus included Jesus Name baptism.
>
> Acts 2:41 Then they that gladly received his word were baptized: and the same day there were added unto them about three thousand souls.

Even on the day of Pentecost, on the birthday of the New Testament Church, there were 3000 baptized in Jesus Name. Those that receive the Word of God get baptized.

Look back just two verses and see that Peter preached Jesus Name baptism.

> Acts 2:38 Then Peter said unto them, Repent, and be baptized every one of you in the name of Jesus Christ for the remission of sins, and ye shall receive the gift of the Holy Ghost.
>
> Acts 2:39 For the promise is unto you, and to your children, and to all that are afar off, even as many as the Lord our God shall call.

I hope and pray that you can see the problem with the trinity heresy. Those who are its victims will die in their sin because they won't be baptized in Jesus Name. Any other water baptism is a worthless rip off!

> Acts 4:12 Neither is there salvation in any other: for there is none other name under heaven given among men, whereby we must be saved.

Remember that the trinity that is worshipped in so many false churches in this hour wasn't even invented till hundreds of years after the Apostles had passed on.

If you want your sins remitted then you need to be baptized in water in the name of the Lord Jesus Christ and not empty trinity titles.

> 1 Peter 3:21 The like figure whereunto even baptism doth also now save us (not the putting away of the filth of the flesh, but the answer of a good conscience toward God,) by the resurrection of Jesus Christ:

Also, baptism is not a "work"! You do no "work" when you get baptized. Jesus did the work on the cross on your behalf. You get baptized to avail yourself of the shed blood of Almighty God.

But those who don't believe that Jesus is the Father, who don't believe that Jesus is the Great "I AM" will see no need to be water baptized in His name.

> John 8:24 I said therefore unto you, that ye shall die in your sins: for if ye believe not that I am he, ye shall die in your sins.

The phrase "he that hath seen me" appears only one time in the entire KJV Bible.

> John 14:9 Jesus saith unto him, Have I been so long time with you, and yet hast thou not known me, Philip? he that hath seen me hath seen the Father; and how sayest thou then, Shew us the Father?

> Mark 16:16 He that believeth and is baptized shall be saved; but he that believeth not shall be damned.

Even with that verse there are false preachers convincing people that baptism doesn't matter, but consider this: Most false preachers can't tell the truth even if they know it. How can they tell their congregations something like, "Well I just found out that Jesus Name is the proper baptism, sorry about your grandma and grandpa etc... No most false preachers are going to keep deceiving souls into hell because they has bills to pay.

> 2 Timothy 3:13 But evil men and seducers shall wax worse and worse, deceiving, and being deceived.

The trinity preacher may be able to scratch your itching ears with all sorts of emotion tweaking fables, but he is not your friend.

> Matthew 7:13 Enter ye in at the strait gate: for wide is the gate, and broad is the way, that leadeth to destruction, and many there be which go in thereat:
>
> 14 Because strait is the gate, and narrow is the way, which leadeth unto life, and few there be that find it.
>
> 15 ¶ Beware of false prophets, which come to you in sheep's clothing, but inwardly they are ravening wolves.

The trinity preacher is not your friend.

Heresy

> Galatians 5:19 Now the works of the flesh are manifest, which are [these]; Adultery, fornication, uncleanness, lasciviousness,
>
> Galatians 5:20 Idolatry, witchcraft, hatred, variance, emulations, wrath, strife, seditions, HERESIES,
>
> Galatians 5:21 Envyings, murders, drunkenness, revellings, and such like: of the which I tell you before, as I have also told [you] in time past, that they which do such things SHALL NOT INHERIT the kingdom of God.

So we see that heresy is right up there with witchcraft! Hello??!

We also must consider that this letter was to the CHURCH, it was written to CHRISTIANS to let them know that if they did certain things that they WOULD BE LOST. Now, this is not to say that these sins are unforgivable, but that anyone who allows these things to remain in their lives will NOT inherit heaven. This means that according to the Bible if two churches are preaching a different doctrine, then NO WAY could they both be going to heaven, ACCORDING TO THE BIBLE.

Those preaching a "post trib" rapture are heretics and not brethren to the real Christian. A preacher teaching heresy might as well be practicing witchcraft.

While a trinitarian is not really a Christian to begin with, the teaching of a trinity or "triunity" is most certainly a heresy.

Now, the trinity claims to teach one god, yet, they teach three separate "persons", that are co-equal and co-eternal. They teach that the Father, son, and Holy Ghost are separate persons, rather than three ways that the ONE person Jesus revealed himself. In fact, they feel that they are wiser than the apostles who always baptized in Jesus name..and they merely "parrot" Matt 28:19, rather than obeying it, as the apostles did..You see, Jesus is the name of the Father:

> John 5:43 I am come in my Father's name, and ye receive me not: if another shall come in his own name, him ye will receive.

Jesus is the name of the son...and Jesus is the name of the Holy Ghost:

> John 14:26 But the Comforter, [which is] the Holy Ghost, whom the Father will send IN MY NAME, he shall teach you all things, and bring all things to your remembrance, whatsoever I have said unto you.
>
> Matthew 28:19 Go ye therefore, and teach all nations, baptizing them in the name of the Father, and of the Son, and of the Holy Ghost:

To OBEY Matt 28:19 the NAME of Jesus MUST be used in baptism. The trinitarian uses a separate "title" for each of the three "god persons" when they baptize, they "parrot" Jesus words INSTEAD of obeying them. If you worship three separate persons, you worship three gods.

Also, if the father and Holy Ghost are two "separate persons" WHICH ONE IS REALLY JESUS' DADDY ??!? We all know that the Father is Jesus' dad, right?? But it was the Holy Ghost that overshadowed Mary!:

> Matthew 1:18 Now the birth of Jesus Christ was on this wise: When as his mother Mary was espoused to Joseph, before they came together, she was found with CHILD OF THE HOLY GHOST.

Oh my! trinitarian!! Which of your god squad persons is really Jesus's dad??? You see, the trinitarian is trying to fit God into their carnal understanding, not realizing that :

> I Timothy 3:16 And without controversy great is the mystery of godliness: GOD WAS MANIFEST IN THE FLESH, justified in the Spirit, seen of angels, preached unto the Gentiles, believed on in the world, received up into glory."

Jesus was not a "second person" but rather, God took on a physical body, He didn't send a "junior god".

> John 2:19 Jesus answered and said unto them, Destroy this temple, and in three days I will raise it up.
>
> John 2:21 But he spake of the TEMPLE OF HIS BODY.

So we see that Jesus raised himself from the dead.

> Galatians 1:1 Paul, an apostle, (not of men, neither by man, but by Jesus Christ, and God the Father, who raised him from the dead;)

Oops, this says that the Father raised him!

> Romans 8:11 But if the Spirit of him that raised up Jesus from the dead dwell in you, he that raised up Christ from the dead shall also quicken your mortal bodies by his Spirit that dwelleth in you.

Oh my ! oh my! This says the Spirit raised Jesus from the dead!!

Now, do we have a Bible full of contradictions?? OR do we have a bunch of Satanic trinity false preachers, teaching a man made trinity.. Heresy is a sin and the only cure is repentance.

> Galatians 1:8 But though we, or an angel from heaven, preach any other gospel unto you than that which we have preached unto you, let him be accursed.
>
> Galatians 1:9 As we said before, so say I now again, If any [man] preach any other gospel unto you than that ye have received, let him be accursed.

Also a dire warning against trinitarianism:

> Colossians 2:8 Beware lest any man spoil you through philosophy and vain deceit, after the tradition of men, after the rudiments of the world, and not after Christ.
>
> 9 For in him dwelleth all the fulness of the Godhead bodily.

> 10 And ye are complete in him, which is the head of all principality and power:
>
> 11 In whom also ye are circumcised with the circumcision made without hands, in putting off the body of the sins of the flesh by the circumcision of Christ:
>
> 12 Buried with him in baptism, wherein also ye are risen with him through the faith of the operation of God, who hath raised him from the dead.

Jesus Name water baptism IS the circumcision of Christ.

Heretic

Titus 3:10 A man that is an heretic after the first and second admonition reject;

Titus 3:11 Knowing that he that is such is subverted, and sinneth, being condemned of himself.

Colossians 2:4 And this I say, lest any man should beguile you with enticing words.

Colossians 2:5 For though I be absent in the flesh, yet am I with you in the spirit, joying and beholding your order, and the stedfastness of your faith in Christ.

Colossians 2:6 As ye have therefore received Christ Jesus the Lord, [so] walk ye in him:

Colossians 2:7 Rooted and built up in him, and stablished in the faith, as ye have been taught, abounding therein with thanksgiving.

Colossians 2:8 Beware lest any man spoil you through philosophy and vain deceit, after the tradition of men, after the rudiments of the world, and not after Christ.

Colossians 2:9 For in him dwelleth all the fulness of the Godhead bodily.

Colossians 2:10 And ye are complete in him, which is the head of all principality and power:

Which

There is only one God and He is ONE person, not three, and his name is Jesus. Sadly, there are many who are not worshiping the Jesus of the Bible, who, according to the scripture IS the everlasting Father. These poor souls are worshiping a figment of carnal human imagination, a man made "Jesus", that is a separate person from God, or just merely a part of God. In their vain imagination they mold their "Jesus" to fit their personal concepts, they manufacture a fable of a "Jesus" that will just overlook unrepented sins and just take any and everything into heaven.

They confuse emotional titillations with spiritual activity...They prefer dewey eyed fables over the Word of God.

An idol need not be a manmade "icon" or statue; a mental concept can also be an idol god, just as much as a statue of a golden calf. It has always been the carnal nature to manufacture a god that fit rather than measuring up to a true Godly standard.

A person worshiping the catholic trinity, might as well worship rocks, or goats, or dogs or trees; they are basing their religion on a figment of human imagination, rather than the God of the Bible.

> Malachi 3:6 For I am the LORD, I change not; therefore ye sons of Jacob are not consumed.
>
> Isaiah 45:6 That they may know from the rising of the sun, and from the west, that there is none beside me. I am the LORD, and there is none else.
>
> Isaiah 45:21 Tell ye, and bring them near; yea, let them take counsel together: who hath declared this from ancient time? who hath told it from that time? have not I the LORD? and there is no God else beside me; a just God and a Saviour; there is none beside me.

The trinity requires two other separate persons here.

Revelation 1:7 Behold, he cometh with clouds; and every eye shall see him, and they [also] which pierced him: and all kindreds of the earth shall wail because of him. Even so, Amen.

(Notice it says HIM not THEM)...

Revelation 1:8 I am Alpha and Omega, the beginning and the ending, saith the Lord, which is, and which was, and which is to come, the Almighty.

(Jesus IS the Almighty)....

Isaiah 43:3 For I am the LORD thy God, the Holy One of Israel, thy Saviour: I gave Egypt for thy ransom, Ethiopia and Seba for thee.

Isaiah 43:10 Ye are my witnesses, sayeth the Lord, and my servant whom I have chosen; that ye may know and believe me, and understand that I am he: before me there was no God formed, neither shall there be after me.

Isaiah 43:11 I, [even] I, [am] the LORD; and beside me [there is] no saviour.

(God came to earth to be the saviour)....

Isaiah 45:21 Tell ye, and bring [them] near; yea, let them take counsel together: who hath declared this from ancient time? [who] hath told it from that time? [have] not I the LORD? and [there is] no God else beside me; a just God and a Saviour; [there is] none beside me.

(Trinity says there are three persons here)...

Hosea 13:4 Yet I [am] the LORD thy God from the land of Egypt, and thou shalt know no god but me: for [there is] no saviour beside me.

(God is the only savior)....

John 14:9 Jesus saith unto him, Have I been so long time with you, and yet hast thou not known me, Philip? he that hath seen me hath seen the Father; and how sayest thou [then], Shew us the Father?

(Of course Jesus IS the Father, come to be the savior)...

Ephesians 4:5 One Lord, one faith, one baptism,

("Which faith are you?" ever heard that?)...

Hebrews 13:8 Jesus Christ the same yesterday, and to day, and for ever.

(Jesus has always been Alpha and Omega)...

Isaiah 9:6 For unto us a child is born, unto us a son is given: and the government shall be upon his shoulder: and his name shall be called Wonderful, Counsellor, The mighty God, The everlasting Father, The Prince of Peace.

(This says that the child to be born is The Mighty God)

Jer 16:20 Shall a man make gods unto himself, and they are no Gods?"

Deut 4:35 Unto thee it was shewed, that thou mightest know that the Lord he is God; there is none else beside him.

Deut 4:39 Know therefore this day, and consider it in thine heart, that the Lord he is God in heaven above, and upon the earth beneath; there is none else.

Deut 32:39 See now that I, even I, am he, and THERE IS NO GOD WITH ME: I kill, and I make alive; I wound and I heal: neither is there any that can deliver out of my hand.

Isaiah 44:6 Thus saith the Lord, the King of Israel, and his redeemer the Lord of hosts: I am the first, and I am the last, and BESIDE ME THERE IS NO GOD.

Isaiah 44:24 Thus saith the Lord, thy redeemer, and he that formed thee from the womb, I am the Lord that maketh all things; that stretcheth forth the heavens ALONE; that spreadeth abroad the earth BY MYSELF;

Isaiah 45:5 ¶ I am the LORD, and there is none else, there is no God beside me: I girded thee, though thou hast not known me:

6 That they may know from the rising of the sun, and from the west, that there is none beside me. I am the LORD, and there is none else.

I Tim 3:16 And without controversy great is the mystery of godliness: GOD WAS MANIFEST IN THE FLESH, justified in the Spirit, seen of angels, preached unto the Gentiles, believed on in the world, received up into glory.

I John 3:16 Hereby perceive we the love of God, because he laid down HIS LIFE for us: and we ought to lay down our lives for the brethren.

John 14:9 Jesus saith unto him, Have I been so long time with you, and yet HAST THOU NOT KNOWN ME, Phillip? HE THAT HATH SEEN ME HATH SEEN THE FATHER; and how sayest thou then, Shew us the Father?

Identity of God

In this hour there are many theories by many honest seekers regarding the identity of God. Some say that God is somehow three separate persons but we need to consider the first of all the commandments.

> Mark 12:29 And Jesus answered him, The first of all the commandments is, Hear, O Israel; The Lord our God is one Lord:

I know that there are many verses that many good people think teach separate persons in a "god squad" as it were, but we need to regard scripture in light of scripture. We need to respect Jesus in his statement regarding the first of all the commandments.

The identity of the God or gods being worshipped is not some side issue but is of foundational importance.

> Exodus 20:5 Thou shalt not bow down thyself to them, nor serve them: for I the LORD thy God am a jealous God, visiting the iniquity of the fathers upon the children unto the third and fourth generation of them that hate me;

> Exodus 34:14 For thou shalt worship no other god: for the LORD, whose name is Jealous, is a jealous God:

> Deuteronomy 4:24 For the LORD thy God is a consuming fire, even a jealous God.

> Deuteronomy 5:9 Thou shalt not bow down thyself unto them, nor serve them: for I the LORD thy God am a jealous God, visiting the iniquity of the fathers upon the children unto the third and fourth generation of them that hate me,

One key to understanding the identity of God is to understand the simple concepts of flesh and spirit.

> 1 Timothy 3:16 And without controversy great is the mystery of godliness: God was manifest in the flesh, justified in the

> Spirit, seen of angels, preached unto the Gentiles, believed on in the world, received up into glory.

Though we humans (created in God's image) have body, soul and spirit we are not each "three separate persons". Though God manifested Himself as "Father, Son, and Holy Ghost" he is not "three separate persons". When society finds someone who is three separate persons do they not lock them up or medicate them (for their protection and protection of society). God is NOT three separate persons!

Allow me to submit to you some foundational truths that I will document from scripture and then use to make my point.

1) God is a Spirit.

> John 4:24 God [is] a Spirit: and they that worship him must worship [him] in spirit and in truth.

2) God is holy.

> I Samuel 2:2 [There is] none holy as the LORD: for [there is] none beside thee: neither [is there] any rock like our God.

3) God is a "Holy Spirit".

4) Jesus is the "Spirit of truth"

> John 14:6 Jesus saith unto him, I am the way, the truth, and the life: no man cometh unto the Father, but by me.

5) Jesus was "dwelling with them" and promised to be "in them".

> John 14:17 [Even] the Spirit of truth; whom the world cannot receive, because it seeth him not, neither knoweth him: but ye know him; for he dwelleth with you, and shall be in you.

6) The "comforter" is the "Spirit of Christ"

John 14:18 I will not leave you comfortless: I will come to you.

7) The "Spirit of Christ" is the "Holy Spirit" is the "Spirit of Truth"

John 14:26 But the Comforter, [which is] the Holy Ghost, whom the Father will send in my name, he shall teach you all things, and bring all things to your remembrance, whatsoever I have said unto you.

8) The Spirit of God visited His creation robed in flesh as the "Son".

I Timothy 3:16 And without controversy great is the mystery of godliness: God was manifest in the flesh, justified in the Spirit, seen of angels, preached unto the Gentiles, believed on in the world, received up into glory.

9) The fullness of God is in Jesus Christ

Colossians 2:9 For in him dwelleth all the fulness of the Godhead bodily.

Colossians 2:10 And ye are complete in him, which is the head of all principality and power:

10) Jesus IS the "everlasting Father".

Isaiah 9:6 For unto us a child is born, unto us a son is given: and the government shall be upon his shoulder: and his name shall be called Wonderful, Counsellor, The mighty God, The everlasting Father, The Prince of Peace.

11) Those who believe that Jesus is a "separate person" from the "Father" don't really know Jesus at all.

John 14:9 Jesus saith unto him, Have I been so long time with you, and yet hast thou not known me, Philip? he that hath seen me hath seen the Father; and how sayest thou [then], Shew us the Father?

We know that Peter was given the keys to the kingdom.

> Matthew 16:19 And I will give unto thee the keys of the kingdom of heaven: and whatsoever thou shalt bind on earth shall be bound in heaven: and whatsoever thou shalt loose on earth shall be loosed in heaven.

Peter used those keys from Jesus to unlock the kingdom of heaven. I really believe that those who think they can reject Peter without rejecting Jesus are not being honest with themselves or others.

> Acts 2:38 Then Peter said unto them, Repent, and be baptized every one of you in the name of Jesus Christ for the remission of sins, and ye shall receive the gift of the Holy Ghost.
>
> 39 For the promise is unto you, and to your children, and to all that are afar off, even as many as the Lord our God shall call.
>
> 40 And with many other words did he testify and exhort, saying, Save yourselves from this untoward generation.
>
> 41 Then they that gladly received his word were baptized: and the same day there were added unto them about three thousand souls.

Three thousand people baptized in Jesus Name hundreds of years before the trinity baptism was even invented by polytheists.

Is not the safe path the Bible path?

> Jeremiah 6:16 Thus saith the LORD, Stand ye in the ways, and see, and ask for the old paths, where is the good way, and walk therein, and ye shall find rest for your souls. But they said, We will not walk therein.
>
> Psalms 119:89 LAMED. For ever, O LORD, thy word is settled in heaven.

No Man Say

> I Corinthians 12:2 Ye know that ye were Gentiles, carried away unto these dumb idols, even as ye were led.
>
> I Corinthians 12:3 Wherefore I give you to understand, that no man speaking by the Spirit of God calleth Jesus accursed: and [that] no man can say that Jesus is the Lord, but by the Holy Ghost.

Folks! This here is one misunderstood and misused scripture. You might just do well to stop and pray right now for the Lord Jesus to bless us with understanding.

Now, I believe that we know that the Bible is a Spiritual Book. It is not open to private interpretation, yet, needs to be rightly divided.

There are some so shallow as to suggest that a person speaking the words "Jesus is the Lord" must be doing so by the Holy Ghost. Well, if you went to a bar and paid a bunch of drunks to repeat those words "Jesus is the Lord", would that be "by the Holy Ghost" ???

> Matthew 7:22 Many will say to me in that day, Lord, Lord, have we not prophesied in thy name? and in thy name have cast out devils? and in thy name done many wonderful works?
>
> Matthew 24:5 For many shall come in my name, saying, I am Christ; and shall deceive many.
>
> Mark 13:6 For many shall come in my name, saying, I am [Christ]; and shall deceive many.
>
> Luke 21:8 And he said, Take heed that ye be not deceived: for many shall come in my name, saying, I am [Christ]; and the time draweth near: go ye not therefore after them.

See what I mean???

There is only one God. His name is Jesus (that's why the apostles used the name "Jesus Christ" when they baptized). One Lord, with one name.

> Zechariah 14:9 And the LORD shall be king over all the earth: in that day shall there be one LORD, and his name one.

OK, one God with one name who manifested Himself as Father (Spirit in creation), son (flesh in redemption), AND as the Holy Ghost (in the Christian, "Christ in you, the hope of glory).

So what that verse is saying is that no man can claim that Jesus is the Lord of his life except that man has the Holy Ghost. Since the Holy Ghost is the form that Jesus is manifesting himself in in this church dispensation. Jesus told the disciples that he would be IN THEM, the only thing that came in them was the Holy Ghost (Jesus' ghost, or "spirit"...the Spirit of the one God also known as the Spirit of Truth)..*

> John 14:17 [Even] the Spirit of truth; whom the world cannot receive, because it seeth him not, neither knoweth him: but ye know him; for he dwelleth with you, and shall be in you.

Jesus was with them, and then he came IN them.

Please don't believe the drivel that just because someone repeats the words "Jesus is Lord" proves that the Holy Spirit is involved.

Puppet

It would be amusing were it not so pathetic that people are so carnal as to believe that when the Bible speaks of the "right hand" that it is referring to one god sitting on another god's "right hand" kinda like "puppet" style.

Can people really be that stupid?? I'm afraid so!

I would think that if one god was sitting on another god's hand that the god in question would have been aware of the other god beside him, eh?

> Isaiah 45:5 I [am] the LORD, and [there is] none else, [there is] no God beside me: I girded thee, though thou hast not known me:

No puppet sitting on Jehovah's right hand.

> Isaiah 45:6 That they may know from the rising of the sun, and from the west, that [there is] none beside me. I [am] the LORD, and [there is] none else.

> Isaiah 45:21 Tell ye, and bring [them] near; yea, let them take counsel together: who hath declared this from ancient time? [who] hath told it from that time? [have] not I the LORD? and [there is] no God else beside me; a just God and a Saviour; [there is] none beside me.

How can people be so carnal and stupid as to be deceived by thinking that the expression "right hand" meant one god sitting puppet style on another god's hand?

Voice from Heaven

Many of the polytheistic false-christians think that verses like John 12:28 justify their polytheism, but what they are doing is really ADMITTING their polytheism when they try to defend it.

> John 12:28 Father, glorify thy name. Then came there a voice from heaven, saying, I have both glorified it, and will glorify it again.
>
> 29 The people therefore, that stood by, and heard it, said that it thundered: others said, An angel spake to him.
>
> 30 Jesus answered and said, This voice came not because of me, but for your sakes.

Those who really know Jesus have no problems with verses like that.

Only One

Jer 16:20 Shall a man make gods unto himself, and they are no Gods?"

Deut 4:35 Unto thee it was shewed, that thou mightest know that the Lord he is God; there is none else beside him.

I believe that the trinity theory proposes that there were 2 other "god person beings" beside Jehovah during this time.

Deut 4:39 Know therefore this day, and consider it in thine heart, that the Lord he is God in heaven above, and upon the earth beneath; there is none else.

I believe it would have said "they" rather than "he" if the trinity theory was scriptural.

Deut 6:4 Hear, O Isriael: The Lord our God is one Lord:

Not "three separate lord persons"

Deut 32:39 See now that I, even I, am he, and THERE IS NO GOD WITH ME: I kill, and I make alive; I wound and I heal: neither is there any that can deliver out of my hand.

According to Rome there were two others with Jehovah Saviour here. Surely Jehovah would have been aware of their presence (especially if they were co-equal, and co-eternal and one of them sitting on His hand?!?)

Psalms 86:10 For thou art great, and doest wonderous things:THOU ART GOD ALONE.

Isaiah 43:3 For I am the LORD thy God, the Holy One of Israel, thy Saviour: I gave Egypt for thy ransom, Ethiopia and Seba for thee.

Well, look right here! Jehovah is claiming to be the "second person" (the savior).

> Isaiah 43:10 Ye are my witnesses, sayeth the Lord, and my servant whom I have chosen; that ye may know and believe me, and understand that I am he: before me there was no God formed, neither shall there be after me.
>
> Isaiah 43:11 I, even I, am the Lord, and BESIDES ME THERE IS NO SAVIOR.

Now surely Jehovah Saviour would have noticed a "second person" hanging around heaven (especially if he was sitting on his right hand).

> Isaiah 44:6 Thus saith the Lord, the King of Israel, and his redeemer the Lord of hosts: I am the first, and I am the last, and BESIDE ME THERE IS NO GOD.
>
> Isaiah 44:24 Thus saith the Lord, thy redeemer, and he that formed thee from the womb, I am the Lord that maketh all things; that stretcheth forth the heavens ALONE; that spreadeth abroad the earth BY MYSELF;

Now why would Jehovah take the credit and not share it with the "second god squad person" of the trinity?

> Isaiah 45:5 ¶ I am the LORD, and there is none else, there is no God beside me: I girded thee, though thou hast not known me:
>
> 6 That they may know from the rising of the sun, and from the west, that there is none beside me. I am the LORD, and there is none else.
>
> Isaiah 45:18 For thus saith the LORD that created the heavens; God himself that formed the earth and made it; he hath established it, he created it not in vain, he formed it to be inhabited: I am the LORD; and there is none else.
>
> Isaiah 45:21 Tell ye, and bring them near; yea, let them take counsel together: who hath declared this from ancient time? who hath told it from that time? have not I the LORD? and there is no God else beside me; a just God and a Saviour; there is none beside me.

> 22 Look unto me, and be ye saved, all the ends of the earth: for I am God, and there is none else.
>
> 23 I have sworn by myself, the word is gone out of my mouth in righteousness, and shall not return, That unto me every knee shall bow, every tongue shall swear.

> Isaiah 46:5 ¶ To whom will ye liken me, and make me equal, and compare me, that we may be like?

Whoa!! The trinity teaches three separate co-equal persons in their god squad.

> Isaiah 46:9 Remember the former things of old: for I am God, and there is none else; I am God, and there is none like me,
>
> Isaiah 47:10 For thou hast trusted in thy wickedness: thou hast said, None seeth me. Thy wisdom and thy knowledge, it hath perverted thee; and thou hast said in thine heart, I am, and none else beside me.
>
> Isaiah 48:11 For mine own sake, even for mine own sake, will I do it: for how should my name be polluted? and I will not give my glory unto another.
>
> 1 Corinthians 2:8 Which none of the princes of this world knew: for had they known it, they would not have crucified the Lord of glory.

It really was the Lord of Glory on that cross! Not some second person of an imaginary god squad of co-equal "persons".

> Titus 1:3 But hath in due times manifested his word through preaching, which is committed unto me according to the commandment of GOD OUR SAVIOR.
>
> Titus 3:4 But after that the kindness and love of GOD OUR SAVIOR toward man appeared, appeared.

Mark 12:29 And Jesus answered him, The first of all the commandments is, Hear, O Israel; the Lord our God is one Lord.

Ephesians 4:5 ONE LORD, one faith, one baptism.

I Tim 3:16 And without controversy great is the mystery of godliness: GOD WAS MANIFEST IN THE FLESH, justified in the Spirit, seen of angels, preached unto the Gentiles, believed on in the world, received up into glory.

I John 3:16 Hereby perceive we the love of God, because he laid down HIS LIFE for us: and we ought to lay down our lives for the brethren.

John 14:9 Jesus saith unto him, Have I been so long time with you, and yet HAST THOU NOT KNOWN ME, Phillip? HE THAT HATH SEEN ME HATH SEEN THE FATHER; and how sayest thou then, Shew us the Father?

Oops, here we have the "second person" of the trinity theory claiming to be the "first person".

Isaiah 9:6 For unto us a CHILD is born, unto us a SON is given: and the government shall be upon his shoulder: and his name shall be called Wonderful, Counsellor, THE MIGHTY GOD, THE EVERLASTING FATHER, the Prince of Peace.

Jude 25 To the only wise GOD OUR SAVIOR, be glory and majesty, dominion and power, both now and forever. Amen.

Identity

After Jesus explained to a man that he would have to be re-born of water and Spirit to be saved, Jesus commented regarding the love of God.

> John 3:3 Jesus answered and said unto him, Verily , verily, I say unto thee, Except a man be born again, he cannot see the kingdom of God.

Jesus often spoke in parables. Many think that this verse speaks of a junior separate "god", but those people are not aware that there is only ONE God.

> John 3:16 For God so loved the world, that he gave his only begotten Son, that whosoever believeth in him should not perish, but have everlasting life.

Those that realize that there is only ONE God do not see a contradiction between John 3:16 and 1 Timothy 3:16, because they realize that the 'Son' was the created (made of a woman) flesh that Jehovah used when He visited His world.

> 1 Timothy 3:16 And without controversy great is the mystery of godliness: God was manifest in the flesh, justified in the Spirit, seen of angels, preached unto the Gentiles, believed on in the world, received up into glory.

Notice that the 'Son' was created or "made". The very word "begotten" means "created". The Spirit of God that inhabited the 'Son' is eternal, the flesh body was made, created, begotten.

> Galatians 4:4 But when the fulness of the time was come, God sent forth his Son, made of a woman, made under the law,

Notice that the 'Son' (the flesh) was begotten, made, created.

> John 8:58 Jesus said unto them, Verily , verily, I say unto you, [Before Abraham was], I am.

Notice here that the "person" inhabiting that "begotten flesh" claimed to pre-exist that created body (and the Jews went to stone Him because they knew that He was claiming to be Jehovah).

For those that *REALLY* believe in only one God, have no problem whatsoever with these verses that cause the trinity cultists to throw fits.

The "Oneness", or "One God" believer is on quite SOLID ground, because:

> Mark 12:29 And Jesus answered him, The [first of all the commandments] <is>, Hear, O Israel; The Lord our God is one Lord:

The Bible gives such a clear warning against the ever so popular trinity cults and their "soul spoiling" characteristics.

> Colossians 2:8 Beware lest any man spoil you through philosophy and vain deceit, after the tradition of men, after the rudiments of the world, and not after Christ.

> Colossians 2:9 For in him dwelleth all the fulness of the Godhead bodily.

> Colossians 2:10 And ye are complete in him, which is the head of all principality and power:

The trinity cultist is clearly preaching a man made philosophy that attempts to convince the gullible that the fullness of the Godhead is somewhere other than in Jesus Christ. They teach that the "fulness" exists in the three imaginary separate persons of their man made trinity idol.

Jesus is God the Father

Jesus is God manifest in the flesh as the son.

> 1Tim 3:16 And without controversy great is the mystery of godliness: God was manifest in the flesh, justified in the Spirit, seen of angels, preached unto the Gentiles, believed on in the world, received up into glory.

Jesus identified Himself as the Father more than once.

> John 8:58 Jesus said unto them, Verily, verily, I say unto you, Before Abraham was, I am.

(The religious filth of that day didn't like the identity of Jesus as all of God much more than the trinity filth of today.)

> John 8:59 Then took they up stones to cast at him: but Jesus hid himself, and went out of the temple, going through the midst of them, and so passed by.

> John 14:9 Jesus saith unto him, Have I been so long time with you, and yet hast thou not known me, Philip? he that hath seen me hath seen the Father; and how sayest thou then, Shew us the Father?

> Rev 1:8 I am Alpha and Omega, the beginning and the ending, saith the Lord, which is, and which was, and which is to come, the Almighty.

> John 1:11 He came unto his own, and his own received him not.

> Acts 9:5 And he said, Who art thou, Lord? And the Lord said, I am Jesus whom thou persecutest: it is hard for thee to kick against the pricks.

> Acts 22:8 And I answered, Who art thou, Lord? And he said unto me, I am Jesus of Nazareth, whom thou persecutest.

> Acts 26:15 And I said, Who art thou, Lord? And he said, I am Jesus whom thou persecutest.

> 1Col 2:8 Which none of the princes of this world knew: for had they known it, they would not have crucified the Lord of glory.

Jesus Christ is the Lord of Glory, not god person #2 in a Roman god squad.

Here is another verse that proves that Jesus Christ is the Everlasting Father and the Mighty God. Trinity filth don't want you to know this.

> Isa 9:6 For unto us a child is born, unto us a son is given: and the government shall be upon his shoulder: and his name shall be called Wonderful, Counsellor, The mighty God, The everlasting Father, The Prince of Peace.

Personagers

If I follow the theory that each manifestation of God theologically requires a personager, I find myself in a quandary. For it leads me to a larger quantity of personagers, even including the plant and animal kingdoms. A couple of examples come to mind, and if manifestation does imply personager, I certainly would not want to bypass such a personager as a theological deity, and theoretically thereby possibly incur the potential wrath of an offended personager. Here are some of the examples that I have found:

> Exodus 3:4 And when the LORD saw that he turned aside to see, God called unto him out of the midst of the bush, and said, Moses, Moses. And he said, Here [am] I.
>
> Exodus 3:5 And he said, Draw not nigh hither: put off thy shoes from off thy feet, for the place whereon thou standest [is] holy ground.
>
> Exodus 3:6 Moreover he said, I [am] the God of thy father, the God of Abraham, the God of Isaac, and the God of Jacob. And Moses hid his face; for he was afraid to look upon God.

* a plant personager *

> Numbers 22:28 And the LORD opened the mouth of the ass, and she said unto Balaam, What have I done unto thee, that thou hast smitten me these three times?

* an animal personager *

> Exodus 13:21 And the LORD went before them by day in a pillar of a cloud, to lead them the way; and by night in a pillar of fire, to give them light; to go by day and night:
>
> Exodus 13:22 He took not away the pillar of the cloud by day, nor the pillar of fire by night, [from] before the people.

Exodus 40:38 For the cloud of the LORD [was] upon the tabernacle by day, and fire was on it by night, in the sight of all the house of Israel, throughout all their journeys.

* Here, there appears to be two more personagers, one for the day and one for the night; or possibly one personager with more than one manifestation...but that would conflict with the theory that each manifestation demands personality.. so I'll count 2 personagers here.

* I believe that adds up to a total so far (if I add the three to the ones I found) of 8 full fledged personagers! Except, to be perfectly honest I have not had the time to do an in depth search for other personagers, so I do not at all present this list as complete. Nor am I presenting the manifestation=personager theory to be truth, just a theory that I have found interesting to explore. *

* So if each "Spirit" demands personality, I found seven more personagers!

Revelation 3:1 And unto the angel of the church in Sardis write; These things saith he that hath the seven Spirits of God, and the seven stars; I know thy works, that thou hast a name that thou livest, and art dead.

* So here are seven more personagers. *

Revelation 4:5 And out of the throne proceeded lightnings and thunderings and voices: and [there were] seven lamps of fire burning before the throne, which are the seven Spirits of God.

* Another seven "lamp personagers" *

Revelation 5:6 And I beheld, and, lo, in the midst of the throne and of the four beasts, and in the midst of the elders, stood a Lamb as it had been slain, having seven horns and seven eyes, which are the seven Spirits of God sent forth into all the earth.

* Seven more "eye personagers" *

* As I look at these verses I perceive that we may even have 14 more, or maybe even 21! Which would be fascinating if it turned out that we had over "thirty separate personagers co-equal and co-eternal" instead of just the aforementioned "three separate personagers". *

* I find it fascinating that the different personagers encompass such great diversity from "spirits to plants, animals and clouds, to furniture" I had no idea that there were so many manifestations demanding personality (assuming, of course that each manifestation is a "separate personager"). *

* I look back in wonder at the old hymn, how it would rhyme? "Gawwddd in thirtytwo peerrrrsons blessed '??????'" I am at a loss as to what the term would be. If 3 personagers = "trinity", what would 32 personagers equal? I guess it might be best to wait and see just how many co-equal, co-eternal personagers that we can find, first.

And of course after all that, the disclaimer: "These 32 are one"

I can't imagine why the trinity cults stop at just 3 gods.

God Squad

I wonder how the god squad folks explain how there could have been a "second person" sitting on Jehovah's hand and Jehovah not been aware of it.

> Isaiah 45:5 I [am] the LORD, and [there is] none else, [there is] no God beside me: I girded thee, though thou hast not known me:
>
> Isaiah 45:6 That they may know from the rising of the sun, and from the west, that [there is] none beside me. I [am] the LORD, and [there is] none else.
>
> Isaiah 45:21 Tell ye, and bring [them] near; yea, let them take counsel together: who hath declared this from ancient time? [who] hath told it from that time? [have] not I the LORD? and [there is] no God else beside me; a just God and a Saviour; [there is] none beside me.

I also wonder how the god squad folks deal with their "first person" claiming to be the "second person" (since they relegate Jesus to being the "second person" of the god squad.)

Jesus is the Father

> 1 Corinthians 2:8 Which none of the princes of this world knew: for had they known it, they would not have crucified the Lord of glory.

Jesus Christ is the Lord of Glory.

> John 14:9 Jesus saith unto him, Have I been so long time with you, and yet hast thou not known me, Philip? he that hath seen me hath seen the Father; and how sayest thou then, Shew us the Father?

Jesus Christ is God the Father, in person, manifest in the flesh.

> 1 Timothy 3:16 And without controversy great is the mystery of godliness: God was manifest in the flesh, justified in the Spirit, seen of angels, preached unto the Gentiles, believed on in the world, received up into glory.

If Jesus Christ was not God the Father how could these verses be in the Bible.

> Revelation 1:8 I am Alpha and Omega, the beginning and the ending, saith the Lord, which is, and which was, and which is to come, the Almighty.
>
> Revelation 1:11 Saying, I am Alpha and Omega, the first and the last: and, What thou seest, write in a book, and send it unto the seven churches which are in Asia; unto Ephesus, and unto Smyrna, and unto Pergamos, and unto Thyatira, and unto Sardis, and unto Philadelphia, and unto Laodicea.
>
> Revelation 21:6 And he said unto me, It is done. I am Alpha and Omega, the beginning and the end. I will give unto him that is athirst of the fountain of the water of life freely.
>
> Revelation 22:13 I am Alpha and Omega, the beginning and the end, the first and the last.

Jesus Christ is the creator of the Earth. Jesus Christ spoke the world into existence.

> John 1:3 All things were made by him; and without him was not any thing made that was made.
>
> John 1:10 He was in the world, and the world was made by him, and the world knew him not.

And, just something to think about, don't expect to find a clean shaven man looking like Caesar on the Great White Throne.

> Isaiah 50:6 I gave my back to the smiters, and my cheeks to them that plucked off the hair: I hid not my face from shame and spitting.

> Revelation 20:11 And I saw a great white throne, and him that sat on it, from whose face the earth and the heaven fled away; and there was found no place for them.

Though we humans (created in God's image) have body, soul and spirit we are not each "three separate persons". Though God manifested Himself as "Father, Son, and Holy Ghost" he is not "three separate persons".

1) God is a Spirit.

> John 4:24 God [is] a Spirit: and they that worship him must worship [him] in spirit and in truth.

2) God is holy.

> I Samuel 2:2 [There is] none holy as the LORD: for [there is] none beside thee: neither [is there] any rock like our God.

3) God is a "Holy Spirit".

4) Jesus is the "Spirit of truth"

> John 14:6 Jesus saith unto him, I am the way, the truth, and the life: no man cometh unto the Father, but by me.

5) Jesus was "dwelling with them" and promised to be "in them".

> John 14:17 [Even] the Spirit of truth; whom the world cannot receive, because it seeth him not, neither knoweth him: but ye know him; for he dwelleth with you, and shall be in you.

6) The "comforter" is the "Spirit of Christ"

> John 14:18 I will not leave you comfortless: I will come to you.

7) The "Spirit of Christ" is the "Holy Spirit" is the "Spirit of Truth"

> John 14:26 But the Comforter, [which is] the Holy Ghost, whom the Father will send in my name, he shall teach you all things, and bring all things to your remembrance, whatsoever I have said unto you.

8) The Spirit of God visited His creation robed in flesh as the "Son".

> I Timothy 3:16 And without controversy great is the mystery of godliness: God was manifest in the flesh, justified in the Spirit, seen of angels, preached unto the Gentiles, believed on in the world, received up into glory.

9) The fullness of God is in Jesus Christ

> Colossians 2:9 For in him dwelleth all the fulness of the Godhead bodily.

> Colossians 2:10 And ye are complete in him, which is the head of all principality and power:

10) Jesus IS the "everlasting Father".

> Isaiah 9:6 For unto us a child is born, unto us a son is given: and the government shall be upon his shoulder: and his name shall be called Wonderful, Counsellor, The mighty God, The everlasting Father, The Prince of Peace.

11) Those who believe that Jesus is a "separate person" from the "Father" don't really know Jesus at all.

> John 14:9 Jesus saith unto him, Have I been so long time with you, and yet hast thou not known me, Philip? he that hath seen me hath seen the Father; and how sayest thou [then], Shew us the Father?

> Genesis 1:27 So God created man in his own image, in the image of God created he him; male and female created he them.

Now when we, a society who are all created in the image of God encounter one who walks among us who is three separate persons, we lock them up for their good and the good of society, right?

There is a commandment in the Word of God for us to know something, for us to be aware of something and it is the FIRST of all the commandments.

> Mark 12:28 And one of the scribes came, and having heard them reasoning together, and perceiving that he had answered them well, asked him, Which is the first commandment of all?

> Mark 12:29 And Jesus answered him, The first of all the commandments is, Hear, O Israel; The Lord our God is one Lord:

There is a dire warning against believing in the trinity.

> Colossians 2:8 Beware lest any man spoil you through philosophy and vain deceit, after the tradition of men, after the rudiments of the world, and not after Christ.

> 9 For in him dwelleth all the fulness of the Godhead bodily.

10 And ye are complete in him, which is the head of all principality and power:

11 In whom also ye are circumcised with the circumcision made without hands, in putting off the body of the sins of the flesh by the circumcision of Christ:

12 Buried with him in baptism, wherein also ye are risen with him through the faith of the operation of God, who hath raised him from the dead.

13 ¶ And you, being dead in your sins and the uncircumcision of your flesh, hath he quickened together with him, having forgiven you all trespasses;

14 Blotting out the handwriting of ordinances that was against us, which was contrary to us, and took it out of the way, nailing it to his cross;

15 And having spoiled principalities and powers, he made a shew of them openly, triumphing over them in it.

The true Oneness Apostolic Pentecostal Holiness Christian will not be ashamed.

The others, well...

Revelation 21:8 But the fearful, and unbelieving, and the abominable, and murderers, and whoremongers, and sorcerers, and idolaters, and all liars, shall have their part in the lake which burneth with fire and brimstone: which is the second death.

Hebrews 2:3 How shall we escape, if we neglect so great salvation; which at the first began to be spoken by the Lord, and was confirmed unto us by them that heard him;

Emperors New Clothes

The Doctrine of the "mystery" trinity asserts that their gods are three separate persons, co-eternal, co-equal. Many are taught that this theory must be accepted, that it is beyond human understanding, and must be accepted by faith. While I believe that the Word of God should be accepted by faith, I don't believe that a human theory that contradicts the word of God need be accepted at all.

In Isaiah Chapter 44-46 God clearly declares that there is no God beside him and no god equal to him, that he is alone. According to the trinity the three separate persons are having fellowship together during this period.

> Isa 44:6 Thus saith the LORD the King of Israel, and his redeemer the LORD of hosts; I [am] the first, and I [am] the last; and beside me [there is] no God.

Where wus that ole "mystery" trinity? Where are the other "mystery" godlets?

> Isaiah 44:8 Fear ye not, neither be afraid: have not I told thee from that time, and have declared [it]? ye [are] even my witnesses. Is there a God beside me? yea, [there is] no God; I know not [any].

Where wus the junior "mystery" godlet sitting on his right hand?

> Isaiah 44:9 They that make a graven image [are] all of them vanity; and their delectable things shall not profit; and they [are] their own witnesses; they see not, nor know; that they may be ashamed.
>
> Isaiah 44:10 Who hath formed a god, or molten a graven image [that] is profitable for nothing?
>
> Isaiah 44:11 Behold, all his fellows shall be ashamed: and the workmen, they [are] of men: let them all be gathered together, let them stand up; [yet] they shall fear, [and] they shall be ashamed together.

Those that make up their own "mystery" IDOLS shall be ASHAMED.

> Isaiah 44:17 And the residue thereof he maketh a god, [even] his graven image: he falleth down unto it, and worshippeth [it], and prayeth unto it, and saith, Deliver me; for thou [art] my god.
>
> Isaiah 44:18 They have not known nor understood: for he hath shut their eyes, that they cannot see; [and] their hearts, that they cannot understand.

Those that make up their own gods lack understanding.

> Isaiah 44:24 Thus saith the LORD, thy redeemer, and he that formed thee from the womb, I [am] the LORD that maketh all [things]; that stretcheth forth the heavens alone; that spreadeth abroad the earth by myself;
>
> Isaiah 44:25 That frustrateth the tokens of the liars, and maketh diviners mad; that turneth wise [men] backward, and maketh their knowledge foolish;

Those "mystery" three god folks gettin' frustrated, they're gettin' mad. (they're starting to appear rather foolish).

> Isaiah 45:5 I [am] the LORD, and [there is] none else, [there is] no God beside me: I girded thee, though thou hast not known me:

Whar's that ole "mystery" trinity? What's he mean sayin' "none else"? (You reckon he might be one o' dem "Jesus only"s?)

> Isaiah 45:6 That they may know from the rising of the sun, and from the west, that [there is] none beside me. I [am] the LORD, and [there is] none else.

Hup! He did it again, denying the other "mystery godlet persons" beside Him! (The trinity is not a "mystery" it is a LIE)

> Isaiah 45:21 Tell ye, and bring [them] near; yea, let them take counsel together: who hath declared this from ancient time? [who] hath told it from that time? [have] not I the LORD? and [there is] no God else beside me; a just God and a Saviour; [there is] none beside me.

Whatsamatter? He can't see the separate, co-equal "saviour person" sitting on his own right hand. Shame on him for denying the second person of trinity.

(Mystery eh? Maybe "mystery BABYLON") The "mystery trinity" can be understood by a quick reading of the children's book "The emperor's new clothes".

> Isaiah 45:22 Look unto me, and be ye saved, all the ends of the earth: for I [am] God, and [there is] none else.

> Isaiah 46:5 To whom will ye liken me, and make [me] equal, and compare me, that we may be like?

Why the two other co-equal, co-eternal, "mystery godlet persons", of course.

Isaiah 9:6 Clearly states that the child that is to be born is the everlasting Father, the Mighty God. In Matt 28:18 Jesus clearly states that he has ALL POWER, so if there were any separate "persons" they would be powerless. Jesus even told Philip "He that hath seen me hath seen the Father." John 14:9 The doctrine of the trinity is simply carnal ungodly men attempting to explain spiritual things to other carnal men.

> In Matt 28:19 Jesus told his disciples to baptise using a name. The apostles did use a name, they used the name of Jesus. Acts 2:38, 8:16, 19:5.

> In Acts 9:5 When Saul cried out to God and asked God who he was, God answered and said, "I AM JESUS". The devil (and his trinity preachers) have many deceived into thinking that Jesus is a junior one third of god, when in fact JESUS IS THE MIGHTY GOD!

Shallow

If we were to follow the shallow and unlearned thinking of the trinitarian, we would end up with a lot more than just three "god persons" in the god squad.

Using their unregenerate flawed logic, we can prove that the "Father" and "God" are TWO SEPARATE PERSONS:

> Gal 1:3 Grace be to you and peace from God the Father, and from our Lord Jesus Christ,

Here they would declare two separate persons, but just look at this next verse:

> Gal 1:4 Who gave himself for our sins, that he might deliver us from this present evil world, according to the will of God and our Father:

OOPS! Now using ignorance and flawed trinitarian logic, we have us another co-equal, co-eternal god person.

The trinitarian is often willingly ignorant of the clear Bible teaching that there is ONLY ONE GOD who is named Jesus. Therefor they are easily confused and manipulated by Satan, because they view the Bible from a foundation of deception and polytheism, rather than from a solid platform of a knowledge of even the first commandment:

> Mark 12:29 And Jesus answered him, The first of all the commandments is, Hear, O Israel; The Lord our God is one Lord:

While they are running around twisting scripture to try and prove 3 or 4 "lords", the Bible still contains Mark 12:29

They brazenly (as is the way of a harlot) spout blasphemy and "three god" philosophy, supported by their twisted and unlearned viewpoint of several misunderstood scriptures, IGNORING that the Bible has a dire warning against them as "soul spoilers".

> Col 2:8 Beware lest any man spoil you through philosophy and vain deceit, after the tradition of men, after the rudiments of the world, and not after Christ.
>
> Col 2:9 For in him dwelleth all the fulness of the Godhead bodily.
>
> Col 2:10 And ye are complete in him, which is the head of all principality and power:

Wrest

Why do so many wrestle with the scripture, but remain in false doctrine?

> II Peter 3:12 Looking for and hasting unto the coming of the day of God, wherein the heavens being on fire shall be dissolved, and the elements shall melt with fervent heat.
>
> II Peter 3:13 Nevertheless we, according to his promise, look for new heavens and a new earth, wherein dwelleth righteousness.
>
> II Peter 3:14 Wherefore, beloved, seeing that ye look for such things, be diligent that ye may be found of him in peace, without spot, and blameless.
>
> II Peter 3:15 And account [that] the longsuffering of our Lord [is] salvation; even as our beloved brother Paul also according to the wisdom given unto him hath written unto you;
>
> * * * * * * * * *
>
> II Peter 3:16 As also in all [his] epistles, speaking in them of these things; in which are some things hard to be understood, which they that are unlearned and unstable wrest, as [they do] also the other scriptures, unto their own destruction.

This is interesting because of Peter's affirmation of Paul and the validity of Paul's writings. Those who reject the teaching of Paul are also rejecting Peter since Peter affirmed Paul.

> II Peter 3:17 Ye therefore, beloved, seeing ye know [these things] before, beware lest ye also, being led away with the error of the wicked, fall from your own stedfastness.

Many false Christians do much study, but are unable to see basic truths, people actually believe that they can be Christian without the Baptism of the Holy Ghost, or they claim to have the Holy Ghost even though they've never spoken in tongues. They really think that their misunderstanding of the scriptures concerning "belief" and "believeth" will save them; and they use that to ignore the truth of the Word of God. They mock at the basic Biblical teachings of holy living and decency, preferring the standards of the "world". And they brazenly lead their families to an eternal hell.

A man that takes his family to a trinity church of any kind is leading his family into eternal torment.

> II Timothy 3:7 Ever learning, and never able to come to the knowledge of the truth.
>
> II Timothy 3:8 Now as Jannes and Jambres withstood Moses, so do these also resist the truth: men of corrupt minds, reprobate concerning the faith.

> II Timothy 3:13 But evil men and seducers shall wax worse and worse, deceiving, and being deceived.
>
> II Timothy 3:14 But continue thou in the things which thou hast learned and hast been assured of, knowing of whom thou hast learned [them];
>
> II Timothy 3:15 And that from a child thou hast known the holy scriptures, which are able to make thee wise unto salvation through faith which is in Christ Jesus.
>
> II Timothy 3:16 All scripture [is] given by inspiration of God, and [is] profitable for doctrine, for reproof, for correction, for instruction in righteousness:

Some just want the scriptures that speak of belief, and feel that they can ignore the rest, at will; but they are not really honest. Often they just feel in their hearts that they are "saved" even though they have never really obeyed Acts 2:38. God uses a special word to describe people like that:

> PRO 28:26 He that trusteth in his own heart is a fool: but whoso walketh wisely, he shall be delivered.

See what God has to say about those who wrest with the scripture rather than simply obeying it because they just know in their heart that they are saved. Did you see what God calls people like that?

Let us review what Peter taught as the plan of salvation for as many as God would ever call.

> Acts 2:38 Then Peter said unto them, Repent, and be baptized every one of you in the name of Jesus Christ for the remission of sins, and ye shall receive the gift of the Holy Ghost.
>
> Acts 2:39 For the promise is unto you, and to your children, and to all that are afar off, even as many as the Lord our God shall call.

Yet look at how the false-christians will wrest the scriptures in their desperate effort to try to justify their disobedience to Acts 2:38.

The Bible is so clear in its warning against trinitarianism or anything even remotely like it.

> Colossians 2:8 Beware lest any man spoil you through philosophy and vain deceit, after the tradition of men, after the rudiments of the world, and not after Christ.
>
> Colossians 2:9 For in him dwelleth all the fulness of the Godhead bodily.
>
> Colossians 2:10 And ye are complete in him, which is the head of all principality and power:

The phrase "for in him" appears only twice in the entire KJV Bible. It is referring to Jesus Christ

Acts 17:28 For in him we live, and move, and have our being; as certain also of your own poets have said, For we are also his offspring.

Colossians 2:9 For in him dwelleth all the fulness of the Godhead bodily.

The true bride of Jesus Christ is the bride of one husband only.

The true bride of Jesus Christ is the bride of "Jesus ONLY".

Yet, the false-church regards the phrase "Jesus Only" as an insult to be hurled at the true Christian. But I like it when they do that, because then I can ask them since they admit they don't worship only Jesus, just who do they worship.

Alpha

I believe that the following study really shows the trinity lie for what it is. I am composing this after preaching from these verses.

> Rev 1:8 I am Alpha and Omega, the beginning and the ending, saith the Lord, which is, and which was, and which is to come, the Almighty.
>
> Rev 1:9 I John, who also am your brother, and companion in tribulation, and in the kingdom and patience of Jesus Christ, was in the isle that is called Patmos, for the word of God, and for the testimony of Jesus Christ.
>
> Rev 1:10 I was in the Spirit on the Lord's day, and heard behind me a great voice, as of a trumpet,
>
> Rev 1:11 Saying, I am Alpha and Omega, the first and the last: and, What thou seest, write in a book, and send it unto the seven churches which are in Asia; unto Ephesus, and unto Smyrna, and unto Pergamos, and unto Thyatira, and unto Sardis, and unto Philadelphia, and unto Laodicea.
>
> Rev 1:12 And I turned to see the voice that spake with me. And being turned, I saw seven golden candlesticks;
>
> Rev 1:13 And in the midst of the seven candlesticks one like unto the Son of man, clothed with a garment down to the foot, and girt about the paps with a golden girdle.

He only saw "one", not three who is Alpha and Omega.

> Rev 1:14 His head and his hairs were white like wool, as white as snow; and his eyes were as a flame of fire;
>
> Rev 1:15 And his feet like unto fine brass, as if they burned in a furnace; and his voice as the sound of many waters.
>
> Rev 1:16 And he had in his right hand seven stars: and out of his mouth went a sharp twoedged sword: and his countenance was as the sun shineth in his strength.

Now that should really throw the trinitarians a loop, because they believe that one junior god is standing on the right hand of another god, but this says that there were seven stars?

> Rev 1:17 And when I saw him, I fell at his feet as dead. And he laid his right hand upon me, saying unto me, Fear not; I am the first and the last:

Here is another one, just think if there were another god on that right hand... and when he turned His hand over, *plop* there went the other god falling off. I mentioned in my sermon that it is OK to mock the trinity; that there is nothing noble or respectable about the trinity lie. Just as the prophet of God mocked the prophets of Baal. When trinity cults do good works it is only to deceive souls into hell.

I mentioned how during the cold war there was a race to provide grain for hungry nations. When the communists would send grain, there was nothing wrong with it, it was nutritional; but it was for the purpose of enslaving the people. When trinity churches do good things it is with the purpose of deceiving souls into hell.

> Rev 1:18 I am he that liveth, and was dead; and, behold, I am alive for evermore, Amen; and have the keys of hell and of death.

Clearly the one described in these verses, the Alpha and Omega, is the Lord Jesus Christ.

Then I read from the previous page a strong anti-trinity verse. I pointed out that it doesn't say God and our Saviour.

> Jude 1:25 To the only wise God our Saviour, be glory and majesty, dominion and power, both now and for ever. Amen.

The trinity is a lie.

Jesus Only

We often hear trinitarians refer to the true monotheistic Church as "Jesus Only". They consider this an insult. They like to claim to "oh how I luuvv Jesus", but they would use His name, the name above every name, as what they perceive to be an insult.

> Acts 4:12 Neither is there salvation in any other: for there is none other name under heaven given among men, whereby we must be saved.

The true Church is the bride of Christ, the bride of "Christ only" and not another. Imagine with me an earthly "bride to be" who declared that she did not want to be married to "husband only", and would mock at the married women and taunt them saying "Ha! You're married to "Jones only." or "you're Smith only"....

There's a word for gals like that who are not "husband only".

They don't want to be married to "Jesus Only", and they often mock at those of us who are betrothed to "Jesus Only". There is something about that name that the world hates.

> Luke 21:17 And ye shall be hated of all men for my name's sake.

I have often asked, that since these folks are admittedly not worshiping "only Jesus", just who are those devils worshiping?

Now here we have a "bride wannabe", but she doesn't want to be married to "husband only", she will mock at true brides and taunt them saying "You're husband only". Well, there is a word for gals like that who are not "husband only" and it is the same word used for the churches that are not "Jesus only".

The Bible speaks of a great false bride, a great church that has daughters that denominated from her. The Bible speaks of this "Great Whore" that is the "Mother of Harlots". Yes, there's a word for gals like that...

The RCC is the "Great Whore"

The "harlot daughters" are the denominations that worship the same false gods as the "Great Whore" (the Catholic trinity). They are not "husband only".

Most of the false christian churches are denominal daughters of the RCC. That is another reason that no one can be saved in a trinity church.

> Revelation 17:1 And there came one of the seven angels which had the seven vials, and talked with me, saying unto me, Come hither; I will shew unto thee the judgment of the great whore that sitteth upon many waters:

The RCC "sitteth on many waters".

> Revelation 17:2 With whom the kings of the earth have committed fornication, and the inhabitants of the earth have been made drunk with the wine of her fornication.

Catholic "indulgences" and false religion have made many "drunk" with her false "trinity" religion.

> Revelation 17:3 So he carried me away in the spirit into the wilderness: and I saw a woman sit upon a scarlet coloured beast, full of names of blasphemy, having seven heads and ten horns.

The "beast" may well be the economic community that the "Whore" (the RCC) rides on. The nations support the Vatican.

> Revelation 17:4 And the woman was arrayed in purple and scarlet colour, and decked with gold and precious stones and pearls, having a golden cup in her hand full of abominations and filthiness of her fornication:

The pomp and jewelry and scarlet robes of the RCC are legendary. But she is most certainly not "Jesus only".

> Revelation 17:5 And upon her forehead [was] a name written, MYSTERY, BABYLON THE GREAT, THE MOTHER OF HARLOTS AND ABOMINATIONS OF THE EARTH.

Yep, there's a word for gals like that.

The RCC is the mother of all of the trinity denominations.

> Revelation 17:6 And I saw the woman drunken with the blood of the saints, and with the blood of the martyrs of Jesus: and when I saw her, I wondered with great admiration.

No organization has murdered (as "heretics") so many real Apostolic Christians as the Roman Catholic Church! History knows no other possible organization than the RCC to fit verse Rev 17:6 and her daughters are the trinity denominations. They are not "Jesus only"; they are not "husband only", and many of them mock and rail at those who , are, "husband only".

So, trinitarian, next time you want to call those who are Acts 2:38 Christians "Jesus only", why not just call us "husband only"? And, well, we know the word for those of you who are not "Jesus only", don't we...

The bride of Jesus is the bride "Jesus Only".

1 Corinthians 10:21 Ye cannot drink the cup of the Lord, and the cup of devils: ye cannot be partakers of the Lord's table, and of the table of devils.

2 Corinthians 6:16 And what agreement hath the temple of God with idols? for ye are the temple of the living God; as God hath said, I will dwell in them, and walk in them; and I will be their God, and they shall be my people.

17 Wherefore come out from among them, and be ye separate, saith the Lord, and touch not the unclean thing; and I will receive you,

18 And will be a Father unto you, and ye shall be my sons and daughters, saith the Lord Almighty.

I hope this helps...

One Husband Only

The true Bride of Christ is the Bride of one husband only.

No trinitarian has been able to answer the simple questions regarding which of their "god persons" is being referred to or is speaking in these verses.

The trinity god squad is simply man making gods unto himself.

> Jer 16:20 Shall a man make gods unto himself, and they are no Gods?"
>
> Deut 4:35 Unto thee it was shewed, that thou mightest know that the Lord he is God; there is none else beside him.

Which one of the god squad members is referred to in the above verse god squad member number 1, god squad member number 2, or god squad member number 3?

I believe that the trinity theory proposes that there were 2 other "god persons" beside Jehovah during this time.

> Deut 4:39 Know therefore this day, and consider it in thine heart, that the Lord he is God in heaven above, and upon the earth beneath; there is none else.

Which one of the god squad members is referred to in the above verse god squad member number 1, god squad member number 2, or god squad member number 3?

I believe it would also have said "they" rather than "he" if the trinity theory was scriptural.

> Deut 6:4 Hear, O Isriael: The Lord our God is one Lord:

Which one of the god squad members is referred to in the above verse god squad member number 1, god squad member number 2, or god squad member number 3?

> Deut 32:39 See now that I, even I, am he, and THERE IS NO GOD WITH ME: I kill, and I make alive; I wound and I heal: neither is there any that can deliver out of my hand.

Which one of the god squad members is speaking to in the above verse god squad member number 1, god squad member number 2, or god squad member number 3?

According to trinity there were two others with Jehovah here, surely Jehovah would have been aware of their presence (especially if they were co-equal, and co-eternal)

> Psalms 86:10 For thou art great, and doest wonderous things: THOU ART GOD ALONE.

Which one of the god squad members is referred to in the above verse god squad member number 1, god squad member number 2, or god squad member number 3?

> Isaiah 43:3 For I am the Lord thy God, the Holy One of Israel, THY SAVIOR:...."

Which one of the god squad members is referred to in the above verse god squad member number 1, god squad member number 2, or god squad member number 3?

> Isaiah 43:10 Ye are my witnesses, sayeth the Lord, and my servant whom I have chosen; that ye may know and believe me, and understand that I am he: before me there was no God formed, neither shall there be after me.

Which one of the god squad members is referred to in the above verse god squad member number 1, god squad member number 2, or god squad member number 3?

> Isaiah 43:11 I, even I, am the Lord, and BESIDES ME THERE IS NO SAVIOR.

Which one of the god squad members is referred to in the above verse god squad member number 1, god squad member number 2, or god squad member number 3?

Now surely Jehovah would have noticed a "second person" hanging around heaven (especially if he was sitting on his right hand).

> Isaiah 44:6 Thus saith the Lord, the King of Israel, and his redeemer the Lord of hosts: I am the first, and I am the last, and BESIDE ME THERE IS NO GOD.

Which one of the god squad members is referred to in the above verse god squad member number 1, god squad member number 2, or god squad member number 3?

> Isaiah 44:24 Thus saith the Lord, thy redeemer, and he that formed thee from the womb, I am the Lord that maketh all things; that stretcheth forth the heavens ALONE; that spreadeth abroad the earth BY MYSELF;

Which one of the god squad members is referred to in the above verse god squad member number 1, god squad member number 2, or god squad member number 3?

Now why would Jehovah take the credit and not share it with the "second person" of the trinity god squad?

> Isaiah 45:5 I am the LORD, and there is none else, there is no God beside me: I girded thee, though thou hast not known me:
>
> 6 That they may know from the rising of the sun, and from the west, that there is none beside me. I am the LORD, and there is none else.
>
> Isaiah 45:18 For thus saith the LORD that created the heavens; God himself that formed the earth and made it; he hath established it, he created it not in vain, he formed it to be inhabited: I am the LORD; and there is none else.
>
> Isaiah 45: 21 Tell ye, and bring them near; yea, let them take counsel together: who hath declared this from ancient time? who hath told it from that time? have not I the LORD? and

there is no God else beside me; a just God and a Saviour; there is none beside me.

22 Look unto me, and be ye saved, all the ends of the earth: for I am God, and there is none else.

Isaiah 46:5 To whom will ye liken me, and make me equal, and compare me, that we may be like?

Isaiah 48:11 For mine own sake, even for mine own sake, will I do it: for how should my name be polluted? and I will not give my glory unto another.

Which one of the god squad members is referred to in the above verses god squad member number 1, god squad member number 2, or god squad member number 3?

Titus 1:3 But hath in due times manifested his word through preaching, which is committed unto me according to the commandment of GOD OUR SAVIOR.

Titus 3:4 But after that the kindness and love of GOD OUR SAVIOR toward man appeared, appeared.

Which one of the god squad members is referred to in the above verses as "savior", god squad member number 1, god squad member number 2, or god squad member number 3?

Mark 12:29 And Jesus answered him, The first of all the commandments is, Hear, O Israel; the Lord our God is one Lord.

Ephesians 4:5 ONE LORD, one faith, one baptism.

I Tim 3:16 And without controversy great is the mystery of godliness: GOD WAS MANIFEST IN THE FLESH, justified in the Spirit, seen of angels, preached unto the Gentiles, believed on in the world, received up into glory.

Which one of the god squad members is referred to in the above verse god squad member number 1, god squad member number 2, or god squad member number 3?

I John 3:16 Hereby perceive we the love of God, because he laid down HIS LIFE for us: and we ought to lay down our lives for the brethren.

St. John 14:9 Jesus saith unto him, Have I been so long time with you, and yet HAST THOU NOT KNOWN ME, Phillip? HE THAT HATH SEEN ME HATH SEEN THE FATHER; and how sayest thou then, Shew us the Father?

Oops, here we have the "second person" of the trinity theory claiming to be the "first person".

Isaiah 9:6 For unto us a CHILD is born, unto us a SON is given: and the government shall be upon his shoulder: and his name shall be called Wonderful, Counsellor, THE MIGHTY GOD, THE EVERLASTING FATHER, the Prince of Peace.

Which one of the god squad members is referred to in the above verse god squad member number 1, god squad member number 2, or god squad member number 3?

Jude 25 To the only wise GOD OUR SAVIOR, be glory and majesty, dominion and power, both now and forever. Amen.

Amazed – False

I am amazed at the audacity of some of the false christians that I believe that the following study really shows the trinity lie for what it is. I am composing this after preaching from these verses.

> Rev 1:8 I am Alpha and Omega, the beginning and the ending, saith the Lord, which is, and which was, and which is to come, the Almighty.
>
> Rev 1:9 I John, who also am your brother, and companion in tribulation, and in the kingdom and patience of Jesus Christ, was in the isle that is called Patmos, for the word of God, and for the testimony of Jesus Christ.
>
> Rev 1:10 I was in the Spirit on the Lord's day, and heard behind me a great voice, as of a trumpet,
>
> Rev 1:11 Saying, I am Alpha and Omega, the first and the last: and, What thou seest, write in a book, and send it unto the seven churches which are in Asia; unto Ephesus, and unto Smyrna, and unto Pergamos, and unto Thyatira, and unto Sardis, and unto Philadelphia, and unto Laodicea.
>
> Rev 1:12 And I turned to see the voice that spake with me. And being turned, I saw seven golden candlesticks;
>
> Rev 1:13 And in the midst of the seven candlesticks one like unto the Son of man, clothed with a garment down to the foot, and girt about the paps with a golden girdle.

He only saw "one", not three who is Alpha and Omega.

> Rev 1:14 His head and his hairs were white like wool, as white as snow; and his eyes were as a flame of fire;
>
> Rev 1:15 And his feet like unto fine brass, as if they burned in a furnace; and his voice as the sound of many waters.
>
> Rev 1:16 And he had in his right hand seven stars: and out of his mouth went a sharp two-edged sword: and his countenance was as the sun shineth in his strength.

Now that should really throw the trinitarians a loop, because they believe that one junior god is standing on the right hand of another god, but this says that there were seven stars?

> Rev 1:17 And when I saw him, I fell at his feet as dead. And he laid his right hand upon me, saying unto me, Fear not; I am the first and the last:

Here is another one, just think if there were another god on that right hand... and when he turned His hand over, *plop* there went the other god falling off. I mentioned in my sermon that it is OK to mock the trinity; that there is nothing noble or respectable about the trinity lie. Just as the prophet of God mocked the prophets of Baal. When trinity cults do good works it is only to deceive souls into hell.

I mentioned how during the cold war there was a race to provide grain for hungry nations. When the communists would send grain, there was nothing wrong with it, it was nutritional; but it was for the purpose of enslaving the people. When trinity churches do good things it is with the purpose of deceiving souls into hell.

> Rev 1:18 I am he that liveth, and was dead; and, behold, I am alive for evermore, Amen; and have the keys of hell and of death.

Clearly the one described in these verses, the Alpha and Omega, is the Lord Jesus Christ.

Then I read from the previous page a strong anti-trinity verse. I pointed out that it doesn't say God and our Saviour.

> Jude 1:25 To the only wise God our Saviour, be glory and majesty, dominion and power, both now and for ever. Amen.

The trinity is a lie.

AntiCHRIST

The word "antichrist" appears 4 time in the Holy Bible in four separate verses.

> 1 John 2:18 Little children, it is the last time: and as ye have heard that antichrist shall come, even now are there many antichrists; whereby we know that it is the last time.
>
> 1 John 2:22 Who is a liar but he that denieth that Jesus<2424> is the Christ? He is antichrist, that denieth the Father and the Son.
>
> 1 John 4:3 And every spirit that confesseth not that Jesus<2424> Christ is come in the flesh is not of God: and this is that spirit of antichrist, whereof ye have heard that it should come; and even now already is it in the world.
>
> 2 John 1:7 For many deceivers are entered into the world, who confess not that Jesus<2424> Christ is come in the flesh. This is a deceiver and an antichrist.

In each of these verses the word translated as Jesus comes from reference 2424

Since words do04 mean things so let us look at the definition of the word. If we are to understand a Bible verse then we need to know the meaning of the words used

in that verse, eh?

2424 Iesous ee-ay-sooce'

> of Hebrew origin 03091; TDNT - 3:284,360; n pr m
>
> AV - Jesus 972, Jesus (Joshua) 2, Jesus (Justus) 1; 975
>
> Jesus = "Jehovah is salvation"

Notice the Hebrew of 03091

03091 Y@howshuwa‘ yeh-ho-shoo’-ah or Y@howshu‘a yeh-ho-shoo’-ah

from 03068 and 03467;

AV - Joshua 218; 218

Joshua or Jehoshua = "Jehovah is salvation" n pr m

Then notice the Hebrew for 03068 referred to above:

03068 Y@hovah yeh-ho-vaw’

from 01961; TWOT - 484a; n pr dei

AV - LORD 6510, GOD 4, JEHOVAH 4, variant 1; 6519

Jehovah = "the existing One"

1) the proper name of the one true God

1a) unpronounced except with the vowel pointings of 0136

The trinity does not teach that "Jehovah savior" came in the flesh, but rather teaches that a "second person", or "junior deity" came in the flesh. Does the trinity teach

that Jehovah died on the cross for your sins or do they teach a "junior person"?

Many are taught John 3:16 but what about 1 John 3:16

> 1 John 3:16 Hereby perceive we the love of God, because he laid down his life for us: and we ought to lay down our lives for the brethren.

That does not say that a junior god person died on the cross now does it?

There is also another group of verses that warn particularly against polytheistic theories, and further declare them capable of "spoiling".

> Colossians 2:8 Beware lest any man spoil you through philosophy and vain deceit, after the tradition of men, after the rudiments of the world, and not after Christ.
>
> Colossians 2:9 For in him dwelleth all the fulness of the Godhead bodily.
>
> Colossians 2:10 And ye are complete in him, which is the head of all principality and power:

Let us review our original verses and simply substitute Jehovah for Jesus since we know that is the definition of the word "Jesus".

> 1 John 2:18 Little children, it is the last time: and as ye have heard that antichrist shall come, even now are there many antichrists; whereby we know that it is the last time.
>
> 1 John 2:22 Who is a liar but he that denieth that Jesus<2424> is the Christ? He is antichrist, that denieth the Father and the Son.
>
> 1 John 4:3 And every spirit that confesseth not that Jesus<2424> Christ is come in the flesh is not of God: and this is that spirit of antichrist, whereof ye have heard that it should come; and even now already is it in the world.
>
> 2 John 1:7 For many deceivers are entered into the world, who confess not that Jesus<2424> Christ is come in the flesh. This is a deceiver and an antichrist.

That's right friend. Trinitarianism is not merely stupid foolish and deceitful,

it really is ANTICHRIST!

Consider also this verse regarding the human tendency that man has to "make up" his own "gods" (If people didn't get a measure of peace and satisfaction they wouldn't have been worshipping creations of their own minds for centuries).

> Jeremiah 5:7 How shall I pardon thee for this? thy children have forsaken me, and sworn by [them that are] no gods: when I had fed them to the full, they then committed adultery, and assembled themselves by troops in the harlots' houses.

> Jeremiah 16:20 Shall a man make gods unto himself, and they [are] no gods?
>
> Genesis 3:8 And they heard the voice of the LORD God walking in the garden in the cool of the day: and Adam and his wife hid themselves from the presence of the LORD God amongst the trees of the garden.

According to the trinity there would have been 5 pair of feet walking in the garden in this verse. 1 pair for Adam, 1 pair for Eve and three pair for the trinity that they were hiding from. Of course the more scholarly of the trinitarians might suggest that there were only 4 pair of feet actually walking because god person #2 was riding on the right hand of god person #1.

Also considering the trinitarian attempt to preach plural gods from Gen 1:26:

> Genesis 1:26 And God said, Let us make man in our image, after our likeness: and let them have dominion over the fish of the sea, and over the fowl of the air, and over the cattle, and over all the earth, and over every creeping thing that creepeth upon the earth.
>
> Genesis 1:27 So God created man in his [own] image, in the image of God created he him; male and female created he them.

Shouldn't verse 27 read "created they them"? And if the "trinity" of three created Adam in "their image", where are the other two Adam persons? We need two other "persons" here. I mean, if one "person" can sit on the other "person"'s right hand then where were Adam's two "co-equal" persons. Then we would need a trinity of wives.

Yet we have trinitarians who claim to be "one god", Biblically Christian, and monotheistic. How can this be?

> 2 Corinthians 11:12 But what I do, that I will do, that I may cut off occasion from them which desire occasion; that wherein they glory, they may be found even as we.

13 For such are false apostles, deceitful workers, transforming themselves into the apostles of Christ.

14 And no marvel; for Satan himself is transformed into an angel of light.

15 Therefore it is no great thing if his ministers also be transformed as the ministers of righteousness; whose end shall be according to their works.

In the above verses Paul says that it is Biblical to try to cut off occasion from the Satanic ministers who will be pretending to be ministers of righteousness.

Revelation 17:1 ¶ And there came one of the seven angels which had the seven vials, and talked with me, saying unto me, Come hither; I will shew unto thee the judgment of the great whore that sitteth upon many waters:

2 With whom the kings of the earth have committed fornication, and the inhabitants of the earth have been made drunk with the wine of her fornication.

3 So he carried me away in the spirit into the wilderness: and I saw a woman sit upon a scarlet coloured beast, full of names of blasphemy, having seven heads and ten horns.

4 And the woman was arrayed in purple and scarlet colour, and decked with gold and precious stones and pearls, having a golden cup in her hand full of abominations and filthiness of her fornication:

5 And upon her forehead was a name written, MYSTERY, BABYLON THE GREAT, THE MOTHER OF HARLOTS AND ABOMINATIONS OF THE EARTH.

6 And I saw the woman drunken with the blood of the saints, and with the blood of the martyrs of Jesus: and when I saw her, I wondered with great admiration.

Know

One should consider the first of all the commandments.

> Mark 12:28 And one of the scribes came, and having heard them reasoning together, and perceiving that he had answered them well, asked him, Which is the first commandment of all?
>
> Mark 12:29 And Jesus answered him, The first of all the commandments [is], Hear, O Israel; The Lord our God is one Lord:

** Many teach that it doesn't matter if you believe in three lords **

> Mark 12:30 And thou shalt love the Lord thy God with all thy heart, and with all thy soul, and with all thy mind, and with all thy strength: this [is] the first commandment.

> Colossians 2:8 Beware lest any man spoil you through philosophy and vain deceit, after the tradition of men, after the rudiments of the world, and not after Christ.
>
> Colossians 2:9 For in him dwelleth all the fulness of the Godhead bodily.
>
> Colossians 2:10 And ye are complete in him, which is the head of all principality and power:

> Mark 14:62 And Jesus said, I am: and ye shall see the Son of man sitting on the right hand of power, and coming in the clouds of heaven.

Right hand does not mean a big ole arm in the sky

> John 4:26 Jesus saith unto her, I that speak unto thee am [he].

John 8:58 Jesus said unto them, Verily, verily, I say unto you, Before Abraham was, I am.

Exodus 3:14 And God said unto Moses, I AM THAT I AM: and he said, Thus shalt thou say unto the children of Israel, I AM hath sent me unto you.

John 14:9 Jesus saith unto him, Have I been so long time with you, and yet hast thou not known me, Philip? he that hath seen me hath seen the Father; and how sayest thou [then], Shew us the Father?

Jude 1:17 But, beloved, remember ye the words which were spoken before of the apostles of our Lord Jesus Christ;

Jude 1:18 How that they told you there should be mockers in the last time, who should walk after their own ungodly lusts.

Jude 1:19 These be they who separate themselves, sensual, having not the Spirit.

Jude 1:20 But ye, beloved, building up yourselves on your most holy faith, praying in the Holy Ghost,

Jude 1:21 Keep yourselves in the love of God, looking for the mercy of our Lord Jesus Christ unto eternal life.

Jude 1:22 And of some have compassion, making a difference:

Jude 1:23 And others save with fear, pulling [them] out of the fire; hating even the garment spotted by the flesh.

Jude 1:24 Now unto him that is able to keep you from falling, and to present [you] faultless before the presence of his glory with exceeding joy,

Jude 1:25 To the only wise God our Saviour, [be] glory and majesty, dominion and power, both now and for ever. Amen.

Isaiah 43:11 I, [even] I, [am] the LORD; and beside me [there is] no saviour.

Isaiah 45:21 Tell ye, and bring [them] near; yea, let them take counsel together: who hath declared this from ancient time? [who] hath told it from that time? [have] not I the LORD? and [there is] no God else beside me; a just God and a Saviour; [there is] none beside me.

Hosea 13:4 Yet I [am] the LORD thy God from the land of Egypt, and thou shalt know no god but me: for [there is] no saviour beside me.

Luke 2:11 For unto you is born this day in the city of David a Saviour, which is Christ the Lord.

Confess

> I John 4:2 Hereby know ye the Spirit of God: Every spirit that confesseth that Jesus Christ is come in the flesh is of God:
>
> I John 4:3 And every spirit that confesseth not that Jesus Christ is come in the flesh is not of God: and this is that [spirit] of antichrist, whereof ye have heard that it should come; and even now already is it in the world.
>
> II John 1:7 For many deceivers are entered into the world, who confess not that Jesus Christ is come in the flesh. This is a deceiver and an antichrist.

Now, I ask you to take a moment and pray and ask Jesus to open our understanding concerning these verses............................

I pray that we can now see beyond the carnal surface "interpretation" of these verses and see what the Lord would have us to see...We have a *lot* of men throwing the name of Jesus around every day, and some who have been recently exposed as totally false preachers, so what is the key to understanding these verses??? Well, it's so simple, really!! We simply look at the definition of the word "Jesus". Jesus means "Jehovah Savior" soooo every spirit that confesseth not that Jehovah is come in the flesh is the antichrist spirit.............

That is why the "trinity" is an antichrist doctrine. They teach that a "second person" came in the flesh, they teach that Jesus is merely one of several separate persons (or gods)....So they don't really believe that Jehovah came to earth "in the flesh"..........

You may also have noticed that the harlot daughters of the trinity mother church are returning home to mama (National Council of Churches etc..) so there will be one great world fellowship of trinitarians to welcome the antichrist to his throne.........

Here are several scriptures, of which, any one of them contradicts the "three separate person" trinity heresy:

> John 10:30 I and [my] Father are one.
>
> John 14:9 Jesus saith unto him, Have I been so long time with you, and yet hast thou not known me, Philip? he that hath seen me hath seen the Father; and how sayest thou [then], Shew us the Father?
>
> I John 3:16 Hereby perceive we the love [of God], because he laid down his life for us: and we ought to lay down [our] lives for the brethren.
>
> John 8:58 Jesus said unto them, Verily, verily, I say unto you, Before Abraham was, I am.
>
> John 1:1 In the beginning was the Word, and the Word was with God, and the Word was God.
>
> John 1:2 The same was in the beginning with God.
>
> John 1:3 All things were made by him; and without him was not any thing made that was made.
>
> John 1:4 In him was life; and the life was the light of men.
>
> John 1:5 And the light shineth in darkness; and the darkness comprehended it not.
>
> John 1:10 He was in the world, and the world was made by him, and the world knew him not.
>
> John 1:11 He came unto his own, and his own received him not.
>
> Malachi 3:1 Behold, I will send my messenger, and he shall prepare the way before me: and the Lord, whom ye seek, shall suddenly come to his temple, even the messenger of the covenant, whom ye delight in: behold, he shall come, saith the LORD of hosts.

(You see the Jews knew that it would be the LORD coming to His temple)

Isaiah 45:21 Tell ye, and bring [them] near; yea, let them take counsel together: who hath declared this from ancient time? [who] hath told it from that time? [have] not I the LORD? and [there is] no God else beside me; a just God and a Saviour; [there is] none beside me.

****

NOTICE THESE TWO VERSES!!:

Isaiah 44:24 Thus saith the LORD, thy redeemer, and he that formed thee from the womb, I [am] the LORD that maketh all [things]; that stretcheth forth the heavens alone; that spreadeth abroad the earth by myself;

John 1:3 All things were made by him; and without him was not any thing made that was made.

****

Acts 9:5 And he said, Who art thou, Lord? And the Lord said, I am Jesus whom thou persecutest: [it is] hard for thee to kick against the pricks. (Who did God say that he was?!?!?!)

Acts 22:8 And I answered, Who art thou, Lord? And he said unto me, I am Jesus of Nazareth, whom thou persecutest. (Who did God say that he was!?!?!)

Acts 26:15 And I said, Who art thou, Lord? And he said, I am Jesus whom thou persecutest.

Revelation 22:12 And, behold, I come quickly; and my reward [is] with me, to give every man according as his work shall be.

Revelation 22:13 I am Alpha and Omega, the beginning and the end, the first and the last.

Jesus is speaking here HE is GOD!! HE IS ALPHA & OMEGA!!!

Revelation 22:14 Blessed [are] they that do his commandments, that they may have right to the tree of life, and may enter in through the gates into the city.

Revelation 22:15 For without [are] dogs, and sorcerers, and whoremongers, and murderers, and idolaters, and whosoever loveth and maketh a lie.

Revelation 22:16 I Jesus have sent mine angel to testify unto you these things in the churches. I am the root and the offspring of David, [and] the bright and morning star.

Revelation 22:20 He which testifieth these things saith, Surely I come quickly. Amen. Even so, come, Lord Jesus.

Revelation 22:21 The grace of our Lord Jesus Christ [be] with you all. Amen.

Know Commandment

There are, of course, many instructions in the New Testament. It is important to know which ones are there to help a person become a Christian and which ones are there to help one who has obeyed the former, to remain a Christian.

In a nutshell, in the book of Acts we discover how to become a Christian and in the epistles (letters to Acts 2:38 Christians) we discover how to "remain" Christian.

I will dwell on issues related to becoming a real Christian that are directly opposed to the polytheistic concepts of trinitarianism.

> Mark 12:28 And one of the scribes came, and having heard them reasoning together, and perceiving that he had answered them well, asked him, Which is the first commandment of all?
>
> Mark 12:29 And Jesus answered him, The first of all the commandments [is], Hear, O Israel; The Lord our God is one Lord:

** Many teach that it doesn't matter if you believe in three lords **

> Mark 12:30 And thou shalt love the Lord thy God with all thy heart, and with all thy soul, and with all thy mind, and with all thy strength: this [is] the first commandment.

Hear that God is only one "person" and love Him (not them) with all your heart. Then we see a dire warning against trinitarianism.

> Colossians 2:8 Beware lest any man spoil you through philosophy and vain deceit, after the tradition of men, after the rudiments of the world, and not after Christ.

> Colossians 2:9 For in him dwelleth all the fulness of the Godhead bodily.

> Colossians 2:10 And ye are complete in him, which is the head of all principality and power:

> Mark 14:62 And Jesus said, I am: and ye shall see the Son of man sitting on the right hand of power, and coming in the clouds of heaven.

Right hand is used throughout the Bible to symbolize power. Right hand does not mean a big ole arm hanging out of the sky.

> John 4:26 Jesus saith unto her, I that speak unto thee am [he].

> John 8:58 Jesus said unto them, Verily, verily, I say unto you, Before Abraham was, I am.

> Exodus 3:14 And God said unto Moses, I AM THAT I AM: and he said, Thus shalt thou say unto the children of Israel, I AM hath sent me unto you.

There is only one "I AM". "I AM" is not three separate persons in a god squad and as stated above, we are commanded to know that.

> John 14:9 Jesus saith unto him, Have I been so long time with you, and yet hast thou not known me, Philip? he that hath seen me hath seen the Father; and how sayest thou [then], Shew us the Father?

Jesus declares Himself.

> John 14:9 Jesus saith unto him, Have I been so long time with you, and yet hast thou not known me, Philip? he that hath seen me hath seen the Father; and how sayest thou [then], Shew us the Father?

Jesus also declares that those who don't realize that He is the Father, don't really know Him at all.

> Jude 1:17 But, beloved, remember ye the words which were spoken before of the apostles of our Lord Jesus Christ;

> Jude 1:18 How that they told you there should be mockers in the last time, who should walk after their own ungodly lusts.
>
> Jude 1:19 These be they who separate themselves, sensual, having not the Spirit.
>
> Jude 1:20 But ye, beloved, building up yourselves on your most holy faith, praying in the Holy Ghost,
>
> Jude 1:21 Keep yourselves in the love of God, looking for the mercy of our Lord Jesus Christ unto eternal life.
>
> Jude 1:22 And of some have compassion, making a difference:
>
> Jude 1:23 And others save with fear, pulling [them] out of the fire; hating even the garment spotted by the flesh.
>
> Jude 1:24 Now unto him that is able to keep you from falling, and to present [you] faultless before the presence of his glory with exceeding joy,
>
> Jude 1:25 To the only wise God our Saviour, [be] glory and majesty, dominion and power, both now and for ever. Amen.

There is only One wise God, the Saviour, Jesus Christ, God manifest in the flesh.

> Isaiah 43:11 I, [even] I, [am] the LORD; and beside me [there is] no saviour.

Jesus (the only Saviour) is the individual speaking in the verse above.

> Isaiah 45:21 Tell ye, and bring [them] near; yea, let them take counsel together: who hath declared this from ancient time? [who] hath told it from that time? [have] not I the LORD? and [there is] no God else beside me; a just God and a Saviour; [there is] none beside me.

Jesus (the only Saviour) is the individual speaking in the verse above.

> Hosea 13:4 Yet I [am] the LORD thy God from the land of Egypt, and thou shalt know no god but me: for [there is] no saviour beside me.

Jesus (the only Saviour) is the individual speaking in the verse above.

> Luke 2:11 For unto you is born this day in the city of David a Saviour, which is Christ the Lord.

So, you see, the trinitarian breaks the first of all the commandments because they teach a god squad of three separate persons. In trinity, God the Father and the "saviour" are two separate persons.

Lettuce

Here we have one of the favorite verses of the trinity/antichrist preachers, except if we keep reading just one verse further; we see that verse 26 couldn't have possibly been referring to a discussion with other gods. God was talking with the angels.

> Genesis 1:26 And God said, Let us make man in our image, after our likeness: and let them have dominion over the fish of the sea, and over the fowl of the air, and over the cattle, and over all the earth, and over every creeping thing that creepeth upon the earth.
>
> Genesis 1:27 So God created man in his [own] image, in the image of God created he him; male and female created he them.

See in verse 27; it says "he" created, not "they" created. But as if that wasn't enough proof, we see in this next verse that God clearly and plainly declares that He did the creating, and I quote "by myself"

> Isaiah 44:24 Thus saith the LORD, thy redeemer, and he that formed thee from the womb, I [am] the LORD that maketh all [things]; that stretcheth forth the heavens alone; that spreadeth abroad the earth by myself;
>
> Isaiah 44:25 That frustrateth the tokens of the liars, and maketh diviners mad; that turneth wise [men] backward, and maketh their knowledge foolish;

God does not seem overly impressed with men's pet theories, does He?

> Isaiah 45:5 I [am] the LORD, and [there is] none else, [there is] no God beside me: I girded thee, though thou hast not known me:
>
> Isaiah 45:6 That they may know from the rising of the sun, and from the west, that [there is] none beside me. I [am] the LORD, and [there is] none else.

Now I have to submit that if there had been any other co-equal, co-eternal 1/3 gods around that Jehovah Saviour would have been aware of them, notice that He states, and I quote "there is none beside me".

> Isaiah 45:23 I have sworn by myself, the word is gone out of my mouth [in] righteousness, and shall not return, That unto me every knee shall bow, every tongue shall swear.
>
> Isaiah 45:23 and Philippians 2:10 & 11 must be referring to the same person, whom all knees will eventually bow to.
>
> Philippians 2:10 That at the name of Jesus every knee should bow, of [things] in heaven, and [things] in earth, and [things] under the earth;
>
> Philippians 2:11 And [that] every tongue should confess that Jesus Christ [is] Lord, to the glory of God the Father.

Now if you're having any trouble at all with thinking that verse 11 speaks of two gods, just take the comma out (the original language didn't have 'em)...and notice the consistent meaning, if we read the verse to mean that Jesus Christ is Lord of the glory of God the Father. If that seems to be stretching things a bit, notice this next verse:

> I Corinthians 2:8 Which none of the princes of this world knew: for had they known [it], they would not have crucified the Lord of glory.

See, it says that Jesus is the Lord of glory, but we see in this next verse that Jehovah Saviour states that He will not share His glory with any other....sooo we see that Jehovah Saviour allowed Himself to be crucified.

> Isaiah 48:11 For mine own sake, [even] for mine own sake, will I do [it]: for how should [my name] be polluted? and I will not give my glory unto another.

And if anyone with even the slightest bit of sincerity has any lingering doubt, Jesus said it about as plain as it could be said.

> John 14:9 Jesus saith unto him, Have I been so long time with you, and yet hast thou not known me, Philip? he that hath seen me hath seen the Father; and how sayest thou [then], Shew us the Father?
>
> John 14:15 If ye love me, keep my commandments.
>
> 16 And I will pray the Father, and he shall give you another Comforter, that he may abide with you for ever;
>
> 17 Even the Spirit of truth; whom the world cannot receive, because it seeth him not, neither knoweth him: but ye know him; for he dwelleth with you, and hall be in you.
>
> 18 I will not leave you comfortless: I will come to you.
>
> Romans 8:9 But ye are not in the flesh, but in the Spirit, if so be that the Spirit of God dwell in you. Now if any man have not the Spirit of Christ, he is none of his.

Notice how the Spirit of God and the Spirit of Christ is the same Spirit. That same Spirit is the Spirit of Truth, or the Holy Ghost.

God is a Spirit.

> John 4:24 God [is] a Spirit: and they that worship him must worship [him] in spirit and in truth.

God is holy.

> I Samuel 2:2 [There is] none holy as the LORD: for [there is] none beside thee: neither [is there] any rock like our God.

God is a "Holy Spirit".

Jesus is the "Spirit of truth"

> John 14:6 Jesus saith unto him, I am the way, the truth, and the life: no man cometh unto the Father, but by me.

Jesus was "dwelling with them" and promised to be "in them".

John 14:17 [Even] the Spirit of truth; whom the world cannot receive, because it seeth him not, neither knoweth him: but ye know him; for he dwelleth with you, and shall be in you.

The "comforter" is the "Spirit of Christ"

John 14:18 I will not leave you comfortless: I will come to you.

The "Spirit of Christ" is the "Holy Spirit" is the "Spirit of Truth"

John 14:26 But the Comforter, [which is] the Holy Ghost, whom the Father will send in my name, he shall teach you all things, and bring all things to your remembrance, whatsoever I have said unto you.

The Spirit of God visited His creation robed in flesh as the "Son".

I Timothy 3:16 And without controversy great is the mystery of godliness: God was manifest in the flesh, justified in the Spirit, seen of angels, preached unto the Gentiles, believed on in the world, received up into glory.

The fullness of God is in Jesus Christ

Colossians 2:9 For in him dwelleth all the fulness of the Godhead bodily.

Colossians 2:10 And ye are complete in him, which is the head of all principality and power:

Jesus IS the "everlasting Father".

Isaiah 9:6 For unto us a child is born, unto us a son is given: and the government shall be upon his shoulder: and his name shall be called Wonderful, Counsellor, The mighty God, The everlasting Father, The Prince of Peace.

Those who believe that Jesus is a "separate person" from the "Father" don't really know Jesus at all.

> John 14:9 Jesus saith unto him, Have I been so long time with you, and yet hast thou not known me, Philip? he that hath seen me hath seen the Father; and how sayest thou [then], Shew us the Father?

Die in Sin

I will explain in this brief post why every trinitarian will die in their sins and spend eternity in a devils' hell. I do this not to condemn souls, because the trinitarian is condemned already, but to warn of the fires of hell.

> Jude 1:23 And others save with fear, pulling them out of the fire; hating even the garment spotted by the flesh.

> 2 Timothy 4:2 Preach the word; be instant in season, out of season; reprove, rebuke, exhort with all longsuffering and doctrine.

Remission of sins is essential for sinful humanity to be "sin free". The word "salvation" means free from sin.

In Acts 2:38 we see that sins are remitted (washed away) by Jesus name baptism. Now the trinitarian is not really worshipping the Jesus of the Bible, so they see no need to be baptized in Jesus name (even though the Bible clearly commands it). They think that their three gods need three separate "titles" in baptism.

> Acts 2:38 Then Peter said unto them, Repent, and be baptized every one of you in the name of Jesus Christ for the remission of sins, and ye shall receive the gift of the Holy Ghost.

> Acts 2:39 For the promise is unto you, and to your children, and to all that are afar off, even as many as the Lord our God shall call.

This is because Jesus is the Great "I AM" of the Bible. His name is the ONLY saving name.

> Acts 4:12 Neither is there salvation in any other: for there is none other name under heaven given among men, whereby we must be saved.

So, you see, trinity preachers really are deceiving people into hell. We don't just say that to be mean, but rather in the service of truth.

Both of the following statements were spoken by the same person:

> Exo 3:14 And God said unto Moses, I AM THAT I AM: and he said, Thus shalt thou say unto the children of Israel, I AM hath sent me unto you.
>
> John 8:58 Jesus said unto them, Verily , verily, I say unto you, Before Abraham was, I am.

Now the false-christian will not accept that Jesus is "I AM". They "don't believe". They are "non-believers". That is why Jesus said that those who would not accept that He really was the "I AM" would die in their sins.

1. Those who do not see Jesus as "I AM" see no need to be baptized in the name of Jesus.

> John 8:24 I said therefore unto you, that ye shall die in your sins: for if ye believe not that I am he, ye shall die in your sins.

2. Sins are remitted by Jesus name baptism.

> Acts 22:16 And now why tarriest thou? arise, and be baptized, and wash away thy sins, calling on the name of the Lord.

3. Those who don't believe in Jesus will refuse Jesus name baptism and will die with their sins UN-REMITTED.

> 1 Timothy 5:24 Some men’s sins are open beforehand, going before to judgment; and some men they follow after.

That is why Jesus said:

> John 8:24 I said therefore unto you, that ye shall die in your sins: for if ye believe not that I am he, ye shall die in your sins.

Mark 16:16 He that believeth and is baptized shall be saved; but he that believeth not shall be damned.

John 3:5 Jesus answered, Verily, verily, I say unto thee, Except a man be born of water and of the Spirit, he cannot enter into the kingdom of God.

Sins are washed away by Jesus name baptism. That is why the Bible commands it, so you can "put on Christ".

Gal 3:27 For as many of you as have been baptized into Christ have put on Christ.

Trinitarians are deceived by their filthy preachers into refusing to "put on Christ".

Mat 1:21 And she shall bring forth a son, and thou shalt call his name JESUS: for he shall save his people from their sins.

Acts 19:4 Then said Paul, John verily baptized with the baptism of repentance, saying unto the people, that they should believe on him which should come after him, that is, on Christ Jesus.

Acts 19:5 When they heard this, they were baptized in the name of the Lord Jesus.

What did the people do immediately when Paul told them to believe on Jesus?

Acts 22:16 And now why tarriest thou? arise, and be baptized, and wash away thy sins, calling on the name of the Lord.

Acts 8:34 And the eunuch answered Philip, and said, I pray thee, of whom speaketh the prophet this? of himself, or of some other man?

35 Then Philip opened his mouth, and began at the same scripture, and preached unto him Jesus.

> 36 And as they went on their way, they came unto a certain water: and the eunuch said, See, here is water; what doth hinder me to be baptized?
>
> 37 And Philip said, If thou believest with all thine heart, thou mayest. And he answered and said, I believe that Jesus Christ is the Son of God.
>
> 38 And he commanded the chariot to stand still: and they went down both into the water, both Philip and the eunuch; and he baptized him.
>
> 39 And when they were come up out of the water, the Spirit of the Lord caught away Philip, that the eunuch saw him no more: and he went on his way rejoicing.

Notice how the eunuch understood that believing on Jesus included being baptized. You now have several examples from the Word of God where hearers of the Word of God knew that belief in Jesus included baptism.

> Acts 2:41 Then they that gladly received his word were baptized: and the same day there were added unto them about three thousand souls.

Even on the day of Pentecost, on the birthday of the New Testament Church, there were 3000 baptized in Jesus Name. Those that receive the Word of God get baptized.

Look back just two verses and see that Peter preached Jesus Name baptism.

> Acts 2:38 Then Peter said unto them, Repent, and be baptized every one of you in the name of Jesus Christ for the remission of sins, and ye shall receive the gift of the Holy Ghost.
>
> Acts 2:39 For the promise is unto you, and to your children, and to all that are afar off, even as many as the Lord our God shall call.

Strong Delusion

We see many servants of the devil promoting their trinity religion with a long running, deep hatred for the truth of the Oneness of God. Some may wonder how they can be so blind and ignorant. I believe that some posting out here have actually crossed the line and God has now written them off and that is why they have such a blindness and bitter hatred for this preacher and the Word of God.

There are some who have rejected the Acts 2:38 message once too often.

> II Thessalonians 2:10 And with all deceivableness of unrighteousness in them that perish; because they received not the love of the truth, that they might be saved.

The true Christian loves the truth!

> II Thessalonians 2:11 And for this cause God shall send them strong delusion, that they should believe a lie:
>
> II Thessalonians 2:12 That they all might be damned who believed not the truth, but had pleasure in unrighteousness.

There is a point where God will reject a truth rejecter and even SEND delusion to them. This is not a game!

> Acts 2:38 Then Peter said unto them, Repent, and be baptized every one of you in the name of Jesus Christ for the remission of sins, and ye shall receive the gift of the Holy Ghost.
>
> Acts 2:39 For the promise is unto you, and to your children, and to all that are afar off, [even] as many as the Lord our God shall call.
>
> Acts 2:40 And with many other words did he testify and exhort, saying, Save yourselves from this untoward generation.

> Acts 2:41 Then they that gladly received his word were baptized: and the same day there were added [unto them] about three thousand souls.

Three thousand baptized in Jesus name, on the birthday of the new testament church, yet the three-god false-christians still reject Jesus Name baptism.

> Acts 2:42 And they continued stedfastly in the apostles' doctrine and fellowship, and in breaking of bread, and in prayers.

> James 1:22 But be ye doers of the word, and not hearers only, deceiving your own selves.

> Acts 22:16 And now why tarriest thou? arise, and be baptized, and wash away thy sins, calling on the name of the Lord.

> Acts 4:12 Neither is there salvation in any other: for there is none other name under heaven given among men, whereby we must be saved.

The trinity religions still reject the only saving name, Jesus!

> Galatians 1:8 But though we, or an angel from heaven, preach any other gospel unto you than that which we have preached unto you, let him be accursed.

It is not merely a suggestion to the real Christian to curse false preachers.

> Galatians 1:9 As we said before, so say I now again, If any [man] preach any other gospel unto you than that ye have received, let him be accursed.

> Galatians 1:10 For do I now persuade men, or God? or do I seek to please men? for if I yet pleased men, I should not be the servant of Christ.

Steadfast in the Faith

The whole armour of God

> Ephesians 6:10 Finally, my brethren, be strong in the Lord, and in the power of his might.

We see that this was written to the Christian. I hope that this will also be informative to the non-Christian an encourage them to obey Acts 2:38 and really become a Biblical Christian.

> Ephesians 6:11 Put on the whole armour of God, that ye may be able to stand against the wiles of the devil.

God provides a way for the saint to be able to stand against the devil.

> Ephesians 6:12 For we wrestle not against flesh and blood, but against principalities, against powers, against the rulers of the darkness of this world, against spiritual wickedness in high [places].

The battle is not a physical, but rather a spiritual one with MULTIPLE foes.

> Ephesians 6:13 Wherefore take unto you the whole armour of God, that ye may be able to withstand in the evil day, and having done all, to stand.

There are times when one has "done all" that one merely needs to stand fast.

> Ephesians 6:14 Stand therefore, having your loins girt about with truth, and having on the breastplate of righteousness;

The TRUTH of the Word of God and the breastplate of righteousness. A Christian that is not living righteously has no breastplate.

> Ephesians 6:15 And your feet shod with the preparation of the gospel of peace;

Feet that are shod with the gospel will not be running to and fro seeking thrills and excitement as the world does.

> Ephesians 6:16 Above all, taking the shield of faith, wherewith ye shall be able to quench all the fiery darts of the wicked.

THEN after all that, it says ABOVE ALL, taking the shield of faith that you would be able to quench some of the fiery darts... NO it says you will be able to quench ALL. That YOU will be able through FAITH!

> Ephesians 6:17 And take the helmet of salvation, and the sword of the Spirit, which is the word of God:

The helmet of salvation.. salvation means freedom from sin. One with sin in their life has no helmet. Study the WORD of God which is the sword of the Spirit. Everything so far was a defensive weapon, but the SWORD is an OFFENSIVE weapon.

> Ephesians 6:18 Praying always with all prayer and supplication in the Spirit, and watching thereunto with all perseverance and supplication for all saints;

PRAY FOR OTHERS! Pray in the Spirit, and WATCHING. Pray always.

Put on the Whole Armour of God. If you are not yet a Christian, obey Acts 2:38 to become a Christian and then you too can put on the full armour of God.

Abner

Let us examine the scenario of a man that LEFT the secure protection that he had been provided by the GRACE of God, via the WORD of God.

> Num 35:11 Then ye shall appoint you cities to be cities of refuge for you; that the slayer may flee thither, which killeth any person at unawares.
>
> Num 35:12 And they shall be unto you cities for refuge from the avenger; that the manslayer die not, until he stand before the congregation in judgment.

Right after a bunch of death penalty statements for murder, there was a provision for what we might consider second degree murder or manslaughter.

> Num 35:22 But if he thrust him suddenly without enmity, or have cast upon him any thing without laying of wait,

Notice here "non-premeditated" murder.

> Num 35:23 Or with any stone, wherewith a man may die, seeing him not, and cast it upon him, that he die, and was not his enemy, neither sought his harm:
>
> Num 35:24 Then the congregation shall judge between the slayer and the revenger of blood according to these judgments:
>
> Num 35:25 And the congregation shall deliver the slayer out of the hand of the revenger of blood, and the congregation shall restore him to the city of his refuge, whither he was fled: and he shall abide in it unto the death of the high priest, which was anointed with the holy oil.
>
> Num 35:26 But if the slayer shall at any time come without the border of the city of his refuge, whither he was fled;

Num 35:27 And the revenger of blood find him without the borders of the city of his refuge, and the revenger of blood kill the slayer; he

shall not be guilty of blood:

Num 35:28 Because he should have remained in the city of his refuge until the death of the high priest: but after the death of the high priest the slayer shall return into the land of his possession.

2 Samuel 2:19 And Asahel pursued after Abner; and in going he turned not to the right hand nor to the left from following Abner.

2 Samuel 2:20 Then Abner looked behind him, and said, Art thou Asahel? And he answered, I am.

2 Samuel 2:21 And Abner said to him, Turn thee aside to thy right hand or to thy left, and lay thee hold on one of the young men, and take thee his armour. But Asahel would not turn aside from following of him.

2 Samuel 2:22 And Abner said again to Asahel, Turn thee aside from following me: wherefore should I smite thee to the ground? how then should I hold up my face to Joab thy brother?

2 Samuel 2:23 Howbeit he refused to turn aside: wherefore Abner with the hinder end of the spear smote him under the fifth rib, that the spear came out behind him; and he fell down there, and died in the same place: and it came to pass, that as many as came to the place where Asahel fell down and died stood still.

Abner LEFT the city of refuge (just a few feet) to speak with Joab. "Come here, friend, I want to speak with you privately".

2 Samuel 3:27 And when Abner was returned to Hebron, Joab took him aside in the gate to speak with him quietly, and smote him there under the

> fifth rib, that he died, for the blood of Asahel his brother.
>
> 2 Samuel 3:30 So Joab and Abishai his brother slew Abner, because he had slain their brother Asahel at Gibeon in the battle.

King David spoke the epitaph.

> 2 Samuel 3:33 And the king lamented over Abner, and said, Died Abner as a fool dieth?
>
> 2 Samuel 3:34 Thy hands were not bound, nor thy feet put into fetters: as a man falleth before wicked men, so fellest thou. And all the people wept again over him.

Look closely, brethren. What exactly was it that motivated Abner in a careless moment to ABANDON the safety of the Word of the Lord (for *just* a few moments)??? Look closely.... Could it be, that it was for:

F E L L O W S H I P

?

Those who engage in fellowship with trinitarians (or the infidels who embrace them) are throwing away their spiritual safety and life.

> 2 Corinthians 6:15 And what concord hath Christ with Belial? or what part hath he that believeth with an infidel?

> 2 Corinthians 6:16 And what agreement hath the temple of God with idols? for ye are the temple of the living God; as God hath said, I will dwell in them, and walk in them; and I will be their God, and they shall be my people.

> 2 Corinthians 6:17 Wherefore come out from among them, and be ye separate, saith the Lord, and touch not the unclean thing; and I will receive you,

> 2 Corinthians 6:18 And will be a Father unto you, and ye shall be my sons and daughters, saith the Lord Almighty.

Those who do not come out from among them, and who are NOT separate, will NOT be received as sons and daughters by the Lord Almighty! DO NOT trade the SAFETY of the Word of God and the NAME of the Lord for the fellowship of devils and infidels.

Separateness and Holiness are NOT "options".

> 1 Corinthians 10:21 Ye cannot drink the cup of the Lord, and the cup of devils: ye cannot be partakers of the Lord's table, and of the table of devils.

Choose ye this day

Choose who ye will serve

> Joshua 24:15 And if it seem evil unto you to serve the LORD, choose you this day whom ye will serve; whether the gods which your fathers served that were on the other side of the flood, or the gods of the Amorites, in whose land ye dwell: but as for me and my house, we will serve the LORD.

The devil has deceived many people into thinking that it is evil to serve the Lord, but the devil is a liar. It is God who has man's best interest at heart.

> Isaiah 1:18 Come now, and let us reason together, saith the LORD: though your sins be as scarlet, they shall be as white as snow; though they be red like crimson, they shall be as wool.
>
> 19 If ye be willing and obedient, ye shall eat the good of the land:
>
> 20 But if ye refuse and rebel, ye shall be devoured with the sword: for the mouth of the LORD hath spoken it.

> Psalms 119:45 And I will walk at liberty: for I seek thy precepts.

> Isaiah 61:1 The Spirit of the Lord GOD is upon me; because the LORD hath anointed me to preach good tidings unto the meek; he hath sent me to bind up the brokenhearted, to proclaim liberty to the captives, and the opening of the prison to them that are bound;

> John 8:34 Jesus answered them, Verily, verily, I say unto you, Whosoever committeth sin is the servant of sin.
>
> 35 And the servant abideth not in the house for ever: but the Son abideth ever.

36 If the Son therefore shall make you free, ye shall be free indeed.

John 10:7 Then said Jesus unto them again, Verily, verily, I say unto you, I am the door of the sheep.

8 All that ever came before me are thieves and robbers: but the sheep did not hear them.

9 I am the door: by me if any man enter in, he shall be saved, and shall go in and out, and find pasture.

10 The thief cometh not, but for to steal, and to kill, and to destroy: I am come that they might have life, and that they might have it more abundantly.

11 I am the good shepherd: the good shepherd giveth his life for the sheep.

12 But he that is an hireling, and not the shepherd, whose own the sheep are not, seeth the wolf coming, and leaveth the sheep, and fleeth: and the wolf catcheth them, and scattereth the sheep.

13 The hireling fleeth, because he is an hireling, and careth not for the sheep.

14 I am the good shepherd, and know my sheep, and am known of mine.

2 Peter 2:17 These are wells without water, clouds that are carried with a tempest; to whom the mist of darkness is reserved for ever.

18 For when they speak great swelling words of vanity, they allure through the lusts of the flesh, through much wantonness, those that were clean escaped from them who live in error.

19 While they promise them liberty, they themselves are the servants of corruption: for of whom a man is overcome, of the same is he brought in bondage.

20 For if after they have escaped the pollutions of the world through the knowledge of the Lord and Saviour Jesus Christ, they are again entangled therein, and overcome, the latter end is worse with them than the beginning.

21 For it had been better for them not to have known the way of righteousness, than, after they have known it, to turn from the holy commandment delivered unto them.

22 But it is happened unto them according to the true proverb, The dog is turned to his own vomit again; and the sow that was washed to her wallowing in the mire.

2 Peter 3:1 ¶ This second epistle, beloved, I now write unto you; in both which I stir up your pure minds by way of remembrance:

2 That ye may be mindful of the words which were spoken before by the holy prophets, and of the commandment of us the apostles of the Lord and Saviour:

3 ¶ Knowing this first, that there shall come in the last days scoffers, walking after their own lusts,

4 And saying, Where is the promise of his coming? for since the fathers fell asleep, all things continue as they were from the beginning of the creation.

5 For this they willingly are ignorant of, that by the word of God the heavens were of old, and the earth standing out of the water and in the water:

6 Whereby the world that then was, being overflowed with water, perished:

7 But the heavens and the earth, which are now, by the same word are kept in store, reserved unto fire against the day of judgment and perdition of ungodly men.

8 ¶ But, beloved, be not ignorant of this one thing, that one day is with the Lord as a thousand years, and a thousand years as one day.

2 Peter 3:9 ¶ The Lord is not slack concerning his promise, as some men count slackness; but is longsuffering to us-ward, not willing that any should perish, but that all should come to repentance.

10 But the day of the Lord will come as a thief in the night; in the which the heavens shall pass away with a great noise, and the elements shall melt with fervent heat, the earth also and the works that are therein shall be burned up.

11 ¶ Seeing then that all these things shall be dissolved, what manner of persons ought ye to be in all holy conversation and godliness,

12 Looking for and hasting unto the coming of the day of God, wherein the heavens being on fire shall be dissolved, and the elements shall melt with fervent heat?

13 Nevertheless we, according to his promise, look for new heavens and a new earth, wherein dwelleth righteousness.

14 Wherefore, beloved, seeing that ye look for such things, be diligent that ye may be found of him in peace, without spot, and blameless.

You are special

You are special. There was never a "you" before and there will never be another "you". Even twins are very different.

> Matthew 10:30 But the very hairs of your head are all numbered.
>
> Luke 12:6 Are not five sparrows sold for two farthings, and not one of them is forgotten before God?
>
> 7 But even the very hairs of your head are all numbered. Fear not therefore: ye are of more value than many sparrows.

All are so important to God that He allowed Himself to be crucified for them.

> 1 John 3:16 Hereby perceive we the love of God, because he laid down his life for us: and we ought to lay down our lives for the brethren.

But we need to know that if God has called us to a purpose and we do not fulfill that calling, God can raise up replacements.

> Luke 19:37 And when he was come nigh, even now at the descent of the mount of Olives, the whole multitude of the disciples began to rejoice and praise God with a loud voice for all the mighty works that they had seen;
>
> 38 Saying, Blessed be the King that cometh in the name of the Lord: peace in heaven, and glory in the highest.
>
> 39 And some of the Pharisees from among the multitude said unto him, Master, rebuke thy disciples.
>
> 40 And he answered and said unto them, I tell you that, if these should hold their peace, the stones would immediately cry out.

What a shame it would be for God to have raised up rocks to praise Him to replace men who "declined". Of course, what are men but dirt finely crafted by the hand of God, eh?

> Genesis 2:7 And the LORD God formed man of the dust of the ground, and breathed into his nostrils the breath of life; and man became a living soul.

Just a thought there... What is dust but little rocks, eh?

Consider Esther. Remember these Biblical characters were people just like you and I with human frailties and human "attitudes".

> Esther 4:5 ¶ Then called Esther for Hatach, one of the king's chamberlains, whom he had appointed to attend upon her, and gave him a commandment to Mordecai, to know what it was, and why it was.
>
> 6 So Hatach went forth to Mordecai unto the street of the city, which was before the king's gate.
>
> 7 And Mordecai told him of all that had happened unto him, and of the sum of the money that Haman had promised to pay to the king's treasuries for the Jews, to destroy them.
>
> 8 Also he gave him the copy of the writing of the decree that was given at Shushan to destroy them, to shew it unto Esther, and to declare it unto her, and to charge her that she should go in unto the king, to make supplication unto him, and to make request before him for her people.
>
> 9 And Hatach came and told Esther the words of Mordecai.
>
> 10 Again Esther spake unto Hatach, and gave him commandment unto Mordecai;
>
> 11 All the king's servants, and the people of the king's provinces, do know, that whosoever, whether man or woman, shall come unto the king into the inner court, who is not called, there is one law of his to put him to death, except such to whom the king shall hold out the golden sceptre, that he may live: but I have not been called to come in unto the king these thirty days.
>
> 12 And they told to Mordecai Esther's words.

> 13 Then Mordecai commanded to answer Esther, Think not with thyself that thou shalt escape in the king's house, more than all the Jews.
>
> 14 For if thou altogether holdest thy peace at this time, then shall there enlargement and deliverance arise to the Jews from another place; but thou and thy father's house shall be destroyed: and who knoweth whether thou art come to the kingdom for such a time as this?

Esther did not want to do her duty, but she did it anyway. Does it matter that she had concerns etc? No, what matters is that she did the will of God and saved herself and her people.

These people, these great heroes of the Bible were men and women just like you and I with fears, likes, dislikes, strengths weaknesses etc and etc, but they OBEYED GOD when the time came in spite of their fears etc...

We in this age are commanded:

> Romans 12:1 ¶ I beseech you therefore, brethren, by the mercies of God, that ye present your bodies a living sacrifice, holy, acceptable unto God, which is your reasonable service.
>
> 2 And be not conformed to this world: but be ye transformed by the renewing of your mind, that ye may prove what is that good, and acceptable, and perfect, will of God.

Now I flat guarantee you that anyone who obeys those verses is going to have to deny themselves part of their own desires and will.

> 1 John 2:15 Love not the world, neither the things that are in the world. If any man love the world, the love of the Father is not in him.
>
> 16 For all that is in the world, the lust of the flesh, and the lust of the eyes, and the pride of life, is not of the Father, but is of the world.
>
> 17 And the world passeth away, and the lust thereof: but he that doeth the will of God abideth for ever.

Bearing With

We see organizational descent into spiritual whoredom, unholiness and compromise. God does not want His ministers "bearing with" or otherwise tolerating false preachers like trinitarians.

Did Paul preach tolerance and fellowship towards deceivers?? Nope!

> II Corinthians 11:12 But what I do, that I will do, that I may cut off occasion from them which desire occasion; that wherein they glory, they may be found even as we.
>
> II Corinthians 11:13 For such [are] false apostles, deceitful workers, transforming themselves into the apostles of Christ.
>
> II Corinthians 11:14 And no marvel; for Satan himself is transformed into an angel of light.
>
> II Corinthians 11:15 Therefore [it is] no great thing if his ministers also be transformed as the ministers of righteousness; whose end shall be according to their works.
>
> II Corinthians 11:16 I say again, Let no man think me a fool; if otherwise, yet as a fool receive me, that I may boast myself a little.
>
> II Corinthians 11:17 That which I speak, I speak [it] not after the Lord, but as it were foolishly, in this confidence of boasting.
>
> II Corinthians 11:18 Seeing that many glory after the flesh, I will glory also.
>
> II Corinthians 11:19 For ye suffer fools gladly, seeing ye [yourselves] are wise.

Let's look back a few verses:

> II Corinthians 11:2 For I am jealous over you with godly jealousy: for I have espoused you to one husband, that I may present [you as] a chaste virgin to Christ.
>
> II Corinthians 11:3 But I fear, lest by any means, as the serpent beguiled Eve through his subtilty, so your minds should be corrupted from the simplicity that is in Christ.

Notice that Paul fears for their LOSS OF CHASTITY and CORRUPTION

> II Corinthians 11:4 For if he that cometh preacheth another Jesus, whom we have not preached, or [if] ye receive another spirit, which ye have not received, or another gospel, which ye have not accepted, ye might well bear with [him].

Just "bearing with" a trinitarian is defined as the manifestation of whoredom and corruption (lack of chastity is "unchaste" or "whorish". One who lacks "fidelity" is an "infidel")

> Galatians 1:8 But though we, or an angel from heaven, preach any other gospel unto you than that which we have preached unto you, let him be accursed.
>
> Galatians 1:9 As we said before, so say I now again, If any [man] preach any other gospel unto you than that ye have received, let him be accursed.
>
> Galatians 1:10 For do I now persuade men, or God? or do I seek to please men? for if I yet pleased men, I should not be the servant of Christ.
>
> II John 1:9 Whosoever transgresseth, and abideth not in the doctrine of Christ, hath not God. He that abideth in the doctrine of Christ, he hath both the Father and the Son.
>
> II John 1:10 If there come any unto you, and bring not this doctrine, receive him not into [your] house, neither bid him God speed:
>
> II John 1:11 For he that biddeth him God speed is partaker of his evil deeds.

Let us look back and see what would be the symptoms of the HIGH RISK group for whoredom and infidelity.

> 2 Cor 10:12 For we dare not make ourselves of the number, or compare ourselves with some that commend themselves: but they measuring themselves by themselves, and comparing themselves among themselves, are not wise.

They COMMEND themselves this "high risk" group. They MEASURE THEMSELVES BY THEMSELVES etc .

> 2 Cor 10:17 But he that glorieth, let him glory in the Lord.
>
> 2 Cor 10:18 For not he that commendeth himself is approved, but whom the Lord commendeth.

Began

Please notice carefully that Jesus told Peter "when" he was converted. This proves that Peter was not yet "converted" (after Peter *was* converted and received the POWER, he NEVER denied Jesus.)

> Luke 22:31 And the Lord said, Simon, Simon, behold, Satan hath desired [to have] you, that he may sift [you] as wheat:
>
> Luke 22:32 But I have prayed for thee, that thy faith fail not: and when thou art converted, strengthen thy brethren.
>
> Luke 22:33 And he said unto him, Lord, I am ready to go with thee, both into prison, and to death.
>
> Luke 22:34 And he said, I tell thee, Peter, the cock shall not crow this day, before that thou shalt thrice deny that thou knowest me.

When Jesus spoke of the "church" He spoke of it in "future tense" (the church was not started until the book of Acts).

> Matthew 16:18 And I say also unto thee, That thou art Peter, and upon this rock I will build my church; and the gates of hell shall not prevail against it.

Jesus gave Peter the keys to unlock the door to the new testament church.

> Matthew 16:19 And I will give unto thee the keys of the kingdom of heaven: and whatsoever thou shalt bind on earth shall be bound in heaven: and whatsoever thou shalt loose on earth shall be loosed in heaven.

Peter unlocked the door to the church on the day of Pentecost in approximately 33 AD.

> Acts 2:38 Then Peter said unto them, Repent, and be baptized every one of you in the name of Jesus Christ for the remission of sins, and ye shall receive the gift of the Holy Ghost.

> Acts 2:39 For the promise is unto you, and to your children, and to all that are afar off, [even] as many as the Lord our God shall call.

The man with the keys declared that Acts 2:38 was for as many as God would call.

> Acts 2:40 And with many other words did he testify and exhort, saying, Save yourselves from this untoward generation.
>
> Acts 2:41 Then they that gladly received his word were baptized: and the same day there were added [unto them] about three thousand souls.

Three thousand had their sins remitted by being baptized in Jesus name.

> Acts 2:42 And they continued stedfastly in the apostles' doctrine and fellowship, and in breaking of bread, and in prayers.

They did not depart from that "Apostles' doctrine". But Paul later gave instructions concerning "men pleasing" deceivers that might come along:

> Galatians 1:8 But though we, or an angel from heaven, preach any other gospel unto you than that which we have preached unto you, let him be accursed.
>
> Galatians 1:9 As we said before, so say I now again, If any [man] preach any other gospel unto you than that ye have received, let him be accursed.
>
> Galatians 1:10 For do I now persuade men, or God? or do I seek to please men? for if I yet pleased men, I should not be the servant of Christ.

Hell 4 You

The people that are willing to point you towards hell for whatever selfish reason, whether social "one-upmanship", or money or anything else associated with false-christianity, are not really your friend at all. Their sugar coated lies will only haunt you in hell.

> Romans 2:5 But after thy hardness and impenitent heart treasurest up unto thyself wrath against the day of wrath and revelation of the righteous judgment of God;
>
> 6 Who will render to every man according to his deeds:
>
> 7 To them who by patient continuance in well doing seek for glory and honour and immortality, eternal life:
>
> 8 But unto them that are contentious, and do not obey the truth, but obey unrighteousness, indignation and wrath,
>
> 9 Tribulation and anguish, upon every soul of man that doeth evil, of the Jew first, and also of the Gentile;
>
> 10 But glory, honour, and peace, to every man that worketh good, to the Jew first, and also to the Gentile:
>
> 11 For there is no respect of persons with God.
>
> 12 For as many as have sinned without law shall also perish without law: and as many as have sinned in the law shall be judged by the law;
>
> 13 (For not the hearers of the law are just before God, but the doers of the law shall be justified.

> James 1:22 But be ye doers of the word, and not hearers only, deceiving your own selves.
>
> 2 Thessalonians 1:7 And to you who are troubled rest with us, when the Lord Jesus shall be revealed from heaven with his mighty angels,
>
> 8 In flaming fire taking vengeance on them that know not God, and that obey not the gospel of our Lord Jesus Christ:

9 Who shall be punished with everlasting destruction from the presence of the Lord, and from the glory of his power;

1 Peter 4:17 For the time is come that judgment must begin at the house of God: and if it first begin at us, what shall the end be of them that obey not the gospel of God?

Revelation 14:10 The same shall drink of the wine of the wrath of God, which is poured out without mixture into the cup of his indignation; and he shall be tormented with fire and brimstone in the presence of the holy angels, and in the presence of the Lamb:

Revelation 20:10 And the devil that deceived them was cast into the lake of fire and brimstone, where the beast and the false prophet [are], and shall be tormented day and night for ever and ever.

Revelation 21:8 But the fearful, and unbelieving, and the abominable, and murderers, and whoremongers, and sorcerers, and idolaters, and all liars, shall have their part in the lake which burneth with fire and brimstone: which is the second death.

Mark 9:43 And if thy hand offend thee, cut it off: it is better for thee to enter into life maimed, than having two hands to go into hell, into the fire that never shall be quenched:

Mark 9:44 Where their worm dieth not, and the fire is not quenched.

Mark 9:45 And if thy foot offend thee, cut it off: it is better for thee to enter halt into life, than having two feet to be cast into hell, into the fire that never shall be quenched.

Mark 9:46 Where their worm dieth not, and the fire is not quenched.

Mark 9:47 And if thine eye offend thee, pluck it out: it is better for

thee to enter into the kingdom of God with one eye, than having two eyes to be cast into hell fire:

Mark 9:48 Where their worm dieth not, and the fire is not quenched.

Hebrews 5:9 And being made perfect, he became the author of eternal salvation unto all them that obey him;

Matthew 7:13 Enter ye in at the strait gate: for wide is the gate, and broad is the way, that leadeth to destruction, and many there be which go in thereat:

Matthew 7:14 Because strait is the gate, and narrow is the way, which leadeth unto life, and few there be that find it.

Isaiah 5:11 Woe unto them that rise up early in the morning, that they may follow strong drink; that continue until night, till wine inflame them!

12 And the harp, and the viol, the tabret, and pipe, and wine, are in their feasts: but they regard not the work of the LORD, neither consider the operation of his hands.

13 Therefore my people are gone into captivity, because they have no knowledge: and their honourable men are famished, and their multitude dried up with thirst.

14 Therefore hell hath enlarged herself, and opened her mouth without measure: and their glory, and their multitude, and their pomp, and he that rejoiceth, shall descend into it.

15 And the mean man shall be brought down, and the mighty man shall be humbled, and the eyes of the lofty shall be humbled:

16 But the LORD of hosts shall be exalted in judgment, and God that is holy shall be sanctified in righteousness.

The false-christian deceiver is NOT your friend!

Luke 16:20 And there was a certain beggar named Lazarus, which was laid at his gate, full of sores,

21 And desiring to be fed with the crumbs which fell from the rich man's table: moreover the dogs came and licked his sores.

22 And it came to pass, that the beggar died, and was carried by the angels into Abraham's bosom: the rich man also died, and was buried;

23 And in hell he lift up his eyes, being in torments, and seeth Abraham afar off, and Lazarus in his bosom.

24 And he cried and said, Father Abraham, have mercy on me, and send Lazarus, that he may dip the tip of his finger in water, and cool my tongue; for I am tormented in this flame.

25 But Abraham said, Son, remember that thou in thy lifetime receivedst thy good things, and likewise Lazarus evil things: but now he is comforted, and thou art tormented.

26 And beside all this, between us and you there is a great gulf fixed: so that they which would pass from hence to you cannot; neither can they pass to us, that would come from thence.

Isaiah 1:18 Come now, and let us reason together, saith the LORD: though your sins be as scarlet, they shall be as white as snow; though they be red like crimson, they shall be as wool.

Seek First

Matthew 6:19 ¶ Lay not up for yourselves treasures upon earth, where moth and rust doth corrupt, and where thieves break through and steal:

20 But lay up for yourselves treasures in heaven, where neither moth nor rust doth corrupt, and where thieves do not break through nor steal:

21 For where your treasure is, there will your heart be also.

22 The light of the body is the eye: if therefore thine eye be single, thy whole body shall be full of light.

23 But if thine eye be evil, thy whole body shall be full of darkness. If therefore the light that is in thee be darkness, how great is that darkness!

24 No man can serve two masters: for either he will hate the one, and love the other; or else he will hold to the one, and despise the other. Ye cannot serve God and mammon.

25 ¶ Therefore I say unto you, Take no thought for your life, what ye shall eat, or what ye shall drink; nor yet for your body, what ye shall put on. Is not the life more than meat, and the body than raiment?

26 Behold the fowls of the air: for they sow not, neither do they reap, nor gather into barns; yet your heavenly Father feedeth them. Are ye not much better than they?

27 Which of you by taking thought can add one cubit unto his stature?

28 And why take ye thought for raiment? Consider the lilies of the field, how they grow; they toil not, neither do they spin:

29 And yet I say unto you, That even Solomon in all his glory was not arrayed like one of these.

30 Wherefore, if God so clothe the grass of the field, which to day is, and to morrow is cast into the oven, shall he not much more clothe you, O ye of little faith?

31 Therefore take no thought, saying, What shall we eat? or, What shall we drink? or, Wherewithal shall we be clothed?

32 (For after all these things do the Gentiles seek:) for your heavenly Father knoweth that ye have need of all these things.

33 But seek ye first the kingdom of God, and his righteousness; and all these things shall be added unto you.

Matthew 22:37 Jesus said unto him, Thou shalt love the Lord thy God with all thy heart, and with all thy soul, and with all thy mind.

Mark 12:30 And thou shalt love the Lord thy God with all thy heart, and with all thy soul, and with all thy mind, and with all thy strength: this is the first commandment.

Luke 10:27 And he answering said, Thou shalt love the Lord thy God with all thy heart, and with all thy soul, and with all thy strength, and with all thy mind; and thy neighbour as thyself.

1 Peter 4:18 And if the righteous scarcely be saved, where shall the ungodly and the sinner appear?

Think (and pray) about that! Even those who do the right things right will barely make it. And this was written to people who have obeyed Acts 2:38 warning them/us. Many in Oneness Churches will not be saved because of their sin.

2 Timothy 3:1 This know also, that in the last days perilous times shall come.

We live in perilous times.

> Ephesians 6:12 For we wrestle not against flesh and blood, but against principalities, against powers, against the rulers of the darkness of this world, against spiritual wickedness in high places.
>
> Exodus 20:3 Thou shalt have no other gods before me.

To some, their position in their organization has become an idol god to them.

> Ezekiel 14:3 Son of man, these men have set up their idols in their heart, and put the stumblingblock of their iniquity before their face: should I be enquired of at all by them?

An "idol" need not be some external thing. For some it is their career (not that we are to be slothful in whatever business we pursue, and to work "as to the Lord".), for some it is their bank account, for some a car, for others a sinful lifestyle, for others a sport, for others a drink, for others drugs, etc and etc.... Anything that a man puts above God in his life is an IDOL IN HIS HEART.

> John 10:10 The thief cometh not, but for to steal, and to kill, and to destroy: I am come that they might have life, and that they might have it more abundantly.

> Matthew 11:28 Come unto me, all ye that labour and are heavy laden, and I will give you rest.
>
> 29 Take my yoke upon you, and learn of me; for I am meek and lowly in heart: and ye shall find rest unto your souls.
>
> 30 For my yoke is easy, and my burden is light.

The true, faithful Christian life is the life of true freedom! For those who really put God and His Word first in their life, they receive the benefits at very low cost.

But there is another frustrating scenario, one cannot ride the fence between good and evil. I think of one of the dimbulbs that was led into sin by a double-married, unqualified licensed UPC preacher. He started out just wanting to be friends with everyone and decided to be "neutral" about that false preacher's sin. Well it hasn't taken the devil long to give that dimbulb a complete makeover. You cannot be neutral about sin.

> James 1:6 But let him ask in faith, nothing wavering. For he that wavereth is like a wave of the sea driven with the wind and tossed.
>
> 7 For let not that man think that he shall receive any thing of the Lord.
>
> 8 A double minded man is unstable in all his ways.

So many are so frustrated in their efforts to be "Christian" because they are double minded. They know that they have sin in their life, but they never will give themselves 100% to God to have power over these things. They have enough commitment to feel guilty but not enough to overcome.

If Church is worth attending at all, then you need to give God PRIORITY in your life and you need to be there every service (if you can do so and still meet other real responsibility). Obviously there are people like doctors, nurses, public safety officers and others whose time is not really their own, but even they, if they are not working need to attend every service.

> Proverbs 13:15 Good understanding giveth favour: but the way of transgressors is hard.

The committed Christian life is the "smart" life.

God is, admittedly demanding, but He gives so much more.

> Romans 12:1 I beseech you therefore, brethren, by the mercies of God, that ye present your bodies a living sacrifice, holy, acceptable unto God, which is your reasonable service.
>
> 2 And be not conformed to this world: but be ye transformed by the renewing of your mind, that ye may prove what is that good, and acceptable, and perfect, will of God.

The Christian is the only proof there is for the World as to what is pleasing to God. We are the ONLY example.

> Titus 2:12 Teaching us that, denying ungodliness and worldly lusts, we should live soberly, righteously, and godly, in this present world;
>
> 13 Looking for that blessed hope, and the glorious appearing of the great God and our Saviour Jesus Christ;
>
> 14 Who gave himself for us, that he might redeem us from all iniquity, and purify unto himself a peculiar people, zealous of good works.

Seek ye FIRST the Kingdom of God AND His righteousness

> Romans 14:17 For the kingdom of God is not meat and drink; but righteousness, and peace, and joy in the Holy Ghost.
>
> 18 For he that in these things serveth Christ is acceptable to God, and approved of men.

Holiness

Are We There Yet?

Are we there yet? Have we arrived? Is the Church all that God wants it to be? Have we learned all there is to learn? Are all of our beliefs and traditions totally and perfectly aligned with the Word of God?

I realize here that I am going to talk about some things that apply to men whose shoes I am not worthy to lace, men that have forgotten more about the Bible than I will ever know, but I must obey God in this matter.

We know from the Word of God that God does not like outward adorning.

> 1 Peter 3:3 Whose adorning let it not be that outward adorning of plaiting the hair, and of wearing of gold, or of putting on of apparel;
>
> 4 But let it be the hidden man of the heart, in that which is not corruptible, even the ornament of a meek and quiet spirit, which is in the sight of God of great price

I believe that these principles of adorning verses apply to both men and women. Note that this is consistent with the above in doctrine but clearly is talking about the women, in LIKE MANNER of the men wear modest apparel.

> 1 Timothy 2:9 In like manner also, that women adorn themselves in modest apparel, with shamefacedness and sobriety; not with broided hair, or gold, or pearls, or costly array;

I come to you with all respect and humility but I must demand of you: Do you really believe that God wants his ministers to look like a gaggle of rich lawyers with expensive suits and a status symbol of a cloth necklace around their necks?

Are ministers to wear an adorning cloth necklace to show their STATUS???

> Romans 12:3 For I say, through the grace given unto me, to every man that is among you, not to think of himself more highly than he ought to think; but to think soberly, according as God hath dealt to every man the measure of faith.

Have we "arrived", are the traditions we have embraced now on equal authority with the Word of God? Do we now have the authority to deck out in costly array and wear adornment of worldly STATUS??? While we preach against jewelry do we wear it ourselves and justify it because it has a clock on it? What about the woman with a necklace that has a little clock on the end?

> Matthew 15:3 But he answered and said unto them, Why do ye also transgress the commandment of God by your tradition?

Is the measuring stick the Bible or what others that we respect and love are doing?

Let me tell you precious Brethren, the phrase "we dare not" appears only one time in the ENTIRE Bible. Only ONE TIME!!!

> 2 Corinthians 10:12 For we dare not make ourselves of the number, or compare ourselves with some that commend themselves: but they measuring themselves by themselves, and comparing themselves among themselves, are not wise.

We must look to the Word of God for our measuring stick.

If we were going to start a new Church and base it totally and exactly upon the Holy Bible. If we were going to base every practice upon the Word of God, what preacher would ever allow a woman to speak out and address the congregation when the Bible says that it is a SHAME for a woman to speak in the Church? What preacher would ever call on a woman to stand up and speak?

When the Bible says:

> 1 Corinthians 14:34 Let your women keep silence in the churches: for it is not permitted unto them to speak; but they are commanded to be under obedience, as also saith the law.
>
> 1 Corinthians 14:35 And if they will learn any thing, let them ask their husbands at home: for it is a shame for women to speak in the church.

Notice that second verse says "AND"; it is ADDING to what was already said. Forget that foolishness about women hollering across the Church. Anytime anyone has to take you away from the Word of God and claim something "historical" as proof the Bible didn't mean what it said, WATCH OUT!!!

Let me just add here that the Bible does NOT forbid a woman from playing music, singing, praying to God, or praising God.

This verse is only talking about speaking in the sense of "speaking out" to address someone other than God. That is a more lengthy study on the word "laleo" (to use words in order to declare one’s mind and disclose one’s thoughts).

If you think God is just kidding about this consider the following!

> 1 Corinthians 14:36 ¶ What? came the word of God out from you? or came it unto you only?
>
> 37 If any man think himself to be a prophet, or spiritual, let him acknowledge that the things that I write unto you are the commandments of the Lord.
>
> 38 But if any man be ignorant, let him be ignorant.

There is no virtue in ignorance.

> Hosea 4:6 My people are destroyed for lack of knowledge: because thou hast rejected knowledge, I will also reject thee, that thou shalt be no priest to me: seeing thou hast forgotten the law of thy God, I will also forget thy children.

> 1 Timothy 2:11 Let the woman learn in silence with all subjection.
>
> 12 But I suffer not a woman to teach, nor to usurp authority over the man, but to be in silence.
>
> 13 For Adam was first formed, then Eve.
>
> 14 And Adam was not deceived, but the woman being deceived was in the transgression.

If we were starting up a Church based totally upon the Word of God who among us would dress up like a rich lawyer and put a ornament around his neck for status and stand up and call on women to stand and testify? Or stand there and tell people not to be conformed to the world or wear costly array?

Think about it brethren, this is REAL!!!

Or who among us would put a gold bracelet or any other kind of bracelet on his wrist and say it was justified because it had a clock on it?

We have an responsibility!

> Romans 12:1 I beseech you therefore, brethren, by the mercies of God, that ye present your bodies a living sacrifice, holy, acceptable unto God, which is your reasonable service.
>
> 2 And be not conformed to this world: but be ye transformed by the renewing of your mind, that ye may prove what is that good, and acceptable, and perfect, will of God.

> 3 For I say, through the grace given unto me, to every man that is among you, not to think of himself more highly than he ought to think; but to think soberly, according as God hath dealt to every man the measure of faith.

Is it the perfect will of God for his ministers to be conformed to this world so that they look like a gaggle of wealthy lawyers with GREAT STATUS with their status ornament hanging around their neck?

Quoting from an online necktie store I found some history of the necktie.

> "The history of neckties dates back a mere hundred years or so, for they came into existence as the direct result of a war. In 1660, in celebration of its hard-fought victory over Turkey, a crack regiment from Croatia (then part of the Austro-Hungarian Empire), visited Paris. There, the soldiers were presented as glorious heroes to Louis XIV, a monarch well known for his eye toward personal adornment. It so happened that the officers of this regiment were wearing brightly colored handkerchiefs fashioned of silk around their necks. These neck cloths, which probably descended from the Roman fascalia worn by orators to warm the vocal chords, struck the fancy of the king, and he soon made them an insignia of royalty as he created a regiment of Royal Cravattes. The word "cravat," incidentally, is derived from the word "Croat."
>
> "How to account for the continued popularity of neckties? For years, fashion historians and sociologists predicted their demise--the one element of a man's attire with no obvious function. Perhaps they are merely part of an inherited tradition. As long as world and business leaders continue to wear ties, the young executives will follow suit and ties will remain a key to the boardroom."

From a Crotian website:

> "Visiting Croatia and neglecting to take back a CROATA tie is like visiting Paris and not seeing the Eiffel Tower, for Croatia is the homeland of cravats."

"The tie, a Croatian invention, was introduced to the world more than 350 years ago.".

"Did you know that Croatia is the mother country of the necktie?"

"Around the year 1650, during the reign of Louis XIV, the Croatian scarf was accepted in France, above all in court, where military ornaments were much admired. The fashionable expression, 'a la croate', soon evolved into a new French word, which still exists today: la cravate. This innovation symbolized the height of culture and elegance. On his return to England from exile, Charles II brought with him this new word in fashion. Over the next ten years, this fashion novelty spread across Europe, as well as across the colonies on the American continent..."

"There might be something you didn't know about Croatia? Many Croatian soldiers were enlisted in the royal regiment during the 17 th century. You could tell them by special scarfs worn around their necks. The same scarfs later came into fashion, at first, in Paris, of course. The French call it cravatte, according to the Croats, and we call it necktie."

WHY DO YOU BRETHREN WANT TO LOOK LIKE THE WORLD????

James 2:1 ¶ My brethren, have not the faith of our Lord Jesus Christ, the Lord of glory, with respect of persons.

2 For if there come unto your assembly a man with a gold ring, in goodly apparel, and there come in also a poor man in vile raiment;

3 And ye have respect to him that weareth the gay clothing, and say unto him, Sit thou here in a good place; and say to the poor, Stand thou there, or sit here under my footstool:

4 Are ye not then partial in yourselves, and are become judges of evil thoughts?

5 Hearken, my beloved brethren, Hath not God chosen the poor of this world rich in faith, and heirs of the kingdom which he hath promised to them that love him?

> 6 But ye have despised the poor. Do not rich men oppress you, and draw you before the judgment seats?
>
> 7 Do not they blaspheme that worthy name by the which ye are called?

Why do you want to look like them, brethren? Why do you feel that you need to look like the rich and powerful of this world? Why would you ever imagine that was pleasing to the Lord?

And one more thing since everyone is probably mad at me by now anyway.

Anyone who doesn't like beards or thinks that beards are sinful is going to have a BIG PROBLEM at the great white throne.

> Revelation 20:11 And I saw a great white throne, and him that sat on it, from whose face the earth and the heaven fled away; and there was found no place for them.

If you think that you are going to be looking at a "clean shaven" face you had better think again. Come on now, do you really think all those young Jewish men shaved their faces to look like Caesar? Do you really believe that you are going to see

a "clean shaven" Roman face on the One on the throne?

It's time for some serious praying, brethren, because we have not arrived yet.

Achen

Joshua 7:1 ¶ But the children of Israel committed a trespass in the accursed thing: for Achan, the son of Carmi, the son of Zabdi, the son of Zerah, of the tribe of Judah, took of the accursed thing: and the anger of the LORD was kindled against the children of Israel.

Joshua 7:18 And he brought his household man by man; and Achan, the son of Carmi, the son of Zabdi, the son of Zerah, of the tribe of Judah, was taken.

Joshua 7:19 And Joshua said unto Achan, My son, give, I pray thee, glory to the LORD God of Israel, and make confession unto him; and tell me now what thou hast done; hide it not from me.

Joshua 7:20 And Achan answered Joshua, and said, Indeed I have sinned against the LORD God of Israel, and thus and thus have I done:

Joshua 7:24 And Joshua, and all Israel with him, took Achan the son of Zerah, and the silver, and the garment, and the wedge of gold, and his sons, and his daughters, and his oxen, and his asses, and his sheep, and his tent, and all that he had: and they brought them unto the valley of Achor.

Joshua 22:20 Did not Achan the son of Zerah commit a trespass in the accursed thing, and wrath fell on all the congregation of Israel? and that man perished not alone in his iniquity.

Ephesians 5:22 Wives, submit yourselves unto your own husbands, as unto the Lord.

Ephesians 5:24 Therefore as the church is subject unto Christ, so let the wives be to their own husbands in every thing.

Ephesians 5:25 Husbands, love your wives, even as Christ also loved the church, and gave himself for it;

Colossians 3:18 ¶ Wives, submit yourselves unto your own husbands, as it is fit in the Lord.

Colossians 3:19 Husbands, love your wives, and be not bitter against them.

1 Timothy 3:12 Let the deacons be the husbands of one wife, ruling their children and their own houses well.

Titus 2:4 That they may teach the young women to be sober, to love their husbands, to love their children,

Titus 2:5 To be discreet, chaste, keepers at home, good, obedient to their own husbands, that the word of God be not blasphemed.

1 Peter 3:1 ¶ Likewise, ye wives, be in subjection to your own husbands; that, if any obey not the word, they also may without the word be won by the conversation of the wives;

1 Timothy 2:11 Let the woman learn in silence with all subjection.

12 But I suffer not a woman to teach, nor to usurp authority over the man, but to be in silence.

13 For Adam was first formed, then Eve.

14 And Adam was not deceived, but the woman being deceived was in the transgression.

15 Notwithstanding she shall be saved in childbearing, if they continue in faith and charity and holiness with sobriety.

1 Corinthians 14:34 ¶ Let your women keep silence in the churches: for it is not permitted unto them to speak; but they are commanded to be under obedience, as also saith the law.

35 And if they will learn any thing, let them ask their husbands at home: for it is a shame for women to speak in the church.

36 ¶ What? came the word of God out from you? or came it unto you only?

37 If any man think himself to be a prophet, or spiritual, let him acknowledge that the things that I write unto you are the commandments of the Lord.

38 But if any man be ignorant, let him be ignorant.

Order in the Church

There are teachings in the Bible that Paul affectionately refers to as 'commandments'. He devotes a whole chapter to the subject of a Christian worship service; that is Corinthians 14. As a foundation, let me point out how Paul ended his exhortation. (I trust that we are mature enough to realize that the book of Corinthians IS the Word of God for the Church, and not merely the Church at Corinth)

> I Corinthians 14:37 If any man think himself to be a prophet, or spiritual, let him acknowledge that the things that I write unto you are the commandments of the Lord.

* Paul gave instructions concerning the "gift of tongues" during a worship service. Of course the "gift of tongues" is not the "other" tongues that a person speaks in when they are filled with the Holy Spirit.

* There is a LIMIT of three messages per service with the "gift of tongues" and that the gift of tongues needs the "gift of interpretation". In every instance that I have witnessed when there is a message in tongues it is one person speaking out with the rest of the church in relative silence. What Paul is teaching is that unless there is "interpretation", a message in unknown tongues does not edify the Body of Christ. However sometimes there are many filled with the Holy Ghost speaking in "other tongues" and several at the same time, and THAT is in order, because a person being filled with the Holy Ghost is NOT the "gift of tongues". *

> I Corinthians 14:13 Wherefore let him that speaketh in an [unknown] tongue pray that he may interpret.

> I Corinthians 14:27 If any man speak in an [unknown] tongue, [let it be] by two, or at the most [by] three, and [that] by course; and let one interpret.
>
> I Corinthians 14:28 But if there be no interpreter, let him keep silence in the church; and let him speak to himself, and to God.

Notice this last verse very closely, please! Paul is saying that the man (given those conditions) is to keep SILENCE, in the sense of "addressing the congregation", now that does NOT forbid that man while not publicly ADDRESSING the church, to pray aloud to God. A person can pray quietly, or in a group QUITE LOUDLY without addressing his words to the whole congregation.

Understanding that Paul is speaking to the issue of a person being the "center of attention" while "addressing the crowd" (which IS the case when the "gift of tongues" is manifested in a worship service.

> I Corinthians 14:34 Let your women keep silence in the churches: for it is not permitted unto them to speak; but [they are commanded] to be under obedience, as also saith the law.

* Women, however, are commanded NOT to address the congregation during a worship service. Paul did not stop there, he added to that commandment that they were also NOT to even ask their husbands questions during a worship service, because a woman speaking in a worship service is SHAME. *

> I Corinthians 14:35 And if they will learn any thing, let them ask their husbands at home: for it is a shame for women to speak in the church.

* Then, notice the VERY NEXT VERSES. Notice that Paul uses the 'C' word. The use of the 'C' word implies that these are more than optional suggestions.*

> I Corinthians 14:37 If any man think himself to be a prophet, or spiritual, let him acknowledge that the things that I write unto you are the commandments of the Lord.
>
> I Corinthians 14:38 But if any man be ignorant, let him be ignorant.

Other areas in the Word of God that also firmly support this doctrine.

> I Timothy 2:8 I will therefore that men pray every where, lifting up holy hands, without wrath and doubting.
>
> I Timothy 2:9 In like manner also, that women adorn themselves in modest apparel, with shamefacedness and sobriety; not with broided hair, or gold, or pearls, or costly array;
>
> I Timothy 2:10 But (which becometh women professing godliness) with good works.
>
> I Timothy 2:11 Let the woman learn in silence with all subjection.
>
> I Timothy 2:12 But I suffer not a woman to teach, nor to usurp authority over the man, but to be in silence.
>
> I Timothy 2:13 For Adam was first formed, then Eve.
>
> I Timothy 2:14 And Adam was not deceived, but the woman being deceived was in the transgression.

It is rebellion against the Word of God to set a woman over a man in authority in the Church, or to appoint women as teachers of men. It does NOT say that a woman cannot teach children or other women or witness and testify the WHOLE remainder of the hours of the week that are spent OUTSIDE of a worship service. REMEMBER, in the true church Christianity, praying, witnessing, testifying, praising, etc. is not just something that you 'go do' several times a week. It is all day long all year long, with times of assembling together with those of like precious faith in a formal worship service. It is THOSE times of formal worship that Paul is addressing in Corinthians 14 *

Pastor, having problems in your church? Have you tried obeying the Bible?

Holiness

> Galatians 5:23 Meekness, temperance: against such there is no law.

> 2 Peter 1:6 And to knowledge temperance; and to temperance patience; and to patience godliness;

So we see that temperance is part of Christianity and that you cannot be "too" temperate. You cannot be "too" holy.

Why women keep silence during a worship service.

From the Zodhiates' Study Bible Dictionary

> 2980. laleo aprol. form of an otherwise obsol. verb: to talk, i.e. utter words: preach, say, speak (after), talk, tell, utter,

Notice carefully that though women are commanded not to laleo at all during a worship service, that there is also a situation where a man is also commanded not to laleo to the congregation. We see here that women are ABSOLUTELY FORBIDDEN to laleo during a worship service:

> 1 Corinthians 14:34. Let your women keep <4601> silence <4601> in the churches: for it is not permitted unto them to speak 2980>; but [they are commanded] to be under obedience, as also saith the law.

Notice also that if there is no interpreter that a man with the gift of tongues is commanded not to use that gift but to laleo to himself and to God.

> 1 Cor 14:28 But if there be no interpreter, let him keep <4601> silence <4601> in the church; and let him speak <2980> to himself, and to God.

Whereas women are commanded NEVER to laleo to the church, men are commanded not to laleo under certain circumstances.

Regardless of popular traditions, the simple fact is that "speak" (laleo) means "speak" and when the Bible says that women are not permitted to speak to the church during a worship service it simply says what it means and means what it says.

> I Corinthians 14:34 Let your women keep silence in the churches: for it is not permitted unto them to speak; but [they are commanded] to be under obedience, as also saith the law.
>
> I Corinthians 14:35 And if they will learn any thing, let them ask their husbands at home: for it is a shame for women to speak in the church.

Certainly "ask" in verse 35 doesn't mean "preach". Speak means "speak"

When the same word "laleo" is used in the verse that limits men to three messages in tongues and further limits that to the situation where there is the gift of interpretation of tongues, it is definitely addressing the situation where the congregation is being addressed from the congregation and not from the pulpit. The word "laleo" INCLUDES preaching but is NOT in any way limited to preaching.

> 1 Corinthians 14:34. Let your women keep <4601> silence <4601> in the churches: for it is not permitted unto them to speak <2980>; but [they are commanded] to be under obedience, as also saith the law.
>
> 2980 laleo lal-eh'-o a prolonged form of an otherwise obsolete verb; TDNT - 4:3/4:69,505; vb
>
> AV - speak (244) - say (15) - tell (12) - talk (11) preach (6) - utter (4) - misc (3) [295]
>
> 1) to utter a voice or emit a sound
>
> 2) to speak, i.e. to use the tongue or the faculty of speech; to utter articulate sounds
>
> 3) to talk
>
> 4) to utter, tell
>
> 5) to use words in order to declare one's mind and disclose one's thoughts; to speak

4601 sigao see-gah'-o

from 4602; TDNT - omitted,omitted; vb

AV - hold (one's) peace (4)

- keep silence (3)

- keep close (1)

- keep secret (1) [9]

1) to keep silence, hold one's peace; to be kept in silence, be concealed

Women are COMMANDED to hold their peace during a worship service. They are COMMANDED not to "declare their thoughts". They are COMMANDED not to "tell". Notice carefully that there are also circumstances when MEN are commanded to keep silence and not give a message in tongues, and this is NOT referring to preaching.

> 1 Cor 14:28 But if there be no interpreter, let him keep <4601> silence <4601> in the church; and let him speak <2980> to himself, and to God.

It is a SIN for a woman to "testify" make a verbal "prayer request" or in ANY way address the congregation during a Christian worship service. Such practices are REBELLIOUS TRADITIONS clearly forbidden by the Word of God. Paul also went on to say:

> I Corinthians 14:37 If any man think himself to be a prophet, or spiritual, let him acknowledge that the things that I write unto you are the commandments of the Lord.

> I Corinthians 14:38 But if any man be ignorant, let him be ignorant.

I hope I haven't violated verse 38 here.

Reasons that Christians do not tell dirty jokes or stories.

Eph 5:11 And have no fellowship with the unfruitful works of darkness, but rather reprove them.

12 For it is a shame even to speak of those things which are done of them in secret.

Ephesians 4:29 Let no corrupt communication proceed out of your mouth, but that which is good to the use of edifying, that it may minister grace unto the hearers.

Regarding jewlrey and more...

1 Timothy 2:8 I will therefore that men pray every where, lifting up holy hands, without wrath and doubting.

9 In like manner also, that women adorn themselves in modest apparel, with shamefacedness and sobriety; not with broided hair, or gold, or pearls, or costly array;

10 But (which becometh women professing godliness) with good works.

11 Let the woman learn in silence with all subjection.

12 But I suffer not a woman to teach, nor to usurp authority over the man, but to be in silence.

13 For Adam was first formed, then Eve.

14 And Adam was not deceived, but the woman being deceived was in the transgression.

Hair style for men and women

Jewlrey is just as much sin as women speaking in Church or cutting her hair or a man having long hair. Shame = sin in these verses

1 Peter 3:1 ¶ Likewise, ye wives, be in subjection to your own husbands; that, if any obey not the word, they also may without the word be won by the conversation of the wives;

2 While they behold your chaste conversation coupled with fear.

3 Whose adorning let it not be that outward adorning of plaiting the hair, and of wearing of gold, or of putting on of apparel;

4 But let it be the hidden man of the heart, in that which is not corruptible, even the ornament of a meek and quiet spirit, which is in the sight of God of great price.

5 For after this manner in the old time the holy women also, who trusted in God, adorned themselves, being in subjection unto their own husbands:

6 Even as Sara obeyed Abraham, calling him lord: whose daughters ye are, as long as ye do well, and are not afraid with any amazement.

7 Likewise, ye husbands, dwell with them according to knowledge, giving honour unto the wife, as unto the weaker vessel, and as being heirs together of the grace of life; that your prayers be not hindered.

Christian men cut their hair short, Christian women do not cut or burn or trim their hair. There is nothing in the Bible that would suggest that God views any types of rings or bracelets differently just because of a wedding or a clock. You won't find rings in any wedding in the Bible. Do you really think that a clock on a gold bracelet makes it less jewelry?

1 Corinthians 11:5 But every woman that prayeth or prophesieth with her head uncovered dishonoureth her head: for that is even all one as if she were shaven.

6 For if the woman be not covered, let her also be shorn: but if it be a shame for a woman to be shorn or shaven, let her be covered.

7 For a man indeed ought not to cover his head, forasmuch as he is the image and glory of God: but the woman is the glory of the man.

8 For the man is not of the woman; but the woman of the man.

9 Neither was the man created for the woman; but the woman for the man.

10 For this cause ought the woman to have power on her head because of the angels.

11 Nevertheless neither is the man without the woman, neither the woman without the man, in the Lord.

12 For as the woman is of the man, even so is the man also by the woman; but all things of God.

13 Judge in yourselves: is it comely that a woman pray unto God uncovered?

14 Doth not even nature itself teach you, that, if a man have long hair, it is a shame unto him?

15 But if a woman have long hair, it is a glory to her: for her hair is given her for a covering.

16 But if any man seem to be contentious, we have no such custom, neither the churches of God.

Isaiah 3:20 The bonnets, and the ornaments of the legs, and the headbands, and the tablets, and the earrings,

21 The rings, and nose jewels,

22 The changeable suits of apparel, and the mantles, and the wimples, and the crisping pins,

23 The glasses, and the fine linen, and the hoods, and the vails.

24 And it shall come to pass, that instead of sweet smell there shall be stink; and instead of a girdle a rent; and instead of well set hair baldness; and instead of a stomacher a girding of sackcloth; and burning instead of beauty.

Romans 12:2 And be not conformed to this world: but be ye transformed by the renewing of your mind, that ye may prove what is that good, and acceptable, and perfect, will of God.

It is notable that if you are sitting under a pastor that is so tradition bound and scripturally ignorant that he calls on women to speak and address the congregation during a worship service, you might as well be sitting under a pastor with hair down to his waist.

<u>Think there are any secrets from God? Think again</u>.

> Ezekiel 8:12 Then said he unto me, Son of man, hast thou seen what the ancients of the house of Israel do in the dark, every man in the chambers of his imagery ? for they say, The LORD seeth us not; the LORD hath forsaken the earth.
>
> Psalms 101:3 I will set no wicked thing before mine eyes: I hate the work of them that turn aside; it shall not cleave to me.
>
> Romans 1:28 And even as they did not like to retain God in their knowledge, God gave them over to a reprobate mind, to do those things which are not convenient;
>
> 29 Being filled with all unrighteousness, fornication, wickedness, covetousness, maliciousness; full of envy, murder, debate, deceit, malignity; whisperers,
>
> 30 Backbiters, haters of God, despiteful, proud, boasters, inventors of evil things, disobedient to parents,
>
> 31 Without understanding, covenantbreakers, without natural affection, implacable, unmerciful:
>
> 32 Who knowing the judgment of God, that they which commit such things are worthy of death, not only do the same, but have pleasure in them that do them.

Having pleasure in them that do them? Does not the last group of scriptures sound like an ad for a soap opera or some super new movie from Hellywood? When people watch TV are they not having pleasure from people sinning?

Real Christians don't own or watch television. If your preacher has a TV or lacks the spiritual integrity to preach strongly against TV and movies, you need to start looking for a real pastor.

Saved?

Paul said

> Corinthians 9:27 But I keep under my body, and bring it into subjection: lest that by any means, when I have preached to others, I myself should be a castaway.

Once saved always saved says that there will be no castaways you can believe them or the Bible.

> Corinthians 10:12 Wherefore let him that thinketh he standeth take heed lest he fall.

Once saved always saved says that no one can fall, You can believe them or the Bible.

> Galatians 6: 7-8 Be not deceived; God is not mocked: for whatsoever a man soweth, that shall he also reap. For he that soweth to his flesh shall of the flesh reap corruption; but he that soweth to the Spirit shall of the Spirit reap life everlasting.

This was written to the church members at Galacia...Once saved always saved says that no believer will reap corruption..You can believe them or the Bible.

> .Galatians 5: 19-21......drunkeness, revellings, and such like: of the which I tell you before, as I have also told you in times past, that they which do such things shall not inherit the kingdom of God.

This was written to "saints in the Galatian church" telling them that if they did certain things that they would NOT inherit the kingdom of God

Hebrews 10: 38,39 Now the just shall live by faith: but if any man draw back, my soul shall have no pleasure in him. But we are not of them that draw back into perdition: but of them that believe to the saving of the soul.

James 1: 21,22 Wherefore, lay apart all filthiness and superfluity of naughtiness, and receive with meekness the engrafted word, which is able to save your souls. But be ye doers of the word, and not hearers only, DECEIVING YOUR OWN SELVES.

For when they speak great swelling words of vanity, they allure through the lusts of the flesh, through much wantonness, those that were clean escaped from them who live in error. (II Peter 2:18)

I John 3:6 Whosoever abideth in him sinneth not: whosoever sinneth hath not seen him neither known him.

Chamber

We have in the Word of God an account of God taking a prophet and showing him a room.

> Ezekiel 8:1 And it came to pass in the sixth year, in the sixth [month], in the fifth [day] of the month, [as] I sat in mine house, and the elders of Judah sat before me, that the hand of the Lord GOD fell there upon me.
>
> Ezekiel 8:2 Then I beheld, and lo a likeness as the appearance of fire: from the appearance of his loins even downward, fire; and from his loins even upward, as the appearance of brightness, as the colour of amber.
>
> Ezekiel 8:3 And he put forth the form of an hand, and took me by a lock of mine head; and the spirit lifted me up between the earth and the heaven, and brought me in the visions of God to Jerusalem, to the door of the inner gate that looketh toward the north; where [was] the seat of the image of jealousy, which provoketh to jealousy.
>
> Ezekiel 8:4 And, behold, the glory of the God of Israel [was] there, according to the vision that I saw in the plain.
>
> Ezekiel 8:5 Then said he unto me, Son of man, lift up thine eyes now the way toward the north. So I lifted up mine eyes the way toward the north, and behold northward at the gate of the altar this image of jealousy in the entry.
>
> Ezekiel 8:6 He said furthermore unto me, Son of man, seest thou what they do? [even] the great abominations that the house of Israel committeth here, that I should go far off from my sanctuary? but turn thee yet again, [and] thou shalt see greater abominations.

* There were various degrees of abomination. *

> Eze 8:7 And he brought me to the door of the court; and when I looked, behold a hole in the wall.

Eze 8:8 Then said he unto me, Son of man, dig now in the wall: and when I had digged in the wall, behold a door.

Eze 8:9 And he said unto me, Go in, and behold the wicked abominations that they do here.

Eze 8:10 So I went in and saw; and behold every form of creeping things, and abominable beasts, and all the idols of the house of Israel, portrayed upon the wall round about.

Eze 8:11 And there stood before them seventy men of the ancients of the house of Israel, and in the midst of them stood Jaazaniah the son of Shaphan, with every man his censer in his hand; and a thick cloud of incense went up.

* Let us notice where these "greater abominations" were committed. *

Eze 8:12 Then said he unto me, Son of man, hast thou seen what the ancients of the house of Israel do in the dark, every man in the chambers of his imagery? for they say, The LORD seeth us not; the LORD hath forsaken the earth.

* The greater abominations were committed by men IN THEIR IMAGINATIONS!*

Eze 8:13 He said also unto me, Turn thee yet again, [and] thou shalt see greater abominations that they do.

Eze 8:14 Then he brought me to the door of the gate of the LORD'S house which [was] toward the north; and, behold, there sat women weeping for Tammuz.

Eze 8:15 Then said he unto me, Hast thou seen [this], O son of man? turn thee yet again, [and] thou shalt see greater abominations than these.

* And progressing we see even greater abomination! *

Eze 8:16 And he brought me into the inner court of the LORD'S house, and, behold, at the door of the temple of the LORD, between the porch and the altar, [were] about five and twenty men, with their backs toward the temple of the

> LORD, and their faces toward the east; and they worshipped the sun toward the east.

* An Easter sunrise service. Think not? Think again! *

* But the Eostre/Ishthar "thing" is not the focus, but rather this verse:*

> Eze 8:12 Then said he unto me, Son of man, hast thou seen what the ancients of the house of Israel do in the dark, every man in the chambers of his imagery? for they say, The LORD seeth us not; the LORD hath forsaken the earth.

* Notice that not only did Jesus (Ezekiel didn't know His name but since I do, I'll just use God's name) know the contents of men's "chamber of imagery" but He was able to even show their contents to His prophet. The point that I am trying to make is that you BE AWARE that you do IN FACT have a "chamber of imagery". Every melodrama or scenario that runs through your mind is in there. Every mental image that you have is in there. Jesus sees in there, and Jesus destroyed the world once because He didn't like the stuff that He was seeing in there.*

> Genesis 6:5 And God saw that the wickedness of man [was] great in the earth, and [that] every imagination of the thoughts of his heart [was] only evil continually.
>
> Genesis 6:6 And it repented the LORD that he had made man on the earth, and it grieved him at his heart.
>
> Genesis 6:7 And the LORD said, I will destroy man whom I have created from the face of the earth; both man, and beast, and the creeping thing, and the fowls of the air; for it repenteth me that I have made them.
>
> Matthew 6:22 The light of the body is the eye: if therefore thine eye be single, thy whole body shall be full of light.
>
> Matthew 6:23 But if thine eye be evil, thy whole body shall be full of darkness. If therefore the light that is in thee be darkness, how great [is] that darkness!

* Everything that you gaze upon goes in to your chamber of imagery and becomes PART OF YOU. The images of Hollywood imported into your

chamber of imagery ARE THERE, and Jesus sees them. Every Gif, or magazine or any such like....can you not remember what it looked like??? You can remember because it is there in the full sight of God in the chamber of your imagery! * When! In the history of man, since the days of Noah, have the chambers of imagery of mankind been so polluted with filth, evil and violence as this TV age? People's chambers of imagery are crammed full of evil from hours a day of images of abominable things. And Jesus SEES it ALL. You REALLY have a "chamber of imagery", and you REALLY ARE responsible for what you put in it.*

> Matthew 24:37 But as the days of Noah [were], so shall also the coming of the Son of man be.

> Luke 17:26 And as it was in the days of Noah, so shall it be also in the days of the Son of man.

Flesh vs Spirit

The Christian life will be a battle of flesh and spirit. This will continue until you endure till the end. The "end" will be your physical death or the rapture of the Church.

> Matthew 24:13 But he that shall endure unto the end, the same shall be saved.
>
> Mark 13:13 And ye shall be hated of all men for my name's sake: but he that shall endure unto the end, the same shall be saved.

Here are some considerations.

> Matthew 11:29 Take my yoke upon you, and learn of me; for I am meek and lowly in heart: and ye shall find rest unto your souls.
>
> Matthew 11:30 For my yoke is easy, and my burden is light.
>
> Proverbs 13:15 Good understanding giveth favour: but the way of transgressors is hard

The Christian life is the far better choice but while the burden is light there is a burden and while the yoke is easy the yoke is there. We need to understand that there is a duty of the Christian.

> Romans 12:1 I beseech you therefore, brethren, by the mercies of God, that ye present your bodies a living sacrifice, holy, acceptable unto God, which is your reasonable service.
>
> Romans 12:2 And be not conformed to this world: but be ye transformed by the renewing of your mind, that ye may prove what is that good, and acceptable, and perfect, will of God.

That is one of the reasons that it is abomination for so called "Oneness Christians" to observe heathen holidays like Xmas and Eostre etc that are based upon lies (you don't honor the Spirit of Truth by making a LIE regardless of how much money some preacher is raking in during the season). It is necessary to be in the world but we do not have to be conformed to the world. Think about this a minute! Where does the buck stop? Who is it whose job it is to prove what is acceptable to God?

Is it some big name preacher? Is it some church that has a talented music program or big choir?

If you have been baptized in Jesus Name and have been filled with the real Holy Ghost of the Bible with the evidence of tongues then it is YOUR responsibility to prove what is that good and acceptable and perfect will of God.

> Romans 7:18 For I know that in me (that is, in my flesh,) dwelleth no good thing: for to will is present with me; but how to perform that which is good I find not.
>
> 19 For the good that I would I do not: but the evil which I would not, that I do.
>
> 20 Now if I do that I would not, it is no more I that do it, but sin that dwelleth in me.

No this does not mean that Paul was a sinner as the false-christian cults teach but is to help us understand that Paul was HUMAN just like we are!

> Romans 7:23 But I see another law in my members, warring against the law of my mind, and bringing me into captivity to the law of sin which is in my members.
>
> 24 O wretched man that I am! who shall deliver me from the body of this death?
>
> 25 I thank God through Jesus Christ our Lord. So then with the mind I myself serve the law of God; but with the flesh the law of sin.

The above verses point out that even the great Apostle Paul had a war between his flesh and Spirit as we all do. Those verses do not mean that Paul was a sinner as some cults teach, but that he had the same battles all humans have. Did you think that you were the only one with fleshly lusts that had to be subjected to the Spirit?

We have some awesome and generous promises from God. Yes we are soldiers in spiritual warfare, but we have God on our side when use our free will to place ourselves on God's side.

> 1 Corinthians 10:13 There hath no temptation taken you but such as is common to man: but God is faithful, who will not suffer you to be tempted above that ye are able; but will with the temptation also make a way to escape, that ye may be able to bear it.
>
> Hebrews 2:18 For in that he himself hath suffered being tempted, he is able to succour them that are tempted.

I would also point out that this wonderful promise from God also is double edged because it also shows us that there is no excuse for sin. This is a beautiful thing about the Word of God that it gives us knowledge and strength to resist the devil.

> James 4:7 Submit yourselves therefore to God. Resist the devil, and he will flee from you.
>
> 8 Draw nigh to God, and he will draw nigh to you. Cleanse your hands, ye sinners; and purify your hearts, ye double minded.

How does one overcome the flesh with its ungodly lusts?

> Romans 6:12 Let not sin therefore reign in your mortal body, that ye should obey it in the lusts thereof.
>
> Romans 13:14 But put ye on the Lord Jesus Christ, and make not provision for the flesh, to fulfil the lusts thereof.

That is one of the reasons that Holiness standards are so important. To keep us out of trouble. That is another reason that real Christians don't have televisions or watch movies or many other worldly entertainments. We don't want to make provision for the flesh for sin. That is why Christian young people don't "date" as the world dates where they practice arousing that which should not be aroused within themselves and then learn to deal with the emotions of breaking up from "relationships" that should never have been ignited to begin with. That pattern gets them in perfect emotional shape for a life of marriage and then DIVORCE!

Holiness is not a burden for the Christian, holiness is a valuable gift from God to keep the burdens OFF OF YOU so that you can keep your FREEDOM and your soul!

The world regards holiness standards as a horrible burden and lack of freedom, but the devil is leading most of them around by the nose and in this hour often with an actual ring in their nose! Sinners that don't care a bit for them sit around in board rooms and dictate what they will wear, how they will talk, what music they will listen to. The sinner is not free. The smoker or drug user is not free. The devil is a liar!

> John 8:34 Jesus answered them, Verily, verily, I say unto you, Whosoever committeth sin is the servant of sin.
>
> 35 And the servant abideth not in the house for ever: but the Son abideth ever.
>
> 36 If the Son therefore shall make you free, ye shall be free indeed.

> 1 Peter 4:12 Beloved, think it not strange concerning the fiery trial which is to try you, as though some strange thing happened unto you:
>
> 13 But rejoice, inasmuch as ye are partakers of Christ's sufferings; that, when his glory shall be revealed, ye may be glad also with exceeding joy.
>
> 14 If ye be reproached for the name of Christ, happy are ye; for the spirit of glory and of God resteth upon you: on their part he is evil spoken of, but on your part he is glorified.
>
> 15 But let none of you suffer as a murderer, or as a thief, or as an evildoer, or as a busybody in other men's matters.
>
> 16 Yet if any man suffer as a Christian, let him not be ashamed; but let him glorify God on this behalf.

17 For the time is come that judgment must begin at the house of God: and if it first begin at us, what shall the end be of them that obey not the gospel of God?

18 And if the righteous scarcely be saved, where shall the ungodly and the sinner appear?

19 Wherefore let them that suffer according to the will of God commit the keeping of their souls to him in well doing, as unto a faithful Creator.

2 Thessalonians 3:3 But the Lord is faithful, who shall stablish you, and keep you from evil.

1 Peter 5:6 Humble yourselves therefore under the mighty hand of God, that he may exalt you in due time:

7 Casting all your care upon him; for he careth for you.

8 ¶ Be sober, be vigilant; because your adversary the devil, as a roaring lion, walketh about, seeking whom he may devour:

9 Whom resist stedfast in the faith, knowing that the same afflictions are accomplished in your brethren that are in the world.

10 ¶ But the God of all grace, who hath called us unto his eternal glory by Christ Jesus, after that ye have suffered a while, make you perfect, stablish, strengthen, settle you.

11 To him be glory and dominion for ever and ever. Amen.

Sin

I John 3:3 And every man that hath this hope in him purifieth himself, even as he is pure.

I John 3:4 Whosoever committeth sin transgresseth also the law: for sin is the transgression of the law.

I John 3:5 And ye know that he was manifested to take away our sins; and in him is no sin.

I John 3:6 Whosoever abideth in him sinneth not: whosoever sinneth hath not seen him, neither known him.

I John 3:7 Little children, let no man deceive you: he that doeth righteousness is righteous, even as he is righteous.

I John 3:8 He that committeth sin is of the devil; for the devil sinneth from the beginning. For this purpose the Son of God was manifested, that he might destroy the works of the devil.

I John 3:9 Whosoever is born of God doth not commit sin; for his seed remaineth in him: and he cannot sin, because he is born of God.

I John 5:18 We know that whosoever is born of God sinneth not; but he that is begotten of God keepeth himself, and that wicked one toucheth him not.

John 5:14 Afterward Jesus findeth him in the temple, and said unto him, Behold, thou art made whole: sin no more, lest a worse thing come unto thee.

John 8:34 Jesus answered them, Verily, verily, I say unto you, Whosoever committeth sin is the servant of sin.

Romans 6:2 God forbid. How shall we, that are dead to sin, live any longer therein?

Romans 6:6 Knowing this, that our old man is crucified with [him], that the body of sin might be destroyed, that henceforth we should not serve sin.

Romans 6:16 Know ye not, that to whom ye yield yourselves servants to obey, his servants ye are to whom ye obey; whether of sin unto death, or of obedience unto righteousness?

Romans 6:17 But God be thanked, that ye were the servants of sin, but ye have obeyed from the heart that form of doctrine which was delivered you.

I Timothy 5:20 Them that sin rebuke before all, that others also may fear.

Hebrews 10:26 For if we sin wilfully after that we have received the knowledge of the truth, there remaineth no more sacrifice for sins,

1 Timothy 5:24 Some men's sins are open beforehand, going before to judgment; and some men they follow after.

John 8:24 I said therefore unto you, that ye shall die in your sins: for if ye believe not that I am he, ye shall die in your sins.

1 John 3:8 He that committeth sin is of the devil; for the devil sinneth from the beginning. For this purpose the Son of God was manifested, that he might destroy the works of the devil.

Chaste

There is a generation that is devoid of the concept that there even be such a thing as spiritual chastity. We even see the reprobate fringe of so called "oneness preachers" who see nothing wrong with attending trinitarian services. Some of these same ones also teach that monogamy is only required of the ministry, though. Yes there are reprobates who are double married (divorced and remarried) who must teach that is what the Bible means when it teaches that a minister must be the husband of only one wife.

Whose job is it to prove what is acceptable to God? Some real spiritual big name preacher off somewhere else, right? Let's have a look...

> Romans 12:2 And be not conformed to this world: but be ye transformed by the renewing of your mind, that ye may prove what is that good, and acceptable, and perfect, will of God.

But notice the method whereby the Jesus Name baptized, Holy Ghost filled saint is to prove the acceptable and perfect will of God.

Does the Word of God really say, "mix with the false brethren and polytheists, bear with them and win them with your tolerance fellowship and love"? or does it say:

> 2 Corinthians 6:17 Wherefore come out from among them, and be ye separate, saith the Lord, and touch not the unclean thing; and I will receive you,

Paul was addressing some Jesus Name baptized, Holy Ghost filled saints and he was afraid for them that they would be corrupted. Just what was this horrible thing that they were doing that Paul feared for their spiritual chastity (or fidelity in other words, that they would be INFIDELS)? What was this horrible thing that Paul was so afraid they might do?

> 2 Corinthians 11:3 But I fear, lest by any means, as the serpent beguiled Eve through his subtilty, so your minds should be corrupted from the simplicity that is in Christ.

Looking back one verse...

> 2 Corinthians 11:2 For I am jealous over you with godly jealousy: for I have espoused you to one husband, that I may present you as a chaste virgin to Christ.

Sure enough, Paul was fearing for their spiritual chastity, their spiritual fidelity.

So let us look at these two verses together

> 2 Corinthians 11:2 For I am jealous over you with godly jealousy: for I have espoused you to one husband, that I may present you as a chaste virgin to Christ.

> 2 Corinthians 11:3 But I fear, lest by any means, as the serpent beguiled Eve through his subtilty, so your minds should be corrupted from the simplicity that is in Christ.

But before we look at this terrible thing that Paul is afraid they would do, let us first look at who might be the "high risk" group for such corruption that Paul is fearful of. Let's back up just a few verses:

> 2 Corinthians 10:12 ¶ For we dare not make ourselves of the number, or compare ourselves with some that commend themselves: but they measuring themselves by themselves, and comparing themselves among themselves, are not wise.

The "high risk" group for spiritual infidelity will be a "mutual admiration society" commending themselves and measuring themselves by themselves, eh?

Now that we have come this far, what is this thing that Paul is so afraid that Jesus Name baptized, Holy Ghost filled saints might do that would render them spiritually corrupt, unchaste" or "whorish". What great evil would they need to do???

> 2 Corinthians 11:4 For if he that cometh preacheth another Jesus, whom we have not preached, or if ye receive another spirit, which ye have not received, or another gospel, which ye have not accepted, ye might well bear with him.

What?! Just for bearing with someone like a trinity preacher or other false christian? What??? Does it really say that a Jesus Name baptized, Holy Ghost filled saint would be corrupted just for "bearing with" a deceiver?

Jesus is coming back for a separate and Holy, spiritually chaste bride.

Here it is again, clearly "in context".

> 2 Corinthians 11:2 For I am jealous over you with godly jealousy: for I have espoused you to one husband, that I may present you as a chaste virgin to Christ.

> 2 Corinthians 11:3 But I fear, lest by any means, as the serpent beguiled Eve through his subtilty, so your minds should be corrupted from the simplicity that is in Christ.
>
> 2 Corinthians 11:4 For if he that cometh preacheth another Jesus, whom we have not preached, or if ye receive another spirit, which ye have not received, or another gospel, which ye have not accepted, ye might well bear with him.

There is nothing "loving" about spiritual corruption.

Just "bear with" a trinitarian teacher or other false christian is spiritual infidelity.

To "bear with" something is quite a passive act, eh? Think of the effort required to merely "bear with" something.

If just "bearing with" trinitarians is whorish, how much more the filth that would entertain at trinitarian services or those who would attend trinitarian services for fellowship?

In closing, let's look at Paul's mean old intolerant attitude towards deceivers.

> 2 Corinthians 11:12 But what I do, that I will do, that I may cut off occasion from them which desire occasion; that wherein they glory, they may be found even as we.
>
> 2 Corinthians 11:13 For such are false apostles, deceitful workers, transforming themselves into the apostles of Christ.
>
> 2 Corinthians 11:14 And no marvel; for Satan himself is transformed into an angel of light.
>
> 2 Corinthians 11:15 Therefore it is no great thing if his ministers also be transformed as the ministers of righteousness; whose end shall be according to their works.

Let the real Children of God remain spiritually separate and chaste.

Real Christianity is not a watered down "passive" religion.

> Mark 12:30 And thou shalt love the Lord thy God with all thy heart, and with all thy soul, and with all thy mind, and with all thy strength: this is the first commandment.

The spiritually unchaste have not obeyed even the first commandment. Or these other commandments either..

> Galatians 1:8 But though we, or an angel from heaven, preach any other gospel unto you than that which we have preached unto you, let him be accursed.

> Galatians 1:9 As we said before, so say I now again, If any man preach any other gospel unto you than that ye have received, let him be accursed.

What other issue is so important that the Word of God repeats the very same commandment in the next verse?

Strange Fire

Why would these individuals who were putting forth effort to please God, incur instead His wrath? What is the principle being taught here?

The reason that Nadab and Abihu were killed is because they offered "strange fire", rather than the "pure" fire from the brazen altar.

> Lev 10:1 And Nadab and Abihu, the sons of Aaron, took either of them his censer, and put fire therein, and put incense thereon, and offered strange fire before the LORD, which he commanded them not.
>
> Lev 10:2 And there went out fire from the LORD, and devoured them, and they died before the LORD.
>
> Lev 10:3 Then Moses said unto Aaron, This is it that the LORD spake, saying, I will be sanctified in them that come nigh me, and before all the people I will be glorified. And Aaron held his peace.
>
> Lev 10:4 And Moses called Mishael and Elzaphan, the sons of Uzziel the uncle of Aaron, and said unto them, Come near, carry your brethren from before the sanctuary out of the camp.
>
> Lev 10:5 So they went near, and carried them in their coats out of the camp; as Moses had said.

Looking back we see that the Lord had just done a great thing:

> Lev 9:23 And Moses and Aaron went into the tabernacle of the congregation, and came out, and blessed the people: and the glory of the LORD appeared unto all the people.
>
> Lev 9:24 And there came a fire out from before the LORD, and consumed upon the altar the burnt offering and the fat: which when all the people saw, they shouted, and fell on their faces.

There had just been a great manifestation of God, but Nadab and Abihu, instead of obeying God, decided to do things their way, and for their efforts incurred the wrath of Jesus.

But what exactly was their error? The Bible teaches that the content of the incense that would be offered to God had to be just so:

> Exo 30:9 Ye shall offer no strange incense thereon, nor burnt sacrifice, nor meat offering; neither shall ye pour drink offering thereon.

Apparently the incense that Nadab and Abihu used was OK. They did not offer "strange incense". The censers that they used were not the problem. Let us look at why they were destroyed.

> Lev 10:1 And Nadab and Abihu, the sons of Aaron, took either of them his censer, and put fire therein, and put incense thereon, and offered strange fire before the LORD, which he commanded them not.

The problem was "strange fire". They were supposed to get the fire for their censers from the brazen altar. The brazen altar was the altar where sacrifices or "sin offerings" were made. It is regarded as a "type and shadow" of the first step in the plan of salvation which is repentance. They offered up worship WITHOUT repentance!

> Acts 2:38 Then Peter said unto them, Repent, and be baptized every one of you in the name of Jesus Christ for the remission of sins, and ye shall receive the gift of the Holy Ghost.

Notice that Acts 2:38 is for all that God will call.

> Acts 2:39 For the promise is unto you, and to your children, and to all that are afar off, even as many as the Lord our God shall call.

> Heb 10:1 For the law having a shadow of good things to come, and not the very image of the things, can never with those sacrifices which they offered year by year continually make the comers thereunto perfect.

Just as Nadab and Abihu tried to worship God their own way and BYPASS the brazen altar and offer "strange fire"; the modern day charismatics bypass repentance and Jesus Name baptism trying to worship God their own way while still being "of the world".

By living worldly and refusing to repent they offer "strange fire" unto the Lord. That is why real Acts 2:38 Christians do not accept the charismatic cults as brethren even if they do obey part of the plan of salvation.

"Almost christian" cults will not even "almost" go to heaven. They offer "strange fire", they don't want the original Apostolic way, though they like the spectacular as did Nadab and Abihu.

Don't be deceived in a charismatic cult. Find a real Apostolic, Pentecostal Church that doesn't offer a sin leavened "strange fire" unto the Lord.

> 1 Cor 5:6 Your glorying is not good. Know ye not that a little leaven leaveneth the whole lump?

Be faithful!

Smote the Rock

Exodus 17:6 Behold, I will stand before thee there upon the rock in Horeb; and thou shalt smite the rock, and there shall come water out of it, that the people may drink. And Moses did so in the sight of the elders of Israel.

Numbers 20:8 Take the rod, and gather thou the assembly together, thou, and Aaron thy brother, and speak ye unto the rock before their eyes; and it shall give forth his water, and thou shalt bring forth to them water out of the rock: so thou shalt give the congregation and their beasts drink.

9 And Moses took the rod from before the LORD, as he commanded him.

10 And Moses and Aaron gathered the congregation together before the rock, and he said unto them, Hear now, ye rebels; must we fetch you water out of this rock?

11 And Moses lifted up his hand, and with his rod he smote the rock twice: and the water came out abundantly, and the congregation drank, and their beasts also.

12 And the LORD spake unto Moses and Aaron, Because ye believed me not, to sanctify me in the eyes of the children of Israel, therefore ye shall not bring this congregation into the land which I have given them.

Obedience

Acts 5:29 Then Peter and the [other] apostles answered and said, We ought to obey God rather than men.

Romans 2:8 But unto them that are contentious, and do not obey the truth, but obey unrighteousness, indignation and wrath,

II Thessalonians 1:7 And to you who are troubled rest with us, when the Lord Jesus shall be revealed from heaven with his mighty angels,

II Thessalonians 1:8 In flaming fire taking vengeance on them that know not God, and that obey not the gospel of our Lord Jesus Christ:

Hebrews 5:9 And being made perfect, he became the author of eternal salvation unto all them that obey him;

I Peter 4:17 For the time [is come] that judgment must begin at the house of God: and if [it] first [begin] at us, what shall the end [be] of them that obey not the gospel of God?

Romans 10:16 But they have not all obeyed the gospel. For Esaias saith, Lord, who hath believed our report?

* The book of Romans labels "non-obeyers" as "non-believers". *

Hebrews 11:7 By faith Noah, being warned of God of things not seen as yet, moved with fear, prepared an ark to the saving of his house; by the which he condemned the world, and became heir of the righteousness which is by faith.

* By FAITH Noah OBEYED. *

Hebrews 11:8 By faith Abraham, when he was called to go out into a place which he should after receive for an inheritance, obeyed; and he went out, not knowing whither he went.

* By FAITH Abraham OBEYED *

James 1:22 But be ye doers of the word, and not hearers only, deceiving your own selves.

Notice the plan of salvation for "as many as the Lord our God shall call.

Acts 2:38 Then Peter said unto them, Repent, and be baptized every one of you in the name of Jesus Christ for the remission of sins, and ye shall receive the gift of the Holy Ghost.

Acts 2:39 For the promise is unto you, and to your children, and to all that are afar off, [even] as many as the Lord our God shall call.

We see the absolute essentiality of obedience in order to be a partaker in the free gift of salvation.

In the New Testament Church the old ceremonial sacrifice of the law has been replaced by the sacrifice of praise.

Psalms 141:2 Let my prayer be set forth before thee as incense; and the lifting up of my hands as the evening sacrifice.

Jeremiah 33:11 The voice of joy, and the voice of gladness, the voice of the bridegroom, and the voice of the bride, the voice of them that shall say, Praise the LORD of hosts: for the LORD is good; for his mercy endureth for ever: and of them that shall bring the sacrifice of praise into the house of the LORD. For I will cause to return the captivity of the land, as at the first, saith the LORD.

We can find confirmation in the New Testament as well regarding the sacrifice of praise in the New Testament Church.

Hebrews 13:15 By him therefore let us offer the sacrifice of praise to God continually, that is, the fruit of our lips giving thanks to his name.

Obedience

With appreciation of the importance of praise and worship to God, there is something that is of greater importance to the Lord Jesus, the one and only Bridegroom of the bride of Christ. (A real bride, is the bride of ONE husband only, the real Church is the bride of only Jesus Christ Himself!)

> Samuel 15:22 And Samuel said, Hath the LORD as great delight in burnt offerings and sacrifices, as in obeying the voice of the LORD? Behold, to obey is better than sacrifice, and to hearken than the fat of rams.

There are many groups that are strong on praise and worship, but are conformed to the world in many areas, even embracing traditions that are contrary to the Word of God.

> James 4:4 Ye adulterers and adulteresses, know ye not that the friendship of the world is enmity with God? whosoever therefore will be a friend of the world is the enemy of God.

I believe that James speaks of spiritual adultery as well as physical sin.

As important as sacrifice (praise and worship) is, obedience is MORE Important.

> Romans 12:2 And be not conformed to this world: but be ye transformed by the renewing of your mind, that ye may prove what is that good, and acceptable, and perfect, will of God.

Spiritual Healing

Spiritual Healing Sermon - 2005

The Bible offers its reader and obeyer more than eternal life after this world and this physical life. There are many benefits of the Christian life in this world. Of course the most important thing is to have obeyed Acts 2:38 and be living holy so as to be ready for eternity. We also need to understand that those in the Bible who were healed or even raised from the dead, later died.

Jesus loved us enough to pay a dear and painful price for our healing in this life.

> Isaiah 53:5 But he was wounded for our transgressions, he was bruised for our iniquities: the chastisement of our peace was upon him; and with his stripes we are healed.

> 1 Peter 2:24 Who his own self bare our sins in his own body on the tree, that we, being dead to sins, should live unto righteousness: by whose stripes ye were healed.

As is the case in so many options the Bible offers us, there is a step of faith required of us. So often that step of faith is to simply take the time and speak the words of our prayers to God.

For healing, though, there are other steps of faith available for the Saints to take. Now I don't say this in any way to diminish simply praying for the sick or for the sick to pray for themselves. Also I believe that God gives extra grace to those who, for good reason, have no local fellowship. Those blessed with a true Church to attend should do so.

> James 5:14 Is any sick among you? let him call for the elders of the church; and let them pray over him, anointing him with oil in the name of the Lord:

> James 5:15 And the prayer of faith shall save the sick, and the Lord shall raise him up; and if he have committed sins, they shall be forgiven him.
>
> James 5:16 Confess your faults one to another, and pray one for another, that ye may be healed. The effectual fervent prayer of a righteous man availeth much.

So we see in the above instructions that they in no way diminish the need for prayer and prayer is even mentioned. Those blessed with a elder (which is another word for Pastor) or elders should avail themselves of their blessing when sickness or infirmity comes their way.

Hearing the Word of God will nourish your soul and increase your faith.

> Romans 10:17 So then faith cometh by hearing, and hearing by the word of God.

So let us study examples of healing in the Word of God to increase our faith that we may be healed of any infirmity.

> Mark 8:22 ¶ And he cometh to Bethsaida; and they bring a blind man unto him, and besought him to touch him.
>
> 23 And he took the blind man by the hand, and led him out of the town; and when he had spit on his eyes, and put his hands upon him, he asked him if he saw ought.
>
> 24 And he looked up, and said, I see men as trees, walking.
>
> 25 After that he put his hands again upon his eyes, and made him look up: and he was restored, and saw every man clearly.
>
> 26 And he sent him away to his house, saying, Neither go into the town, nor tell it to any in the town.
>
> 27 ¶ And Jesus went out, and his disciples, into the towns of Caesarea Philippi: and by the way he asked his disciples, saying unto them, Whom do men say that I am?

> 28 And they answered, John the Baptist: but some say, Elias; and others, One of the prophets.
>
> 29 And he saith unto them, But whom say ye that I am? And Peter answereth and saith unto him, Thou art the Christ.
>
> 30 And he charged them that they should tell no man of him.

Here is an example from the Old Testament of a man obeying God and a healing taking place.

> 2 Kings 20:6 And I will add unto thy days fifteen years; and I will deliver thee and this city out of the hand of the king of Assyria; and I will defend this city for mine own sake, and for my servant David's sake.
>
> 7 And Isaiah said, Take a lump of figs. And they took and laid it on the boil, and he recovered.

Now some will teach that Christians should not use doctors. That doctrine is not supported by the Bible. Now I will say that one should use prayer as the first thing when there is injury or sickness.

> Matthew 9:12 But when Jesus heard that, he said unto them, They that be whole need not a physician, but they that are sick.

If Jesus Himself said the above words, how can any follower of Jesus teach against doctors?

> Luke 5:31 And Jesus answering said unto them, They that are whole need not a physician; but they that are sick.

> Colossians 4:14 Luke, the beloved physician, and Demas, greet you.

It would appear from the above verse that Luke was continuing as a physician after becoming a Christian and following Jesus.

> Mark 5:25 And a certain woman, which had an issue of blood twelve years,
>
> 26 And had suffered many things of many physicians, and had spent all that she had, and was nothing bettered, but rather grew worse,
>
> 27 When she had heard of Jesus, came in the press behind, and touched his garment.
>
> 28 For she said, If I may touch but his clothes, I shall be whole.
>
> 29 And straightway the fountain of her blood was dried up; and she felt in her body that she was healed of that plague.
>
> 30 And Jesus, immediately knowing in himself that virtue had gone out of him, turned him about in the press, and said, Who touched my clothes?
>
> 31 And his disciples said unto him, Thou seest the multitude thronging thee, and sayest thou, Who touched me?
>
> 32 And he looked round about to see her that had done this thing.
>
> 33 But the woman fearing and trembling, knowing what was done in her, came and fell down before him, and told him all the truth.
>
> 34 And he said unto her, Daughter, thy faith hath made thee whole; go in peace, and be whole of thy plague.

We who are Apostolic Christians know that the same Jesus who healed that lady is the same Jesus who indwells us as the Holy Spirit.

> John 14:17 Even the Spirit of truth; whom the world cannot receive, because it seeth him not, neither knoweth him: but ye know him; for he dwelleth with you, and shall be in you.

8 ¶ I will not leave you comfortless: I will come to you.

Jesus is now the Spirit of truth and the comforter.

The Word of God also gives examples of followers of Jesus Christ taking a step of faith by speaking words and healing being the result. This is important for our faith. It is one thing for Jesus Himself to heal people, it is quite another for his followers to also be able to use that power. What a wonderful and loving God Jesus is!

> Acts 3:1 Now Peter and John went up together into the temple at the hour of prayer, being the ninth hour.
>
> 2 And a certain man lame from his mother's womb was carried, whom they laid daily at the gate of the temple which is called Beautiful, to ask alms of them that entered into the temple;
>
> 3 Who seeing Peter and John about to go into the temple asked an alms.
>
> 4 And Peter, fastening his eyes upon him with John, said, Look on us.
>
> 5 And he gave heed unto them, expecting to receive something of them.
>
> 6 Then Peter said, Silver and gold have I none; but such as I have give I thee: In the name of Jesus Christ of Nazareth rise up and walk.
>
> 7 And he took him by the right hand, and lifted him up: and immediately his feet and ankle bones received strength.
>
> 8 And he leaping up stood, and walked, and entered with them into the temple, walking, and leaping, and praising God.
>
> 9 And all the people saw him walking and praising God:
>
> 10 And they knew that it was he which sat for alms at the Beautiful gate of the temple: and they were filled with wonder and amazement at that which had happened unto him.

> 11 And as the lame man which was healed held Peter and John, all the people ran together unto them in the porch that is called Solomon's, greatly wondering.
>
> 12 ¶ And when Peter saw it, he answered unto the people, Ye men of Israel, why marvel ye at this? or why look ye so earnestly on us, as though by our own power or holiness we had made this man to walk?

Peter went on to give Jesus credit for the healing. This is an interesting account because the lame man did not even ask for healing, but simply cooperated with the man of God who had compassion on him.

There are many accounts of healing in the Bible and I won't attempt to read all of them now, but the basics are the same that healing comes by the power of God.

It is generally not based upon whether the individual deserves healing, but rather based upon their asking, though with the account in James there is the implication

that in some cases there was sin in the life of the sick person. It does say "if" though so while sickness may well be the fruit of sin it is not a sign of sin. Many have sickness who do not have unrepentant sin. So beware any doctrine that would teach that illness was a sign of sin. There are certainly many very healthy sinners, eh?

In closing I again read these Biblical instructions:

> James 5:14 Is any sick among you? let him call for the elders of the church; and let them pray over him, anointing him with oil in the name of the Lord:
>
> James 5:15 And the prayer of faith shall save the sick, and the Lord shall raise him up; and if he have committed sins, they shall be forgiven him.
>
> James 5:16 Confess your faults one to another, and pray one for another, that ye may be healed. The effectual fervent prayer of a righteous man availeth much.

Laleo

From the Zodhiates' Study Bible Dictionary

> 2980. laleo aprol. form of an otherwise obsol. verb: to talk, i.e. utter words: preach, say, speak (after), talk, tell, utter,

Notice carefully that though women are commanded not to laleo at all during a worship service, that there is also a situation where a man is also commanded not to laleo to the congregation.

We see here that women are ABSOLUTELY FORBIDDEN to laleo during a worship service:

> 1 Corinthians 14:34. Let your women keep <4601> silence <4601> in the churches: for it is not permitted unto them to speak <2980>; but [they are commanded] to be under obedience, as also saith the law.

Notice also that if there is no interpreter that a man with the gift of tongues is commanded not to use that gift but to laleo to himself and to God.

> 1 Cor 14:28 But if there be no interpreter, let him keep <4601> silence <4601> in the church; and let him speak <2980> to himself, and to God.

Whereas women are commanded NEVER to laleo to the church, men are commanded not to laleo under certain circumstances.

Regardless of popular traditions, the simple fact is that "speak"(laleo) means "speak" and when the Bible says that women are not permitted to speak to the church during a worship service it simply says what it means and means what it says.

> I Corinthians 14:34 Let your women keep silence in the churches: for it is not permitted unto them to speak; but [they are commanded] to be under obedience, as also saith the law.

> I Corinthians 14:35 And if they will learn any thing, let them ask their husbands at home: for it is a shame for women to speak in the church.

Certainly "ask" in verse 35 doesn't mean "preach".

Speak means "speak"

Preachers

I felt to publish this study to clear up a lot of the confusion being published for and by men who are Biblically disqualified from the ministry but who are taking advantage of corruption in religious organizations and their deviation away from the Bible.

> 1 Corinthians 1:21 For after that in the wisdom of God the world by wisdom knew not God, it pleased God by the foolishness of preaching to save them that believe.
>
> 22 For the Jews require a sign, and the Greeks seek after wisdom:
>
> 23 But we preach Christ crucified, unto the Jews a stumblingblock, and unto the Greeks foolishness;
>
> 24 But unto them which are called, both Jews and Greeks, Christ the power of God, and the wisdom of God.
>
> 25 Because the foolishness of God is wiser than men; and the weakness of God is stronger than men.
>
> 26 For ye see your calling, brethren, how that not many wise men after the flesh, not many mighty, not many noble, are called:
>
> 27 But God hath chosen the foolish things of the world to confound the wise; and God hath chosen the weak things of the world to confound the things which are mighty;
>
> 28 And base things of the world, and things which are despised, hath God chosen, yea, and things which are not, to bring to nought things that are:

There are requirements for the ministry that exceed the requirements for salvation. That means that there are those who will be saved who are not qualified for the ministry. Also consider that of those qualified for the ministry only a few will actually be chosen by God. Also, it is God who calls men to preach, not families or organizations.

Notice that a deacon (a young preacher), an elder, or a bishop; all must be the husband of only one wife. So if a man has a living ex-wife and has re-married; he is disqualified from the ministry. Also if his wife and children are not in subjection to him, then he is disqualified from being a pastor...

So, you see, there are many filling pulpits who have no business there, and I speak of the true Church and not the false church.

Consider that marriage is not a sin that is washed away by Jesus Name baptism, but rather it is a covenant. If a married sinner man comes and obeys Acts 2:38 without his wife is that marriage suddenly washed away?

> 1 Corinthians 7:12 But to the rest speak I, not the Lord: If any brother hath a wife that believeth not, and she be pleased to dwell with him, let him not put her away.
>
> 1 Corinthians 7:13 And the woman which hath an husband that believeth not, and if he be pleased to dwell with her, let her not leave him.

A divorced man who obeys Acts 2:38 still has an ex-wife when he comes up out of the waters of baptism. If he owed alimony before he was baptized, he still owes it after baptism. If he had children from his first wife they are STILL his children. Baptism does not wash away an ex-wife, nor does it wash away children. Corrupt religious organizations are defying the Word of God when they license divorced and remarried men to preach.

Remember marriage is a covenant not a sin.

> I Timothy 3:2 A bishop then must be blameless, the husband of one wife, vigilant, sober, of good behaviour, given to hospitality, apt to teach;
>
> I Timothy 3:3 Not given to wine, no striker, not greedy of filthy lucre; but patient, not a brawler, not covetous;
>
> I Timothy 3:4 One that ruleth well his own house, having his children in subjection with all gravity;

> I Timothy 3:5 (For if a man know not how to rule his own house, how shall he take care of the church of God?)
>
> I Timothy 3:6 Not a novice, lest being lifted up with pride he fall into the condemnation of the devil.
>
> I Timothy 3:10 And let these also first be proved; then let them use the office of a deacon, being [found] blameless.
>
> I Timothy 3:11 Even so [must their] wives [be] grave, not slanderers, sober, faithful in all things.

A man's immediate family members can, by their unfaithfulness disqualify a man from the ministry.

> I Timothy 3:12 Let the deacons be the husbands of one wife, ruling their children and their own houses well.

> Titus 1:5 For this cause left I thee in Crete, that thou shouldest set in order the things that are wanting, and ordain elders in every city, as I had appointed thee:

While God calls men to preach it is not out of order for those in the ministry to recognize God's calling on other men. But notice again the requirements. We can also be confident that Paul is not speaking of false accusations here considering some of the charges that had been leveled against him in the past.

> Titus 1:6 If any be blameless, the husband of one wife, having faithful children not accused of riot or unruly.
>
> Titus 1:7 For a bishop must be blameless, as the steward of God; not selfwilled, not soon angry, not given to wine, no striker, not given to filthy lucre;

All through we see one issue coming up that a minister must be the husband of only one wife. That does not mean one at a time and it does not mean that polygamy is acceptable in the Church membership. The issue is divorce and remarriage.

I have heard so many excuses from those who violate the Word of God, but I can find no where in the Bible where God ever accepted an excuse.

Some of the looser in this hour suggest that if a person was married before they came to the Lord then it doesn't matter, BUT, a man owing alimony before baptism still owes it after baptism. Baptism does not wash away a marriage or divorce.

Marriage is a covenant, not a sin.

Also we must remember that if any preacher is preaching any variation from the apostolic doctrine (Acts 2:38).....

> Galatians 1:8 But though we, or an angel from heaven, preach any other gospel unto you than that which we have preached unto you, let him be accursed.
>
> Galatians 1:9 As we said before, so say I now again, If any [man] preach any other gospel unto you than that ye have received, let him be accursed.

A glance at Acts 19 will verify that Paul adhered faithfully to the Apostolic Acts 2:38 doctrine. (The Church at Ephesus was founded in Acts 19).

> Acts 19:1 And it came to pass, that, while Apollos was at Corinth, Paul having passed through the upper coasts came to Ephesus: and finding certain disciples,
>
> 2 He said unto them, Have ye received the Holy Ghost since ye believed? And they said unto him, We have not so much as heard whether there be any Holy Ghost.
>
> 3 And he said unto them, Unto what then were ye baptized? And they said, Unto John's baptism.
>
> 4 Then said Paul, John verily baptized with the baptism of repentance, saying unto the people, that they should believe on him which should come after him, that is, on Christ Jesus.

5 When they heard this, they were baptized in the name of the Lord Jesus.

6 And when Paul had laid his hands upon them, the Holy Ghost came on them; and they spake with tongues, and prophesied.

7 And all the men were about twelve.

8 ¶ And he went into the synagogue, and spake boldly for the space of three months, disputing and persuading the things concerning the kingdom of God.

9 But when divers were hardened, and believed not, but spake evil of that way before the multitude, he departed from them, and separated the disciples, disputing daily in the school of one Tyrannus.

Men and Women

Genesis 2:15 And the LORD God took the man, and put him into the garden of Eden to dress it and to keep it.

16 ¶ And the LORD God commanded the man, saying, Of every tree of the garden thou mayest freely eat:

17 But of the tree of the knowledge of good and evil, thou shalt not eat of it: for in the day that thou eatest thereof thou shalt surely die.

18 ¶ And the LORD God said, It is not good that the man should be alone; I will make him an help meet for him.

19 And out of the ground the LORD God formed every beast of the field, and every fowl of the air; and brought them unto Adam to see what he would call them: and whatsoever Adam called every living creature, that was the name thereof.

20 And Adam gave names to all cattle, and to the fowl of the air, and to every beast of the field; but for Adam there was not found an help meet for him.

21 ¶ And the LORD God caused a deep sleep to fall upon Adam, and he slept: and he took one of his ribs, and closed up the flesh instead thereof;

22 And the rib, which the LORD God had taken from man, made he a woman, and brought her unto the man.

23 And Adam said, This is now bone of my bones, and flesh of my flesh: she shall be called Woman, because she was taken out of Man.

24 Therefore shall a man leave his father and his mother, and shall cleave unto his wife: and they shall be one flesh.

25 And they were both naked, the man and his wife, and were not ashamed.

Genesis 3:1 ¶ Now the serpent was more subtil than any beast of the field which the LORD God had made. And he said unto the woman, Yea, hath God said, Ye shall not eat of every tree of the garden?

2 And the woman said unto the serpent, We may eat of the fruit of the trees of the garden:

3 But of the fruit of the tree which is in the midst of the garden, God hath said, Ye shall not eat of it, neither shall ye touch it, lest ye die.

4 And the serpent said unto the woman, Ye shall not surely die:

5 For God doth know that in the day ye eat thereof, then your eyes shall be opened, and ye shall be as gods, knowing good and evil.

6 ¶ And when the woman saw that the tree was good for food, and that it was pleasant to the eyes, and a tree to be desired to make one wise, she took of the fruit thereof, and did eat, and gave also unto her husband with her; and he did eat.

7 And the eyes of them both were opened, and they knew that they were naked; and they sewed fig leaves together, and made themselves aprons.

8 And they heard the voice of the LORD God walking in the garden in the cool of the day: and Adam and his wife hid themselves from the presence of the LORD God amongst the trees of the garden.

9 ¶ And the LORD God called unto Adam, and said unto him, Where art thou?

10 And he said, I heard thy voice in the garden, and I was afraid, because I was naked; and I hid myself.

11 ¶ And he said, Who told thee that thou wast naked? Hast thou eaten of the tree, whereof I commanded thee that thou shouldest not eat?

12 And the man said, The woman whom thou gavest to be with me, she gave me of the tree, and I did eat.

> 13 And the LORD God said unto the woman, What is this that thou hast done? And the woman said, The serpent beguiled me, and I did eat.
>
> 14 ¶ And the LORD God said unto the serpent, Because thou hast done this, thou art cursed above all cattle, and above every beast of the field; upon thy belly shalt thou go, and dust shalt thou eat all the days of thy life:
>
> 15 And I will put enmity between thee and the woman, and between thy seed and her seed; it shall bruise thy head, and thou shalt bruise his heel.
>
> 16 ¶ Unto the woman he said, I will greatly multiply thy sorrow and thy conception; in sorrow thou shalt bring forth children; and thy desire shall be to thy husband, and he shall rule over thee.
>
> 17 ¶ And unto Adam he said, Because thou hast hearkened unto the voice of thy wife, and hast eaten of the tree, of which I commanded thee, saying, Thou shalt not eat of it: cursed is the ground for thy sake; in sorrow shalt thou eat of it all the days of thy life;
>
> 18 Thorns also and thistles shall it bring forth to thee; and thou shalt eat the herb of the field;
>
> 19 In the sweat of thy face shalt thou eat bread, till thou return unto the ground; for out of it wast thou taken: for dust thou art, and unto dust shalt thou return.
>
> 20 ¶ And Adam called his wife's name Eve; because she was the mother of all living.
>
> 21 ¶ Unto Adam also and to his wife did the LORD God make coats of skins, and clothed them.

Note that the aprons were not adequate and that God made them coats.

> 2 Corinthians 11:3 But I fear, lest by any means, as the serpent beguiled Eve through his subtilty, so your minds should be corrupted from the simplicity that is in Christ.

What a sad thing indeed to be the the person that sets the example that the Bible gives to avoid.

1 Timothy 2:7 Whereunto I am ordained a preacher, and an apostle, (I speak the truth in Christ, and lie not;) a teacher of the Gentiles in faith and verity.

8 I will therefore that men pray every where, lifting up holy hands, without wrath and doubting.

9 ¶ In like manner also, that women adorn themselves in modest apparel, with shamefacedness and sobriety; not with broided hair, or gold, or pearls, or costly array;

10 But (which becometh women professing godliness) with good works.

11 Let the woman learn in silence with all subjection.

12 But I suffer not a woman to teach, nor to usurp authority over the man, but to be in silence.

13 For Adam was first formed, then Eve.

14 And Adam was not deceived, but the woman being deceived was in the transgression.

15 Notwithstanding she shall be saved in childbearing, if they continue in faith and charity and holiness with sobriety.

There are reasons that God has different commands for women than men in the Church.

1 Corinthians 11:3 But I would have you know, that the head of every man is Christ; and the head of the woman is the man; and the head of Christ is God.

4 Every man praying or prophesying, having his head covered, dishonoureth his head.

5 But every woman that prayeth or prophesieth with her head uncovered dishonoureth her head: for that is even all one as if she were shaven.

6 For if the woman be not covered, let her also be shorn: but if it be a shame for a woman to be shorn or shaven, let her be covered.

7 For a man indeed ought not to cover his head, forasmuch as he is the image and glory of God: but the woman is the glory of the man.

8 For the man is not of the woman; but the woman of the man.

9 Neither was the man created for the woman; but the woman for the man.

10 For this cause ought the woman to have power on her head because of the angels.

11 Nevertheless neither is the man without the woman, neither the woman without the man, in the Lord.

12 For as the woman is of the man, even so is the man also by the woman; but all things of God.

13 Judge in yourselves: is it comely that a woman pray unto God uncovered?

14 Doth not even nature itself teach you, that, if a man have long hair, it is a shame unto him?

15 But if a woman have long hair, it is a glory to her: for her hair is given her for a covering.

16 But if any man seem to be contentious, we have no such custom, neither the churches of God.

God simply has different roles for women than men.

1 Corinthians 14:34 Let your women keep silence in the churches: for it is not permitted unto them to speak; but they are commanded to be under obedience, as also saith the law.

1 Corinthians 14:35 And if they will learn any thing, let them ask their husbands at home: for it is a shame for women to speak in the church.

Love and Marriage

Matthew 26:26 And as they were eating, Jesus took bread, and blessed it, and brake it, and gave it to the disciples, and said, Take, eat; this is my body.

27 And he took the cup, and gave thanks, and gave it to them, saying, Drink ye all of it;

28 For this is my blood of the new testament, which is shed for many for the remission of sins.

29 But I say unto you, I will not drink henceforth of this fruit of the vine, until that day when I drink it new with you in my Father's kingdom.

Mark 14:22 And as they did eat, Jesus took bread, and blessed, and brake it, and gave to them, and said, Take, eat: this is my body.

23 And he took the cup, and when he had given thanks, he gave it to them: and they all drank of it.

24 And he said unto them, This is my blood of the new testament, which is shed for many.

25 Verily I say unto you, I will drink no more of the fruit of the vine, until that day that I drink it new in the kingdom of God.

Luke 22:19 And he took bread, and gave thanks, and brake it, and gave unto them, saying, This is my body which is given for you: this do in remembrance of me.

20 Likewise also the cup after supper, saying, This cup is the new testament in my blood, which is shed for you.

John 13:1 Now before the feast of the passover, when Jesus knew that his hour was come that he should depart out of this world unto the Father, having loved his own which were in the world, he loved them unto the end.

2 And supper being ended, the devil having now put into the heart of Judas Iscariot, Simon's son, to betray him;

3 Jesus knowing that the Father had given all things into his hands, and that he was come from God, and went to God;

4 He riseth from supper, and laid aside his garments; and took a towel, and girded himself.

5 After that he poureth water into a bason, and began to wash the disciples' feet, and to wipe them with the towel wherewith he was girded.

6 Then cometh he to Simon Peter: and Peter saith unto him, Lord, dost thou wash my feet? Peter saith: Gr. he saith

7 Jesus answered and said unto him, What I do thou knowest not now; but thou shalt know hereafter.

8 Peter saith unto him, Thou shalt never wash my feet. Jesus answered him, If I wash thee not, thou hast no part with me.

9 Simon Peter saith unto him, Lord, not my feet only, but also my hands and my head.

10 Jesus saith to him, He that is washed needeth not save to wash his feet, but is clean every whit: and ye are clean, but not all.

11 For he knew who should betray him; therefore said he, Ye are not all clean.

12 So after he had washed their feet, and had taken his garments, and was set down again, he said unto them, Know ye what I have done to you?

13 Ye call me Master and Lord: and ye say well; for so I am.

14 If I then, your Lord and Master, have washed your feet; ye also ought to wash one another's feet.

15 For I have given you an example, that ye should do as I have done to you.

16 Verily, verily, I say unto you, The servant is not greater than his lord; neither he that is sent greater than he that sent him.

17 If ye know these things, happy are ye if ye do them.

1 Corinthians 11:23 For I have received of the Lord that which also I delivered unto you, That the Lord Jesus the same night in which he was betrayed took bread:

24 And when he had given thanks, he brake it, and said, Take, eat: this is my body, which is broken for you: this do in remembrance of me. in…: or, for a remembrance

25 After the same manner also he took the cup, when he had supped, saying, This cup is the new testament in my blood: this do ye, as oft as ye drink it, in remembrance of me.

26 For as often as ye eat this bread, and drink this cup, ye do shew the Lord's death till he come. ye do…: or, shew ye

27 Wherefore whosoever shall eat this bread, and drink this cup of the Lord, unworthily, shall be guilty of the body and blood of the Lord.

28 But let a man examine himself, and so let him eat of that bread, and drink of that cup.

29 For he that eateth and drinketh unworthily, eateth and drinketh damnation to himself, not discerning the Lord's body. damnation: or, judgment

30 For this cause many are weak and sickly among you, and many sleep.

31 For if we would judge ourselves, we should not be judged.

Roles

Ephesians 5:20 Giving thanks always for all things unto God and the Father in the name of our Lord Jesus Christ;

21 ¶ Submitting yourselves one to another in the fear of God.

22 Wives, submit yourselves unto your own husbands, as unto the Lord.

23 For the husband is the head of the wife, even as Christ is the head of the church: and he is the saviour of the body.

24 Therefore as the church is subject unto Christ, so let the wives be to their own husbands in every thing.

25 Husbands, love your wives, even as Christ also loved the church, and gave himself for it;

26 That he might sanctify and cleanse it with the washing of water by the word,

27 That he might present it to himself a glorious church, not having spot, or wrinkle, or any such thing; but that it should be holy and without blemish.

28 So ought men to love their wives as their own bodies. He that loveth his wife loveth himself.

29 For no man ever yet hated his own flesh; but nourisheth and cherisheth it, even as the Lord the church:

30 For we are members of his body, of his flesh, and of his bones.

31 For this cause shall a man leave his father and mother, and shall be joined unto his wife, and they two shall be one flesh.

32 This is a great mystery: but I speak concerning Christ and the church.

33 Nevertheless let every one of you in particular so love his wife even as himself; and the wife see that she reverence her husband.

Colossians 3:18 ¶ Wives, submit yourselves unto your own husbands, as it is fit in the Lord.

19 Husbands, love your wives, and be not bitter against them.

20 Children, obey your parents in all things: for this is well pleasing unto the Lord.

21 Fathers, provoke not your children to anger, lest they be discouraged.

22 Servants, obey in all things your masters according to the flesh; not with eyeservice, as menpleasers; but in singleness of heart, fearing God:

23 And whatsoever ye do, do it heartily, as to the Lord, and not unto men;

24 Knowing that of the Lord ye shall receive the reward of the inheritance: for ye serve the Lord Christ.

25 But he that doeth wrong shall receive for the wrong which he hath done: and there is no respect of persons.

I Peter 3:1 ¶ Likewise, ye wives, be in subjection to your own husbands; that, if any obey not the word, they also may without the word be won by the conversation of the wives;

2 While they behold your chaste conversation coupled with fear.

3 Whose adorning let it not be that outward adorning of plaiting the hair, and of wearing of gold, or of putting on of apparel;

4 But let it be the hidden man of the heart, in that which is not corruptible, even the ornament of a meek and quiet spirit, which is in the sight of God of great price.

5 For after this manner in the old time the holy women also, who trusted in God, adorned themselves, being in subjection
unto their own husbands: 6 Even as Sara obeyed Abraham,
calling him lord: whose daughters ye are, as long as ye do well, and are not afraid with any amazement.

7 Likewise, ye husbands, dwell with them according to knowledge, giving honour unto the wife, as unto the weaker vessel, and as being heirs together of the grace of life; that your prayers be not hindered.

8 ¶ Finally, be ye all of one mind, having compassion one of another, love as brethren, be pitiful, be courteous:

9 Not rendering evil for evil, or railing for railing: but contrariwise blessing; knowing that ye are thereunto called, that ye should inherit a blessing.

10 For he that will love life, and see good days, let him refrain his tongue from evil, and his lips that they speak no guile:

11 Let him eschew evil, and do good; let him seek peace, and ensue it.

12 For the eyes of the Lord are over the righteous, and his ears are open unto their prayers: but the face of the Lord is against them that do evil.

13 And who is he that will harm you, if ye be followers of that which is good?

14 But and if ye suffer for righteousness' sake, happy are ye: and be not afraid of their terror, neither be troubled;

Revelation 19:7 Let us be glad and rejoice, and give honour to him: for the marriage of the Lamb is come, and his wife hath made herself ready.

Revelation 21:9 ¶ And there came unto me one of the seven angels which had the seven vials full of the seven last plagues, and talked with me, saying, Come hither, I will shew thee the bride, the Lamb's wife.

Fornication

Acts 15:29 That ye abstain from meats offered to idols, and from blood, and from things strangled, and from fornication: from which if ye keep yourselves, ye shall do well. Fare ye well.

Romans 1:29 Being filled with all unrighteousness, fornication, wickedness, covetousness, maliciousness; full of envy, murder, debate, deceit, malignity; whisperers,

30 Backbiters, haters of God, despiteful, proud, boasters, inventors of evil things, disobedient to parents,

31 Without understanding, covenant breakers, without natural affection, implacable, unmerciful:

32 Who knowing the judgment of God, that they which commit such things are worthy of death, not only do the same, but have pleasure in them that do them.

1 Corinthians 6:9 ¶ Know ye not that the unrighteous shall not inherit the kingdom of God? Be not deceived: neither fornicators, nor idolaters, nor adulterers, nor effeminate, nor abusers of themselves with mankind,

10 Nor thieves, nor covetous, nor drunkards, nor revilers, nor extortioners, shall inherit the kingdom of God.

11 And such were some of you: but ye are washed, but ye are sanctified, but ye are justified in the name of the Lord Jesus, and by the Spirit of our God.

12 ¶ All things are lawful unto me, but all things are not expedient: all things are lawful for me, but I will not be brought under the power of any.

13 Meats for the belly, and the belly for meats: but God shall destroy both it and them. Now the body is not for fornication, but for the Lord; and the Lord for the body.

14 And God hath both raised up the Lord, and will also raise up us by his own power.

15 Know ye not that your bodies are the members of Christ? shall I then take the members of Christ, and make them the members of an harlot? God forbid.

16 What? know ye not that he which is joined to an harlot is one body? for two, saith he, shall be one flesh.

17 But he that is joined unto the Lord is one spirit.

18 Flee fornication. Every sin that a man doeth is without the body; but he that committeth fornication sinneth against his own body.

19 What? know ye not that your body is the temple of the Holy Ghost which is in you, which ye have of God, and ye are not your own?

20 For ye are bought with a price: therefore glorify God in your body, and in your spirit, which are God's.

Galatians 5:19 Now the works of the flesh are manifest, which are these; Adultery, fornication, uncleanness, lasciviousness,

20 Idolatry, witchcraft, hatred, variance, emulations, wrath, strife, seditions, heresies,

21 Envyings, murders, drunkenness, revellings, and such like: of the which I tell you before, as I have also told you in time past, that they which do such things shall not inherit the kingdom of God.

Ephesians 5:3 But fornication, and all uncleanness, or covetousness, let it not be once named among you, as becometh saints;

Colossians 3:5 Mortify therefore your members which are upon the earth; fornication, uncleanness, inordinate affection, evil concupiscence, and covetousness, which is idolatry:

1 Thessalonians 4:3 For this is the will of God, even your sanctification, that ye should abstain from fornication:

Jude 1:7 Even as Sodom and Gomorrha, and the cities about them in like manner, giving themselves over to fornication, and going after strange flesh, are set forth for an example, suffering the vengeance of eternal fire.

Revelation 2:14 But I have a few things against thee, because thou hast there them that hold the doctrine of Balaam, who taught Balac to cast a stumbling block before the children of Israel, to eat things sacrificed unto idols, and to commit fornication.

Revelation 2:20 Notwithstanding I have a few things against thee, because thou sufferest that woman Jezebel, which calleth herself a prophetess, to teach and to seduce my servants to commit fornication, and to eat things sacrificed unto idols.

Revelation 2:21 And I gave her space to repent of her fornication; and she repented not.

Revelation 9:21 Neither repented they of their murders, nor of their sorceries, nor of their fornication, nor of their thefts.

Fornication and Adultery

Consider that these verses were written to people who had obeyed Acts 2:38, people who were real Christians. There is both a physical fornication and adultery, and a spiritual fornication (such as if a real Christian would visit a trinity church).

> Rom 1:28 And even as they did not like to retain God in their knowledge, God gave them over to a reprobate mind, to do those things which are not convenient;
>
> Rom 1:29 Being filled with all unrighteousness, fornication, wickedness, covetousness, maliciousness; full of envy, murder, debate, deceit, malignity; whisperers,
>
> Rom 1:30 Backbiters, haters of God, despiteful, proud, boasters, inventors of evil things, disobedient to parents,
>
> 1 Cor 6:13 Meats for the belly, and the belly for meats: but God shall destroy both it and them. Now the body is not for fornication, but for the Lord; and the Lord for the body.
>
> 1 Cor 6:15 Know ye not that your bodies are the members of Christ? shall I then take the members of Christ, and make them the members of an harlot? God forbid.
>
> 1 Cor 6:16 What? know ye not that he which is joined to an harlot is one body? for two, saith he, shall be one flesh.
>
> 1 Cor 6:17 But he that is joined unto the Lord is one spirit.
>
> 1 Cor 6:18 Flee fornication. Every sin that a man doeth is without the body; but he that committeth fornication sinneth against his own body.

Flee both physical AND spiritual fornication.

> 1 Cor 6:19 What? know ye not that your body is the temple of the Holy Ghost which is in you, which ye have of God, and ye are not your own?
>
> 1 Cor 6:20 For ye are bought with a price: therefore glorify God in your body, and in your spirit, which are God's.

Gal 5:19 Now the works of the flesh are manifest, which are these; Adultery, fornication, uncleanness, lasciviousness,

Gal 5:20 Idolatry, witchcraft, hatred, variance, emulations, wrath, strife, seditions, heresies,

Gal 5:21 Envyings, murders, drunkenness, revellings, and such like: of the which I tell you before, as I have also told you in time past, that they which do such things shall not inherit the kingdom of God.

Eph 5:3 But fornication, and all uncleanness, or covetousness, let it not be once named among you, as becometh saints;

1 Th 4:3 For this is the will of God, even your sanctification, that ye should abstain from fornication:

1 Th 4:4 That every one of you should know how to possess his vessel in sanctification and honour;

Repent or Perish

Repentance involves a change! When someone repents of something there is a change. When a smoker repents they quit. When a fornicator repents they STOP committing fornication. etc and etc. True repentance produces a drastic change in behavior.

> Luke 13:3 I tell you, Nay: but, except ye repent, ye shall all likewise perish.
>
> 2 And Jesus answering said unto them, Suppose ye that these Galilaeans were sinners above all the Galilaeans, because they suffered such things?
>
> 3 I tell you, Nay: but, except ye repent, ye shall all likewise perish.
>
> 4 Or those eighteen, upon whom the tower in Siloam fell, and slew them, think ye that they were sinners above all men that dwelt in Jerusalem?
>
> 5 I tell you, Nay: but, except ye repent, ye shall all likewise perish.
>
> 6 ¶ He spake also this parable; A certain man had a fig tree planted in his vineyard; and he came and sought fruit thereon, and found none.
>
> 7 Then said he unto the dresser of his vineyard, Behold, these three years I come seeking fruit on this fig tree, and find none: cut it down; why cumbereth it the ground?
>
> 8 And he answering said unto him, Lord, let it alone this year also, till I shall dig about it, and dung it:
>
> 9 And if it bear fruit, well: and if not, then after that thou shalt cut it down.
>
> 10 ¶ And he was teaching in one of the synagogues on the sabbath.

11 And, behold, there was a woman which had a spirit of infirmity eighteen years, and was bowed together, and could in no wise lift up herself.

12 And when Jesus saw her, he called her to him, and said unto her, Woman, thou art loosed from thine infirmity.

13 And he laid his hands on her: and immediately she was made straight, and glorified God.

14 And the ruler of the synagogue answered with indignation, because that Jesus had healed on the sabbath day, and said unto the people, There are six days in which men ought to work: in them therefore come and be healed, and not on the sabbath day.

15 The Lord then answered him, and said, Thou hypocrite, doth not each one of you on the sabbath loose his ox or his ass from the stall, and lead him away to watering?

16 And ought not this woman, being a daughter of Abraham, whom Satan hath bound, lo, these eighteen years, be loosed from this bond on the sabbath day?

17 And when he had said these things, all his adversaries were ashamed: and all the people rejoiced for all the glorious things that were done by him.

Revelation 2:13 I know thy works, and where thou dwellest, even where Satan's seat is: and thou holdest fast my name, and hast not denied my faith, even in those days wherein Antipas was my faithful martyr, who was slain among you, where Satan dwelleth.

14 But I have a few things against thee, because thou hast there them that hold the doctrine of Balaam, who taught Balac to cast a stumblingblock before the children of Israel, to eat things sacrificed unto idols, and to commit fornication.

15 So hast thou also them that hold the doctrine of the Nicolaitans, which thing I hate.

16 Repent; or else I will come unto thee quickly, and will fight against them with the sword of my mouth.

> 17 He that hath an ear, let him hear what the Spirit saith unto the churches; To him that overcometh will I give to eat of the hidden manna, and will give him a white stone, and in the stone a new name written, which no man knoweth saving he that receiveth it.

Even real Churches that have gone bad and have departed from the Word of God, measuring themselves by themselves rather than by the Word of God, their only hope is REPENTANCE. They have to STOP defying the Word of God.

> Jeremiah 18:10 If it do evil in my sight, that it obey not my voice, then I will repent of the good, wherewith I said I would benefit them.
>
> Jeremiah 26:3 If so be they will hearken, and turn every man from his evil way, that I may repent me of the evil, which I purpose to do unto them because of the evil of their doings.

God will repent of his judgments for those who repent of their transgressions.

God has such wonderful promises for those who obey His Word!

> Revelation 21:1 ¶ And I saw a new heaven and a new earth: for the first heaven and the first earth were passed away; and there was no more sea.
>
> 2 And I John saw the holy city, new Jerusalem, coming down from God out of heaven, prepared as a bride adorned for her husband.
>
> 3 And I heard a great voice out of heaven saying, Behold, the tabernacle of God is with men, and he will dwell with them, and they shall be his people, and God himself shall be with them, and be their God.
>
> 4 And God shall wipe away all tears from their eyes; and there shall be no more death, neither sorrow, nor crying,

neither shall there be any more pain: for the former things are passed away.

5 And he that sat upon the throne said, Behold, I make all things new. And he said unto me, Write: for these words are true and faithful.

6 And he said unto me, It is done. I am Alpha and Omega, the beginning and the end. I will give unto him that is athirst of the fountain of the water of life freely.

7 He that overcometh shall inherit all things; and I will be his God, and he shall be my son.

8 But the fearful, and unbelieving, and the abominable, and murderers, and whoremongers, and sorcerers, and idolaters, and all liars, shall have their part in the lake which burneth with fire and brimstone: which is the second death.

We are reading the wonderful things of God and then it says "BUT"!

Acts 26:12 Whereupon as I went to Damascus with authority and commission from the chief priests,

13 At midday, O king, I saw in the way a light from heaven, above the brightness of the sun, shining round about me and them which journeyed with me.

14 And when we were all fallen to the earth, I heard a voice speaking unto me, and saying in the Hebrew tongue, Saul, Saul, why persecutest thou me? it is hard for thee to kick against the pricks.

15 And I said, Who art thou, Lord? And he said, I am Jesus whom thou persecutest.

16 But rise, and stand upon thy feet: for I have appeared unto thee for this purpose, to make thee a minister and a witness both of these things which thou hast seen, and of those things in the which I will appear unto thee;

17 Delivering thee from the people, and from the Gentiles, unto whom now I send thee,

> 18 To open their eyes, and to turn them from darkness to light, and from the power of Satan unto God, that they may receive forgiveness of sins, and inheritance among them which are sanctified by faith that is in me.
>
> 19 Whereupon, O king Agrippa, I was not disobedient unto the heavenly vision:
>
> 20 But shewed first unto them of Damascus, and at Jerusalem, and throughout all the coasts of Judaea, and then to the Gentiles, that they should repent and turn to God, and do works meet for repentance.

Works meet for repentance! REAL repentance produces a drastic change in a person.

> Ezekiel 14:6 Therefore say unto the house of Israel, Thus saith the Lord GOD; Repent, and turn yourselves from your idols; and turn away your faces from all your abominations.
>
> 7 For every one of the house of Israel, or of the stranger that sojourneth in Israel, which separateth himself from me, and setteth up his idols in his heart, and putteth the stumblingblock of his iniquity before his face, and cometh to a prophet to enquire of him concerning me; I the LORD will answer him by myself:
>
> 8 And I will set my face against that man, and will make him a sign and a proverb, and I will cut him off from the midst of my people; and ye shall know that I am the LORD.

Turn your faces away from evil! Real Christians do not sit in front of a TV or a movie and put abominations in front of their faces.

> Acts 2:38 Then Peter said unto them, Repent, and be baptized every one of you in the name of Jesus Christ for the remission of sins, and ye shall receive the gift of the Holy Ghost.

39 For the promise is unto you, and to your children, and to all that are afar off, even as many as the Lord our God shall call.

40 And with many other words did he testify and exhort, saying, Save yourselves from this untoward generation.

41 Then they that gladly received his word were baptized: and the same day there were added unto them about three thousand souls.

42 ¶ And they continued stedfastly in the apostles' doctrine and fellowship, and in breaking of bread, and in prayers.

Snuff

From the scriptures I discern that a person in hell would prefer to warn of their fate rather than to soothe others with same destination. Here is the scriptural basis for this:

> Luke 16:25 But Abraham said, Son, remember that thou in thy lifetime receivedst thy good things, and likewise Lazarus evil things: but now he is comforted, and thou art tormented.
>
> Luke 16:26 And beside all this, between us and you there is a great gulf fixed: so that they which would pass from hence to you cannot; neither can they pass to us, that [would come] from thence.
>
> Luke 16:27 Then he said, I pray thee therefore, father, that thou wouldest send him to my father's house:
>
> Luke 16:28 For I have five brethren; that he may testify unto them, lest they also come into this place of torment.

* Assuming a person had obeyed the Gospel and had become a Christian, then the book of Corinthians would apply to them. There are also many ways short of suicide for one to defile oneself. *

> I Corinthians 3:16 Know ye not that ye are the temple of God, and [that] the Spirit of God dwelleth in you?
>
> I Corinthians 3:17 If any man defile the temple of God, him shall God destroy; for the temple of God is holy, which [temple] ye are.

* Among those who do really become Christians, only those that "endure to the end" will be saved. *

> Matthew 10:22 And ye shall be hated of all [men] for my name's sake: but he that endureth to the end shall be saved.
>
> I Corinthians 6:9 Know ye not that the unrighteous shall not inherit the kingdom of God? Be not deceived: neither

fornicators, nor idolaters, nor adulterers, nor effeminate, nor abusers of themselves with mankind,

I Corinthians 6:10 Nor thieves, nor covetous, nor drunkards, nor revilers, nor extortioners, shall inherit the kingdom of God.

* I see no kindness or love in offering sugar coated lies. *

Holy Hair

I Corinthians 11:14 Doth not even nature itself teach you, that, if a man have long hair, it is a shame unto him?

I Corinthians 11:15 But if a woman have long hair, it is a glory to her: for [her] hair is given her for a covering.

** What true Christian woman is going to remove a portion of her "glory" to conform to the worldly dictates? **

I Timothy 2:9 In like manner also, that women adorn themselves inmodest apparel, with shamefacedness and sobriety; not with broided hair, or gold, or pearls, or costly array;

I Timothy 2:10 But (which becometh women professing godliness) with good works.

*** "Shamefaced" = "Plainfaced"

Modest = covering the body, not partially naked.

I Timothy 2:11 Let the woman learn in silence with all subjection.

I Peter 3:3 Whose adorning let it not be that outward [adorning] of plaiting the hair, and of wearing of gold, or of putting on of apparel;

I Peter 3:4 But [let it be] the hidden man of the heart, in that which is not corruptible, [even the ornament] of a meek and quiet spirit, which is in the sight of God of great price.

I Peter 3:5 For after this manner in the old time the holy women also, who trusted in God, adorned themselves, being in subjection unto their own husbands:

I Peter 3:6 Even as Sara obeyed Abraham, calling him lord: whose daughters ye are, as long as ye do well, and are not afraid with any amazement.

Deuteronomy 22:5 The woman shall not wear that which pertaineth unto a man, neither shall a man put on a woman's garment: for all that do so [are] abomination unto the LORD thy God.

** If it was abomination then, it is abomination now...***

Psalms 101:3 I will set no wicked thing before mine eyes: I hate the work of them that turn aside; [it] shall not cleave to me.

** TV, Movies etc.. **

Romans 1:32 Who knowing the judgment of God, that they which commit such things are worthy of death, not only do the same, but have pleasure in them that do them.

Matthew 6:21 For where your treasure is, there will your heart be also.

Matthew 6:22 The light of the body is the eye: if therefore thine eye be single, thy whole body shall be full of light.

Matthew 6:23 But if thine eye be evil, thy whole body shall be full of darkness. If therefore the light that is in thee be darkness, how great [is] that darkness!

Matthew 6:24 No man can serve two masters: for either he will hate the one, and love the other; or else he will hold to the one, and despise the other. Ye cannot serve God and mammon.

I Corinthians 11:6 For if the woman be not covered, let her also be shorn: but if it be a shame for a woman to be shorn or shaven, let her be covered.

** If a woman even trims her hair she might as well shave it all in the sight of God **

I Corinthians 11:7 For a man indeed ought not to cover [his] head, forasmuch as he is the image and glory of God: but the woman is the glory of the man.

I Corinthians 11:8 For the man is not of the woman; but the woman of the man.

I Corinthians 11:9 Neither was the man created for the woman; but the woman for the man.

I Corinthians 11:11 Nevertheless neither is the man without the woman, neither the woman without the man, in the Lord.

I Corinthians 11:15 But if a woman have long hair, it is a glory to her: for [her] hair is given her for a covering.

** What is a woman's covering? Her hair.

Hebrews 12:14 Follow peace with all men, and holiness, without which no man shall see the Lord:

Hair

I Timothy 2:9 In like manner also, that women adorn themselves in modest apparel, with shamefacedness and sobriety; not with broided hair, or gold, or pearls, or costly array;

I Timothy 2:10 But (which becometh women professing godliness) with good works.

Shamefacedness means "plain faced, not "painted up" in the worldly style, not wearing gold or pearls etc...Modest apparel also means clothes that cover the body, that do not expose nakedness, that do not generate lust, modest apparel: Christians don't wear shorts they don't expose their bodies by mixed bathing (swimming)...they don't run the streets naked with the heathen (remember, to Adam & Eve the fig leaf was sufficient, BUT GOD MADE THEM COATS! THE FIG LEAF APRON WASN'T ENOUGH!!

I Corinthians 11:5 But every woman that prayeth or prophesieth with [her] head uncovered dishonoureth her head: for that is even all one as if she were shaven.

I Corinthians 11:6 For if the woman be not covered, let her also be shorn: but if it be a shame for a woman to be shorn or shaven, let her be covered.

Now 11:15 says what the covering is, it's HAIR, so it's saying that if she is going to cut her hair, she might as well be shaved bald, but since it would be a shame for her to be shaved bald, let her remain covered (covered with hair, UNCUT).

I Corinthians 11:14 Doth not even nature itself teach you, that, if a man have long hair, it is a shame unto him?

I Corinthians 11:15 But if a woman have long hair, it is a glory to her: for [her] hair is given her for a covering.

No woman that *really* loves God with all her heart, soul, and strength (which is part of the first commandment), is going to brazenly trim off her glory to fit the worldly *styles*.

> Deuteronomy 22:5 The woman shall not wear that which pertaineth unto a man, neither shall a man put on a woman's garment: for ALL that do so [are] abomination unto the LORD thy God.

Women who wear pants, pantsuits, or any other form of trousers are abomination to God just as much as men who wear dresses.

> II Timothy 3:16 All scripture [is] given by inspiration of God, and [is] profitable for doctrine, for reproof, for correction, for instruction in righteousness:

ALL SCRIPTURE!!! ALL SCRIPTURE!!!

> II Timothy 3:17 That the man of God may be perfect, throughly furnished unto all good works.
>
> II Timothy 4:2 Preach the word; be instant in season, out of season; reprove, rebuke, exhort with all longsuffering and doctrine.
>
> II Timothy 4:3 For the time will come when they will not endure sound doctrine; but after their own lusts shall they heap to themselves teachers, having itching ears;
>
> II Timothy 4:4 And they shall turn away [their] ears from the truth, and shall be turned unto fables.

It's always been the devil's business to convince men that God's word doesn't really mean what it says; likewise it's the job of the false preacher to keep the "damned" comfortable and secure in their fake "salvation"

Beards

This is a study for Acts 2:38 Christians, especially preachers. If you have not obeyed Acts 2:38 to become a Christian I encourage you to do so since it is the plan of salvation for as many as the Lord will call.

> Acts 2:38 Then Peter said unto them, Repent, and be baptized every one of you in the name of Jesus Christ for the remission of sins, and ye shall receive the gift of the Holy Ghost.
>
> 39 For the promise is unto you, and to your children, and to all that are afar off, even as many as the Lord our God shall call.

It says: "As many as the Lord our God shall call." so you do the math.

Moving along.

It has become a tradition among some Acts 2:38 Churches to teach a lie that there is something wrong with having a beard, that it is somehow not holy.

The Bible does teach that it is a shame for a man to have long hair but that is clearly referring to the hair on his head. The Bible clearly distinguishes between a beard and head hair length.

> 1 Corinthians 11:14 Doth not even nature itself teach you, that, if a man have long hair, it is a shame unto him?
>
> 1 Corinthians 11:15 But if a woman have long hair, it is a glory to her: for her hair is given her for a covering.

Clearly the Bible is talking about hair on the head. That is also part of the reason why real Christian women don't cut their hair, but that is another topic.

A study of the Bible regarding beards and the Jewish history simply proves that the normal thing for a man is to have a beard.

I don't have time in this study to read every Bible verse that simply proves how normal it is throughout Bible history for a man to have a beard.

We don't really think that the Jewish men including Jesus shaved their faces to look like Caesar, do we? We know from the scripture that Jesus Himself had a beard.

> Isaiah 50:6 I gave my back to the smiters, and my cheeks to them that
>
> plucked off the hair: I hid not my face from shame and spitting.

Some of you doubters might want to look at some photos of the founders of some of the modern Oneness organizations.

It has become a tradition to teach a lie that there is something wrong with having a beard. I do not teach that it is a sin for a man to shave (unless he did it for effeminate reasons).

The more serious spiritual issue is actually not about beards, but rather about lying since if a preacher teaches that a beard is somehow unholy or sinful, that man is a liar and all liars will have their part in the lake of fire.

So really the issue is not beards, but about lying.

Just look at the corruption and sin in the leadership of some of the biggest Oneness organizations. They have been measuring themselves by themselves for a long long time. The phrase "we dare not" appears only once in the entire Bible!

> 2 Corinthians 10:12 For we dare not make ourselves of the number, or compare ourselves with some that commend themselves: but they measuring themselves by themselves, and comparing themselves among themselves, are not wise.
>
> 1 Chronicles 19:4 Wherefore Hanun took David's servants, and shaved them, and cut off their garments in the midst hard by their buttocks, and sent them away.

Men without beards in many cases were ASHAMED! That proves that beards were/are NORMAL for a MAN!

> 2 Samuel 10:5 When they told it unto David, he sent to meet them, because the men were greatly ashamed: and the king said, Tarry at Jericho until your beards be grown, and then return.
>
> 1 Chronicles 19:5 Then there went certain, and told David how the men were served. And he sent to meet them: for the men were greatly ashamed. And the king said, Tarry at Jericho until your beards be grown, and then return.

Someone has been lying to someone about beards being unholy, and all liars will have their part in the lake of fire. If you reject a man because he has a beard, let me point out another that you also reject.

> Isaiah 50:6 I gave my back to the smiters, and my cheeks to them that plucked off the hair: I hid not my face from shame and spitting.

So the real issue here has not to do with beards but rather with lying and heresy. Preaching against beards is quite simply heresy and it is lying.

So let's look at what God has promised for all unrepentant liars (regardless of whether they carry cards from any organization).

> Revelation 21:8 But the fearful, and unbelieving, and the abominable, and murderers, and whoremongers, and sorcerers, and idolaters, and all liars, shall have their part in the lake which burneth with fire and brimstone: which is the second death.

So what does God have in store for these men who preach against beards?

It will be no "clean shaven" Caesar looking individual who casts them into the lake of fire because we know that Jesus Christ had a beard (which is simply the normal state of a man).

Amazing the number of so called "churches" where neither Jesus Christ nor any of His Apostles would be allowed on their platforms!

Lying and heresy are SINS!

> Galatians 5:20 Idolatry, witchcraft, hatred, variance, emulations, wrath, strife, seditions, heresies,
>
> 21 Envyings, murders, drunkenness, revellings, and such like: of the which I tell you before, as I have also told you in time past, that they which do such things shall not inherit the kingdom of God.

So we see basically that a preacher teaching against beards might as well be practicing witchcraft.

A preacher is ordered to "preach the Word", not his personal whim and fancy based upon his tradition!

> 2 Timothy 4:2 Preach the word; be instant in season, out of season; reprove, rebuke, exhort with all longsuffering and doctrine.

So if you are a preacher and you have ever preached against beards you need to repent of your lying and heresy and beg God for forgiveness. You might want to keep in mind that the Lord Jesus Christ you are praying to also wears a beard.

Unrepented lying and heresy will send anyone to hell regardless of their organizational position or traditional whim and fancy.

Meats

I understand that to have dedicated oneself to a premise and to discover that it was a false premise can be painful, but it is still better to know the truth. I spent quite a few years as a vegetarian myself before I became a Christian. There are things that are important to God and other things that are not important.

> John 8:32 And ye shall know the truth, and the truth shall make you free.

Here we see that Jesus asked for meat to eat, was given fish and then ate it. I fear that someone has misled some of you about what the Bible teaches about diet.

> Luke 24:36 ¶ And as they thus spake, Jesus himself stood in the midst of them, and saith unto them, Peace be unto you.
>
> 37 But they were terrified and affrighted, and supposed that they had seen a spirit.
>
> 38 And he said unto them, Why are ye troubled? and why do thoughts arise in your hearts?
>
> 39 Behold my hands and my feet, that it is I myself: handle me, and see; for a spirit hath not flesh and bones, as ye see me have.
>
> 40 And when he had thus spoken, he shewed them his hands and his feet.
>
> 41 And while they yet believed not for joy, and wondered, he said unto them, Have ye here any meat?
>
> 42 And they gave him a piece of a broiled fish, and of an honeycomb.
>
> 43 And he took it, and did eat before them.

> John 21:13 Jesus then cometh, and taketh bread, and giveth them, and fish likewise.

14 This is now the third time that Jesus shewed himself to his disciples, after that he was risen from the dead.

15 ¶ So when they had dined, Jesus saith to Simon Peter, Simon, son of Jonas, lovest thou me more than these? He saith unto him, Yea, Lord; thou knowest that I love thee. He saith unto him, Feed my lambs.

1 Corinthians 8:8 But meat commendeth us not to God: for neither, if we eat, are we the better; neither, if we eat not, are we the worse.

Romans 14:¶ Him that is weak in the faith receive ye, but not to doubtful disputations.

2 For one believeth that he may eat all things: another, who is weak, eateth herbs.

Here is a warning regarding any group that would teach one to abstain from meats. I encourage you to look these verses up in greater context.

1 Timothy 4:3 Forbidding to marry, and commanding to abstain from meats, which God hath created to be received with thanksgiving of them which believe and know the truth.

1 Timothy 4:4 For every creature of God is good, and nothing to be refused, if it be received with thanksgiving:

All of this is moot unless a person has obeyed Acts 2:38 to really become a Biblical Christian. That is something that IS of Great importance to God. Notice how Acts 2:38 is for as many as the Lord will call.

Acts 2:38 Then Peter said unto them, Repent, and be baptized every one of you in the name of Jesus Christ for the remission of sins, and ye shall receive the gift of the Holy Ghost.

39 For the promise is unto you, and to your children, and to all that are afar off, even as many as the Lord our God shall call.

40 And with many other words did he testify and exhort, saying, Save yourselves from this untoward generation.

41 Then they that gladly received his word were baptized: and the same day there were added unto them about three thousand souls.

Goats

The Bible speaks of a true church that is the bride of Christ. It also speaks of a false church "the Great Whore" and her harlot daughters, or the churches that denominated from her.

> Rev 17:5 And upon her forehead was a name written, MYSTERY, BABYLON THE GREAT, THE MOTHER OF HARLOTS AND ABOMINATIONS OF THE EARTH.

The Bible also speaks of sheep and goats, referring to those of like spirit.

> Mat 25:33 And he shall set the sheep on his right hand, but the goats on the left.

A true bride is looking for ways to please the groom, she does not have to be constantly berated with his wishes. A hint that something is offensive to the groom is enough..

> Mark 12:30 And thou shalt love the Lord thy God with all thy heart, and with all thy soul, and with all thy mind, and with all thy strength: this is the first commandment.

A whore on the other hand sees very little wrong in anything, as the modern day charismatic false Christian. Spiritual whores that ignore the principles of holy living, clinging to their former loves (the ways of the world)...They assume that if the Bible doesn't expressly forbid something, that they have license to wallow in it; ignoring the basic principles set forth in the Word of God...

> Prov 30:20 Such is the way of an adulterous woman; she eateth, and wipeth her mouth, and saith, I have done no wickedness.

And the whores see no real need for real pastors, they see no need to submit to a true Christian spiritual leader, if anything they want a mealy figurehead. They draw to themselves many teachers having itching ears...They love a false preacher to twist the Word of God and tell them that they're OK...

> 2 Tim 4:3 For the time will come when they will not endure sound doctrine; but after their own lusts shall they heap to themselves teachers, having itching ears;
>
> 2 Tim 4:4 And they shall turn away their ears from the truth, and shall be turned unto fables.

As the whore sees no need in being married and taking on the name of the man, the harlot churches see no real need in taking on Jesus' name in baptism.

> Gal 3:27 For as many of you as have been baptized into Christ have put on Christ.

Just a few thoughts about spirits I wanted to share, because the goats and sheep will one day be separated, and all the scholarship and education in the world won't be a consideration at all...only the spirit of the individual. The obedient sheep on one side, and the rebellious goats on another. The bride without spot or blemish on one side, and the whorish, worldly, brazen false church on the other.

> Rev 21:8 But the fearful, and unbelieving, and the abominable, and murderers, and whoremongers, and sorcerers, and idolaters, and all liars, shall have their part in the lake which burneth with fire and brimstone: which is the second death.

I hope this helps.

Separate

> 2 Corinthians 6:14 Be ye not unequally yoked together with unbelievers: for what fellowship hath righteousness with unrighteousness? and what communion hath light with darkness?
>
> 15 And what concord hath Christ with Belial? or what part hath he that believeth with an infidel?
>
> 16 And what agreement hath the temple of God with idols? for ye are the temple of the living God; as God hath said, I will dwell in them, and walk in them; and I will be their God, and they shall be my people.
>
> 17 Wherefore come out from among them, and be ye separate, saith the Lord, and touch not the unclean thing; and I will receive you,
>
> 18 And will be a Father unto you, and ye shall be my sons and daughters, saith the Lord Almighty.
>
> 1 ¶ Having therefore these promises, dearly beloved, let us cleanse ourselves from all filthiness of the flesh and spirit, perfecting holiness in the fear of God.

Many teach that verse 14 speaks of being married to a non-believer and I wholeheartedly agree. That verse certainly teaches that, but it also teaches much more. For example a Christian would not be wise to enter into a business partnership with a non-believer. That is not to say that Christians would not do business with non-believers but I would hope all would be able to see the difference between shopping at someones store and going into partnership with them.

When it comes to one who teaches a false doctrine the Bible has different commandments.

> Galatians 1:8 But though we, or an angel from heaven, preach any other gospel unto you than that which we have preached unto you, let him be accursed.

> Galatians 1:9 As we said before, so say I now again, If any man preach any other gospel unto you than that ye have received, let him be accursed.

Many spiritually unchaste would deny that the above verses were commandments, but if they are not then what are they, helpful suggestions? What other commandment in the Bible is actually repeated in the next verse? How can any Saint who has had kin deceived into hell by some trinity preacher not understand the importance of those commandments?

> 2 Corinthians 11:1 Would to God ye could bear with me a little in my folly: and indeed bear with me.
>
> 2 For I am jealous over you with godly jealousy: for I have espoused you to one husband, that I may present you as a chaste virgin to Christ.
>
> 3 But I fear, lest by any means, as the serpent beguiled Eve through his subtilty, so your minds should be corrupted from the simplicity that is in Christ.
>
> 4 For if he that cometh preacheth another Jesus, whom we have not preached, or if ye receive another spirit, which ye have not received, or another gospel, which ye have not accepted, ye might well bear with him.
>
> 5 ¶ For I suppose I was not a whit behind the very chiefest apostles.
>
> 6 But though I be rude in speech, yet not in knowledge; but we have been throughly made manifest among you in all things.

How does God define spiritual unchastity? Can it be that simply "bearing with" a deceiver is considered by God Himself to be "unchaste behaviour"?

> Romans 12:1 I beseech you therefore, brethren, by the mercies of God, that ye present your bodies a living sacrifice, holy, acceptable unto God, which is your reasonable service.

> 2 And be not conformed to this world: but be ye transformed by the renewing of your mind, that ye may prove what is that good, and acceptable, and perfect, will of God.

We are in a time when even so called "Oneness" Christians will conform to the world in heathen celebration that has nothing to do with Jesus.

> Revelation 21:27 And there shall in no wise enter into it any thing that defileth, neither whatsoever worketh abomination, or maketh a lie: but they which are written in the Lamb's book of life.

> Revelation 22:15 For without are dogs, and sorcerers, and whoremongers, and murderers, and idolaters, and whosoever loveth and maketh a lie.

Bearing

God does not want His ministers "bearing with" or otherwise tolerating false preachers.

> II Corinthians 11:12 But what I do, that I will do, that I may cut off occasion from them which desire occasion; that wherein they glory, they may be found even as we.
>
> II Corinthians 11:13 For such [are] false apostles, deceitful workers, transforming themselves into the apostles of Christ.
>
> II Corinthians 11:14 And no marvel; for Satan himself is transformed into an angel of light.
>
> II Corinthians 11:15 Therefore [it is] no great thing if his ministers also be transformed as the ministers of righteousness; whose end shall be according to their works.
>
> II Corinthians 11:16 I say again, Let no man think me a fool; if otherwise, yet as a fool receive me, that I may boast myself a little.
>
> II Corinthians 11:17 That which I speak, I speak [it] not after the Lord, but as it were foolishly, in this confidence of boasting.
>
> II Corinthians 11:18 Seeing that many glory after the flesh, I will glory also.
>
> II Corinthians 11:19 For ye suffer fools gladly, seeing ye [yourselves] are wise.
>
> II Corinthians 11:2 For I am jealous over you with godly jealousy: for I have espoused you to one husband, that I may present [you as] a chaste virgin to Christ.
>
> II Corinthians 11:3 But I fear, lest by any means, as the serpent beguiled Eve through his subtilty, so your minds should be corrupted from the simplicity that is in Christ.

II Corinthians 11:4 For if he that cometh preacheth another Jesus, whom we have not preached, or [if] ye receive another spirit, which ye

have not received, or another gospel, which ye have not accepted, ye might well bear with [him].

Galatians 1:8 But though we, or an angel from heaven, preach any other gospel unto you than that which we have preached unto you, let him be accursed.

Galatians 1:9 As we said before, so say I now again, If any [man] preach any other gospel unto you than that ye have received, let him be accursed.

Galatians 1:10 For do I now persuade men, or God? or do I seek to please men? for if I yet pleased men, I should not be the servant of Christ.

II John 1:9 Whosoever transgresseth, and abideth not in the doctrine of Christ, hath not God. He that abideth in the doctrine of Christ, he hath both the Father and the Son.

II John 1:10 If there come any unto you, and bring not this doctrine, receive him not into [your] house, neither bid him God speed:

II John 1:11 For he that biddeth him God speed is partaker of his evil deeds.

Lying

Many find that it is the easy way when facing a difficult or even inconvenient situation to simply lie. I know of a United Pentecostal Church International preacher that not only will lie, but encourages others to lie as well.

There are some who feel that lying can be the "kind" thing to do in order to avoid conflict. But lying is a very serious matter. Trust lost may never be regained and so many will lie much more than they originally intended to try to cover their "small" lie. They have to keep telling bigger lies to cover their previous lying.

The devil himself is the father of lies.

> John 8:44 Ye are of your father the devil, and the lusts of your father ye will do. He was a murderer from the beginning, and abode not in the truth, because there is no truth in him. When he speaketh a lie, he speaketh of his own: for he is a liar, and the father of it.

There is not much sin warned against in the Word of God more serious than lying. I believe that there is not much that is more offensive to God than a liar.

> Isaiah 44:25 That frustrateth the tokens of the liars, and maketh diviners mad; that turneth wise men backward, and maketh their knowledge foolish;

Consider the company that liars are listed among in the Word of God.

> 1 Timothy 1:10 For whoremongers, for them that defile themselves with mankind, for menstealers, for liars, for perjured persons, and if there be any other thing that is contrary to sound doctrine;

No unrepentant liar should in their remotest dreams think that they will be saved.

So does that mean there is no hope for the liar? No, but the only hope of the liar is to REPENT of their lying and repentance means QUITTING. A smoker that repents of smoking QUITS SMOKING! If they don't quit, then they didn't really repent!

> Luke 13:3 I tell you, Nay: but, except ye repent, ye shall all likewise perish.
>
> Revelation 21:8 But the fearful, and unbelieving, and the abominable, and murderers, and whoremongers, and sorcerers, and idolaters, and all liars, shall have their part in the lake which burneth with fire and brimstone: which is the second death.

There are very few cases in the New Testament of individuals being actually struck down dead by God on the spot. Consider this study and the sin that was committed.

> Acts 5:1 ¶ But a certain man named Ananias, with Sapphira his wife, sold a possession,
>
> 2 And kept back part of the price, his wife also being privy to it, and brought a certain part, and laid it at the apostles' feet.
>
> 3 But Peter said, Ananias, why hath Satan filled thine heart to lie to the Holy Ghost, and to keep back part of the price of the land?
>
> 4 Whiles it remained, was it not thine own? and after it was sold, was it not in thine own power? why hast thou conceived this thing in thine heart? thou hast not lied unto men, but unto God.
>
> 5 And Ananias hearing these words fell down, and gave up the ghost: and great fear came on all them that heard these things.
>
> 6 And the young men arose, wound him up, and carried him out, and buried him.
>
> 7 And it was about the space of three hours after, when his wife, not knowing what was done, came in.

> 8 And Peter answered unto her, Tell me whether ye sold the land for so much? And she said, Yea, for so much.
>
> 9 Then Peter said unto her, How is it that ye have agreed together to tempt the Spirit of the Lord? behold, the feet of them which have buried thy husband are at the door, and shall carry thee out.
>
> 10 Then fell she down straightway at his feet, and yielded up the ghost: and the young men came in, and found her dead, and, carrying her forth, buried her by her husband.
>
> 11 And great fear came upon all the church, and upon as many as heard these things.

Notice when Peter spoke to Ananias in verse 4. Why did they lie if not just so people would feel a certain way about them? Did they not lie and die for fellowship, popularity? Think about that point. What a shame! They were under no obligation or anything; this was a voluntary giving situation. They lied just for popularity!

There are a lot of modern day people, even so called "preachers" that need to consider how God feels about lying.

> Proverbs 22:1 A good name is rather to be chosen than great riches, and loving favour rather than silver and gold.

This does not mean that lying is some unforgivable sin. All have lied at some point in their life, all have been sinners at some point in their life but for someone to deliberately lie after having obeyed Acts 2:38, is a grievous matter. The cure for lying is repentance as it is for other sin.

But for an obeyer of Acts 2:38 to deliberately sin is a dangerous thing.

> Hebrews 10:26 For if we sin wilfully after that we have received the knowledge of the truth, there remaineth no more sacrifice for sins,
>
> 27 But a certain fearful looking for of judgment and fiery indignation, which shall devour the adversaries.
>
> 28 He that despised Moses' law died without mercy under two or three witnesses:

29 Of how much sorer punishment, suppose ye, shall he be thought worthy, who hath trodden under foot the Son of God, and hath counted the blood of the covenant, wherewith he was sanctified, an unholy thing, and hath done despite unto the Spirit of grace?

That is the grievous situation of the reprobate and the infidel and others who deliberately engage in sinful activity after obeying Acts 2:38 and why we almost never see a reprobate or infidel come to repentance. I don't know of any!

God draws a distinction between regular sinners and sinners who are pretending to be Christians.

1 Cor 5:9 I wrote unto you in an epistle not to company with fornicators:

10 Yet not altogether with the fornicators of this world, or with the covetous, or extortioners, or with idolaters; for then must ye needs go out of the world.

11 But now I have written unto you not to keep company, if any man that is called a brother be a fornicator, or covetous, or an idolater, or a railer, or a drunkard, or an extortioner; with such an one no not to eat.

12 For what have I to do to judge them also that are without? do not ye judge them that are within?

13 But them that are without God judgeth. Therefore put away from among yourselves that wicked person.

Is there any of age past infancy who has not at some point had someone deliberately lie to them? Once that happened it is hard if not impossible to ever trust that person. Trust that is betrayed is rarely restored.

Psalms 101:7 He that worketh deceit shall not dwell within my house: he that telleth lies shall not tarry in my sight.

Again, according to Jesus Christ who is the father of lies?

> John 8:44 Ye are of your father the devil, and the lusts of your father ye will do. He was a murderer from the beginning, and abode not in the truth, because there is no truth in him. When he speaketh a lie, he speaketh of his own: for he is a liar, and the father of it.

Now I don't mean to say that everyone who is mistaken or misled is necessarily a liar, just like every mistake is not necessarily a sin. But deliberate lying and other deliberate sin is a grievous thing.

Prayer

When Jehovah Saviour (the ONLY Saviour) took it upon Himself to come to earth in human form to offer Himself as a perfect sacrifice and to set a perfect example for us to follow; he spent much time in his flesh praying to His Spirit.

> I Timothy 3:16 And without controversy great is the mystery of godliness: God was manifest in the flesh, justified in the Spirit, seen of angels, preached unto the Gentiles, believed on in the world, received up into glory.

When Jehovah came in the flesh, he really came in flesh that was "carnal" and "killable". His suffering on earth and on the cross was REAL. He really did become FLESH. He had to keep his flesh in subjection just as any other man. In his flesh, He prayed to His Spirit.

> Heb 4:15 For we have not an high priest which cannot be touched with the feeling of our infirmities; but was in all points tempted like as we are, yet without sin.
>
> Acts 1:11 Which also said, Ye men of Galilee, why stand ye gazing up into heaven? this same Jesus, which is taken up from you into heaven, shall so come in like manner as ye have seen him go into heaven.

* The apostles asked Jesus to teach them how to pray, and Jesus answered them with a pattern or "format" for prayer, a manner of prayer. *

> Matthew 6:9 After this manner therefore pray ye: Our Father which art in heaven, Hallowed be thy name.

Notice that the first part of the prayer acknowledges God, and places GREAT significance on His NAME. (His name is Jesus). Those that have denied His name by refusing it in baptism, or by whatever other method need not continue with this prayer, since they have rejected His name. It is brazen hypocrisy for a trinitarian to pray the Lord's prayer.

> Matthew 6:10 Thy kingdom come. Thy will be done in earth, as [it is] in heaven.

* His earthly kingdom is now "in the Holy Ghost"

> Romans 14:17 For the kingdom of God is not meat and drink; but righteousness, and peace, and joy in the Holy Ghost.

* Then a prayer that His will be done in earth (we are made of earth), noticeL 'IN' earth. *

> Matthew 6:11 Give us this day our daily bread.

* Then after all that, we bring our personal physical needs to Him *

> Matthew 6:12 And forgive us our debts, as we forgive our debtors.

* Then a little soul searching. *

> Matthew 6:13 And lead us not into temptation, but deliver us from evil: For thine is the kingdom, and the power, and the glory, for ever. Amen.

* Of course, to pray to be "not lead into temptation" and "delivered from evil" and then to sit and watch a television or movie is the epitome of sham and hypocrisy. *

> Matthew 6:22 The light of the body is the eye: if therefore thine eye be single, thy whole body shall be full of light.

> Matthew 6:23 But if thine eye be evil, thy whole body shall be full of darkness. If therefore the light that is in thee be darkness, how great [is] that darkness!

> Matthew 6:14 For if ye forgive men their trespasses, your heavenly Father will also forgive you:
>
> Matthew 6:15 But if ye forgive not men their trespasses, neither will your Father forgive your trespasses.

* Then a clear admonition from the Lord. *

There is a pattern to the "Lord's prayer". We must first acknowledge Him as the Father, we then reverence His NAME. Then we pray for His kingdom to be manifest, and His will to be done. We do all that before we even arrive at "presenting our needs".

Infidel

"Infidels" what does that mean?

Consider the term infidelity? See the association? Consider also the related concepts of "chaste" vs. "unchaste". This is also related to "holy" and "unholy".

Can someone who is spiritually unchaste be holy at the same time? Can an unholy, unchaste person be saved? (I speak of the unrepentant here).

We see so called "preachers" licensed by the United Pentecostal Church advocating lying and we see so called "christians" supporting such sin.

> Isaiah 35:8 And an highway shall be there, and a way, and it shall be called The way of holiness; the unclean shall not pass over it; but it shall be for those: the wayfaring men, though fools, shall not err therein.
>
> Romans 1:4 And declared to be the Son of God with power, according to the spirit of holiness, by the resurrection from the dead:
>
> Romans 6:19 I speak after the manner of men because of the infirmity of your flesh: for as ye have yielded your members servants to uncleanness and to iniquity unto iniquity; even so now yield your members servants to righteousness unto holiness.
>
> Romans 6:22 But now being made free from sin, and become servants to God, ye have your fruit unto holiness, and the end everlasting life.
>
> 2 Corinthians 7:1 Having therefore these promises, dearly beloved, let us cleanse ourselves from all filthiness of the flesh and spirit, perfecting holiness in the fear of God.
>
> Ephesians 4:24 And that ye put on the new man, which after God is created in righteousness and true holiness.

Holiness is not some optional issue! Salvation depends on it.

The Bible teaches that merely "bearing with" a teacher of false doctrine makes one "unchaste". Note carefully how Paul is concerned for their chastity.

Keep in mind the relationship of chastity, fidelity and holiness. If that is not enough to convince you notice that Paul is talking about Christians being corrupted!

> 2 Corinthians 11:2 For I am jealous over you with godly jealousy: for I have espoused you to one husband, that I may present you as a chaste virgin to Christ.
>
> 3 But I fear, lest by any means, as the serpent beguiled Eve through his subtilty, so your minds should be corrupted from the simplicity that is in Christ.
>
> 4 For if he that cometh preacheth another Jesus, whom we have not preached, or if ye receive another spirit, which ye have not received, or another gospel, which ye have not accepted, ye might well bear with him.

Now see that the great thing that Paul is so fearful of here is also sin of omission as well. What does it mean to "bear with" someone? Does it not mean to tolerate? Let's look at Strongs. It does not mean that we believe Strong was a Christian to accept that he was an adequate linguist.

> 430 anechomai an-ekh'-om-ahee
>
> middle voice from 303 and 2192; TDNT - 1:359,*; v
>
> AV - suffer 7, bear with 4, forbear 2, endure 2; 15
>
> 1) to hold up
>
> 2) to hold one's self erect and firm
>
> 3) to sustain, to bear, to endure

Consider Paul's fear for the Church that they would become unchaste and corrupt just for "bearing with" a deceiver like a trinitarian.

There is a generation of so called "Oneness Christians" who are devoid of even the concept that there exists such a thing a spiritual chastity, but that is were we get "infidel" from! This generation is a manifestation of the fruits of a generation measuring themselves by themselves and their traditions.

> 2 Corinthians 10:12 For we dare not make ourselves of the number, or compare ourselves with some that commend themselves: but they measuring themselves by themselves, and comparing themselves among themselves, are not wise.

Paul gives the Church commandments as well regarding what to do regarding those who bring false religion to you.

> Galatians 1:8 But though we, or an angel from heaven, preach any other gospel unto you than that which we have preached unto you, let him be accursed.
>
> Galatians 1:9 As we said before, so say I now again, If any man preach any other gospel unto you than that ye have received, let him be accursed.

Let me mention that the phrase "let him be accursed" appears only twice in the Bible. Also note that Paul's commandment is the only commandment that the Bible repeats twice. Some teach that it is not a commandment but these also, in my experience also believe in women preachers, double married preachers and that it is OK for a Saint to attend trinitarian worship services among other things.

It is a sin to merely "bear with" a trinitarian preacher. Now, it is important to realize that every trinitarian is not a preacher, but if a trinitarian is promoting false doctrines, then they are a "preacher". The same individual that I might invite into my home for a visit if they just dropped by, I would probably curse on my doorstep if they came bringing false-christian tracts on behalf of their cult.

The way some of those Mormon boys look at me wide eyed you would think I was the first one to ever curse them in the Name of the Lord Jesus Christ!

> Colossians 3:17 And whatsoever ye do in word or deed, do all in the name of the Lord Jesus, giving thanks to God and the Father by him.

And, if you do not have the scriptural foundation to curse them in the Name of the Lord Jesus, then you better not do it.

Remember, just to bear with someone teaching a false religion is spiritual whoredom. That's right! What do you thing that "unchaste" means?

There is a wedding supper coming up. There is also Great Whore, the mother of all trinity denominations! God chose that terminology, not me!

> Revelation 17:1 And there came one of the seven angels which had the seven vials, and talked with me, saying unto me, Come hither; I will shew unto thee the judgment of the great whore that sitteth upon many waters:
>
> Revelation 17:5 And upon her forehead was a name written, MYSTERY, BABYLON THE GREAT, THE MOTHER OF HARLOTS AND ABOMINATIONS OF THE EARTH.

That's right the trinity really is a "mystery" as most trinitarians will admit because they themselves can't begin to understand the confusion. It is MYSTERY BABYLON! God is not the author of confusion!

Keeping the Sabbath?

Unless one is an Acts 2:38 Christian it doesn't really matter what they do. Many fruitcakes claim to be "keeping the sabbath" not realizing that if they have even turned on a light switch they have "broken the sabbath". The New Testament Christian is to keep every day holy.

> Exodus 16:29 See, for that the LORD hath given you the sabbath, therefore he giveth you on the sixth day the bread of two days; abide ye every man in his place, let no man go out of his place on the seventh day.
>
> Exodus 20:10 But the seventh day [is] the sabbath of the LORD thy God: [in it] thou shalt not do any work, thou, nor thy son, nor thy daughter, thy manservant, nor thy maidservant, nor thy cattle, nor thy stranger that [is] within thy gates:
>
> Exodus 31:14 Ye shall keep the sabbath therefore; for it [is] holy unto you: every one that defileth it shall surely be put to death: for whosoever doeth [any] work therein, that soul shall be cut off from among his people.
>
> Exodus 31:15 Six days may work be done; but in the seventh [is] the sabbath of rest, holy to the LORD: whosoever doeth [any] work in the sabbath day, he shall surely be put to death.
>
> Exodus 35:3 Ye shall kindle no fire throughout your habitations upon the sabbath day.
>
> Numbers 15:32 And while the children of Israel were in the wilderness, they found a man that gathered sticks upon the sabbath day.
>
> Numbers 15:35 And the LORD said unto Moses, The man shall be surely put to death: all the congregation shall stone him with stones without the camp.

Jeremiah 17:21 Thus saith the LORD; Take heed to yourselves, and bear no burden on the sabbath day, nor bring [it] in by the gates of Jerusalem;

Jeremiah 17:22 Neither carry forth a burden out of your houses on the sabbath day, neither do ye any work, but hallow ye the sabbath day, as I commanded your fathers.

Matthew 11:30 For my yoke [is] easy, and my burden is light.

Matthew 12:1 At that time Jesus went on the sabbath day through the corn; and his disciples were an hungred, and began to pluck the ears of corn, and to eat.

Matthew 12:2 But when the Pharisees saw [it], they said unto him, Behold, thy disciples do that which is not lawful to do upon the sabbath day.

Matthew 12:3 But he said unto them, Have ye not read what David did, when he was an hungred, and they that were with him;

Matthew 12:4 How he entered into the house of God, and did eat the shewbread, which was not lawful for him to eat, neither for them which were with him, but only for the priests?

Matthew 12:5 Or have ye not read in the law, how that on the sabbath days the priests in the temple profane the sabbath, and are blameless?

Matthew 12:6 But I say unto you, That in this place is [one] greater than the temple.

Matthew 12:7 But if ye had known what [this] meaneth, I will have mercy, and not sacrifice, ye would not have condemned the guiltless.

Matthew 12:8 For the Son of man is Lord even of the sabbath day.

Matthew 12:9-12 And when he was departed thence, he went into their synagogue: 10 And, behold, there was a man which had [his] hand withered. And they asked him, saying, Is it lawful to heal on the sabbath days? that they might accuse him. 11 And he said unto them, What man shall there be among you, that shall have one sheep, and if it fall into a pit on the sabbath day, will he not lay hold on it, and lift [it] out? 12 How much then is a man better than a sheep? Wherefore it is lawful to do well on the sabbath days.

John 5:10 The Jews therefore said unto him that was cured, It is the sabbath day: it is not lawful for thee to carry [thy] bed.

John 5:16 And therefore did the Jews persecute Jesus, and sought to slay him, because he had done these things on the sabbath day.

John 5:18 Therefore the Jews sought the more to kill him, because he not only had broken the sabbath, but said also that God was his Father, making himself equal with God.

John 9:16 Therefore said some of the Pharisees, This man is not of God, because he keepeth not the sabbath day. Others said, How can a man that is a sinner do such miracles? And there was a division among them.

Colossians 2:16 Let no man therefore judge you in meat, or in drink, or in respect of an holyday, or of the new moon, or of the sabbath [days]:

1 Peter 2:5 Ye also, as lively stones, are built up a spiritual house, an holy priesthood, to offer up spiritual sacrifices, acceptable to God by Jesus Christ.

1 Peter 2:9 But ye are a chosen generation, a royal priesthood, an holy nation, a peculiar people; that ye should shew forth the praises of him who hath called you out of darkness into his marvellous light:

The real Acts 2:38 Christian is a part of a royal priesthood.

Matthew 12:5 Or have ye not read in the law, how that on the sabbath days the priests in the temple profane the sabbath, and are blameless?

Xmas, "Christ mass"

Tis the season for even otherwise "Saints" to go a whoring led by knowing compromisers wanting those extra donations and attendance.

Hey, what's wrong with a little whoring with the world here and there, eh?

> 2 Corinthians 10:12 ¶ For we dare not make ourselves of the number, or compare ourselves with some that commend themselves: but they measuring themselves by themselves, and comparing themselves among themselves, are not wise.
>
> Romans 12:2 And be not conformed to this world: but be ye transformed by the renewing of your mind, that ye may prove what is that good, and acceptable, and perfect, will of God.

Tis the season for even "Oneness", so called "holiness" churches to celebrate a Roman Catholic mass that has NOTHING WHATSOEVER to do with Jesus Christ other than to defy His Word in a plethora of ways.

There is, however, one "Christmas" style celebration is mentioned in the Bible, though, did you know that? (other than the tree worship stuff, I mean).

> Revelation 11:7 And when they shall have finished their testimony, the beast that ascendeth out of the bottomless pit shall make war against them, and shall overcome them, and kill them.
>
> 8 And their dead bodies shall lie in the street of the great city, which spiritually is called Sodom and Egypt, where also our Lord was crucified.
>
> 9 And they of the people and kindreds and tongues and nations shall see their dead bodies three days and an half, and shall not suffer their dead bodies to be put in graves.
>
> Revelation 11:10 And they that dwell upon the earth shall rejoice over them, and make merry, and shall send gifts one to another; because these two prophets tormented them that dwelt on the earth.

Related scriptures:

> Exodus 20:5 Thou shalt not bow down thyself to them, nor serve them: for I the LORD thy God am a jealous God, visiting the iniquity of the fathers upon the children unto the third and fourth generation of them that hate me;
>
> Exodus 34:14 For thou shalt worship no other god: for the LORD, whose name is Jealous, is a jealous God:
>
> Deuteronomy 4:24 For the LORD thy God is a consuming fire, even a jealous God.
>
> Deuteronomy 5:9 Thou shalt not bow down thyself unto them, nor serve them: for I the LORD thy God am a jealous God, visiting the iniquity of the fathers upon the children unto the third and fourth generation of them that hate me,
>
> Deuteronomy 6:15 (For the LORD thy God is a jealous God among you) lest the anger of the LORD thy God be kindled against thee, and destroy thee from off the face of the earth.
>
> Joshua 24:19 And Joshua said unto the people, Ye cannot serve the LORD: for he is an holy God; he is a jealous God; he will not forgive your transgressions nor your sins.

And, of course, the tree thing...

> Jer 10:2 Thus saith the LORD, Learn not the way of the heathen, and be not dismayed at the signs of heaven; for the heathen are dismayed at them.
>
> Jer 10:3 For the customs of the people [are] vain: for [one] cutteth a tree out of the forest, the work of the hands of the workman, with the axe.
>
> Jer 10:4 They deck it with silver and with gold; they fasten it with nails and with hammers, that it move not.

Genealogies

I Timothy 1:4 Neither give heed to fables and endless genealogies, which minister questions, rather than godly edifying which is in faith: [so do].

Titus 3:9 But avoid foolish questions, and genealogies, and contentions, and strivings about the law; for they are unprofitable and vain.

Serve

Joshua 24:15 And if it seem evil unto you to serve the LORD, choose you this day whom ye will serve; whether the gods which your fathers served that were on the other side of the flood, or the gods of the Amorites, in whose land ye dwell: but as for me and my house, we will serve the LORD.

Isaiah 1:18 Come now, and let us reason together, saith the LORD: though your sins be as scarlet, they shall be as white as snow; though they be red like crimson, they shall be as wool.

Deuteronomy 11:26 Behold, I set before you this day a blessing and a curse;

27 A blessing, if ye obey the commandments of the LORD your God, which I command you this day:

28 And a curse, if ye will not obey the commandments of the LORD your God, but turn aside out of the way which I command you this day, to go after other gods, which ye have not known.

Proverbs 13:15 Good understanding giveth favour: but the way of transgressors is hard.

John 10:10 The thief cometh not, but for to steal, and to kill, and to destroy: I am come that they might have life, and that they might have it more abundantly.

Matthew 11:28 Come unto me, all ye that labour and are heavy laden, and I will give you rest.

29 Take my yoke upon you, and learn of me; for I am meek and lowly in heart: and ye shall find rest unto your souls.

30 For my yoke is easy, and my burden is light.

Hebrews 5:9 And being made perfect, he became the author of eternal salvation unto all them that obey him;

3 John 1:2 Beloved, I wish above all things that thou mayest prosper and be in health, even as thy soul prospereth.

Matthew 6:24 No man can serve two masters: for either he will hate the one, and love the other; or else he will hold to the one, and despise the other. Ye cannot serve God and mammon.

Luke 16:13 No servant can serve two masters: for either he will hate the one, and love the other; or else he will hold to the one, and despise the other. Ye cannot serve God and mammon.

Hebrews 12:28 Wherefore we receiving a kingdom which cannot be moved, let us have grace, whereby we may serve God acceptably with reverence and godly fear:

Romans 12:11 Not slothful in business; fervent in spirit; serving the Lord;

Righteousness

James 5:16 Confess your faults one to another, and pray one for another, that ye may be healed. The effectual fervent prayer of a righteous man availeth much.

There are many benefits from God for the righteous. Many got their names in the Bible because God found them to be righteous

Genesis 7:1 And the LORD said unto Noah, Come thou and all thy house into the ark; for thee have I seen righteous before me in this generation.

Think about this next one in light of current events. Some wonder how God can keep from destroying the world because of the rampant sin.

Genesis 18:20 And the LORD said, Because the cry of Sodom and Gomorrah is great, and because their sin is very grievous;

21 I will go down now, and see whether they have done altogether according to the cry of it, which is come unto me; and if not, I will know.

22 And the men turned their faces from thence, and went toward Sodom: but Abraham stood yet before the LORD.

23 ¶ And Abraham drew near, and said, Wilt thou also destroy the righteous with the wicked?

24 Peradventure there be fifty righteous within the city: wilt thou also destroy and not spare the place for the fifty righteous that are therein?

25 That be far from thee to do after this manner, to slay the righteous with the wicked: and that the righteous should be as the wicked, that be far from thee: Shall not the Judge of all the earth do right?

26 And the LORD said, If I find in Sodom fifty righteous within the city, then I will spare all the place for their sakes.

Abraham continued his negotiations with the God of the universe.

Genesis 18:32 And he said, Oh let not the Lord be angry, and I will speak yet but this once: Peradventure ten shall be found there. And he said, I will not destroy it for ten's sake.

Consider this! Sodom would have been spared if there could have been found 10 rightous people.

Psalms 5:12 For thou, LORD, wilt bless the righteous; with favour wilt thou compass him as with a shield.

What is this "rightousness" thing? It carries a lot of weight with God!

Psalms 1:5 Therefore the ungodly shall not stand in the judgment, nor sinners in the congregation of the righteous.

We see that righteousness includes freedom from sin.

Psalms 1:6 For the LORD knoweth the way of the righteous: but the way of the ungodly shall perish.

We see that rightousness includes godliness.

Psalms 7:9 Oh let the wickedness of the wicked come to an end; but establish the just: for the righteous God trieth the hearts and reins.

Psalms 11:7 For the righteous LORD loveth righteousness; his countenance doth behold the upright.

We see that rightousness cannot be faked.

> Psalms 32:11 Be glad in the LORD, and rejoice, ye righteous: and shout for joy, all ye that are upright in heart.

The righteous are upright in heart.

> Psalms 34:15 The eyes of the LORD are upon the righteous, and his ears are open unto their cry.
>
> 16 The face of the LORD is against them that do evil, to cut off the remembrance of them from the earth.
>
> 17 The righteous cry, and the LORD heareth, and delivereth them out of all their troubles.

Righteousness does not mean freedom from troubles or afflictions or persecution or hatred.

> Psalms 34:19 Many are the afflictions of the righteous: but the LORD delivereth him out of them all.
>
> Psalms 34:21 Evil shall slay the wicked: and they that hate the righteous shall be desolate.

There is a price to pay for hating the righteous.

> Psalms 37:25 I have been young, and now am old; yet have I not seen the righteous forsaken, nor his seed begging bread.
>
> Proverbs 10:24 The fear of the wicked, it shall come upon him: but the desire of the righteous shall be granted.

Some think that those living for God are in some sort of bondage. The God of this world has blinded them.

What is righteousness?

> 1 John 3:7 Little children, let no man deceive you: he that doeth righteousness is righteous, even as he is righteous.

8 He that committeth sin is of the devil; for the devil sinneth from the beginning. For this purpose the Son of God was manifested, that he might destroy the works of the devil.

9 Whosoever is born of God doth not commit sin; for his seed remaineth in him: and he cannot sin, because he is born of God.

10 In this the children of God are manifest, and the children of the devil: whosoever doeth not righteousness is not of God, neither he that loveth not his brother.

Revelation 22:11 He that is unjust, let him be unjust still: and he which is filthy, let him be filthy still: and he that is righteous, let him be righteous still: and he that is holy, let him be holy still.

Your righteousness is determined simply by what you use your God given free will to do and you cannot be righteous without the Holy Ghost.

Romans 14:17 For the kingdom of God is not meat and drink; but righteousness, and peace, and joy in the Holy Ghost.

18 For he that in these things serveth Christ is acceptable to God, and approved of men.

Psalms 15:1 ¶ <<A Psalm of David.>> LORD, who shall abide in thy tabernacle? who shall dwell in thy holy hill?

2 He that walketh uprightly, and worketh righteousness, and speaketh the truth in his heart.

3 He that backbiteth not with his tongue, nor doeth evil to his neighbour, nor taketh up a reproach against his neighbour.

Lord's Supper

Matthew 26:26 And as they were eating, Jesus took bread, and blessed it, and brake it, and gave it to the disciples, and said, Take, eat; this is my body.

27 And he took the cup, and gave thanks, and gave it to them, saying, Drink ye all of it;

28 For this is my blood of the new testament, which is shed for many for the remission of sins.

29 But I say unto you, I will not drink henceforth of this fruit of the vine, until that day when I drink it new with you in my Father's kingdom.

Mark 14:22 And as they did eat, Jesus took bread, and blessed, and brake it, and gave to them, and said, Take, eat: this is my body.

23 And he took the cup, and when he had given thanks, he gave it to them: and they all drank of it.

24 And he said unto them, This is my blood of the new testament, which is shed for many.

25 Verily I say unto you, I will drink no more of the fruit of the vine, until that day that I drink it new in the kingdom of God.

Luke 22:19 And he took bread, and gave thanks, and brake it, and gave unto them, saying, This is my body which is given for you: this do in remembrance of me.

20 Likewise also the cup after supper, saying, This cup is the new testament in my blood, which is shed for you.

John 13:1 Now before the feast of the passover, when Jesus knew that his hour was come that he should depart out of this world unto the Father, having loved his own which were in the world, he loved them unto the end.

2 And supper being ended, the devil having now put into the heart of Judas Iscariot, Simon's son, to betray him;

3 Jesus knowing that the Father had given all things into his hands, and that he was come from God, and went to God;

4 He riseth from supper, and laid aside his garments; and took a towel, and girded himself.

5 After that he poureth water into a bason, and began to wash the disciples' feet, and to wipe them with the towel wherewith he was girded.

6 Then cometh he to Simon Peter: and Peter saith unto him, Lord, dost thou wash my feet? Peter saith: Gr. he saith

7 Jesus answered and said unto him, What I do thou knowest not now; but thou shalt know hereafter.

8 Peter saith unto him, Thou shalt never wash my feet. Jesus answered him, If I wash thee not, thou hast no part with me.

9 Simon Peter saith unto him, Lord, not my feet only, but also my hands and my head.

10 Jesus saith to him, He that is washed needeth not save to wash his feet, but is clean every whit: and ye are clean, but not all.

11 For he knew who should betray him; therefore said he, Ye are not all clean.

12 So after he had washed their feet, and had taken his garments, and was set down again, he said unto them, Know ye what I have done to you?

13 Ye call me Master and Lord: and ye say well; for so I am.

14 If I then, your Lord and Master, have washed your feet; ye also ought to wash one another's feet.

15 For I have given you an example, that ye should do as I have done to you.

16 Verily, verily, I say unto you, The servant is not greater than his lord; neither he that is sent greater than he that sent him.

17 If ye know these things, happy are ye if ye do them.

1 Corinthians 11:23 For I have received of the Lord that which also I delivered unto you, That the Lord Jesus the same night in which he was betrayed took bread:

24 And when he had given thanks, he brake it, and said, Take, eat: this is my body, which is broken for you: this do in remembrance of me. in…: or, for a remembrance

25 After the same manner also he took the cup, when he had supped, saying, This cup is the new testament in my blood: this do ye, as oft as ye drink it, in remembrance of me.

26 For as often as ye eat this bread, and drink this cup, ye do shew the Lord's death till he come. ye do…: or, shew ye

27 Wherefore whosoever shall eat this bread, and drink this cup of the Lord, unworthily, shall be guilty of the body and blood of the Lord.

28 But let a man examine himself, and so let him eat of that bread, and drink of that cup.

29 For he that eateth and drinketh unworthily, eateth and drinketh damnation to himself, not discerning the Lord's body. damnation: or, judgment

30 For this cause many are weak and sickly among you, and many sleep.

31 For if we would judge ourselves, we should not be judged.

Love

Many speak of love. Some use the word love to speak of compromise for the sake of "pleasantness".

If am man was asleep in a burning building would soft kind reassuring words gently whispered in his ear be "love"?

Are the kind reassuring lies of the trinity preacher preached to his/her/its lost congregation "love"?

Are the compromises and worldliness of some Oneness preacher gone reprobate to build a bigger congregation, "love"

Are organizations like the UPCI licensing Biblically disqualified men to preach, practicing love?

How does God, Himself define the word "love".

> Exodus 20:6 And shewing mercy unto thousands of them that love me, and keep my commandments.
>
> Deuteronomy 5:10 And shewing mercy unto thousands of them that love me and keep my commandments.
>
> Deuteronomy 7:9 Know therefore that the LORD thy God, he [is] God, the faithful God, which keepeth covenant and mercy with them that love him and keep his commandments to a thousand generations;

There is a saying that I believe is in harmony with the scripture that says, "Love is not an emotion, but rather a commitment". Does not the high and Godly love of marriage involve a serious lifetime commitment?

> Deuteronomy 11:1 Therefore thou shalt love the LORD thy God, and keep his charge, and his statutes, and his judgments, and his commandments, alway.
>
> Deuteronomy 11:13 And it shall come to pass, if ye shall hearken diligently unto my commandments which I command you this day, to love the LORD your God, and to serve him with all your heart and with all your soul, Deuteronomy 11:22 For if ye shall diligently keep all these

> commandments which I command you, to do them, to love the LORD your God, to walk in all his ways, and to cleave unto him;

The people in these false christian cults like trinity etc who claim to love God while disregarding his Word are really really stupid in the most ultimate eternal way.

> Deuteronomy 19:9 If thou shalt keep all these commandments to do them, which I command thee this day, to love the LORD thy God, and to walk ever in his ways; then shalt thou add three cities more for thee, beside these three:
>
> Deuteronomy 30:16 In that I command thee this day to love the LORD thy God, to walk in his ways, and to keep his commandments and his statutes and his judgments, that thou mayest live and multiply: and the LORD thy God shall bless thee in the land whither thou goest to possess it.
>
> Joshua 22:5 But take diligent heed to do the commandment and the law, which Moses the servant of the LORD charged you, to love the LORD your God, and to walk in all his ways, and to keep his commandments, and to cleave unto him, and to serve him with all your heart and with all your soul.
>
> Nehemiah 1:5 And said, I beseech thee, O LORD God of heaven, the great and terrible God, that keepeth covenant and mercy for them that love him and observe his commandments:
>
> Psalms 119:127 Therefore I love thy commandments above gold; yea, above fine gold.

Why would the Psalmist write the above? Well, he perceived that it is a PRIVLEDGE to even be aware of the commandments of God.

> Daniel 9:4 And I prayed unto the LORD my God, and made my confession, and said, O Lord, the great and dreadful God, keeping the covenant and mercy to them that love him, and to them that keep his commandments;
>
> John 14:15 If ye love me, keep my commandments.

> John 14:21 He that hath my commandments, and keepeth them, he it is that loveth me: and he that loveth me shall be loved of my Father, and I will love him, and will manifest myself to him.

No, that verse does not support a belief in plural gods as some false-christians would imagine in their delusions and polytheism.

> John 15:10 If ye keep my commandments, ye shall abide in my love; even as I have kept my Father's commandments, and abide in his love.

> I John 5:2 By this we know that we love the children of God, when we love God, and keep his commandments.

> I John 5:3 For this is the love of God, that we keep his commandments: and his commandments are not grievous.

Note carefully here. How does the Word of God define the love of God?

> II John 1:6 And this is love, that we walk after his commandments. This is the commandment, That, as ye have heard from the beginning, ye should walk in it.

How does your Bible define the word "love"?

If you are deceived in some false-christian cult like trinity or any of the other sin cults or backslidden and worldly even among Oneness, I hope this brief study will cause you to "come out from among them" and find yourself a real holiness Oneness Church. When all is said and done, that will be the only major decision you ever made that really mattered. The rest is just "details".

Praise, Music and Dance

There are many examples of the importance of praise and worship to God. There are also many references to musical instruments used to praise the Lord.

I also believe that the Bible teaches a whole hearted exuberant enthusiastic music and praise, even dance to the Lord.

> Psalms 9:11 Sing praises to the LORD, which dwelleth in Zion: declare among the people his doings.
>
> Psalms 18:49 Therefore will I give thanks unto thee, O LORD, among the heathen, and sing praises unto thy name.
>
> Psalms 22:3 But thou art holy, O thou that inhabitest the praises of Israel.
>
> Psalms 27:6 And now shall mine head be lifted up above mine enemies round about me: therefore will I offer in his tabernacle sacrifices of joy; I will sing, yea, I will sing praises unto the LORD.
>
> Psalms 47:6 Sing praises to God, sing praises: sing praises unto our King, sing praises.
>
> Psalms 47:7 For God is the King of all the earth: sing ye praises with understanding.
>
> Psalms 56:12 Thy vows are upon me, O God: I will render praises unto thee.
>
> Psalms 68:4 Sing unto God, sing praises to his name: extol him that rideth upon the heavens by his name JAH, and rejoice before him.
>
> Psalms 68:32 Sing unto God, ye kingdoms of the earth; O sing praises unto the Lord; Selah:
>
> Psalms 75:9 But I will declare for ever; I will sing praises to the God of Jacob.

Psalms 78:4 We will not hide them from their children, shewing to the generation to come the praises of the LORD, and his strength, and his wonderful works that he hath done.

Psalms 92:1 <<A Psalm or Song for the sabbath day.>> It is a good thing to give thanks unto the LORD, and to sing praises unto thy name, O most High:

Psalms 108:3 I will praise thee, O LORD, among the people: and I will sing praises unto thee among the nations.

Psalms 135:3 Praise the LORD; for the LORD is good: sing praises unto his name; for it is pleasant.

Psalms 144:9 I will sing a new song unto thee, O God: upon a psaltery and an instrument of ten strings will I sing praises unto thee.

Psalms 146:2 While I live will I praise the LORD: I will sing praises unto my God while I have any being.

Psalms 147:1 Praise ye the LORD: for it is good to sing praises unto our God; for it is pleasant; and praise is comely.

Psalms 149:3 Let them praise his name in the dance: let them sing praises unto him with the timbrel and harp.

Psalms 148:4 Praise him, ye heavens of heavens, and ye waters that be above the heavens.

Psalms 148:5 Let them praise the name of the LORD: for he commanded, and they were created.

Psalms 149:1 ¶ Praise ye the LORD. Sing unto the LORD a new song, and his praise in the congregation of saints.

Psalms 150:1 ¶ Praise ye the LORD. Praise God in his sanctuary: praise him in the firmament of his power.

2 Praise him for his mighty acts: praise him according to his excellent greatness.

> 3 Praise him with the sound of the trumpet: praise him with the psaltery and harp.
>
> 4 Praise him with the timbrel and dance: praise him with stringed instruments and organs.
>
> 5 Praise him upon the loud cymbals: praise him upon the high sounding cymbals.
>
> 6 Let every thing that hath breath praise the LORD. Praise ye the LORD.

> Psalms 141:1 ¶ <<A Psalm of David.>> LORD, I cry unto thee: make haste unto me; give ear unto my voice, when I cry unto thee.
>
> 2 Let my prayer be set forth before thee as incense; and the lifting up of my hands as the evening sacrifice.

It is scriptural that we offer sacrifice to God in the form of our praise and worship.

But there is something else to consider. As important as praise and worship are, there is something more important. Many churches are strong in praise and worship but neglect the greater matter.

> 1 Samuel 15:22 And Samuel said, Hath the LORD as great delight in burnt offerings and sacrifices, as in obeying the voice of the LORD? Behold, to obey is better than sacrifice, and to hearken than the fat of rams.
>
> 23 For rebellion is as the sin of witchcraft, and stubbornness is as iniquity and idolatry. Because thou hast rejected the word of the LORD, he hath also rejected thee from being king.
>
> 24 ¶ And Saul said unto Samuel, I have sinned: for I have transgressed the commandment of the LORD, and thy words: because I feared the people, and obeyed their voice.

> 25 Now therefore, I pray thee, pardon my sin, and turn again with me, that I may worship the LORD.
>
> 26 And Samuel said unto Saul, I will not return with thee: for thou hast rejected the word of the LORD, and the LORD hath rejected thee from being king over Israel.

Note something here that is of great importance. Repentance is not guaranteed. There are Biblical examples of people who went too far and God did NOT accept their repentance.

Obedience is more important than praise and worship, but blessed is the Church that offers praise and worship to God from a foundation of Obedience to His Word.

> Hebrews 5:9 And being made perfect, he became the author of eternal salvation unto all them that obey him;

Jesus is only the author of salvation to those who obey His Word.

Make sure that your praise and worship is built on a foundation of Obedience. Otherwise, according to the Word of God, you might as well be practicing witchcraft. Think about that! Churches that disregard the Word of God might as well be practicing witchcraft.

> Proverbs 28:9 He that turneth away his ear from hearing the law, even his prayer shall be abomination.

People in false-christian cults or even "Oneness" that have turned their backs on the Word of God are only deceiving themselves.

> James 1:22 But be ye doers of the word, and not hearers only, deceiving your own selves.

End Times

Rapture

Rather than try to address every heretical misunderstanding that is being propagated by sensationalist heretic so-called prophecy specialists, I will try to provide you a simple basic foundation of truth. I do not consider myself a "prophecy preacher", but most of this stuff is very basic and elementary.

Because there are disasters, earthquakes etc as never before is certainly a sign of the end time, but it does not mean that the vials in Rev are being poured out.

> Matthew 24:5 For many shall come in my name, saying, I am Christ ; and shall deceive many.
>
> 6 And ye shall hear of wars and rumours of wars: see that ye be not troubled: for all these things must come to pass, but the end is not yet.
>
> 7 For nation shall rise against nation, and kingdom against kingdom: and there shall be famines, and pestilences, and earthquakes, in divers places.
>
> 8 All these are the beginning of sorrows.
>
> 9 Then shall they deliver you up to be afflicted, and shall kill you: and ye shall be hated of all nations for my name's sake.
>
> 10 And then shall many be offended, and shall betray one another, and shall hate one another.
>
> 11 And many false prophets shall rise, and shall deceive many.
>
> 12 And because iniquity shall abound, the love of many shall wax cold.
>
> 13 But he that shall endure unto the end, the same shall be saved.

Notice that it does not say that the wrath of God is poured out. It is notable that one of the things it mentions is that the real Christian will be hated for His "Name's sake". The trinitarian hatred for the Name of Jesus in baptism comes to mind.

We have some promises from Jesus. Those real Oneness Christians who know that Jesus IS the Holy Ghost will be able to understand this.

> John 14:7 Even the Spirit of truth; whom the world cannot receive, because it seeth him not, neither knoweth him: but ye know him; for he dwelleth with you, and shall be in you.
>
> 18 I will not leave you comfortless: I will come to you.

Jesus is the Truth! Jesus was telling them that He was with them but would be IN them. That is a strong sermon for monotheism right there. Remember that the Spirit of Jesus IS the Holy Spirit and He promised that He would NOT leave us comfortless. Remember that promise from the Comforter.

Now another basic foundational point is that, while the antichrist system is at work and the antichrist is probably walking this earth right now, he CANNOT be revealed until the Holy Spirit is taken out of the way.

> 2 Thessalonians 2:7 For the mystery of iniquity doth already work: only he who now letteth will let, until he be taken out of the way.

I trust that we can agree that the only one with the power to "letteth" regarding the antichrist is Jesus Christ (Oneness Christians understanding that Jesus IS the Father, Son, AND Holy Ghost.)

> 2 Thessalonians 2:1 Now we beseech you, brethren, by the coming of our Lord Jesus Christ, and by our gathering together unto him,

2 That ye be not soon shaken in mind, or be troubled, neither by spirit, nor by word, nor by letter as from us, as that the day of Christ is at hand.

3 ¶ Let no man deceive you by any means: for that day shall not come, except there come a falling away first, and that man of sin be revealed, the son of perdition;

4 Who opposeth and exalteth himself above all that is called God, or that is worshipped; so that he as God sitteth in the temple of God, shewing himself that he is God.

5 Remember ye not, that, when I was yet with you, I told you these things?

6 And now ye know what withholdeth that he might be revealed in his time.

7 For the mystery of iniquity doth already work: only he who now letteth will let, until he be taken out of the way.

8 And then shall that Wicked be revealed, whom the Lord shall consume with the spirit of his mouth, and shall destroy with the brightness of his coming:

9 Even him, whose coming is after the working of Satan with all power and signs and lying wonders,

Now hopefully by this time we see two points proven from the scripture.

1. Jesus has promised that He will not leave the Church comfortless

and

2. The antichrist cannot be revealed until the Spirit of God is taken out of the way.

Revelation 13:14 And deceiveth them that dwell on the earth by the means of those miracles which he had power to do in the sight of the beast; saying to them that dwell on the earth, that they should make an image to the beast, which had the wound by a sword, and did live.

15 And he had power to give life unto the image of the beast, that the image of the beast should both speak, and cause that as many as would not worship the image of the beast should be killed.

16 And he causeth all, both small and great, rich and poor, free and bond, to receive a mark in their right hand, or in their foreheads:

17 And that no man might buy or sell, save he that had the mark, or the name of the beast, or the number of his name.

18 Here is wisdom. Let him that hath understanding count the number of the beast: for it is the number of a man; and his number is Six hundred threescore and six.

I believe that before the antichrist can be revealed and implement his mark, that the Gentile Church will be gone.

I believe that when the Spirit of Christ leaves, that the Church goes with Him.

1 Thessalonians 4:10 And indeed ye do it toward all the brethren which are in all Macedonia: but we beseech you, brethren, that ye increase more and more;

11 And that ye study to be quiet, and to do your own business, and to work with your own hands, as we commanded you;

12 That ye may walk honestly toward them that are without, and that ye may have lack of nothing.

13 ¶ But I would not have you to be ignorant, brethren, concerning them which are asleep, that ye sorrow not, even as others which have no hope.

14 For if we believe that Jesus died and rose again, even so them also which sleep in Jesus will God bring with him.

> 15 For this we say unto you by the word of the Lord, that we which are alive and remain unto the coming of the Lord shall not prevent them which are asleep.
>
> 16 For the Lord himself shall descend from heaven with a shout, with the voice of the archangel, and with the trump of God: and the dead in Christ shall rise first:
>
> 17 Then we which are alive and remain shall be caught up together with them in the clouds, to meet the Lord in the air: and so shall we ever be with the Lord.
>
> 18 Wherefore comfort one another with these words.

> 1 Thessalonians 5:1 ¶ But of the times and the seasos, brethren, ye have no need that I write unto you.
>
> 2 For yourselves know perfectly that the day of the Lord so cometh as a thief in the night.
>
> 3 For when they shall say, Peace and safety; then sudden destruction cometh upon them, as travail upon a woman with child; and they shall not escape.

Would sudden destruction coming be a "comfort" to the Church if same was going to happen to the Church.

Does the bridegroom come to beat up the bride right before the wedding supper? Did Noah get wet? Did Lot get singed?

> Matthew 24:37 But as the days of Noe were, so shall also the coming of the Son of man be.

> Luke 17:26 And as it was in the days of Noe, so shall it be also in the days of the Son of man.
>
> 27 They did eat, they drank, they married wives, they were given in marriage, until the day that Noe entered into the ark, and the flood came, and destroyed them all.

> 28 Likewise also as it was in the days of Lot; they did eat, they drank, they bought, they sold, they planted, they builded;
>
> 29 But the same day that Lot went out of Sodom it rained fire and brimstone from heaven, and destroyed them all.
>
> 30 Even thus shall it be in the day when the Son of man is revealed.

Think about what happened in Sodom right after Lot left. Think about what happened right after Noah left. Then look at the verses in 1 Thessalonians. It speaks of the Rapture and then great destruction.

> 29 But the same day that Lot went out of Sodom it rained fire and brimstone from heaven, and destroyed them all.
>
> 30 Even thus shall it be in the day when the Son of man is revealed.

God comes for His Bride, then WHAM!!

The Day

The "day of the Lord" should NEVER be confused with the rapture of the Church. To do so is a very serious and grievous error. The rapture of the church is something for the Christian to look forward to, but the "day of the Lord" is another matter.

> Amos 5:18 Woe unto you that desire the day of the LORD! to what end is it for you? the day of the LORD is darkness, and not light.

The "day of the Lord" is a terrible judgment that will come AFTER the rapture of the true Church.

> Isa 2:12 For the day of the LORD of hosts shall be upon every one that is proud and lofty, and upon every one that is lifted up; and he shall be brought low:

> Isa 13:6 Howl ye; for the day of the LORD is at hand; it shall come as a destruction from the Almighty.
>
> Isa 13:7 Therefore shall all hands be faint, and every man's heart shall melt:
>
> Isa 13:8 And they shall be afraid: pangs and sorrows shall take hold of them; they shall be in pain as a woman that travaileth: they shall be amazed one at another; their faces shall be as flames.
>
> Isa 13:9 Behold, the day of the LORD cometh, cruel both with wrath and fierce anger, to lay the land desolate: and he shall destroy the sinners thereof out of it.
>
> Isa 13:10 For the stars of heaven and the constellations thereof shall not give their light: the sun shall be darkened in his going forth, and the moon shall not cause her light to shine.

Isa 13:11 And I will punish the world for their evil, and the wicked for their iniquity; and I will cause the arrogancy of the proud to cease, and will lay low the haughtiness of the terrible.

Jer 46:10 For this is the day of the Lord GOD of hosts, a day of vengeance, that he may avenge him of his adversaries: and the sword shall devour, and it shall be satiate and made drunk with their blood: for the Lord GOD of hosts hath a sacrifice in the north country by the river Euphrates.

Ezek 13:5 Ye have not gone up into the gaps, neither made up the hedge for the house of Israel to stand in the battle in the day of the LORD.

Ezek 30:3 For the day is near, even the day of the LORD is near, a cloudy day; it shall be the time of the heathen.

Joel 1:15 Alas for the day! for the day of the LORD is at hand, and as a destruction from the Almighty shall it come.

Joel 2:1 Blow ye the trumpet in Zion, and sound an alarm in my holy mountain: let all the inhabitants of the land tremble: for the day of the LORD cometh, for it is nigh at hand;

Joel 2:11 And the LORD shall utter his voice before his army: for his camp is very great: for he is strong that executeth his word: for the day of the LORD is great and very terrible; and who can abide it?

Joel 2:31 The sun shall be turned into darkness, and the moon into blood, before the great and the terrible day of the LORD come.

Joel 3:14 Multitudes, multitudes in the valley of decision: for the day of the LORD is near in the valley of decision.

Amos 5:18 Woe unto you that desire the day of the LORD! to what end is it for you? the day of the LORD is darkness, and not light.

Amos 5:19 As if a man did flee from a lion, and a bear met him; or went into the house, and leaned his hand on the wall, and a serpent bit him.

> Amos 5:20 Shall not the day of the LORD be darkness, and not light? even very dark, and no brightness in it?

How could these verses above be referring to the coming of the Lord to be united with His true Church? No brightness in it!

Yet the coming of the Lord for the Church will be a glorious moment for the real Christian (and interesting "news" for the denominations to read about).

> 1 Th 4:15 For this we say unto you by the word of the Lord, that we which are alive and remain unto the coming of the Lord shall not prevent them which are asleep.
>
> 1 Th 4:16 For the Lord himself shall descend from heaven with a shout, with the voice of the archangel, and with the trump of God: and the dead in Christ shall rise first:
>
> 1 Th 4:17 Then we which are alive and remain shall be caught up together with them in the clouds, to meet the Lord in the air: and so shall we ever be with the Lord.
>
> 1 Th 4:18 Wherefore comfort one another with these words.

Notice the contrast between the rapture that the saint is to look forward to, and be comforted by, and the "day of the Lord".

> Amos 5:18 Woe unto you that desire the day of the LORD! to what end is it for you? the day of the LORD is darkness, and not light.

See? The "rapture" and the "Day of the Lord" are COMPLETELY DIFFERENT EVENTS.

Day of the Lord

I know that many are being taught a false doctrine of the Church going through the wrath of God. That is not consistent with the days of Noah or Lot. Noah did not get soaked and Lot did not get toasted.

The "day of the Lord" should NEVER be confused with the rapture of the Church. To do so is a very serious and grievous error. The rapture of the church is something for the Christian to look forward to, but the "day of the Lord" is another matter.

> Amos 5:18 Woe unto you that desire the day of the LORD! to what end is it for you? the day of the LORD is darkness, and not light.

The "day of the Lord" is a terrible judgment that will come AFTER the rapture of the true Church.

> Isa 2:12 For the day of the LORD of hosts shall be upon every one that is proud and lofty, and upon every one that is lifted up; and he shall be brought low:
>
> Isa 13:6 Howl ye; for the day of the LORD is at hand; it shall come as a destruction from the Almighty.
>
> Isa 13:7 Therefore shall all hands be faint, and every man's heart shall melt:
>
> Isa 13:8 And they shall be afraid: pangs and sorrows shall take hold of them; they shall be in pain as a woman that travaileth: they shall be amazed one at another; their faces shall be as flames.
>
> Isa 13:9 Behold, the day of the LORD cometh, cruel both with wrath and fierce anger, to lay the land desolate: and he shall destroy the sinners thereof out of it.
>
> Isa 13:10 For the stars of heaven and the constellations thereof shall not give their light: the sun shall be darkened in his going forth, and the moon shall not cause her light to shine.

Isa 13:11 And I will punish the world for their evil, and the wicked for their iniquity; and I will cause the arrogancy of the proud to cease, and will lay low the haughtiness of the terrible.

Jer 46:10 For this is the day of the Lord GOD of hosts, a day of vengeance, that he may avenge him of his adversaries: and the sword shall devour, and it shall be satiate and made drunk with their blood: for the Lord GOD of hosts hath a sacrifice in the north country by the river Euphrates.

Ezek 13:5 Ye have not gone up into the gaps, neither made up the hedge for the house of Israel to stand in the battle in the day of the LORD.

Ezek 30:3 For the day is near, even the day of the LORD is near, a cloudy day; it shall be the time of the heathen.

Joel 1:15 Alas for the day! for the day of the LORD is at hand, and as a destruction from the Almighty shall it come.

Joel 2:1 Blow ye the trumpet in Zion, and sound an alarm in my holy mountain: let all the inhabitants of the land tremble: for the day of the LORD cometh, for it is nigh at hand;

Joel 2:11 And the LORD shall utter his voice before his army: for his camp is very great: for he is strong that executeth his word: for the day of the LORD is great and very terrible; and who can abide it?

> Joel 2:31 The sun shall be turned into darkness, and the moon into blood, before the great and the terrible day of the LORD come.
>
> Joel 3:14 Multitudes, multitudes in the valley of decision: for the day of the LORD is near in the valley of decision.
>
> Amos 5:18 Woe unto you that desire the day of the LORD! to what end is it for you? the day of the LORD is darkness, and not light.
>
> Amos 5:19 As if a man did flee from a lion, and a bear met him; or went into the house, and leaned his hand on the wall, and a serpent bit him.
>
> Amos 5:20 Shall not the day of the LORD be darkness, and not light? even very dark, and no brightness in it?

How could these verses above be referring to the coming of the Lord to be united with His true Church? No brightness in it!

Yet the coming of the Lord for the Church will be a glorious moment for the real Christian (and interesting "news" for the denominations to read about).

> 1 Th 4:15 For this we say unto you by the word of the Lord, that we which are alive and remain unto the coming of the Lord shall not prevent them which are asleep.
>
> 1 Th 4:16 For the Lord himself shall descend from heaven with a shout, with the voice of the archangel, and with the trump of God: and the dead in Christ shall rise first:
>
> 1 Th 4:17 Then we which are alive and remain shall be caught up together with them in the clouds, to meet the Lord in the air: and so shall we ever be with the Lord.
>
> 1 Th 4:18 Wherefore comfort one another with these words.

Notice the contrast between the rapture that the saint is to look forward to, and be comforted by, and the "day of the Lord".

> Amos 5:18 Woe unto you that desire the day of the LORD! to what end is it for you? the day of the LORD is darkness, and not light.

See? The "rapture" and the "Day of the Lord" are COMPLETELY DIFFERENT EVENTS.

The End

Matthew 13:40 As therefore the tares are gathered and burned in the fire; so shall it be in the end of this world.

Matthew 13:49 So shall it be at the end of the world: the angels shall come forth, and sever the wicked from among the just,

Matthew 24:3 And as he sat upon the mount of Olives, the disciples came unto him privately, saying, Tell us, when shall these things be? and what [shall be] the sign of thy coming, and of the end of the world?

Matthew 24:4 And Jesus answered and said unto them, Take heed that no man deceive you.

Matthew 24:5 For many shall come in my name, saying, I am Christ; and shall deceive many.

Matthew 24:6 And ye shall hear of wars and rumours of wars: see that ye be not troubled: for all [these things] must come to pass, but the end is not yet.

Matthew 24:7 For nation shall rise against nation, and kingdom against kingdom: and there shall be famines, and pestilences, and earthquakes, in divers places.

These things have all happened in history, but never all so greatly in one single generation.

Matthew 24:8 All these [are] the beginning of sorrows.

Matthew 24:9 Then shall they deliver you up to be afflicted, and shall kill you: and ye shall be hated of all nations for my name's sake.

Most false churches HATE Jesus name (especially in baptism).

> Matthew 24:11 And many false prophets shall rise, and shall deceive many.

So many deceived by false preachers these days.

> Matthew 24:12 And because iniquity shall abound, the love of many shall wax cold.
>
> Matthew 24:13 But he that shall endure unto the end, the same shall be saved.
>
> Matthew 24:34 Verily I say unto you, This generation shall not pass, till all these things be fulfilled.

This is THAT generation, the end of all things is at hand.

> Matthew 24:37 But as the days of Noe [were], so shall also the coming of the Son of man be.
>
> Matthew 24:38 For as in the days that were before the flood they were eating and drinking, marrying and giving in marriage, until the day that Noe entered into the ark,
>
> Matthew 24:39 And knew not until the flood came, and took them all away; so shall also the coming of the Son of man be.

The worldly were skeptical then, as they are now.

> Luke 21:24 And they shall fall by the edge of the sword, and shall be led away captive into all nations: and Jerusalem shall be trodden down of the Gentiles, until the times of the Gentiles be fulfilled.

The time of the Gentiles is almost fulfilled.

Luke 21:25 And there shall be signs in the sun, and in the moon, and in the stars; and upon the earth distress of nations, with perplexity; the sea and the waves roaring;

Luke 21:26 Men's hearts failing them for fear, and for looking after those things which are coming on the earth: for the powers of heaven shall be shaken.

Nervous breakdowns etc..Anxiety attacks...the time is NOW.

Jeremiah 51:6 Flee out of the midst of Babylon, and deliver every man his soul: be not cut off in her iniquity; for this [is] the time of the LORD'S vengeance; he will render unto her a recompence.

Jeremiah 51:7 Babylon [hath been] a golden cup in the LORD'S hand, that made all the earth drunken: the nations have drunken of her wine; therefore the nations are mad.

Jeremiah 51:8 Babylon is suddenly fallen and destroyed: howl for her; take balm for her pain, if so be she may be healed.

Jeremiah 51:9 We would have healed Babylon, but she is not healed: forsake her, and let us go every one into his own country: for her judgment reacheth unto heaven, and is lifted up [even] to the skies.

Jeremiah 50:40 As God overthrew Sodom and Gomorrah and the neighbour [cities] thereof, saith the LORD; [so] shall no man abide there, neither shall any son of man dwell therein.

Fire from the sky, so that no one can abide there. Nuclear War?

I Thessalonians 5:3 For when they shall say, Peace and safety; then sudden destruction cometh upon them, as travail upon a woman with child; and they shall not escape.

Safety

I Thessalonians 4:16 For the Lord himself shall descend from heaven with a shout, with the voice of the archangel, and with the trump of God: and the dead in Christ shall rise first:

* Notice it says "Lord himself" rather than "Lord's themselves" *

I Thessalonians 4:17 Then we which are alive [and] remain shall be caught up together with them in the clouds, to meet the Lord in the air: and so shall we ever be with the Lord.

* This is referring to the true Christians. *

I Thessalonians 4:18 Wherefore comfort one another with these words.

I Thessalonians 5:1 But of the times and the seasons, brethren, ye have no need that I write unto you.

* The "brethren" were those who had obeyed Acts 2:38, since Acts 2:38 was the salvation plan that Paul preached, (See Acts 19) *

I Thessalonians 5:2 For yourselves know perfectly that the day of the Lord so cometh as a thief in the night.

I Thessalonians 5:3 For when they shall say, Peace and safety; then sudden destruction cometh upon them, as travail upon a woman with child; and they shall not escape.

When the world thinks that it has "arrived" at peace....

II Peter 3:10 But the day of the Lord will come as a thief in the night; in the which the heavens shall pass away with a great noise, and the elements shall melt with fervent heat, the earth also and the works that are therein shall be burned up.

II Peter 3:11 [Seeing] then [that] all these things shall be dissolved, what manner [of persons] ought ye to be in [all] holy conversation and godliness,

II Peter 3:12 Looking for and hasting unto the coming of the day of God, wherein the heavens being on fire shall be dissolved, and the elements shall melt with fervent heat?

II Peter 3:13 Nevertheless we, according to his promise, look for new heavens and a new earth, wherein dwelleth righteousness.

* The "we" are those who had obeyed Acts 2:38. *

II Peter 3:14 Wherefore, beloved, seeing that ye look for such things, be diligent that ye may be found of him in peace, without spot, and blameless.

* Just doesn't sound like the modern "sin everyday but be saved" false religion, does it? *

II Peter 3:15 And account [that] the longsuffering of our Lord [is] salvation; even as our beloved brother Paul also according to the wisdom given unto him hath written unto you;

II Peter 3:16 As also in all [his] epistles, speaking in them of these things; in which are some things hard to be understood, which they that are unlearned and unstable wrest, as [they do] also the other scriptures, unto their own destruction.

* We have certainly seen the unlearned and unstable wrestle the scriptures to their own destruction. *

> II Peter 3:17 Ye therefore, beloved, seeing ye know [these things] before, beware lest ye also, being led away with the error of the wicked, fall from your own stedfastness.

* Just doesn't quite fit the "once saved always saved" cry of the false church, does it? *

> II Peter 3:18 But grow in grace, and [in] the knowledge of our Lord and Saviour Jesus Christ. To him [be] glory both now and for ever. Amen.

* Notice that it says "to him" and not "to them" *

Seek Death

Revelation 13:16 And he causeth all, both small and great, rich and poor, free and bond, to receive a mark <5480> in their right hand, or in their foreheads:

17 And that no man might buy or sell, save he that had the mark, or the name of the beast, or the number of his name.

18 Here is wisdom. Let him that hath understanding count the number of the beast: for it is the number of a man; and his number is Six hundred threescore and six.

5480 charagma khar'-ag-mah

AV - mark 8, graven 1; 9

1) a stamp, an imprinted mark

1a) of the mark stamped on the forehead or the right hand as the badge of the followers of the Antichrist

1b) the mark branded upon horses

2) thing carved, sculpture, graven work

2a) of idolatrous images

We live in a time where the things spoken of regarding the mark are close to being feasible with technology. Cars offer as a feature various GPS devices where one can have their exact location pinpointed. Whole industries have great concerns for fraud prevention which come down to various methods of people identifying themselves. We pass little coded cards or key chain tags over scanners at grocery stores to get our discounted price. Is it that huge of a step to have that barcode or one of the other "marks" that have replaced it or whatever tattooed onto one's hand. Would a society that wears jewelry pierced through their bodies and tattoos all over be "concerned" about one more little mark on their body to prevent fraud? This are the end times. Don't kid yourself. This IS the time to get right with God!

> Revelation 9:1 ¶ And the fifth angel sounded, and I saw a star fall from heaven unto the earth: and to him was given the key of the bottomless pit.
>
> 2 And he opened the bottomless pit; and there arose a smoke out of the pit, as the smoke of a great furnace; and the sun and the air were darkened by reason of the smoke of the pit.
>
> 3 And there came out of the smoke locusts upon the earth: and unto them was given power, as the scorpions of the earth have power.
>
> 4 And it was commanded them that they should not hurt the grass of the earth, neither any green thing, neither any tree; but only those men which have not the seal of God in their foreheads.
>
> 5 And to them it was given that they should not kill them, but that they should be tormented five months: and their torment was as the torment of a scorpion, when he striketh a man.
>
> 6 And in those days shall men seek death, and shall not find it; and shall desire to die, and death shall flee from them.

Of course the real Christians will already be gone from the earth. There are of course many mysteries that we cannot understand, but some things the Bible is clear about. If the coming of the Lord for His Church was going to be a time of horror for the Church why would such a thing be a "comfort"?

> Revelation 9:6 And in those days shall men seek death, and shall not find it; and shall desire to die, and death shall flee from them.

Can we comprehend the horror of a time when men are actually seeking DEATH and cannot die? Is that hard to believe when now we see people being kept alive by machines, sometimes against their will?

> 1 Thessalonians 4:16 For the Lord himself shall descend from heaven with a shout, with the voice of the archangel,

and with the trump of God: and the dead in Christ shall rise first:

17 Then we which are alive and remain shall be caught up together with them in the clouds, to meet the Lord in the air: and so shall we ever be with the Lord.

18 Wherefore comfort one another with these words.

The true Christians can comfort one another regarding the Rapture.

John 6:44 No man can come to me, except the Father which hath sent me draw him: and I will raise him up at the last day.

God is Holy, God is a Spirit, God is a Holy Spirit.

2 Thessalonians 2:3 ¶ Let no man deceive you by any means: for that day shall not come, except there come a falling away first, and that man of sin be revealed, the son of perdition;

4 Who opposeth and exalteth himself above all that is called God, or that is worshipped; so that he as God sitteth in the temple of God, shewing himself that he is God.

5 Remember ye not, that, when I was yet with you, I told you these things?

6 And now ye know what withholdeth that he might be revealed in his time.

7 For the mystery of iniquity doth already work: only he who now letteth will let, until he be taken out of the way.

8 And then shall that Wicked be revealed, whom the Lord shall consume with the spirit of his mouth, and shall destroy with the brightness of his coming:

9 Even him, whose coming is after the working of Satan with all power and signs and lying wonders,

10 And with all deceivableness of unrighteousness in them that perish; because they received not the love of the truth, that they might be saved.

> 11 And for this cause God shall send them strong delusion, that they should believe a lie:
>
> 12 That they all might be damned who believed not the truth, but had pleasure in unrighteousness.

Notice this verse:

> 2 Thessalonians 2:7 For the mystery of iniquity doth already work: only he who now letteth will let, until he be taken out of the way.

No power other than the Holy Spirit could hold back the antichrist, so when will the Holy Spirit be taken away from the Earth so that the antichrist can be revealed?

Those of us who are Christians know that Jesus is the Holy Spirit.

> John 14:17 Even the Spirit of truth; whom the world cannot receive, because it seeth him not, neither knoweth him: but ye know him; for he dwelleth with you, and shall be in you.
>
> 18 I will not leave you comfortless: I will come to you.

> Hebrews 13:5 Let your conversation be without covetousness; and be content with such things as ye have: for he hath said, I will never leave thee, nor forsake thee.

When the Church is raptured the Spirit of Christ will be "out of the way" and then the antichrist will be revealed.

Those who put their faith into the things of this world will be sorely disappointed.

> 2 Peter 3:10 But the day of the Lord will come as a thief in the night; in the which the heavens shall pass away with a

great noise, and the elements shall melt with fervent heat, the earth also and the works that are therein shall be burned up.

11 ¶ Seeing then that all these things shall be dissolved, what manner of persons ought ye to be in all holy conversation and godliness,

12 Looking for and hasting unto the coming of the day of God, wherein the heavens being on fire shall be dissolved, and the elements shall melt with fervent heat?

13 Nevertheless we, according to his promise, look for new heavens and a new earth, wherein dwelleth righteousness.

14 Wherefore, beloved, seeing that ye look for such things, be diligent that ye may be found of him in peace, without spot, and blameless.

How could the Bible be any plainer?

Luke 17:26 And as it was in the days of Noe, so shall it be also in the days of the Son of man.

27 They did eat, they drank, they married wives, they were given in marriage, until the day that Noe entered into the ark, and the flood came, and destroyed them all.

28 Likewise also as it was in the days of Lot; they did eat, they drank, they bought, they sold, they planted, they builded;

29 But the same day that Lot went out of Sodom it rained fire and brimstone from heaven, and destroyed them all.

30 Even thus shall it be in the day when the Son of man is revealed.

In the days of Noah it was a very wicked society, kind of like reading a current newspaper on just about any day you could pick.

Genesis 6:11 ¶ The earth also was corrupt before God, and the earth was filled with violence.

12 And God looked upon the earth, and, behold, it was corrupt; for all flesh had corrupted his way upon the earth.

Get right or get left

I Thessalonians 4:14-5:4 For if we believe that Jesus died and rose again, even so them also which sleep in Jesus will God bring with him. For this we say unto you by the word of the Lord, that we which are alive [and] remain unto the coming of the Lord shall not prevent them which are asleep. For the Lord himself shall descend from heaven with a shout, with the voice of the archangel, and with the trump of God: and the dead in Christ shall rise first: Then we which are alive [and] remain shall be caught up together with them in the clouds, to meet the Lord in the air: and so shall we ever be with the Lord. Wherefore comfort one another with these words. But of the times and the seasons, brethren, ye have no need that

I write unto you. For yourselves know perfectly that the day of the Lord so cometh as a thief in the night. For when they shall say, Peace and safety; then sudden destruction cometh upon them, as travail upon a woman with child; and they shall not escape. But ye, brethren, are not in darkness, that day should overtake you as a thief.

Hebrews 10:24-25 And let us consider one another to provoke unto love and to good works: Not forsaking the assembling of ourselves together, as the manner of some [is]; but exhorting [one another]: and so much the more, as ye see the day approaching.

Acts 2:38-40 Then Peter said unto them, Repent, and be baptized every one of you in the name of Jesus Christ for the remission of sins, and ye shall receive the gift of the Holy Ghost. For the promise is unto you, and to your children, and to all that are afar off, [even] as many as the Lord our God shall call. And with many other words did he testify and exhort, saying, Save yourselves from this untoward generation.

> Psalms 150:1-5 Praise ye the LORD. Praise God in his sanctuary: praise him in the firmament of his power. Praise him for his mighty acts: praise him according to his excellent greatness. Praise him with the sound of the trumpet: praise him with the psaltery and harp. Praise him with the timbrel and dance: praise him with stringed instruments and organs. Praise him upon the loud cymbals: praise him upon the high sounding cymbals. Let every thing that hath breath praise the LORD.

A person need not be a Biblical scholar to perceive that current events are fulfilling Bible prophesy concerning the time of the return to earth of Jesus Christ to remove his True church before pouring out his judgments upon the earth. There has never been a day such as the one we are living in, except in the days of Noah, and the days of Sodom and Gomorrah.

The Bible has predicted many, many things that have all come to pass, and, according to the Bible; the return of the Lord will take place in the time frame of a twinkling of an eye. We would be of all men most foolish to allow such a moment to catch us unprepared, and considering current events; we would surely be found without excuse. The end of all things is at hand.

Days of Noah (Noe)

Matthew 24:37 But as the days of Noe were, so shall also the coming of the Son of man be.

Luke 17:20 ¶ And when he was demanded of the Pharisees, when the kingdom of God should come, he answered them and said, The kingdom of God cometh not with observation:

21 Neither shall they say, Lo here! or, lo there! for, behold, the kingdom of God is within you.

22 And he said unto the disciples, The days will come, when ye shall desire to see one of the days of the Son of man, and ye shall not see it.

23 And they shall say to you, See here; or, see there: go not after them, nor follow them.

24 For as the lightning, that lighteneth out of the one part under heaven, shineth unto the other part under heaven; so shall also the Son of man be in his day.

25 But first must he suffer many things, and be rejected of this generation.

26 And as it was in the days of Noe, so shall it be also in the days of the Son of man.

27 They did eat, they drank, they married wives, they were given in marriage, until the day that Noe entered into the ark, and the flood came, and destroyed them all.

28 Likewise also as it was in the days of Lot; they did eat, they drank, they bought, they sold, they planted, they builded;

29 But the same day that Lot went out of Sodom it rained fire and brimstone from heaven, and destroyed them all.

30 Even thus shall it be in the day when the Son of man is revealed.

Soon

I'm just going to post a few scriptures concerning what life will be like for those who choose the sugar coated soothing lies of the false preachers. Right now the true church is still on the earth, but this is the "rapture generation" when the real Christians will....

> I Thessalonians 4:16 For the Lord himself shall descend from heaven with a shout, with the voice of the archangel, and with the trump of God: and the dead in Christ shall rise first:

> I Thessalonians 4:17 Then we which are alive [and] remain shall be caught up together with them in the clouds, to meet the Lord in the air: and so shall we ever be with the Lord.

It is not hard for me to believe that right after this that there will be a preacher massacre, as people see how they've been deceived, but most of the churches will be having services as usual. Soon they will be delighted to hear of this great leader that is finally bringing peace to the world. The trinity harlots will return to mama and they will embrace this great new leader with all the answers.

I even imagine that some preachers will suggest that the rapture never really happened and offer the fact that they are all still here as "proof".

Anyway, within about four years there will be some problems. All this will probably take place within the next 10 or 15 years.

> Revelation 6:4 And there went out another horse [that was] red: and [power] was given to him that sat thereon to take peace from the earth, and that they should kill one another: and there was given unto him a great sword.

> Revelation 6:8 And I looked, and behold a pale horse: and his name that sat on him was Death, and Hell followed with him. And power was given unto them over the fourth part of the earth, to kill with sword, and with hunger, and with death, and with the beasts of the earth.

Revelation 6:12 And I beheld when he had opened the sixth seal, and, lo, there was a great earthquake; and the sun became black as sackcloth of hair, and the moon became as blood;

Revelation 6:13 And the stars of heaven fell unto the earth, even as a fig tree casteth her untimely figs, when she is shaken of a mighty wind.

Revelation 6:14 And the heaven departed as a scroll when it is rolled together; and every mountain and island were moved out of their places.

Revelation 6:15 And the kings of the earth, and the great men, and the rich men, and the chief captains, and the mighty men, and every bondman, and every free man, hid themselves in the dens and in the rocks of the mountains;

Revelation 6:16 And said to the mountains and rocks, Fall on us, and hide us from the face of him that sitteth on the throne, and from the wrath of the Lamb:

Revelation 6:17 For the great day of his wrath is come; and who shall be able to stand?

Revelation 8:7 The first angel sounded, and there followed hail and fire mingled with blood, and they were cast upon the earth: and the third part of trees was burnt up, and all green grass was burnt up.

Revelation 8:8 And the second angel sounded, and as it were a great mountain burning with fire was cast into the sea: and the third part of the sea became blood;

Revelation 8:9 And the third part of the creatures which were in the sea, and had life, died; and the third part of the ships were destroyed.

Revelation 8:10 And the third angel sounded, and there fell a great star from heaven, burning as it were a lamp, and it fell upon the third part of the rivers, and upon the fountains of waters;

Revelation 8:11 And the name of the star is called Wormwood: and the third part of the waters became wormwood; and many men died of the waters, because they were made bitter.

Revelation 8:12 And the fourth angel sounded, and the third part of the sun was smitten, and the third part of the moon, and the third part of the stars; so as the third part of them was darkened, and the day shone not for a third part of it, and the night likewise.

Revelation 8:13 And I beheld, and heard an angel flying through the midst of heaven, saying with a loud voice, Woe, woe, woe, to the inhabiters of the earth by reason of the other voices of the trumpet of the three angels, which are yet to sound!

Revelation 9:1 And the fifth angel sounded, and I saw a star fall from heaven unto the earth: and to him was given the key of the bottomless pit.

Revelation 9:2 And he opened the bottomless pit; and there arose a smoke out of the pit, as the smoke of a great furnace; and the sun and the air were darkened by reason of the smoke of the pit.

Revelation 9:3 And there came out of the smoke locusts upon the earth: and unto them was given power, as the scorpions of the earth have power.

Revelation 9:4 And it was commanded them that they should not hurt the grass of the earth, neither any green thing, neither any tree; but only those men which have not the seal of God in their foreheads.

Revelation 9:5 And to them it was given that they should not kill them, but that they should be tormented five months: and their torment [was] as the torment of a scorpion, when he striketh a man.

Revelation 9:6 And in those days shall men seek death, and shall not find it; and shall desire to die, and death shall flee from them.

Soon

Men are living today who will experience Revelation 9:6. Men are currently highly respected members of false churches today, that will experience Revelation 9:6. There are people reading here who may very well experience Revelation 9:6.

If you wonder why I curse false preachers, you should consider Revelations 9:6. Can you even imagine the horror so bad? God will not even let men die? Think about it, it's real.

It's coming in YOUR generation. If your religion is not the religion that Jesus Apostles preached, you will experience the wrath of God firsthand. Better take another look at

Acts 2:38, better take a long hard look....

Last Days

II Timothy 3:1 This know also, that in the last days perilous times shall come.

II Timothy 3:2 For men shall be lovers of their own selves, covetous, boasters, proud, blasphemers, disobedient to parents, unthankful, unholy,

II Timothy 3:3 Without natural affection, trucebreakers, false accusers, incontinent, fierce, despisers of those that are good,

II Timothy 3:4 Traitors, heady, highminded, lovers of pleasures more than lovers of God;

II Timothy 3:5 Having a form of godliness, but denying the power thereof: from such turn away.

II Timothy 3:6 For of this sort are they which creep into houses, and lead captive silly women laden with sins, led away with divers lusts,

II Timothy 3:7 Ever learning, and never able to come to the knowledge of the truth.

II Peter 3:3 Knowing this first, that there shall come in the last days scoffers, walking after their own lusts,

II Peter 3:4 And saying, Where is the promise of his coming? for since the fathers fell asleep, all things continue as [they were] from the beginning of the creation.

II Peter 3:5 For this they willingly are ignorant of, that by the word of God the heavens were of old, and the earth standing out of the water and in the water:

II Peter 3:6 Whereby the world that then was, being overflowed with water, perished:

II Peter 3:7 But the heavens and the earth, which are now, by the same word are kept in store, reserved unto fire against the day of judgment and perdition of ungodly men.

II Peter 3:8 But, beloved, be not ignorant of this one thing, that one day [is] with the Lord as a thousand years, and a thousand years as one day.

II Peter 3:9 The Lord is not slack concerning his promise, as some men count slackness; but is longsuffering to us-ward, not willing that any should perish, but that all should come to repentance.

II Peter 3:10 But the day of the Lord will come as a thief in the night; in the which the heavens shall pass away with a great noise, and the elements shall melt with fervent heat, the earth also and the works that are therein shall be burned up.

II Peter 3:11 [Seeing] then [that] all these things shall be dissolved, what manner [of persons] ought ye to be in [all] holy conversation and godliness,

II Peter 3:12 Looking for and hasting unto the coming of the day of God, wherein the heavens being on fire shall be dissolved, and the elements shall melt with fervent heat?

II Peter 3:13 Nevertheless we, according to his promise, look for new heavens and a new earth, wherein dwelleth righteousness.

II Peter 3:14 Wherefore, beloved, seeing that ye look for such things, be diligent that ye may be found of him in peace, without spot, and blameless.

Jude 1:17 But, beloved, remember ye the words which were spoken before of the apostles of our Lord Jesus Christ;

Jude 1:18 How that they told you there should be mockers in the last time, who should walk after their own ungodly lusts.

Jude 1:19 These be they who separate themselves, sensual, having not the Spirit.

Jude 1:20 But ye, beloved, building up yourselves on your most holy faith, praying in the Holy Ghost,

II Peter 2:4 For if God spared not the angels that sinned, but cast [them] down to hell, and delivered [them] into chains of darkness, to be reserved unto judgment;

II Peter 2:5 And spared not the old world, but saved Noah the eighth [person], a preacher of righteousness, bringing in the flood upon the world of the ungodly;

II Peter 2:6 And turning the cities of Sodom and Gomorrha into ashes condemned [them] with an overthrow, making [them] an ensample unto those that after should live ungodly;

II Peter 2:7 And delivered just Lot, vexed with the filthy conversation of the wicked:

II Peter 2:8 (For that righteous man dwelling among them, in seeing and hearing, vexed [his] righteous soul from day to day with [their] unlawful deeds;)

II Peter 2:9 The Lord knoweth how to deliver the godly out of temptations, and to reserve the unjust unto the day of judgment to be punished:

II Peter 2:12 But these, as natural brute beasts, made to be taken and destroyed, speak evil of the things that they understand not; and shall utterly perish in their own corruption;

II Peter 2:13 And shall receive the reward of unrighteousness, [as] they that count it pleasure to riot in the day time. Spots [they are] and blemishes, sporting themselves with their own deceivings while they feast with you;

Revelation 20:11 And I saw a great white throne, and him that sat on it, from whose face the earth and the heaven fled away; and there was found no place for them.

Revelation 20:12 And I saw the dead, small and great, stand before God; and the books were opened: and another book was opened, which is [the book] of life: and the dead were judged out of those things which were written in the books, according to their works.

Revelation 20:13 And the sea gave up the dead which were in it; and death and hell delivered up the dead which were in them: and they were judged every man according to their works.

Revelation 20:14 And death and hell were cast into the lake of fire. This is the second death.

Revelation 20:15 And whosoever was not found written in the book of life was cast into the lake of fire.

Revelation 21:8 But the fearful, and unbelieving, and the abominable, and murderers, and whoremongers, and sorcerers, and idolaters, and all liars, shall have their part in the lake which burneth with fire and brimstone: which is the second death.

End of The World

Sermon preached 03/31/2007

I don't consider myself a prophecy preacher, but one doesn't have to be a prophecy preacher to read the newspaper and notice a few things.

> 2 Timothy 3:1 This know also, that in the last days perilous times shall come.
>
> 2 For men shall be lovers of their own selves, covetous, boasters, proud, blasphemers, disobedient to parents, unthankful, unholy,
>
> 3 Without natural affection, trucebreakers, false accusers, incontinent, fierce, despisers of those that are good,
>
> 4 Traitors, heady, high-minded, lovers of pleasures more than lovers of God;
>
> 5 Having a form of godliness, but denying the power thereof: from such turn away.

Have you ever noticed the churches where they teach that people live a life of sin but that they are somehow saved by grace even though they live in sin? They teach that no one can help but live a sinful life and they take some out of context verses to support that premise. They deny the power of the Holy Ghost! They have a form of godliness, they go to some church, they hold

to a "form" of religion, but they deny the POWER! They teach people that they will be saved in their sin rather than preaching deliverance from sin. It's the con game of con games!

> 2 Peter 3:3 Knowing this first, that there shall come in the last days scoffers, walking after their own lusts,
>
> 4 And saying, Where is the promise of his coming? for since the fathers fell asleep, all things continue as they were from the beginning of the creation.

5 For this they willingly are ignorant of, that by the word of God the heavens were of old, and the earth standing out of the water and in the water:

6 Whereby the world that then was, being overflowed with water, perished:

7 But the heavens and the earth, which are now, by the same word are kept in store, reserved unto fire against the day of judgment and perdition of ungodly men.

8 ¶ But, beloved, be not ignorant of this one thing, that one day is with the Lord as a thousand years, and a thousand years as one day.

9 ¶ The Lord is not slack concerning his promise, as some men count slackness; but is longsuffering to us-ward, not willing that any should perish, but that all should come to repentance.

10 But the day of the Lord will come as a thief in the night; in the which the heavens shall pass away with a great noise, and the elements shall melt with fervent heat, the earth also and the works that are therein shall be burned up.

11 ¶ Seeing then that all these things shall be dissolved, what manner of persons ought ye to be in all holy conversation and godliness,

12 Looking for and hasting unto the coming of the day of God, wherein the heavens being on fire shall be dissolved, and the elements shall melt with fervent heat?

13 Nevertheless we, according to his promise, look for new heavens and a new earth, wherein dwelleth righteousness.

14 Wherefore, beloved, seeing that ye look for such things, be diligent that ye may be found of him in peace, without spot, and blameless.

1 Peter 4:7 But the end of all things is at hand: be ye therefore sober, and watch unto prayer.

8 And above all things have fervent charity among yourselves: for charity shall cover the multitude of sins.

> Matthew 24:37 But as the days of Noe were, so shall also the coming of the Son of man be.
>
> 38 For as in the days that were before the flood they were eating and drinking, marrying and giving in marriage, until the day that Noe entered into the ark,
>
> 39 And knew not until the flood came, and took them all away; so shall also the coming of the Son of man be.

We live in a time where there are eating and drinking establishments everywhere you look. People are marrying and giving in marriage (some over and over again). The world doesn't have a clue!

> Luke 17:26 And as it was in the days of Noe, so shall it be also in the days of the Son of man.
>
> 27 They did eat, they drank, they married wives, they were given in marriage, until the day that Noe entered into the ark, and the flood came, and destroyed them all.
>
> 28 Likewise also as it was in the days of Lot; they did eat, they drank, they bought, they sold, they planted, they builded;
>
> 29 But the same day that Lot went out of Sodom it rained fire and brimstone from heaven, and destroyed them all.
>
> 30 Even thus shall it be in the day when the Son of man is revealed.

I don't need to prove to you the similarities between the days of Lot and this hour in which we live. In some countries it is a crime to even preach against Sodomy and related sins. It is contemptible that rank abominable sinners would attempt to ride the coattails of legitimate civil rights struggles.

Sodomy has become an accepted lifestyle choice in this hour, just like in Sodom and Gomorrah.

How many of you think that the Lord will come for His Church in the next few minutes? Raise your hand if you do.

> Matthew 24:44 Therefore be ye also ready: for in such an hour as ye think not the Son of man cometh.
>
> Luke 12:40 Be ye therefore ready also: for the Son of man cometh at an hour when ye think not.

So what does being ready mean in this day and age? It means having obeyed Acts 2:38 which is the Biblical plan of salvation and it means to be living holy and full of the Spirit.

> Acts 2:38 Then Peter said unto them, Repent, and be baptized every one of you in the name of Jesus Christ for the remission of sins, and ye shall receive the gift of the Holy Ghost.

Some may ask how we know that Acts 2:38 is the plan of salvation for everyone. Just read Acts 2:39

> Acts 2:39 For the promise is unto you, and to your children, and to all that are afar off, even as many as the Lord our God shall call.

"As many as the Lord our God shall call" doesn't leave a whole lot of "wiggle room" for the honest hearted among us. Also, why would anyone who really loved Jesus Christ not want to obey the Biblical plan of salvation that was preached on the birthday of His Church? I must preach this straight and pure. There is too much at stake to play popularity games with the social religions.

We baptize in Jesus Name because:

> Acts 4:12 Neither is there salvation in any other: for there is none other name under heaven given among men, whereby we must be saved.

We are living in the end times. There are so many signs such as the fact that Israel exists. Many say well there have always been earthquakes and famines and wars and things like that, but we have NEVER seen so many all at the SAME TIME in history.

The true Church awaits a great promise from God (remember here that Noah didn't get soaked and Lot didn't get half burned, the Rapture is before the Great Tribulation, but there is not time to get into all that tonight.

> 1 Thessalonians 4:16 For the Lord himself shall descend from heaven with a shout, with the voice of the archangel, and with the trump of God: and the dead in Christ shall rise first:
>
> 17 Then we which are alive and remain shall be caught up together with them in the clouds, to meet the Lord in the air: and so shall we ever be with the Lord.
>
> 18 Wherefore comfort one another with these words.

> 1 Thessalonians 5:1 ¶ But of the times and the seasons, brethren, ye have no need that I write unto you.
>
> 2 For yourselves know perfectly that the day of the Lord so cometh as a thief in the night.
>
> 3 For when they shall say, Peace and safety; then sudden destruction cometh upon them, as travail upon a woman with child; and they shall not escape.

> 2 Corinthians 6:2 (For he saith, I have heard thee in a time accepted, and in the day of salvation have I succoured thee: behold, now is the accepted time; behold, now is the day of salvation.)

This is not the time in history to gamble with your salvation, planning to obey God some day down the road.

Hell

Revelation 14:10 The same shall drink of the wine of the wrath of God, which is poured out without mixture into the cup of his indignation; and he shall be tormented with fire and brimstone in the presence of the holy angels, and in the presence of the Lamb:

Revelation 20:10 And the devil that deceived them was cast into the lake of fire and brimstone, where the beast and the false prophet [are], and shall be tormented day and night for ever and ever.

Revelation 21:8 But the fearful, and unbelieving, and the abominable, and murderers, and whoremongers, and sorcerers, and idolaters, and all liars, shall have their part in the lake which burneth with fire and brimstone: which is the second death.

Mark 9:43 And if thy hand offend thee, cut it off: it is better for thee to enter into life maimed, than having two hands to go into hell, into the fire that never shall be quenched:

Mark 9:44 Where their worm dieth not, and the fire is not quenched.

Mark 9:45 And if thy foot offend thee, cut it off: it is better for thee to enter halt into life, than having two feet to be cast into hell, into the fire that never shall be quenched:

Mark 9:46 Where their worm dieth not, and the fire is not quenched.

Mark 9:47 And if thine eye offend thee, pluck it out: it is better for thee to enter into the kingdom of God with one eye, than having two eyes to be cast into hell fire:

Mark 9:48 Where their worm dieth not, and the fire is not quenched.

Heaven

This started out as a study on heaven, but I noticed a couple of other blessings.

> 1 Cor 2:8 Which none of the princes of this world knew: for had they known it, they would not have crucified the Lord of glory.

Notice that right after Jesus is described as the Lord of glory (which blows away the trinity garbage), a hint of what awaits those who obey God.

> 1 Cor 2:9 But as it is written, Eye hath not seen, nor ear heard, neither have entered into the heart of man, the things which God hath prepared for them that love him.
>
> 1 Cor 2:10 But God hath revealed them unto us by his Spirit: for the Spirit searcheth all things, yea, the deep things of God.
>
> 1 Cor 2:11 For what man knoweth the things of a man, save the spirit of man which is in him? even so the things of God knoweth no man, but the Spirit of God.
>
> 1 Cor 2:12 Now we have received, not the spirit of the world, but the spirit which is of God; that we might know the things that are freely given to us of God.
>
> 1 Cor 2:13 Which things also we speak, not in the words which man's wisdom teacheth, but which the Holy Ghost teacheth; comparing spiritual things with spiritual.
>
> 1 Cor 2:14 But the natural man receiveth not the things of the Spirit of God: for they are foolishness unto him: neither can he know them, because they are spiritually discerned.

Then an answer to the false christian whine of "oh you're judging me" when they are confronted by the Word of God that exposes them as fakes.

1 Cor 2:15 But he that is spiritual judgeth all things, yet he himself is judged of no man.

1 Cor 2:16 For who hath known the mind of the Lord, that he may instruct him? But we have the mind of Christ.

Glory to God for His unfathomable generosity, Praise the name of Jesus!

Rev 21:10 And he carried me away in the spirit to a great and high mountain, and showed me that great city, the holy Jerusalem, descending out of heaven from God,

Rev 21:11 Having the glory of God: and her light was like unto a stone most precious, even like a jasper stone, clear as crystal;

Rev 21:12 And had a wall great and high, and had twelve gates, and at the gates twelve angels, and names written thereon, which are the names of the twelve tribes of the children of Israel:

Rev 21:13 On the east three gates; on the north three gates; on the south three gates; and on the west three gates.

Rev 21:13 On the east three gates; on the north three gates; on the south three gates; and on the west three gates.

Rev 21:14 And the wall of the city had twelve foundations, and in them the names of the twelve apostles of the Lamb.

Rev 21:15 And he that talked with me had a golden reed to measure the city, and the gates thereof, and the wall thereof.

Rev 21:16 And the city lieth foursquare, and the length is as large as the breadth: and he measured the city with the reed, twelve thousand furlongs. The length and the breadth and the height of it are equal.

Rev 21:17 And he measured the wall thereof, an hundred and forty and four cubits, according to the measure of a man, that is, of the angel.

Rev 21:18 And the building of the wall of it was of jasper: and the city was pure gold, like unto clear glass.

> Rev 21:19 And the foundations of the wall of the city were garnished with all manner of precious stones. The first foundation was jasper; the second, sapphire; the third, a chalcedony; the fourth, an emerald;
>
> Rev 21:20 The fifth, sardonyx; the sixth, sardius; the seventh, chrysolyte; the eighth, beryl; the ninth, a topaz; the tenth, a chrysoprasus; the eleventh, a jacinth; the twelfth, an amethyst.
>
> Rev 21:21 And the twelve gates were twelve pearls: every several gate was of one pearl: and the street of the city was pure gold, as it were transparent glass.

I believe that science only recently discovered that totally pure gold is TRANSPARENT like glass.

> Rev 21:22 And I saw no temple therein: for the Lord God Almighty and the Lamb are the temple of it.
>
> Rev 21:23 And the city had no need of the sun, neither of the moon, to shine in it: for the glory of God did lighten it, and the Lamb is the light thereof.
>
> Rev 21:24 And the nations of them which are saved shall walk in the light of it: and the kings of the earth do bring their glory and honour into it.
>
> Rev 21:25 And the gates of it shall not be shut at all by day: for there shall be no night there.

And, notice that, there will be no night in heaven.

What a small and tiny price that God asks of a man, only asking man to renounce a path of self-destruction and death by obeying Acts 2:38.

> 2 Pet 1:16 For we have not followed cunningly devised fables, when we made known unto you the power and coming of our Lord Jesus Christ, but were eyewitnesses of his majesty.

Isa 1:18 Come now, and let us reason together, saith the LORD: though your sins be as scarlet, they shall be as white as snow; though they be red like crimson, they shall be as wool.

Isa 1:19 If ye be willing and obedient, ye shall eat the good of the land:

That same Jehovah God was manifest in the flesh.

1 Tim 3:16 And without controversy great is the mystery of godliness: God was manifest in the flesh, justified in the Spirit, seen of angels, preached unto the Gentiles, believed on in the world, received up into glory.

Heb 5:9 And being made perfect, he became the author of eternal salvation unto all them that obey him;

Josh 24:15 And if it seem evil unto you to serve the LORD, choose you this day whom ye will serve; whether the gods which your fathers served that were on the other side of the flood, or the gods of the Amorites, in whose land ye dwell: but as for me and my house, we will serve the LORD.

The End

Made in the USA
Middletown, DE
17 March 2023